Innovation and Transformation of Public Health

Muhammad Farooq Umer
Department of Preventive Dental Sciences, College of Dentistry, King Faisal University, Al Hofuf, Saudi Arabia

IGI Global
Scientific Publishing
Publishing Tomorrow's Research Today

Vice President of Editorial	Melissa Wagner
Director of Acquisitions	Mikaela Felty
Director of Book Development	Jocelynn Hessler
Production Manager	Mike Brehm
Cover Design	Jose Rosado

Published in the United States of America by
IGI Global Scientific Publishing
701 East Chocolate Avenue
Hershey, PA, 17033, USA
Tel: 717-533-8845
Fax: 717-533-7115
Website: https://www.igi-global.com E-mail: cust@igi-global.com

Library of Congress Cataloging-in-Publication Data

Names: Umer, Muhammad Farooq, 1979- editor
Title: Innovation and transformation of public health / edited by Muhammad Farooq Umer.
Description: Hershey, PA : IGI Global Scientific Publishing, [2026] | Includes bibliographical references and index. | Summary: "This book aims to serve as a definitive academic resource, fostering critical dialogue, advancing scholarship, and inspiring innovative solutions to the pressing public health challenges of our time"-- Provided by publisher.
Identifiers: LCCN 2025010769 (print) | LCCN 2025010770 (ebook) | ISBN 9798337319926 h/c | ISBN 9798337319933 s/c | ISBN 9798337319940 ebook
Subjects: LCSH: Public health--Technological innovations | Public health administration--Technological innovations | Public health--Moral and ethical aspects | Artificial intelligence--Medical applications
Classification: LCC RA394 .I555 2025 (print) | LCC RA394 (ebook)
LC record available at https://lccn.loc.gov/2025010769
LC ebook record available at https://lccn.loc.gov/2025010770

British Cataloguing in Publication Data
A Cataloguing in Publication record for this book is available from the British Library.

This book is dedicated with profound respect and heartfelt gratitude to Professor Guihua Zhuang, Dean, School of Public Health, and Professor of Epidemiology and Health Statistics, School of Public Health, Xi'an Jiaotong University, Xi'an, Shaanxi, China.

Your unwavering mentorship, scholarly guidance, and inspirational leadership during my doctoral journey have left an indelible mark on my academic and professional life. Your commitment to scientific rigor, intellectual curiosity, and public health advancement continues to inspire generations of researchers. It is an honor to dedicate this work to you in recognition of your enduring impact on my growth as a scholar and on the broader field of epidemiology and public health.

With Regards

Dr. Muhammad Farooq Umer

Table of Contents

Detailed Table of Contents

Universal health coverage is key to meeting the health-related goals and addressing health inequities. If trends continue, up to 5 billion of the world's population will not be covered by essential health services in 2030, as highlighted in the Universal Health Coverage: Global Monitoring Report, released last week by WHO. Their aim is to engage with countries better to identify priorities, plan and implement together. Accelerate progress in countries through joint actions under 7 accelerator themes, which represent common challenges for many countries and where the agencies' mandates, expertise and resources offer solutions, namely: 1) Primary health care 2) Sustainable health financing 3) Community and civil society engagement 4) Determinants of health 5) Innovative programming in fragile and vulnerable settings and for disease outbreak responses 6) Research and development, innovation and access, and 7) Data and digital health. They will also work together to advance gender equality and support the delivery of global public goods.

Universal Health Coverage (UHC) aims to ensure that all individuals have access to essential healthcare services without financial hardship. While significant progress has been made globally, challenges such as funding gaps, healthcare disparities, and infrastructure limitations hinder its full implementation. The objective of this chapter is to analyze the progress, challenges, and lessons learned in achieving UHC while proposing strategies for overcoming existing barriers. To achieve this, a comprehensive approach was adopted, including a review of policy frameworks, quantitative analysis of healthcare access metrics, and case studies from countries with successful UHC models. This chapter contributes by providing a comparative analysis of UHC implementation across different healthcare systems, identifying effective policy interventions, and recommending scalable strategies for overcoming financial and infrastructural barriers. This also integrates real-world case studies and quantitative evaluations to offer actionable insights.

Environmental inequalities exacerbate global health disparities, particularly in low- and middle-income countries (LMICs). Air, water, and land pollution disproportionately affect marginalized communities, increasing the burden of communicable diseases like malaria and diarrhea, as well as non-communicable diseases such as COPD and cardiovascular disorders. Environmental factors also contribute to mental health issues due to natural disasters and climate change. This chapter examines environmental injustice and disease burden through epidemiological data, case studies, and policy evaluations. Solutions include community-based interventions, stronger regulations, innovative technologies, and multilateral cooperation. The chapter highlights the need for a holistic approach involving governments, organizations, and civil society to create equitable policies protecting vulnerable populations.

The rapid adoption of Artificial Intelligence (AI) in healthcare has revolutionized diagnostics, treatment planning, and patient care, but it has also raised critical ethical concerns, particularly regarding health equity. Algorithmic biases, often stemming from imbalanced datasets, result in unequal performance, with marginalized communities experiencing reduced accuracy and higher misdiagnosis rates. This chapter aims to investigate the impact of such biases and propose strategies to mitigate them. Using a structured methodology, the chapter analysed AI models in diagnostic and treatment prediction tasks with diverse datasets, implemented data augmentation, re-sampling, and fairness-aware algorithms, and evaluated improvements using equity metrics. However, applying these mitigation strategies reduced biases and improved equity metrics. Finally, the chapter underscores the need for ethical frameworks and inclusive data practices to balance innovation with fairness and ensure equitable healthcare outcomes for all.

This chapter, The Pandemic's Wake: Public Health Systems Under Scrutiny Analysis of global health systems' strengths and vulnerabilities revealed by COVID-19, seeks to analyze the lessons learned from the COVID-19 pandemic, focusing on how it revealed the capabilities and shortcomings of global health systems. By examining the responses of various nations, the role of international collaboration, and the disproportionate impacts on vulnerable populations, this chapter aims to provide a comprehensive understanding of what worked, what failed, and what must be done to build stronger, more equitable public health systems for the future. The pandemic underscored the critical importance of robust public health infrastructure, science-driven policies, and global solidarity. At the same time, it exposed deep-seated inequities, underfunding, and systemic weaknesses that hindered effective responses.

This chapter examines the psychological and philosophical aspects of health behaviors during pandemics. It examines how fear, uncertainty, and collective trauma shape responses to public health measures, risk perception, and moral reasoning. Psychological theories—such as cognitive dissonance, behavioural economics, and social identity—are used to understand how individuals navigate conflicting information and emotional stress. Philosophically, the study engages with ethical frameworks like utilitarianism, deontology, and virtue ethics to assess justifications for health policies and personal choices. The tension between autonomy and the common good is critically analysed, offering insights for ethically grounded, effective health interventions in future crises.

This chapter explores the critical intersection of emotional intelligence (EI) and post-pandemic resilience within the field of public health nursing. In the wake of COVID-19, nurses have faced profound emotional, ethical, and systemic challenges that have strained traditional coping strategies. Drawing on the socio-cognitive and affective frameworks, this chapter proposes a transformative, evidence-based model that positions EI as a pivotal competency for fostering resilience in public health nurses, especially in the care for older adults. Through a synthesis of contemporary theory, qualitative insights, and pedagogical strategies, the chapter outlines a framework for developing emotionally intelligent nursing professionals capable of thriving amid crises and contributing to resilient public health systems. Implications for leadership, education, and interprofessional collaboration are discussed.

This chapter explores the growing role of artificial intelligence (AI) in the healthcare sector, highlighting its applications in key areas such as medical imaging, chronic disease management, pharmaceutical research and massive data analysis. AI, through techniques such as machine learning (ML) and explainable AI (XAI), is helping to transform healthcare practices by offering more personalised and efficient solutions, while reducing costs and optimising processes. However, its adoption raises a number of challenges, including technical, organisational and ethical obstacles relating to the management of sensitive data, the transparency of algorithmic decisions and the problem of bias. The chapter also discusses the drawbacks of AI, such as the black box problem and the risks of exacerbating inequalities in access to care. In conclusion, it emphasises the importance of ethical, responsible and transparent implementation of AI to ensure sustainable improvements in healthcare and the sustainability of healthcare systems.

This chapter explores the role of artificial intelligence in epidemiology, focusing on its application in early outbreak detection and disease spread prediction. It examines how machine learning, natural language processing, and predictive analytics are applied to real-time data from clinical, environmental, and digital sources. The chapter demonstrates the integration of AI into public health surveillance systems and discusses the ethical, technical, and infrastructural challenges involved. It highlights the potential of AI to process large, heterogeneous datasets at speed and scale, enabling earlier intervention and resource allocation during emerging health crises. By analyzing historical trends and identifying hidden patterns, AI models offer critical support to decision-makers in managing uncertainty and enhancing response strategies. This chapter argues for an interdisciplinary and transparent approach to algorithm design, data governance, and stakeholder collaboration.

Chronic diseases significantly contribute to global morbidity and mortality, highlighting the need for advanced solutions . This project introduces a Synergistic Mobile Informatics Framework, integrating real-time data acquisition, predictive analytics, and personalized treatment recommendations for proactive chronic disease management . Leveraging wearable devices, mobile apps, and cloud-based machine learning, the framework enables continuous health monitoring, early detection of disease exacerbations, and tailored interventions . By analyzing physiological, behavioral, and environmental data in real time, advanced predictive models identify high-risk trends, triggering early alerts for patients and healthcare providers . These alerts reduce complications, hospitalizations, and healthcare costs . This approach fosters collaboration between patients, providers, and technology, empowering individuals to manage their health effectively while transforming chronic disease care through precision, efficiency, and innovation .

Hasan Mujtaba, School of Dentistry, Shaheed Zulfiqar Ali Bhutto Medical University, Islamabad, Pakistan
Muhammad Mohsin Javaid, School of Dentistry, Shaheed Zulfiqar Ali Bhutto Medical University, Islamabad, Pakistan

Oral health is increasingly recognized as a critical component of overall well-being, with growing evidence linking oral diseases to systemic health conditions. This chapter explores the biological mechanisms underlying the relationship between oral and systemic health, including the role of chronic inflammation, the oral microbiome, and immune system dysregulation in the development and progression of systemic diseases. We examine how periodontal disease, a prevalent inflammatory condition affecting the gums and supporting structures of the teeth, serves as a model for understanding this connection, with links to atherosclerosis, insulin resistance, and inflammatory-mediated disorders. Through an analysis of epidemiological studies, clinical trials, and emerging research, this chapter highlights the bidirectional influence between oral and systemic diseases, emphasizing how poor oral health can exacerbate systemic conditions. This chapter advocates for a comprehensive, patient-centered approach to health that recognizes the mouth as a gateway to overall wellness.

Muhammad Farooq Umer, Department of Preventive Dental Sciences, College of Dentistry, King Faisal University, Hofuf, Saudi Arabia

This chapter explores the transformative impact of artificial intelligence (AI) on oral health diagnostics, highlighting its growing role in enhancing diagnostic accuracy, efficiency, and personalized patient care. It outlines how machine learning algorithms, particularly deep learning and convolutional neural networks, are being applied to detect dental caries, periodontal disease, and oral cancers with increasing precision. The chapter discusses current trends in AI integration within dental imaging, predictive analytics, and tele-dentistry, while also addressing critical challenges such as data privacy, integration barriers, ethical concerns, and clinician training. Through case studies and literature synthesis, it evaluates the effectiveness and limitations of AI tools in real-world settings. Emphasis is placed on collaborative, ethical, and patient-centered approaches for successful adoption. The chapter concludes by suggesting future directions for regulatory frameworks, public trust, and interdisciplinary innovation to optimize AI-driven oral health diagnostics.

Access to oral health care remains a significant global challenge, for marginalized populations. We explored structural, socioeconomic, and systemic barriers contributing to oral health disparities, with a focus on low-income groups, rural communities, ethnic minorities, and individuals with disabilities. We examined the inadequacies in oral health policies, workforce distribution, insurance coverage, and health literacy that limit equitable service delivery. Drawing on global evidence and case studies, the chapter proposes multi-sectoral and community-based strategies to enhance accessibility, including mobile dental clinics, task shifting, tele-dentistry, and culturally responsive care models. Policy recommendations emphasize integration of oral health into primary healthcare, sustainable financing mechanisms, and educational reforms. The chapter underscores the urgent need for innovative, inclusive, and equity-driven approaches to ensure universal access to oral health services, aligning with Sustainable Development Goals and the WHO Global Oral Health Action Plan 2023–2030.

This chapter explores the evolving landscape of dental public health, focusing on the critical roles of policy innovation, digital technology, and workforce transformation in advancing equitable oral health systems globally. It highlights the persistent burden of oral diseases, particularly in low- and middle-income countries, and the urgent need for integrated public health responses aligned with the WHO Global Oral Health Action Plan (2023–2030) and the UN Sustainable Development Goals. The

Preface

INTRODUCTION

In an era marked by rapid transformation, persistent health disparities, and unprecedented global crises, the field of public health stands at a pivotal crossroads. *Contemporary Public Health: Advancements, Challenges, and Innovations* emerges from this critical juncture as a timely and essential contribution to the growing body of knowledge that seeks not only to understand but also to shape the future of public health.

The COVID-19 pandemic served as a stark reminder of the interconnectedness of health systems worldwide and the urgent need for resilient, equitable, and adaptive public health infrastructures. Yet, it also accelerated innovation—propelling the integration of digital technologies, artificial intelligence, and data-driven strategies into public health practice. At the same time, longstanding challenges such as healthcare inequities, access to oral health services, and gaps in global cooperation demand renewed attention and innovative responses.

This edited volume was conceptualized to capture and catalyze the multifaceted evolution of public health. Organized into four thematically distinct but interrelated sections—*Public Health Post-COVID-19*, *Modern Global Public Health*, *AI in Public Health*, and *Dental Public Health*—the book offers a panoramic yet focused view of the critical domains shaping public health discourse and practice today.

The first section, *Public Health Post-COVID-19*, investigates the global health system's vulnerabilities laid bare by the pandemic and presents a roadmap for future preparedness and system reform. The second section, *Modern Global Public Health*, shifts focus to enduring inequalities and the imperative of strengthening international partnerships to address persistent and emerging health threats. The third section, *AI in Public Health*, explores the transformative potential of emerging technologies, emphasizing both their promise and the ethical complexities they entail. Finally,

Dental Public Health brings attention to a frequently overlooked but integral aspect of health, examining the connection between oral and systemic health, and proposing innovative models for inclusive dental care delivery.

This volume aims to serve as more than just an academic text—it is designed to be a dynamic resource that bridges theory and practice. By bringing together scholarly insight, practical strategies, and interdisciplinary perspectives, this book aspires to influence policy development, professional practice, and academic inquiry alike.

Our contributors—diverse in expertise, geography, and professional background—address critical goals throughout the chapters. These include examining post-pandemic resilience, reducing global health inequalities, highlighting emergent threats like climate change and infectious disease, advancing health technologies, promoting oral health equity, and envisioning a more inclusive, collaborative future for global public health. Each chapter contributes to a broader narrative that champions innovation, critical reflection, and actionable solutions.

The intended audience for this book is equally diverse. Researchers and academicians will find a rich source of data, frameworks, and research trajectories. Public health professionals and practitioners will gain access to case studies and strategic insights to inform their interventions. Policymakers, health planners, and leaders of international organizations will discover guidance rooted in evidence and shaped by global perspectives. Technologists and innovators at the intersection of healthcare and AI will be challenged to consider ethical, equitable, and impactful applications of emerging tools. And for students, this volume offers both foundational knowledge and forward-looking perspectives on a rapidly evolving field.

As Editor, I envision this book as a cornerstone contribution to the next generation of public health scholarship and practice. It is our hope that *Contemporary Public Health: Advancements, Challenges, and Innovations* will foster critical dialogue, encourage cross-sector collaboration, and inspire innovation to address the most pressing health challenges of our time.

Let this be a step forward—toward a healthier, more equitable, and more resilient world.

ORGANIZATION OF THE BOOK

Chapter 1: The Role of Multilateral Organizations' Contributions of WHO, UNICEF, and Other Bodies to Advancing Global Health

In this foundational chapter, we examine the indispensable contributions of multilateral organizations such as WHO and UNICEF in promoting global health through social innovation, strategic advocacy, and collaborative research. The chapter outlines how these organizations work synergistically under seven accelerator themes—including primary healthcare, sustainable financing, civil society engagement, and digital health—to help countries identify priorities and implement scalable interventions. It underscores the collective mission to achieve Universal Health Coverage (UHC) while emphasizing gender equality, global public goods delivery, and the need for cohesive international cooperation in the face of complex global health challenges.

Chapter 2: Universal Health Coverage: Progress Toward Achieving Universal Health Coverage and Lessons Learned

This chapter provides a critical assessment of the global journey toward Universal Health Coverage (UHC), evaluating both progress and persistent barriers. Drawing upon quantitative metrics, policy analysis, and country case studies, the chapter dissects the structural and financial impediments to achieving UHC. It further offers comparative insights into effective policy frameworks and proposes adaptable strategies to bridge gaps in access and equity. By combining empirical evidence with real-world examples, the chapter aims to inspire scalable, system-level reforms that align with health equity and economic sustainability.

Chapter 3: Environmental Inequities and Global Health: Bridging the Gap in Vulnerable Communities

Environmental injustice is an overlooked but profound determinant of global health disparities. This chapter explores how pollution and climate change disproportionately affect marginalized populations in LMICs, exacerbating both infectious and chronic diseases. Through the lens of epidemiological data and policy evaluation, it advocates for community-based interventions, technological innovation, and cross-sectoral cooperation. The chapter calls for a rights-based, holistic approach to environmental and health governance—urging policymakers and stakeholders to create conditions that protect and empower the most vulnerable communities.

Chapter 4: Challenges in Health Equity: Balancing Innovation with Fairness and Addressing Algorithmic Biases

As AI systems become integral to healthcare delivery, this chapter critically evaluates their unintended consequences, particularly algorithmic biases that undermine equity. With robust methodological analysis, the chapter investigates the unequal outcomes stemming from imbalanced training data and proposes technological solutions such as fairness-aware algorithms and inclusive datasets. It challenges us to align innovation with justice, emphasizing the need for ethical AI frameworks that promote fairness, transparency, and equal treatment across all patient demographics.

Chapter 5: The Pandemic's Wake: Global Health Systems' Strengths and Vulnerabilities

COVID-19 served as both a mirror and a magnifying glass, revealing the strengths and fragilities of global health systems. This chapter analyzes national responses, global coordination efforts, and systemic inequities laid bare by the pandemic. Through cross-national comparisons, it identifies key lessons and policy failures while advocating for stronger public health infrastructure and resilient, equity-centered systems. The narrative compels readers to reflect on the urgent reforms needed to fortify our collective defenses against future global health emergencies.

Chapter 6: Psychological and Philosophical Aspects of Pandemics and Related Health Behaviors

Pandemics are as much psychological and moral events as they are medical crises. This chapter explores the intersection of psychology and philosophy in shaping health behavior, focusing on how fear, identity, and ethical reasoning inform public compliance and resistance. Integrating cognitive theories and normative ethics, it unpacks the societal tensions between individual autonomy and collective responsibility. The chapter offers a profound understanding of the human condition in times of crisis, guiding more compassionate and effective health policy development.

Chapter 7: Emotional Intelligence and Post-Pandemic Resilience: A Framework for Public Health Nursing

In this compelling chapter, we spotlight the critical role of emotional intelligence (EI) in nurturing resilience among public health nurses, especially in the post-pandemic landscape. Rooted in affective science and grounded in real-world nursing experiences, the chapter presents a framework that equips nurses to navigate emotional fatigue, ethical dilemmas, and interprofessional challenges. It positions EI not only as a coping mechanism but as a transformative leadership competency for future-proofing the public health workforce.

Chapter 8: Artificial Intelligence in Healthcare: Roles, Challenges and Disadvantages

Artificial Intelligence (AI) promises transformative improvements in healthcare, yet its integration is not without consequence. This chapter surveys AI's key applications—ranging from imaging to data analytics—while critically addressing challenges such as data governance, algorithmic transparency, and ethical deployment. Highlighting the "black box" dilemma and the risk of systemic bias, it urges a cautious, human-centered approach to AI adoption. The chapter emphasizes that sustainability in healthcare innovation must be built on principles of equity, responsibility, and accountability.

Chapter 9: AI in Epidemiology: Predicting the Unpredictable

Harnessing the predictive power of AI, this chapter investigates its role in real-time disease surveillance and outbreak forecasting. By integrating data from clinical, environmental, and digital sources, AI emerges as a powerful ally in public health decision-making. Yet, challenges in ethics, infrastructure, and governance persist. The chapter advocates for a transparent and interdisciplinary approach to AI development, calling for inclusive data practices and robust stakeholder collaboration to ensure technology serves the many, not the few.

Chapter 10: A Synergistic Mobile Informatics Framework for Proactive Chronic Disease Prognostication and Therapeutic Optimization

This chapter introduces an innovative mobile informatics framework designed to revolutionize chronic disease management through predictive analytics and real-time health monitoring. Leveraging wearable technologies, machine learning, and cloud-based platforms, the framework facilitates early intervention, personalized therapy, and patient empowerment. With a strong emphasis on precision medicine and preventative care, the chapter illustrates how digital tools can dramatically improve outcomes and reduce healthcare burdens for chronic disease patients worldwide.

Chapter 11: Implications of Poor Oral Health on Systemic Conditions

Oral health is a gateway to general health—this chapter explores that biological and clinical connection in depth. By examining the mechanisms linking oral diseases like periodontitis to systemic conditions such as cardiovascular disease and diabetes, the chapter elevates the importance of integrated care. Through a review of clinical and epidemiological evidence, it emphasizes a patient-centered approach that recognizes oral health as a fundamental component of holistic healthcare delivery.

Chapter 12: Impact of Artificial Intelligence on Oral Health Diagnostics

AI is reshaping oral health diagnostics, enabling more precise and efficient detection of dental conditions. This chapter explores applications of machine learning in imaging, diagnostics, and tele-dentistry, while also scrutinizing associated risks such as data security, algorithmic opacity, and practitioner readiness. It calls for collaborative models that balance innovation with patient trust and safety. Through case studies and best practices, the chapter provides a blueprint for ethical and impactful AI adoption in dentistry.

Chapter 13: Improving Access to Oral Health Care for Underserved Populations

Equity in oral healthcare remains an unmet global goal, particularly among marginalized populations. This chapter examines the systemic, financial, and social barriers that limit access, especially in rural and low-income communities. It proposes targeted solutions, including mobile clinics, tele-dentistry, and culturally competent care models. Policy recommendations are grounded in global evidence and advocate for the integration of oral health into primary care systems. The chapter champions inclusive and innovative approaches aligned with global development agendas.

Chapter 14: The Future of Dental Public Health: Its Policy, Innovation, and Workforce Development

Looking ahead, this chapter maps the future trajectory of dental public health by interlinking policy innovation, digital transformation, and workforce evolution. It discusses how integrated care models, AI, and remote technologies can expand access and improve quality. Simultaneously, it highlights the urgent need to restructure dental education and workforce models to align with global health priorities. Through this holistic vision, the chapter provides a forward-thinking roadmap for equitable and sustainable oral health systems.

Chapter 15: Emerging Infectious Control Technologies: A Global Perspective

This chapter addresses the global challenge of hospital-acquired infections (HAIs) and introduces innovative technologies aimed at controlling these risks. From antimicrobial coatings to UV-C disinfection and nanomaterials, the chapter evaluates a spectrum of solutions through the lens of efficacy, cost, and sustainability. Field applications and policy implications are discussed in detail, with recommendations for global implementation. By situating infection control within broader health system resilience, the chapter underscores the potential of technology to safeguard patient safety worldwide.

CONCLUSION

As we conclude this volume, *Contemporary Public Health: Advancements, Challenges, and Innovations*, we reflect on the collective urgency and shared responsibility that define the public health mission today. The chapters within this book do not merely recount the state of public health—they interrogate its foundations, illuminate its inequities, and reimagine its future.

From navigating the aftermath of a global pandemic to harnessing artificial intelligence for early disease detection, from closing the gaps in oral healthcare to strengthening global partnerships, our contributors have offered insight, critique, and vision. Their work underscores a profound truth: that public health is both a science and a social contract—rooted in evidence, yet dependent on collaboration, empathy, and justice.

What emerges from these pages is not a single prescription, but a mosaic of strategies, innovations, and reflections that equip stakeholders across disciplines to respond to current realities and future uncertainties. Whether read as a whole or in parts, this volume is designed to provoke dialogue, deepen understanding, and inspire informed action among scholars, practitioners, policymakers, and students alike.

As Editor, I am deeply grateful to the authors, peer reviewers, and supporting institutions whose commitment to advancing public health has shaped this work. May this book serve as both a mirror and a map—a mirror that reflects the complexities of our global health landscape, and a map that helps guide the way toward a more equitable, responsive, and resilient public health future.

Acknowledgement

Funding Statement

The Deanship of Scientific Research, Vice Presidency supported this Book for Graduate Studies and Scientific Research, King Faisal University, Saudi Arabia. [Project Number: KFU251553].

Chapter 1
The Role of Multilateral Organizations' Contributions of WHO, UNICEF, and Other Bodies to Advancing Global Health:
Promotion of Social Innovation, Support Research, and Advocacy for Health Globally

Ayesha Babar Kawish
https://orcid.org/0000-0002-3077-3237
Al-Shifa School of Public Health, Al-Shifa Trust Eye Hospital, Pakistan

Syema Awais
https://orcid.org/0000-0002-9797-7066
WHO, Pakistan

ABSTRACT

Universal health coverage is key to meeting the health-related goals and addressing health inequities. If trends continue, up to 5 billion of the world's population will not be covered by essential health services in 2030, as highlighted in the Universal Health Coverage: Global Monitoring Report, released last week by WHO. Their aim is to engage with countries better to identify priorities, plan and implement together.

DOI: 10.4018/979-8-3373-1992-6.ch001

Accelerate progress in countries through joint actions under 7 accelerator themes, which represent common challenges for many countries and where the agencies' mandates, expertise and resources offer solutions, namely: 1) Primary health care 2) Sustainable health financing 3) Community and civil society engagement 4) Determinants of health 5) Innovative programming in fragile and vulnerable settings and for disease outbreak responses 6) Research and development, innovation and access, and 7) Data and digital health. They will also work together to advance gender equality and support the delivery of global public goods.

CONTEXT

Multilateral organizations like Gavi, UNAIDS, UNDP,UNFPA,UNICEF, UNITAID, UN Women, World Bank Group, WFP and WHO all work with Governments to improve global health. They promote social innovation, support research, and advocate for health care delivery. They work together to accelerate progress towards the health-related Sustainable Development Goals (SDGs) by 2030.

Healthy Lives and Well-being for All is the ultimate goal in health. Healthy people are essential for sustainable development and for ending poverty, promoting peaceful and inclusive societies as well as protecting the environment. Over the last few decades, significant gains have been made in key areas of health, but the 2030 targets will not be met without redoubled efforts.

Universal health coverage is key to meeting the health-related goals and addressing health inequities. If trends continue, up to 5 billion of the world's population will not be covered by essential health services in 2030, as highlighted in the Universal Health Coverage: Global Monitoring Report 2023, released by WHO. To leave no one behind, countries need to address health inequities. Improved collaboration and coordination can help countries tackle complex health challenges and bring innovative solutions.

The aim of multilateral organizations is to engage better with countries to identify priorities, plan and implement together. Accelerate progress in countries through joint actions under 7 accelerator themes, which represent common challenges for many countries and where the agencies' mandates, expertise and resources offer solutions, namely: 1) Primary health care 2) Sustainable health financing 3) Community and civil society engagement 4) Determinants of health 5) Innovative programming in fragile and vulnerable settings and for disease outbreak responses 6) Research and development, innovation and access, and 7) Data and digital health. They will also collaborate to promote gender equality and help deliver global public goods.

INTRODUCTION TO MULTILATERAL ORGANIZATIONS IN GLOBAL HEALTH

Multilateral organizations are international groups that are made for collaboration between multiple countries aimed at achieving common objectives. In the area of global public health, they are instrumental in uniting countries to advance collaboration, information exchange, resource allocation, and lobbying for health as a right for all citizens. In light of the increasing complexity and interconnectivity of global health issues—transcending borders and impacting communities around the world—these organizations are more critical, now, than ever. They assist in militarizing the concept of global health that no single country should face challenges alone and that universal good health is a right to all people.

Global Health has radically changed in the last 100 years. The discourse about global health has been framed by multilateral organizations, which have spanned topics like the control of infectious diseases, including smallpox and polio, and today's issues of pandemics, non-communicable diseases (NCDs), and mental health. Organizations not only promote a worldwide consensus on the norms, strategies, and priorities of global health. They are also seen as a way to lessen the gap between countries that have shown different capacities to implement effective health interventions.

This cooperation paradigm is rooted in the recognition that health is a global public good, which is relevant as health does not know national borders and so should not the nature of interventions to prevent disease or treat disease. Therefore, multilateral organizations can allow for international solidarity and catalyze approaches that promote inclusive, equitable and sustainable health interventions.

The Sustainable Development Goals (SDGs) that capture the high-level political commitment to health, with the goal most closely linked to the health sector being Goal 3 which is called: "Ensure healthy lives and promote well-being for all at all ages" is a representation of the centrality of health to human development. Realizing this particular goal will require not only national commitments to health, but also international commitments that support national health but do so in a coordinated way, potentially drawn together via the support of multilateral organizations which act as both catalysts and convenors (United Nations, 2015).

Multilateral organizations can be described as organizations which are created by three or more countries, to engage and interact regarding issues that are of common interest and global priority. Multilateral organizations access funding for projects from many governments for the projects that are funded. Some examples include countries working together at United Nations, the World Trade Organization and funding from the World Bank. The United Nations Organization is an intergovernmental organization whose primary aims is to maintain international peace and security.

Transparency

Transparency is imperative for the credibility and effectiveness of multilateral health institutions in the spaces of WHO and UNICEF. Multilateral health organizations need to act transparently with stakeholders, member states, and the public regarding the organization's processes, funders, and decision making.

Multilateral organizations responded to criticism for their slow response to the Ebola outbreak a second time in 2014-2016 by providing mechanisms for real-time data sharing and public dashboards to increase accountability for public health emergencies [Lancet, 2015]. UNICEF has developed transparency in an open data format with open data sites like the “Transparency Portal” that publishes financial and programmatic data in real-time [UNICEF]. However, there remain concerns over data opacity in politically sensitive regions, reports not released in a timely manner, and lack of clarity on feedback opportunities for local actors. By improving internal audit functions and external reviews, multilateral health organizations can mitigate these issues and help restore public trust [WHO, 2016].

Geopolitical Dynamics

Multilateral health organizations function within a political environment, influenced by geopolitics, which affects funding decisions, influences the decisions of organizations, and impacts the implementation of programs. For example, the U.S. and China, often referred to as major funders, have both used their funding to affect strategic health diplomacy agendas through WHO platforms for the goals of their own health agendas [Global Health Centre, 2019]. Geopolitical strains can inhibit unified responses to global health threats. A pertinent example is the controversy of Taiwan's exclusion from WHO meetings despite the fact they have the most successful response to COVID-19 to date, due to China's political pressure [BMJ, 2004]. Also, the distribution of vaccines during COVID-19 highlighted inequities relating to global power, which resulted in WHO developing programs such as COVAX to ensure equitable access [GAVI. The COVAX Facility, 2020]. To navigate these power dynamics represents a constant challenge for multilateral organizations in attempting to ensure equity and solidarity, while also maintaining neutrality.

Funding Sustainability

Sustainable and predictable financing is an ongoing dilemma for multilateral health agencies. WHO's core budget is over 80% dependent on voluntary contributions, which are often earmarked according to the priorities of donors, rather than global priorities [WHO, 2014]. UNICEF is broader in scope and has less dependence on voluntary funding, but nonetheless faces challenges. Use of UNICEF's services in low-income countries are frequently negatively impacted by being underfunded or at risk of delay due to donor fatigue or political maneuvers [UNICEF, 2023]. Recommendations provided for ameliorating the challenges include: diversifying funding sources, increasing (mandatory) assessed contributions from member states, and improve financial planning through multi-year commitments [N Engl J Med., 2013]. Although mechanisms like WHO's Contingency Fund for Emergencies provide progress towards improved funding conditions, appropriate replenishment mechanisms and governance mechanisms must be in place to establish efficacy.

KEY PLAYERS IN MULTILATERAL HEALTH ARCHITECTURE

World Health Organization (WHO)

Founded in 1948, the World Health Organization (WHO) is the premier global health agency of the United Nations system. With a mandate to “promote health, keep the world safe, and serve the vulnerable,” WHO provides leadership on health matters, shapes the health research agenda, sets norms and standards, articulates evidence-based policy options, provides technical support to countries, and monitors health trends (WHO, 2023).

WHO’s work spans a vast range of activities, including emergency response, disease surveillance, health systems strengthening, and setting guidelines for clinical practice and public health. The organization’s International Health Regulations (IHR) serve as a legal framework for global health security, compelling countries to detect, report, and respond to public health emergencies (WHO, 2021).

In the aftermath of the West African Ebola outbreak (2014-2016), WHO instituted wide-ranging reforms to its operations, including the establishment of the Organization’s Health Emergent Program, and the Contingency Fund for Emergencies (The Milbank Quarterly, 2023).

WHO was an integral coordinating body in response to the COVID-19 pandemic, supplying vital information, stimulating action and providing leadership to the worldwide effort through global vaccine distribution with COVAX. WHO is frequently criticized in number of areas, and continues to have substantial issues, but it remains instrumental in global health governance (Lancet, 2020). Among the top achievements of WHO are:

1) Smallpox eradication,
2) Malarial elimination in Europe,
3) Near eradication of Polio,

4) Management of the Covid-19 pandemic.

Case Study 4: WHO and Digital Health Surveillance in Southeast Asia

WHO is actively driving and enhancing digital health surveillance in the region through the WHO South-East Asia Regional Office (SEARO) to strengthen their health information systems, and their ability to surveil, and prepare for pandemics. This work involves implementing digital technologies to help with surveillance and contact tracing and building resilient health systems. Some important aspects of the WHO's digital health activities in SEARO are:

Strengthening Health Information Systems

The World Health Organization (WHO) advocates national health information systems (HIS) and civil registration and vital statistics systems (CRVS), important systems for health data collection and analysis.

Adopting Digital Technologies

WHO is also supportive of the use of tools for surveillance as applied to digital disease detection, genetic surveillance, and sewage surveillance, to assist with identifying and tracking new threats.

Improving Contact Tracing

Digital surveillance systems are also used in support of contact tracing, particularly in response to a pandemic.

Building Resilience

WHO's ongoing work focuses on supporting the strengthening of Member State emergency response capacities related to public health emergencies, including building the skills of health workforce in field epidemiology and emergency management.

Collaboration and Partnerships

WHO collaborates with Member States, development partners, and other actors to foster innovation and promote best practice sharing across many areas of digital health.

Community Engagement

WHO emphasizes the importance of community engagement in public health surveillance and response, ensuring that primary healthcare facilities and communities are well-prepared.

Learning from COVID-19

WHO is drawing lessons from the COVID-19 pandemic to improve surveillance and contact tracing systems, including the use of digital technologies.

Multi-Sectoral Approach

WHO promotes a multi-sectoral approach to surveillance, involving stakeholders from the health sector and beyond.

Focus on Equity and Access

WHO aims to ensure that digital health solutions are accessible and equitable for all, promoting universal health coverage.

United Nations Children's Fund (UNICEF)

UNICEF focuses on the health and well-being of children and mothers. Established in 1946, UNICEF has become a global leader in child health, nutrition, education, and protection. In the health sector, UNICEF works to reduce child mortality, improve maternal health, and combat diseases through immunization, nutrition programs, and emergency health responses (UNICEF, 2022).

UNICEF collaborates closely with governments, NGOs, and other UN agencies to implement large-scale programs. It plays a critical role in health supply chains, delivering vaccines, medical supplies, and nutritional supplements to the most remote and underserved regions.

UNICEF, the United Nations agency for children, works to protect the rights of every child, especially the most disadvantaged and those hardest to reach. Across more than 190 countries and territories, we do whatever it takes to help children survive, thrive and fulfil their potential. The world's largest provider of vaccines, UNICEF also runs the world's largest humanitarian warehouse. By mandate from the United Nations General Assembly, UNICEF works to protect the rights of every child, in times of peace or crisis. The right to childhood is universal.

UNICEF's Nutrition Program in Sub-Saharan Africa

UNICEF works to address all forms of malnutrition in Eastern and Southern Africa, firstly by preventing it before it occurs. This means acting early to address the drivers of malnutrition in early childhood, middle childhood and adolescence and among women. We work to prevent all forms of malnutrition by improving children's and women's access to nutritious, safe, affordable and sustainable diets. We support quality nutrition services – such as support for breastfeeding, complementary feeding, micronutrient supplementation, deworming and dietary counselling – that keep children and women well nourished. And we promote optimal feeding, hygiene and care practices for children and women. Where prevention efforts fall short, we work to ensure the early detection and treatment of wasting and other forms of life- threatening malnutrition in early childhood.

To do this UNICEF works with governments and multiple partners across the 21 countries in Sub-Saharan Africa to develop:

- **Health systems**, including community platforms, that deliver malnutrition prevention services to all children and identify and treat child wasting. All countries deliver these services.
- **Food systems** that support nutritious foods, healthy food environments and healthy food practices for all children. In ESAR we are implementing the "first foods" for children in Africa initiative in 15 countries so far.
- **Social protection systems** that address child poverty as a key driver of malnutrition, with systematic linkages to nutrition services in the health system and to food system initiatives. To date 12 countries are delivering or developing social protection services within national systems that have synergies with nutrition services.
- **Water and sanitation systems** that ensure healthy environments where children live, play and learn.
- **Education systems** that provide nutritious meals, nutrition education and healthy food environments within and outside of schools. So far 15 countries have initiated nutrition interventions in the education system.

United Nations Fund for Population (UNFPA)

UNFPA is the United Nations sexual and reproductive health agency. Our mission is to deliver a world where every pregnancy is wanted, every childbirth is safe and every young person's potential is fulfilled. We promote gender equality and empower women, girls and young people to take control of their bodies and their futures. We work with partners in more than 150 countries to provide access to a wide range of sexual and reproductive health services. Our goal is ending unmet need for family planning, preventable maternal death, and gender-based violence and harmful practices including child marriage and female genital mutilation by 2030. The agency began operating in 1969 as the United Nations Fund for Population Activities, the same year the United Nations General Assembly declared "parents have the exclusive right to determine freely and responsibly the number and spacing of their children." While its name was changed to the United Nations Population Fund in 1987, the original acronym remains. The goal of UNFPA is to ensure sexual and reproductive rights and choices for all, especially women and young people, so that they can access high-quality sexual and reproductive health services, including voluntary family planning, maternal health care and comprehensive sexuality education. The International Conference on Population and Development (ICPD), held in Cairo in 1994, made women's empowerment and autonomy a basis for sustainable economic and social progress. The ICPD Program of Action adopted by 179 governments in Cairo and the 2019 Nairobi Statement, a recommitment to that program within the context of the 2030 Agenda for Sustainable Development, has guided our work since. Our programs, which operate in more than 150 countries and territories with 80 per cent of the world's population, further the realization of sexual and reproductive rights and choices.

In 2018, UNFPA launched efforts to achieve three transformative results, also known as the three zeros, by 2030:

Ending Unmet Need for Family Planning

Zero unmet need for family planning. We are the world's single-largest provider of donated contraceptives to developing countries, and our programmes increase the availability of contraceptives and dismantle barriers to services.

Ending Preventable Maternal Death

Zero preventable maternal deaths. We help strengthen health systems, train and educate health workers and midwives, and improve access to a full range of reproductive health services. Our support for women's maternal health is especially significant in 32 countries with the highest rates of maternal mortality and morbidity.

Ending Gender-Based Violence and Harmful Practices

Zero gender-based violence and harmful practices. We work with policymakers, justice systems and health systems and engage men and boys to advance gender equality. We protect survivors of gender-based violence by providing a combination of essential services, including in humanitarian crises.

Case Study: UNFPA's Maternal Health Support in Conflict Zones

DEEM funded by UNFPA has started implementing providing maternal and newborn health services (RH) for conflict-affected areas project since January 2019. In 2021, Deem for Development Organization implemented RH project within 14 HFs (4 CEmONC and 10 BEmONC HFs) in Taiz governorate.

CEmONC and BEmONC Health Facilities (Health Facilities) are two levels of emergency obstetric and newborn care including CEmONC at the highest level, with more comprehensive services including surgery and blood transfusion in addition to the basic services offered in BEmONC. BEmONC includes BEmONC essential services such as administration of parenteral oxytocic drugs and newborn resuscitation, and CEmONC includes surgical capacity and blood transfusion.

Elaboration

- **BEmONC (Basic Emergency Obstetric and Newborn Care):**

This level provides essential life-saving services for obstetric and newborn emergencies, to include administering parenteral oxytocic drugs (to stop bleeding) providing parenteral antibiotic loading doses, and newborn resuscitation.

- **CEmONC (Comprehensive Emergency Obstetric and Newborn Care):**

This level serves as an add-on to BEmONC by providing the ability to perform surgery for emergencies such as C-sections and transfusions. This extra capaciaty is essential for managing more complex and severe complications during the childbirth process and postpartum.

- **Importance of CEmONC:**

The availability of CEmONC services is crucial for reducing maternal and newborn mortality, especially in areas where access to advanced medical care may be limited.

UNDP (United Nations Development Program):

Addresses health through the lens of development, focusing on the social, economic, and environmental determinants of health. UNDP supports governance, resilience, and health-related policy reform (UNDP, 2023). UNDP works in about

170 countries and territories, helping to eradicate poverty, reduce inequalities and exclusion, and build resilience so countries can sustain progress. As the UN's development agency, UNDP plays a critical role in helping countries achieve the Sustainable Development Goals.

A global pandemic, conflicts, disasters and other crises have set back progress towards the Sustainable Development Goals (SDGs) and reversed human development for the first time in decades. With the rest of the UN family, UNDP is committed to accelerating action to get the world back on track to achieve the 17 Goals to end extreme poverty, guarantee human rights and secure the environment for all of humanity.

UNITAID

Funds and facilitates access to innovative health technologies and interventions, especially for HIV, TB, and malaria. UNITAID shapes markets to ensure affordable prices and sustainable supply chains for medicines, equipment and vaccines for the above-mentioned diseases. (UNITAID, 2022).

Its committed workforce of some 110 employees from more than 40 countries is responsible for finding new and innovative ways to prevent, diagnose and treat diseases more quickly, effectively and affordably. The secretariat is led by Executive Director, while the secretariat staff manage the day-to-day operations of the organization and implement policies approved by the Executive Board. Its office is hosted by the World Health Organization and based out of Geneva, Switzerland, operations are administered in accordance with its constitution and WHO rules.

Their efforts are supported by the executive board, the decision-making body of the organization, which provides strategic guidance, monitors progress and oversees the finances. The focus areas include

UNAIDS

UNAIDS is leading the global effort to end AIDS as a public health threat by 2030 as part of the Sustainable Development Goals. Since the first cases of HIV were reported more than 40 years ago, 88 million people have become infected with HIV and 42 million have died from AIDS-related illnesses. Since it started operations in 1996, UNAIDS has led and inspired global, regional, national and local leadership, innovation and partnership to ultimately consign HIV to history. UNAIDS is a problem-solver. It places people living with HIV and people affected by the virus at the decision-making table and at the centre of designing, delivering and monitoring the AIDS response. It charts paths for countries and communities to get on the Fast-Track to ending AIDS and is a bold advocate for addressing the legal and policy barriers to the AIDS response.

UNAIDS provides the strategic direction, advocacy, coordination and technical support needed to catalyze and connect leadership from governments, the private sector and communities to deliver life-saving HIV services. Without UNAIDS, there would be no strategic vision for the AIDS response.

In 2021, at the United Nations General Assembly on HIV, member states committed to a set of global targets that would set countries on the path to achieve the Sustainable Development Goal (SDG) of ending AIDS as a public health threat by 2030. These targets were to be reached by 2025.

In March 2024, the UNAIDS Executive Director established a Global Task Team of experts across government, civil society, donors, academic and public health institutes, to recommend a new set of global targets for the HIV response beyond 2025. These targets define what is required to reach the global goal of ending AIDS as a public health threat by 2030 and will be proposed for adoption by United Nations Member States at the 2026 United Nations High-Level Meeting on HIV/AIDS. Finalization of the recommended targets will be followed by the development of the next Global AIDS Strategy that will outline how these targets can be achieved.

GAVI, the Vaccine Alliance

Public-private partnership that increases access to immunization in low-income countries. Gavi has helped vaccinate over 800 million children since its inception in 2000 (Gavi, 2023). In 1999, the Global Alliance for Vaccines and Immunization (now Gavi, the Vaccine Alliance) was established. The Alliance consists of major players in global immunization, including WHO, other key UN agencies, leaders of the vaccine industry, government representatives and major foundations. Its role is to overcome barriers preventing millions of children from receiving vaccines. As part of its mission to save lives and protect people's health by increasing equitable and sustainable use of vaccines, Gavi has helped vaccinate more than 1.1 billion children in 78 lower-income countries, preventing more than 18.8 million future deaths. The Vaccine Alliance's mission is: to save lives and protect people's health by increasing equitable and sustainable use of vaccines.

Gavi also plays a key role in improving global health security by supporting health systems as well as funding global stockpiles for Ebola, cholera, meningococcal and yellow fever vaccines. After two decades of progress, Gavi is now focused on protecting the next generation, above all the zero-dose children who have not received even a single vaccine shot. The Vaccine Alliance employs innovative finance and the latest technology from drones to biometrics to save lives, prevent outbreaks before they can spread and help countries on the road to self-sufficiency.

Case Study 1: Gavi and Polio Eradication in Pakistan

Gavi, the Vaccine Alliance has championed overall polio eradication initiatives in Pakistan by supporting the re-establishment of the Global Polio Eradication Initiative (GPEI). Gavi has also offered financial and technical support in order to strengthen the routine immunization program and allow for immunization service introductions like the inactivated polio vaccination (IPV). The Gavi support has been instrumental for improved allocation as health budget financing and planning indicators for vaccination campaigns improved.

Elaboration

Gavi's Support:

Gavi has provided financial support for IPV procurement and IPV supply support for immunization efforts as well.

Synergy with Routine Immunization:

Gavi collaborates with Health Ministries to assist in integrating the delivery of polio vaccination with routine vaccination programs.

Global Collaboration:

Gavi collaborates with partners including UNICEF and WHO and the Government of Pakistan to work towards the eradication of polio, and other vaccine preventable diseases.

Addressing Challenges:

Gavi recognizes that there is a multitude of issues in Pakistan that contribute to lower vaccination coverage in certain areas, and we will be addressing these challenges with innovative methods and taking into account stakeholder concerns around security.

Impact

Gavi resources and funding has helped achieve some global decline in terms of the number of reported polio cases, and Pakistan has also been on a gradual trajectory to eradicate polio with only 1 child paralyzed by wild poliovirus in 2021, down from 306 in 2014.

Continued Commitment

Although Gavi continues to support the government of Pakistan's polio eradication efforts, it participates as part of the Polio Eradication Strategy 2022–2026 with a shared vision of a world without polio.

WFP (World Food Program)

WFP tackles hunger and malnutrition, both of which are critical determinants of health. WFP supports maternal and child nutrition programs and provides food aid in emergencies (WFP, 2023). The World Food Program is the largest humanitarian agency saving lives in emergencies and using assistance to help communities become self-sufficient and resilient to shocks It was established in 1961. In 1963, the first development project was launched in 1963 and in 2020 WFP was awarded the Nobel Peace Prize. It recognizes WFP's role in addressing food insecurity, improving conditions for peace and acting as a driving force to prevent the use of hunger as a weapon of war and conflict.

Powered by the passion, dedication and professionalism of 23,000 staff worldwide, the World Food Program (WFP) has a presence in over 120 countries and territories to carry out its mission. We bring life-saving food to people displaced by conflict and made destitute by disasters, and help individuals and communities find life-changing solutions to the multiple challenges they face in building better futures.

Their work is to enhance nutrition in women and children, support small holder farmers in improving productivity and reducing losses, help countries and communities prepare for and cope with climate-related shocks, and boost human capital through school feeding programs.

In conflict situations, we bring relief to exhausted populations and use food assistance to build pathways to peace and stability work for which WFP was awarded the Nobel Peace Prize in 2020.

UN Women

UN Women is the UN organization delivering programs, policies and standards that uphold women's human rights and ensure that every woman and girl lives up to her full potential.

For many years, the United Nations faced serious challenges in its efforts to promote gender equality globally, including inadequate funding and no single recognized driver to direct UN activities on gender equality issues. In July 2010, the United Nations General Assembly created UN Women, the United Nations Entity for Gender Equality and the Empowerment of Women, to address such challenges.

In doing so, UN Member States took an historic step in accelerating the Organization's goals on gender equality and the empowerment of women.

The creation of UN Women came about as part of the UN reform agenda, bringing together resources and mandates for greater impact. It merges and builds on the important work of four previously distinct parts of the UN system, which focused exclusively on gender equality and women's empowerment:

1) Division for the Advancement of Women (DAW),
2) International Research and Training Institute for the Advancement of Women (INSTRAW),
3) Office of the Special Adviser on Gender Issues and Advancement of Women (OSAGI),
4) United Nations Development Fund for Women (UNIFEM)

UN Women supports UN Member States as they set global standards for achieving gender equality and works with governments and civil society to design laws, policies, programmes and services needed to ensure that the standards are effectively implemented and truly benefit women and girls worldwide. It works globally to make the vision of the Sustainable Development Goals a reality for women and girls and stands behind women's equal participation in all aspects of life, focusing on four strategic priorities:

1) Women lead, participate in and benefit equally from governance systems
2) Women have income security, decent work and economic autonomy
3) All women and girls live a life free from all forms of violence
4) Women and girls contribute to and have greater influence in building sustainable peace and resilience, and benefit equally from the prevention of natural disasters and conflicts and humanitarian action

UN Women also coordinates and promotes the UN system's work in advancing gender equality, and in all deliberations and agreements linked to the 2030 Agenda. The entity works to position gender equality as fundamental to the Sustainable Development Goals, and a more inclusive world.

Over many decades, the United Nations has made significant progress in advancing gender equality, including through landmark agreements such as the Beijing Declaration and Platform for Action and the Convention on the Elimination of All Forms of Discrimination against Women (CEDAW).

Working for the empowerment and rights of women and girls globally, UN Women's main roles are:

- To support inter-governmental bodies, such as the Commission on the Status of Women, in their formulation of policies, global standards and norms.
- To help Member States implement these standards, standing ready to provide suitable technical and financial support to those countries that request it, and to forge effective partnerships with civil society.
- To lead and coordinate the UN system's work on gender equality, as well as promote accountability, including through regular monitoring of system-wide progress.

World Bank Group

A major financier of global health programs. The World Bank provides loans, grants, and technical assistance to support health system reforms, infrastructure development, and health financing mechanisms (World Bank, 2023).

Health is a fundamental human right essential for societal progress, yet millions worldwide face financial hardship from out-of-pocket healthcare costs. In low- and middle-income countries, these payments often force households to choose between healthcare and basic necessities, delaying treatment, worsening health outcomes, and risking impoverishment. The lack of comprehensive healthcare financing systems and affordable services further exacerbates this challenge. The World Bank's mission is to end extreme poverty and boost shared prosperity on a livable planet.

The World Bank Group works in every major area of development and provides a wide array of financial products, technical assistance and hence, helps countries share and apply innovative knowledge and solutions to tackle today's intertwined development challenges. The World Bank has funded over 15,000 development projects via traditional loans, interest-free credits, and grants.

Protection for the Poorest

Social safety nets, such as cash transfers, pensions or public works programs, are essential for improving the livelihoods of people in developing countries, particularly in the face of risks from systemic shocks. The World Bank Group is committed to improving health outcomes, responding to epidemics and other emergencies, and providing the full range of preventive, curative or palliative services, aiming to strengthen human capital and allow people to reach their full potential.

Improving Health Service Delivery

The World Bank Group is working to ensure that all individuals can access quality healthcare services without financial hardship by helping countries better understand, measure, and address the drivers of out-of-pocket payments. This in turn helps countries strengthen healthcare systems by improving service quality, establishing effective care pathways, and emphasizing preventive and promotive services. Additionally, the WBG helps leverage private sector innovation and capital to lower healthcare costs. However, a lack of reliable data presents a challenge as achieving financial protection in health requires continuous assessment, feedback loops, and adjustments rather than one-off policy reform.

Many countries are on an unsustainable debt path due to weak domestic revenue generation and reliance on costly external borrowing. Following recent crises, increased government spending has not been matched by efforts to mobilize revenue or rein in expenditures, causing debt levels to surge. The World Bank Group helps countries strengthen their fiscal and debt management, by conducting broad fiscal analyses, enhancing debt transparency, providing technical assistance on tax administration and debt management, and delivering training and tools so governments can better evaluate the fiscal impact of policies. However, implementing reforms requires sustained efforts, especially as many emerging markets and developing economies face global macroeconomic pressures beyond their control. Rising interest rates have increased the cost of debt servicing for these countries while also leading investors to move money out of riskier investments. This has raised financing costs for all borrowers, making multilateral financing increasingly vital.

IDA

With IDA's help, hundreds of millions of people have escaped poverty through the creation of jobs, access to clean water, schools, roads, nutrition, electricity, and more.

IFC

A member of the World Bank Group is the largest global development institution focused on the private sector in emerging markets. We work in more than 100 countries, using our capital, expertise, and influence to create markets and opportunities in developing countries. In fiscal year 2024, IFC committed a record $56 billion to private companies and financial institutions in developing countries, leveraging private sector solutions and mobilizing private capital to create a world free of poverty on a livable planet.

MIGA

Support governments in attracting private sector investments for infrastructure, health care, education, and other development priorities. The platform is your single point of contact in collaborating on how guarantees can be coupled with your existing products to support developing countries in addressing an unparalleled set of overlapping global crises companies invest in emerging markets and developing economies with confidence by mitigating political and commercial risks. The platform is your point of contact for all World Bank Group guarantee options.

ICSID

International Centre for settlement of disputes

IOM International Organization for Migration

Established in 1951, IOM is part of the United Nations System and stands as the leading intergovernmental organization in the field of migration.

With 175 member states, a further 8 states holding observer status and offices in 172 countries, IOM is dedicated to promoting humane and orderly migration for the benefit of all. It does so by providing support to migrants across the world, developing effective responses to the shifting dynamics of migration and providing advice on migration policy and practice.

The organization collaborates with governmental, intergovernmental and non-governmental partners to improve the resilience of people on the move, particularly those in situations of vulnerability. It also works closely with governments to manage all forms of mobility, and their impacts. This work includes operations in some of the most complex emergency settings in the world.

The IOM Constitution recognizes the link between migration and economic, social and cultural development, as well as to the right of freedom of movement.

IOM's work is focused on the following three objectives:

1) **Saving lives and protecting people on the move**: To fulfill this objective, IOM puts the safety, dignity and protection of people first in the most challenging crisis response contexts in the world.

2)**Driving solutions to displacement**: In response to this aim, IOM endeavors to reduce the risks and impacts of climate change, environmental degradation, conflict and instability for communities affected by or at risk of displacement.

3)**Facilitating pathways for regular migration**: To address this pursuit, IOM prioritizes whole-of-government, whole-of-society approaches to safely connect people, goods, services, knowledge and innovation.

Comparative Evaluations Among Organizations

Multilateral health organizations vary in their mandates, operational models, geographic scope, and strategic priorities. A comparative evaluation highlights both complementarities and overlaps, enabling better coordination and role clarity in global health governance.

WHO's normative authority is complemented by UNICEF's strong logistics and advocacy capacity, while GAVI and the Global Fund bring financing power and vertical programming. Regionally, PAHO and Africa CDC contextualize global policies and strengthen regional health systems.

Regional and Global Trend Analyses

Global health trends increasingly reflect complex interlinkages among climate change, pandemics, conflict, migration, and chronic disease burdens. Multilateral organizations must adapt to these evolving patterns.

Global Trends

- **Pandemic Preparedness and Response:** COVID-19 exposed systemic fragilities, prompting WHO to develop the Pandemic Accord and expand its Health Emergencies Programme [WHO, 2023].
- **Shift Toward Universal Health Coverage (UHC):** WHO and World Bank report slow but steady global progress toward UHC goals, with significant gaps in financing and service quality [WHO & World Bank Global Monitoring Report, 2023].
- **Climate and Health Nexus:** UNICEF, UNEP, and WHO are increasingly integrating climate risk into maternal and child health strategies [WHO. COP28 Special Report on Climate Change and Health. 2023].

Regional Trends

- **Africa:** Africa CDC is championing health sovereignty, leading efforts on vaccine production, surveillance, and workforce development [Africa CDC, 2022].
- **South-East Asia:** WHO SEARO supports regional digital health strategies and cross-border outbreak containment [WHO South-East Asia. Regional Digital Health Strategy 2021–2025].

- **Americas:** PAHO is focused on noncommunicable disease control and health equity, driven by post-COVID recovery efforts [PAHO. Strategic Plan 2020–2025].

These trends reflect a growing shift from vertical, disease-specific programs to integrated, system-strengthening approaches. Multilateral organizations are evolving to meet the demands of a multipolar, climate-stressed, and demographically shifting world.

Evolution of Multilateral Health Organizations

Table 1. Conceptual framework: from norms to networks

Organization	Mandate	Key Strengths	Limitations
WHO	Normative guidance, health policy, emergencies	Global legitimacy, standard-setting, technical expertise	Underfunded core budget, slow reform pace [WHO, 2014]
UNICEF	Child and maternal health, immunization, nutrition	Field presence, supply delivery, equity-focused	Program dependence on donor trends [UNICEF, 2016]
GAVI	Vaccine access in LMICs	Public-private partnerships, rapid scale-up	Focus limited to vaccines [GAVI]
The Global Fund	Fight against AIDS, TB, Malaria	Results-based funding, civil society engagement	Disease-specific vertical programming [Global Fund, 2023]
PAHO	Health development in the Americas	Regional capacity-building, disease surveillance	Resource constraints, political interference [PAHO, 2020]
Africa CDC	Coordination of Africa's health responses	African ownership, outbreak response, training	Young institution, dependent on external funds [Africa CDC, 2022]

MULTILATERALISM AND THE SDGS: HEALTHY LIVES AND WELL-BEING FOR ALL

Alignment with SDG 3 and Interlinkages with Other Goals

Multilateralism plays a crucial role in achieving SDG 3 (Good Health and Well-being) by promoting collaboration and resource sharing among nations. SDG 3, in turn, is deeply interconnected with other SDGs, particularly those related to social, economic, and environmental dimensions. Effectively, progress on one SDG can positively impact others, and vice versa.

Alignment with SDG 3 and Interlinkages

SDG 3: Good Health and Well-being: The intention of this aim is to prevent disease and prevent premature death, as well to limit health risks. Linkages to the other SDGs:

Interlinkages with other SDGs

SDG 1 (No Poverty): Poverty creates health concern and threat to health, pollution and environmental degradation will limit SDG 3 progress.

SDG 2 (Zero Hunger): Food security and nutrition key elements of good health and wellbeing.

SDG 4 (Quality Education): Health outcomes are critical to learning and educational success.

SDG 5 (Gender Equality): Gender inequality will limit access to health care access and thereby women's health outcomes.

SDG 6 (Clean Water and Sanitation): Clean water and sanitation must be considered basic health needs.

SDG 8 (Decent Work and Economic Growth): Healthy workforce is basis for success and development.

SDG 13 (Climate Action): Climate change already has health risk and health impacts; it will be necessary to act across all SDGs.

Multilateralism's Role

Strengthening Collaboration

The World Health Organization (WHO) and the United Nations Development Program (UNDP) are international organizations which create opportunities to collectively learn from each other's successes and lessons in a manner which could enable faster traction across SDG 3 and in turn support global health.

Resource Mobilization

International organizations can collaborate on how to improve financial and technical support to support health programs/projects in developing countries.

Knowledge Sharing

There are several ways knowledge sharing can occur in connecting effective practice across countries that may allow for faster progress on SDG 3.

Monitoring and Evaluation

International organizations are involved in monitoring and evaluation of progress being made against SDG 3 targets and indicators. In summary, SDG 3, and all of the SDGs, are interconnected and mutually reinforcing. Multilateralism has a very important role to play in developing these interconnectedness, facilitating collaboration as is necessary, and speeding progress towards a sustainable and healthier future for all as envisioned by the WHO.

Importance of UHC (Universal Health Coverage)

Universal Health Coverage (UHC) represents multilateralism as it relates to global health priorities, sustainable development, and ultimately builds health systems in all countries. UHC builds sustainable health system development to enable everyone to access essential health services without cost and without suffering financial hardship. UHC is part of the Sustainable Development Goals (SDGs), as the broader aspects of health are connected to other international health commitments.

Elaboration

Global Health Goals:

Universal Health Coverage (UHC) is a unifying goal for global health and the health community to galvanize around the notion that every person, everywhere is able to access the health care they need, when they need it at little or no financial cost.

Sustainable Development:

Universal Health Coverage (UHC) relates to the Sustainable Development Goals (SDGs), and particularly SDG 3 (Good Health and Well-being), which is to ensure healthy lives and promote well-being for all people at all ages.

Strengthening Health Systems:

Achievement of UHC equate with strengthening health systems to build access to quality health services with the focus on primary health care, while reducing financial risk which has the co-benefit of contributing to health systems strengthening.

Multilateralism and Collaboration:

Achievement of UHC requires collaboration between countries, international agencies (the World Health Organization), and stakeholders to build commonality to share information and knowledge, share resources, and share best practices.

Benefits Beyond Health:

Achievement of UHC has health and actual physical health benefits, but has the same community social benefits such as economic benefits, improved social cohesion, and reduced poverty.

Financial Protection:

UHC aims to protect individuals and families from financial hardship due to healthcare costs, which is a major barrier to accessing care, especially in low- and middle-income countries.

THE SEVEN ACCELERATOR THEMES FOR HEALTH PROGRESS

Accelerator discussion frames have been developed to present the central role of accelerators in driving progress towards the health-related SDGs, opportunities and bottlenecks to closer coordination, roles of and implications for relevant organizations and initial frameworks for joint action. The accelerators are aimed toward identifying collectively shaped, country-relevant, concrete actions at global, regional and country level.

1) Sustainable health financing
2) Primary health care
3) Community and civil society engagement
4) Determinants of health
5) Research and development, innovation and access
6) Data and digital health
7) Innovative programming in fragile and vulnerable settings and for disease outbreak responses

Sustainable Health Financing

Sustainable health financing ensures long-term funding for healthcare, preventing catastrophic health-related costs and financial hardship for individuals and families.

It involves strategies like prepaid contributions, risk-sharing, and government support to build robust health systems.

Key Aspects of Sustainable Health Financing

i. **Risk Sharing:** Creating mechanisms to share financial risk across the population, protecting individuals from catastrophic health expenditures that could lead to poverty or financial ruin.
ii. **Social health insurance**, so that the financial costs can be allocated between a large part of the population
iii. **Government Support:** Providing a strong foundation of public financing and investing in the health system to ensure that it can effectively serve the population.
iv. **Universal Health Coverage (UHC):** Advancing towards UHC, which requires a well-funded, sustainable health financing system.
v. **Monitoring and Evaluation:** Strengthening the monitoring and evaluation of health financing, including development assistance and domestic financing flows, to improve efficiency and visibility.
vi. **Technical Assistance and Capacity Building:** Assisting countries with developing prioritized national health financing road maps and providing technical assistance to build capacity.
vii. **Engaging with Stakeholders:** Working with all manners of stakeholders, including, the private sector, civil society organisations, and international development partners, to achieve sustainable financing for healthcare.
viii. **Transparency and Accountability:** Increasing transparency and accountability in health financing to ensure that funds are used effectively and efficiently.

Examples of Sustainable Financing Strategies

1. **Social Health Insurance:** includes a contributory mechanism where individuals/ employers contribute to a fund which is used for healthcare coverage.
2. **Government Subsidies:** government funding for health specifically for the poor and for those unable to pay for insurance.
3. **Tax Revenue:** tax revenue or taxes are used as a main source of health system funding.
4. **Private Sector Involvement:** The role of the private sector in financing healthcare is through collaborations, or private insurance companies. These potential sources could help countries work toward sustainable and equitable health financing systems that enable access to effective and quality health services for all.

Primary Health Care (PHC) as a Foundation for UHC

Primary Health Care (PHC) is the basis on which Universal Health Coverage (UHC) can be achieved as it provides the first interface with health services, and ensures vulnerable populations get access to health services equitably. PHC aims to provide comprehensive, integrated, and accessible health services at a geographic community level, making it the most effective and efficient approach to achieving UHC.

Definition of PHC

PHC is the first level of contact within a healthcare system, acting as the entry point for individuals to access health services. It includes a range of services like health promotion, disease prevention, treatment, rehabilitation, and palliative care.

Significance UHC

PHC provides the necessary foundation for UHC by:

- Ensuring access to essential health services for all, regardless of socioeconomic status or location.
- Strengthening health systems by focusing on building capacity at the primary care level, including workforce development and resource allocation.
- Promoting a people-centered approach to healthcare, empowering individuals and communities to participate in their health and well-being.

How Does PHC Contribute to UHC?

- Through the policy reform of health systems towards PHC, countries can increase access to essential quality health services, mitigate health inequities, and decrease health service costs.
- Investment in PHC has an impact on health improvements for groups facing the greatest barriers to access, such as vulnerable populations in rural locations or in marginalized communities.
- Strengthening PHC can also help to create more flexible and responsive health systems that can respond well to health emergencies in terms of public health threats.
- WHO is involved in supporting countries to strengthen PHC through initiatives such as PHC4UHC mission, with emphasis on the development of a PHC oriented model of care to accompany rollout of UHC.

- The primary care oriented model of care being piloted in Islamabad and Charsadda is piloting the implementation of a comprehensive UHC benefit package while showcasing how this model can be scaled nationally in Pakistan.

Principles of PHC for UHC

- **Accessibility:** Making health services available for all persons in every location and socio-economic status.
- **Equity:** Reducing health inequities, addressing the needs of marginalized populations, and ensuring equitable access to essential health services for all.
- **Integration:** Delivering comprehensive, integrated, health services for physical and mental health and the social determinants of health.
- **Participation:** Empowering individual and community participation in health and wellbeing by encouraging self-care and community-based solutions.
- **Multisectoral approach:** Recognizing that health is influenced by a number of determinants, and that different sectors must collaborate to achieve UHC goals.

Community and Civil Society Engagement

Sustainable health financing guarantees ongoing funding for enhancing the health care system, offering protection against catastrophic health expenses and financial problems for families and individuals. It encompasses ideas like prepayment, sharing of risks involved, assistance from governments, and it is an essential aspect of future-proofing our health care systems.

Social and Environmental Determinants of Health

Social and Environmental Determinants of Health are the "non-medical" factors that provide the majority of health-producing outcomes that an individual receives. They encapsulate different aspects of people's lives that are unconcerned about their medical care, and will impact the conditions in which someone lives and dies, as well as health and well-being as a whole. Non-medical factors are numerous, such as: person's socioeconomic status, education level, housing, food security, and physical environment.

Social Determinants of Health

- **Socioeconomic Status:** Although it differs from health determinants, income, working conditions, and/or social class aligns with good health outcomes, in general, income, social status, and other aspects help determine good health.
- **Education:** Access to quality education and learning opportunities can empower individuals to make informed decisions about their health and improve their overall well-being.
- **Housing:** Safe and stable housing is crucial for health, as inadequate housing can lead to various health problems.
- **Food Security:** Access to nutritious and affordable food is essential for good health, and food insecurity can have significant negative impacts on individuals' health.
- **Social Support:** Strong social networks and community connections can buffer against stress and promote positive health outcomes.
- **Healthcare Access:** The availability of timely access to good quality, reasonably priced health care services to assist with prevention and/or treatment of illness is critical for optimal health, and without this, health inequities can emerge.
- **Transportation:** Access to reliable and affordable transportation can impact individuals' ability to access healthcare, work, and other essential services.
- **Social and Community Context:** Many aspects create social context, including, the relationships an individual can build, their ability to join or belong to communities, and understanding social cohesion can all impact individual health.

Environmental Determinants of Health

- **Physical Environment:** Safe and clean environments, including air and water quality, healthy workplaces, and safe communities, are essential for good health.
- **Built Environment:** The design and layout of buildings and communities can influence physical activity levels, access to healthy food, and overall health.
- **Climate Change:** Climate change can exacerbate environmental hazards, such as air pollution and water scarcity, leading to various health problems.
- **Pollution:** Exposure to pollutants, such as air and water pollution, can have significant negative impacts on health.

- **Food and Environment:** The production and distribution of food, as well as the environment in which it is grown, can influence health through food security, food safety, and nutrition

Climate Change and Health: Urgency for Multisectoral Response

Climate change is no longer a future risk—it is a present and intensifying health emergency. From rising vector-borne diseases to food insecurity and heat-related mortality, its impacts are multidimensional and disproportionally affect vulnerable populations in low- and middle-income countries (LMICs).

Multilateral organizations such as WHO, UNICEF, and UNEP have begun integrating climate concerns into health programming. WHO's "COP28 Special Report on Climate Change and Health" underscored the need for climate-resilient health systems and called for stronger alignment between environmental and health governance frameworks [WHO. COP28 Special Report on Climate Change and Health. 2023]. UNICEF, through its Children's Climate Risk Index, has revealed that over 1 billion children are at "extremely high risk" of climate impacts, necessitating urgent investments in water, sanitation, nutrition, and mental health [UNICEF, 2021].

However, efforts remain fragmented. Cross-sectoral collaboration with urban planning, agriculture, disaster risk management, and energy sectors is essential. Programs like the Alliance for Transformative Action on Climate and Health (ATACH) aim to bridge these gaps but require expanded funding and institutional commitment [WHO, 2023].

Migration and Health: The Overlooked Crisis in Global Health Governance

The rising incidence of forced displacement around the world has continued to increase to more than 110 million people and is leading to novel health vulnerabilities and systemic pressures both on transit and destination (or host) countries [UNHCR, 2023]. Migrants and refugees are particularly susceptible to inequitable access to healthcare, discrimination in healthcare, and exposure to communicable diseases associated with overcrowded housing and shelter conditions. WHO's Global Action Plan on Promoting the Health of Refugees and Migrants (2019-2023) provides opportunities and actions towards coherent, inclusive policies, mobile health approaches, and culturally informed healthcare policies that countries can employ to address the health needs of migrants and refugees [WHO. GLOBAL ACTION PLAN, 2019-2023].

Member states have different levels of political will and temporal constraints that have caused them to implement some of WHO's global call statements but have not adapted them to acknowledge the practical conditions on the ground facing refugees and migrants. Coordination between multilateral organizations has been insufficient within the domains of vaccine passports and global coordinate plans to address COVID-19.

UNICEFF has lead child- based programming in displacement locations while UNHCR provides emergency relief to migratory shocks or emergencies. Health, housing, legal protection, and education across sectors and context have not mobilized under any coherent integration framework where population or individual wellbeing were a precondition of providing a coherent support system. Gaining governance for integrated care and or collaborative approaches to improving health and social capitals in the International Organization for Migration (IOM) is imperative, but IOM has yet to determine a decisive governance role and or positive interrelationship with WHO stakeholders [IOM, 2022]

Embracing Cross-Sectoral Integration

The intersectionality between climate change and migration and health outcomes suggests a need to adopt non-silo policy mechanisms, policy coherence, and a global cross-sectoral governance framework. Multilateral organizations can lead the sectoral approaches and processes that leverage their normative, operational, and convening expertise and resources to facilitate coherent enhancements to improve wellbeing opportunities. Future approaches should emphasize:

- **Policy coherence** across health, environment, labor, and humanitarian sectors.
- **Integrated data systems** that track overlapping vulnerabilities.
- **Joint funding mechanisms** to support multi-dimensional interventions.

Without addressing these urgent and interconnected issues holistically, global health progress will remain uneven and vulnerable to systemic shocks.

Research, Development, Innovation, and Access

Research, Development, Innovation, and Access (RDIA), is a cyclic continuum whereby each phase leads to the next phase culminating in the last phase back to the first phase of the cycle. The RDIA cycle is important in the advancement of work in several areas such as, technology, business, and public policy.

Research: The first step, or stage, is to adequately investigate it to seek new knowledge or understanding.

Development: This is to take what is obtained from research and develop or design or implement it into a new product, processes, or services.

Innovation: This is to implement (i.e., market in a sense) new ideas, processes, and/or products, often utilizing previous research and development.

Access: This is principally making clear that everyone can access those innovative products, processes, and/or services that can be put to use by those in need of the services, thus increasing equity and amplifying the take-up.

Examples

Scientific Research:

Basic research into areas such as medicine can result in new drugs, therapies or medical practices, and improved access to healthcare, and the health benefits that come with it.

Business Innovation:

The R&D (Research and Development) in business can translate into new products, improved production processes, enhanced experiences for customers, and greater market innovations and access to those innovations.

Public Policy:

Research can lead to new policies and regulation and subsequently innovation in infrastructure, environment, and social programs with greater access to those public channels of advancement.

Key Considerations

Funding:

Research and development typically require significant financial commitment from both the public sector and private sector.

Intellectual Property:

Patents and trademarks are mechanisms of protecting efforts for innovation encouraging more R&D is made in the public interest and society benefits.

Collaboration:

Collaboration among researchers, developers, and innovators is a requirement for the development and successful implementation of any potential innovation.

Accessibility:

Increased access to any innovations is desirable for everyone, but especially for those that would lead to social and economic growth, advancement, and equality.

Data and Digital Health Transformation

Digital health transformation is the process of using data and digital technologies for the enhancement of health delivery processes and improved patient outcomes. Digital health transformation also involves a number of usages/dimensions. i.e. telehealth, artificial intelligence (AI) and digital health platforms developed which provide opportunities for improved accessibility, efficiency, and effectiveness of health care systems. The World Health Organization (WHO) and organizations, like Capgemini, are placing effort on digital health transformation initiatives, as well as further the global health agenda. Key aspects of digital and data health transformation:

- **Data-driven decision making:**

AI and machine-learning tools can analyze large data sets quickly and predict possible patient outcomes, tailor the treatment and care plan, and optimize allocated resources in the health care system.

- **Enhanced accessibility:**

Telemedicine and mobile health apps eliminate geographical boundaries to provide rural, distant, or neglected populations with health care.

- **Improved patient experience:**

Digital health patient tools give patients more agency with their own health by allowing them to monitor their own progress and connect with their health care providers.

- **Increased efficiency:**

Digital health solutions can support efficiency by reducing administrative burden, reducing paperwork, and reducing communication barriers for health systems.

- **Data privacy and security:**

Data governance frameworks and accountable systems for storing data are important steps to protect patient data and provide for responsible use of data.

- **Policy and regulatory frameworks:**

A strong policy framework and a clear regulatory pathway for acquisition and deployment are important to ensure adoption of digital health technologies.

A few examples of digital health applications:

1) **Telemedicine**: enabling patients to receive treatment, consultation, and monitoring over video, mobile app, and wearable devices.
2) **AI used on diagnosing and treating patients**: for early detection of diseases, drug discovery, and individualized medicine.
3) **Wearable Technologies**: Wearable technologies used to track a user's exercise, sleep, and other health measures in order to provide insights for patient-centered care.
4) **EHRs are secure, accessible digital records** enabling information to be exchanged among caregivers.
5) **Public health surveillance**: Used to surveil disease outbreaks and health trends, to take action through the use of digital data.

Innovation in Fragile and Vulnerable Settings

Dealing with the sophisticated difficulties faced by frail and Conflicted areas, refugee camps, and other places with resource scarcity all define vulnerable environments. Using scientific breakthroughs, creative funding models, and local involvement, these areas can get more resilience and sustainable progress.

Specific Areas Where Creativity is Transforming

- **Resilient Food Systems:** Systems for food, land, and water in vulnerable areas tackling problems including displacement, conflict, and climate change.
- **Humanitarian Financing:** creative funding methods including Humanitarian Innovative Financing (HIF) helps to open bigger and More sustainable sources of finance to meet long-run needs in weak environs.
- **Quality of Care:** enhancing fragile healthcare A multifaced approach, including engaging settings, is needed. The World Health Organization says that patients, families, and communities as well as tackling problems including accessibility to infrastructure and clinical care. WHO, organizational (WHO).

- **Data Collection:** Innovative data gathering techniques are vital for knowing the particular needs and vulnerabilities of people in A SpringerLink report claims that fragile environments.
- **Climate Change Adaptation:** Changing fragile environments demands creative solutions, including targeted climate funding for the requirements of these areas.

Essential factors to be considered in fragile settings for innovation:

Context-Specific Solutions: Innovations have to be modified for the particular context of the weak scene given its particular problems and weaknesses.

Community Engagement: Including local communities in the development and execution of inventions is vital to guarantee their success and longevity.

Collaboration and Partnerships: Good innovation demands cooperation among several parties: partnerships and collaboration Several parties—including humanitarian organizations, governments, research institutes, and private sector players.

Sustainability: Over time, inventions should be created to be sustainable. tackling not only current demands but also aiding in longrun growth.

Learning and Adaptation: Continuous learning and adaptation are critical to guarantee learning and adaptation. that in ever-changing, fragile surroundings, inventions stay pertinent and successful.

Limitations in Funding and Donor Exhaustion

Early in 2025, the worldwide aid network was shaken when the United States government (USG) declared an executive order that abruptly reduced or stopped most of USAID's operations. In Total, it is estimated that USG has cut $60 billion in foreign assistance, and much uncertainty around the future of the US's foreign assistance remains.

Formerly the world's largest donor, in 2024 the US had contributed nearly 30% of total aid from Development Assistance Committee (DAC) countries. This rupture sent shockwaves through the humanitarian and development sectors, creating an immediate funding gap that is affecting both international and local actors. Many international non-governmental organizations (INGOs) have been hit hard, losing major funding agreements and seeing large-scale programs halted or frozen overnight. Some have been forced to scale back operations in multiple countries, shut down regional and country offices, and pause planned expansions. But the ripple effects don't stop there. Local and national organizations - many of which rely on INGOs as their main donors and partners - were (and still are) also facing severe challenges. INGOs had projects terminated overnight, staff laid off, and critical services like healthcare, education, and protection disrupted. The most serious impact, however, is on the communities those organizations served. Millions of people have already lost access to essential support and millions more will lose services as the full effects of the cuts are felt.

The United States is not the only donor reducing aid, even if their cuts are the most staggering and abrupt. Almost all Global North donors have already announced reductions to their 2025 budgets, with some forecasting further decreases over the coming years. Data now shows that humanitarian funding from Western governments began declining in 2024.

The international organizations are trying to maintain financial sustainability while continuing to deliver aid effectively to vulnerable populations. To address this funding gap, organizations can adopt alternative financing models and maximize impact through the following approaches:

- Promote localization – strengthen local non-governmental organizations (NGOs), community-based organizations (CBOs), and small and medium enterprises (SMEs) to take the lead in aid delivery. This reduces costs while ensuring a community-driven approach to meet the needs of vulnerable people.
- Support social enterprises – encourage business models that generate revenue and reinvest profits into essential services such as healthcare, WASH, and education.
- Minimize operational costs – shift the role of international NGOs towards the capacity-building of local actors, enabling them to efficiently implement programs on the ground.
- Enhance collaboration – establish joint country programs among international organizations to reduce costs and improve effectiveness through networking and policy advocacy.
- Diversifying revenue streams through service delivery fees, public-private partnerships, and institutional fundraising can further reduce reliance on diminishing donor contributions.
- International organizations can also reduce spending on non-essential services such as workshops and foreign trips and opt for virtual meetings instead, without spending money on travelling and accommodation
- Funds can also be raised by harnessing remittances from the diaspora communities so that they can sponsor NGO activities in their own countries.
- By leveraging innovation in ICT and fintech, and expanding geographically and thematically, organizations can navigate the funding shifts and thrive in today's evolving aid landscape

INGOs can sustain their mission, optimize resources, and create long-term impact serving vulnerable communities despite the funding challenges by embracing these strategies.

Strengthening South-South Cooperation

Developing nations working together on many topics like knowledgesharing, economic partnerships, and capacity building will help to strengthen SouthSouth Cooperation (SSC). reach shared objectives. This approach is regarded as a method by which one can exploit the particular needs and Global South encounters that encourage solidarity and collective self-dependence. SSC Addresses the particular problems faced by developing nations in fields like climate change, sustainable development, and reduction in poverty.

Important parts of building SSC:

- **Knowledge sharing and capacity building:**

Developing nations might gain knowledge from one another's triumphs and lessons. Enhancing their skills in several fields.

- **Economic partnerships:**

Working together on trade, investment, and economic integration can generate fresh opportunities and bolster regional economies.

- **Addressing global challenges:**

Dealing with common problems like climate change can be greatly aided by SSC. health crises and poverty.

- **South-South-Triangular Cooperation:**

Including a Northern partner to assist SouthSouth projects can tap into resources and knowledge, so amplifying the effect of such efforts.

- **Policy and advocacy:**

SSC can enhance the shared voice of the Global South in global forums, thereby advancing their interests and priorities.

Examples of SSC Initiatives:

- **Climate change adaptation:**

SouthSouth Collaboration can promote the knowledge and technology sharing for climate resilience.

- **Agricultural development:**

To raise food security, developing countries can disseminate proven agricultural techniques and inventions.

- **Health initiatives:**

Through knowledge sharing and, SSC may assist with worldwide health issues. cooperative research.

- **Technology transfer:**

From one another, developing nations may acquire knowledge of technical developments and fit them to their unique needs.

Benefits of Strengthening SSC:

- **Increased self-reliance:**

SSC helps developing countries discover their own answers and increase their capacity.

- **Enhanced collective bargaining power:**

Working together, developing nations can carry greater weight on the international stage. discussions.

- **More effective development outcomes:**

Often more affordable, SSC helps development considerably.

- **Greater equity and inclusion:**

SSC can promote more equitable and inclusive development by addressing the specific needs of the Global South.

Geopolitical Influence in Global Health: The Role of Non-Western Alliances

Multilateral health interventions are not insulated from geopolitics. While Western donors have historically shaped global health priorities through organizations like WHO, GAVI, and The Global Fund, non-Western alliances—such as BRICS, ASEAN, and the Shanghai Cooperation Organization (SCO)—are increasingly asserting influence.

BRICS and Alternative Global Health Diplomacy

The BRICS countries (Brazil, Russia, India, China, South Africa) have actively promoted South-South cooperation as an alternative to Western-dominated aid paradigms. China, for example, has established bilateral medical aid programs in Africa, often bypassing traditional multilateral channels. These efforts emphasize infrastructure, biotechnology transfer, and non-interference, contrasting with the more conditional funding models of Western donors [*Glob Health Gov.*, 2008].

> *"China's approach to global health emphasizes bilateralism and capacity-building, often through infrastructural investment rather than normative frameworks." [Glob Health Gov., 2017]*

India's pharmaceutical diplomacy—providing affordable generics and vaccines during COVID-19—also challenged the dominance of Western pharma and COVAX-led distributions [*J Asian Afr Stud.*, 2022].

However, critics argue that such geopolitical initiatives are strategic rather than altruistic, serving diplomatic visibility and economic interests.

> *"Non-Western health diplomacy often mirrors the strategic motives of the West, albeit through different rhetoric." [Glob Public Health, 2012]*

Public–Private Partnerships (PPPs): Promise and Pitfalls

Public–Private Partnerships have become a cornerstone of multilateral global health efforts, especially for financing innovation, accelerating access, and strengthening delivery systems. However, they raise critical concerns about transparency, accountability, and equity.

Successful Case Example: GAVI Alliance

GAVI—the Global Alliance for Vaccines and Immunization—is widely cited as a successful PPP involving WHO, UNICEF, the World Bank, Bill & Melinda Gates Foundation, and private vaccine manufacturers.

- It helped immunize over 888 million children between 2000 and 2023 [GAVI, 2023].
- Leveraged advance market commitments to lower vaccine prices and stimulate production.

"GAVI represents a hybrid governance model that mobilizes resources and leverages market mechanisms to achieve public health objectives." [Glob Public Health, 2014]

Critique: Power Asymmetries and Corporate Influence

However, PPPs can reinforce power asymmetries by embedding corporate interests into public decision-making:

- The Bill & Melinda Gates Foundation, though non-state, is one of WHO's top funders—raising concerns about agenda-setting skewed toward technological fixes over structural determinants of health [Health Policy Plan, 2009].
- There is often a lack of transparency in how private actors influence procurement, pricing, and evaluation processes.

"The increasing role of private foundations in global health threatens to erode democratic oversight and public accountability." [Glob Soc Policy, 2012]

Additionally, small or local pharmaceutical firms in LMICs are often excluded from these partnerships, undermining domestic innovation ecosystems.

Policy Implication: Toward Equitable Governance

To address these issues, scholars recommend:

- Establishing conflict-of-interest frameworks in PPPs (especially for WHO)
- Enhancing LMIC representation in PPP governance boards
- Conducting independent evaluations of health PPPs beyond output metrics

"Accountable PPPs should integrate civic voices, especially from the global South, to rebalance current governance asymmetries." (Buse & Walt, 2000) [Bull World Health Organ., 2000]

CONCLUSION AND KEY TAKEAWAYS

Recap of Multilateral Organizations' Vital Roles

Multilateral organizations face ongoing challenges and must adapt to a changing world. The way forward for these organizations involves strengthening their effectiveness, addressing emerging issues, and adapting to new realities. This includes enhancing public diplomacy, strengthening multilateral participation, and restructuring their constitutive and functional aspects to accommodate new actors and reengage with ideals that have become everyday life.

A more comprehensive view of the way forward is presented here:

Enhance Effectiveness and Adaptability

- **Strengthen Multilateral Participation:**

Multilateral institutions have to guarantee member states' enthusiastic participation, regular representation and engagement in discussions pertinent to their interests.

- **Restructure and Adapt:**

Organizations must modify their approach to account for the shifting worldwide scene. layouts and features to fit fresh actors and problems. This could Revisit the ideas guiding their work here.

- **Address Emerging Issues:**

Organizations should be aggressive in spotting and resolving new problems including climate change, sustainable development, and human preservation rights.

- **Enhance Public Diplomacy:**

Creating a complete public diplomacy plan will enable groups Encourage knowledge, develop relationships, and express their message.

- **Promote Peace and Security:**

Prevention and resolution of conflicts depend critically on multilateral institutions. upholding international law and advancing peace and security.

- Integrated, equity-focused, and accountable global health governance

Advancing health equity depends on developing strong local government systems to encourage equity-oriented management in all industries. Formalization of systems that allow cooperation among governmental agencies, civil society, and people in vulnerable situations is the aim of this central area, therefore guaranteeing that judgments satisfy the linked needs of many communities. This field of research helps to foster open, clear responsibility by giving equity top importance. Inclusive governance mechanisms that empower local players to guide change are accountable. properly.

- Urgency of collective action to meet 2030 SDG targets

Collective action to meet the Sustainable Development Goals (SDGs) by 2030 is urgently needed because time is running out, progress is lagging behind, and the challenges are interconnected, requiring a coordinated global effort to address issues like poverty, inequality, climate change, and health disparities across all countries. Here's why urgent action is crucial:

- **Time is limited:**

With only a few years left until 2030, the window to achieve the SDGs is narrowing significantly.

- **Progress is stalling:**

Despite progress made, many countries are not on track to achieve the SDGs by 2030, particularly in areas like poverty reduction, gender equality, and climate action.

- **Interconnectedness of the goals:**

The SDGs are linked, so progress on one objective depends on progress on others. Fighting climate change (SDG 13), for instance, is vital for general sustainable development.

- **Global challenges:**

The planet is beset with major difficulties including the COVID19 epidemic, war, economic crises and climate change, which further impede advancement toward the SDGs.

- **Need for collective action:**

To solve these problems well, every player including governments should consider: Businesses, civil society, and global organizations must cooperate in a systematic and concerted manner. Try adding the response options in your search to get a more useful explanation for multiple choice questions.

Ways ahead to guarantee no one is left behind

Nations must prioritize social equality and inclusiveness to make sure no one is left behind. making sure that women, minorities, and disabled people among other vulnerable groups, have chances and resources available to everyone. This entails tackling prejudice, inequality and the underlying reasons of exclusion via focused policies and projects.

Key Pathways Forward

1. Identify and Address Marginalized Groups:

One essential first step, considering factors like poverty, lack of access to healthcare and education, and prejudice, is to clarify who is left behind and why.

2. Implement Inclusive Policies and Programs:

Create plans and policies targeting the particular needs of underprivileged communities. guaranteeing availability to basic services including social security, education, and healthcare.

3. Promote Gender Equality:

A fundamental development objective, gender equality calls for empowering women and girls to advance general inclusion and progress.

4. Strengthen Social Safety Nets:

Develop robust social safety nets to shield weak people and families from financial upheavals and guarantee a minimum quality of life.

5. Promote Inclusive Economic Growth:

Concentrate on people-centered economic changes like those involving digital investing. change and opening doors for small enterprises especially in neglected regions.

6. Address Root Causes of Inequality:

Tackle discrimination and injustice at their root, which entails correcting attitudes that are hostile. stigmas and stereotyping.

7. Engage with Civil Society and Communities:

Include communities in the development project planning and execution to: Make certain their needs are met and their voices are heard.

8. Monitor and Evaluate Progress:

Regularly check and assess the development of LNOB projects to find areas needing development and guarantee responsibility.

By using these techniques, nations will be able to create a more inclusive and just society in which everyone has equal opportunity to flourish and benefit from the benefits of development.

REFERENCES

Africa C. D. C. (2022). Framework for Public Health Workforce Development. Available from: https://africacdc.org

Buse, K., & Walt, G. (2000). Global public–private partnerships: Part I – a new development in health? *Bulletin of the World Health Organization*, *78*(4), 549–561. PMID: 10885184

GAVI. (2020). The COVAX Facility. Available from: https://www.gavi.org/covax-facility

GAVI. (2023). Impact Report 2023. Available from: https://www.gavi.org

GAVI. About Gavi. Available from: https://www.gavi.org/our-alliance/about

Global Fund. (2023). Results Report 2023. Available from: https://www.theglobalfund.org

IOM. Migration Health Annual Report 2022. Available from: https://www.iom.int

PAHO. (2020). Strategic Plan 2020–2025. Available from: https://www.paho.org/en/documents/strategic-plan

WHO South-East Asia. Regional Digital Health Strategy 2021–2025.

UNHCR. (2023). Global Trends: Forced Displacement in 2023.

UNICEF. (2021). The Climate Crisis Is a Child Rights Crisis: Introduction to the Children's Climate Risk Index.

UNICEF. (2023). Annual Report 2023. Available from: https://www.unicef.org/reports/annual-report-2023

UNICEF. Transparency Portal. Available from: https://open.unicef.org

UNICEF. Strategy for Health 2016–2030. Available from: https://www.unicef.org/documents/health-strategy-2016-2030

WHO. (2023). Strengthening WHO preparedness for and response to health emergencies. Executive Board Report;

WHO. (2023). COP28 Special Report on Climate Change and Health.

WHO. (2023). COP28 Special Report on Climate Change and Health.

WHO. Alliance for Transformative Action on Climate and Health (ATACH). Available from: https://www.who.int/initiatives/atach

WHO. Promoting the Health of Refugees and Migrants: Global Action Plan 2019–2023.

WHO & World Bank. (2023). Tracking Universal Health Coverage: 2023 Global Monitoring Report.

Chapter 2
Universal Health Coverage:
Progress Toward Achieving Universal Health Coverage and Lessons Learned

Muhammad Arshed
https://orcid.org/0009-0005-0683-9610
Baqai Medical University, Pakistan

Abdul Kabeer Kazi
https://orcid.org/0000-0001-9860-2891
Baqai Medical University, Pakistan

Waseela Ashraf
https://orcid.org/0000-0002-2236-8581
University of Europe for Applied Sciences, UAE

Mehwish Kiran
Baqai Medical University, Pakistan

ABSTRACT

Universal Health Coverage (UHC) aims to ensure that all individuals have access to essential healthcare services without financial hardship. While significant progress has been made globally, challenges such as funding gaps, healthcare disparities, and infrastructure limitations hinder its full implementation. The objective of this chapter is to analyze the progress, challenges, and lessons learned in achieving UHC while proposing strategies for overcoming existing barriers. To achieve this, a comprehensive approach was adopted, including a review of policy frameworks,

DOI: 10.4018/979-8-3373-1992-6.ch002

quantitative analysis of healthcare access metrics, and case studies from countries with successful UHC models. This chapter contributes by providing a comparative analysis of UHC implementation across different healthcare systems, identifying effective policy interventions, and recommending scalable strategies for overcoming financial and infrastructural barriers. This also integrates real-world case studies and quantitative evaluations to offer actionable insights.

INTRODUCTION

Definition and Concept of Universal Health Coverage (UHC)

Universal Health Coverage (UHC) is a foundational principle of global health equity. It ensures all individuals and communities receive the health services they need, ranging from health promotion to prevention, treatment, rehabilitation, and palliative care, without suffering financial hardship. The concept is deeply rooted in the human right to health and serves as a key objective in achieving sustainable development goals (World Health Organization, 2022a). UHC does not imply free healthcare for all, but rather equitable access to essential, high-quality services that are financially accessible and provided through a well-functioning health system.

Globally, UHC has gained traction as a guiding framework for health system reforms. It requires robust health financing mechanisms that promote risk pooling and prepayment, while minimizing out-of-pocket expenses that disproportionately affect vulnerable populations (Ifeagwu et al., 2021). Importantly, the COVID-19 pandemic underscored systemic inequities and reignited the global urgency to invest in resilient health systems that can withstand shocks while maintaining core services (Verguet et al., 2021).

Efforts toward UHC must also address the broader determinants of health and ensure inclusivity across regions, particularly in low- and middle-income countries where access gaps are more pronounced. Oral health, mental health, and non-communicable diseases, often overlooked, must be fully integrated into UHC agendas (World Health Organization, 2022b). Ultimately, UHC is not just about coverage, it is about care that is available, affordable, and acceptable to all, irrespective of socioeconomic status, geography, or background.

Historical Evolution of UHC

The journey of Universal Health Coverage (UHC) is one of progressive realization, rooted in human rights, shaped by global crises, and driven by shifting public expectations. Its origins trace back to the post-World War II era, when the devastating consequences of inequality and poor access to healthcare inspired nations to envision health as a public good. The establishment of the World Health Organization (WHO) in 1948 marked a turning point, embedding the right to health in international discourse and laying the foundation for UHC (World Health Organization, 2022a).

The concept gained further traction in the 1978 Alma-Ata Declaration, which underscored primary healthcare as central to achieving “Health for All.” However, global commitment wavered during the 1980s and 1990s amid structural adjustment programs and privatization trends, particularly in low-income countries. The early 2000s saw a revival, spurred by mounting evidence on health disparities and the rise of global health initiatives (Ranabhat et al., 2023).

In 2012, the United Nations officially endorsed UHC as a global development goal, which later became enshrined in the Sustainable Development Goals (SDG 3.8). Since then, UHC has evolved into a multidimensional framework encompassing financial protection, service coverage, and equity (World Health Organization, 2022b).

Today, UHC is no longer an abstract ideal; it is a political commitment and a practical imperative. The WHO now promotes a competency-based framework to strengthen health systems and workforce capacities to make UHC not only a promise, but a lived reality for future generations (World Health Organization, 2022b).

UHC in the Context of the Sustainable Development Goals (SDG 3.8)

Universal Health Coverage (UHC) has emerged not just as a healthcare ideal, but as a cornerstone of the global development agenda, anchored firmly in Sustainable Development Goal 3.8 (SDG 3.8). This specific target under SDG 3 seeks to “achieve universal health coverage, including financial risk protection, access to quality essential healthcare services, and access to safe, effective, quality, and affordable essential medicines and vaccines for all.” It signals a global promise: health without impoverishment, care without exclusion.

Introduced in the 2015 United Nations 2030 Agenda, SDG 3.8 redefined health as a fundamental enabler of economic stability, gender equality, and social inclusion (Kipo-Sunyehzi, 2024). The COVID-19 pandemic, however, stress-tested this vision, exposing vulnerabilities in health systems and underscoring the urgency to accelerate UHC efforts, particularly in the domains of non-communicable disease control and health financing (Takian et al., 2022).

UHC under SDG 3.8 is not just about expanding insurance schemes; it demands integrated policies, robust health workforces, and equitable service delivery. The World Health Organization has reinforced this through global competency frameworks and policy guidance designed to help countries monitor progress and build resilient systems (World Health Organization, 2022a, 2022b).

As we advance toward 2030, SDG 3.8 serves as both a benchmark and moral imperative, urging nations to transform health promises into measurable outcomes, ensuring that no one is left behind in the pursuit of wellbeing.

Conceptual Frameworks for UHC

Achieving UHC requires a clear conceptual framework to analyze complex dimensions of health systems. The UHC Cube and WHO Health System Building Blocks are two widely recognized models that can provide essential guide for understanding and comparing UHC progress across different countries (World Health Organization, 2010; Kutzin, 2013). The UHC cube is a simple but powerful tool that captures the following three core dimensions of UHC:

- Population coverage: Who is covered?
- Service coverage: Which health services are included?
- Financial Protection: What proportion of the costs are covered, and to what extent are individuals protected from financial hardship?

This framework highlights the trade-offs and challenges inherent in expanding UHC, such as reaching marginalized groups, including a wider range of essential services, and ensuring no one faces catastrophic health spending. It serves as a reference point through this chapter to assess how different countries approach the expansion of coverage along these three axes. Whereas the WHO Health System Building Blocks framework (Harrington & Voehl, 2016) further dissect the complex machinery that underpins health system, identifying six key components:

- Service Delivery
- Health workforce
- Health Information Systems
- Access to Essential Medicines and Technologies
- Health Financing
- Leadership and Governance

By exploring case studies, reforms, and challenges to these building blocks, we will systematically analyze how progress toward UHC depends on strengthening the entire system.

THE PROMISE OF UNIVERSAL HEALTH COVERAGE

Equity and Social Justice

At its core, Universal Health Coverage (UHC) embodies a commitment to equity and social justice. It challenges the notion that access to healthcare should depend on one's ability to pay or social standing. In practical terms, this means designing systems where vulnerable populations, rural communities, women, minorities, and the poor, receive the same quality of care as urban elites (Sakas, 2024). Without this moral compass, UHC becomes a hollow promise.

Equity in health is not just a goal; it is a process of actively identifying and dismantling barriers. For instance, Rwanda's community-based health insurance scheme has achieved remarkable inclusion of the poor by tiering premiums based on income (Kipo-Sunyehzi, 2024). However, global realities differ; market-driven reforms often dilute social justice in favor of efficiency, especially in the Global South, where donor influence can shift priorities away from local equity needs (Prince, 2024). Across diverse contexts, certain groups remain persistently underserved, even within countries committed to UHC. Identifying these groups and targeting their unique barriers is essential for translating equity from principle into practice. Table 1 summarizes key populations at risk of exclusion and practical "last-mile" strategies to reach them.

Table 1. Groups at risk of exclusion and "last-mile" solutions for universal health coverage

Group at Risk of Exclusion	Key Barriers	Effective "Last-Mile" Solutions	Examples/References
Rural populations	Geographic isolation, few health facilities, transport costs	Mobile health clinics, community health workers, outreach visits	India, Ethiopia, Kenya, Brazil (Braniff & Hanouch, 2018; Macinko & Harris, 2015; Wang et al., 2016)
Migrants and refugees	Language barriers, lack of legal status, discrimination	Interpreter services, legal aid clinics, mobile outreach teams	UNHCR, Bangladesh Rohingya clinics(United Nations, 2019)
Persons with disabilities	Physical inaccessibility, lack of trained staff, stigma	Disability-friendly clinics, targeted outreach, CHWs	Afghanistan (Trani et al., 2011)

continued on following page

Table 1. Continued

Group at Risk of Exclusion	Key Barriers	Effective "Last-Mile" Solutions	Examples/References
Poor/low-income groups	Out-of-pocket costs, informal employment, lack of insurance	Subsidized insurance, cash transfers, community-based financing	Rwanda, Thailand, Pakistan SSP (Tangcharoensathien et al., 2018)
Ethnic minorities/ indigenous peoples	Cultural barriers, remote locations, mistrust	Culturally tailored services, hiring local CHWs, mobile units	Brazil (Macinko & Harris, 2015)
Urban slum dwellers	Overcrowding, poor infrastructure, lack of formal registration	Slum outreach programs, mobile clinics, pop-up health camps	Kenya, India (Park et al., 2022)
Women and children	Gender discrimination, transport, financial dependency	Maternal health outreach, vouchers, CHW home visits	Brazil, Ethiopia, Pakistan LHWs (Douthwaite & Ward, 2005)
Elderly	Limited mobility, chronic conditions, social isolation	Home-based care, telemedicine, mobile screening units	Thailand, Brazil, global PHC (Kruk et al., 2018)

Implementing these targeted strategies is critical, as COVID-19 pandemic spotlighted these disparities. In high-income nations, vaccines were swiftly distributed, while low-income countries faced fatal delays, demonstrating how equity cannot be assumed in global health frameworks (Takian et al., 2022). Moreover, health equity is not a static concept. It evolves with social dynamics, requiring constant reflection and course correction (Loewenson, 2022).

True UHC cannot thrive in a system skewed toward market justice over human rights. Equitable UHC demands legal frameworks that guarantee protection for all, not just access, but fair access. Justice, in this context, is not an ideal; it's an operational necessity (Foster et al., 2025).

The Centrality of Primary Health Care (PHC)

PHC is the cornerstone of equitable and cost effective UHC. PHC brings essential services close to communities, emphasizing prevention, early intervention, and health promotion. This people centered-approach is important for addressing the diverse needs of different populations including those who were at most risk of exclusion (World Health Organization & UNICEF, 2018). For example, Brazil's Family Health strategy deploys multidisciplinary teams to provide comprehensive PHC services. The teams constitute doctors, nurses, and community health agents (3-4) and sometimes dentists, psychologists, or nutritionists to a specific geographic area and population (usually ~ 1,000 families) and helped in significant reduction in infant mortality and improved health equity in both urban and rural settings (Macinko & Harris, 2015). Similarly, Thailand strengthened its PHC and build a strong foundation for its Universal Coverage Scheme (UCS) by first investing in rural health centers and training health workers. When UCS was launched in 2001, it ensured that nearly the entire population could access health services, especially the poor in remote areas. Primary care became the first point of contact, helping people avoid unnecessary hospital visits. This approach improved health outcomes and protected families from high medical costs (Tangcharoensathien et al., 2018). These two examples showed guaranteed outcomes in if countries are investing in PHC. Countries can achieve better health outcomes, greater equity, and lower capita health spending compared to those with hospital-centric systems (Kruk et al., 2018).

Financial Risk Protection

One of the most compelling promises of Universal Health Coverage (UHC) is shielding individuals and families from catastrophic health expenditures. In many parts of the world, illness still triggers financial ruin, forcing families to choose between food and medicine or selling assets to afford treatment. UHC, when effectively implemented, breaks this cycle by ensuring that healthcare costs do not translate into poverty (Foster et al., 2025).

This protection goes beyond simply offering insurance, it requires thoughtful policy design and implementation. In South Africa, the National Health Insurance (NHI) framework seeks to pool risks and resources across the population, reducing out-of-pocket expenses and promoting equitable access (Kipo-Sunyehzi, 2024). However, success hinges on sustainability and inclusivity; schemes that neglect the informal sector or the unemployed often leave the most vulnerable exposed.

The pandemic further amplified the urgency of financial protection. In many countries, individuals delayed or skipped care due to costs, exacerbating preventable conditions and overwhelming health systems later (Takian et al., 2022). Moreover, out-of-pocket spending during COVID-19 highlighted structural inequities in countries without universal or subsidized care.

Global lessons reveal that integrating financial risk protection into UHC must address both supply- and demand-side barriers. Subsidies, smart benefit packages, and regulatory mechanisms are essential, but so is building trust in public systems (Jensen et al., 2022). Financial protection is not just an economic policy; it is a human right. Without it, UHC becomes exclusionary, undermining its foundational promise of care without hardship (Sakas, 2024).

Improving Health Outcomes and Well-being

Universal Health Coverage (UHC) is not just about expanding access, it is fundamentally about improving health outcomes and enhancing overall well-being. When people receive the care they need without delay, morbidity and mortality decline, quality of life increases, and societies become more resilient. UHC directly contributes to this by integrating preventive, curative, rehabilitative, and palliative care into a cohesive system (Takian et al., 2022).

Evidence from across the globe supports this. For instance, Ghana's National Health Insurance Scheme has increased utilization of maternal and child health services, reducing neonatal mortality and boosting early immunization rates (Kipo-Sunyehzi, 2024).

UHC also fosters long-term well-being by addressing non-medical determinants of health. Policies that extend coverage to mental health, chronic disease management, and oral care, often overlooked in traditional systems, demonstrate a commitment to holistic well-being (World Health Organization, 2022a). This broad spectrum approach is vital in ensuring not just survival, but flourishing lives.

COVID-19 reminded the world that fragmented health systems result in avoidable deaths, especially in marginalized communities. The failure to provide basic care led to surges in untreated conditions, mental health crises, and lower life expectancy in underserved populations (Takian et al., 2022).

Improved outcomes are not incidental, they are the deliberate result of inclusive, people-centered care. UHC, when effectively implemented, reduces disparities and nurtures healthier societies, where well-being is not a privilege but a public good (Jensen et al., 2022; Sakas, 2024).

Strengthening Health Systems

Universal Health Coverage (UHC) serves as both a goal and a catalyst for health system strengthening. By prioritizing equitable access, financial protection, and quality care, UHC demands the overhaul of fragmented infrastructures and inefficiencies that plague many healthcare systems, especially in low- and middle-income countries (Jensen et al., 2022). It calls for cohesive strategies that unify public health, clinical services, human resources, governance, and financing mechanisms.

In countries like Rwanda and Tanzania, the push for UHC has led to major investments in health worker training, digital health systems, and performance-based financing models (Kipo-Sunyehzi, 2024). These investments not only enhance service delivery but also build resilience, enabling systems to respond more effectively to public health emergencies, as evidenced during the COVID-19 pandemic (Takian et al., 2022).

A well-functioning UHC model depends on the reliability of its foundational pillars: supply chain management, health information systems, accountability frameworks, and primary care networks (Loewenson, 2022). These components must be integrated, adequately funded, and politically supported to ensure sustainable transformation.

UHC also demands a shift from disease-centered models to people-centered systems. This shift enables proactive health promotion, continuity of care, and community engagement, strengthening trust between populations and health institutions (Sakas, 2024). Importantly, it encourages intersectoral collaboration, linking healthcare with education, housing, and social services for comprehensive well-being.

Economic and Social Benefits

Universal Health Coverage (UHC) is not merely a health initiative; it is a strategic investment in a nation's economic and social development. By reducing the economic burden of out-of-pocket health expenses and increasing access to care, UHC enhances workforce productivity, lowers poverty rates, and fosters greater societal cohesion (Takian et al., 2022).

Healthy populations are more economically active. When individuals are not financially crippled by illness or excluded from care due to cost, they can contribute meaningfully to economic output. Countries that have implemented UHC frameworks, such as South Africa through its National Health Insurance, are observing long-term improvements in labor participation and reduced absenteeism due to preventable diseases (Kipo-Sunyehzi, 2024).

Moreover, UHC promotes social equity by reducing disparities in health access and outcomes. This fosters social stability, strengthens public trust in institutions, and mitigates the societal divisions that often accompany inequitable health systems (Prince, 2024).

The ripple effects extend further. UHC encourages innovation, regulatory reform, and intersectoral collaboration, creating an enabling environment for sustainable development. In doing so, it aligns health policy with broader economic strategies, creating a virtuous cycle of growth and well-being (Foster et al., 2025; Sakas, 2024).

KEY DIMENSIONS OF UHC

The following three subsections directly correspond to the core dimensions of the UHC Cube conceptual framework: population, services, financial protection. Structuring our analysis in this way enables a systematic assessment of both progress and persistent challenges, especially when comparing different country experiences.

Each dimension represents a unique axis of UHC expansion and highlights specific policy tradeoffs like reaching marginalized groups, ensuring comprehensive service inclusion, and preventing financial hardship due to health costs. To monitor these dimensions consistently at global and national levels, international agencies such as WHO and the World Bank use standardized indicators, including the UHC Service Coverage Index and measures of financial risk protection. These monitoring tools and their practical application are discussed in detail in section 4.

Population Coverage

Population coverage is a fundamental pillar of Universal Health Coverage (UHC), reflecting the proportion of individuals who have access to essential health services. Achieving comprehensive population coverage is crucial for ensuring equitable health outcomes across different demographics.

Pakistan

Pakistan faces significant challenges in expanding population coverage. As of 2023, approximately 50% of the population lacked access to essential health services, highlighting substantial disparities in healthcare accessibility (Arshed, Kiran, et al., 2025). The country's physician density stands at 1.1 per 1,000 population, below the global average of 1.7, indicating a shortage of healthcare professionals. Additionally, the UHC service coverage index for Pakistan was reported at 53.9 in 2023, showing gradual improvement from previous years but still indicating room for significant progress (NHSRC, 2024).

United States

In contrast, the United States has achieved higher levels of population coverage. In 2023, 92% of Americans had health insurance for all or part of the year, with private insurance covering 65.4% and public programs like Medicare and Medicaid covering 36.3%. Despite this high coverage rate, disparities persist, particularly among certain age groups and ethnic minorities. For instance, young adults aged 19 to 25 had the highest uninsured rate at 14.1%, and Hispanic adults experienced an uninsured rate of 23.6%, more than three times that of white adults (World Health Organization, 2024).

Table 2. Comparative overview

Country	Population Coverage (%)	Physician Density (per 1,000)	UHC Service Coverage Index (2023)
Pakistan	~50	1.1	53.9
United States	92	2.6	83.0 (Estimated)

Source: *(WHO, 2024; NHSRC, 2024)*

Service Coverage

Service coverage under Universal Health Coverage (UHC) measures the range and quality of health services that populations can access without financial hardship. It goes beyond mere insurance enrollment and assesses whether individuals actually receive needed care, from preventive services to rehabilitation (Takian et al., 2022).

Pakistan

Pakistan's service coverage has expanded modestly but still shows critical gaps. The UHC service coverage index, which reflects access to essential health services such as reproductive, maternal, newborn, and child health; infectious diseases; and non-communicable diseases, stood at 53.9 in 2023 (NHSRC, 2024). Immunization rates, a key service coverage indicator, have improved, 76% of children received full basic vaccinations in 2022, up from 66% in 2017 (UNICEF Pakistan). However, access to mental health, rehabilitation, and chronic disease management remains extremely limited, especially in rural areas.

Primary healthcare (PHC) in Pakistan, despite being crucial for UHC, suffers from underfunding, workforce shortages, and poor supply chain systems (Jaca et al., 2022). Only 45% of primary health facilities offer all basic services, reflecting a need for systemic reform (World Health Organization, 2024).

United States

The United States, although a high-income nation, presents a paradox. While the technical availability of services is high, affordability, administrative barriers, and inequities limit actual service coverage (Foster et al., 2025). In 2023, despite having world-class healthcare facilities, about 9.2% of Americans delayed or avoided medical care due to cost (CDC, 2025). Preventive services, such as cancer screenings and vaccinations, remain underutilized only 70% of eligible women received a mammogram in the last two years.

Moreover, rural America faces healthcare deserts, where fewer providers serve vast geographic areas. The U.S. also struggles with chronic disease management: 6 in 10 adults have at least one chronic disease, and 4 in 10 have two or more (CDC, 2025).

Table 3. Comparative overview

Country	Service Coverage Index (2023)	Key Service Gap
Pakistan	53.9	Mental health, rural chronic disease care
United States	83.0 (Estimated)	Cost barriers, rural healthcare deserts

Source: (CDC, 2025)

Service coverage requires more than infrastructure; it demands equitable access, high-quality service delivery, and the removal of systemic barriers, a lesson applicable globally (Kipo-Sunyehzi, 2024; Prince, 2024).

Financial Coverage

Financial coverage under Universal Health Coverage (UHC) ensures that individuals can access necessary healthcare services without suffering financial hardship. It is a fundamental dimension of UHC that directly links health to social protection and equity (Foster et al., 2025).

Pakistan

Pakistan faces serious challenges in achieving adequate financial protection. Out-of-pocket (OOP) health expenditure remains alarmingly high, comprising 58% of the total health expenditure as of 2022 (World Bank Data). Only about 3% of the population is covered under formal health insurance schemes, and catastrophic health expenditures push nearly 4 million Pakistanis into poverty every year (Endalamaw et al., 2022).

The Sehat Sahulat Program (SSP), a landmark initiative launched by the government, aims to improve financial coverage. As of late 2023, it expanded to cover over 40 million families nationwide (nhsrc.gov.pk). However, gaps remain in implementation, particularly in rural and underserved regions.

Moreover, public health spending remains critically low at just 1.2% of GDP, compared to the WHO's recommended 5% benchmark. Consequently, patients often rely on unregulated private providers, exposing them to variable quality and costs (Jaca et al., 2022).

United States

The United States spends approximately 17.3% of its GDP on healthcare, the highest among OECD countries (OECD Health Data 2024). Despite this, financial coverage gaps persist. Roughly 8.4% of the population remained uninsured in 2023, predominantly impacting minority groups and low-income individuals (cdc.gov) (OECD, 2022).

Underinsurance is another major issue. In 2023, about 23% of insured adults were considered underinsured, meaning their insurance did not adequately protect them from high out-of-pocket costs (Commonwealth Fund, 2024).

While programs like Medicaid and Medicare offer financial protection to specific groups, coverage varies widely by state, and administrative complexities deter full realization of UHC principles (Prince, 2024).

GLOBAL PROGRESS TOWARD UHC

Universal Health Coverage (UHC) has become a global priority, with international agencies, governments, and civil societies striving to close health gaps and guarantee equitable access to services. Despite notable achievements, disparities in progress remain significant, particularly between high-income countries and low- and middle-income countries (LMICs) (Endalamaw et al., 2022).

Indicators for Monitoring UHC

To systematically track UHC advancement, the World Health Organization (WHO) and World Bank have established a set of core indicators. These indicators assess two dimensions: (1) service coverage (essential health services delivered across population groups) and (2) financial protection (reduction in the financial burden due to healthcare costs) (WHO, 2024). The UHC Service Coverage Index (SCI), developed by WHO and the World Bank, is the principal tool to quantify progress. It ranges from 0 (worst) to 100 (best), summarizing coverage across four main health service areas.

- The service coverage indicators span several domains:
- Reproductive, maternal, newborn, and child health
- Infectious diseases (such as tuberculosis and HIV)

- Non-communicable diseases (NCDs) management

Financial protection indicators measure the proportion of the population facing catastrophic health expenditures, typically defined as spending more than 10% or 25% of household income on health (NHSRC, 2024). Monitoring these indicators is crucial for identifying gaps, evaluating interventions, and informing policy actions to achieve equitable health outcomes (Jensen et al., 2022). These measures are described in more detailing major reports by WHO and the World Bank, which form the backbone of global UHC tracking (World Health Organization, 2021).

WHO and World Bank UHC Service Coverage Index

The SCI and financial protection metrics together allow policymakers and researchers to monitor progress, compare between countries, and evaluate the impact of reforms on equity and access. As of 2023, the global average UHC SCI was 68 out of 100, with major regional and income-group disparities (WHO, 2024). High-income countries typically achieve SCI scores above 80, while many LMICs lag below 50 (NHSRC, 2024).

For example:

China has made remarkable improvements, increasing its SCI from 44 in 2003 to 79 in 2018, largely through robust investments in primary healthcare and social health insurance expansion(Zhou et al., 2022).

Sub-Saharan Africa remains the region with the lowest SCI, hindered by weak health systems, limited financing, and workforce shortages (Jaca et al., 2022).

In Pakistan, the SCI improved modestly from 42 in 2015 to 50 in 2022, indicating incremental progress but highlighting persistent systemic weaknesses (NHSRC, 2024).

Regional Trends and Variations

High-Income Countries

High-income countries such as Japan, Australia, and many European nations boast near-universal service coverage, underpinned by strong public financing, robust primary care networks, and effective social protection systems (Allen et al., 2023).

Middle-Income Countries

Middle-income countries exhibit mixed progress. China's near-universal insurance coverage contrasts sharply with countries like South Africa and Brazil, where service quality and equity challenges persist despite widespread insurance schemes (Jaca et al., 2022; Zhou et al., 2022).

Low-Income Countries

Low-income regions, particularly in sub-Saharan Africa and parts of South Asia, face entrenched barriers:

- Inadequate health workforce density
- Inconsistent availability of essential medicines
- Insufficient government health expenditure (Jaca et al., 2022)
- Socio-political instability affecting healthcare delivery

While donor-driven programs (e.g., Gavi, Global Fund) have improved access to specific services (e.g., immunization, HIV treatment), comprehensive UHC remains a distant goal.

UHC in Low- and Middle-Income Countries (LMICs)

Achieving UHC in LMICs necessitates overcoming deeply rooted structural and economic challenges. Many LMICs rely heavily on out-of-pocket payments, exposing households to catastrophic health expenditures and medical impoverishment (Endalamaw et al., 2022; Kaiser et al., 2023).

Key Challenges Include:

- **Health Financing Gaps.** Limited fiscal space to expand health insurance schemes to informal workers (Kaiser et al., 2023).
- **Health Workforce Shortages.** Inadequate distribution and training of healthcare professionals, particularly in rural areas (Koohpayehzadeh et al., 2021).
- **Infrastructure Deficits.** Poor health facility infrastructure, diagnostic capabilities, and pharmaceutical supply chains.
- **Policy Fragmentation.** Lack of coherent national strategies for UHC implementation.

However, successful LMIC examples offer valuable lessons:

- **Thailand's UHC program** drastically reduced catastrophic expenditures and improved service access through tax-financed universal schemes.
- **Rwanda** achieved over 90% health insurance coverage through community-based health insurance models (Koohpayehzadeh et al., 2021).

These examples underscore that political commitment, innovative financing, and primary care strengthening are critical to LMICs' UHC advancement (Allen et al., 2023).

Role of Public-Private Partnerships

Public-private partnerships (PPPs) are increasingly recognized as instrumental for accelerating progress toward UHC, particularly in resource-constrained environments.

Strategic Advantages of PPPs Include:

- Mobilizing private sector investments to supplement limited public resources
- Expanding service delivery networks into underserved areas
- Leveraging private sector expertise in technology, logistics, and management
- Enhancing innovation and efficiency in health systems (Koohpayehzadeh et al., 2021).

Countries like India (via Ayushman Bharat) and Kenya (through various PPP-based hospital management models) have successfully integrated PPPs into their UHC strategies, achieving expanded service coverage and improved patient outcomes.

Nonetheless, PPPs require:

- Strong governance and regulatory frameworks
- Clear alignment of public health goals with private sector incentives
- Continuous monitoring to ensure equity, quality, and accountability (Jensen et al., 2022)

When designed and managed effectively, PPPs can serve as a catalyst for achieving health equity and financial protection goals, especially in complex LMIC contexts (Allen et al., 2023).

Emerging Global Trends Affecting UHC

While monitoring frameworks capture key coverage and financial trends, a set of powerful global forces are reshaping the path to UHC:

- **Urban-Rural Divide:** Service access and health outcomes remain highly unequal between urban and rural populations in both high- and low-income countries. Rural residents often experience fewer facilities, staff shortages, and greater travel times, highlighting the need for innovative delivery models such as mobile clinics and telemedicine (World Health Organization & UNICEF, 2018).
- **Migration and Displacement:** Increasing migration, both internal (rural to urban) and international, as well as refugee flows, present major challenges for UHC—requiring flexible, inclusive policies to ensure coverage regardless of legal status or location (United Nations, 2019).
- **Aging Populations:** As life expectancy rises, more countries confront the twin pressures of chronic disease management and long-term care, which require shifting service models and financing approaches to sustain UHC (World Health Organization, 2015).
- **Climate Change:** Extreme weather, disease outbreaks, and environmental hazards are stressing health systems, creating new needs for resilience, surveillance, and adaptation in UHC planning (Romanello et al., 2021).
- **COVID-19 Pandemic:** The pandemic exposed both the vulnerabilities and strengths of health systems globally. It revealed critical gaps in surge capacity, health worker protection, and equitable service delivery. Yet, it also accelerated innovations—such as digital health, remote consultations, and flexible insurance schemes—that are now integral to UHC (World Health Organization, 2021).

Addressing these trends is essential for countries aiming to not only achieve, but also sustain and adapt UHC in a rapidly changing world.

CHALLENGES AND BARRIERS TO ACHIEVING UHC

While Universal Health Coverage (UHC) remains a global aspiration, its realization is hindered by numerous challenges. These barriers are deeply entrenched in political, financial, systemic, and societal domains, affecting progress unevenly across countries (WHO, 2024). Understanding these barriers is crucial for developing resilient and equitable health systems.

Political and Policy Constraints

Political instability, weak governance, and fragmented policy frameworks significantly obstruct UHC progress. In many countries, healthcare reform lacks sustained political will, often influenced by short-term electoral cycles rather than long-term public health goals (Allen et al., 2023). Frequent changes in leadership lead to inconsistent policy implementation, undermining the continuity required for UHC initiatives. Additionally, vested interests and lobbying by private healthcare stakeholders can skew policy priorities, leading to inequitable service models. In fragile or conflict-affected states, healthcare systems are often under-resourced and incapable of strategic planning or nationwide coverage (Endalamaw et al., 2022). Therefore, robust political commitment, evidence-based policymaking, and inclusive governance structures are indispensable for overcoming political and policy barriers to UHC.

Effective governance is key to overcoming political and policy barriers to UHC. Decentralization, as seen in countries like Brazil, Indonesia, and India, can make health systems more responsive and accountable—but only if strong oversight and capacity-building are in place to prevent new disparities (World Health Organization, 2011). Multisectoral partnerships, including collaboration between health, finance, and social sectors, enable coordinated action on health determinants and better resource mobilization. Building institutional capacity and ensuring transparent, inclusive decision-making are also critical for successful UHC reform (Greer et al., 2016).

Inadequate Financing and Out-of-Pocket Expenditures

Sustainable financing remains a cornerstone of UHC, yet many nations—especially LMICs—suffer from chronic underfunding of health systems. Public health expenditure often falls below the recommended 5% of GDP, leading to significant resource gaps (WHO, 2024). Consequently, health systems rely heavily on out-of-pocket (OOP) payments, exposing individuals and families to catastrophic financial risks. In many countries, OOP expenditures account for over 40% of total health spending, pushing millions into poverty annually (Jensen et al., 2022). High OOP costs deter timely healthcare seeking, exacerbating disease burdens and health inequities. Inadequate health financing also limits investments in infrastructure, technology, workforce development, and essential medicines, further weakening service delivery capacity. Expanding fiscal space for health, introducing progressive taxation, and strategically pooling resources are critical measures for achieving equitable, affordable healthcare access under UHC frameworks (Kaiser et al., 2023).

Health Workforce Shortages and Misdistribution

An effective health workforce is foundational to delivering essential services, yet severe shortages and uneven distribution of healthcare workers continue to undermine UHC. According to WHO (2024), there is a projected global shortfall of 10 million health workers by 2030, disproportionately affecting low-income countries. Rural and underserved areas suffer the most, with critical shortages of doctors, nurses, midwives, and allied health professionals (Koohpayehzadeh et al., 2021). Urban-centric workforce concentration results in substantial access barriers for rural and marginalized populations. Without addressing workforce planning, education, retention, and equitable distribution, achieving UHC will remain elusive. Strategic investments in health professional education, incentive-based rural deployment, continuous professional development, and ethical international recruitment practices are essential to build resilient and responsive health systems capable of delivering UHC.

Addressing workforce gaps requires more than just increasing numbers. Countries are increasingly using task-shifting—delegating certain clinical roles to nurses or community health workers—to extend coverage in underserved areas. Ethiopia's Health Extension Program and nurse-led clinics in Brazil and South Africa are proven examples (Macinko & Harris, 2015; Wang et al., 2016). Sustainable UHC depends on investments in workforce training, fair compensation, supportive supervision, and strong retention strategies, especially for rural postings.

Quality and Accountability Gaps

Expanding healthcare coverage without ensuring quality and accountability leads to ineffective and inequitable outcomes. Numerous studies reveal that poor-quality care is now a greater barrier to mortality reduction than insufficient access alone (Jensen et al., 2022). A focus solely on expanding coverage risks perpetuating a "quantity over quality" paradigm. Strengthening health system governance, enforcing clinical guidelines, enhancing health information systems, and fostering a culture of continuous quality improvement are critical steps toward ensuring that UHC efforts translate into meaningful health gains for populations (Allen et al., 2023). Equally important is building patient trust through respectful, culturally competent care and accountability mechanisms, ensuring that expanded coverage leads to real improvements in people's lives.

Inequities in Access and Health Outcomes

Despite national-level advances, profound disparities persist in healthcare access and outcomes across socioeconomic, geographic, gender, and ethnic lines. Marginalized populations—such as rural communities, indigenous groups, refugees, and informal sector workers—often face systemic exclusion from health services (Endalamaw et al., 2022). Social determinants of health, including poverty, education, housing, and discrimination, exacerbate these inequities. Urban residents generally enjoy better service availability and health outcomes compared to rural dwellers. Additionally, women and children in low-resource settings continue to experience disproportionately high mortality and morbidity rates due to inadequate maternal and child health services. Health interventions that do not explicitly address these social gradients risk reinforcing, rather than reducing, disparities. Achieving UHC requires embedding equity at the core of health policy design and implementation. This includes disaggregated data monitoring, targeted interventions for vulnerable groups, financial protection measures, and deliberate strategies to close the rural-urban and rich-poor gaps in health outcomes WHO (2024).

Social determinants such as poverty, education, housing, gender, and employment have a profound effect on health equity and UHC outcomes. For example, higher educational attainment especially among women is linked to better health-seeking behaviors and outcomes. Tackling these root causes requires coordinated action beyond the health sector, including social protection programs and inclusive public policies. Only by addressing these social determinants can UHC truly close gaps in access and health outcomes.

INNOVATIONS AND REFORMS TO ADVANCE UHC

Strategic Purchasing and Health Financing Reforms

Strategic purchasing reforms have emerged as pivotal innovations for advancing Universal Health Coverage (UHC). Strategic purchasing refers to the deliberate allocation of pooled funds to healthcare providers based on population needs, quality performance, and cost-effectiveness, rather than simply funding services (Verguet et al., 2021). In Sub-Saharan Africa, health financing reforms focusing on risk pooling and strategic purchasing, such as Rwanda's Mutuelles de Santé, have significantly expanded service access (Ifeagwu et al., 2021; Kipo-Sunyehzi, 2024). By shifting from input-based financing to output-based mechanisms, countries can incentivize efficiency, accountability, and equity. Reforms must ensure that funding prioritizes primary healthcare services, preventive interventions, and underserved populations (Bayarsaikhan et al., 2022). However, challenges such as weak regulatory frameworks, fragmented health insurance schemes, and political resistance often impede implementation (Odoch et al., 2023). Key insights reveal that countries adopting transparent contracting processes, robust monitoring systems, and citizen engagement mechanisms achieve better outcomes. Moving forward, embedding strategic purchasing within broader public financial management reforms remains crucial for sustaining UHC gains, particularly in low- and middle-income countries (Sparkes et al., 2021). Pakistan's UHC Service Coverage Index trajectory also emphasizes the need for continued financing reforms to improve quality and accessibility (NHSRC, 2024).

Leveraging Digital Health and Telemedicine

Digital health and telemedicine have redefined pathways to achieving UHC, particularly by addressing geographical, infrastructural, and workforce barriers (Arshed et al., 2024; Arshed, Mahmud, et al., 2023). Telemedicine platforms enable remote consultations, diagnosis, treatment, and follow-ups, significantly extending healthcare access to underserved areas. For example, Bangladesh's Portable Health Clinic demonstrated that telemedicine could effectively deliver preventive and primary care to remote populations (Islam-Maruf et al., 2021). The WHO Global Digital Health Strategy (2020) urges countries to invest in digital platforms, mobile health, and interoperable health information systems to bridge care gaps. Global models abound: India's eSanjeevani enables millions of remote consultations; Rwanda's Babyl platform integrates AI-powered triage and telemedicine into national PHC; and China's telehealth reforms have extended specialist access to rural populations.

COVID-19 further accelerated digital health adoption globally, highlighting its role in maintaining service continuity (Takian et al., 2022). However, digital divides—caused by poor internet infrastructure, digital illiteracy, and affordability issues—remain critical barriers (Upreti et al., 2024). Key insights suggest that equitable digital health strategies must prioritize data security, interoperability, user-centric design, and capacity-building for healthcare workers (Jensen et al., 2022). Successful models, such as China's integration of telehealth within its primary healthcare reforms, demonstrate how digital innovations can strengthen UHC (Zhou et al., 2022). Policy frameworks must also address licensing, reimbursement, and regulatory gaps to sustain the growth of telehealth ecosystems (Arshed et al., 2024). Ultimately, leveraging digital health innovations requires a balanced approach that combines technology deployment with strong governance and social inclusivity measures (Arshed, Zakar, et al., 2023; Arshed, Mahmud, et al., 2025). Robust governance, user-centric design, and ongoing health worker training are critical for ensuring digital innovations improve equity and service quality.

Community-Based Health Insurance and Social Protection Schemes

Community-Based Health Insurance (CBHI) and broader social protection schemes are vital instruments in advancing UHC, particularly among informal sector workers and rural communities. CBHI models pool resources at the community level, offering risk protection and improving healthcare affordability (Ifeagwu et al., 2021;

Kaiser et al., 2023). Rwanda's CBHI scheme, covering over 80% of its population, is a widely cited success story, reflecting how decentralized, community-managed programs can effectively contribute to UHC (Kipo-Sunyehzi, 2024). Social protection measures, including subsidized insurance and direct cash transfers, further enhance financial risk protection (Foster et al., 2025). However, challenges such as adverse selection, limited financial sustainability, and weak governance structures often threaten the long-term viability of CBHI schemes (Ranabhat et al., 2023). Key insights suggest that successful schemes ensure government subsidies for the poorest, effective integration with national health financing systems, and community participation in governance (Prince, 2024). To maximize impact, CBHI must be linked with broader national financing reforms, government subsidies for the poorest, and active community engagement—ensuring that no population is left behind as coverage expands. Well-designed schemes, like Rwanda's Mutuelles de Santé, demonstrate how inclusion and solidarity can be embedded in UHC reforms. Furthermore, international experiences emphasize that CBHI must not replace national health insurance efforts but should complement them in a harmonized framework (Bayarsaikhan et al., 2022).

Decentralization and Local Health Governance

Decentralization—transferring authority and resources from central governments to local authorities—has been recognized as a key reform for strengthening health systems and promoting UHC. Decentralized governance enables more responsive, culturally sensitive, and efficient healthcare delivery tailored to local population needs (Jaca et al., 2022; Loewenson, 2022). For instance, the Philippines' devolution of healthcare services to local government units facilitated improved access to primary care and maternal health services (Koohpayehzadeh et al., 2021). Decentralization enhances community ownership, accountability, and participatory decision-making—elements critical for achieving equity in health (Endalamaw et al., 2022). However, challenges include disparities in administrative capacity across regions, financial resource imbalances, and risks of local political interference (Ranabhat et al., 2023). Key insights indicate that decentralization must be accompanied by strong capacity-building, clear delineation of roles, adequate funding mechanisms, and transparent performance monitoring (Allen et al., 2023). Successful examples show that local governance innovations, such as community health councils and participatory budgeting processes, significantly improve service delivery quality and responsiveness (World Health Organization, 2022b). In the post-COVID-19 era, empowering local health systems with resources, autonomy, and accountability will be vital to achieving resilient, equitable UHC worldwide (Verguet et al., 2021).

Decentralization of health governance supports innovation by allowing local adaptation of services and greater responsiveness to community needs. Local authorities can pilot new service models, involve community councils in decision-making, and quickly scale effective solutions. This bottom-up approach fosters equity by directly addressing local determinants of health and empowering populations to demand quality and accountability. Successful reforms, such as participatory budgeting in Brazil or local health committees in Kenya, illustrate how decentralized systems when backed by strong national frameworks and adequate funding can drive both equity and innovation in the pursuit of UHC.

COUNTRY CASE STUDIES AND LESSONS LEARNED

Thailand: Health Security through Universal Coverage Scheme

This case illustrates: Financial risk protection, equity, and primary care innovation

Context

In the late 1990s, Thailand faced significant disparities in healthcare access, particularly among low-income and rural populations. Prior to reforms, around 30% of the population remained uninsured.

Intervention

In 2001, Thailand launched the Universal Coverage Scheme (UCS), famously known as the "30 Baht Scheme," where citizens paid only 30 Baht (~USD 0.70) per visit for medical services. Funded primarily through general taxation, the UCS targeted the uninsured population and aimed to eliminate financial barriers to health services (Verguet et al., 2021).

Outcomes

The UCS dramatically improved healthcare access, achieving over 98% population coverage by 2011. Catastrophic health spending fell sharply, and maternal and child mortality rates also declined. Public satisfaction with health services increased significantly, even in remote areas.

Lessons Learned

Thailand's success highlights the importance of political commitment, a tax-based financing model, and a focus on primary care strengthening. The scheme's equity-driven design helped reduce health inequalities nationwide. The case study has been extracted from the work of Verguet et al., (2021). Thailand faced significant healthcare disparities in the late 1990s, with around 30% of the population uninsured, particularly in rural and low-income areas. To address these gaps, Thailand launched the Universal Coverage Scheme (UCS) in 2001, known as the "30 Baht Scheme." This initiative allowed citizens to access medical services for a minimal fee of just 30 Baht (~USD 0.70) per visit. Funded primarily through general taxation, the UCS was specifically designed to target the uninsured population and eliminate financial barriers to healthcare (Verguet et al., 2021).

By 2011, the UCS had achieved remarkable success, extending coverage to over 98% of the population. It significantly reduced catastrophic health expenditures and contributed to declines in maternal and child mortality rates. Additionally, public satisfaction with healthcare services rose, even in remote regions. The UCS's success can be attributed to its political commitment, a tax-based financing model, and a focus on strengthening primary healthcare (Koohpayehzadeh et al., 2021). The equity-driven design of the UCS helped reduce health inequalities, ensuring that even the most marginalized populations had access to essential healthcare services (Jaca et al., 2022).

The case of Thailand demonstrates that universal health coverage can be effectively implemented in low- and middle-income countries through strong political will, inclusive financing mechanisms, and a commitment to primary care. These elements are critical in ensuring equitable healthcare access and improving population health outcomes (Kaiser et al., 2023; Verguet et al., 2021).

Rwanda: Community-Based Insurance and Equity

This case illustrates: Equity, community participation, and financial risk protection in low resource settings

Context

Post-genocide Rwanda in the 1990s suffered from devastated health infrastructure and extreme poverty. Health outcomes were among the poorest globally, with life expectancy barely reaching 40 years.

Intervention

Rwanda introduced Mutuelles de Santé, a community-based health insurance model, in 2003. The program required affordable annual premiums, adjusted for income levels, and government subsidies for the poorest (Kipo-Sunyehzi, 2024).

Outcomes

By 2010, insurance coverage reached over 90% of the population. Health service utilization rates soared, maternal mortality rates halved, and child immunization rates exceeded 90%. Financial protection improved markedly, with a sharp decline in catastrophic health expenditures.

Lessons Learned

Rwanda's experience shows that universal health coverage can be rapidly advanced even in low-resource settings through strong leadership, community participation, and cross-subsidization mechanisms.

The above case has been derived from the work of Kipo-Sunyehzi, (2024).

Rwanda's post-genocide recovery in the 1990s was marked by severe challenges in healthcare infrastructure and extreme poverty. At the time, health outcomes were among the poorest globally, with life expectancy barely reaching 40 years. To address these challenges, Rwanda introduced the Mutuelles de Santé program in 2003, a community-based health insurance model. This initiative required affordable annual premiums adjusted according to income levels, with government subsidies supporting the poorest households (Kipo-Sunyehzi, 2024).

By 2010, the program had achieved remarkable success, covering over 90% of the population. Health service utilization rates surged, maternal mortality rates were halved, and child immunization rates exceeded 90%. These improvements were accompanied by a significant reduction in catastrophic health expenditures, demonstrating enhanced financial protection for the population. Rwanda's model highlighted the critical role of strong leadership, community engagement, and cross-subsidization in achieving universal health coverage (UHC) even in a low-resource setting. The success of this initiative underscored the potential for rapid health improvements through strategic financing and inclusive policies (Kaiser et al., 2023).

The Rwandan case offers valuable lessons on the importance of local ownership, political will, and targeted financing mechanisms in expanding health coverage. It also emphasizes the need for continuous monitoring and adapting to local contexts to ensure sustainability and equity in UHC programs (Kipo-Sunyehzi, 2024; WHO, 2024).

Pakistan: Sehat Sahulat Program and Public Health Challenges

This case illustrates: Financial protection expansion, public-private partnership, and persistent equity/services quality challenges

Context

Pakistan has historically faced significant gaps in healthcare access, particularly among rural and low-income populations. Out-of-pocket expenditure accounts for over 60% of total health spending.

Intervention

The Sehat Sahulat Program (SSP), launched nationally in 2019, provides health insurance cards to eligible families, covering hospitalization costs up to PKR 1 million per year. The program primarily targets low-income households, with government funding and private hospital empanelment (NHSRC, 2024).

Outcomes

By 2023, millions of families were enrolled, with usage rates steadily increasing. However, issues related to quality assurance, fraud, and limited-service availability in rural areas persist. Public awareness and utilization in marginalized areas remain below expectations.

Lessons Learned

Pakistan's case shows that political will and targeted financing can rapidly expand financial protection, but parallel investments in service delivery capacity and monitoring systems are critical for success.

The NHSRC, (2024) report analyzes Pakistan's progress on the UHC Service Coverage Index, highlighting improvements and persistent health system challenges.

Pakistan has historically struggled with inequitable healthcare access, particularly for rural and low-income populations, exacerbated by high out-of-pocket (OOP) expenditures, which account for over 60% of health spending (NHSRC, 2024). In response, the government launched the Sehat Sahulat Program (SSP) nationally in 2019 to provide financial protection through health insurance cards, covering up to PKR 1 million annually per family. This initiative, targeting the poorest segments, marked a major policy shift aligning with broader global trends favoring universal health coverage (UHC) through strategic public-private partnerships (Atim et al., 2021).

By 2023, millions of families had enrolled, and service utilization steadily increased, demonstrating the program's success in expanding coverage (NHSRC, 2024). However, significant challenges remain. Issues such as limited hospital availability in rural areas, inconsistent service quality, fraud, and low public awareness in marginalized regions have constrained the program's full potential (Bayarsaikhan et al., 2022). The case of Pakistan reinforces global evidence that financial risk protection must be coupled with systemic investments in service delivery, infrastructure, and regulatory oversight to achieve meaningful health equity (Smithers & Waitzkin, 2022).

Moreover, Pakistan's experience aligns with concerns raised globally about the risks of health financing reforms being derailed without sustained political commitment and rigorous monitoring (Sparkes et al., 2021). Community engagement, capacity building, and strengthening primary care are critical for the SSP to evolve into a robust pillar for achieving UHC (Hossain et al., 2024; Odoch et al., 2023). Overall, Pakistan's model reflects both the promise and the complexities inherent in expanding health security under resource-constrained conditions.

Table 4. Comparative overview of UHC reforms: dimensions, challenges, and solutions

Country	Key Dimension(s)	Main Challenge Addressed	Core Innovation/Lesson
Thailand	Financial protection, Equity, Primary Care	Reducing out-of-pocket spending, rural/urban health gaps	Tax-based financing, universal scheme, PHC focus
Rwanda	Equity, Community Participation, Financial Protection	Access for the poor, system rebuilding post-conflict	Community-based insurance, subsidies, leadership
Pakistan	Financial Protection, Public-Private Partnerships, Service Quality	Inequitable access, rural-urban gaps	Targeted insurance, private sector engagement, need for quality/ awareness

These case studies collectively demonstrate that achieving UHC is possible across a variety of contexts by focusing on financial risk protection, health equity, and system innovation. Thailand's universal scheme leveraged tax-based financing and strong political commitment to close equity gaps. Rwanda showed how community participation and targeted subsidies can rapidly rebuild and expand health coverage even after crisis. Pakistan's experience reveals that rapid gains in financial protection must be matched with investments in service quality, awareness, and infrastructure especially for marginalized groups. Across all cases, success depended on adaptive policy design, robust governance, and a continuous focus on the core dimensions of the UHC Cube.

WAY FORWARD AND STRATEGIC RECOMMENDATIONS

Strengthening Governance and Political Commitment

Governance and political commitment are crucial to achieving Universal Health Coverage (UHC), as they lay the foundation for the necessary reforms and resource allocation. Governments must prioritize healthcare and demonstrate unwavering political will to ensure its accessibility for all citizens. Strong leadership ensures that UHC becomes an integral part of national health policies and is supported by legal frameworks and budgetary allocations.

For example, Rwanda has demonstrated outstanding political commitment in healthcare. The country's President, Paul Kagame, championed reforms that led to the successful implementation of a community-based health insurance scheme, covering 80% of the population. This initiative has significantly reduced out-of-pocket expenditures and improved health access. In contrast, countries like Nigeria have faced difficulties in achieving UHC due to inconsistent political support and unstable governance (Kipo-Sunyehzi, 2024).

Data from the World Health Organization (WHO) highlights that in 2023, countries with strong political commitment to health saw better progress in UHC coverage, particularly those in Sub-Saharan Africa, where coverage has increased by 18% over the last decade (WHO, 2024).

Ensuring Sustainable Financing and Investment

Sustainable financing is the backbone of UHC, ensuring that systems can provide equitable healthcare services without causing financial hardship for individuals. Public health financing models based on general taxation or social health insurance have proven successful in achieving UHC. According to the WHO, (2024), countries with high government investment in health, such as Sweden and Finland, boast some of the best health outcomes, with life expectancy exceeding 82 years.

In contrast, low-income countries often struggle with insufficient healthcare funding, leading to inequality in health service delivery. A sustainable financing model should focus on expanding public funds, improving tax collection systems, and exploring innovative financing mechanisms like micro-insurance and international aid (Kaiser et al., 2023). For instance, Thailand's "30 Baht Scheme" illustrates the power of low-cost contributions from citizens, enabling universal access to healthcare. This scheme has dramatically reduced financial barriers, covering over 98% of the population by 2011 (Verguet et al., 2021).

Countries like South Korea have utilized a single-payer system funded by taxes, which ensures equitable access for all citizens. Research by Takian et al., (2022) shows that countries that achieve UHC have a well-defined, diversified funding strategy.

Promoting Health Equity and Inclusive Policies

Promoting health equity is a central goal of UHC, ensuring that all individuals, regardless of their socio-economic status, geographic location, or gender, have access to quality healthcare services. Equity-driven policies must address the social determinants of health and seek to eliminate disparities in healthcare access. Countries like Cuba have exemplified the benefits of inclusive policies, where healthcare is universally accessible, irrespective of income.

Recent studies highlight that low-income and rural populations face the most significant barriers to healthcare, including financial constraints, lack of infrastructure, and cultural discrimination. According to the WHO, inequalities in healthcare access have worsened in many countries during the COVID-19 pandemic, exacerbating pre-existing disparities (Takian et al., 2022). A concerted effort is needed to target vulnerable populations, such as refugees, migrants, and informal workers, to ensure that they are not excluded from UHC initiatives.

Moreover, incorporating health equity into policy requires a multi-sectoral approach, involving collaboration between health and other sectors like education, social protection, and housing. For example, Kenya's UHC strategy integrates health policies with programs targeting poverty reduction and education, significantly improving health outcomes in marginalized communities (Kipo-Sunyehzi, 2024). By embedding equity into every aspect of healthcare policy, governments can ensure the inclusivity of UHC.

Data-Driven Decision-Making, Digital Transformation, and System Resilience

Digital health has become indispensable in the wake of COVID-19, accelerating the adoption of telemedicine, real-time data analytics, and remote care. Post-pandemic, countries must build on these gains by integrating digital tools into everyday health system operations, it is not only for efficiency but for equity and preparedness. For example, India's use of digital immunization tracking and Rwanda's real-time health data systems both enabled faster, targeted responses to outbreaks and routine care needs (Jaca et al., 2022).

The pandemic also exposed health system vulnerabilities, highlighting the need for adaptive and resilient infrastructures. Robust supply chains, surge capacity planning, and flexible service delivery models such as mobile clinics and telehealth are now essential elements for safeguarding health during crises and climate-related shocks. Building resilience must include investments in digital infrastructure, health workforce capacity, and multisectoral emergency preparedness (Romanello et al., 2021)

Table 5. Global digital health and resilience implementation

Country	Digital Health System	Impact
India	National Health Mission Data Tracking	Improved immunization and health access tracking
Rwanda	Digital health platforms for real-time medical data	Enhanced resource allocation, reduced healthcare costs
United States	Telemedicine expansion during COVID-19	Increased access to healthcare in rural areas, cost savings

Global Solidarity, Climate Adaptation and Learning from Success Stories

Achieving UHC requires global solidarity, cross-sectoral learning, and proactive adaptation to climate change, particularly in low- and middle-income countries (LMICs), where resources are limited, and the burden of disease is highest. Climate shocks including heatwaves, flooding, and disease outbreaks require health systems to build adaptive capacities, from early warning surveillance to climate-resilient infrastructure. International cooperation and learning from success stories are key to accelerating progress towards UHC. For instance, the success of Thailand's Universal Coverage Scheme, which achieved 98% population coverage by 2011, provides valuable lessons for other countries in the region (Verguet et al., 2021).

Similarly, Rwanda's community-based health insurance system has reduced out-of-pocket expenses and improved health outcomes, serving as a model for many African nations. The collaboration between South Africa and international donors has led to improved health financing, allowing the country to extend coverage to informal sector workers (Koohpayehzadeh et al., 2021). These success stories illustrate that with the right policy mix, UHC can be achieved even in resource-constrained settings.

Moreover, learning from global experiences is essential for adapting strategies to local contexts. Countries can utilize international frameworks like the WHO's UHC Service Coverage Index to assess their progress and identify areas for improvement (WHO, 2024). By fostering collaboration, sharing resources, and providing technical assistance, countries can accelerate their UHC goals and work towards universal access to quality healthcare for all.

Recommendation: Future Research and Monitoring

To ensure sustained progress toward UHC, countries must invest in continuous research, innovation, and robust monitoring systems. Future work should focus on:

- Evaluating the long-term impacts of digital health and telemedicine on equity
- Assessing the resilience of health systems to pandemics and climate shocks
- Improving data quality and indicator frameworks for real-time decision-making
- Studying cross-sectoral interventions that address the social determinants of health

Ongoing investment in research, transparent reporting, and international data sharing will be essential for adapting UHC strategies to evolving challenges and opportunities.

CONCLUSION

Reaffirming the Value of UHC

Universal Health Coverage (UHC) is foundational to equitable, sustainable health systems worldwide. By guaranteeing access to essential health services without financial hardship, UHC promotes social justice, reduces poverty, and upholds human dignity. The COVID-19 pandemic underscored the vital importance of robust, inclusive healthcare by reinforcing UHC's role in health security and crisis resilience (Takian et al., 2022). Country experiences, from Rwanda's community insurance to Thailand's universal scheme, demonstrate that political commitment, financial protection, and primary care innovation drive success (Kipo-Sunyehzi, 2024). Aligning UHC with the Sustainable Development Goals, especially SDG 3, further anchors its value as both a health and moral imperative.

Transforming Health Systems for Resilience and Inclusion

Achieving truly universal coverage requires resilient, inclusive, and adaptable health systems. The pandemic revealed the need for rapid emergency response, data-driven resource allocation, and sustained essential services, especially for marginalized groups (Koohpayehzadeh et al., 2021; Loewenson, 2022). Investment in digital health, workforce training, and infrastructure could combined with targeted policies to reach women, refugees, and people with disabilities. It also builds systems that can withstand future shocks. Examples from South Korea, New Zealand,

and Rwanda show the value of flexible, inclusive reforms supported by strong leadership and technology.

UHC as a Pathway to Health and Human Development

Universal Health Coverage is not only a pathway to improved health outcomes but also a driver of human development. Achieving UHC provides economic benefits, improves social equity, and enhances the well-being of individuals and communities. By reducing out-of-pocket expenditures on health, UHC ensures that families are not pushed into poverty due to medical costs, a major concern in many low-and-middle-income countries (LMICs) (Atim et al., 2021). Furthermore, UHC contributes to long-term economic growth by creating healthier, more productive populations. Evidence from countries like Thailand and Costa Rica demonstrates that expanding access to healthcare has a direct correlation with enhanced workforce productivity and overall economic performance (Foster et al., 2025).

However, the pathway to achieving UHC is complex and requires coordinated action across various sectors, including health, finance, education, and social protection. Successful UHC implementation must be underpinned by policies that integrate health with other social determinants, such as access to clean water, sanitation, and education, all of which contribute to better health outcomes (Bayarsaikhan et al., 2022). Furthermore, UHC is closely linked to human rights and social justice. It ensures that health services are not only available but also affordable and of high quality, thereby advancing human development and reducing inequality (Sakas, 2024).

As countries continue to move toward UHC, global cooperation and the sharing of best practices will be essential. The experiences of nations such as Japan, which has one of the longest life expectancies in the world due to its efficient and inclusive healthcare system, offer valuable lessons for low-resource settings (Kaiser et al., 2023). To achieve UHC and its related benefits, it is crucial that governments, international organizations, and the private sector work together to create a sustainable and inclusive healthcare model. This includes increasing domestic health financing, strengthening health systems, and fostering innovation in healthcare delivery (Loewenson, 2022).

Table 6. Comparative UHC performance in select countries

Country	UHC Coverage Index (UHC SCI)	Key UHC Strategies	Key Outcomes
Rwanda	87%	Community-based health insurance, mobile health tech	Reduced maternal mortality, high immunization rates
Thailand	95%	Universal health insurance, primary healthcare focus	Significant reduction in poverty due to healthcare costs
Brazil	90%	Public healthcare system (SUS), decentralized approach	Improved health equity and reduced healthcare disparities
Japan	100%	National Health Insurance, high quality primary care	Longest life expectancy globally, low healthcare costs

UHC is an essential component of global health policy, with profound implications for health outcomes and human development. The transition to UHC demands not only political will and strategic investment but also a collective commitment to health equity, resilience, and inclusion. Achieving UHC is a journey that requires the involvement of all sectors and stakeholders, with a shared focus on building a future where health services are accessible to all, regardless of economic status or geographic location. As demonstrated by successful global examples, UHC offers a sustainable pathway to enhanced health, economic stability, and human development for all.

Looking Forward: Adapting UHC for a Changing World

Looking ahead, sustaining and advancing UHC will require health systems to continuously adapt to major global shifts included demographic transitions, migration patterns, the health effects of climate change, and rapid technological innovation. Policymakers must embrace flexible strategies that build system resilience, address the needs of aging and mobile populations, and integrate climate adaptation into health planning. Harnessing digital health, fostering cross-sectoral partnerships, and investing in ongoing research and robust monitoring frameworks will be essential to ensure UHC remains inclusive, equitable, and responsive. Ultimately, the journey toward UHC is a dynamic, collective effort that requires political will, social solidarity, and innovative thinking to deliver health and human development for all, in every context.

REFERENCES

Allen, L. N., Pettigrew, L. M., Exley, J., Nugent, R., Balabanova, D., Villar-Uribe, M., Baatiema, L., Shubber, Z., Mugambi, J., Kidd, M., Zewdie, A., Padula, I., & Abimbola, S. (2023). The role of Primary Health Care, primary care and hospitals in advancing Universal Health Coverage. *BMJ Global Health*, *8*(12), 10–12. DOI: 10.1136/bmjgh-2023-014442 PMID: 38084496

Arshed, M., Kiran, M., Umer, M. F., Samkari, J. A., hassan, S. M., Qamer, S., Gillani, A. H., Hameed, S., Ashraf, W., Mujtaba, H., & Khan, M. N. (2025). Prevalence and associated factors of adherence to antihypertensive medication: A nationwide cross-sectional study. *BMC Public Health*, *25*(1), 2364. Advance online publication. DOI: 10.1186/s12889-025-21456-6 PMID: 40610935

Arshed, M., Mahmud, A. B., Minhat, H. S., Ying, L. P., & Umer, M. F. (2023). Effectiveness of mHealth Interventions in Medication Adherence among Patients with Cardiovascular Diseases: A Systematic Review. *Diseases (Basel, Switzerland)*, *11*(1), 41. Advance online publication. DOI: 10.3390/diseases11010041 PMID: 36975590

Arshed, M., Mahmud, A. B., Umer, M. F., Mashhadi, F., & Kawish, A. B. (2025). Study protocol for a randomized control trial investigating the effectiveness of a multifaceted mHealth approach on adherence to antihypertensive treatment among patients in Pakistan. *Pakistan Journal of Medical Sciences*, *41*(1), 22–28. DOI: 10.12669/pjms.41.1.9272 PMID: 39867791

Arshed, M., Umer, M. F., Kiran, M., Akhter, A. M., Gillani, A. H., Qamer, S., Kawish, A. B., Zofeen, S., Farid, A., & Khan, M. N. (2024). Prevalence and associated factors of non-adherence to antihyperlipidemic medication: A nationwide cross sectional survey in Pakistan. *Scientific Reports*, *14*(1), 20613. DOI: 10.1038/s41598-024-71120-z PMID: 39232055

Arshed, M., Zakar, R., Umer, M. F., Kiran, M., Ullah, N., Iftikhar, G., & Fischer, F. (2023). Efficacy of mHealth and education-led peer counseling for patients with hypertension and coronary artery disease in Pakistan: Study protocol for a double-blinded pragmatic randomized-controlled trial with factorial design. *Trials*, *24*(1), 448. DOI: 10.1186/s13063-023-07472-0 PMID: 37424031

Atim, C., Koduah, A., & Kwon, S. (2021). How and why do countries make Universal Health Care policies? Interplay of country and global factors. *Journal of Global Health*, *11*, 1–12. DOI: 10.7189/jogh.11.16003 PMID: 34912556

Bayarsaikhan, D., Tessier, L., & Ron, A. (2022). Universal Health Coverage and Social Health Protection: Policy relevance to health system financing reforms. *International Social Security Review, 75*(2), 75–95. https://doi.org/https://doi.org/10.1111/issr.12295. DOI: 10.1111/issr.12295

Braniff, L., & Hanouch, M. (2018, July 10). *Bringing Health Microinsurance to Kenyans via Mobile Phone | Blog | CGAP*. https://www.cgap.org/blog/bringing-health-microinsurance-to-kenyans-mobile-phone

CDC. (2025). *Chronic Disease*. https://www.cdc.gov/chronic-disease/index.html

Commonwealth Fund. (2024). *Underinsurance is a growing problem in US healthcare*. https://www.emarketer.com/content/underinsurance-growing-problem-us-healthcare

Douthwaite, M., & Ward, P. (2005). Increasing Contraceptive Use in Rural Pakistan: An Evaluation of the Lady Health Worker Programme. *Health Policy and Planning, 20*(2), 117–123. DOI: 10.1093/heapol/czi014 PMID: 15746220

Endalamaw, A., Gilks, C. F., Ambaw, F., & Assefa, Y. (2022). Universality of universal health coverage: A scoping review. *PLoS ONE, 17*(8 August), 1–15. DOI: 10.1371/journal.pone.0269507

Foster, N. D., Benjamin, K., Parwani, P., & Perehudoff, K. (2025). Universal Health Coverage and Social Protection: Evolution and Future Opportunities for Global Health Law and Equity. *The Journal of Law, Medicine & Ethics, 1–5*(S1), 35–39. Advance online publication. DOI: 10.1017/jme.2025.3 PMID: 40237133

Greer, S. L., Wismar, M., & Figueras, J. (2016). *Edited by Strengthening Health System Governance Better policies, stronger performance*. European Observatory on Health Systems and Policies Series.

Harrington, H. J., & Voehl, F. (2016). The innovation tools handbook: Organizational and operational tools, methods, and techniques that every innovator must know. *The Innovation Tools Handbook: Organizational and Operational Tools, Methods, and Techniques That Every Innovator Must Know, 1*, 1–435. DOI: 10.1201/b21448

Hossain, F., Islam, R., Osugi, T., Shah, F., Mine, T., Nakashima, N., & Ahmed, A. (2024). Concept of Micro Healthcare Entrepreneurship (MHE) to Facilitate Universal Health Coverage (UHC): Prospects and Challenges. *Sustainability (Basel), 16*(6), 2268. Advance online publication. DOI: 10.3390/su16062268

Ifeagwu, S. C., Yang, J. C., Parkes-Ratanshi, R., & Brayne, C. (2021). Health financing for universal health coverage in Sub-Saharan Africa: A systematic review. *Global Health Research and Policy, 6*(1), 8. Advance online publication. DOI: 10.1186/s41256-021-00190-7 PMID: 33641673

Islam-Maruf, R., Ahmed, A., Yokota, F., Kikuchi, K., Nishikitani, M., Izukura, R., Sato, Y., Nohara, Y., & Nakashim, N. (2021). Portable health clinic as a telemedicine system with appropriate technologies for unreached communities. *Studies in Health Technology and Informatics*, *2020*(0), 57–67. DOI: 10.3233/SHTI210028

Jaca, A., Malinga, T., Iwu-Jaja, C. J., Nnaji, C. A., Okeibunor, J. C., Kamuya, D., & Wiysonge, C. S. (2022). Strengthening the Health System as a Strategy to Achieving a Universal Health Coverage in Underprivileged Communities in Africa: A Scoping Review. *International Journal of Environmental Research and Public Health*, *19*(1), 587. Advance online publication. DOI: 10.3390/ijerph19010587 PMID: 35010844

Jensen, N., Kelly, A. H., & Avendano, M. (2022). Health equity and health system strengthening–Time for a WHO re-think. *Global Public Health: An International Journal for Research, Policy and Practice*, *17*(3), 377–390. DOI: 10.1080/17441692.2020.1867881 PMID: 33427084

Kaiser, A. H., Rotigliano, N., Flessa, S., Ekman, B., & Sundewall, J. (2023). Extending universal health coverage to informal workers: A systematic review of health financing schemes in low- and middle-income countries in Southeast Asia. *PLoS One*, *18*(7), 1–31. DOI: 10.1371/journal.pone.0288269 PMID: 37432943

Kipo-Sunyehzi, D. D. (2024). Sustainable Development Goal 3.8 Universal Health Coverage from global perspectives: An analysis of the health insurance policies in Rwanda, Tanzania, South Africa, and Ghana. *Health Sciences Investigations Journal*, *6*(1), 814–822. DOI: 10.46829/hsijournal.2024.7.6.1.814-822

Koohpayehzadeh, J., Azami-Aghhdash, S., Derakhshani, N., Rezapour, A., Kalajahi, R. A., Khasraghi, J. S., Nikoomanesh, M., Sabetrohani, H., & Soleimanpour, S. (2021). Best Practices in Achieving Unive ersal Health Cove erage: A Scoping Review. *Medical Journal of the Islamic Republic of Iran*, •••, 1–35. PMID: 36042832

Kruk, M. E., Gage, A. D., Arsenault, C., Jordan, K., Leslie, H. H., Roder-DeWan, S., Adeyi, O., Barker, P., Daelmans, B., Doubova, S. V., English, M., García-Elorrio, E., Guanais, F., Gureje, O., Hirschhorn, L. R., Jiang, L., Kelley, E., Lemango, E. T., Liljestrand, J., & Pate, M. (2018). High-quality health systems in the Sustainable Development Goals era: Time for a revolution. *The Lancet. Global Health*, *6*(11), e1196–e1252. DOI: 10.1016/S2214-109X(18)30386-3 PMID: 30196093

Kutzin, J. (2013). Health financing for universal coverage and health system performance: Concepts and implications for policy. *Bulletin of the World Health Organization*, *91*(8), 602–611. DOI: 10.2471/BLT.12.113985 PMID: 23940408

Loewenson, R. (2022). Which UHC? Features for Equity and Universalism Comment on "Universal Health Coverage for Non-Communicable Diseases and Health Equity: Lessons From Australian Primary Healthcare.". *International Journal of Health Policy and Management, 11*(5), 704–707. DOI: 10.34172/ijhpm.2021.89 PMID: 34380201

Macinko, J., & Harris, M. J. (2015). Brazil's Family Health Strategy — Delivering Community-Based Primary Care in a Universal Health System. *The New England Journal of Medicine, 372*(23), 2177–2181. DOI: 10.1056/NEJMp1501140 PMID: 26039598

NHSRC. (2024). *Trend Analysis of the UHC Service Coverage Index (UHC Index).* Government of Pakistan, Ministry of National Health Services, Regulations and Coordination. https://lmis.gov.pk/docs/uhc/30 04 2022-Brief Trend Analysis of UHC Index at National and Provincial Area Level.pdf

Odoch, W. D., Senkubuge, F., Masese, A. B., & Hongoro, C. (2023). A critical review of literature on health financing reforms in Uganda – progress, challenges and opportunities for achieving UHC. *African Health Sciences, 23*(1), 736–746. DOI: 10.4314/ahs.v23i1.78 PMID: 37545949

OECD. (2022). *Understanding differences in health expenditure between the United States and OECD countries.* Organisation for Economic Co-Operation and Development., DOI: 10.1787/ae3016b9-

Organization, W. H. (2010). *World Health Report: Health systems financing: the path to universal coverage.* WHO Press. https://www.who.int/publications/i/item/9789241564021

Park, J. E., Kibe, P., Yeboah, G., Oyebode, O., Harris, B., Ajisola, M. M., Griffiths, F., Aujla, N., Gill, P., Lilford, R. J., & Chen, Y. F. (2022). Factors associated with accessing and utilisation of healthcare and provision of health services for residents of slums in low and middle-income countries: A scoping review of recent literature. *BMJ Open, 12*(5), 1–18. DOI: 10.1136/bmjopen-2021-055415 PMID: 35613790

Prince, R. J. (2024). Blurring 'social justice' with 'market justice' in recent experiments with healthcare and social protection in the Global South. *Global Social Policy, 24*(2), 331–335. DOI: 10.1177/14680181241261476

Ranabhat, C. L., Acharya, S. P., Adhikari, C., & Kim, C. B. (2023). Universal health coverage evolution, ongoing trend, and future challenge: A conceptual and historical policy review. *Frontiers in Public Health, 11*, 1041459. Advance online publication. DOI: 10.3389/fpubh.2023.1041459 PMID: 36815156

Romanello, M., McGushin, A., Di Napoli, C., Drummond, P., Hughes, N., Jamart, L., Kennard, H., Lampard, P., Solano Rodriguez, B., Arnell, N., Ayeb-Karlsson, S., Belesova, K., Cai, W., Campbell-Lendrum, D., Capstick, S., Chambers, J., Chu, L., Ciampi, L., Dalin, C., & Hamilton, I. (2021). The 2021 report of the <em>Lancet</em> Countdown on health and climate change: Code red for a healthy future. *Lancet, 398*(10311), 1619–1662. DOI: 10.1016/S0140-6736(21)01787-6 PMID: 34687662

Sakas, N. (2024). Advancing Social Justice and Equity in Health and Wellness: A Global Perspective. *Journal of International Social Research, 17*(117).

Smithers, D., & Waitzkin, H. (2022). Universal health coverage as hegemonic health policy in low- and middle-income countries: A mixed-methods analysis. *Social Science and Medicine, 302*(August 2021), 114961. DOI: 10.1016/j.socscimed.2022.114961

Sparkes, S. P., Eozenou, P. H. V., Evans, D., Kurowski, C., Kutzin, J., & Tandon, A. (2021). Will the Quest for UHC be Derailed? *Health Systems and Reform, 7*(2), e1929796. Advance online publication. DOI: 10.1080/23288604.2021.1929796 PMID: 34402407

Takian, A., Raoofi, A., & Haghighi, H. (2022). COVID-19 pandemic: The fears and hopes for SDG 3, with focus on prevention and control of noncommunicable diseases (SDG 3.4) and universal health coverage (SDG 3.8). *COVID-19 and the Sustainable Development Goals, January*, 211–234. DOI: 10.1016/B978-0-323-91307-2.00014-6

Tangcharoensathien, V., Witthayapipopsakul, W., Panichkriangkrai, W., Patcharanarumol, W., & Mills, A. (2018). Health systems development in Thailand: A solid platform for successful implementation of universal health coverage. *Lancet, 391*(10126), 1205–1223. DOI: 10.1016/S0140-6736(18)30198-3 PMID: 29397200

Trani, J. F., Kett, M., Bakhshi, P., & Bailey, N. (2011). Disability, vulnerability and citizenship: To what extent is education a protective mechanism for children with disabilities in countries affected by conflict? *International Journal of Inclusive Education, 15*(10), 1187–1203. DOI: 10.1080/13603116.2011.555078

United Nations. (2019). *The Sustainable Development Goals Report 2019.* United Nations Publication Issued by the Department of Economic and Social Affairs. https://unstats.un.org/sdgs/report/2019/The-Sustainable-Development-Goals-Report-2019.pdf

Upreti, K., Malik, K., Kapoor, A., Patel, N., & Tiwari, P. (2024). Revolutionizing healthcare telemedicine's global technological integration. *Improving Security, Privacy, and Connectivity Among Telemedicine Platforms*, 71–92. DOI: 10.4018/979-8-3693-2141-6.ch004

Verguet, S., Hailu, A., Eregata, G. T., Memirie, S. T., Johansson, K. A., & Norheim, O. F. (2021). Toward universal health coverage in the post-COVID-19 era. *Nature Medicine, 27*(3), 380–387. DOI: 10.1038/s41591-021-01268-y PMID: 33723458

Wang, H., Tesfaye, R., Ramana, G. N. V., & Chekagn, C. T. (2016). *Ethiopia Health Extension Program: An Institutionalized Community Approach for Universal Health Coverage*. World Bank Publications.

WHO. (2024, January 8). *UHC service coverage index*. DOI: 10.1787/80546e4a-en

World Health Organization. (2021). *Tracking Universal Health Coverage: 2021 Global Monitoring Report*. Tracking Universal Health Coverage: 2017 Global Monitoring Report. DOI: 10.1596/978-92-4-151355-5

World Health Organization. (2011). *Governance for Health in The 21st Century*. WHO., DOI: 10.1111/j.1865-1682.2011.01225.x

World Health Organization. (2015). *World Report on Ageing and Health*. Who.Int.

World Health Organization. (2022a). Global Competency and Outcomes Framework for Universal Health Coverage. In *WHO*. https://www.who.int/publications/i/item/9789240034662

World Health Organization. (2022b). *Global oral health status report Towards universal health coverage for oral health by 2030*. World Health Organization. https://www.who.int/publications/i/item/9789240061484

World Health Organization & UNICEF. (2018). A vision for Primary health care in the 21st Century. *World Health Organizarion*, 1–64. https://www.who.int/docs/default-source/primary-health/vision.pdf?sfvrsn=c3119034_2

Zhou, Y., Li, C., Wang, M., Xu, S., Wang, L., Hu, J., Ding, L., & Wang, W. (2022). Universal health coverage in China: A serial national cross-sectional study of surveys from 2003 to 2018. *The Lancet. Public Health, 7*(12), e1051–e1063. DOI: 10.1016/S2468-2667(22)00251-1 PMID: 36462516

Chapter 3
Environmental Inequities and Global Health:
Bridging the Gap in Vulnerable Communities

Kholis Kholis Ernawati
https://orcid.org/0000-0002-3582-5294
Universitas YARSI, Indonesia

ABSTRACT

Environmental inequalities exacerbate global health disparities, particularly in low- and middle-income countries (LMICs). Air, water, and land pollution disproportionately affect marginalized communities, increasing the burden of communicable diseases like malaria and diarrhea, as well as non-communicable diseases such as COPD and cardiovascular disorders. Environmental factors also contribute to mental health issues due to natural disasters and climate change. This chapter examines environmental injustice and disease burden through epidemiological data, case studies, and policy evaluations. Solutions include community-based interventions, stronger regulations, innovative technologies, and multilateral cooperation. The chapter highlights the need for a holistic approach involving governments, organizations, and civil society to create equitable policies protecting vulnerable populations.

INTRODUCTION

Environmental inequalities drive health disparities, especially in Low- and Middle-Income Countries (LMICs), where multiple environmental risks worsen socioeconomic challenges. Pollution and environmental hazards are unevenly

DOI: 10.4018/979-8-3373-1992-6.ch003

distributed, with marginalized groups facing greater exposure. Studies, including Liu et al. (2021), show that racial and ethnic minorities are over twice as likely as non-Hispanic whites to live in highly polluted areas. These inequalities are further exacerbated in urban contexts, where low-income neighborhoods often face higher exposure to pollutants from industrial activity and motor vehicle emissions (Bangkara et al., 2022a; Jiao et al., 2018).

Environmental degradation—marked by deforestation, soil erosion, and biodiversity loss—significantly harms public health in marginalized communities, especially as agricultural expansion and industrial pollution destroy habitats and heighten disaster risks like floods and landslides that disproportionately impact people with low incomes (Baudet et al., 2022). Climate change further worsens these vulnerabilities through extreme weather and shifting disease patterns, affecting populations with limited adaptive capacity (Achmadi & Ernawati, 2017). Rapid urbanization adds to the burden by fostering informal settlements with inadequate sanitation, where low-income communities face higher exposure to pollution and greater disease risk due to poor infrastructure and waste management (Bangkara et al., 2022; Jiao et al., 2018)

One of the key approaches to addressing health disparities due to environmental inequities is to strengthen regulatory frameworks to reduce sources of pollution, particularly in residential and urban environments. As Asikainen et al. suggested, increasing ventilation rates can partially mitigate indoor air quality challenges. However, attention must be paid to the potential infiltration of air pollution from outside (Asikainen et al., 2016). Effective policies should consider the specific pollution profile faced by each community, with a multifaceted approach that integrates community-based data (Evangelopoulos et al., 2021).

This article analyzes environmental injustice as a significant factor exacerbating global health disparities, particularly in low- and middle-income countries (LMICs). Using a multidisciplinary approach, it explores the relationship between environmental factors and disease burden distribution through epidemiological data, case studies, and environmental and health policy evaluation. The article also proposes community-based solutions, strengthening environmental regulations, and utilizing innovative technologies to bridge the gap in access to healthy environments. This article contributes to formulating more inclusive and equitable policies to protect the most vulnerable communities from adverse environmental impacts through a holistic approach involving governments, international organizations, the private sector, and civil society.

METHODOLOGY

This article employs a multidisciplinary literature review approach to explore environmental inequalities and their impact on global health comprehensively. The review involved systematic searches of peer-reviewed scientific literature through electronic databases such as PubMed, Scopus, Web of Science, and Google Scholar, covering publications from 2015 to 2025. Specific search terms included combinations of keywords such as "environmental inequalities," "global health," "air pollution," "water contamination," "land degradation," "artificial intelligence (AI)," "machine learning," "health policy," and "environmental injustice."

Inclusion criteria for literature selection encompassed studies explicitly addressing the relationship between environmental factors and global health disparities, emphasizing vulnerable communities. The review considered articles detailing quantitative analyses of epidemiological data from recognized global databases, notably the Global Burden of Disease (GBD) and the World Health Organization's (WHO) World Health Statistics, to capture morbidity and mortality trends associated with environmental conditions. Studies providing qualitative insights through case studies in Asia, Africa, and Latin America, including stakeholder experiences and community perceptions of environmental health impacts and policy barriers, were also prioritized.

Additionally, literature was systematically reviewed on the role and effectiveness of environmental health policies, such as vehicle emission standards, water quality regulations, and waste management practices across various countries. A comparative policy analysis approach was utilized to understand the diversity of policy effectiveness in addressing environmental injustices globally.

Particular attention was paid to reviewing literature on applications of Artificial Intelligence (AI) in monitoring and predicting environmental health impacts. The review included studies utilizing machine learning algorithms such as Random Forest, Neural Networks, Convolutional Neural Networks (CNN), and Recurrent Neural Networks (RNN). Literature demonstrating the use of these AI models in analyzing historical environmental and public health data, predicting disease risk, or enhancing early warning systems for environmental hazards was critically evaluated. Cross-validation methodologies, accuracy metrics, and robustness assessments reported within these studies were also examined to provide insights into the validity, strengths, and limitations of AI-driven environmental health monitoring.

The synthesis from this multidisciplinary literature review highlights gaps, strengths, and areas for future research, providing comprehensive recommendations for addressing global environmental health inequalities through policy, community interventions, and technological innovation.

RESULTS AND DISCUSSION

Identifying Patterns of Environmental Injustice

Disparities in the distribution of environmental risks and their impacts on disadvantaged populations are an important highlight in environmental justice studies. Research shows that marginalized groups, often as a result of discriminatory policies, face higher environmental stresses, such as poor air quality and limited access to clean water, as well as greater vulnerability to natural disasters. Ren and Giang explain that historical urban planning and segregation policies, such as redlining, have created patterns of inequitable risk distribution, with minority populations often concentrated in areas with worse environmental conditions and limited access to vital resources (Ren & Giang, 2024).

Another important element is the interaction between environmental justice and social vulnerability. Bishop & Reed suggest that populations facing higher environmental risks also experience slower recovery from disasters; this stage is closely related to health determinants influenced by their socioeconomic conditions (Bishop & Reed, 2022). Communities with limited resources are more vulnerable to disasters and have less access to post-disaster support, including health services and recovery infrastructure. Therefore, it is important to understand the systemic and holistic approach to addressing environmental justice challenges.

Recent advances in artificial intelligence (AI), particularly with models such as Vision Transformers (ViT) and Graph Neural Networks (GNN), have significantly enhanced the identification and mapping of environmental injustices. ViT has outperformed conventional methods in analyzing satellite imagery, providing high accuracy in locating vulnerable regions such as slums and areas prone to flooding, often at risk for environmentally-related diseases (Kala et al., 2020). In parallel, GNNs excel in illustrating intricate spatial relationships between socioeconomic factors, environmental quality, and potential public health risks. This capability facilitates a more holistic approach to decision-making in environmental health policies (Moyano-Fernández et al., 2024). Moreover, the ethical implications associated with these AI models necessitate cautious development to ensure transparency and fairness, particularly as they scale in application within public health (Murphy et al., 2021). Combining socioeconomic and environmental components through AI tools can lead to better identification of health disparities and aid in formulating effective interventions, thus promoting environmental justice (Castro et al., 2024).

Research by Zolitschka et al. showed a spatial correlation between health outcomes and environmental stressors experienced by populations, which is an important indicator in understanding health inequalities (Zolitschka et al., 2022). They found that social mechanisms at the neighborhood level can exacerbate differences in health outcomes, confirming that inequities in the distribution of environmental stressors and quality of life, more generally in socio-economically deprived regions, contribute to health inequalities. Exposure to environmental stressors is not only a physical problem but also a social problem that requires multidisciplinary interventions to address multiple interacting factors. Data from various studies show that communities with high social inequality, while facing multiple environmental challenges, develop unfavorable patterns of health and well-being. Without adequate attention to these inequalities, public welfare outcomes will remain unbalanced. By studying social interactions within specific groups, we can identify ways social support can reduce the negative impact of environmental stressors.

A data-driven approach to mapping environmental risks and their impacts, as suggested by Eccles et al. (2023), is crucial for effective mitigation strategies. Many factors are interrelated, including exposure to hazardous chemicals and quality of daily life, so the approach should consider multiple dimensions of risk. An interdisciplinary approach to understanding environmental exposures improves our understanding of physical risks and how social inequities can shape collective mindsets, behaviors, and community health outcomes.

Applying artificial intelligence (AI) technologies to identify patterns of environmental injustice presents several critical challenges. Firstly, data bias, typically due to unrepresentative datasets, leads to inaccurate predictions, which can perpetuate societal inequalities. This concern regarding algorithmic bias and its implications has been emphasized in the literature by Intahchomphoo & Gundersen (2020). Additionally, data privacy issues arise, particularly when handling sensitive personal information for environmental models, which mandates a careful approach to ensure ethical compliance, as highlighted by Dahlin (2024). Furthermore, Intahchomphoo & Gundersen (2020) also discuss the risk of algorithmic discrimination affecting vulnerable communities, reinforcing the need for an ethical framework and community involvement in AI deployment. Recent advancements in AI, such as convolutional neural networks (CNNs) for analyzing satellite imagery, show promise in addressing specific environmental health challenges. While specialized AI models can mitigate ecological impacts, they must be cautiously implemented to foster algorithmic justice and equitable outcomes. Integrating AI and IoT-driven technologies for environmental monitoring shows potential for significant advancements, but these technologies must be carefully managed to address related challenges (Davariashtiyani et al., 2024).

Air Pollution in Urban Slums

One of the most common forms of environmental injustice is exposure to high levels of air pollution in urban slums, especially in low- and middle-income countries

(LMICs). Exposure to air pollution in urban slums is a critical issue many countries face, especially in low- and middle-income countries (LMICs). These settlements are often located near industrial zones that produce toxic emissions, along highways congested with vehicles, or near poorly managed landfills. One of the leading causes of air pollution in these areas is emissions from transportation. In many areas with weak environmental regulations, older vehicles that do not meet emissions standards continue to be used, resulting in dangerous levels of pollutants such as nitrogen dioxide (NO_2) and fine particulate matter (PM2.5). According to research, decarbonizing the transport sector can reduce Greenhouse Gas (GHG) Emissions and significantly improve air quality, positively impacting public health, especially in areas with large populations exposed to high pollution (Berberian et al., 2024).

The use of solid fuels for cooking and heating is also a critical factor contributing to high levels of air pollution in slums. Many low-income households rely on firewood, charcoal, or other biomass as an energy source, which produces harmful emissions indoors and outdoors. Research has found that prolonged exposure to this pollution can increase the risk of serious illness and affect people's overall quality of life (N'gattia et al., 2020).

All these factors are interrelated and contribute to a situation that defines environmental injustice in slums. For example, inequities in the placement of industrial facilities and highways are directly proportional to the environmental impacts felt by the surrounding residents. This injustice is further exacerbated by environmental politics that often ignore the needs and voices of the poor communities affected. A study shows that despite efforts to improve emissions from specific sectors, inequity in air quality impacts remains unsolved, especially for marginalized communities (Sergi et al., 2020). Research shows that good air quality has implications for physical health and contributes to the mental and emotional well-being of individuals living there. Decreased air quality can trigger stress, anxiety, and other mental health issues, further exacerbating the socioeconomic situation in already vulnerable communities (Polonik et al., 2023).

Research shows a direct correlation between air pollution levels and the incidence of respiratory diseases in New Delhi. A Geographic Information System (GIS)-based study showed a strong association between emergency room visits due to acute respiratory symptoms and high levels of air pollution (Yadav et al., 2024). Further analysis revealed that despite pollution control efforts, PM2.5 concentrations remain high throughout the year, contributing to increased morbidity and mortality rates (Ashutosh Deshpande et al., 2024; Dutta & Jinsart, 2022). Long-term exposure to air pollutants is also associated with increased hospitalizations due to respiratory diseases such as asthma and Chronic Obstructive Pulmonary Disease (COPD). The impact can be seen in various health indicators, including a high prevalence of diseases such as asthma and pneumonia, which are disproportionately more prevalent in low-income populations that have limited access to health services. Long-term exposure to particulate pollution is a significant risk factor for chronic health problems, highlighting the importance of effective public health policies to reduce the health impacts of air pollution in the National Capital Region (NCR) (Deshpande et al., 2024; Brajer, 2022)

Contaminated Water Sources

The impact of inequalities in access to clean water reflects one of the most fundamental facets of environmental injustice, significantly impacting public health, especially among poor communities often dependent on polluted water sources. This unequal access is not only an issue of resource distribution but is also closely linked to social, economic, and policy factors that exacerbate conditions. In this context, pollution of water sources is one of the most important challenges faced. One of the leading causes of pollution in the global context is the poorly managed disposal of industrial waste. Industrial processes that produce goods often leave a heavy trail of pollution, mainly through effluents containing hazardous chemicals discharged into rivers and water sources without adequate treatment processes (Baba, 2024).

Poor sanitation also contributes significantly to water contamination. In communities lacking adequate sanitation infrastructure, such as efficient sewage systems, groundwater becomes saturated with harmful pathogens. For example, Escherichia coli can contaminate water sources, potentially triggering infectious disease epidemics. These problems are limited to poor communities in developing countries and present in more complex forms in developed countries, where infrastructure failures can cause severe health impacts (Sharma et al., 2024).

Poor domestic waste management services result in more pollution problems. In areas with high population density, directly discharging garbage and sewage into waterways intensifies the problem. This is reflected in studies showing that inefficient waste management reduces water quality and increases the risk of public exposure to hazardous substances. Better management and mapping of pollution sources can improve water quality and provide more equitable access for communities.

A case in point is the pollution of the Citarum River in Indonesia. It is widely regarded as one of the most polluted rivers in the world, mainly due to effluents from the textile industry flowing untreated. Environmental impact assessments recorded high levels of heavy metals and toxic chemicals in the river ecosystem. The health impacts on the river-dependent population are very real, with reports of skin diseases and nervous system disorders as long-term effects of exposure to polluted water. Through the right public policy approach, the government has organized a plan to clean up the Citarum River in the context of sustainability, although challenges remain in implementation (Fridayani, 2020).

The water crisis in Flint, Michigan, provides an important additional perspective on how contamination diseases can arise even in more developed contexts. Here, problems arose when the city's water source was diverted without adequate corrosion protection, resulting in dangerous lead contamination for residents, including children, who are more vulnerable to permanent neurological damage. The Flint case shows that water structures and policies are a problem in the developing world and a crisis in the developed world, signaling that environmental injustice crosses geographic and economic boundaries (Chen et al., 2021)

Natural Disasters and Socioeconomic Vulnerability

Marginalized communities are disproportionately affected by natural disasters due to various socioeconomic vulnerabilities, especially in comparison to wealthier populations who have the means to avoid high-risk environments or recover more quickly from disaster impacts. The relationship between socioeconomic status and disaster vulnerability has been extensively documented in academic literature, highlighting the interconnection between poverty, inadequate infrastructure, and the geographical locations of vulnerable communities.

One of the primary factors contributing to the vulnerability of marginalized groups is their place of residence. Many informal settlements are in disaster-prone areas, such as riverbanks, steep slopes, and coastal regions with high flooding risks, landslides, and storms. For example, a case study in Koyra Upazila, Bangladesh, revealed that recurrent disasters prevent communities from fully recovering before the next disaster occurs, creating a cycle of helplessness and poverty. Residents face significant challenges in disaster management due to their limited adaptive capacity, which is further exacerbated by their geographical and socioeconomic conditions (Tashmin & Islam, 2023).

The absence of resilient infrastructure worsens the risks faced by these communities. Research indicates that poor drainage systems, poorly constructed housing, and a lack of disaster preparedness measures significantly increase the likelihood of fatalities and injuries during disaster events. For instance, Hage et al. emphasize that socioeconomic factors must be considered in post-disaster reconstruction processes, as both the physical damage experienced and a community's poverty level significantly affect recovery outcomes (El Hage et al., 2023). These findings align with Blockstein et al., who highlight that social capital within marginalized communities plays a crucial role in disaster resilience. Many community members rely on local social networks, such as religious organizations, for post-disaster support. While these social connections are beneficial, dependence on limited resources also indicates constraints in community recovery capacity (Blockstein et al., 2024).

The lack of post-disaster assistance is another dimension of vulnerability in marginalized communities. Studies show that communities with low political representation or visibility tend to receive less aid, and often with delays, following disasters. Consequently, they experience prolonged recovery and remain more vulnerable to subsequent crises. The 2015-2030 Disaster Risk Reduction Framework underscores the importance of community empowerment, suggesting that mutual assistance among communities can enhance resilience and accelerate recovery, mainly when supported by local governance structures (Chandra et al., 2020). Conversely, communities with low levels of disaster preparedness education and risk management awareness often lack adequate emergency readiness, worsening their vulnerability (Yuwanto et al., 2021).

Difficult economic conditions limit individuals' and families' ability to invest in disaster protection measures. Research on socioeconomic vulnerability in Koyra Upazila highlighted that financial constraints often prevent individuals from adopting disaster-resistant building practices or relocating to safer areas. These resource limitations create a cycle of poverty that is difficult to break, as families struggle to meet their basic needs without a safety net in the form of support systems or adequate infrastructure (Tashmin & Islam, 2023).

The flooding situation in South Asia, particularly in countries such as Bangladesh, India, and Pakistan, poses a serious challenge that has been exacerbated by changing rainfall patterns and unplanned urbanization. Almazroui et al. revealed that projected increases in rainfall and high temperatures in northwestern South Asia will lead to extreme flash floods due to glacier melt and higher summer precipitation. These projections emphasize the region's growing vulnerability to climate change (Almazroui et al., 2020).

Flood disasters between 2004 and 2016 have caused massive economic losses. Matheswaran et al. highlight the need for more integrated risk reduction strategies, particularly for small-scale farmers who serve as the backbone of rural economies (Matheswaran et al., 2019). For instance, the severe flooding in August 2022 underscored the recurring flood crisis in Pakistan. Reports indicate that more than one billion people in South Asia have been affected by floods over the past two decades, reflecting the immense impact of these disasters on communities (Nanditha et al., 2023). Flooding not only leads to the immediate loss of housing but also disrupts livelihoods, further exacerbating poverty, especially for vulnerable populations living in lowland areas. The socioeconomic conditions of affected communities play a crucial role in their adaptive capacity, making the relationship between economic vulnerability and climate variability a key aspect of analyzing the ongoing flood situation (Rhaman et al., 2022).

THE RELATIONSHIP BETWEEN ENVIRONMENTAL INJUSTICE AND DISEASE BURDEN

Environmental injustice significantly impacts public health, particularly in the spread of infectious diseases. In this context, communities exposed to higher environmental risks—such as pollution, limited access to clean water, and failing sanitation systems—bear a much more significant disease burden than those living in healthier environments. Research indicates that unhealthy environments directly contribute to the rising incidence of infectious diseases, including malaria and dengue fever. Inadequate waste management, lack of access to clean water, and the effects of climate change all contribute to the creation of environments that support the reproduction of disease vectors, such as mosquitoes (Suresh et al., 2023; X. Wang, 2022).

Vector-Borne Infectious Diseases

One example of how environmental injustice exacerbates infectious disease epidemics is malaria transmission by *Anopheles* mosquitoes (Ernawati et al., 2014; Susanna et al., 2012). Studies show that deforestation—often occurring in developing countries due to agricultural expansion and natural resource exploitation—increases the risk of malaria spread. In the Amazon, for example, research has documented that deforestation has significantly contributed to rising malaria cases by altering ecosystems to favor mosquito vector development. Climate change also expands the geographical range of vector-borne diseases by increasing temperatures and altering rainfall patterns; both create favorable conditions for mosquito reproduction, allowing them to migrate to previously low-risk areas (Wu & Huang, 2022).

Dengue fever, caused by the Aedes aegypti mosquito, also demonstrates a strong link to environmental injustice. Poor sanitation and stagnant water often serve as breeding grounds for this mosquito species. According to recent studies, unplanned urbanization and inadequate infrastructure development worsen this issue, leading to demographic and social changes that further deepen inequities in access to healthcare resources (Connolly et al., 2021; Ernawati et al., 2021). Degraded environments increase the likelihood of disease transmission, and inadequate public health responses in policy and practice only exacerbate the disease burden.

Statistics indicate that approximately 80% of the global population is currently at risk of infection from vector-borne diseases, with over 700,000 deaths occurring annually (Wu & Huang, 2022). This burden is exceptionally high in underdeveloped regions, where resources for risk mitigation and vector control efforts are severely limited. As a result, a cycle of injustice emerges, worsening public health conditions and increasing the incidence of infectious diseases. Adopting a One Health approach that integrates human, animal, and environmental health is crucial to developing more effective and sustainable prevention strategies (Magalhaes et al., 2024).

Recognizing the link between environmental injustice and disease burden underscores the need for targeted interventions, including infrastructure improvements, climate change mitigation, and the enforcement of inclusive health policies. Without such measures, environmental injustices and their associated health effects will persist, placing the most vulnerable communities at heightened risk of infectious disease outbreaks. Further research is needed to deepen our understanding of these factors and formulate more effective strategies to combat health inequities stemming from poor environmental conditions.

Waterborne Diseases

The relationship between environmental injustice and disease burden, particularly waterborne diseases, is highly complex and deeply rooted in socioeconomic disparities. Diseases such as cholera, acute diarrhea, and hepatitis A predominantly affect communities with limited access to clean water and sanitation, a condition often worsened by environmental injustice. In Africa and South Asia, recurring cholera epidemics are closely linked to the contamination of drinking water sources by *Vibrio cholerae*, which thrives in environments with poor sanitation infrastructure (Patel et al., 2023).

The high incidence of diarrhea among children, a leading cause of infant and under-five mortality worldwide, underscores the urgency of addressing environmental injustice (Parris et al., 2021). Poor sanitation facilities and water contamination are key factors driving these health problems. Inequitable distribution of clean water manifests environmental injustice, where impoverished communities often rely on contaminated water sources. At the same time, wealthier areas enjoy access to safe drinking water, further exacerbating health disparities (Brooks & Fields, 2021; Tundjungsari et al., 2020).

Environmental injustice directly impacts public health and is shaped by sociopolitical landscapes, determining access to health resources. Studies indicate that structural inequalities create recurring patterns of health disparities, negatively affecting minority groups and low-income communities. The Environmental Justice Index (EJI), developed by the Centers for Disease Control and Prevention (CDC), serves as a crucial tool for measuring these disparities by assessing environmental conditions and social vulnerability at the community level (Nogueira & Yabroff, 2024).

Considering the social-environmental determinants of health in the context of waterborne diseases, it is essential to acknowledge the lived experiences of affected communities. Brooks and Fields emphasize how health disparities reflect broader social injustices that disproportionately impact marginalized racial and ethnic groups (Brooks & Fields, 2021). These disparities are not random but result from historical discrimination and social exclusion, leading to higher exposure to environmental pollutants and inadequate access to healthcare resources. The connection between social injustice and health equity initiatives highlights the need for evidence-based policymaking, incorporating affected communities' voices and experiences to improve public health outcomes.

Pollution Exposure and Chronic Health Conditions

Non-communicable diseases (NCDs) are increasingly recognized as a significant public health challenge, closely linked to environmental factors, particularly pollution exposure. Environmental injustice provides a key analytical framework for understanding how air pollution, hazardous chemicals, and unhealthy working conditions disproportionately impact specific populations, increasing their risk of chronic diseases. Chronic respiratory diseases such as Chronic Obstructive Pulmonary Disease (COPD) and asthma are among the most common NCDs associated with air pollution. Data from the World Health Organization (WHO) indicate that over 90% of deaths attributed to air pollution occur in low- and middle-income countries (LMICs) (Shrestha et al., 2024). Vulnerable groups, including children and the elderly, face heightened risks due to their physiological and social conditions, which limit their resilience to environmental hazards (Tsocheva et al., 2023).

Chronic respiratory diseases are primarily triggered by exposure to airborne particulate matter (PM2.5, PM10) and other pollutants from motor vehicles, industrial activities, and biomass combustion. For example, in Beijing, declining air quality due to vehicle emissions and industrial pollution has been correlated with increased asthma cases among children and respiratory illnesses in the elderly. Research also highlights that indoor air quality is often worse than outdoor air, yet it receives little attention in discussions about pollution (Martins et al., 2024).

The double burden of infectious and non-communicable diseases in sub-Saharan Africa adds complexity to understanding environmental health determinants. The region faces significant challenges due to poor environmental conditions, contributing to rising chronic diseases amidst limited healthcare policies and medical infrastructure. Environmental health studies in the region show a strong statistical correlation between environmental exposure and health deterioration. Thus, understanding environmental injustice in the context of air pollution and its relationship with NCDs is crucial, as it reveals systemic inequalities in health risks experienced by different population groups (Bishoge et al., 2023).

Cardiovascular Diseases

Long-term exposure to air pollution is correlated with an increased risk of various cardiovascular diseases (CVD), including hypertension, stroke, and coronary heart disease. Research indicates that delicate particulate matter (PM2.5), one of the primary components of air pollution, plays a critical role in this relationship by entering the bloodstream and triggering systemic inflammation, a precursor to atherosclerosis, one of the leading causes of cardiovascular disease. This relationship's implications are extensive, affecting individual health outcomes and influencing public health policies and urban planning strategies (Wolf et al., 2021; Yen & Chen, 2021).

Exposure to delicate particulate matter can induce an inflammatory response that leads to endothelial damage, creating conditions that promote the formation of arterial plaques (Kraus & Murphy, 2021; Wolf et al., 2021). A study by Wolf et al. supports these findings, stating that long-term exposure to low levels of ambient air pollution is significantly associated with increased stroke and coronary heart disease in several European cohorts. This research reinforces that sustained environmental exposure is a serious risk factor for cardiovascular morbidity (Wolf et al., 2021).

A landmark study in India illustrated stark differences in cardiovascular disease incidence based on air quality. Individuals living in highly polluted areas had a significantly higher risk of heart attacks than those in regions with better air quality. These findings highlight the tangible health risks associated with poor air quality, where heart disease incidence rises in environments with high pollution levels (Yen & Chen, 2021).

Cancer and Exposure to Hazardous Chemicals

The relationship between environmental contamination by hazardous chemicals and increased cancer risk has been well-established in various studies. Heavy metals such as mercury, lead, and arsenic, as well as persistent organic pollutants (POPs), have been linked to different types of cancer due to their toxic effects on human health. This phenomenon is particularly evident in industrial areas, where exposure to harmful chemicals is significantly higher, posing significant public health challenges.

Numerous studies have shown that exposure to environmental contaminants increases the risk of various types of cancer. Rickard et al. highlight that per- and poly-fluoroalkyl substances (PFAS) can trigger chemotherapy drug resistance in ovarian cancer cells, indicating that environmental contaminants not only raise cancer risk but also affect cancer treatment outcomes (Rickard et al., 2022). In a comprehensive review, Rojas-Rueda et al. found a strong link between pollutant exposure and multiple cancers, including lung and cervical cancer (Rojas-Rueda et al., 2021). These findings align with research by Korsakov et al., which reported an increased incidence of endometrial cancer in populations residing in areas with significant chemical contamination, confirming the correlation between environmental toxicity and cancer risk (Korsakov et al., 2022).

Beyond general environmental exposure, occupational exposure to hazardous chemicals has also been associated with increased cancer risk. Sectors such as mining and manufacturing show higher susceptibility to cancer, particularly lung cancer, due to prolonged exposure to heavy metals and toxic substances (Rojas-Rueda et al., 2021). Additionally, research by Koual et al. indicates that environmental chemical exposure can contribute to therapy resistance in cancer treatment, including breast cancer treatment (Koual et al., 2020).

Impacts on Mental Health

The relationship between environmental injustice and mental health issues is increasingly recognized in public health and environmental studies. The psychological effects of exposure to hazardous environments, particularly in communities with high pollution levels or those at risk of natural disasters, often manifest as heightened stress and anxiety. Numerous studies have shown that poor environmental conditions contribute to mental health disorders, particularly in urban areas with high levels of air pollution.

Air pollution is widely linked to various health issues, including respiratory and cardiovascular diseases. However, its impact on mental health is equally concerning. A systematic review found that prolonged exposure to air pollutants, such as fine particulate matter (PM2.5), is significantly associated with increased anxiety and depression in densely populated cities, including New Delhi and Mexico City. The psychological distress caused by living in such hazardous environments stems from long-term concerns about health impacts, creating a cycle of chronic anxiety (Carballo et al., 2022).

Environmental crisis-related stress is further exacerbated by continuous exposure to hazardous conditions. Wang et al. highlighted that during health crises, such as the COVID-19 pandemic, psychological stress in the general population increased due to misinformation and limited access to accurate health data. This situation mirrors the psychological impact experienced by communities facing environmental injustice, where a lack of information about pollution and disaster preparedness contributes to heightened anxiety and stress (C. Wang et al., 2020).

Limited access to a healthy environment can trigger more significant emotional distress. Wagener et al. found that the absence of access to comfortable and green spaces significantly contributes to increased emotional strain. The researchers emphasized the need for interventions to enhance psychological resilience in communities affected by environmental injustice. They proposed educational strategies focusing on increasing awareness of environmental hazards and promoting adaptive coping mechanisms, which can help alleviate mental health burdens in vulnerable populations (Wagener et al., 2022).

SOLUTIONS TO OVERCOMING ENVIRONMENTAL INJUSTICE

A multifaceted approach is required to address environmental injustice, exacerbating global health disparities. This includes community-based interventions, strengthening environmental regulations, technological innovations, and multilateral collaboration. These solutions must be holistic and sustainable, considering social, economic, and political factors influencing access to a healthy environment.

Community-Based Interventions

Community-based interventions are crucial in raising public awareness and promoting collective action to tackle environmental issues. By empowering local communities to monitor, advocate, and implement environmental solutions, disparities in access to a healthy environment can be reduced.

One successful example of this approach is the Clean Air Initiative in Southeast Asia, which effectively increased public awareness of urban air pollution and influenced policy changes regarding vehicle emissions in major cities (Rebeiro-Hargrave et al., 2021). Initiatives like this demonstrate that community engagement in data collection plays a vital role in environmental monitoring strategies, where educators and facilitators equip residents with low-cost air quality monitoring tools (Griswold et al., 2024). Through this approach, environmental health awareness improves, and communities become more proactive in advocating for change based on accurate data from their environment (Dirgantara et al., 2023).

Community-Based Economic Empowerment

Environment-based economic empowerment initiatives enhance the objectives of community-based interventions by creating local economic opportunities that align with environmental sustainability. Communities are encouraged to develop environmentally friendly businesses, such as waste banks and community-managed waste systems (Tommy et al., 2024). For instance, various initiatives in Brazil have demonstrated that community-based recycling programs help reduce environmental pollution and create job opportunities for residents (Rebeiro-Hargrave et al., 2021).

This dual impact proves that engaging communities in environmental action benefits them economically and makes them active agents of environmental management.

Environmental Communication as a Key Factor in Public Participation

Effective environmental communication is crucial in encouraging community participation in conservation efforts. Through verbal and non-verbal communication, communities can articulate environmental problems and mobilize collective action (Dirgantara et al., 2023). By integrating educational interventions and participatory monitoring, communities not only become recipients of information but also active participants in developing solutions, thereby increasing the impact of environmental education (Griswold et al., 2024).

Strengthening Environmental Regulations

Environmental injustice is a pressing issue exacerbated by weak regulations and inadequate environmental policy enforcement. To comprehensively address this problem, governments worldwide must adopt a multifaceted approach to strengthen environmental regulations, particularly in industrial pollution control, waste management, and protecting vulnerable ecosystems.

Industrial Pollution Control Through Strict Regulations

Governments must establish and enforce stringent emission standards supported by robust monitoring mechanisms in industrial pollution control. Research shows that stricter vehicle emission regulations positively impact air quality. For example, a study revealed that reducing total hydrocarbons (THC) in vehicle emissions is directly linked to implementing stricter emission standards (Drozd et al., 2016).

The success of such regulations is further demonstrated by Sweden, where industrial pollution levels have significantly declined due to strict regulations and incentives for industries adopting environmentally friendly technologies (Ravi et al., 2023). This regulatory model can be adopted globally to reduce pollution levels effectively. Evidence suggests that higher regulatory intensity can enhance manufacturing performance, particularly in the green sector. A comparative study in South Korea shows that the impact of environmental regulations varies across industries, necessitating tailored regulatory approaches. This strategy helps reduce pollution and maintains economic productivity in the manufacturing sector (Yoo & Heshmati, 2019).

Strengthening Waste Management Through Effective Policies

Environmental regulations must also be enhanced to oversee industrial waste treatment. Costa Rica is an example of a country with effective waste management policies. The nation has implemented incentives for industries actively reducing hazardous waste production while committing to innovation in recycling and waste treatment (Yoo & Heshmati, 2019). Governments can mitigate water and soil pollution by enforcing stricter waste management regulations and promoting sustainable industry practices. Furthermore, imposing penalties on violators and providing incentives for compliant companies will enhance the effectiveness of these policies, encouraging industries to adapt to stricter waste management standards.

Protecting Vulnerable Ecosystems From Resource Exploitation

Safeguarding areas vulnerable to resource exploitation is crucial to strengthening environmental regulations. Restricting land conversion for industrial purposes is essential to preserving local ecosystems. Various studies have assessed the environmental impact of resource extraction and land-use changes, emphasizing the need for regulations to prevent excessive industrialization (Xue, 2022). Such regulations must be enforced to conserve fragile ecosystems and ensure that the rights and health of local communities are prioritized over unsustainable industrial expansion.

The Importance of International Cooperation in Environmental Regulation

International collaboration is essential for strengthening environmental regulations. Since pollution and environmental degradation transcend national borders, a cooperative approach involving shared standards and best practices can enhance the effectiveness of local regulations. This global perspective facilitates the exchange of successful case studies, such as those from Sweden and Costa Rica, encouraging other countries to implement similar strategies for improving environmental regulations (Ravi et al., 2023).

Public and Community Involvement in the Regulatory Process

Public engagement in the regulatory process is critical in addressing environmental injustice. Communities affected by industrial pollution often have unique insights that can provide valuable input in shaping environmental policies. Therefore, platforms must be established to enable communities to participate in decision-making processes actively, ensuring that regulations are more responsive and accountable to their needs (Ravi et al., 2023).

CONCLUSION

Environmental inequality significantly contributes to global health disparities, particularly among marginalized communities. Uneven exposure to risks like air and water pollution and land degradation increases the burden of both communicable and non-communicable diseases, especially in low-income groups and areas with limited healthcare access. In LMICs, poor infrastructure and weak regulations exacerbate these conditions.

Urban air pollution and industrial emissions are major drivers of chronic respiratory and cardiovascular diseases, while water contamination and poor sanitation raise infection risks, especially among children. Populations in disaster-prone regions also face rising mental health issues due to environmental stress and displacement. Climate change, unregulated urbanization, and resource exploitation further worsen environmental inequality by spreading vector-borne diseases, increasing slum settlements, and accelerating ecosystem degradation.

Addressing these challenges requires community engagement, stronger regulations, technological innovation, and international collaboration. Solutions include participatory environmental monitoring, stricter pollution control, digital technologies for early warnings, and global support for vulnerable countries. Ultimately, environmental inequality is an ecological concern and a public health and social justice crisis. Multidisciplinary, evidence-based strategies involving governments, global institutions, and civil society are essential to ensure equitable environmental health for all.

RECOMMENDATIONS

Based on the analysis in this chapter, several strategic measures can be taken to address environmental injustice and mitigate its impact on public health:

Enhancing Community Participation and Awareness

One of the most effective ways to combat environmental injustice is by actively empowering local communities to monitor and advocate for their environment. Educational programs that raise awareness about environmental hazards and mitigation strategies should be strengthened, particularly in high-risk areas.

Strengthening Regulations and Law Enforcement

Stricter pollution and waste management regulations are essential to protect vulnerable communities from hazardous environmental exposures. Governments must increase oversight of industrial emissions and enforce stricter environmental standards.

Promoting Technological Innovation for Environmental Monitoring and Risk Mitigation

Technology can enhance the effectiveness of environmental monitoring and risk mitigation. Governments and the private sector should encourage the adoption of technologies such as IoT sensors, digital health applications, and renewable energy solutions to reduce environmental health impacts.

Strengthening Multilateral Cooperation to Address Global Environmental Injustice

Since the effects of environmental injustice are global, international cooperation is needed to tackle this issue. Organizations like the WHO, UNEP, and the World Bank should continue strengthening programs linking environmental justice to public health.

Integrating Environmental Justice into Global Health Policies

Environmental injustice must be recognized as a key determinant of global health, and public health policies should reflect this connection.

By implementing these recommendations, gaps in environmental health can be reduced, and the most vulnerable populations can receive better protection from the adverse effects of environmental degradation. An inclusive and sustainable approach will be key to ensuring that environmental justice and global health equity are realized in a tangible and lasting manner.

REFERENCES

Achmadi, U. F., & Ernawati, K. (2017). Climate Change Globalization and Emerging Disease, Challenges and Good Pracitces for Environmental Health Specialist. *International Journal of Public Health and Clinical Sciences*, *4*(2), 2289–7577.

Almazroui, M., Saeed, S., Saeed, F., Islam, M. N., & Ismail, M. (2020). Projections of Precipitation and Temperature over the South Asian Countries in CMIP6. *Earth Systems and Environment*, *4*(2), 297–320. DOI: 10.1007/s41748-020-00157-7

Asikainen, A., Carrer, P., Kephalopoulos, S., Fernandes, E. de O., Wargocki, P., & Hänninen, O. (2016). Reducing burden of disease from residential indoor air exposures in Europe (HEALTHVENT project). *Environmental Health: A Global Access Science Source*, *15*(S1), S35. DOI: 10.1186/s12940-016-0101-8 PMID: 26961383

Baba, F. A. (2024). Water Pollution: Causes, Impacts, and Solutions: a critical review. J*ournal of Sciences and Humanities*. 1-18. DOI: 10.37376/jsh.vi76.5785

Bangkara, B. M. A. S. A., Maruf, I. R., Ernawati, K., Fatmawati, E., & Manullang, S. O. (2022). Identification of the impact of the pandemic on the life of urban slums in Indonesia and solutions to solve it. *International Journal of Health Sciences*, 3331–3344. DOI: 10.53730/ijhs.v6nS1.5488

Baudet, A., Baurès, E., Blanchard, O., Le Cann, P., Gangneux, J.-P., & Florentin, A. (2022). Indoor Carbon Dioxide, Fine Particulate Matter and Total Volatile Organic Compounds in Private Healthcare and Elderly Care Facilities. *Toxics*, *10*(3), 136. DOI: 10.3390/toxics10030136 PMID: 35324761

Berberian, A. G., Perera, F., Arunachalam, S., Levy, J. I., Buckley, L., Arter, C., Coomes, K. E., & Buonocore, J. J. (2024). Children's health impacts from a proposed decarbonization policy in the transportation sector in the Eastern United States. *Environmental Research Letters*, *19*(4), 044001. DOI: 10.1088/1748-9326/ad2e73

Bishoge, O. K., Ajayi, D. D., Mfinanga, S. G., & Aremu, A. K. (2023). Students' perceptions of the nature and magnitude of environmental health concerns in Mtwara town, Tanzania. *Environmental Quality Management*, *32*(3), 263–274. DOI: 10.1002/tqem.21915

Bishop, J. A., & Reed, P. (2022). Defining Success: Establishing Clarity of Purpose and a Measurement Framework to Advance Health Equity. *Journal of Public Health Management and Practice*, *28*(5), 559–561. DOI: 10.1097/PHH.0000000000001577 PMID: 35867505

Blockstein, J., Tilt, J. H., & Botello Salgado, B. (2024). Daily vulnerability and disaster resilience: A case study of preferred community assets and social capital for Latinx coastal residents. *Disaster Prevention and Management, 33*(6), 57–72. DOI: 10.1108/DPM-02-2024-0048

Brajer, R. A. (2022). Effects of Air Pollution on the Development of Respiratory Diseases among Residents in New Delhi, India. *Journal of Medicine, Nursing & Public Health, 5*(2), 1–11. DOI: 10.53819/81018102t5070

Brooks, M., & Fields, E. (2021). Community Partnered Participatory Research methods as tools for racial justice and health equity. *Perspectives in Public Health, 141*(5), 261–262. DOI: 10.1177/1757913921989377 PMID: 34431390

Chandra, Y. A., Kawamura, Y., Paudel, S., & Nishigawa, M. (2020). Value of mutual assistance for disaster risk reduction in Japan, Indonesia, and Nepal: A preliminary study. *Health Emergency and Disaster Nursing, 7*(1), 9–16. DOI: 10.24298/hedn.2018-0010

Chen, C., Chen, J., Fang, R., Ye, F., Yang, Z., Wang, Z., Shi, F., & Tan, W. (2021). What medical waste management system may cope With COVID-19 pandemic: Lessons from Wuhan. *Resources, Conservation and Recycling, 170*, 105600. DOI: 10.1016/j.resconrec.2021.105600 PMID: 33821099

Connolly, C., Keil, R., & Ali, S. H. (2021). Extended urbanisation and the spatialities of infectious disease: Demographic change, infrastructure and governance. *Urban Studies (Edinburgh, Scotland), 58*(2), 245–263. DOI: 10.1177/0042098020910873

Dahlin, E. (2024). Who Says Artificial Intelligence Is Stealing Our Jobs? *Socius: Sociological Research for a Dynamic World, 10*, 23780231241259672. Advance online publication. DOI: 10.1177/23780231241259672

Davariashtiyani, A., Wang, B., Hajinazar, S., Zurek, E., & Kadkhodaei, S. (2024). Impact of data bias on machine learning for crystal compound synthesizability predictions. *Machine Learning: Science and Technology, 5*(4), 040501. DOI: 10.1088/2632-2153/ad9378

de Castro, Y. V. C., Morii, K. Y., Santos, I. A., Destefani, A. C., & Destefani, V. C. (2024). Beyond Black Boxes: Interpretabel AI for Enhanced Risk Assesment and Ethical Decision-Making in Forensic Psychiatry. *Revista Ibero-Americana de Humanidades. Ciência & Educação (Bauru), 10*(8), 2475–2479. DOI: 10.51891/rease.v10i8.15298

Deshpande, A., Tomar, A., & Pagare, A. (2024). Quantitative analysis of air pollution levels and its health implications in Delhi-NCR: A longitudinal study. *International Journal of Science and Research Archive, 11*(2), 759–768. DOI: 10.30574/ijsra.2024.11.2.0488

Dirgantara, P., Kalaloi, A. F., & Dianita, I. A. (2023). Environmental communication in community-based conservation movement: Lesson from the Masigit Kareumbi Hunting Park, Indonesia. *IOP Conference Series. Earth and Environmental Science, 1211*(1), 012004. DOI: 10.1088/1755-1315/1211/1/012004

Drozd, G. T., Zhao, Y., Saliba, G., Frodin, B., Maddox, C., Weber, R. J., Chang, M.-C. O., Maldonado, H., Sardar, S., Robinson, A. L., & Goldstein, A. H. (2016). Time Resolved Measurements of Speciated Tailpipe Emissions from Motor Vehicles: Trends with Emission Control Technology, Cold Start Effects, and Speciation. *Environmental Science & Technology, 50*(24), 13592–13599. DOI: 10.1021/acs.est.6b04513 PMID: 27993057

Dutta, A., & Jinsart, W. (2022). Air pollution in Delhi, India: It's status and association with respiratory diseases. *PLoS One, 17*(9), e0274444. DOI: 10.1371/journal.pone.0274444 PMID: 36126064

Eccles, K. M., Karmaus, A. L., Kleinstreuer, N. C., Parham, F., Rider, C. V., Wambaugh, J. F., & Messier, K. P. (2023). A geospatial modeling approach to quantifying the risk of exposure to environmental chemical mixtures via a common molecular target. *The Science of the Total Environment, 855*, 158905. DOI: 10.1016/j.scitotenv.2022.158905 PMID: 36152849

El Hage, J., Shahrour, I., Hage Chehade, F., & Abi Farraj, F. (2023). A Comprehensive Assessment of Buildings for Post-Disaster Sustainable Reconstruction: A Case Study of Beirut Port. *Sustainability (Basel), 15*(18), 13433. DOI: 10.3390/su151813433

Ernawati, K., Achmadi, U., & Hayurani, H. (2014). Relationship Between Mosquito Breeding Places With Malaria in Pesawaran. *Jurnal Ilmu Kesehatan Masyarakat, 5*(3), 202–210.

Ernawati, K., Farras, R. M., Zakiyyah, A., Hayu, M., Salsabila, A. P., Aulia, M. L., Kurnianingsih, I., & Rifqatussa'adah, . (2021). Community Behavior in Controlling Aedes aegypti Mosquito Breeding Places before and during the Covid-19 Pandemic. *IOP Conference Series. Earth and Environmental Science, 940*(1), 012081. DOI: 10.1088/1755-1315/940/1/012081

Evangelopoulos, D., Chatzidiakou, L., Walton, H., Katsouyanni, K., Kelly, F. J., Quint, J. K., Jones, R. L., & Barratt, B. (2021). Personal exposure to air pollution and respiratory health of COPD patients in London. *The European Respiratory Journal, 58*(1), 2003432. DOI: 10.1183/13993003.03432-2020 PMID: 33542053

Fridayani, H. D. (2020). The Government's Role in Facing SDGs 2030 Citarum River Clean-up Program, Indonesia: An Analysis. *Journal of Governance and Public Policy, 7*(1). Advance online publication. DOI: 10.18196/jgpp.71120

Griswold, W., Patel, M., & Gnanadass, E. (2024). 'One Person Cannot Change It; It's Going to Take a Community': Addressing Inequity through Community Environmental Education. *Adult Learning, 35*(1), 23–33. DOI: 10.1177/10451595221145206

Hernandez Carballo, I., Bakola, M., & Stuckler, D. (2022). The impact of air pollution on COVID-19 incidence, severity, and mortality: A systematic review of studies in Europe and North America. *Environmental Research, 215*, 114155. DOI: 10.1016/j.envres.2022.114155 PMID: 36030916

Intahchomphoo, C., & Gundersen, O. E. (2020). Artificial Intelligence and Race: A Systematic Review. *Legal Information Management, 20*(2), 74–84. DOI: 10.1017/S1472669620000183

Jiao, K., Xu, M., & Liu, M. (2018). Health status and air pollution related socioeconomic concerns in urban China. *International Journal for Equity in Health, 17*(1), 18. DOI: 10.1186/s12939-018-0719-y PMID: 29402280

Kala, A. K., Atkinson, S. F., & Tiwari, C. (2020). Exploring the socioeconomic and environmental components of infectious diseases using multivariate geovisualization: West Nile Virus. *PeerJ, 8*, e9577. DOI: 10.7717/peerj.9577 PMID: 33194330

Korsakov, A. V., Kryukova, A. E., Troshin, V. P., Milushkina, O. Yu., & Lagerev, D. G. (2022). Cervical and Endometrial Cancer Incidence in the Female Population from the Bryansk Region Living in Conditions of Chemical, Radioactive and Combined Environmental Contamination (2000–2020). *Life (Chicago, Ill.), 12*(10), 1488. DOI: 10.3390/life12101488 PMID: 36294923

Koual, M., Tomkiewicz, C., Cano-Sancho, G., Antignac, J.-P., Bats, A.-S., & Coumoul, X. (2020). Environmental chemicals, breast cancer progression and drug resistance. *Environmental Health : A Global Access Science Source, 19*(1), 117. DOI: 10.1186/s12940-020-00670-2 PMID: 33203443

Kraus, L., & Murphy, H. (2021). The long term effects of outdoor air pollution in urban environments on cardiovascular health: A global review. *Commonhealth (Philadelphia, Pa.), 2*(3), 122–133. DOI: 10.15367/ch.v2i3.493

Liu, J., Clark, L. P., Bechle, M. J., Hajat, A., Kim, S.-Y., Robinson, A. L., Sheppard, L., Szpiro, A. A., & Marshall, J. D. (2021). Disparities in Air Pollution Exposure in the United States by Race/Ethnicity and Income, 1990–2010. *Environmental Health Perspectives*, *129*(12), 127005. Advance online publication. DOI: 10.1289/EHP8584 PMID: 34908495

Magalhaes, T., Barreto, A., Mesquita-Silva, J., Serravalle, K. M. L., Valente de Andrade, M., Gomes, R. C. L., Nazaré, R. J., Calado, R. M. G. A., Ribeiro, G. S., & Kitron, U. (2024). Tailoring a One Health course for an established non-One Health graduate program in Brazil. *Frontiers in Tropical Diseases*, *4*, 1317092. Advance online publication. DOI: 10.3389/fitd.2023.1317092

Martins, C., Rufo, J., Padrão, A., Fonseca, H., Batista, L., Santos, M. P., Zacca, R., Silva, J. P., & Ribeiro, A. I. (2024). *Movement behaviours, air pollution and health in school-aged children: a cross-sectional study to guide the co- creation of healthier environments - The MOVE-AIR Project*. DOI: 10.21203/rs.3.rs-5312146/v1

Matheswaran, K., Alahacoon, N., Pandey, R., & Amarnath, G. (2019). Flood risk assessment in South Asia to prioritize flood index insurance applications in Bihar, India. *Geomatics, Natural Hazards & Risk*, *10*(1), 26–48. DOI: 10.1080/19475705.2018.1500495

Moyano-Fernández, C., Rueda, J., Delgado, J., & Ausín, T. (2024). May Artificial Intelligence take health and sustainability on a honeymoon? Towards green technologies for multidimensional health and environmental justice. *Global Bioethics = Problemi di Bioetica*, *35*(1), 2322208. Advance online publication. DOI: 10.1080/11287462.2024.2322208 PMID: 38476503

Murphy, K., Di Ruggiero, E., Upshur, R., Willison, D. J., Malhotra, N., Cai, J. C., Malhotra, N., Lui, V., & Gibson, J. (2021). Artificial intelligence for good health: A scoping review of the ethics literature. *BMC Medical Ethics*, *22*(1), 14. DOI: 10.1186/s12910-021-00577-8 PMID: 33588803

N'gattia, K. A., Kouassi, D. P., Coulibaly, D., Chérif, D., & Tiembré, I. (2020). Perception of Inhabitants in Urban Slums of Bouake (Cote D' Ivoire) About The Health Risks of Unsanitary Environments. *African Journal of Health. Safety and Environment*, *1*(1), 73–80. DOI: 10.52417/ajhse.v1i1.34

Nanditha, J. S., Kushwaha, A. P., Singh, R., Malik, I., Solanki, H., Chuphal, D. S., Dangar, S., Mahto, S. S., Vegad, U., & Mishra, V. (2023). The Pakistan Flood of August 2022: Causes and Implications. *Earth's Future*, *11*(3), e2022EF003230. Advance online publication. DOI: 10.1029/2022EF003230

Nogueira, L. M., & Yabroff, K. R. (2024). Climate change and cancer: The Environmental Justice perspective. *Journal of the National Cancer Institute, 116*(1), 15–25. DOI: 10.1093/jnci/djad185 PMID: 37813679

Parris, C. L., Hegtvedt, K. A., & Johnson, C. (2021). Assessments of Environmental Injustice among Black Americans. *Social Currents, 8*(1), 45–63. DOI: 10.1177/2329496520950808 PMID: 36199976

Patel, V. R., Jella, T., Gupta, A., Nassel, A., Ibrahim, A., & Hussaini, S. M. Q. (2023). Association of Neighborhood-Level Environmental Injustice With Health Status in the US. *JAMA Internal Medicine, 183*(10), 1162. DOI: 10.1001/jamainternmed.2023.2835 PMID: 37578753

Polonik, P., Ricke, K., Reese, S., & Burney, J. (2023). Air quality equity in US climate policy. *Proceedings of the National Academy of Sciences of the United States of America, 120*(26), e2217124120. Advance online publication. DOI: 10.1073/pnas.2217124120 PMID: 37339204

Ravi, S. S., Osipov, S., & Turner, J. W. G. (2023). Impact of Modern Vehicular Technologies and Emission Regulations on Improving Global Air Quality. *Atmosphere (Basel), 14*(7), 1164. DOI: 10.3390/atmos14071164

Rebeiro-Hargrave, A., Fung, P. L., Varjonen, S., Huertas, A., Sillanpää, S., Luoma, K., Hussein, T., Petäjä, T., Timonen, H., Limo, J., Nousiainen, V., & Tarkoma, S. (2021). City Wide Participatory Sensing of Air Quality. *Frontiers in Environmental Science, 9*, 773778. Advance online publication. DOI: 10.3389/fenvs.2021.773778

Ren, S., & Giang, A. (2024). Inequitable Spatial and Temporal Patterns in the Distribution of Multiple Environmental Risks and Benefits in Metro Vancouver. *GeoHealth, 8*(12), e2024GH001157. Advance online publication. DOI: 10.1029/2024GH001157 PMID: 39712528

Rickard, B. P., Tan, X., Fenton, S. E., & Rizvi, I. (2022). Select Per- and Polyfluoroalkyl Substances (PFAS) Induce Resistance to Carboplatin in Ovarian Cancer Cell Lines. *International Journal of Molecular Sciences, 23*(9), 5176. DOI: 10.3390/ijms23095176 PMID: 35563566

Rojas-Rueda, D., Morales-Zamora, E., Alsufyani, W. A., Herbst, C. H., AlBalawi, S. M., Alsukait, R., & Alomran, M. (2021). Environmental Risk Factors and Health: An Umbrella Review of Meta-Analyses. *International Journal of Environmental Research and Public Health, 18*(2), 704. DOI: 10.3390/ijerph18020704 PMID: 33467516

Saidur Rhaman, M., Tahjib-Ul-Arif, , Golam Kibria, M., & Hoque, A. (2022). Climate Change and Its Adverse Impacts on Plant Growth in South Asia: Current Status and Upcoming Challenges. *Phyton, 91*(4), 695–711. DOI: 10.32604/phyton.2022.018898

Sergi, B. J., Adams, P. J., Muller, N. Z., Robinson, A. L., Davis, S. J., Marshall, J. D., & Azevedo, I. L. (2020). Optimizing Emissions Reductions from the U.S. Power Sector for Climate and Health Benefits. *Environmental Science & Technology, 54*(12), 7513–7523. DOI: 10.1021/acs.est.9b06936 PMID: 32392045

Sharma, S., Paudel, M., Singh, A., Milligan, L., & Singh, G. B. (2024). Environmental Justice Education in Nepal: Policies and Practices. *Prithvi Academic Journal, 7*, 41–56. DOI: 10.3126/paj.v7i1.65762

Shrestha, N., Shah, S., Khanal, G., & Ghimire, P. (2024). Prevalence of non-communicable disease risk factor among the adult population of Bharatpur Metropolitan City, Chitwan, Nepal. *Journal of Chitwan Medical College, 14*(1), 49–54. DOI: 10.54530/jcmc.1469

Suresh, S., Meraj, G., Kumar, P., Singh, D., Khan, I. D., Gupta, A., Yadav, T., Kouser, A., & Avtar, R. (2023). *Disease Dynamics in a Changing Climate: Impact of Urbanization and Temperature Variability on Infectious Diseases in Coimbatore*. DOI: 10.21203/rs.3.rs-3065785/v1

Susanna, D., Ernawati, K., & Achmadi, U. F. (2012). Sustainable planning in a malaria vector control program: A study in Pesawaran, Indonesia. *Malaria Journal, 11*(S1), 1–2. DOI: 10.1186/1475-2875-11-S1-P129

Tashmin, N., & Islam, M. S. (2023). Climate Change Induced Socioeconomic Vulnerability- A Case Study for Koyra Upazila, Khulna, Bangladesh. *The Dhaka University Journal of Earth and Environmental Sciences, 11*(2), 67–79. DOI: 10.3329/dujees.v11i2.68858

Tommy, S., Sujianto, Rusli, Z., & Heriyanto, M. (2024). Grand design policy for economic empowerment through waste management: A case study of Pekanbaru City's environmental and energy strategies. *E3S Web of Conferences, 506*, 02003. DOI: 10.1051/e3sconf/202450602003

Tsocheva, I., Scales, J., Dove, R., Chavda, J., Kalsi, H., Wood, H. E., Colligan, G., Cross, L., Newby, C., Hall, A., Keating, M., Sartori, L., Moon, J., Thomson, A., Tomini, F., Murray, A., Hamad, W., Tijm, S., Hirst, A., & Griffiths, C. J. (2023). Investigating the impact of London's ultra low emission zone on children's health: Children's health in London and Luton (CHILL) protocol for a prospective parallel cohort study. *BMC Pediatrics, 23*(1), 556. DOI: 10.1186/s12887-023-04384-5 PMID: 37925402

Tundjungsari, V., Ernawati, K., & Mutia, N. (2020). *Public Health Surveillance to Promote Clean and Healthy Life Behaviours Using Big Data Approach (An Indonesian Case Study)* (pp. 761–775). DOI: 10.1007/978-3-030-23162-0_69

Wagener, A., Stassart, C., & Etienne, A.-M. (2022). COVID-19 and Its Lockdown in Belgium: How Limited Access to Environmental Satisfaction Impacts Emotions? *Psychologica Belgica, 62*(1), 34–46. DOI: 10.5334/pb.1082 PMID: 35087679

Wang, C., Pan, R., Wan, X., Tan, Y., Xu, L., Ho, C. S., & Ho, R. C. (2020). Immediate Psychological Responses and Associated Factors during the Initial Stage of the 2019 Coronavirus Disease (COVID-19) Epidemic among the General Population in China. *International Journal of Environmental Research and Public Health, 17*(5), 1729. DOI: 10.3390/ijerph17051729 PMID: 32155789

Wang, X. (2022). Can Environmental Health Play a Key Role in Prevention of Infectious Diseases? *Journal of Innovations in Medical Research, 1*(3). Advance online publication. DOI: 10.56397/JIMR/2022.10.03

Wolf, K., Hoffmann, B., Andersen, Z. J., Atkinson, R. W., Bauwelinck, M., Bellander, T., Brandt, J., Brunekreef, B., Cesaroni, G., Chen, J., de Faire, U., de Hoogh, K., Fecht, D., Forastiere, F., Gulliver, J., Hertel, O., Hvidtfeldt, U. A., Janssen, N. A. H., Jørgensen, J. T., & Ljungman, P. L. S. (2021). Long-term exposure to low-level ambient air pollution and incidence of stroke and coronary heart disease: A pooled analysis of six European cohorts within the ELAPSE project. *The Lancet. Planetary Health, 5*(9), e620–e632. DOI: 10.1016/S2542-5196(21)00195-9 PMID: 34508683

Wu, Y., & Huang, C. (2022). Climate Change and Vector-Borne Diseases in China: A Review of Evidence and Implications for Risk Management. *Biology (Basel), 11*(3), 370. DOI: 10.3390/biology11030370 PMID: 35336744

Xue, Y. (2022). Evaluation analysis on industrial green total factor productivity and energy transition policy in resource-based region. *Energy & Environment, 33*(3), 419–434. DOI: 10.1177/0958305X211005428

Yadav, B., Gupta, A., Sharma, N., & Sharma, Y. (2024). IoT-Enabled Health Monitoring Systems: Transforming Healthcare Delivery. *International Journal for Research in Applied Science and Engineering Technology, 12*(2), 1108–1116. DOI: 10.22214/ijraset.2024.58516

Yen, C.-C., & Chen, P.-L. (2021). *Regional air pollution severity affects the incidence of acute myocardial infarction triggered by short-term pollutant exposure: A time-stratified case-crossover analysis*. DOI: 10.21203/rs.3.rs-432348/v1

Yoo, S., & Heshmati, A. (2019). The Effects of Environmental Regulations on the Manufacturing Industry's Performance: A Comparison of Green and Non-Green Sectors in Korea. *Energies*, *12*(12), 2296. DOI: 10.3390/en12122296

Yuwanto, L., Handoko, R., & Maduwinarti, A. (2021). Implementation of Disaster Risk Reduction Policy: Moderating Effect of Community Participation. *Journal of Public Policy and Administration*, *5*(4), 163. DOI: 10.11648/j.jppa.20210504.17

Zolitschka, K. A., Razum, O., & Sauzet, O. (2022). Using agent-based modelling to test hypotheses on the role of neighbourhood social mechanisms in the development of small-area health inequalities. *Journal of Epidemiology and Community Health*, *76*(8), 750–755. DOI: 10.1136/jech-2021-218310 PMID: 35568396

Chapter 4
Challenges in Health Equity:
Balancing Innovation With Fairness and Addressing Algorithmic Biases

Muhammad Arshed
https://orcid.org/0009-0005-0683-9610
Baqai Medical University, Pakistan

Abdul Kabeer Kazi
https://orcid.org/0000-0001-9860-2891
Baqai Medical University, Pakistan

Mehwish Kiran
Baqai Medical University, Pakistan

Syed Muhammad Fauzan Ali
https://orcid.org/0000-0002-7838-2622
Baqai Medical University, Pakistan

ABSTRACT

The rapid adoption of Artificial Intelligence (AI) in healthcare has revolutionized diagnostics, treatment planning, and patient care, but it has also raised critical ethical concerns, particularly regarding health equity. Algorithmic biases, often stemming from imbalanced datasets, result in unequal performance, with marginalized communities experiencing reduced accuracy and higher misdiagnosis rates. This chapter aims to investigate the impact of such biases and propose strategies to mitigate them. Using a structured methodology, the chapter analysed AI models

DOI: 10.4018/979-8-3373-1992-6.ch004

in diagnostic and treatment prediction tasks with diverse datasets, implemented data augmentation, re-sampling, and fairness-aware algorithms, and evaluated improvements using equity metrics. However, applying these mitigation strategies reduced biases and improved equity metrics. Finally, the chapter underscores the need for ethical frameworks and inclusive data practices to balance innovation with fairness and ensure equitable healthcare outcomes for all.

INTRODUCTION TO ETHICAL AI IN HEALTHCARE

Overview of Artificial Intelligence in Healthcare

Artificial intelligence is rapidly revolutionizing healthcare, driven by the growing availability of health data and advancements in analytical techniques (Al Kuwaiti et al., 2023). AI in healthcare entails the application of advanced technologies and algorithms to emulate human cognition and decision-making in the analysis, interpretation, and management of medical data (Yelne et al., 2023). It's not a monolithic technology but a range of computational models and algorithms that simulate cognitive processes, such as learning, reasoning, and adaptation (Al Kuwaiti et al., 2023).

AI's applications encompass virtually all domains of healthcare, from clinical decision support at the point of care to patient self-management of chronic conditions at home and drug research (M. Chen & Decary, 2020). AI can be integrated with existing technologies to facilitate routine diagnoses (Sadiku et al., 2020). Natural language processing, a subset of AI, is used to analyze unstructured textual data like doctors' notes and lab reports (M. Chen & Decary, 2020). Deep learning, another AI technique, utilizes multi-layered neural networks to process heterogeneous datasets, allowing algorithms to handle intricate and diverse data types (Jiang et al., 2017). AI greatly enhances the nature of operations, diagnostics, and clinical procedures (Dailah et al., 2024).

Importance of Ethics in AI Applications

The importance of ethics in AI applications within healthcare cannot be overstated. As AI systems become growingly integrated into clinical practice, diagnostics, and patient care, the ethical implications become more pronounced and demand careful consideration (Elendu et al., 2023). Ethical considerations are crucial in ensuring that AI serves to improve healthcare outcomes without compromising patient rights, privacy, or exacerbating existing inequalities (Farhud & Zokaei, 2021).

One of the primary reasons ethics is paramount is the potential for algorithmic bias. AI algorithms are trained on data, and if that data reflects existing societal biases, the AI system will likely perpetuate and even amplify those biases (Elendu et al., 2023). This can lead to unequal or unfair treatment decisions, particularly for vulnerable populations. Ensuring fairness requires careful attention to the data used to train AI models, as well as ongoing monitoring and auditing of algorithms to detect and correct any biases (Elendu et al., 2023).

Defining Health Equity in the Context of AI

Health equity, as defined by the World Health Organization, is "the absence of unfair and avoidable or remediable differences in health among population groups defined socially, economically, demographically, or geographically" (Berdahl et al., 2023). In the context of AI, achieving health equity means ensuring that AI systems do not exacerbate existing health disparities or create new ones (Cestonaro et al., 2023). It requires careful attention to how AI technologies are developed, deployed, and used, with a focus on mitigating bias and promoting fairness across all population groups (Smith & Heath Jeffery, 2020).

To achieve health equity in the context of AI, it is essential to address the root causes of health disparities and to ensure that AI systems are designed and used in ways that promote fairness and inclusivity. This includes:

- **Diverse and representative data:** AI systems should be trained on diverse datasets that accurately reflect the populations they are intended to serve (Gurevich et al., 2023).
- **Algorithmic auditing:** AI systems should be regularly audited to identify and correct biases (Smith & Heath Jeffery, 2020).
- **Transparency and Explainability:** AI systems should be transparent and explainable, allowing stakeholders to understand how decisions are made.
- **Human oversight:** Human oversight is important to ensure that AI systems complement, rather than replace, the empathy, compassion, and clinical judgment of healthcare professionals
- **Stakeholder engagement:** Involving patients, healthcare providers, ethicists, and policymakers in the development and deployment of AI systems (Smith & Heath Jeffery, 2020).

Objectives and Scope of the Chapter

This chapter aims to provide a comprehensive and nuanced exploration of the challenges and opportunities at the intersection of health equity and artificial intelligence (Elendu et al., 2023). It seeks to equip researchers, healthcare practitioners, policymakers, and technologists with the knowledge and tools necessary to navigate the complex ethical landscape surrounding AI in healthcare. The objectives of this book are to:

1. **Define and contextualize health equity in the age of AI:** Provide a clear and accessible definition of health equity and examine how AI can both exacerbate and alleviate existing health disparities.
2. **Explore the ethical dimensions of AI in healthcare:** Investigate the ethical considerations of AI and robotics in healthcare, including privacy and data security, bias and fairness, accountability and transparency, autonomy and human oversight, impact on healthcare professionals, societal implications, and regulatory challenges (Elendu et al., 2023).
3. **Identify and analyze algorithmic biases:** Provide strategies for identifying and mitigating algorithmic biases in AI systems, with a focus on ensuring fairness and inclusivity across diverse population groups (Panch et al., 2019)
4. **Evaluate the potential risks and benefits of AI in healthcare ethically**: Considering the impact on patients, healthcare professionals, and the broader healthcare system(Elendu et al., 2023).
5. **Examine existing ethical frameworks and guidelines:** Assess their adequacy and applicability in real-world healthcare settings (Elendu et al., 2023).
6. **Offer strategies for promoting fairness and inclusivity in AI development and deployment:** Provide concrete recommendations for promoting health equity through the responsible design, implementation, and evaluation of AI systems
7. **Highlight the importance of stakeholder engagement:** Emphasize the need for collaboration among patients, clinicians, ethicists, policymakers, and industry representatives in shaping the future of AI in healthcare (Nyariro et al., 2023).

The role of AI in addressing health disparities related to race, ethnicity, socioeconomic status, gender, geography, and other social determinants of health.

- The ethical implications of using AI in clinical decision-making, diagnostics, and treatment.
- The challenges of ensuring data privacy and security in AI-driven healthcare systems.
- The importance of transparency and explainability in AI algorithms.
- The need for human oversight and accountability in AI decision-making processes.
- The impact of AI on the doctor-patient relationship and the future of the healthcare workforce.

AI IN HEALTHCARE – INNOVATIONS AND OPPORTUNITIES

The Role of AI in Diagnosis and Treatment

AI is rapidly transforming the landscape of diagnosis and treatment in healthcare (Alowais et al., 2023). By leveraging machine learning algorithms, AI can analyze complex medical data with enhanced efficiency and precision than ever before (Bekbolatova et al., 2024). This leads to earlier and more precise diagnoses, which are crucial for effective treatment (Alowais et al., 2023). For instance, AI can assist in the early detection of life-threatening diseases, allowing clinicians to initiate prompt interventions (Alowais et al., 2023). The ability to interpret clinical data faster is especially critical in emergency departments, where timely intervention can significantly impact patient outcomes (Alowais et al., 2023).

Figure 1. AI workflow in clinical diagnosis and treatment planning

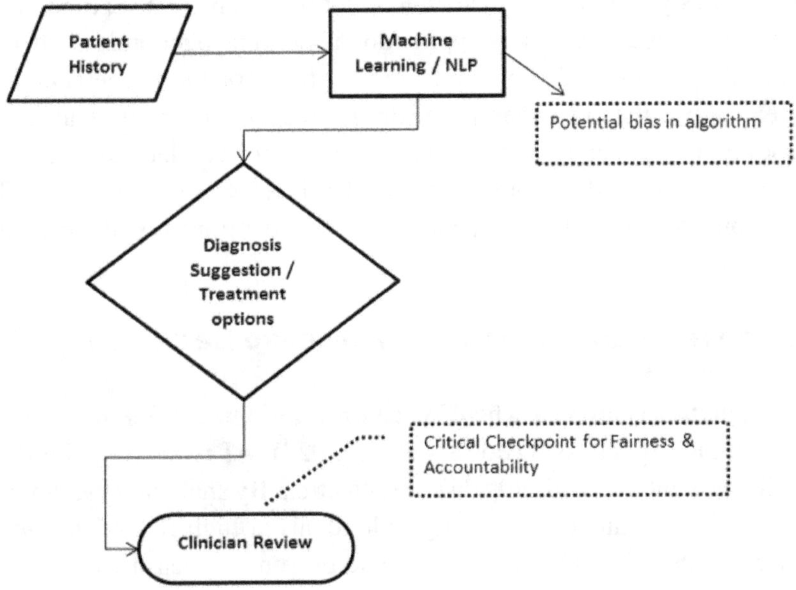

AI's capabilities extend to creating personalized treatment plans. By analyzing individual patient data, including genetic information and lifestyle factors, AI algorithms can tailor treatments to a patient's unique needs (Alowais et al., 2023). This approach not only optimizes treatment outcomes but also minimizes potential side effects (Alowais et al., 2023). In the realm of oncology, AI algorithms can delve into the intricate details of tumor genomics, proteomics, and other molecular profiles, providing a deeper understanding of the mechanisms driving cancer (Bongurala et al., 2025).

AI-Driven Drug Discovery and Personalized Medicine

AI is revolutionizing drug discovery by significantly accelerating the identification of potential drug candidates and predicting their behavior within the body (Alowais et al., 2023; Will Heaven, 2023). Traditionally, drug discovery is a protracted and resource-intensive process, often taking over 10 years and billions of dollars to bring a new drug to market (Will Heaven, 2023). AI streamlines this process by analyzing vast amounts of biological data to identify viable therapeutic candidates and predict their efficacy, thus reducing the need for extensive lab work (Will Heaven, 2023). Machine-learning models can predict how potential drugs might behave in the body and eliminate non-viable candidates early on (Will Heaven, 2023).

In personalized medicine, AI algorithms analyze individual patient data, including genetic makeup, lifestyle, and other factors, to tailor treatment plans to their unique needs (Serrano et al., 2024). One key application is pharmacogenomics, where AI predicts a patient's response to different medications based on their genetic makeup, guiding the selection of the most appropriate drug and dosage (Serrano et al., 2024). By understanding the human genome, AI helps improve our understanding of how diseases occur, are prevented, and are treated (Taherdoost & Ghofrani, 2024). This personalized approach optimizes treatment outcomes and minimizes adverse effects (Alowais et al., 2023).

AI for Predictive Analytics and Early Disease Detection

Predictive analytics is an area where AI can revolutionize different aspects of health care, including diagnosis (Alowais et al., 2023). AI is making significant strides in predictive analytics and early disease detection. By analyzing vast amounts of patient data, AI algorithms can identify individuals at high risk of developing certain diseases, enabling timely intervention and preventive measures (*5 Ways AI Is Transforming Health Systems*, 2025). This proactive approach has the potential to significantly improve patient outcomes and reduce healthcare costs (*5 Ways AI Is Transforming Health Systems*, 2025).

AI's analytical capabilities extend to various data types, including medical records, genetic information, and lifestyle factors. By integrating these diverse data points, AI can generate more accurate and personalized risk assessments (Kurant, 2023). For instance, AI can interrogate genomic datasets to predict the likelihood of developing conditions like Alzheimer's disease (Raju, 2023). This allows for early intervention strategies, such as lifestyle changes or medication, to mitigate or delay the onset of the disease (Kurant, 2023; M et al., 2025). The technology is expected to grow rapidly in the coming years (Arshed, Mahmud, et al., 2023; Arshed, Zakar, et al., 2023; Arshed, Mahmud, et al., 2024; Arshed et al., 2025).

Digital Health and Telemedicine: AI's Contribution

AI is significantly enhancing digital health and telemedicine, transforming how healthcare is delivered and accessed (Chang, 2020). Telemedicine uses innovative technology to improve access to and quality of healthcare (Arshed, Mahmud, et al., 2024; Arshed et al., 2025; Pacis et al., 2018). AI contributes by enabling AI-driven virtual agents that can address patient inquiries, schedule appointments, and remotely monitor health conditions, thereby growing efficiency (Raju, 2023).

One of the most promising applications of AI in this field is in remote patient monitoring. AI systems can analyze data collected from wearable devices and other remote sensors to detect clinically significant alterations in a patient's condition (Artificial Intelligence in Telehealth: Current Applications and Future Possibilities, 2024). AI tools are not yet authorized to diagnose patients, but AI-powered diagnostic tools can analyze medical images and provide preliminary diagnoses, enhancing the efficiency and accuracy of remote consultations (Alowais et al., 2023; Bill Siwicki, 2023).

AI's role in digital health also extends to personalized care. Machine learning algorithms can analyze patient data to anticipate health complications and tailor personalized care plans (Arshed, Mahmud, et al., 2023; Arshed, Umer, et al., 2024; Arshed, Zakar, et al., 2023). Furthermore, AI-driven virtual assistants in telemedicine are redefining patient-provider interactions, offering patients convenient access to healthcare information and resources and communication with healthcare professionals in an efficient and personalized manner (Y.-H. Li et al., 2024).

UNDERSTANDING ALGORITHMIC BIAS IN HEALTHCARE AI

What is Algorithmic Bias?

Algorithmic bias in healthcare refers to systematic and unfair disparities in how AI models perform across different patient groups. These biases often stem from unrepresentative or imbalanced training data, flawed model design, or unintended consequences of real-world implementation. When left unchecked, algorithmic bias can lead to misdiagnoses, unequal treatment recommendations, and the reinforcement of existing health disparities. For instance, an AI tool trained mostly on data from a single ethnic group may perform poorly when applied to other populations, compromising patient safety and fairness (McCall et al., 2022).

As healthcare systems increasingly rely on AI, addressing bias becomes critical for ensuring equitable care. Researchers advocate for rigorous model evaluation, diverse datasets, and ethical frameworks that center on fairness and transparency (R. J. Chen et al., 2023). Beyond technical fixes, a deeper ethical reflection is required to redefine fairness in AI systems used in medicine (Ogbodu, 2023), aligning technology with inclusive and patient-centred values.

Types of Bias in AI Systems

As artificial intelligence (AI) becomes more embedded in healthcare and other critical domains, understanding the different types of bias in AI systems is crucial. These biases not only undermine algorithmic efficacy but can also reinforce social inequities, particularly when affecting high-stakes decisions like diagnosis, treatment, or access to care (Mittermaier et al., 2023).

Figure 2. Sources and types of bias in healthcare AI

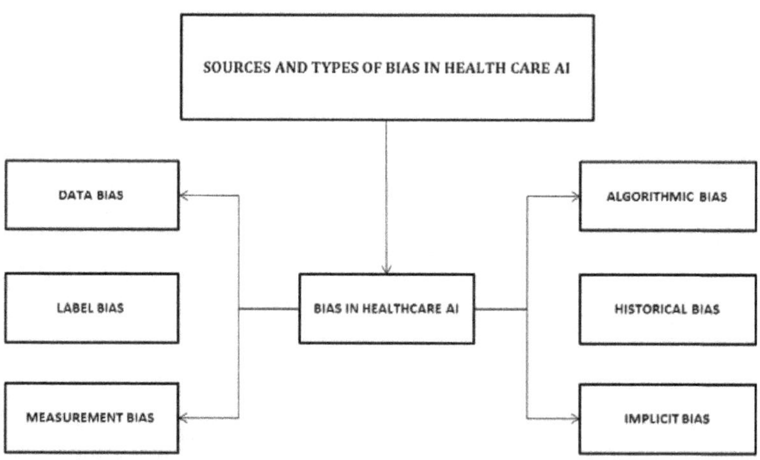

- **Data Biases**: Data bias occurs when the dataset used to train an AI model is unrepresentative of the population it aims to serve. This can result from historical underrepresentation of certain groups, poor sampling techniques, or outdated information. In healthcare, for instance, if a model is primarily trained on data from urban male patients, it may perform poorly on rural or female populations (Fazil et al., 2024) argue that data bias is one of the most common and impactful forms of bias, often serving as the root cause for downstream algorithmic disparities.

- **Label Bias**: Label bias arises when the labels, or outcomes, used to train AI are themselves biased. This typically reflects human errors or social prejudices embedded in historical decision-making. For example, if past diagnostic decisions were influenced by racial stereotypes, these biases are encoded into the AI system (Ferrara, 2024).
- **Measurement Bias**: Measurement bias refers to errors or inconsistencies in how data is recorded or captured. In healthcare, different hospitals might use varying standards for measuring blood pressure, or electronic health records may inconsistently document symptoms. When AI models learn from such noisy or non-standardized data, their performance becomes unreliable across different environments (Mittermaier et al., 2023). This type of bias can be subtle yet significantly affect clinical accuracy.
- **Algorithmic Design Bias**: Sometimes bias is baked into the design choices of the algorithm itself. From selecting features to tuning parameters, design decisions can unintentionally privilege one group over another. Kordzadeh and Ghasemaghaei (2022) emphasize that developers often optimize for overall accuracy, which can obscure poor performance in minority subgroups, a form of statistical invisibility that reinforces systemic disadvantage (Kordzadeh & and Ghasemaghaei, 2022).
- **Historical Bias**: Historical bias reflects structural and societal inequalities embedded in the data itself, even if collected and processed correctly. AI systems trained on such data risk reproducing and legitimizing existing disparities. For example, healthcare access disparities between income groups may be reflected in treatment recommendations if not addressed explicitly (Fazil et al., 2024; Ferrara, 2024).
- **Implicit Bias**: Implicit bias, a form of cognitive bias, is introduced when developers unconsciously embed their worldviews into algorithms. As Johnson (2021) points out, even the framing of a problem, what to predict, and what constitutes success, can reflect cultural assumptions and power dynamics (Johnson et al., 2021).

How Bias Manifests in Healthcare AI

Bias in healthcare AI often shows up in subtle but harmful ways, and it has real consequences for patients. It's not just about technical errors, it's about how the data and systems we rely on can unintentionally leave people behind. One of the biggest issues is that AI models are often trained on limited or non-diverse data. For example, if an AI tool is built using health records mostly from White male patients, it might not perform well when used to diagnose conditions in women or ethnic minorities. This kind of bias can lead to missed diagnoses or improper treatment (Byrne, 2021).

Another area where bias surfaces is in digital tools that prioritize care. AI systems might suggest different treatment paths based on data that doesn't account for socioeconomic differences or varying access to care. These decisions can disproportionately affect patients who already face barriers in the healthcare system (Albahri et al., 2023).

Healthcare professionals are increasingly aware of this issue. A recent online survey showed that many see AI bias as a serious concern that needs to be addressed before wider adoption can happen (Vorisek et al., 2023). The takeaway is clear: if AI is going to improve healthcare, it must be built and tested with fairness at its core.

Ethical and Legal Implications of Algorithmic Bias

Algorithmic bias in healthcare AI raises profound ethical and legal concerns, particularly in countries like Pakistan, where digital policy and AI regulations are still taking shape. Ethically, the core issue lies in how biased algorithms can widen health disparities by misrepresenting or excluding specific populations, especially minorities, women, and rural communities. This contradicts the core ethical principles of healthcare: equity, justice, and non-maleficence (Vorisek et al., 2023).

From a legal standpoint, Pakistan currently lacks a dedicated, enforceable framework governing the use of AI in healthcare. While some policy discussions have begun, including recent efforts to draft digital and AI-specific laws (I. Ahmad et al., 2024), these are still in early stages and lack implementation mechanisms. This absence of regulation leaves space for misuse, data privacy violations, and unaccountable decision-making in clinical environments.

Globally, legal instruments like the GDPR and AI Act in the EU are setting standards for transparency, fairness, and explainability. These principles are especially crucial in healthcare, where patient outcomes depend on trust and accurate diagnostics. There is also growing focus on building AI that is trustworthy and explainable to clinicians and patients alike (Albahri et al., 2023).

To move forward, countries still in the development phase must accelerate the expansion of AI governance within healthcare, grounded in both legal safeguards and ethical training for health professionals. This includes embedding AI ethics in medical education and establishing oversight bodies to audit AI systems for bias and fairness.

HEALTH DISPARITIES AND AI – CHALLENGES IN EQUITY

Defining Health Disparities

Health disparities refer to systemic inequities in health outcomes and access to care across different population groups, often shaped by social, economic, and environmental disadvantages. These disparities are not random; they are deeply embedded in systems of power, policies, and historical injustices that perpetuate unequal treatment and outcomes in healthcare (Farahani & Ghasemi, 2024).

At the core, health disparities are driven by a combination of structural racism, socioeconomic inequality, and systemic barriers in education, housing, and employment. These social determinants directly impact health behaviours, chronic disease risks, and access to timely and quality medical care (Konstantopoulos et al., 2023). For instance, individuals from marginalized communities are more likely to live in areas with poor environmental conditions, limited healthcare facilities, and lower health literacy, factors that converge to elevate disease susceptibility.

Understanding the root causes of these disparities requires more than just statistics; it demands an examination of how systems operate unequally. Causal diagrams and other epidemiological tools have proven useful in mapping the influence of race, policy, and environment on health outcomes, helping researchers move beyond correlation to uncover actual pathways of inequity (Howe et al., 2022).

Tackling these disparities calls for a shift in healthcare priorities, from reactive treatment to proactive, equity-driven reform. Only by addressing the underlying structural issues can we hope to close the gap in health outcomes and build a more just healthcare system.

AI's Potential to Widen or Reduce Health Inequities

Artificial Intelligence (AI) holds both opportunities and risks when it comes to addressing health inequities. On one hand, AI can enhance diagnostic precision, streamline clinical workflows, and extend healthcare access to underserved areas through telemedicine and predictive analytics. However, if not rigorously validated and regulated, AI risks reinforcing existing disparities, particularly for marginalized populations who are often underrepresented in the data used to train these systems (Konstantopoulos et al., 2023).

The challenge lies in the fact that AI learns from historical data, data that may already be biased due to systemic inequalities in healthcare delivery. This means that algorithms might unintentionally encode and perpetuate disparities unless they are explicitly audited for fairness and inclusivity. For instance, if an AI tool is trained primarily on urban populations, it may perform poorly for rural communities, widening the access and quality gap.

Yet, there's enormous potential for AI to drive equity. When embedded within well-designed, place-based interventions, AI can support general practice in identifying at-risk groups and tailoring care to their specific needs (d'Elia et al., 2022; Gkiouleka et al., 2023). Furthermore, lessons from global initiatives show that equitable health outcomes are achievable when technology is aligned with policies aimed at social upliftment (Bambra, 2022).

Ultimately, the key lies in intentional design. AI must be developed with equity as a central pillar, not an afterthought. That means involving diverse voices, addressing data gaps, and holding systems accountable to ensure technology becomes a bridge, not a barrier, to health justice.

Data Quality and Representation Issues

In the realm of healthcare AI, the saying "garbage in, garbage out" couldn't be more true. The quality and representativeness of data used to train AI models directly affect the accuracy, safety, and fairness of their outcomes. Unfortunately, much of the data currently used in health-related machine learning systems is riddled with inaccuracies, inconsistencies, and underrepresentation of minority groups (Mohammed et al., 2024).

Poor data quality can stem from a range of issues, including incorrect labels, missing values, or biased sampling methods. In healthcare, even minor errors in labelling diagnoses or recording symptoms can lead to serious consequences when algorithms make clinical decisions based on flawed inputs (Wu et al., 2021). Moreover, underrepresentation of certain populations, be it due to geography, ethnicity, gender, or socioeconomic status, can create representational gaps in AI systems, ultimately marginalizing the very groups that need care the most.

Deep learning, often considered the gold standard for predictive analytics, is especially data-hungry. Yet, it's highly sensitive to noise and imbalances within datasets. This makes the data collection process, not just model development, a critical component of AI design (Wang et al., 2022).

Ethical Considerations in Health Data Collection

Collecting health data for AI applications isn't just a technical challenge, it's a deeply ethical one. The sensitive nature of health information requires that patient autonomy, privacy, and informed consent be strictly upheld. One of the core concerns lies in who owns the data and how transparently it is being used. Patients often remain unaware of how their health records are utilized, raising significant issues of data ownership and control (Chiruvella & Guddati, 2021).

Ethical dilemmas further intensify when data is collected without clear, ongoing consent or when it's reused in secondary research without patient knowledge. In qualitative settings, such as interviews or focus groups, the potential for ethical breaches increases, especially if consent protocols are unclear or culturally insensitive (Laryeafio & Ogbewe, 2023).

With AI models depending heavily on large, often unstructured datasets, the temptation to overlook ethical safeguards for the sake of scale or speed is real. However, such shortcuts risk eroding public trust and compromising the integrity of healthcare systems (Wang et al., 2022). Moreover, the integration of AI in medicine must be governed by strict frameworks to avoid exploitation and ensure data is collected, stored, and applied with transparency and fairness (Farhud & Zokaei, 2021).

FAIRNESS IN AI – ETHICAL AND REGULATORY FRAMEWORKS

Principles of Fairness in AI Development

The principle of fairness in artificial intelligence (AI) development centres on ensuring that AI systems operate equitably, without reinforcing existing societal biases or creating new forms of discrimination. In the context of healthcare, employment, legal systems, and public services, fairness is fundamental to maintaining trust, legitimacy, and social justice.

Fairness begins with data integrity. Machine learning models trained on biased, incomplete, or non-representative datasets are likely to reproduce these biases in real-world decisions (Giovanola & Tiribelli, 2023). Therefore, the pursuit of fairness requires methodical evaluation of data sources, representation, and labelling practices. However, fairness is not merely a technical concern, it is a multidisciplinary challenge that intersects with ethics, law, and public policy.

According to Leslie et al. (2024), fairness must be embedded throughout the AI lifecycle, from conceptualization and design to deployment and post-deployment monitoring. This includes involving diverse stakeholders, ensuring transparency in algorithmic decision-making, and conducting ongoing impact assessments to identify unintended harms (Leslie et al., 2024).

Bateni et al. (2022) highlight that operationalizing fairness involves trade-offs, between accuracy and equity, or individual and group outcomes, which must be navigated with care and accountability (Bateni et al., 2022). Studies advocate for robust governance frameworks to enforce ethical standards and hold developers and institutions responsible for the consequences of their AI systems (Almeida et al., 2021).

Global Ethical Guidelines for AI in Healthcare

As artificial intelligence (AI) becomes growingly embedded in healthcare systems worldwide, global ethical guidelines have emerged to ensure its development and use align with principles of human dignity, equity, safety, and accountability. The World Health Organization (2021) has outlined six core principles to guide AI in health: protecting autonomy, promoting human well-being and safety, ensuring transparency, fostering responsibility, promoting inclusiveness, and sustaining responsiveness. These principles provide a methodical evaluation for integrating AI into clinical and public health settings (WHO, 2021).

Across global healthcare systems, these guidelines are being gradually operationalized. For instance, the United Kingdom's National Health Service has adopted AI solutions such as DeepMind's Streams app, with strict ethical oversight regarding data usage and patient consent. In South Korea, AI tools are used for early cancer detection, but only after undergoing rigorous ethical review processes that include fairness audits and stakeholder consultation (F. Li et al., 2023).

A truly global ethical framework must also recognize local health system capacities, data protection laws, and cultural sensitivities. As the integration of AI in healthcare accelerates, the global community must not only develop standards but also commit to enforcing them, ensuring that innovation enhances care without compromising human rights.

Regulatory Approaches: GDPR, HIPAA, and AI Acts

Making sure artificial intelligence is used responsibly and safely, there are clear and strong regulations guiding its application. These legal frameworks are not simply bureaucratic guidelines, they represent our collective commitment to uphold patient rights, protect sensitive data, and hold technology to human-centered standards.

One of the most influential examples is the General Data Protection Regulation (GDPR) in the European Union. This regulation requires transparency in how personal data is used, offers individuals the right to access or challenge automated decisions, and demands that consent be informed and freely given. In healthcare AI, where data is both personal and predictive, GDPR encourages a culture of accountability and respect for individual autonomy (Mohammad Amini et al., 2023).

Meanwhile, in the United States, the Health Insurance Portability and Accountability Act (HIPAA) governs how health information is stored, shared, and secured. Although originally developed before AI's emergence, HIPAA's emphasis on safeguarding patient data is now being applied to digital health tools, such as mobile health apps and remote monitoring technologies (Mia et al., 2022).

More recently, the European Union's proposed AI Act has marked a major shift toward regulating AI-specific risks. It classifies AI systems based on potential harm and places stricter rules on high-risk applications like those in healthcare. The act emphasizes human oversight, data quality, and system transparency, reinforcing the need to balance innovation with public trust (Ruschemeier, 2023).

Accountability and Transparency in AI Models

Accountability and transparency are fundamental components of responsible AI development, especially in sectors like healthcare where the stakes are high. These concepts ensure that artificial intelligence systems not only function correctly but also remain understandable and open to scrutiny. In the context of AI, accountability refers to the obligation of developers, organizations, and policymakers to take responsibility for the outcomes produced by AI systems, including addressing any unintended consequences or biases (Mensah, 2023). Transparency, on the other hand, involves providing clear insights into how AI models make decisions, ensuring that these processes are comprehensible and traceable to humans (Novelli et al., 2024).

The growing use of AI in healthcare has amplified the need for robust accountability frameworks. The European Union's Artificial Intelligence Act, for example, aims to regulate AI systems, particularly high-risk applications, ensuring they are not only effective but also accountable (Hacker, 2020). It mandates that AI systems, especially in critical fields, undergo rigorous oversight, with a clear path to accountability for any issues that arise.

In practice, accountability and transparency require AI developers to document and explain their models' decision-making processes, making it easier to identify and correct any biases or errors (Lechterman, 2022).

MITIGATING BIAS AND ENSURING FAIRNESS IN AI

Bias in artificial intelligence is often a mirror of real-world inequalities, reflecting gaps in data, design, and decision-making. In sensitive sectors like healthcare, unchecked bias can lead to serious consequences, such as misdiagnosis or unequal access to treatment. Addressing this issue goes beyond technical tweaks; it demands a deeper commitment to fairness from those who create and manage AI systems.

Fairness starts with asking the right questions: Who is being represented in the data? Whose voice is missing? Technical solutions like diverse datasets and algorithm audits can help, but without input from stakeholders, especially those affected, true fairness remains out of reach. Organizations must involve ethicists, clinicians, and patient communities early in development to create systems that serve everyone equally.

Figure 3. Bias mitigation strategies across the AI lifecycle

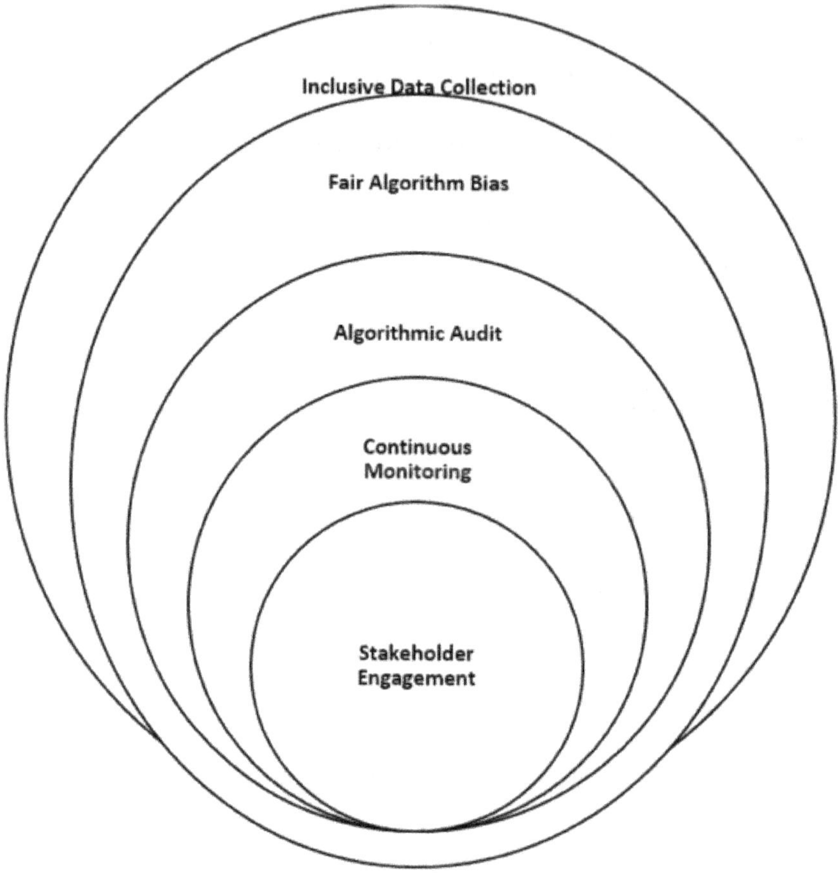

Bias Detection and Correction Techniques

In the development and deployment of artificial intelligence systems, particularly in healthcare, bias is one of the most pressing ethical challenges. Left unchecked, biased AI can reinforce systemic inequalities, misdiagnose patients, and offer treatment suggestions that disproportionately harm already vulnerable populations.

Detecting and correcting these biases is therefore not just a technical issue, it is a moral and social responsibility.

Bias often originates from imbalanced datasets that do not reflect diverse patient populations or historical data that carries embedded societal prejudices (Agarwal et al., 2023). Detection involves statistical audits, fairness testing, and analyzing model performance across different demographic groups. Once identified, correction techniques may include reweighting datasets, synthetic data generation to fill representation gaps, and algorithmic adjustments such as adversarial debiasing or fairness constraints.

Importantly, the process of bias mitigation must involve continuous monitoring, not just at model training but throughout deployment. A growing body of research has emphasized the need for transparent, explainable AI systems that allow stakeholders to scrutinize decisions (Albahri et al., 2023).

In regions like Pakistan, scholars are calling for robust legal frameworks to guide responsible AI use and address algorithmic discrimination in sensitive domains like law and healthcare (I. Ahmad et al., 2024; J. B. Ahmad et al., 2024). Mitigating bias, therefore, is a shared responsibility that spans technology, ethics, law, and governance.

Fair Machine Learning Algorithms and Their Applications

The pursuit of fairness in machine learning (ML) has become a cornerstone in designing ethical AI systems, especially in sectors like healthcare where decisions can significantly impact human lives. Fair ML algorithms aim to ensure that predictive outcomes do not disadvantage individuals or groups based on race, gender, or other protected attributes.

However, defining fairness in machine learning is far from straightforward. Different models adopt various fairness criteria, such as demographic parity, equal opportunity, or individual fairness, each with its trade-offs between accuracy and equity (Gao et al., 2024). For instance, algorithms that optimize for accuracy alone may inadvertently favour majority populations while underrepresenting minorities, leading to skewed diagnostics and treatment plans.

Real-world studies have demonstrated these pitfalls. A recent analysis revealed that ChatGPT exhibited racial and gender biases in managing acute coronary syndrome cases, showcasing how even advanced AI tools can produce inequitable medical recommendations. Furthermore, algorithms deemed "fair" in theory often fall short in practice when deployed within complex, real-life contexts (Fu et al., 2022).

Developers must, therefore, go beyond technical adjustments and integrate fairness into the entire ML lifecycle, from data collection and model training to validation and ongoing assessment (Valdivia et al., 2021). Fair machine learning is not a destination but a continual process that demands vigilance, ethical intent, and inclusive design.

Algorithmic Audits and Explainability in AI

As AI systems growingly shape decisions in healthcare, finance, and public policy, the demand for transparency and trust has never been more urgent. Algorithmic audits and explainability stand at the core of ethical AI governance, serving as vital tools to ensure systems are not just accurate, but also accountable.

Algorithmic audits involve systematically inspecting AI models to uncover hidden biases, discriminatory patterns, and flawed assumptions. These audits can be conducted internally or externally, though the independence of external audits often lends greater credibility. However, as Costanza-Chock, Raji, emphasize, a major concern is, "who audits the auditors?" Without standardized practices and regulatory oversight, auditing efforts risk becoming superficial checks rather than deep evaluations (Costanza-Chock et al., 2022).

Understanding AI from the outside in, known as black-box auditing, is essential, particularly when access to proprietary algorithms is limited. Such audits rely on observing outputs in varied conditions to infer underlying logic. Explainability complements these efforts by making AI decisions interpretable for end-users, regulators, and affected individuals.

THE FUTURE OF ETHICAL AI IN HEALTH EQUITY

As artificial intelligence continues to shape the healthcare landscape, its future will depend not just on technological advances but on how ethically and equitably it is implemented. At its core, the future of ethical AI in health equity is contingent upon transparency, accountability, and inclusivity, factors that are currently under scrutiny.

Ultimately, the future of ethical AI in health equity lies not in flawless code but in ethical foresight. It will require interdisciplinary collaboration, strong governance, and a relentless focus on fairness to ensure AI becomes a bridge to better healthcare, not a barrier.

Emerging Trends in AI and Healthcare

Artificial Intelligence in healthcare is no longer a futuristic promise, it's a fast-evolving reality, reshaping how we diagnose, treat, and manage diseases. As of 2025, AI stands at a dynamic midpoint in its evolution: past its experimental infancy but not yet fully mature. It's transitioning from pilot studies and isolated tools to integrated systems embedded across clinical workflows, diagnostics, and patient engagement platforms.

Current trends reveal a surge in real-time predictive analytics, AI-powered diagnostics, and personalized treatment planning. AI is not just identifying disease patterns; it's forecasting outbreaks, flagging health risks, and optimizing surgical precision (Khang, 2024). Wearable health devices, backed by AI algorithms, are enabling continuous monitoring and early intervention for chronic conditions.

Another breakthrough lies in natural language processing (NLP), allowing AI to extract actionable insights from unstructured medical records, improving efficiency and reducing physician burnout. This is especially transformative in telehealth, where AI Chatbots and virtual assistants are becoming the first line of mental and physical health support (Alzubaidi & Ravikanth, 2025).

Looking ahead, the integration of AI with genomics, robotics, and digital twins will redefine precision medicine. The future holds intelligent systems capable of learning from every clinical interaction, adapting to patient diversity, and delivering hyper-personalized care.

Policy Recommendations for Ethical AI in Healthcare

The ethical use of Artificial Intelligence (AI) in healthcare, much like any technology, is contingent upon the strength and clarity of the policies that govern it. A piece of technology in itself is neutral; it is neither inherently good nor bad. The outcomes it produces, however, depend entirely on how and by whom it is used. Consider a car: when it crashes due to reckless driving, we don't blame the vehicle, we blame the driver. Similarly, when AI is used irresponsibly, it is not the algorithm but the human decisions behind its design, implementation, or oversight that are at fault. Therefore, ethical AI isn't a technical challenge alone; it's a policy and governance issue at its core.

To ensure AI remains a force for good in healthcare, robust policy frameworks are non-negotiable. These policies must address the lifecycle of AI, from data collection and algorithm design to deployment and monitoring, focusing on transparency, accountability, equity, and patient safety. Importantly, the rise of generative AI tools such as ChatGPT, DeepSeek, and MedGPT is revolutionizing healthcare communication, medical education, documentation, and decision support. These tools can simulate doctor-patient conversations, generate medical summaries, and assist in diagnostics.

Many high-income countries are now taking strides to establish ethical boundaries for AI. For instance, the European Union's AI Act outlines risk-based classifications and mandates human oversight for high-risk AI systems, particularly those used in healthcare (Palaniappan et al., 2024). Likewise, the U.S. FDA has issued regulatory guidelines on AI/ML-based Software as a Medical Device (SaMD), aiming to create adaptive yet safe environments for AI development.

However, major gaps remain, especially in low- and middle-income countries. Folorunso et al. (2024) argue that without contextualized AI policies, developing nations may adopt imported systems that reinforce bias, compromise patient privacy, or fail to address local health challenges. What's needed is a grounded, inclusive, and adaptive approach to regulation that factors in the socio-economic, infrastructural, and ethical nuances of different healthcare systems (Folorunso et al., 2024).

Collaborative Efforts for Redefining the Use of AI

The path to ethical and equitable AI in healthcare is not one to be walked alone. It demands a dynamic and committed alliance among healthcare practitioners, academic institutions, and the industry. At the heart of this collaboration lies a shared responsibility: to ensure that AI technologies, particularly generative AI, are developed and deployed to serve all patients fairly, without bias, misinformation, or inequity.

Healthcare professionals are uniquely positioned to influence how AI systems are designed and applied. Their on-the-ground experience offers valuable insights into clinical workflows, patient sensitivities, and the ethical dilemmas that arise in real-time. When clinicians actively contribute to AI development, they ensure that models are trained with real-world context, thus enhancing both fairness and functionality.

Academia, particularly medical universities and research institutions, must now play a dual role. First, as educators, they must integrate AI ethics, data literacy, and human-AI collaboration into medical and healthcare curricula. Second, as innovators, they must push forward research that explores AI's limitations, sociotechnical impacts, and ethical frameworks (Pinzolits, 2023). The academic setting is the ideal Launchpad for cultivating future healthcare professionals who are not just users of AI but informed and ethical evaluators.

The ideal starting point is cross-disciplinary collaboration. Medical schools should engage with computer science departments; hospitals should partner with AI startups; and policy researchers should work with clinicians. Industry-academia collaborations like that of Hippocratic AI with Chamberlain University and Walden University provide a compelling case study.

Such partnerships set the standard: ethical AI begins with co-ownership. By shaping AI tools together, through joint research, pilot programs, and shared curricula, academia and industry can ensure that technology amplifies equity rather than exacerbates gaps (Palaniappan et al., 2024).

Concluding Thoughts: Balancing Innovation with Ethical Responsibility

As this book draws to a close, one message remains crystal clear: the future of healthcare will not be defined solely by technological capability, but by our collective ethical will. Artificial Intelligence, particularly in healthcare, is not just a scientific milestone, it is an ethical juncture. The question is no longer whether we can build powerful AI tools, but whether we should, and how we should, responsibly and inclusively.

Healthcare is not an industry like any other. It is deeply human. It touches lives at their most vulnerable. In this space, innovation without ethical grounding is not progress, it is peril. It demands a commitment to fairness, transparency, and above all, compassion. As Agarwal et al. rightly argue, addressing algorithmic bias is not a technical tweak, it's a moral imperative. If left unchecked, these systems risk amplifying health disparities rather than alleviating them (Agarwal et al., 2023).

This is where collaboration becomes essential. Industry leaders, academic institutions, medical universities, and frontline practitioners must form a united front. Healthcare professionals bring the empathy, academic researchers bring the rigor, and the tech industry brings the innovation. But it is only in synergy that these strengths will translate into ethical, practical, and inclusive AI systems.

This chapter has repeatedly emphasized that we must move beyond the hype. We must look AI in the eye, not as a panacea, but as a tool that mirrors our values, choices, and biases. And as Giovanola and Tiribelli argue, redefining fairness in healthcare AI must go beyond metrics, it must resonate with justice, respect, and equity (Giovanola & Tiribelli, 2023).

The true measure of progress will not be in how fast AI evolves, but in how wisely it is governed. Our duty is not just to innovate, but to safeguard the sanctity of care in the process. Let this book be more than an academic document. Let it serve as a call to conscience, for developers, educators, regulators, and caregivers alike.

In the end, the future of healthcare AI will not be written in code alone. It will be authored by the courage, compassion, and clarity of those who choose to lead with ethics first.

REFERENCES

Agarwal, R., Bjarnadottir, M., Rhue, L., Dugas, M., Crowley, K., Clark, J., & Gao, G. (2023). Addressing algorithmic bias and the perpetuation of health inequities: An AI bias aware framework. *Health Policy and Technology*, *12*(1), 100702. DOI: 10.1016/j.hlpt.2022.100702

Ahmad, I., Bakhsh, D. F., Faisal, M., & Sultan, S. (2024). Regulatory Framework for Artificial Intelligence in the Legal System of Pakistan. *The Critical Review of Social Sciences Studies*, *2*(2), 2. Advance online publication. DOI: 10.59075/ewvavd86

Ahmad, J. B., Hussain, M. A., & Mir, H. A. (2024). Developing a Legal Framework for Digital Policy: A Roadmap for AI Regulations in Pakistan. *Law and Policy Review*, *3*(1), 1. Advance online publication. DOI: 10.32350/lpr.31.08

Al Kuwaiti, A., Nazer, K., Al-Reedy, A., Al-Shehri, S., Al-Muhanna, A., Subbarayalu, A. V., Al Muhanna, D., & Al-Muhanna, F. A. (2023). A Review of the Role of Artificial Intelligence in Healthcare. *Journal of Personalized Medicine*, *13*(6), 951. DOI: 10.3390/jpm13060951 PMID: 37373940

Albahri, A. S., Duhaim, A. M., Fadhel, M. A., Alnoor, A., Baqer, N. S., Alzubaidi, L., Albahri, O. S., Alamoodi, A. H., Bai, J., Salhi, A., Santamaría, J., Ouyang, C., Gupta, A., Gu, Y., & Deveci, M. (2023). A systematic review of trustworthy and explainable artificial intelligence in healthcare: Assessment of quality, bias risk, and data fusion. *Information Fusion*, *96*, 156–191. DOI: 10.1016/j.inffus.2023.03.008

Almeida, P., Santos, C.Jr, & Farias, J. (2021). Artificial Intelligence Regulation: A framework for governance. *Ethics and Information Technology*, *23*(3), 505–525. Advance online publication. DOI: 10.1007/s10676-021-09593-z

Alowais, S. A., Alghamdi, S. S., Alsuhebany, N., Alqahtani, T., Alshaya, A. I., Almohareb, S. N., Aldairem, A., Alrashed, M., Bin Saleh, K., Badreldin, H. A., Al Yami, M. S., Al Harbi, S., & Albekairy, A. M. (2023). Revolutionizing healthcare: The role of artificial intelligence in clinical practice. *BMC Medical Education*, *23*(1), 689. DOI: 10.1186/s12909-023-04698-z PMID: 37740191

Alzubaidi, L. H., & Ravikanth, P. (2025). The Future of Healthcare: Emerging Technologies and Trends. In *Advances in Sports Science and Technology*. CRC Press. DOI: 10.1201/9781003616283-11

Arshed, M., Mahmud, A., Minhat, H. S., Lim, P. Y., & Zakar, R. (2024). Effectiveness of a Multifaceted Mobile Health Intervention (Multi-Aid-Package) in Medication Adherence and Treatment Outcomes Among Patients With Hypertension in a Low- to Middle-Income Country: Randomized Controlled Trial. *JMIR mHealth and uHealth, 12*, e50248. DOI: 10.2196/50248 PMID: 38896837

Arshed, M., Mahmud, A. B., Minhat, H. S., Ying, L. P., & Umer, M. F. (2023). Effectiveness of mHealth Interventions in Medication Adherence among Patients with Cardiovascular Diseases: A Systematic Review. *Diseases (Basel, Switzerland), 11*(1), 41. DOI: 10.3390/diseases11010041 PMID: 36975590

Arshed, M., Mahmud, A. B., Umer, M. F., Mashhadi, F., & Kawish, A. B. (2025). Study protocol for a randomized control trial investigating the effectiveness of a multifaceted mHealth approach on adherence to antihypertensive treatment among patients in Pakistan. *Pakistan Journal of Medical Sciences, 41*(1), 1. Advance online publication. DOI: 10.12669/pjms.41.1.9272 PMID: 39867791

Arshed, M., Umer, M. F., Kiran, M., Akhter, A. M., Gillani, A. H., Qamer, S., Kawish, A. B., Zofeen, S., Farid, A., & Khan, M. N. (2024). Prevalence and associated factors of non-adherence to antihyperlipidemic medication: A nationwide cross sectional survey in Pakistan. *Scientific Reports, 14*(1), 20613. DOI: 10.1038/s41598-024-71120-z PMID: 39232055

Arshed, M., Zakar, R., Umer, M. F., Kiran, M., Ullah, N., Iftikhar, G., & Fischer, F. (2023). Efficacy of mHealth and education-led peer counseling for patients with hypertension and coronary artery disease in Pakistan: Study protocol for a double-blinded pragmatic randomized-controlled trial with factorial design. *Trials, 24*(1), 448. DOI: 10.1186/s13063-023-07472-0 PMID: 37424031

Bambra, C. (2022). Levelling up: Global examples of reducing health inequalities. *Scandinavian Journal of Public Health, 50*(7), 908–913. DOI: 10.1177/14034948211022428 PMID: 34148458

Bateni, A., Chan, M. C., & Eitel-Porter, R. (2022). *AI Fairness: From Principles to Practice* (arXiv:2207.09833). arXiv. https://doi.org//arXiv.2207.09833DOI: 10.48550

Bekbolatova, M., Mayer, J., Ong, C. W., & Toma, M. (2024). Transformative Potential of AI in Healthcare: Definitions, Applications, and Navigating the Ethical Landscape and Public Perspectives. *Healthcare (Basel), 12*(2), 125. DOI: 10.3390/healthcare12020125 PMID: 38255014

Berdahl, C. T., Baker, L., Mann, S., Osoba, O., & Girosi, F. (2023). Strategies to Improve the Impact of Artificial Intelligence on Health Equity: Scoping Review. *JMIR AI, 2*, e42936. DOI: 10.2196/42936 PMID: 38875587

Bill Siwicki. (2023). *The intersection of telehealth and AI: How can they reinforce each other? | Healthcare IT News*. https://www.healthcareitnews.com/news/intersection-telehealth-and-ai-how-can-they-reinforce-each-other

Bongurala, A. R., Save, D., & Virmani, A. (2025). Progressive role of artificial intelligence in treatment decision-making in the field of medical oncology. *Frontiers in Medicine, 12*, 1533910. DOI: 10.3389/fmed.2025.1533910 PMID: 40018354

Byrne, M. D. (2021). Reducing Bias in Healthcare Artificial Intelligence. *Journal of Perianesthesia Nursing, 36*(3), 313–316. DOI: 10.1016/j.jopan.2021.03.009 PMID: 34112365

Cestonaro, C., Delicati, A., Marcante, B., Caenazzo, L., & Tozzo, P. (2023). Defining medical liability when artificial intelligence is applied on diagnostic algorithms: A systematic review. *Frontiers in Medicine, 10*, 1305756. DOI: 10.3389/fmed.2023.1305756 PMID: 38089864

Chang, A. (2020). *The Role of Artificial Intelligence in Digital Health.*, DOI: 10.1007/978-3-030-12719-0_7

Chen, M., & Decary, M. (2020). Artificial intelligence in healthcare: An essential guide for health leaders. *Healthcare Management Forum, 33*(1), 10–18. DOI: 10.1177/0840470419873123 PMID: 31550922

Chen, R. J., Wang, J. J., Williamson, D. F. K., Chen, T. Y., Lipkova, J., Lu, M. Y., Sahai, S., & Mahmood, F. (2023). Algorithmic fairness in artificial intelligence for medicine and healthcare. *Nature Biomedical Engineering, 7*(6), 719–742. DOI: 10.1038/s41551-023-01056-8 PMID: 37380750

Chiruvella, V., & Guddati, A. K. (2021). Ethical Issues in Patient Data Ownership. *Interactive Journal of Medical Research, 10*(2), e22269. DOI: 10.2196/22269 PMID: 34018968

Costanza-Chock, S., Raji, I. D., & Buolamwini, J. (2022). Who Audits the Auditors? Recommendations from a field scan of the algorithmic auditing ecosystem. *Proceedings of the 2022 ACM Conference on Fairness, Accountability, and Transparency*, 1571–1583. DOI: 10.1145/3531146.3533213

d'Elia, A., Gabbay, M., Rodgers, S., Kierans, C., Jones, E., Durrani, I., Thomas, A., & Frith, L. (2022). Artificial intelligence and health inequities in primary care: A systematic scoping review and framework. *Family Medicine and Community Health, 10*(Suppl 1), e001670. DOI: 10.1136/fmch-2022-001670 PMID: 36450391

Dailah, H. G., Koriri, M., Sabei, A., Kriry, T., & Zakri, M. (2024). Artificial Intelligence in Nursing: Technological Benefits to Nurse's Mental Health and Patient Care Quality. *Health Care*, *12*(24), 24. Advance online publication. DOI: 10.3390/healthcare12242555 PMID: 39765983

Elendu, C., Amaechi, D. C., Elendu, T. C., Jingwa, K. A., Okoye, O. K., John Okah, M., Ladele, J. A., Farah, A. H., & Alimi, H. A. (2023). Ethical implications of AI and robotics in healthcare. *Revista de Medicina (São Paulo)*, *102*(50), e36671. DOI: 10.1097/MD.0000000000036671 PMID: 38115340

Farahani, M., & Ghasemi, G. (2024). *Artificial Intelligence and Inequality: Challenges and Opportunities*. Qeios., DOI: 10.32388/7HWUZ2

Farhud, D. D., & Zokaei, S. (2021). Ethical Issues of Artificial Intelligence in Medicine and Healthcare. *Iranian Journal of Public Health*, *50*(11), i–v. DOI: 10.18502/ijph.v50i11.7600 PMID: 35223619

Fazil, A. W., Hakimi, M., Shahidzay, A., & Hasas, A. (2024). Exploring the Broad Impact of AI Technologies on Student Engagement and Academic Performance in University Settings in Afghanistan. *RIGGS Journal of Artificial Intelligence and Digital Business*, *2*(2), 56–63. DOI: 10.31004/riggs.v2i2.268

Ferrara, E. (2024). Fairness and Bias in Artificial Intelligence: A Brief Survey of Sources, Impacts, and Mitigation Strategies. *Sci*, *6*(1), 1. Advance online publication. DOI: 10.3390/sci6010003

Folorunso, A., Olanipekun, K., Adewumi, T., & Samuel, B. (2024). *A policy framework on AI usage in developing countries and its impact*. 154–166. DOI: 10.30574/gjeta.2024.21.1.0192

Fu, R., Aseri, M., Singh, P. V., & Srinivasan, K. (2022). "Un"Fair Machine Learning Algorithms. *Management Science*, *68*(6), 4173–4195. DOI: 10.1287/mnsc.2021.4065

Gao, J., Chou, B., McCaw, Z. R., Thurston, H., Varghese, P., Hong, C., & Gronsbell, J. (2024). *What is Fair? Defining Fairness in Machine Learning for Health* (arXiv:2406.09307). arXiv. https://doi.org//arXiv.2406.09307DOI: 10.48550

Giovanola, B., & Tiribelli, S. (2023). Beyond bias and discrimination: Redefining the AI ethics principle of fairness in healthcare machine-learning algorithms. *AI & Society*, *38*(2), 549–563. DOI: 10.1007/s00146-022-01455-6 PMID: 35615443

Gkiouleka, A., Wong, G., Sowden, S., Bambra, C., Siersbaek, R., Manji, S., Moseley, A., Harmston, R., Kuhn, I., & Ford, J. (2023). Reducing health inequalities through general practice. *The Lancet. Public Health*, *8*(6), e463–e472. DOI: 10.1016/S2468-2667(23)00093-2 PMID: 37244675

Gurevich, E., El Hassan, B., & El Morr, C. (2023). Equity within AI systems: What can health leaders expect? *Healthcare Management Forum*, *36*(2), 119–124. DOI: 10.1177/08404704221125368 PMID: 36226507

Hacker, P. (2020). *AI Regulation in Europe* (SSRN Scholarly Paper 3556532). Social Science Research Network. DOI: 10.2139/ssrn.3556532

Howe, L. J., Nivard, M. G., Morris, T. T., Hansen, A. F., Rasheed, H., Cho, Y., Chittoor, G., Ahlskog, R., Lind, P. A., Palviainen, T., van der Zee, M. D., Cheesman, R., Mangino, M., Wang, Y., Li, S., Klaric, L., Ratliff, S. M., Bielak, L. F., Nygaard, M., & Davies, N. M. (2022). Within-sibship genome-wide association analyses decrease bias in estimates of direct genetic effects. *Nature Genetics*, *54*(5), 581–592. DOI: 10.1038/s41588-022-01062-7 PMID: 35534559

Jiang, F., Jiang, Y., Zhi, H., Dong, Y., Li, H., Ma, S., Wang, Y., Dong, Q., Shen, H., & Wang, Y. (2017). Artificial intelligence in healthcare: Past, present and future. *Stroke and Vascular Neurology*, *2*(4), 230–243. DOI: 10.1136/svn-2017-000101 PMID: 29507784

Johnson, K. B., Wei, W.-Q., Weeraratne, D., Frisse, M. E., Misulis, K., Rhee, K., Zhao, J., & Snowdon, J. L. (2021). Precision Medicine, AI, and the Future of Personalized Health Care. *Clinical and Translational Science*, *14*(1), 86–93. DOI: 10.1111/cts.12884 PMID: 32961010

Khang, A. (Ed.). (2024). *AI and IoT Technology and Applications for Smart Healthcare Systems*. Auerbach Publications., DOI: 10.1201/9781032686745

Konstantopoulos, W., Collins, K., Diaz, R., Duber, H., Edwards, C., Hsu, A., Ranney, M., Riviello, R., Wettstein, Z., & Sachs, C. (2023). Race, Healthcare, and Health Disparities: A Critical Review and Recommendations for Advancing Health Equity. *The Western Journal of Emergency Medicine*, *24*(5). Advance online publication. DOI: 10.5811/WESTJEM.58408 PMID: 37788031

Kordzadeh, N., & Ghasemaghaei, M. (2022). Algorithmic bias: Review, synthesis, and future research directions. *European Journal of Information Systems*, *31*(3), 388–409. DOI: 10.1080/0960085X.2021.1927212

Kurant, D. E. (2023). Opportunities and Challenges with Artificial Intelligence in Genomics. *Clinics in Laboratory Medicine*, *43*(1), 87–97. DOI: 10.1016/j.cll.2022.09.007 PMID: 36764810

Laryeafio, M., & Ogbewe, O. (2023). Ethical consideration dilemma: Systematic review of ethics in qualitative data collection through interviews. *Journal of Ethics in Entrepreneurship and Technology*, *3*(2), 94–110. DOI: 10.1108/JEET-09-2022-0014

Lechterman, T. M. (2022). *The concept of accountability in AI ethics and governance* (1st ed.). Oxford University Press., https://ora.ox.ac.uk/objects/uuid:c954516e-9139-47ed-941e-978a82f7d84e

Leslie, D., Ashurst, C., González, N., Griffiths, F., Jayadeva, S., Jorgensen, M., Katell, M., Krishna, S., Kwiatkowski, D., Martins, C., Mohammed, S., Mougan, C., Pandit, S., Richey, M., Sakshaug, J., Vallor, S., & Vilain, L. (2024). 'Frontier AI,' Power, and the Public Interest: Who Benefits, Who Decides? *Harvard Data Science Review*, (Special Issue 5). Advance online publication. DOI: 10.1162/99608f92.4a42495c

Li, F., Ruijs, N., & Lu, Y. (2023). Ethics & AI: A Systematic Review on Ethical Concerns and Related Strategies for Designing with AI in Healthcare. *AI*, *4*(1), 1. Advance online publication. DOI: 10.3390/ai4010003

Li, Y.-H., Li, Y.-L., Wei, M.-Y., & Li, G.-Y. (2024). Innovation and challenges of artificial intelligence technology in personalized healthcare. *Scientific Reports*, *14*(1), 18994. DOI: 10.1038/s41598-024-70073-7 PMID: 39152194

McCall, C. J., DeCaprio, D., & Gartner, J. (2022). The Measurement and Mitigation of Algorithmic Bias and Unfairness in Healthcare AI Models Developed for the CMS AI Health Outcomes Challenge (p. 2022.09.29.22280537). *medRxiv*. DOI: 10.1101/2022.09.29.22280537

Mia, M. R., Shahriar, H., Valero, M., Sakib, N., Saha, B., Barek, M. A., Faruk, M. J. H., Goodman, B., Khan, R. A., & Ahamed, S. I. (2022). A comparative study on HIPAA technical safeguards assessment of android mHealth applications. *Smart Health (Amsterdam, Netherlands)*, *26*, 100349. DOI: 10.1016/j.smhl.2022.100349 PMID: 39086849

Mittermaier, M., Raza, M. M., & Kvedar, J. C. (2023). Bias in AI-based models for medical applications: Challenges and mitigation strategies. *NPJ Digital Medicine*, *6*(1), 113. DOI: 10.1038/s41746-023-00858-z PMID: 37311802

Mohammad Amini, M., Jesus, M., Fanaei Sheikholeslami, D., Alves, P., Hassanzadeh Benam, A., & Hariri, F. (2023). Artificial Intelligence Ethics and Challenges in Healthcare Applications: A Comprehensive Review in the Context of the European GDPR Mandate. *Machine Learning and Knowledge Extraction*, *5*(3), 3. Advance online publication. DOI: 10.3390/make5030053

Mohammed, S., Budach, L., Feuerpfeil, M., Ihde, N., Nathansen, A., Noack, N., Patzlaff, H., Naumann, F., & Harmouch, H. (2024). *The Effects of Data Quality on Machine Learning Performance* (arXiv:2207.14529). arXiv. https://doi.org//arXiv.2207.14529DOI: 10.48550

Novelli, C., Taddeo, M., & Floridi, L. (2024). Accountability in artificial intelligence: What it is and how it works. *AI & Society*, *39*(4), 1871–1882. DOI: 10.1007/s00146-023-01635-y

Nyariro, M., Emami, E., Caidor, P., & Abbasgholizadeh Rahimi, S. (2023). Integrating equity, diversity and inclusion throughout the lifecycle of AI within healthcare: A scoping review protocol. *BMJ Open*, *13*(9), e072069. DOI: 10.1136/bmjopen-2023-072069 PMID: 37751956

Ogbodu, C. (2023). *Fairness and Bias in Big Data Analytics: An Ethical Framework for Decision Making*.

Pacis, D., Subido, E. J., & Bugtai, N. (2018). Trends in telemedicine utilizing artificial intelligence. In *AIP Conference Proceedings* (Vol. 1933). DOI: 10.1063/1.5023979

Palaniappan, K., Lin, E. Y. T., & Vogel, S. (2024). Global Regulatory Frameworks for the Use of Artificial Intelligence (AI) in the Healthcare Services Sector. *Healthcare (Basel)*, *12*(5), 562. DOI: 10.3390/healthcare12050562 PMID: 38470673

Panch, T., Mattie, H., & Atun, R. (2019). Artificial intelligence and algorithmic bias: Implications for health systems. *Journal of Global Health*, *9*(2), 020318. DOI: 10.7189/jogh.09.020318 PMID: 31788229

Pinzolits, R. (2023). AI in academia: An overview of selected tools and their areas of application. *MAP Education and Humanities*, *4*, 37–50. DOI: 10.53880/2744-2373.2023.4.37

Raju, N. (2023, May 2). *How AI and Digital Health are shaping Global Healthcare*. CXOToday.Com. https://cxotoday.com/cxo-bytes/how-ai-and-digital-health-are-shaping-global-healthcare/

Ruschemeier, H. (2023). *The Problems of the Automation Bias in the Public Sector – A Legal Perspective* (SSRN Scholarly Paper 4521474). Social Science Research Network. https://papers.ssrn.com/abstract=4521474

Sadiku, M., Fagbohungbe, O., & Musa, S. (2020). Artificial Intelligence in Food Industry. *International Journal of Engineering Research and Advanced Technology*, *06*(10), 12–19. DOI: 10.31695/IJERAT.2020.3649

Serrano, D. R., Luciano, F. C., Anaya, B. J., Ongoren, B., Kara, A., Molina, G., Ramirez, B. I., Sánchez-Guirales, S. A., Simon, J. A., Tomietto, G., Rapti, C., Ruiz, H. K., Rawat, S., Kumar, D., & Lalatsa, A. (2024). Artificial Intelligence (AI) Applications in Drug Discovery and Drug Delivery: Revolutionizing Personalized Medicine. *Pharmaceutics*, *16*(10), 1328. DOI: 10.3390/pharmaceutics16101328 PMID: 39458657

Smith, M., & Heath Jeffery, R. C. (2020). Addressing the challenges of artificial intelligence in medicine. *Internal Medicine Journal*, *50*(10), 1278–1281. DOI: 10.1111/imj.15017 PMID: 33111408

Taherdoost, H., & Ghofrani, A. (2024). AI's role in revolutionizing personalized medicine by reshaping pharmacogenomics and drug therapy. *Intelligent Pharmacy*, *2*(5), 643–650. DOI: 10.1016/j.ipha.2024.08.005

Valdivia, A., Sánchez-Monedero, J., & Casillas, J. (2021). How fair can we go in machine learning? Assessing the boundaries of accuracy and fairness. *International Journal of Intelligent Systems*, *36*(4), 1619–1643. DOI: 10.1002/int.22354

Vorisek, C. N., Stellmach, C., Mayer, P. J., Klopfenstein, S. A. I., Bures, D. M., Diehl, A., Henningsen, M., Ritter, K., & Thun, S. (2023). Artificial Intelligence Bias in Health Care: Web-Based Survey. *Journal of Medical Internet Research*, *25*, e41089. DOI: 10.2196/41089 PMID: 37347528

Wang, X., Lin, X., & Shao, B. (2022). Artificial intelligence changes the way we work: A close look at innovating with chatbots. *Journal of the Association for Information Science and Technology*, *74*(3), 339–353. Advance online publication. DOI: 10.1002/asi.24621

5. *Ways AI is Transforming Health Systems*. (2025). https://www.medtronic.com/en-us/our-company/ai-healthcare-technology-solutions.html

WHO. (2021). *WHO issues first global report on Artificial Intelligence (AI) in health and six guiding principles for its design and use*. https://www.who.int/news/item/28-06-2021-who-issues-first-global-report-on-ai-in-health-and-six-guiding-principles-for-its-design-and-use

Will Heaven. (2023). *AI is dreaming up drugs that no one has ever seen. Now we've got to see if they work. | MIT Technology Review*. https://www.technologyreview.com/2023/02/15/1067904/ai-automation-drug-development/

Wu, E., Wu, K., Daneshjou, R., Ouyang, D., Ho, D. E., & Zou, J. (2021). How medical AI devices are evaluated: Limitations and recommendations from an analysis of FDA approvals. *Nature Medicine*, *27*(4), 582–584. DOI: 10.1038/s41591-021-01312-x PMID: 33820998

Yelne, S., Chaudhary, M., Dod, K., Sayyad, A., & Sharma, R. (2023). Harnessing the Power of AI: A Comprehensive Review of Its Impact and Challenges in Nursing Science and Healthcare. *Cureus*, *15*(11), e49252. DOI: 10.7759/cureus.49252 PMID: 38143615

Chapter 5
The Pandemic's Wake:
Global Health Systems' Strengths and Vulnerabilities

Mingwang Shen
https://orcid.org/0000-0003-4553-800X
Xi'an Jiaotong University, China

ABSTRACT

This chapter, The Pandemic's Wake: Public Health Systems Under Scrutiny Analysis of global health systems' strengths and vulnerabilities revealed by COVID-19, seeks to analyze the lessons learned from the COVID-19 pandemic, focusing on how it revealed the capabilities and shortcomings of global health systems. By examining the responses of various nations, the role of international collaboration, and the disproportionate impacts on vulnerable populations, this chapter aims to provide a comprehensive understanding of what worked, what failed, and what must be done to build stronger, more equitable public health systems for the future. The pandemic underscored the critical importance of robust public health infrastructure, science-driven policies, and global solidarity. At the same time, it exposed deep-seated inequities, underfunding, and systemic weaknesses that hindered effective responses.

SECTION 1: GLOBAL HEALTH SYSTEMS BEFORE COVID-19

The emergence of the COVID-19 pandemic in late 2019 and its subsequent global spread in 2020 subjected national and international health systems to an unprecedented stress test. To comprehend the profound impact of this crisis and to draw meaningful lessons for the future, it is imperative to first establish a clear understanding of the global public health landscape as it existed prior to this watershed event. This section will delineate the key components of global public health

DOI: 10.4018/979-8-3373-1992-6.ch005

infrastructure, explore the dominant healthcare models and philosophies prevalent at the time, and critically examine the pre-existing challenges and undercurrents of vulnerability that, in many respects, set the stage for the difficulties that were to follow. While advancements in medical science and health service delivery had been significant in preceding decades, the pre-pandemic world was, as events would tragically demonstrate, far from uniformly prepared for a public health emergency of such magnitude and complexity. To systematically assess this state of preparedness and the subsequent pandemic responses, this chapter adopts a composite analytical framework drawing on core concepts from Health System Resilience, Crisis Governance, and Public Health Preparedness theories. The health system resilience lens allows for an examination of the capacity of health systems to absorb, adapt, and transform in the face of shocks. Crisis governance theory provides tools to analyze decision-making processes, leadership, inter-agency coordination, and the political dynamics that unfold under uncertainty. Finally, frameworks of public health preparedness, informed by scholarly analysis of past outbreaks like the 2003 SARS epidemic and the 2009 H1N1 pandemic, emphasize the criticality of early warning, risk communication, and non-pharmaceutical interventions. By leveraging this multi-faceted framework, we can move beyond merely describing 'what happened' to critically analyzing 'why it happened,' thereby revealing the deep-seated structural strengths and vulnerabilities that were not fully appreciated before the pandemic.

The Landscape of Global Public Health Infrastructure Pre-2020

The architecture of global public health prior to 2020 was a complex web of international organizations, national health systems, non-governmental entities, and academic institutions, all contributing to varying degrees to health policy, surveillance, and response. At the apex of this system stood the World Health Organization (WHO), the United Nations' specialized agency for health, tasked with providing leadership on global health matters, shaping the health research agenda, setting norms and standards, articulating evidence-based policy options, providing technical support to countries, and monitoring and assessing health trends. Alongside the WHO, organizations like the Organization for Economic Co-operation and Development (OECD) played a crucial role in collecting and analyzing comparative data on health system performance across its member states, offering valuable insights into spending, access, and outcomes. (OECD, 2021)

An examination of OECD health data from the period immediately preceding the pandemic reveals critical aspects of prevailing health system priorities. The OECD's "Health at a Glance 2021" report indicated that, on average, only 2.7% of health spending in member countries was allocated to prevention (OECD, 2021). While this comparative data provides a valuable high-level benchmark, it is important to recognize its limitations as a secondary data summary. As an aggregation of national statistics, it can mask significant regional variations within countries and relies on standardized reporting that may not fully capture the nuances of diverse health financing systems. Nonetheless, the overarching trend it revealed—a systemic underinvestment in proactive public health—represented a significant latent vulnerability (OECD, 2021). While most OECD countries had achieved some form of universal health coverage, their operational focus and spending priorities demonstrated a system that was inherently more reactive than proactive. This is substantiated by several key data points within the pre-pandemic landscape. First, health spending was overwhelmingly directed at curative care, with an average of only 2.7% of all health expenditure in OECD countries allocated to proactive disease prevention. Second, a failure to proactively invest in preparedness was widespread, with the 2019 GHS Index finding that 155 out of 195 countries had not dedicated specific funding to strengthen their epidemic preparedness in the preceding three years. Finally, funding often followed a reactive "panic-and-neglect" cycle, particularly in the United States, where temporary increases for emergencies like H1N1 were followed by cuts once the threat subsided. While most OECD countries had achieved some form of universal health coverage, ensuring that the majority of their populations had access to healthcare services, persistent barriers to access remained, and these were often more pronounced for disadvantaged groups.(OECD, 2021) This focus on treatment over prevention meant that many health systems were inherently more reactive than proactive, a characteristic that would be severely tested by a novel pathogen requiring robust preventative and early control measures.

Further insight into the state of global preparedness came from the Global Health Security (GHS) Index. The findings of the inaugural 2019 Global Health Security (GHS) Index were sobering, leading to its conclusion that, despite varying levels of economic development, all countries remained "dangerously unprepared" for future epidemic and pandemic threats. This assessment was supported by several key pieces of evidence from the report itself. Critically, no country scored in the top tier of preparedness, and the average country score was a mere 38.9 out of 100 (GHS Index, 2021). The GHS Index highlighted specific, widespread areas of weakness, including insufficient health system capacity to treat the sick and protect health workers, a lack of dedicated financial investment in strengthening epidemic preparedness, and a failure to adequately plan for the needs of vulnerable populations during a health emergency (GHS Index, 2021). The GHS Index highlighted specific areas of weakness, including insufficient health system capacity to treat the sick and protect health workers, a lack of dedicated financial investment in strengthening epidemic or pandemic preparedness, and a failure to adequately plan for the needs of vulnerable populations during a health emergency.(GHS Index, 2021)

The financial landscape underpinning global health initiatives, particularly in low- and middle-income countries (LMICs), also presented challenges. Trends in Official Development Assistance (ODA) for health programs were a concern even before COVID-19. While total ODA remained below the UN's 0.7% GNI target, analysis from private sector firms like McKinsey indicated a more troubling trend of decreasing foreign aid volumes pre-pandemic, with projections for further reductions (McKinsey, 2025). It should be noted that as a private sector analysis, McKinsey's projections are based on proprietary models, and while influential, they represent one specific forecast. Nonetheless, the trend they identified was a significant concern, as ODA, though a small part of a recipient's overall budget, often serves as a uniquely stable and vital funding source for specific health sectors in countries with limited domestic resources (McKinsey, 2025). A decline in such aid would inevitably place additional strain on already fragile health systems, diminishing their capacity to invest in preparedness and respond effectively to emerging health threats. Several major donor countries had, in fact, announced upcoming reductions to their foreign aid budgets even before the full economic impact of the pandemic was felt.(McKinsey, 2025)

Comparative Healthcare Models: Pre-Existing Strains and Vulnerabilities

The approaches to organizing, financing, and delivering healthcare varied significantly across the globe pre-2020, broadly falling into categories such as universal health coverage (UHC) systems (achieved through single-payer or multi-payer mechanisms), socialized medicine, and predominantly private insurance-based models.(Verywell health, 2025)

Universal Health Coverage (UHC) refers to a system where every individual has health coverage, ensuring access to necessary health services without facing financial hardship. This can be achieved through various mechanisms, including government-run systems, mandatory private insurance, or a combination thereof. (Verywell health, 2025) Many developed nations, and an increasing number of LMICs, had embraced UHC as a policy goal, recognizing health as a fundamental human right.

A single-payer system is a specific model for achieving UHC, where the government (typically through taxes) is the primary entity responsible for financing healthcare and paying claims, though the delivery of care may still be through public and/or private providers.(Verywell health, 2025) Socialized medicine takes this a step further, with the government not only financing care but also owning and operating healthcare facilities and employing medical staff. (Verywell health, 2025)

Table 1. Comparison of dominant healthcare system models

Model Type	Key Example Country	Primary Funding	Key Pre-Pandemic Challenge
Socialized Medicine	United Kingdom	Predominantly tax-funded	Persistent staff shortages, growing waiting lists, financial instability
Single-Payer	Canada	Financed through general taxation	Long waiting times for specialist care, shortage of family doctors
Multi-Payer Social Insurance	Germany	"Sickness funds" co-financed by employee and employer contributions	Rising pharmaceutical costs, complexities of governance
Private-Based Hybrid	United States	Patchwork of private insurance and public programs (e.g., Medicare/Medicaid)	High per capita spending with poorer health outcomes, significant uninsured/ underinsured population

In contrast, private insurance models rely on individuals, employers, or a combination to purchase health coverage from private insurance companies, with varying degrees of government regulation and subsidization.

A comparative look at several key countries illustrates these models and their pre-pandemic states:

- **United States:** The U.S. stood as a notable outlier among developed nations for not having a system of universal healthcare. Its healthcare system was a fragmented patchwork of private employer-sponsored insurance, individual private insurance (some purchased via government-run marketplaces established by the Affordable Care Act), and public single-payer programs like Medicare (for the elderly and disabled) and Medicaid (for low-income individuals, jointly funded by federal and state governments).(Verywell health, 2025) Despite spending significantly more on healthcare per capita and as a percentage of GDP than any other OECD country, the U.S. consistently reported poorer health outcomes, including lower life expectancy and higher rates of avoidable mortality, compared to its peers. A significant portion of its population remained uninsured or underinsured, facing substantial financial barriers to care.(Verywell health, 2025)
- **United Kingdom:** The National Health Service (NHS) in the UK is a quintessential example of a UHC system achieved through socialized medicine. It is a classic tax-funded model where the government both finances care and directly runs hospitals and employs staff, providing comprehensive services largely free at the point of service.(Verywell health, 2025) However, the pre-2020 pressures of chronic staff shortages, long waiting lists, and recurring deficits highlight a core structural vulnerability of such highly centralized, government-run systems. (UK Parliament, 2025) (Gainsbury & Julian, 2025)

Their direct exposure to political funding cycles and potential for bureaucratic inertia makes them susceptible to chronic under-resourcing and challenges in nimble adaptation, even while fulfilling the promise of universal access.

- **Canada:** Canada's healthcare system, often referred to as Medicare, provides UHC through a publicly funded, provincially administered model where essential physician and hospital services are covered by a single-payer system in each province/territory, financed through general taxation.(Verywell health, 2025) Private insurance typically covers services not included in public plans, such as prescription drugs (outside hospitals), dental, and vision care. Pre-pandemic, Canada grappled with issues such as long waiting times for specialist care, a shortage of family doctors, and underinvestment in primary care relative to its peers. These challenges reveal a structural trade-off inherent in many single-payer systems. While they control system-wide costs through a powerful central payer, this monopsony power can lead to supply-side rationing, chronic wait times, and efficiency hurdles that signal a system struggling with capacity despite ensuring financial access for its citizens. (Glazier, 2023) These factors contributed to pressures on emergency departments and challenges in chronic disease management.(Glazier, 2023)
- **Germany:** Germany achieves UHC through a multi-payer system built on principles of social insurance. It mandates health coverage for all residents, primarily through a system of competing, non-profit "sickness funds" (statutory health insurance), co-financed by employee and employer contributions, with an option for higher earners and certain groups to opt for private health insurance.(Verywell health, 2025) The German system is characterized by high levels of health expenditure, a high density of physicians, and relatively low out-of-pocket payments for patients. However, its pre-2020 challenges included rising pharmaceutical costs and significant demographic pressures. More fundamentally, the system's complexity illustrates the core challenge of the multi-payer social insurance model: its inherently fragmented governance structure. With responsibilities divided between federal, state, and numerous self-governing associations of payers and providers, implementing swift, unified national health policy and driving systemic reforms can become exceedingly complex and slow.

This comparative analysis reveals a critical insight: while no single healthcare model was free from pre-existing pressures, the nature of their vulnerabilities differed systemically. The country cases show that universal systems like the UK's and Canada's primarily faced capacity and efficiency challenges (e.g., wait times, staff shortages), whereas the fragmented, high-expenditure US system struggled with more fundamental equity and access challenges. This distinction is crucial for understanding why different systems buckled in different ways under the uniform stress of the pandemic.. While UHC systems aimed to ensure access and financial protection, their operational capacities and specific areas of vulnerability varied. The fragmented nature of the US system, despite its high expenditure, presented unique challenges related to equity and coordinated public health action. These diverse starting points would significantly influence how each nation navigated the unfolding pandemic.

Pre-Existing Challenges and Undercurrents of Vulnerability

Beyond the structural features of healthcare models, several underlying challenges and vulnerabilities were pervasive across the global health landscape before COVID-19, contributing to a state of latent fragility that the pandemic would starkly expose.

Underfunding and Resource Allocation for Public Health and Prevention

A critical and widespread vulnerability was the chronic underinvestment in public health infrastructure and preventative services. This systemic de-prioritization of proactive measures was a critical and widespread vulnerability, evidenced by the previously cited OECD data showing that a mere 2.7% of total health expenditure was dedicated to prevention. This figure starkly illustrates a systemic de-prioritization of proactive measures designed to keep populations healthy and mitigate the risk of outbreaks. Instead, the overwhelming focus of health spending was on curative care, treating illness after it occurred.

In the United States, this underinvestment was particularly acute and well-documented. Federal investment in public health capabilities had declined over decades, following a reactive "ebb-and-flow" cycle of temporary funding increases during emergencies (like H1N1 or Ebola) followed by cuts. This reactive pattern runs directly contrary to the core lesson from the 2003 SARS outbreak—the necessity of sustained, proactive investment in preparedness—and resulted in a long-term hollowing out of public health infrastructure.(Serchen et al., 2023) In the United States, this underinvestment was particularly acute. Federal funding for public health had declined over decades, often following a reactive "ebb-and-flow" cycle of temporary increases during emergencies (like H1N1 or Ebola) followed by cuts once the threat subsided (DeSalvo et al., 2021). This inconsistent approach left state and local health departments with persistent resource gaps, outdated IT and data systems, and a diminished capacity for core functions, as public health constituted a meager 2-3% of total government health spending (Maani & Galea, 2020). The persistence of this underinvestment can be attributed to several mutually reinforcing factors. A core issue is the "prevention paradox": when public health works, crises are averted, and its success is therefore invisible, making it a difficult sell for political leaders seeking credit for tangible results. This is compounded by powerful economic incentives, as the vast and profitable curative care industry (hospitals, pharmaceuticals) holds significantly more lobbying power than the diffuse, under-resourced public health sector. Finally, the short-term nature of political and budget cycles encourages a focus on immediate problems rather than on abstract, long-term investments in preparedness for low-probability, high-consequence events, perpetuating the "panic-and-neglect" funding cycle.

Workforce Shortages and Capacity Gaps

The human resources available to public health and healthcare systems were another area of significant concern globally. The WHO had projected, even before COVID-19, a global shortage of 18 million health workers by 2030 (this estimate was later revised downward to 10 million, but still represents a substantial gap). (Boniol et al., 2022) This shortage was not evenly distributed, with a staggering 6.5-fold difference in the density of health workers (physicians, nurses, midwives, etc.) between high-income and low-income countries (Boniol et al., 2022), underscoring profound global inequities in health system capacity. Specific shortages were identified in critical areas such as general practitioners, psychiatrists, and particularly nurses in various regions.(Simeonova-Ganeva & Ganev, 2023)

In the United States, the public health workforce had been shrinking. Local health departments had shed over 56,000 jobs in the decade prior to the pandemic. (DeSalvo et al., 2021) The remaining workforce often lacked specialized public health training, and recruitment and retention were significant challenges due to factors like non-competitive salaries and limited opportunities for career advancement.(DeSalvo et al., 2021) This erosion of the public health workforce meant fewer personnel were available for crucial tasks like disease surveillance, contact tracing, health education, and emergency response when COVID-19 arrived.

Health Inequities: Socioeconomic, Racial, and Geographic Disparities

Deep-seated health inequities were a pervasive feature of many societies pre-pandemic. The OECD noted a clear social gradient in health outcomes, with disadvantaged individuals, those living in deprived areas, and most ethnic minorities experiencing higher risks of infection and death from various causes even before COVID-19.(OECD, 2021)

In the United States, long-standing racial and socioeconomic inequities in healthcare access, the quality of care received, and overall health outcomes were well-documented.(DeSalvo et al., 2021) These disparities were driven by a complex interplay of factors including systemic racism, economic inequality, differences in educational attainment, housing conditions, and environmental exposures. These pre-existing inequities meant that certain communities entered the pandemic already bearing a disproportionate burden of chronic diseases and facing greater barriers to health-protective resources, making them exceptionally vulnerable to the impacts of a novel infectious disease.

Global Health Security (GHS) Index: Preparedness Assessments vs. Reality

The 2019 GHS Index, while a pioneering effort to systematically assess global health security capacities, inadvertently highlighted a critical disjuncture between perceived preparedness and actual operational readiness. As noted, no country was deemed fully prepared, and the average global score was alarmingly low.(GHS Index, 2021) The Index pointed to widespread deficiencies in crucial areas: 70% of countries lacked sufficient health capacity in clinics, hospitals, and community health centers; a vast majority (155 out of 195) had not made dedicated financial investments in epidemic preparedness in the preceding three years; and most had failed to adequately incorporate the needs of vulnerable populations into their emergency plans.(GHS Index, 2021)

Perhaps most tellingly, the United States, which received the highest overall score in the 2019 GHS Index, subsequently mounted a response that was widely criticized. This disconnects between perceived preparedness and actual response effectiveness highlights the inherent limitations of assessment tools like the GHS Index, a critique that echoes scholarly reflections on prior outbreaks such as H1N1. For instance, numerous studies argue that while such indices are adept at quantifying 'on-paper' technical capacities (e.g., laboratory systems, existing legislation), they often fail to capture the critical 'soft infrastructure' of ‘crisis governance’, such as political will, social trust, and the operational ability to translate plans into effective action. This “illusion of preparedness” in some high-scoring nations may have engendered a false sense of security, masking the deep-seated vulnerabilities that the pandemic would soon lay bare. (GHS Index, 2021)

The pre-pandemic landscape was thus characterized by a complex interplay of advancements and significant, often normalized, vulnerabilities. The systemic underinvestment in prevention and public health, coupled with workforce shortages and pervasive inequities, created a global health environment that was, in retrospect, precariously balanced. While UHC models aimed to provide a safety net, they too faced internal pressures that could compromise their resilience. The declining trend in ODA for health further threatened the capacity of LMICs to strengthen their foundational health systems. Collectively, these factors suggest that the world, despite its scientific progress, was inadequately prepared for the scale and nature of the shock that COVID-19 would deliver. The pandemic did not so much create new weaknesses as it ruthlessly exposed and amplified those that had long been present, often hidden beneath the surface of everyday health system operations. In summary, the pre-pandemic landscape demonstrates a profound failure to apply existing preparedness frameworks in a meaningful way. While frameworks like the GHS Index existed and international health regulations were in place, they were not matched with the necessary political will, sustained financial investment, or operational readiness. The systemic focus on curative care over prevention, coupled with a depleted public health workforce and a false sense of security in some high-scoring nations, meant that the world's on-paper preparedness was a fragile veneer. This gap between theoretical frameworks and on-the-ground reality was the most critical underlying vulnerability, setting a global stage that was dangerously unprepared for the shock that was to come.

SECTION 2: THE PANDEMIC UNFOLDS: EARLY RESPONSES AND CHALLENGES

The final days of 2019 marked the emergence of a novel respiratory illness in Wuhan, China, an event that would rapidly escalate into a global crisis of unprecedented scale and complexity. The initial phase of the COVID-19 pandemic, spanning roughly from January to June 2020, was characterized by the swift international spread of the SARS-CoV-2 virus, a wide spectrum of national responses, and the immediate, often overwhelming, challenges faced by public health systems worldwide. This section chronicles this critical period, examining the timeline of the virus's dissemination, the key decisions made by international bodies like the WHO, and the diverse strategies adopted by countries in their attempts to contain the burgeoning threat. It will particularly focus on the implementation and impact of non-pharmaceutical interventions (NPIs), the crucial role of public health messaging, and the significant hurdles encountered in scaling up testing and contact tracing efforts.

Emergence and Initial Spread of SARS-CoV-2

The emergence of the novel coronavirus followed a now-familiar pattern of rapid escalation. First identified as a cluster of atypical pneumonia cases in Wuhan, China in December 2019, the causative agent, SARS-CoV-2, was identified by January 7, 2020. Despite China's swift sharing of the virus's genome sequence, which enabled global diagnostic development, the pathogen quickly outpaced containment efforts. By mid-January, cases were confirmed in Thailand, Japan, and the United States, and evidence of human-to-human transmission was undeniable. China's unprecedented lockdown of Wuhan on January 23 marked a critical moment, yet the virus was already seeded globally, setting the stage for an international crisis.(Yale Medicine, 2021)(Centers for Disease Control and Prevention, 2024)For example, in Senegal, community health workers and volunteers were pivotal in early case detection and reporting. In the United States, partnerships between public health departments and local entities. This leveraging of local infrastructure was particularly evident in several African nations, offering a crucial counter-narrative to the high-tech responses often highlighted in the West. In Senegal, for example, the government drew upon its experience with Ebola, activating a network of trusted community health workers for surveillance, contact tracing, and public education. This community-centric model, built on pre-existing relationships and local trust, proved highly effective for early case detection and management with limited resources, showcasing a resilient, low-cost approach. This leveraging of local infrastructure was particularly evident in several African nations. In Senegal, for example, the government drew upon its experience with Ebola, activating a network of trusted community health workers for surveillance, contact tracing, and public education. This community-centric model, built on pre-existing relationships and local trust, proved highly effective for early case detection and management with limited resources, showcasing a resilient, low-cost approach often overlooked in Global North analyses.

The World Health Organization's role during this initial phase was pivotal, yet it also became a subject of considerable scrutiny. The WHO convened its International Health Regulations (IHR) Emergency Committee on January 22-23 but initially decided against declaring the outbreak a Public Health Emergency of International Concern (PHEIC).(Centers for Disease Control and Prevention, 2024) However, as the situation evolved rapidly, the committee reconvened and, on January 30, 2020, declared COVID-19 a PHEIC, signaling the formal recognition of an "extraordinary event" constituting a public health risk to other states through international spread, potentially requiring a coordinated international response. Despite this declaration, the global response was varied. It was not until March 11, 2020, after the virus had spread to 114 countries with over 118,000 cases and 4,291 deaths, that the WHO officially characterized COVID-19 as a pandemic.(Yale Medicine, 2021)

Criticisms of the WHO's early response centered on the timeliness of its declarations and the nature of its guidance, particularly concerning travel restrictions and mask usage. For instance, as late as February 3, 2020, the WHO Director-General advised against measures that would "unnecessarily interfere with international travel and trade," a stance consistent with the WHO's traditional position that travel restrictions are generally ineffective but one that drew criticism as the virus spread globally. Similarly, early WHO guidance on face masks, such as that issued on March 30, 2020, recommended their use primarily for individuals who were symptomatic or caring for someone with COVID-19, not for the general public. This advice would evolve as understanding of asymptomatic and presymptomatic transmission grew, but the initial hesitancy was a point of contention. Some critics argued that the WHO was too deferential to China in the early stages, potentially delaying a more robust global alert. These specific criticisms of the WHO's early actions were symptomatic of a larger, systemic problem: delayed multilateral coordination. The critical window in January and February 2020 was marked by a lack of unified global leadership and a failure to swiftly implement coordinated international travel policies and resource-sharing mechanisms. This reflects an enduring vulnerability in the global health security architecture, where the WHO's limited authority under the International Health Regulations (IHR) can be undermined by the political and economic interests of powerful member states, ultimately hindering a rapid, cohesive global response to an emergent threat.

A Tale of Two Responses: Comparing Proactive Containment with Reactive Mitigation

As SARS-CoV-2 spread globally, countries adopted a wide array of strategies in an attempt to mitigate its impact. These responses varied significantly in their timing, intensity, and nature, reflecting diverse political contexts, healthcare system capacities, past experiences with epidemics, and evolving understandings of the virus.

Non-Pharmaceutical Interventions (NPIs): Lockdowns, Travel Restrictions, Social Distancing, Mask Guidance

A comparative look at the use of movement restrictions reveals a critical divergence in timing and strategy. A few countries acted with preemptive decisiveness. China implemented an unprecedentedly strict lockdown of Wuhan, a city of 11 million people, on January 23, 2020. (Centers for Disease Control and Prevention, 2024)(Yang et al., 2022) Following a different model (Konishi, 2024), New Zealand and Australia later adopted strict, early lockdown measures that were credited with initially suppressing transmission. In sharp contrast, most Western nations hesitated.

The majority of countries implemented their strictest travel restrictions, including border closures, only after the WHO declared a pandemic in March, by which point the virus was already spreading extensively within their communities. The evidence suggests that while early and stringent controls could significantly delay the epidemic's peak and buy valuable time for preparedness, the delayed implementation in many Western countries turned lockdowns from a proactive containment tool into a blunt, economically damaging instrument of last resort Table 2 shows the key non-pharmacological interventions (NPIs) in the US, UK, New Zealand and South Korea by early 2020 and their timelines.

Table 2. Key non-pharmacological interventions (NPIs) in the US, UK, New Zealand and South

Country	Key Non-Pharmaceutical Interventions - NPIs	Approximate Timeline - Early 2020
United States	- A state of public health emergency is declared. - Travel restrictions: Progressive restrictions on entry of travellers from China, Iran and the Schengen area of Europe. - National Emergency: A national state of emergency is declared. - Social Distancing: "Mitigating the Spread" guidelines are issued recommending restrictions on gatherings. - Lockdowns: No national lockdown, left to the discretion of state and local governments, resulting in inconsistent responses. - Mask Policy: Official messages were inconsistent, and early on the public was not even advised to wear masks.	- 31 January: public health emergency - February-13 March: travel restrictions in force - 13 March: National emergency - Mid-March: Social distance guidelines issued
United Kingdom	- Social Distance: It is recommended that non-essential contacts and travelling be stopped. - School Closures: Nationwide closure of schools. - Nationwide lockdown: The first nationwide lockdown is declared and people are asked to "stay home". - Contact tracing: Early attempts were abandoned in mid-March due to a spike in cases.	- Mar 16: Social Distance Advice - 20 March: School closures - 23 March: National lockdown declared
New Zealand	- Travel restrictions: Mandatory 14-day self-imposed quarantine for all persons entering the country. - Border closures: Borders are closed to almost all non-citizens. - Alert system: Activation of a four-tier alert system with rapidly escalating alert levels. - Nationwide lockdown: A strict "Level 4" nationwide lockdown was imposed, the centrepiece of its "Go Hard, Go Early" strategy.	- 14 March: mandatory quarantine on entry - 19 March: border closure - 25 March: national blockade
South Korea	- Core strategy: Focus on Test, Trace, and Isolate rather than mandatory national blockades. - Mass Testing: Rapidly expand PCR testing capacity. - Technology Tracking: Active contact tracing and isolation management using digital technology such as GPS applications. - Social Distance: Conduct a "Social Distance Enhancement Campaign". - Mask supply: Implement a mask rationing system to ensure supply.	- From late January: testing and tracking initiated - 6 March: Rationing of masks - 22nd March: Intensified social distance exercise

Korea by early 2020 and their timelines

Guidance on the use of face masks by the general public was a particularly contentious and evolving aspect of the early response. As mentioned, initial WHO recommendations were limited. In the United States, inconsistent messaging from public health officials and political leaders, coupled with initial advice against general public mask use (partly driven by concerns about PPE shortages for healthcare workers), led to widespread confusion and hampered adoption.(Committee on Oversight and Government Reform, 2024) By September 2020, 14 US states still had not implemented any form of mask mandate.(British Medical Association, 2024) The UK also experienced significant delays in implementing advice on face coverings.(Chun-Chien Kuo, n.d.) This evolving and often contradictory guidance on masks underscored the challenge of adapting public health recommendations swiftly in the face of new scientific evidence, particularly regarding asymptomatic transmission and the potential for aerosol spread.

Public Health Messaging: Strategies, Effectiveness, And Trust-Building Efforts

The critical role of public health communication became immediately apparent when comparing national responses. The critical role of public health communication became immediately apparent when comparing national responses. Countries that achieved early success, such as New Zealand, implemented clear, consistent messaging through a simple alert system, framing the response as a collective societal effort to build public trust (Quach et al., 2021). Similarly, Vietnam's government used transparent updates and patriotic messaging to foster community cooperation (Quach et al., 2021). In stark contrast, the United States and the United Kingdom were plagued by significant challenges, including conflicting messages from different authorities, the perceived politicization of public health guidance, and a failure to effectively counter a burgeoning "infodemic" (Committee on Oversight and Government Reform, 2024)(Quach et al., 2021)(Schuh et al., 2025)(Chun-Chien Kuo, n.d.)(Méndiz-Noguero et al., 2023). This comparison demonstrates that successful communication was less about the volume of information and more about the consistency, transparency, and trustworthiness of its source.

(Bhingarde et al., 2021) Vietnam's government prioritized health over economic growth, employed patriotic messaging to encourage adherence to public health measures, and provided financial support for those in quarantine, fostering community cooperation.(Quach et al., 2021) Key elements of these successful strategies included transparency, consistency, decisive leadership, multi-channel dissemination, and efforts to build and maintain public trust.

In contrast, many Western nations, including the US and UK, faced significant challenges in public health messaging.(Committee on Oversight and Government Reform, 2024) These challenges were often characterized by conflicting messages from different authorities, perceived politicization of public health guidance, and a failure to effectively counter a burgeoning "infodemic" of misinformation and disinformation.(Committee on Oversight and Government Reform, 2024) In the US, for example, a significant portion of the population believed the news media exaggerated the risks of COVID-19.(Schuh et al., 2025) In the UK, public health messaging during the summer of 2020 became mixed, with a political narrative emphasizing the easing of restrictions rather than sustained caution, which damaged public trust.(Chun-Chien Kuo, n.d.) Studies also revealed that limited public health literacy among the populace could hinder the effectiveness of even well-intentioned messages.(Christina M. Potter,Aishwarya Nagar,Erin R. Fink, Vanessa Grégoire,Jessica Malaty Rivera, Alex Zhu, 2024) The rapid spread of false or misleading information via social media and other channels actively undermined public health efforts, highlighting the urgent need for strategies to manage the information environment and proactively build trust.(Méndiz-Noguero et al., 2023)

Testing and Contact Tracing: Scale-Up Efforts and Operational Challenges

The strategic divide in early pandemic response is starkly illustrated by a comparison of national testing and contact tracing capabilities (Konishi, 2024). On one hand, nations like South Korea leveraged prior experience with MERS to rapidly develop and deploy PCR tests, achieving a capacity of 15,000 tests per day by April 2020 and coupling it with aggressive, technology-driven contact tracing. By March 11, South Korea had tested over 3,600 people per million (Quach et al., 2021). Vietnam and Taiwan similarly benefited from past epidemic experiences, implementing proactive, data-informed tracing systems from the outset (Jui Bhingarde, Kacy Nowak, Dr. Robert F. Breiman, 2021)(Quach et al., 2021). On the other hand, the United States and the United Kingdom faced immense challenges. The US response was crippled by significant delays in deploying functional test kits and overly restrictive testing guidelines that missed widespread community transmission, while the UK's limited initial testing capacity led it to abandon community contact tracing entirely in mid-March. This comparative failure highlights that effective testing and tracing depended not on wealth, but on pre-existing public health infrastructure, logistical readiness, and a political willingness to act decisively—foundations that had been weakened by chronic underinvestment in some Western nations. A comparative analysis of these initial responses offers a critical insight for policymakers. The cases of South Korea and New Zealand, when contrasted with the US and UK, demonstrate that a country's governance model and its reservoir of social trust were more predictive of an effective early response than its economic standing. This suggests that policy interventions aimed at building public trust and streamlining public health governance during non-crisis periods are a high-yield investment for future pandemic preparedness. Using these country responses as comparative evidence highlights a key determinant of early success: governance and social cohesion. The cases of South Korea, Taiwan, and New Zealand demonstrate that nations with recent epidemic experience, high levels of public trust, and decisive, centralized public health leadership were able to rapidly implement proactive, society-wide strategies. In contrast, the initial responses in the US and UK were characterized by fragmented authority, inconsistent messaging, and lower social buy-in. This comparison suggests that a country's governance model and its reservoir of social trust were more predictive of an effective early response than its economic standing or on-paper preparedness.

However, many countries in Europe and North America faced immense challenges in implementing effective testing and tracing strategies at the necessary scale and speed.(Serchen et al., 2023) The United States, for example, experienced significant delays in deploying functional diagnostic tests due to issues with the initial CDC-developed test kits and bottlenecks created by centralized testing protocols.(Serchen et al., 2023) Early testing guidelines were also overly restrictive, focusing on individuals with travel history to China, thereby missing widespread community transmission. By March 11, 2020, the US had tested only 23 people per million, compared to South Korea's over 3,600 per million.(Areal & Sheppy, 2021) Furthermore, long turnaround times for test results in the US, often exceeding seven days, severely limited their utility for timely contact tracing and isolation. (Angelici et al., 2023) Chronic underinvestment in public health infrastructure was a key contributing factor to these failures.(Serchen et al., 2023) Federal investment in public health capabilities had declined over decades, and funding often followed a reactive 'ebb-and-flow' cycle, with temporary increases in response to specific emergencies (like H1N1 or Ebola) followed by subsequent cuts once the immediate threat subsided. This reactive pattern runs contrary to the core lesson from the SARS outbreak—the necessity of sustained, proactive investment—and resulted in a long-term hollowing out of public health infrastructure.

The United Kingdom similarly struggled. Initial contact tracing efforts were abandoned in mid-March 2020 as cases surged, and the country's testing capacity was initially very limited (around 1,500 tests per day), constraining tracing efforts primarily to high-risk settings like hospitals and care homes.(Chun-Chien Kuo, n.d.) Later attempts to scale up, including the outsourcing of contact tracing services, were criticized as costly and ineffective.(Chun-Chien Kuo, n.d.) The testing failures in the U.S. and many European countries were not simply operational missteps but symptoms of deeper, structural weaknesses. In the United States, significant delays were caused by regulatory and bureaucratic hurdles, such as the initial distribution of flawed CDC-developed test kits and centralized protocols that created bottlenecks. This stood in stark contrast to countries like South Korea, which leveraged its centralized biotech sector for rapid, mass-scale test deployment. Ultimately, these immediate problems were rooted in a more profound issue: the chronic underinvestment in public health infrastructure. Decades of neglect had left these nations with insufficient laboratory capacity, outdated data systems, and a diminished public health workforce, creating a system with no surge capacity to handle the unprecedented demand of a pandemic. The development and rollout of the NHS contact tracing app also faced significant technical challenges, privacy concerns, and delays, with the initial version being discontinued.(Atkinson et al., 2020)

In continental Europe, countries like Italy and Spain, which were hit hard and early by the pandemic, saw their healthcare systems rapidly overwhelmed, making comprehensive testing and tracing exceedingly difficult amidst surging caseloads. (Juan Rodríguez Teruel, Eloísa del Pino, José Real-Dato, 2023) While Germany was notable for its early development of a diagnostic test and rapid scaling of PCR testing capacity through a network of public and private laboratories (Wieler et al., 2023), it later faced challenges related to siloed data systems that hindered efficient information exchange.(Or et al., 2022) France also experienced initial shortages of masks and PPE, and while testing eventually became widely available and fully funded, its contact tracing app, "TousAntiCovid," launched in June 2020, saw limited uptake for actual contact tracing purposes due to public concerns about battery consumption and data privacy.(Wieler et al., n.d.)

The WHO's initial guidelines in May 2020 suggested that at least 80% of new cases should have their close contacts traced and quarantined within 72 hours of case confirmation.(Feachem et al., n.d.) However, achieving this target proved immensely challenging for many nations, particularly those with widespread community transmission, limited public health workforce capacity, and underdeveloped data infrastructure. The period between the WHO's PHEIC declaration in late January and the widespread implementation of stringent measures in many Western countries in mid-to-late March represented a critical window of missed opportunity. This delay allowed the virus to seed extensively within communities, exponentially increasing the scale of the challenge and rendering subsequent containment efforts, including contact tracing, far more difficult and less effective. The failure to rapidly establish and scale effective testing and contact tracing systems in many Western nations during this initial wave was a fundamental strategic misstep, leading to greater reliance on prolonged and economically damaging lockdowns and contributing to higher overall caseloads and mortality in these regions. Crucially, this overview of initial responses fails to capture the inequitable application of these measures. Non-pharmaceutical interventions like social distancing, remote work, and school closures were not neutral; they were privileges largely available to higher-income, white-collar households. For low-income essential workers, who were disproportionately from ethnic minority communities, "staying at home" was not an option, forcing them into high-exposure environments. Similarly, access to testing was often faster and easier in wealthier neighborhoods, while contact tracing proved less effective in dense, low-income communities or among populations with precarious work situations. Thus, the public health response itself, while designed to be universal, was experienced in a highly stratified manner, reinforcing the pre-existing vulnerabilities that would define the pandemic's unequal burden.

Early Challenges and Systemic Strains

The initial onslaught of the COVID-19 pandemic subjected health systems globally to immense and often overwhelming pressure, revealing deep-seated systemic strains and immediate operational challenges.

Overwhelmed Healthcare Capacity: PPE Shortages, ICU Bed Crises, Staff Burnout

One of the most immediate and visible consequences of the rapid spread of SARS-CoV-2 was the overwhelming of healthcare capacity in many regions.(Serchen et al., 2023) Hospitals, particularly in early hotspots, were inundated with patients requiring acute and intensive care, far exceeding their normal operational capacities. This surge led to critical shortages of essential resources. Personal Protective Equipment (PPE) for healthcare workers, including masks, gowns, and gloves, became scarce globally, leaving frontline staff dangerously exposed to infection.(Serchen et al., 2023) This was a particularly acute problem in Spain (Madrid and Cataluña), contributing to high anxiety and infection rates among healthcare professionals. The Strategic National Stockpile in the US, intended to provide such resources during emergencies, was found to be under-resourced and insufficiently replenished from previous public health events.(Serchen et al., 2023)

Intensive Care Unit (ICU) beds and mechanical ventilators, critical for managing severe respiratory distress associated with COVID-19, were also in short supply. (Serchen et al., 2023) This forced many healthcare systems to resort to crisis standards of care, making agonizing decisions about rationing life-saving interventions. (Serchen et al., 2023) The catastrophic potential of a health system exceeding its surge capacity was starkly illustrated during the Delta variant wave in India in early 2021. The surge completely overwhelmed the nation's healthcare infrastructure, leading to a critical, nationwide shortage of medical oxygen. Hospitals, both urban and rural, were forced to turn away patients, and the crisis resulted in an immense death toll that was widely considered to be significantly undercounted. This case provides a harrowing, large-scale example of how a major health system can collapse when faced with a sufficiently virulent and transmissible pathogen. The strain on healthcare staff was immense. Already facing pre-existing workforce shortages in some areas, medical professionals worked under extreme pressure, often with inadequate resources and facing high risks of personal infection. This led to widespread physical exhaustion, moral distress from being unable to provide optimal care to all patients, and significant psychological trauma, contributing to high rates of burnout, anxiety, and PTSD among healthcare workers.(Serchen et al., 2023)

Failures in International Coordination and Data Sharing

The global nature of the pandemic demanded unprecedented international coordination and rapid, transparent data sharing. However, the early phase was marked by significant failures in this regard.(Committee on Oversight and Government Reform, 2024) The Lancet COVID-19 Commission, among others, highlighted failures in the timely notification of the initial outbreak by China and a subsequent lack of timely, accurate, and systematic sharing of data on infections, deaths, and viral variants by many countries.(Gavi, the Vaccine Alliance, 2025) This hampered a unified global understanding of the virus's characteristics, its spread, and the effectiveness of different interventions. The WHO's own response was criticized by some for being slow or overly influenced by political pressures, particularly from China, which allegedly delayed the sharing of critical information. These failures in global cooperation and data transparency hindered the ability of the international community to mount a swift, cohesive, and optimally informed response.

The Infodemic: Misinformation and its Impact on Public Health Efforts

Concurrent with the viral pandemic, a global "infodemic"—an overwhelming deluge of information, much of it false or misleading—spread rapidly, primarily through social media and other digital platforms.(Committee on Oversight and Government Reform, 2024) This infodemic had a profoundly negative impact on public health efforts. Misinformation about the virus's origin, severity, modes of transmission, and the efficacy (or supposed dangers) of preventive measures and treatments fueled public confusion, anxiety, and distrust in official health guidance and scientific expertise.(Committee on Oversight and Government Reform, 2024) In some instances, public health officials and political leaders themselves contributed to the confusion through conflicting messaging, premature pronouncements, or a perceived lack of transparency.(Committee on Oversight and Government Reform, 2024) The politicization of public health measures, such as mask-wearing or social distancing, further exacerbated the problem, making it difficult to achieve broad public compliance with recommended interventions.(Schuh et al., 2025) The infodemic was not merely a nuisance; it was a direct impediment to effective pandemic control. It actively eroded public trust in science and government, polarized societies, and, in some cases, led to direct harm from the promotion of unproven treatments. This phenomenon highlighted a critical vulnerability in the 21st-century public health landscape: the battle for narrative control. Effectively countering it requires more than reactive fact-checking; it demands proactive, transparent, and empathetic health communication, investment in media literacy education, and collaboration with technology platforms to curb the spread of dangerous falsehoods, thereby building long-term societal resilience against harmful narratives..

The early phase of the COVID-19 pandemic thus revealed a world caught off guard, with health systems struggling to cope with a novel pathogen that spread with alarming speed. While some countries demonstrated initial success through decisive action and effective use of public health tools, many others faced overwhelming challenges related to resource shortages, coordination failures, and a debilitating infodemic. The experiences of these first six months laid bare the critical importance of preparedness, agile governance, public trust, and international solidarity in the face of a global health threat.

SECTION 3: STRENGTHS AND VULNERABILITIES OF PUBLIC HEALTH SYSTEMS REVEALED BY COVID-19

The COVID-19 pandemic acted as an unsparing crucible for global health systems, subjecting them to pressures far exceeding those encountered in recent memory. This intense stress test had a dual effect: it brought to light certain latent strengths and capacities for innovation within these systems, but more starkly, it exposed a wide array of profound and often interconnected vulnerabilities. This section moves beyond the chronicle of early crisis responses to dissect the deeper systemic attributes applying the aforementioned frameworks of health system resilience and crisis governance to understand how these factors shaped countries' experiences. It will analyze how factors such as scientific ingenuity, healthcare adaptability, and community resilience emerged as strengths, while simultaneously examining how issues like fragmented governance, chronic underinvestment, supply chain fragilities, data system inadequacies, workforce strain, and, critically, pervasive health inequities were magnified, defining the pandemic's devastating and unequal trajectory.

Unveiled Strengths: Resilience and Innovation

Despite the overwhelming challenges, the COVID-19 pandemic also catalyzed and revealed significant strengths within the global scientific community and various public health systems. These areas of resilience and innovation were crucial in mitigating the pandemic's impact and offered valuable lessons for future preparedness.

Rapid Scientific Advancements (Vaccines, Therapeutics, Diagnostics)

One of the most remarkable achievements during the pandemic was the unprecedented speed of scientific advancement, particularly in the development of vaccines, therapeutics, and diagnostics. The development of multiple effective COVID-19 vaccines, most notably mRNA vaccines, within approximately 11 months of the virus's genetic sequencing was a monumental scientific feat.(Marta Angelici, Paolo Berta, Joan Costa-Font, GilbertoTurati, 2023) This rapid development was built upon decades of prior research into vaccine platforms, including mRNA technology, and was facilitated by intense global scientific collaboration, significant public and private investment, and expedited regulatory pathways.(Marta Angelici, Paolo Berta, Joan Costa-Font, GilbertoTurati, 2023)

Similarly, the biomedical research community moved swiftly to identify and develop diagnostic tools. Germany's Charité hospital, for example, developed one of the earliest diagnostic tests for SARS-CoV-2.(Wieler et al., 2023) Private and public laboratories globally worked to scale up testing capacities, although the success and speed of this scale-up varied considerably by country.(Wieler et al., 2023) In the realm of therapeutics, existing drugs like dexamethasone were identified through clinical trials (such as the RECOVERY trial in the UK) as effective in reducing mortality in severe cases, while new antiviral treatments like Remdesivir received emergency use authorizations.(Keshta et al., 2021) The ability of the global scientific and pharmaceutical sectors to innovate and adapt at such speed demonstrated a powerful latent capacity, offering a critical tool in combating the virus.

Adaptability of Healthcare Delivery (e.g., Telehealth, Repurposed Infrastructure):

Healthcare systems demonstrated considerable adaptability in service delivery in response to the pandemic's pressures. The most notable shift was the dramatic expansion of telehealth services.(Maani & Galea, 2020)As in-person consultations became risky or restricted, regulatory barriers to telemedicine were lowered in many countries, leading to a surge in virtual consultations. This shift not only helped maintain access to care for many patients, particularly those in remote areas or with chronic conditions requiring ongoing management, but also reshaped patient and provider expectations for healthcare delivery.(Marta Angelici, Paolo Berta, Joan Costa-Font, GilbertoTurati, 2023)

Healthcare infrastructure also showed adaptability, albeit often under duress. Hospitals rapidly repurposed existing wards into COVID-19 units, expanded ICU capacities where possible, and developed protocols for managing surges of critically ill patients.(Serchen et al., 2023) While the implementation of "crisis standards of care" in overwhelmed systems signified a failure to meet normal care levels, the ability to formally adapt protocols and triage mechanisms under extreme circumstances was, in itself, a form of operational resilience aimed at maximizing benefit with severely constrained resources.(Serchen et al., 2023)

Community Engagement and Solidarity

In many instances, community engagement and solidarity emerged as vital strengths. Community-based surveillance and support networks played a crucial role in some settings. For example, in Senegal, community health workers and volunteers were pivotal in early case detection and reporting.(Sanger Institute, n.d.) In the United States, partnerships between public health departments and local entities like faith-based organizations helped to increase access to testing in underserved communities.(DeSalvo et al., 2021) This highlighted the power of leveraging existing local networks and trusted community figures to extend the reach of public health interventions. This leveraging of local infrastructure was particularly evident in several African nations, offering a crucial counter-narrative to the high-tech responses often highlighted in the West. In Senegal, for example, the government drew upon its experience with Ebola, activating a network of trusted community health workers for surveillance, contact tracing, and public education. This community-centric model, built on pre-existing relationships and local trust, proved highly effective for early case detection and management with limited resources. It underscored a key strength often overlooked in global health: the resilience and adaptability of community-based systems, which can succeed where technology-heavy or top-down approaches may fail, especially in under-resourced settings.

Furthermore, in countries that mounted successful early responses, such as New Zealand, high levels of public adherence to NPIs were critical.(Quach et al., 2021) This compliance was often fostered by clear, consistent government communication, a sense of shared purpose, and public trust in leadership. Spontaneous acts of community support, volunteerism, and mutual aid also demonstrated societal resilience in many parts of the world.

Strengthened Surveillance and Genomic Sequencing Capabilities

The pandemic spurred significant advancements in public health surveillance, particularly in the realm of genomic sequencing. The establishment and rapid scaling of national and international genomic surveillance networks, such as the COVID-19 Genomics UK (COG-UK) consortium, were instrumental.(Marjanovic et al., 2022) COG-UK, a partnership of NHS organizations, public health agencies, and academic institutions, sequenced hundreds of thousands of SARS-CoV-2 genomes, providing crucial data for tracking viral evolution, identifying new variants of concern (like Alpha and Delta), and informing public health responses and vaccine development strategies.(Marjanovic et al., 2022) The commitment to open data sharing through platforms like GISAID (Global Initiative on Sharing Avian Influenza Data) facilitated global collaboration among scientists and public health officials.(Rito et al., 2023) This real-time application of genomics to a public health crisis represented a paradigm shift in infectious disease surveillance. This leadership in genomic surveillance was not limited to high-income nations. Indeed, scientific institutions in South Africa played a pivotal global role in identifying and transparently sharing data on new variants of concern, including the Beta and Omicron variants. This demonstrated significant scientific capacity within a non-OECD context, providing critical early warnings to the entire world.

Wastewater surveillance also emerged as a powerful, non-invasive tool for monitoring community-level spread of SARS-CoV-2.(Marta Angelici, Paolo Berta, Joan Costa-Font, GilbertoTurati, 2023) By detecting viral RNA in sewage, public health authorities could often anticipate clinical surges by several days, providing an early warning system to inform resource allocation and public health interventions. The CDC's National Wastewater Surveillance System in the US, for example, expanded rapidly during the pandemic.(Marta Angelici, Paolo Berta, Joan Costa-Font, GilbertoTurati, 2023) Additionally, efforts were made in some regions to improve data linkages between different parts of the health system, such as connecting contact tracing data with case management and laboratory results, enhancing the coherence of surveillance efforts.(Sanger Institute, n.d.) However, the rapid deployment of these digital health strategies also raised critical questions of equity and ethics. Technology-driven surveillance, while powerful, brought significant concerns regarding data privacy, potential for government overreach, and the risk of stigmatizing certain communities. Furthermore, the pivot to telehealth and digital contact tracing highlighted the "digital divide," where marginalized populations, including the elderly, low-income individuals, and those in rural areas with poor connectivity, faced significant barriers to accessing these essential services. This underscored the lesson that technological solutions must be designed and implemented with a strong equity lens to avoid exacerbating the very disparities they are meant to address. These innovations and adaptations in surveillance provided critical intelligence for navigating the pandemic's complex dynamics.

Systemic Failures Laid Bare: From Governance to Global Supply Chains

While the pandemic showcased instances of resilience and innovation, it more profoundly exposed and exacerbated a multitude of pre-existing systemic weaknesses within public health and healthcare systems globally. These vulnerabilities often proved to be critical determinants of a country's ability to effectively respond to the crisis.

Governance and Leadership: Fragmented Decision-Making, Political Interference, Lack of Trust

Building on the divergent initial responses discussed earlier, the systemic nature of these failures in governance and leadership became even more apparent as the pandemic progressed. In countries like the United States, the federal response was widely criticized. The response in the United States, for instance, serves as a textbook case of failed crisis governance. Its federalist system, normally a source of local autonomy, became a critical vulnerability. The lack of a centralized, science-led command structure, coupled with the significant politicization of public health guidance, resulted in a chaotic patchwork of contradictory state and local policies, representing a fundamental breakdown in the principles of effective crisis management..(Serchen et al., 2023) This fragmentation, a critical failure of federalist governance models under the intense pressure of a national emergency, led to a chaotic patchwork of inconsistent responses, fueled public confusion, and severely eroded trust in both scientific advice and official institutions.(Committee on Oversight and Government Reform, 2024) It is noteworthy that the 2019 GHS Index had already identified low public confidence in the US government as a potential vulnerability.(Serchen et al., 2023) This pattern of governance failure was tragically mirrored in parts of Latin America, most notably Brazil. There, a combination of presidential denialism, intense political polarization between federal and state authorities, and the deliberate promotion of misinformation created a perfect storm for uncontrolled viral spread. The rejection of scientific advice and the downplaying of the virus's severity by top leadership directly undermined public health efforts, leading to one of the world's highest death tolls. The Brazilian case serves as a stark example of how, similar to the US, internal political dysfunction and a leadership vacuum can cripple a nation's pandemic response, regardless of the underlying capacity of its health system.

At the global level, the governance of health security also revealed significant weaknesses. The World Health Organization, despite its crucial mandate, faced limitations in its authority and resources, and its response was criticized by some for delays and perceived susceptibility to political pressures from member states. The Council on Foreign Relations Task Force report highlighted that effective global health security ultimately depends on the actions of sovereign states, which are often reluctant to cede authority to international bodies.(House Oversight Committee, 2024) The CompCoRe Interim Report (January 2021) categorized several nations, including the US, Brazil, India, Italy, and the UK, as "Chaos Countries" due to their experiences with policy incoherence and significant conflict over policy goals, often linked to polarized political environments and a pervasive distrust in expertise. (Mathai Mammen et al., n.d.) This "soft infrastructure" gap—encompassing trust, communication, and governance—proved to be a critical vulnerability, as technical capacity and resources are insufficient if not supported by strong leadership and societal consensus.

Chronic Underinvestment: Impact on Surge Capacity and Core Functions

The decades of chronic underinvestment in public health infrastructure, discussed in Section 1, had a direct and devastating impact on the ability of health systems to cope with the surge in demand created by COVID-19.(OECD, 2021) This underfunding translated directly into insufficient surge capacity in hospitals, including shortages of ICU beds, ventilators, and, critically, trained staff to manage the influx of severely ill patients.(Serchen et al., 2023) Core public health functions essential for pandemic response—such as robust surveillance systems, laboratory capacity, contact tracing programs, and health education campaigns—were often under-resourced and quickly overwhelmed. The pandemic starkly illustrated that neglecting public health investment during inter-crisis periods is a false economy, leading to far greater human and economic costs when a major health threat emerges.

Supply Chain Fragility for Essential Medical Goods

The pandemic exposed extreme vulnerabilities in global supply chains for essential medical goods, particularly PPE, testing reagents, and certain critical care medications.(Serchen et al., 2023) Widespread shortages occurred globally as demand skyrocketed and production, often concentrated in a few countries (notably China for PPE), was disrupted or redirected by national priorities.(Serchen et al., 2023) The "just-in-time" inventory systems prevalent in many healthcare organizations, designed for efficiency in normal times, proved inadequate for the sustained surge in demand during a pandemic. Even well-resourced countries like Germany experienced shortages of PPE.(Wieler et al., 2023) The US Strategic National Stockpile was found to be insufficiently stocked to meet national needs, leading to chaotic competition among states for limited supplies.(Serchen et al., 2023) This fragility highlighted the risks of over-reliance on distant and concentrated sources for critical supplies and the need for greater diversification and strategic stockpiling. This fragility exposed a fundamental vulnerability of the modern globalized economy: the "just-in-time" logistics model, optimized for efficiency, is inherently brittle in a crisis. The pandemic revealed that the hyper-concentration of manufacturing for essential goods like PPE in a few countries is not just a market feature but a critical national and global security risk. This dependency created a zero-sum scramble for resources, highlighting the need to rethink global supply chains by prioritizing resilience, diversification, and strategic regional stockpiling over pure cost efficiency.

Data Systems and Interoperability: Gaps in Real-Time Information

Effective pandemic response relies on timely, accurate, and comprehensive data. However, the pandemic revealed significant deficiencies in public health data systems in many countries.(Serchen et al., 2023) In the United States, outdated, fragmented, and non-interoperable data systems at local, state, and federal levels severely hampered real-time surveillance, case tracking, and the reporting of crucial epidemiological information.(Serchen et al., 2023) Many health departments relied on manual data entry and antiquated technologies, leading to delays and inaccuracies. Germany, despite its advanced healthcare system, also faced challenges due to highly siloed data systems that made information exchange and comprehensive analysis difficult.(Or et al., 2022) Globally, the lack of standardized data collection and reporting protocols, and delays in sharing information on infections, deaths, and viral variants, impeded a clear and timely understanding of the pandemic's trajectory and impact.(House Oversight Committee, 2024) These data gaps critically undermined the ability of public health authorities to make informed decisions and target interventions effectively.

Workforce Resilience and Mental Health

The health workforce, the backbone of any pandemic response, was stretched to its limits and beyond. Pre-existing global shortages of health workers were exacerbated by the demands of COVID-19.(Boniol et al., 2022) Healthcare professionals on the front lines faced enormous physical and emotional burdens, including extreme workloads, high risk of infection (often compounded by PPE shortages), the moral distress of making life-or-death decisions under conditions of scarcity, and the psychological trauma of witnessing widespread suffering and death.(Glazier, 2023) This led to alarming rates of burnout, anxiety, depression, and PTSD among healthcare workers globally, as documented in countries like Spain and Canada.

(Glazier, 2023) The pandemic underscored the urgent need not only to expand the health workforce but also to implement robust systems for supporting their mental health and well-being, particularly during prolonged crises. Beyond the direct strain on the health workforce, the pandemic inflicted a devastating toll on the mental health and socio-economic well-being of the general population. Prolonged lockdowns, social isolation, fear of the virus, and grief created a parallel mental health crisis, with surging rates of anxiety, depression, and other psychological distress reported globally. Simultaneously, public health measures, while necessary, triggered a severe economic downturn. Widespread job losses, business closures, and disruptions to education disproportionately affected low-wage workers, women, and young people, exacerbating poverty and inequality and demonstrating that a public health crisis is inextricably linked to a socio-economic one.

The paradox of the pandemic lies in this coexistence of remarkable innovation, particularly in the biomedical sphere, with catastrophic failures in many fundamental public health functions. The rapid development of vaccines, for instance, showcased scientific prowess, yet this occurred alongside fragmented governance, broken data systems, and inequitable resource distribution that hampered the effective deployment of these and other interventions. This suggests a critical disconnect: while societies could mobilize high-level scientific and technological capacity, this did not automatically translate into effective system-wide performance or equitable outcomes, largely because the foundational public health infrastructure and the "soft" infrastructure of trust and governance were often deeply compromised.

The Pandemic's Unequal Burden: Health Inequities Laid Bare

One of the most profound and disturbing revelations of the COVID-19 pandemic was its grossly unequal impact. The virus and its societal consequences did not affect all populations equally; rather, it disproportionately burdened those already marginalized by social, economic, and health disparities. The pandemic acted as an accelerant and amplifier of these pre-existing inequities, turning them into critical determinants of COVID-19 infection, severity, and mortality.

Disproportionate Impact on Vulnerable Populations (Elderly, Low-Income, Ethnic Minorities, Pre-Existing Conditions)

Globally, older adults and individuals with underlying health conditions (such as diabetes, heart disease, and chronic respiratory illnesses) were quickly identified as being at significantly higher risk for severe outcomes from COVID-19, including hospitalization and death.(OECD, 2021) However, the pandemic's unequal toll extended far beyond these groups, deeply cleaving along lines of socioeconomic status, race, and ethnicity.

Low-income communities worldwide faced a confluence of risk factors. Residents often lived in more crowded housing conditions, making physical distancing difficult. Many were employed in essential frontline jobs that could not be performed remotely, increasing their exposure to the virus.(House Oversight Committee, 2024) They also frequently experienced greater barriers to accessing healthcare, testing, and, later, vaccines. In the United States, data from the Centers for Disease Control and Prevention (CDC) and other sources starkly illustrated these disparities. Black, Indigenous, Latino, and Pacific Islander populations experienced significantly higher rates of COVID-19 infection, hospitalization, and death compared to their White counterparts.(Serchen et al., 2023) For example, a CDC MMWR report focusing on Los Angeles County showed that during the surges before vaccines were widely available (July 2020 and January 2021), COVID-19 incidence was substantially higher in communities with the lowest median household income compared to those with the highest.(Schuh et al., 2025) The COVID-19 infection rate was found to be three times higher in predominantly Black counties than in predominantly White ones, with the mortality rate being six times higher.(House Oversight Committee, 2024) The CDC even developed the Minority Health Social Vulnerability Index (SVI) to help identify racial and ethnic minority communities at greatest risk during public health emergencies.(Rudiger, 2023) These patterns were not unique to the US; similar disparities were observed in many countries, reflecting how deeply social and economic fault lines determined vulnerability to the pandemic. A significant dimension of this unequal burden was its gendered impact. Globally, women constitute the vast majority of the frontline health and social care workforce, placing them at a significantly higher risk of exposure to the virus. Furthermore, lockdown measures and school closures precipitated a massive increase in unpaid care work—including childcare and tending to sick family members—a burden that fell disproportionately on women, forcing millions to reduce their work hours or leave the labor force entirely. The isolation of lockdowns also fueled a "shadow pandemic" of increased domestic violence, leaving many women trapped in unsafe homes. This failure to account for gender-specific impacts in pandemic planning represents a critical flaw in health system preparedness.

The Role of Universal Health Coverage (UHC) In Mitigating or Exacerbating Inequities

The concept of Universal Health Coverage (UHC)—ensuring that all people have access to the quality health services they need without suffering financial hardship—is fundamentally linked to health equity.(World Health Organization (WHO), 2025) In theory, robust UHC systems should provide a crucial buffer against the inequitable impacts of a pandemic by ensuring broader access to prevention, testing, treatment, and care. Some analyses suggested that UHC could have significantly reduced mortality; one estimate proposed that a single-payer UHC system in the US might have saved over 200,000 lives in 2020 alone.(World Health Organization (WHO), 2025)

However, the empirical evidence on the actual performance of UHC systems during COVID-19 in terms of equitable outcomes was mixed and complex.(OECD, 2021) While most OECD countries had some form of UHC, many still faced pre-existing access barriers and underinvestment in prevention.(OECD, 2021) Comparative studies yielded inconsistent results: some indicated that UHC countries experienced lower infection rates or, conversely, higher case fatality rates than non-UHC countries, while others found no significant difference.(Dongarwar & Salihu, 2020) Countries with strong UHC systems, such as the UK, Italy, and Spain, nonetheless struggled significantly with high caseloads, overwhelmed healthcare systems, and substantial mortality during certain waves of the pandemic. Furthermore, the pandemic itself caused massive disruptions to essential health services in 92% of countries in 2021, thereby stalling or reversing progress towards UHC goals.(Endalamaw et al., 2025)

This complex picture suggests that while UHC provides a necessary foundation, its mere existence did not automatically guarantee an effective or equitable pandemic response. The specific design and comprehensiveness of UHC systems, the strength of their underlying public health infrastructure, the level of investment in preparedness and surge capacity, and the political and societal commitment to proactively addressing social determinants of health proved to be more decisive factors. The pandemic revealed that for UHC to truly translate into better and more equitable outcomes during a major health crisis, it must be deeply integrated with robust public health capabilities, agile governance, and targeted interventions to protect the most vulnerable. The quality, comprehensiveness, and actual accessibility of services under UHC, rather than its simple presence, were what mattered most. The pandemic underscored that health security is indivisible from health equity; A system that fails to protect its most vulnerable members is, by definition, not secure. The long-term implication of this failure is not just a moral catastrophe but a strategic one. Failing to address deep-seated health inequities during a crisis permanently scars the social fabric, deepens distrust between communities and the state, and leaves behind a sicker, less productive, and more divided society long after the virus recedes, thereby locking in a cycle of vulnerability for generations to come. Ultimately, drawing together the comparative evidence from the varied country experiences in this chapter reveals a central paradox of the pandemic. While scientific and technical capacity (e.g., vaccine development, genomic sequencing) proved to be a global strength, its effective deployment was entirely contingent on the “soft infrastructure” of governance, political stability, and public trust. Countries that possessed this soft infrastructure were able to translate technical prowess into better health outcomes. Those that did not, despite their wealth or scientific leadership, saw their technical capacities squandered. This illustrates the most profound systemic lesson: in a global health crisis, societal cohesion and effective governance are the most critical assets of all.3.4. The Amplified Crisis in Low- and Middle-Income Countries (LMICs)

The pandemic's impact was profoundly amplified in LMICs, where pre-existing structural constraints created a cascade of interlocking crises that high-income countries did not face to the same degree. Chronically limited fiscal space, often compounded by high external debt burdens, made it impossible for most LMICs to deploy the massive economic stimulus and social safety net packages seen in the West. This financial reality meant that prolonged lockdowns, while a potential public health tool, were an economic impossibility, forcing a devastating choice between controlling the virus and averting widespread poverty and hunger. Furthermore, their limited purchasing power and position in the global hierarchy left them at a severe disadvantage in the scramble for essential medical goods, from PPE to, most critically, vaccines, exacerbating their inability to mount an effective response.

Beyond the immediate financial constraints, the pandemic inflicted severe collateral damage on already fragile primary healthcare systems in LMICs. The necessary diversion of limited resources and personnel to combat COVID-19 had a catastrophic effect on essential, routine health services. This resulted in dramatic declines in childhood immunization coverage, disruptions to maternal and child health programs, and a significant setback in the fight against endemic diseases like HIV, tuberculosis, and malaria. For many LMICs, the long-term health consequences of these disruptions may ultimately prove to be as, or even more, devastating than the direct mortality from COVID-19 itself, showcasing a critical vulnerability of systems with no inbuilt redundancy.

SECTION 4: LESSONS LEARNED AND RECOMMENDATIONS FOR THE FUTURE

The COVID-19 pandemic, a global crisis of historic proportions, has served as a profound and painful learning experience for public health systems, governments, and societies worldwide. Its wake has left an indelible mark, compelling a critical re-evaluation of how nations and the international community prepare for and respond to large-scale health threats. This concluding section synthesizes the overarching lessons derived from this global ordeal and articulates a comprehensive set of recommendations aimed at fostering more resilient, equitable, and effective public health systems and a strengthened global health security architecture. Drawing upon the analyses of major post-pandemic commissions, expert bodies, and research initiatives, the objective is to provide a forward-looking roadmap for policymakers, healthcare leaders, and global health advocates to better navigate the inevitable health challenges of the future.

Synthesizing Key Lessons from the Global COVID-19 Experience

The multifaceted global response to COVID-19, with its patchwork of successes and failures, has yielded several undeniable lessons that must inform future strategies.

The Imperative of Proactive and Sustained Investment in Public Health Infrastructure

Perhaps the most glaring lesson is that chronic underfunding of public health infrastructure is a catastrophic false economy. The pandemic starkly demonstrated that systems weakened by insufficient investment are ill-equipped to withstand a major crisis. The long-term implication of this neglect extends beyond vulnerability to the next pandemic; it cripples the system's ability to address routine public health challenges, from chronic disease to environmental hazards, and perpetuates a cycle of costly, reactive crisis management that erodes public trust and economic stability.(DeSalvo et al., 2021) Reactive, crisis-driven funding, often characterized by cycles of "panic and neglect," is demonstrably inadequate for building the sustained resilience required.(Serchen et al., 2023) Proactive, predictable, and substantial investment in these core public health functions is not merely an expenditure but a critical investment in national and global security and economic stability.(DeSalvo et al., 2021)

The Critical Role of Agile Governance, Clear Communication, and Public Trust

The effectiveness of pandemic responses was inextricably linked to the quality of governance, the clarity and consistency of public health communication, and the level of public trust in institutions and leadership. Countries that mounted more successful responses, particularly in the early stages, often exhibited decisive leadership, coherent and adaptable governance structures, and the ability to communicate transparently and effectively with their populations, thereby fostering cooperation and adherence to public health measures.(Jui Bhingarde, Kacy Nowak, Dr. Robert F. Breiman, 2021) Conversely, where governance was fragmented, decision-making politicized, communication inconsistent or contradictory, and public trust eroded, pandemic responses faltered, leading to confusion, non-compliance, and ultimately, poorer health outcomes.(Serchen et al., 2023) The concurrent "infodemic" of misinformation and disinformation further underscored the necessity of proactive strategies for building and maintaining public trust and ensuring the integrity of health information.(Méndiz-Noguero et al., 2023)

The Necessity of Robust Global Collaboration and Solidarity

Pandemics, by their very nature, transcend national borders and demand a globally coordinated response. The COVID-19 experience painfully highlighted the consequences of failures in international cooperation. "Vaccine nationalism" and inadequate data sharing not only prolonged the pandemic but also revealed deep fissures in the global order. The critical long-term implication of these coordination failures is a profound "trust deficit" in multilateral institutions like the WHO. This erosion of trust encourages nationalist, go-it-alone approaches, making future collaboration on shared threats—from climate change to the next pandemic—exponentially more difficult and undermining the very foundation of global health security..(House Oversight Committee, 2024) A profound lesson is the urgent need for strengthened multilateral institutions and robust mechanisms that ensure equitable resource distribution, foster genuine collaboration in research and development, and promote a shared sense of responsibility for global health security.

Reforming National Public Health Systems

Building on these overarching lessons, comprehensive reforms are needed at the national level to create public health systems capable of effectively preventing, detecting, and responding to future health threats.

Strengthening Core Public Health Functions: Surveillance, Laboratory Capacity, Emergency Preparedness

Nations must prioritize the modernization and reinforcement of their core public health functions. A core critical assessment of the COVID-19 response is that most existing national pandemic preparedness plans were inadequate, proving to be static, "on-paper" documents that failed under real-world stress (National Academy of Medicine, n.d.-b). It is not enough for these plans to simply exist; they must be transformed into living systems. This means they must be funded, continually pressure-tested through realistic, multi-sectoral simulation exercises, and updated to explicitly address the specific failures seen in 2020, such as planning for the needs of vulnerable populations and ensuring clear lines of authority in fragmented governance systems (DeSalvo et al., 2021).

Building a Resilient and Well-Supported Health Workforce

The immense strain on the health workforce underscored the need for strategic investment in its recruitment, retention, and well-being. The long-term implication of inaction is severe: continued burnout will trigger a "brain drain" from the public health and medical fields, leading to a critical loss of skills and institutional memory. This depletes the capacity to respond not only to future pandemics but also to the everyday health needs of the population, creating a fragile system vulnerable to collapse under even minor stress. A critical assessment is that the "just-in-time" global supply chain model fundamentally failed during the pandemic, proving to be a catastrophic vulnerability for essential medical goods. The reliance on distant, concentrated sources for PPE and other supplies led to a chaotic global scramble. Therefore, nations must shift their strategic approach, treating supply chain resilience as a matter of national security. This requires policies that encourage the diversification of suppliers, support domestic or regional manufacturing of critical items, and mandate the creation and proper management of robust national stockpiles. (The Joint Commission, n.d.)

Modernizing Data Infrastructure and Promoting Data-Driven Decision-Making

The pandemic exposed critical deficiencies in public health data infrastructure. Modernization of public health data systems to be integrated, interoperable, and equity-focused is essential. A critical component of this is closing the "digital health gap." The long-term implication of failing to ensure equitable access to digital health tools and data infrastructure is the cementing of a two-tiered health system. This would permanently disadvantage elderly, low-income, and rural populations, locking in healthcare inequities and undermining the goal of universal health coverage for the next generation..(The Royal Society, 2023)

Addressing Health Inequities as a Central Pillar of Preparedness

The disproportionate impact of COVID-19 on vulnerable populations has made it unequivocally clear that health equity must be a central and non-negotiable component of all pandemic preparedness and response efforts.(Schuh et al., 2025) This requires moving beyond rhetoric to implement concrete strategies that address the social determinants of health, ensure equitable access to health services and countermeasures, and protect the rights and needs of marginalized communities. Meaningful community engagement in the planning, implementation, and evaluation of public health interventions is essential for building trust and ensuring that strategies are culturally appropriate and effective.(National Academy of Medicine, n.d.-a)

Enhancing Global Health Governance and Security

Given the transboundary nature of pandemics, national reforms alone are insufficient. Strengthening global health governance and security is equally vital.

Reforming the WHO and Strengthening the International Health Regulations (IHR)

There is a broad consensus on the need to reform and strengthen the World Health Organization, providing it with greater authority, political independence, and sustainable, flexible financing to effectively lead and coordinate global health emergency responses.(The Independent Panel for Pandemic, n.d.) Recommendations from bodies like the Independent Panel for Pandemic Preparedness and Response (IPPPR) include measures such as a single, longer term for the WHO Director-General to enhance independence and increasing assessed contributions from member states to ensure more predictable funding.(The Independent Panel for Pandemic, n.d.) The International Health Regulations (IHR 2005), the key legal framework for global health security, also require strengthening to improve compliance, ensure timely and transparent reporting of outbreaks by member states, and empower the WHO to investigate potential threats more rapidly and declare emergencies based on the precautionary principle when necessary.(The Independent Panel for Pandemic, n.d.) The amendments to the IHR agreed upon in June 2024, which include introducing a definition of a "pandemic emergency" and establishing a Coordinating Financial Mechanism, represent steps in this direction.(Juneja Gandhi et al., 2023)

Developing and Implementing a Robust International Pandemic Accord/Treaty

To address gaps not fully covered by the IHR and to secure high-level political commitment, negotiations are underway for a new international pandemic accord or treaty.(The Independent Panel for Pandemic, n.d.) The aim of such an instrument is to establish clear roles and responsibilities, promote equitable access to medical countermeasures (vaccines, therapeutics, diagnostics), enhance global surveillance and data sharing, and ensure more coordinated and effective international action during pandemics. These negotiations, targeted for completion by 2025 or earlier, must address the concerns of all nations, particularly LMICs, regarding issues of transparency, benefit-sharing from pathogen data, technology transfer, and enforceability to ensure the resulting agreement is both effective and equitable.(Thomas Cueni, 2023)

Ensuring Equitable Access to Medical Countermeasures (Vaccines, Therapeutics, Diagnostics)

A critical failure of the global response was the profound inequity in access to life-saving medical countermeasures, a problem starkly illustrated by the lack of vaccine equity. High-income nations engaged in "vaccine nationalism," securing doses far in excess of their populations' needs, while low- and middle-income countries were left waiting, prolonging the pandemic and deepening global disparities. This inequity was perfectly illustrated by the case of South Africa. Despite its scientists providing the world with critical data on new variants, the country struggled to procure adequate vaccine supplies for its own population in a timely manner, starkly demonstrating that scientific contribution did not translate into equitable access to life-saving countermeasures. Future frameworks must establish robust mechanisms for the research, development, scaled-up manufacturing, and equitable allocation of pandemic products, moving decisively beyond purely market-driven models that prioritize wealthier nations.(The Independent Panel for Pandemic, n.d.) Proposals include transforming initiatives like the Access to COVID-19 Tools (ACT) Accelerator into permanent, end-to-end platforms for global public goods, ensuring commitments to technology transfer in publicly funded R&D agreements, and reserving a portion of real-time production for LMICs.(The Independent Panel for Pandemic, n.d.)

A Call to Action: Fostering Political Will and Sustained Commitment

The lessons from COVID-19 are numerous and profound, and the path to a more secure future requires more than technical fixes; it demands sustained political will, adequate and predictable financing, and a fundamental shift in how societies prioritize public health and global cooperation. A striking feature of the post-COVID-19 landscape is the remarkable degree of consensus among major international commissions and expert bodies on the core failures of the pandemic response and the essential pillars of necessary reforms. Reports from the Lancet COVID-19 Commission, the IPPPR, the G20 High Level Independent Panel (HLIP) on Financing, the CFR Task Force, and the WHO itself, despite their diverse origins and specific remits, converge on several key themes: the need for stronger and more independent global health governance (particularly a reformed WHO), significantly increased and sustained financing for pandemic preparedness at both national and international levels, a central focus on health equity, enhanced surveillance and early warning systems, mechanisms for equitable research and development and access to countermeasures, and deeper international cooperation.(House Oversight Committee, 2024) This convergence provides a powerful, evidence-informed mandate for global action. The challenge now lies less in identifying *what* needs to be done and more in mustering the collective political will and resources to implement these widely endorsed strategic directions.

A core challenge will be to overcome the "preparedness paradox"—the inherent difficulty in maintaining political focus and financial investment on low-probability, high-consequence events like pandemics, especially as the immediate sense of crisis fades. The historical cycle of "panic and neglect" must be broken. Recommendations to elevate pandemic preparedness to a national security priority, to embed preparedness assessments into routine international financial evaluations (e.g., by the IMF) (The Independent Panel for Pandemic, n.d.), and to establish dedicated international financing facilities with long-term commitments (The Independent Panel for Pandemic, n.d.) are all aimed at institutionalizing this commitment and ensuring that the lessons of COVID-19 translate into enduring change rather than transient concern.

Furthermore, the pandemic has inextricably linked health equity with health security. Future preparedness and response efforts will be fundamentally flawed if they do not systematically identify and address the underlying social, economic, and health disparities that render certain populations disproportionately vulnerable. (Schuh et al., 2025) Equity can no longer be an afterthought; it must be a non-negotiable prerequisite and a central organizing principle for all local, national, and global health security initiatives. This involves not only ensuring equitable access to medical countermeasures but also tackling the root causes of vulnerability through intersectoral action and community engagement.

Finally, the concerted push for a new pandemic treaty and significant amendments to the IHR signals a global recognition that aspirational guidelines and informal cooperation are insufficient. There is a clear movement towards codifying the lessons of COVID-19 into stronger, more binding international legal obligations to enhance accountability and ensure more consistent and effective global responses. (The Independent Panel for Pandemic, n.d.) The success of this endeavor will hinge on navigating complex geopolitical landscapes, ensuring genuine commitment from all nations—particularly the most powerful—and designing these instruments to be both ambitious in scope and practical and equitable in their implementation, especially for the LMICs that often bear the heaviest burden of pandemics and systemic global inequities.

The evidence presented in this chapter constitutes a direct call to action for its intended audience. For scholars, the analysis compels a move beyond measuring on-paper capacities to developing new metrics for governance quality and social trust—the true determinants of resilience. For policymakers, the devastating cost of inaction must translate into concrete policy: breaking the "panic-and-neglect" funding cycle by treating public health as a core national security interest. Finally, for public health professionals, the lesson is clear: technical expertise is insufficient without community trust. The foremost task is to rebuild that trust through radical transparency and deep community engagement, ensuring that when the next crisis arrives, the public is a partner, not a bystander.

REFERENCES

Angelici, M., Berta, P., Costa-Font, J., & Turati, G. (2023, April 11). Gilberto-Turati. (2023). Divided we survive? Multilevel governance during the COVID-19 pandemic in italy and spain. *Publius*, *53*(2), 227–250. Advance online publication. DOI: 10.1093/publius/pjad002

Areal, A. G., & Sheppy, B. (2021). A crisis of governance—Or an opportunity? *Health Services Insights*, *14*, 11786329211033845. DOI: 10.1177/11786329211033845 PMID: 34366672

Atkinson, P., Gobat, N., Lant, S., Mableson, H., Pilbeam, C., Solomon, T., Tonkin-Crine, S., & Sheard, S. (2020). Understanding the policy dynamics of COVID-19 in the UK: Early findings from interviews with policy makers and health care professionals. Social Science & Medicine (1982), 266, 113423. DOI: 10.1016/j.socscimed.2020.113423

Bhingarde, J., & Nowak, K., Breiman, R. (2021). How Vietnam, South Korea, Singapore, and New Zealand fought – and nearly defeated – COVID-19. https://www.exemplars.health/stories/how-vietnam-south-korea-singapore-and-new-zealand

Boniol, M., Kunjumen, T., Nair, T. S., Siyam, A., Campbell, J., & Diallo, K. (2022). The global health workforce stock and distribution in 2020 and 2030: A threat to equity and "universal" health coverage? *BMJ Global Health*, *7*(6), e009316. DOI: 10.1136/bmjgh-2022-009316 PMID: 35760437

British Medical Association. (2024). The public health response by UK governments to COVID-19. https://www.bma.org.uk/advice-and-support/covid-19/what-the-bma-is-doing/the-public-health-response-by-uk-governments-to-covid-19

Centers for Disease Control and Prevention. (2024). CDC Museum COVID-19 Timeline. https://www.cdc.gov/museum/timeline/covid19.html

Potter, C.M., Nagar, A., Fink, E.R., Grégoire, V., Rivera, J.M., & Zhu, A. (2024). Checklist to Build Trust, Improve Public Health Communication, and Anticipate Misinformation During Public Health Emergencies.https://centerforhealthsecurity.org/sites/default/files/2024-07/2024-07-12-checklist.pdf

Chun-Chien Kuo. (n.d.). COVID-19 active cases: Taiwan, New Zealand, and neighboring Asian countries. https://www.researchgate.net/figure/COVID-19-active-cases-Taiwan-New-Zealand-and-neighboring-Asian-countries_fig2_347165952

Committee on Oversight and Government Reform. (2024). FINAL REPORT: COVID Select Concludes 2-Year Investigation, Issues 500+ Page Final Report on Lessons Learned and the Path Forward. https://oversight.house.gov/release/final-report-covid-select-concludes-2-year-investigation-issues-500-page-final-report-on-lessons-learned-and-the-path-forward/

Cueni, T. (2023). Five priorities for future pandemic preparedness and response. https://www.ifpma.org/insights/five-priorities-for-future-pandemic-preparedness-and-response/

DeSalvo, K., Hughes, B., Bassett, M., Benjamin, G., Fraser, M., Galea, S., Gracia, J. N., & Howard, J. (2021). Public health COVID-19 impact assessment: Lessons learned and compelling needs. *NAM Perspectives, 2021*. Advance online publication. DOI: 10.31478/202104c PMID: 34532688

Dongarwar, D., & Salihu, H. M. (2020). COVID-19 pandemic: Marked global disparities in fatalities according to geographic location and universal health care. *International Journal of MCH and AIDS*, *9*(2), 213–216. DOI: 10.21106/ijma.389 PMID: 32461818

Endalamaw, A., Mengistu, T. S., Khatri, R. B., Wolka, E., Erku, D., Zewdie, A., & Assefa, Y. (2025). Universal health coverage-exploring the what, how, and why using realist review. *PLOS Global Public Health*, *5*(3), e0003330. DOI: 10.1371/journal.pgph.0003330 PMID: 40100795

Gainsbury, S., & Julian, S. (2025). NHS provider deficits are back: How bad is the situation? https://www.nuffieldtrust.org.uk/news-item/nhs-provider-deficits-are-back-how-bad-is-the-situation

Gavi, the Vaccine Alliance. (2025). When it comes to health information, who should you trust? 4 ways to spot a dodgy 'expert.' https://www.gavi.org/vaccineswork/when-it-comes-health-information-who-should-you-trust-4-ways-spot-dodgy-expert

Glazier, R. H. (2023). Our role in making the canadian health care system one of the world's best: How family medicine and primary care can transform—and bring the rest of the system with us. *Canadian Family Physician Médecin de Famille Canadien*, *69*(1), 11–16. DOI: 10.46747/cfp.690111 PMID: 36693751

House Oversight Committee. (2024). After action review of the covid-19 pandemic: The lessons learned and a path forward. https://oversight.house.gov/wp-content/uploads/2024/12/2024.12.04-SSCP-FINAL-REPORT-ANS.pdf

Index, G. H. S. (2021). The GHS Index measures the capacities of 195 countries to prepare for epidemics and pandemics. https://ghsindex.org/

Juneja Gandhi, T., Dumka, N., & Kotwal, A. (2023). Is the proposed global treaty an answer for public health emergencies? *BMJ Global Health*, *8*(9), e012759. DOI: 10.1136/bmjgh-2023-012759 PMID: 37709300

Keshta, A. S., Mallah, S. I., Al Zubaidi, K., Ghorab, O. K., Keshta, M. S., Alarabi, D., Abousaleh, M. A., Salman, M. T., Taha, O. E., Zeidan, A. A., Elsaid, M. F., & Tang, P. (2021). COVID-19 versus SARS: A comparative review. *Journal of Infection and Public Health*, *14*(7), 967–977. DOI: 10.1016/j.jiph.2021.04.007 PMID: 34130121

Konishi, T. (2024). A comparative analysis of COVID-19 response measures and their impact on mortality rate. *COVID*, *4*(2), 130–150. DOI: 10.3390/covid4020012

Maani, N., & Galea, S. (2020). COVID-19 and underinvestment in the public health infrastructure of the united states. *The Milbank Quarterly*, *98*(2), 250–259. DOI: 10.1111/1468-0009.12463 PMID: 32333418

Marjanovic, S., Romanelli, R. J., Ali, G.-C., Leach, B., Bonsu, M., Rodriguez-Rincon, D., & Ling, T. (2022). COVID-19 genomics UK (COG-UK) consortium: Final report. *Rand Health Quarterly*, *9*(4), 24. PMID: 36238008

Mammen, H., Narasimhan, V., Kuntz, R. Lewis-Hall, F. Poul, M. & Schechter, A.H. (n.d.). Health Product Manufacturers and Innovators COVID-19 Impact Assessment: Lessons Learned and Compelling Needs. https://nam.edu/perspectives/health-product-manufacturers-and-innovators-covid-19-impact-assessment-lessons-learned-and-compelling-needs/

McKinsey. (2025). A generational shift: The future of foreign aid. https://www.mckinsey.com/industries/social-sector/our-insights/a-generational-shift-the-future-of-foreign-aid

Méndiz-Noguero, A., Wennberg-Capellades, L., Regadera-González, E., & Goni-Fuste, B. (2023). Public health communication and the covid-19: A review of the literature during the first wave. *El Profesional de la Información*, *320313*, e320313. Advance online publication. DOI: 10.3145/epi.2023.may.13

National Academy of Medicine. (n.d.-a). Lessons for Public Health Excellence from the COVID-19 Pandemic: A Perspective from New York City. https://nam.edu/perspectives/lessons-for-public-health-excellence-from-the-covid-19-pandemic-a-perspective-from-new-york-city/

National Academy of Medicine. (n.d.-b). Public Health COVID-19 Impact Assessment: Lessons Learned and Compelling Needs. https://nam.edu/perspectives/public-health-covid-19-impact-assessment-lessons-learned-and-compelling-needs/

Feachem, N.S., Sanders, K., & Barker, F. (n.d.). The United States' Response to COVID-19: A Case Study, Synopsis. https://globalhealthsciences.ucsf.edu/wp-content/uploads/2024/02/summary_us_case_study5.pdf

OECD. (2021). Health at a Glance 2021: OECD Indicators. OECD. DOI: 10.1787/ae3016b9-en

Or, Z., Gandré, C., Durand Zaleski, I., & Steffen, M. (2022). France's response to the covid-19 pandemic: Between a rock and a hard place. *Health Economics, Policy, and Law*, *17*(1), 14–26. DOI: 10.1017/S1744133121000165 PMID: 33662232

Parliament, U. K. (2025). Fifth Report of Session 2024–25. https://publications.parliament.uk/pa/cm5901/cmselect/cmpubacc/350/report.html

Quach, H.-L., Nguyen, K. C., Hoang, N.-A., Pham, T. Q., Tran, D. N., Le, M. T. Q., Do, H. T., Vien, C. C., Phan, L. T., Ngu, N. D., Tran, T. A., Phung, D. C., Tran, Q. D., Dang, T. Q., Dang, D.-A., & Vogt, F. (2021). Association of public health interventions and COVID-19 incidence in vietnam, january to december 2020. *International Journal of Infectious Diseases*, *110*(Suppl 1), S28–S43. DOI: 10.1016/j.ijid.2021.07.044 PMID: 34332082

Simeonova-Ganeva, R. & Ganev, K. (2023). Health workforce shortages. Unpublished. DOI: 10.13140/RG.2.2.33416.53768

Rito, T., Fernandes, P., Duarte, R., & Soares, P. (2023). Evaluating data sharing of SARS-CoV-2 genomes for molecular epidemiology across the COVID-19 pandemic. *Viruses*, *15*(2), 560. DOI: 10.3390/v15020560 PMID: 36851774

Rudiger, A. (2023). The equity effect of universal health care. *Health and Human Rights*, *25*(2), 171–176. PMID: 38145143

Sanger Institute. (n.d.). COVID-19 Genomics UK (COG-UK) Consortium. https://www.sanger.ac.uk/collaboration/covid-19-genomics-uk-cog-uk-consortium/

Schuh, J. S., Prus, E. C., Abello, C., Evans, K., Walker, K., Miller, M., & Castrucci, B. C. (2025). Public health communication and trust: Opportunities for understanding. Journal of Health Communication, 30(sup1), 76–89. DOI: 10.1080/10810730.2025.2466098

Serchen, J., Cline, K., Mathew, S., Hilden, D., Mathew, S., Hilden, D., Beachy, M., Curry, W., Hollon, M., Jumper, C., Mellacheruvu, P., Parshley, M., Sagar, A., Slocum, J., Tan, M., Van Doren, V., & Yousef, E. (2023). Preparing for future pandemics and public health emergencies: An American college of physicians policy position paper. *Annals of Internal Medicine*, *176*(9), 1240–1244. DOI: 10.7326/M23-0768 PMID: 37487216

Teruel, J.R., del Pino, E., & Real-Dato, J. (2023). The Limits of Power Concentration and Expert Knowledge in Emergency Management: Spain's Government Response during the First Phase of the Covid-19 Pandemic. South European Society and Politics.

The Independent Panel for Pandemic. (n.d.). Main Report & accompanying work. https://theindependentpanel.org/mainreport/

The Joint Commission. (n.d.). Our-Priorities. https://www.jointcommission.org/our-priorities/

The Royal Society. (2023). COVID-19: Examining the effectiveness of non-pharmaceutical interventions. https://royalsociety.org/news-resources/projects/impact-non-pharmaceutical-interventions-on-covid-19-transmission/

Verywell health. (2025). Single-Payer Healthcare vs. Universal Coverage. https://www.verywellhealth.com/difference-between-universal-coverage-and-single-payer-system-1738546

Wieler, L. H., Antao, E.-M., & Hanefeld, J. (2023). Reflections from the COVID-19 pandemic in germany: Lessons for global health. *BMJ Global Health*, *8*(9), e013913. DOI: 10.1136/bmjgh-2023-013913 PMID: 37748795

Wieler, L. H., & Gottschalk, R. (2020). *Emerging COVID-19 success story: the challenge of maintaining progress*. Exemplars in Global Health.

World Health Organization (WHO). (2025). Universal health coverage (UHC). https://www.who.int/news-room/fact-sheets/detail/universal-health-coverage-(uhc)

Yale Medicine. (2021). Our Pandemic Year— [Timeline. https://www.yalemedicine.org/news/covid-timeline]. *COVID*, *19*, •••.

Yang, B., Sullivan, S. G., Du, Z., Tsang, T. K., & Cowling, B. J. (2022). Effectiveness of international travel controls for delaying local outbreaks of COVID-19. *Emerging Infectious Diseases*, *28*(1), 251–253. DOI: 10.3201/eid2801.211944 PMID: 34647863

Chapter 6
Psychological and Philosophical Aspects of Pandemics and Related Health Behaviors

Carlo Lazzari
https://orcid.org/0000-0002-9253-4610
International Centre for Healthcare and Medical Education, London, UK

Marco Rabottini
International Centre for Healthcare and Medical Education, London, UK

ABSTRACT

This chapter examines the psychological and philosophical aspects of health behaviors during pandemics. It examines how fear, uncertainty, and collective trauma shape responses to public health measures, risk perception, and moral reasoning. Psychological theories—such as cognitive dissonance, behavioural economics, and social identity—are used to understand how individuals navigate conflicting information and emotional stress. Philosophically, the study engages with ethical frameworks like utilitarianism, deontology, and virtue ethics to assess justifications for health policies and personal choices. The tension between autonomy and the common good is critically analysed, offering insights for ethically grounded, effective health interventions in future crises.

DOI: 10.4018/979-8-3373-1992-6.ch006

BACKGROUND

Cognitive Biases and Group Dynamics in Pandemic Risk Perception and Health Behaviour

The emergence of pandemics like COVID-19 has highlighted the importance of cognitive processes in shaping how individuals and groups perceive health risks. It is essential to understand how cognitive biases can cause people to overestimate their ability to avoid disease or underestimate the threats posed by infectious agents. These mental distortions are further influenced by social dynamics, especially peer pressure, which can greatly impact health behaviors. The interaction between individual thoughts and group norms creates a complex framework for analyzing behavior during pandemics, such as COVID-19 and AIDS. This chapter examines how personal cognitive biases and social pressures influence health behaviors and perceptions during infectious disease outbreaks. It aims to explore how cognitive biases and group influences—particularly peer pressure and social norms—affect risk perception and health actions during such crises. By studying the psychological and social factors involved in pandemics like COVID-19 and AIDS, the research seeks to improve understanding of behavioral responses to health threats and guide the development of more ethical and scientifically grounded public health strategies.

Cognitive and Social Constructions of Pandemic Risk Perception and Behaviour

Perception of health risks during infectious disease outbreaks is heavily influenced by cognitive biases and their amplification through social interactions. These biases, such as optimism bias, availability heuristic, and confirmation bias, are not isolated errors but interconnected processes that skew judgment and behavior in predictable patterns. On an individual level, optimism bias creates a false sense of invulnerability, causing people to underestimate their vulnerability to infection (Weinstein, 1980; Betsch et al., 2020). This feeling is reinforced by the availability heuristic, which influences risk assessment based on how salient and familiar certain information is. When people see repeated media reports about COVID-19 but lack personal experience with illness, their perception of risk may lessen rather than grow (Tversky & Kahneman, 1973; Fletcher & Rauscher, 2021). These distortions are further amplified through confirmation bias, where individuals seek out and interpret information to confirm their existing beliefs (Klayman, 1995; Peters, 2022). In a pandemic, such biases create self-sustaining loops of misperception, encouraging risky behaviors and reducing compliance with protective measures (Liu et al., 2020). Their influence extends beyond individual minds into social environments. Social settings act as amplifiers of cognitive distortion. Peer pressure can lead individuals to adjust their behavior to align with group norms—often prioritizing social cohesion over health guidelines (Cialdini & Trost, 1998; Hale et al., 2020). In communities where COVID-19 risks were collectively downplayed, individual biases were socially reinforced, resulting in coordinated resistance to interventions. This social contagion spreads beliefs and actions through networks much like a virus (Bikhchandani, Hirshleifer & Welch, 1992). Misperceptions are internalized and externalized, validated through imitation and a desire to belong. The need for social conformity further entrenches biased thinking. In high-stakes social situations, people often override rational judgment to maintain group identity and avoid exclusion. During the COVID-19 pandemic, this was clear among younger groups who prioritized social interaction over safety, despite the epidemiological risks (Anson & Eritsyan, 2023). These interconnected psychological and social mechanisms form a dynamic framework for understanding pandemic behaviors. Biases influence perception, but it is through social interactions that they translate into behavior. Effective public health responses must address both cognitive distortions and the social structures that sustain and spread them.

Cognitive, Social, and Developmental Determinants of Health Behaviour in Pandemic Contexts

Understanding personal health behavior during pandemics requires a multifaceted analysis that integrates cognitive psychology, social influence, and developmental history. Cognitive biases such as optimism bias, availability heuristic, and confirmation bias distort individual judgment, while social dynamics—particularly peer norms and relational pressures—intensify or reshape these distortions. However, beneath these situational drivers lie deeper psychological structures formed during early developmental experiences. At the behavioral level, individuals often misjudge risk through biased cognition: they perceive themselves as less vulnerable (optimism bias), miscalculate likelihood based on media saturation (availability heuristic), and seek affirming information (confirmation bias). These distortions are not merely intrapsychic; they become socially contagious. Through peer pressure, groups validate and amplify misperceptions, leading to collective noncompliance. Social psychological frameworks such as the Theory of Planned Behavior illustrate how even positive attitudes toward protective actions may be negated when subjective norms within one's community discourage them (Ajzen, 1991; Gollust et al., 2020). The bystander effect similarly worsens the problem: when responsibility is spread among many, individuals are less likely to take initiative, especially in public health settings (Darley & Latane, 1968). These socially amplified biases are not isolated phenomena; they are embedded within developmental dispositions. Attachment theory provides crucial insight: individuals with secure attachment styles—rooted in early caregiving experiences—are more likely to trust health authorities and internalize protective messages ("I take care of myself as others have taken care of me") (Lazzari & Masino, 2015). Conversely, those with anxious-avoidant attachments may struggle to accept public health guidance, lacking foundational trust in figures of authority ("I do not take care of myself because no one has ever taken care of me"). These internalized patterns can shape lifelong attitudes toward health and risk. The implications for public health strategy are clear: interventions must address not only informational gaps and cognitive distortions but also relational and developmental contexts. Strategies that use positive peer modeling—highlighting trusted community leaders—can shift subjective norms and encourage protective behavior (Austin & Harkins, 2008). Campaigns that promote collective responsibility may reframe individual actions as socially meaningful, bridging the gap between cognition and community. Tailored communication that considers attachment styles and relational trust can further improve message acceptance, especially among groups historically disengaged from institutional health efforts. Together, these layers of influence form a dynamic and impactful framework for understanding health behavior: cognition shapes perception, social forces influence actions, and developmental history determines receptivity. Incorporating these elements provides a deeper foundation for fostering behavioral change during public health crises.

Society and Pandemics: A Quadruplex Helix of Health Belief and Behavior

Pandemics exert multidimensional pressure on societies, prompting a complex interplay of individual cognition, relational dynamics, collective norms, and cultural narratives. To explore these interactions, we propose a four-stage framework—the quadruplex helix model—which places pandemic health behaviors within ascending layers of existential orientation and social organization. This model shows how solipsism, irrationalism, and biased rationality influence human responses to health crises across broader social domains, from the self to extended culture (see Table 1). At the micro level, health beliefs are shaped by solipsistic reasoning, where individuals see their own subjective convictions as the only truth. This aligns with classical definitions of solipsism, which suggest that the self can only know its own perceptions and that external reality is ultimately unknowable (Merriam-Webster Dictionary, 2024; The Editors of Encyclopaedia Britannica, 2024). During a pandemic, such inward thinking leads to unhealthy behaviors, including denying personal vulnerability, overestimating immunity, and ignoring communal guidelines. These tendencies often stem from cognitive biases like optimism bias and the illusion of control, which distort risk perception and undermine prevention efforts (Eldidgre,

2024). The meso level involves dyadic relationships, especially within couples or close partnerships. Here, shared health beliefs may develop but are vulnerable to uneven influence. One person might dominate the way they understand knowledge, leading to phenomena similar to folie à deux, where false beliefs are reinforced through emotional and cognitive bonds (Lazzari et al., 1995). This stage demonstrates how fragile interpersonal understanding can be during crises, where joint reasoning can either strengthen or weaken adherence to preventive behaviors, depending on the influence and trust between partners. At the macro level, individuals act within peer groups and generational collectives that shape normative views on health. Beliefs like "only weak people wear masks" show how group norms override personal judgment, enforcing behaviors through symbolic identity and social pressure. Health practices at this stage are driven by conformity and perceived in-group values, often leading to rejection of preventive measures if they clash with group beliefs. Common biases like groupthink and social desirability bias distort objective reasoning in favor of cohesion and group loyalty (Eldidgre, 2024). The mega stage covers cultural and national belief systems, where public perceptions of illness and immunity are influenced by propaganda, collective myths, and institutional narratives. Claims such as "our nation is immune" reveal how cultural exceptionalism and health nationalism create epistemic bubbles that resist global evidence and hamper international cooperation. Behaviors at this level are also influenced by mistrust of institutions and politicized messaging, further reinforced by cognitive biases like confirmation bias, in-group favoritism, and fundamental attribution error (Eldidgre, 2024). Collectively, these stages show how health beliefs and behaviors in pandemics are shaped by systemic flaws in reasoning—biases that originate from subjective views of reality and spread through social systems. By mapping these biases onto existential positions within the quadruplex helix, we help explain how individuals create meaning, respond to threats, and engage with public health efforts. Understanding this helix is vital for developing public health strategies that address both epistemic and symbolic aspects of behavior. Interventions must consider the emotional, cognitive, and relational structures that influence pandemic responses—recognizing that health behavior is not just about scientific compliance but also a culturally and philosophically meaningful act of interpretation.

Impact of Pandemics on Society

Pandemics rupture the fabric of human experience, destabilizing the physical, psychological, and ontological conditions through which life is normally navigated. While public health literature often focuses on biological contagion and institutional responses, it is equally important to explore the existential landscape that crisis reveals. Drawing on the ontological framework developed by Lazzari et al.

(1995), this narrative traces how individuals move through fear, isolation, coping, resilience, and reflection—not as separate stages, but as a fluid and interconnected arc of meaning-making under stress.

Fear and Anxiety

The onset of a pandemic triggers widespread fear and anxiety, primarily due to concerns about personal and community vulnerability. As Lazzari et al. (1995) observe, this fear extends beyond just disease transmission to include the disruption of routines and the breakdown of social trust. Kierkegaard's idea of anxiety as the "dizziness of freedom" (1844) fits here: people face the uncertain nature of existence, where familiar norms are upended, leaving the self vulnerable to a sense of ontological vertigo.

Isolation and Loneliness

As a direct result of public health measures like social distancing and quarantine, isolation has become a defining experience. According to Lazzari et al. (1995), this state worsens psychological distress, especially for those living alone or lacking strong support systems. But its importance goes even further—Heidegger's concept of Mitsein (being-with) is broken, forcing the individual into a liminal space where relational identity is no longer maintained through physical presence. Loneliness becomes an ontological condition, symbolizing disconnection from the shared world.

Coping Mechanisms and Resilience

Faced with this existential vacuum, individuals develop coping strategies that, as Lazzari et al. (1995) describe, include mindfulness, creative engagement, and family connection. These actions do not merely reduce discomfort—they represent a reassertion of agency and the will to create meaning again. Viktor Frankl's existential psychology suggests that suffering is not just endured but can become a place for purposeful meaning-making (1946). From these actions, resilience emerges—not as a fixed trait, but as an ongoing response that reflects ontological flexibility. The adaptability observed during prolonged crises is rooted in these symbolic efforts to restore coherence.

Reflection and Introspection

As resilience develops, it creates space for deeper self-examination. Lazzari et al. (1995) note that many people start to reevaluate their values and goals, engaging in a process of existential self-reflection. This shift toward reflection is strengthened by Sartre's insistence that freedom comes with responsibility—not only to oneself but to others (1946). In the context of a pandemic, such introspection often leads to increased ethical awareness and relational responsibility, echoing modern public health ethics that emphasize solidarity and moral accountability (Jennings et al., 2016).

Taken together, these ontological dimensions depict a dynamic process: fear triggers dislocation; isolation heightens it; coping restores agency; resilience adjusts lived experience; and introspection reshapes existential outlook. This framework, developed by Lazzari et al. (1995), positions the pandemic not only as a biomedical event but as a philosophical challenge—a test through which individuals reinterpret their being-in-the-world. Public health must address not only the epidemiological crisis but also the symbolic and existential upheaval it causes.

Philosophical and Psychological Aspects of Pandemic Experience and Behavioral Response

This model describes pandemic behavior as a layered interaction among existential disruption, cognitive architecture, symbolic meaning, and social ecology. Building on the ontological trajectory outlined by Lazzari et al. (1995), it views human responses to pandemics as a dynamic process rooted in interconnected areas of lived experience.

Ontological Grounding

At its core, the existential shock caused by crisis involves a sudden break in the flow of time, connection with others, and stable embodiment. Fear and anxiety surface as basic signs of ontological disconnection, worsened by isolation and the breaking apart of being-with (Heidegger, Being and Time, 1927). This area reflects the personal destabilization that happens before behavioral reasoning begins.

Cognitive-Epistemic Layer

Superimposed upon this ontological foundation is a cognitive layer, where biases such as optimism bias, availability heuristic, and confirmation bias distort risk perception and impede adaptive reasoning (Lazzari et al., 1995). These epistemic distortions are not merely irrational—they are products of bounded cognition interacting with emotionally charged contexts, filtered through symbolic and affective cues.

Symbolic-Moral Domain

Behavior arises within systems of symbolic meaning and moral orientation. Public health measures hold not only practical value but also moral and cultural significance. Acceptance or rejection of vaccination, distancing, or masking is often influenced by social allegiance, identity frameworks, and ethical narratives. Sartre's concept of moral freedom and responsibility (1946) intersects here with Frankl's theory of meaning-making amid suffering (1946), framing behavior as a symbolic act within a broader moral ecology.

Socio-Relational Field

At the macro-social level, group dynamics—including peer pressure, community norms, and relational accountability—shape individual behavior. The socio-ecological perspective argues that individuals are part of networks of influence where compliance depends on visibility, solidarity, and the desire for moral consistency (Jennings et al., 2016). In this context, resilience is not just an individual trait but shared, arising from collective stories of care and adaptation.

Model Implications

Understanding pandemic behavior through this multi-layered model goes beyond simplified ideas of rational choice or behavioral compliance. It asserts that to change public behavior, interventions must target:

a) Ontological distress by fostering existential coherence and emotional validation;
b) Cognitive bias by deploying reflective education and epistemic scaffolding;
c) Symbolic meaning by aligning public health messaging with culturally resonant moral frameworks;
d) Social ecology by engaging relational networks and leveraging normative momentum.

Public health, ethics, and philosophy are thus called into coaction—constructing a response that honors the full spectrum of what it means to live, relate, and act in a world punctured by crisis.

ONTOLOGICAL AND PSYCHOLOGICAL FOUNDATIONS OF PANDEMIC BEHAVIOR

Pandemic response cannot be fully understood through biomedical rationalism or isolated psychological models alone. Instead, it must be viewed within a layered framework that considers the ontological instability caused by crisis and the socio-ecological systems through which behavior is shaped. Ontology, as the philosophical study of being, provides essential insight into how people interpret reality during health emergencies. This interpretive process influences not only how knowledge is perceived but also behavioral patterns, especially when the routine fabric of life is disrupted by threats (Simons, 1998; Cambridge Dictionary Online, 2024). From this ontological perspective, human nature appears as contingent, adaptable, and emotionally receptive. Research by Lazzari and Costigliola (1993) shows instances where individuals knowingly engage in risky behaviors despite awareness of potential harm, challenging traditional views of rationality as purely decision-making based on reason (Cambridge Dictionary, 2025). This creates the idea of inverted rationality, where emotional responses override cognitive evaluation, often leading to non-compliance or delays in adopting preventive actions (Lazzari et al., 1994). Such behavior demonstrates that responses to contagion are driven more by existential conditions—like fear, loss of control, and symbolic dislocation—than by factual information alone. The socio-ecological model builds on this ontological basis by tracking how behavior is influenced across different levels of human interaction. At the individual level, cognitive biases—such as optimism bias, availability heuristic, and confirmation bias—hamper accurate risk assessment and lead to epistemic distortion (Lazzari et al., 1994). These biases are not isolated; they are rooted in emotional states like anxiety and helplessness, which influence judgment and actions (Kumar and Preetha, 2018). At the interpersonal level, relationships can serve as both protective and harmful channels of health information. Supportive messaging encourages preventive behavior (Van Bavel et al., 2020), while social contagion within skeptical groups can spread misinformation and foster resistance (Cohen et al., 2021). Social identity and group loyalty further complicate this process, determining whether people accept or reject public health measures based on perceived social norms (Trifiletti et al., 2022). Role models—whether institutional or personal—are especially influential when individuals face cognitive doubt or emotional vulnerability. During moments of existential uncertainty, these figures can act as symbols of stability or, if conflicting, heighten dissonance and defiance (Lazzari et al., 2020). Therefore, pandemic-related behaviors are best understood by combining ontological models—which reveal internal dislocation and existential recalibration caused by crisis—and socio-ecological frameworks, which illustrate the external symbolic, cognitive, and relational forces shaping responses. This integrated approach emphasizes that adherence to health measures results from a mix of emotional states, symbolic meanings, societal norms, and knowledge orientations. It encourages public health efforts to shift from simply sharing instructions to engaging with lived experiences—reframing health communication and intervention as processes of existential healing and symbolic alignment. If you want, I can help develop an abstract and subsections for this as part of a broader manuscript—possibly connecting it to epistemic governance or symbolic anthropology. Would you like to proceed with that?

Role Modelling During Pandemics: Ontological and Socio-Ecological Interactions

During pandemics, decisions about preventive health behaviors are influenced not only by empirical data but also by layered relational, cognitive, and symbolic factors. Key among these are role models, who serve as mediators between institutional knowledge and public interpretation—operating within both ontological and socio-ecological domains. These figures, including public health officials, celebrities, community leaders, and family members, help translate scientific messages into emotionally and morally understandable forms, guiding behavioral adoption. Bandura's (1977) social learning theory highlights this process, noting that individuals tend to imitate behaviors observed in trusted figures—especially during times of uncertainty and threat. Role models proved especially vital during the COVID-19 pandemic. For instance, communicators like Dr. Anthony Fauci provided consistent and accessible information, helping align public behaviors with institutional guidelines (Centers for Disease Control and Prevention [CDC], 2020). Such figures reinforce ontological stability by creating a coherent narrative through which people interpret risk, responsibility, and agency. However, this influence is not universal. The development of cognitive hesitancy—defined as reluctance or delay in accepting scientific knowledge due to epistemic mistrust or emotional uncertainty—can significantly weaken the impact of even credible role models (Rosenstock, Strecher, & Becker, 1994). Hesitancy becomes more pronounced when authoritative figures deliver conflicting messages, leading to cognitive dissonance—a psychological state where individuals experience stress when trying to reconcile contradictory information (Festinger, 1957). This dissonance often results in selective adherence based on pre-existing beliefs, fracturing collective responses and undermining prevention efforts. For example, inconsistent messaging from political leaders early in COVID-19, particularly about mask effectiveness and viral severity, created widespread confusion and non-compliance (World Health Organization [WHO], 2020). In such instances, the individual's ontological coherence—already destabilized by crisis—is further compromised by epistemic contradictions. When role models' symbolic authority conflicts with scientific consensus, it can unintentionally reinforce skepticism and hinder protective behaviors. These dynamics are further influenced by socio-cultural mechanisms. When figures express doubt or dismiss preventive measures, their followers may adopt these cues—leading to behavioral non-compliance. High-profile celebrities expressing anti-vaccine sentiments have notably affected public attitudes, decreasing vaccination rates (Dubé et al., 2013). Within the socio-ecological framework, this behavioral spread occurs across intrapersonal, interpersonal, and community levels—where individual cognition, relational dynamics, and social norms interact to shape health choices. To mitigate these risks, public health campaigns must focus on credibility, consistency, and symbolic alignment when choosing role models. Such initiatives should highlight scientifically informed voices capable of bridging ontological vulnerability with epistemic skepticism. Addressing root causes of cognitive hesitancy—such as institutional mistrust and limited scientific understanding—is crucial (Lewandowsky, Ecker, & Cook, 2017). Promoting dialogical engagement, community involvement, and culturally resonant messaging helps build relational trust and stabilizes personal meaning within the broader ecological system. In conclusion, role modeling during pandemics operates within a complex interplay of human nature, ontology, and social ecology. The influence of role models depends not only on their messages but also on how they are perceived, internalized, and symbolically positioned. To foster adaptive health behaviors, public health strategies must recognize that role models are existential figures whose impact is shaped by emotional states, moral identities, and the socio-symbolic landscape. Interventions grounded in both ontological understanding and socio-ecological awareness are essential to navigate the epistemic fragility and moral uncertainty inherent in pandemics.

Solipsism During Pandemics: Psychological, Philosophical, and Preventive Implications

During pandemics, especially under lockdown conditions, increasing social isolation can heighten solipsistic tendencies and limit exposure to additional information crucial for disease prevention. Solipsism, in philosophical terms, argues that the self is the only entity that can be known to exist and that knowledge beyond one's own mental states is inherently uncertain (Merriam-Webster Dictionary, 2024; The Editors of Encyclopaedia Britannica, 2024). This extreme form of subjective idealism provides a critical perspective for evaluating human responses to crises such as pandemics. As individuals face disruptions, they often align their health perceptions more with personal experience than with collective advice. If solipsism dominates, health behaviors could diverge from public health guidelines, as cognition turns inward, focusing on belief rather than evidence. This disconnect between personal judgment and institutional goals undermines primary prevention efforts (Merriam-Webster Dictionary, 2024). Evidence from recent pandemics shows that people frequently interpret risks based on personal perceptions when making health decisions. The immediacy of individual experience can override broader knowledge systems, resulting in fragmented responses rooted in incomplete information (Pettigrew et al., 2020). This is especially problematic with new pathogens like SARS-CoV-2, where feelings of risk—shaped by emotion, bias, and social influence—may conflict with scientific evidence or health authority directives (Lazzari et al., 1995). The concept of solipsism is relevant here. During crises, emotional states heavily influence thinking, often causing those who feel personally invulnerable to downplay the pandemic's severity or dismiss guidelines as unnecessary (Leventhal et al., 1997). During the initial stages of COVID-19, people who saw themselves at low risk often ignored measures like mask-wearing or physical distancing, reflecting a solipsistic view that prioritizes personal belief over community responsibility (Lazzari & Rabottini, 2020). Digital platforms further reinforce these tendencies. Social media, while enabling communication, also spreads both factual information and misinformation, creating a jumble of conflicting narratives that can complicate risk assessment (Cinelli et al., 2020). People in echo chambers might strengthen solipsistic beliefs by trusting personal judgment over expert advice, weakening consistent health behaviors across groups. Extended periods of isolation can intensify this inward focus. Research indicates that prolonged solitude increases anxiety and fosters self-centered thinking, which can reduce responsiveness to community health efforts (Cacioppo & Cacioppo, 2014). In such cases, emotional comfort and personal safety may take precedence over collective well-being, reducing adherence to protocols meant for community safety. Public health officials and policymakers need to consider these solipsistic influences when designing responses. Differences between expected and actual behaviors often come from misinformation and the dominance of personal experience. Vaccination efforts have highlighted significant gaps between scientific evidence and personal beliefs—where some reject vaccines based on anecdotal reasoning despite strong proof of their effectiveness (Schmid et al., 2017). These decisions show how solipsistic thinking can obscure broader ethical and social concerns. To address this, public health messages should engage both individual views and collective stories. Messages emphasizing shared experiences, social interdependence, and moral responsibility can help counteract solipsistic biases. Educational programs that illustrate how personal choices affect community health may foster greater solidarity. Creating environments that promote empathy and mutual care can realign individual behaviors with public health goals, strengthening primary prevention during future health crises. In summary, solipsism subtly but powerfully influences risk perception and health actions during pandemics. Its focus on personal experience and self-reliance makes it harder to encourage compliance with preventive measures. Combating solipsistic tendencies requires a combination of philosophical understanding, psychological sensitivity, and social engagement—approaches that recognize how individual cognition and community needs intersect during times of shared vulnerability.

EXISTENTIAL ASPECTS OF PANDEMICS

The Existential and Philosophical Implications of Pandemics on Mankind

Throughout history, pandemics have repeatedly sparked deep existential and philosophical reflection within individuals and societies. Whether examining the devastation caused by the Black Death, the disorientation of the Spanish Flu, or the global shock of COVID-19, such events significantly disrupt daily life and force humanity to confront fundamental questions about fragility, purpose, and interconnection. As a result, pandemics trigger both collective and personal reevaluations of what it means to exist, which values guide us, and how we position ourselves in a world suddenly filled with uncertainty. At the heart of this reflection lies the framework of existentialism—a philosophical movement focused on finding meaning in a universe that may seem indifferent or absurd (Sartre, 2007). In pandemic contexts, existentialism becomes even more urgent as mortality looms large and suffering increases. The widespread unpredictability, illness, and upheaval reveal the fragility of human life, echoing Camus's (1948) discussion of existential vulnerability and absurdity, where people face the limits of rational explanation and the universe's indifference. This philosophical landscape is further enriched by the theme of death anxiety, explored extensively by Heidegger (1962) in Being and Time. He argues that authentic existence emerges when individuals confront their mortality. During pandemics, this confrontation is often unavoidable, leading to feelings of existential dread. However, in its aftermath, people are often pushed— or compelled—to rethink their lives, reevaluate their priorities and values, and reconsider ways of being that once seemed unchangeable (Heidegger, 1962).

Extending this argument, Kierkegaard's concept of the leap of faith presents a way through uncertainty. Amid the ontological chaos of pandemics, faith surfaces not just as religious belief but as a personal commitment to finding meaning despite the lack of empirical proof (Kierkegaard, 1980). In this context, spiritual practices and metaphysical reflection act as anchors for many seeking stability during crises. By turning inward toward transcendent meaning, individuals navigate the absurdity of their circumstances and regain control over their interpretation of reality (Kierkegaard, 1980). Closely related is the effect of enforced isolation and the pursuit of authenticity, where Sartre's (1943) idea that existence precedes essence becomes especially relevant. Pandemic-driven social distancing and lockdowns break down familiar social roles and prompt introspection. In this solitude, people reconnect with their identities and face the possibility that pre-pandemic lifestyles might have been shaped more by habit or social expectation than true desire. Isolation, then, becomes a testing ground for authenticity, prompting new ways of self-definition (Sartre, 1943). From there, the focus naturally shifts outward to the interconnectedness of human life. As Harari (2016) notes, pandemics reveal the shared biological vulnerability of humans across geography, culture, and class. The rapid spread of disease and the need for coordinated public responses highlight the limits of individualism and emphasize the moral importance of solidarity. Through collective action—based on compassion and empathy—societies rediscover the relational side of survival and the moral stakes involved. At the same time, pandemics trigger reflection on the inherent absurdity of existence, as Camus (1948) discusses in The Plague. By depicting human suffering as detached from moral purpose or logical cause-and-effect, Camus underscores the irrationality of crisis and the human effort to assign meaning to it. But instead of giving in to despair, his absurdist ethics suggest that defiance—through solidarity and moral resolve—can bring a sense of purpose even amid futility.

Building on this foundation, pandemics put ethical frameworks under renewed scrutiny. As Jonas (1974) argues, the imperative of responsibility in ethics demands considering the long-term consequences of our actions. In pandemics, resource allocation, policy enforcement, and public compliance reveal tensions between individual liberties and collective welfare. Ethical dilemmas such as triage, vaccination equity, and economic shutdowns highlight the need for forward-thinking, intergenerational ethical reasoning (Jonas, 1974). At a more structural level, Foucault (1975) examines how institutions seek to manage populations through biopolitical mechanisms—surveillance, discipline, and regulation. Pandemics stress-test these systems, exposing the limits of centralized control and the unpredictability inherent in human biology and environmental systems. Foucault's critique shows how the illusion of mastery over nature gives way to the need for humility, shifting human self-understanding from dominance toward ecological embeddedness (Foucault, 1975). In contrast to these critiques, Frankl's (2006) concept of logotherapy offers a hopeful existential tool. He argues that meaning can be created even through suffering, as long as individuals engage with their experiences purposefully. In the context of pandemics, acts of creativity, care, and altruism serve as pathways through which individuals reaffirm identity, transcend despair, and contribute to a greater good. Meaning-making thus becomes a psychological and philosophical foundation for resilience (Frankl, 2006). Finally, pandemics highlight the ongoing tension between individualism and collectivism. Measures such as lockdowns, mask mandates, and vaccination campaigns starkly contrast personal autonomy with communal responsibility. Rawls's (1971) theory of justice provides a philosophical basis for balancing these demands by emphasizing fairness through social cooperation and equitable resource distribution. In practice, the pandemic underscores the importance of trust, transparency, and reciprocity in navigating collective crises and maintaining ethical governance. Taken together, these reflections reveal pandemics as moments of deep philosophical significance. They challenge individuals to confront mortality, grapple with absurdity, pursue authenticity, and embrace interconnectedness. In doing so, pandemics expose the vulnerabilities of modern civilization and the latent strength of human meaning-making. Through existential inquiry and ethical awareness, humanity gains an opportunity—not only to endure—but to transform, reaffirming its resilience in an unpredictable and often indifferent world.

Fatalism and Meaning-Making in Pandemic Society: A Quadruplex Helix Perspective

Pandemics act as profound fault lines that reveal how individuals and societies understand meaning, agency, and vulnerability. One of the most common responses during crises is fatalism—the belief that events are predetermined and that personal action has little effect (Cambridge Dictionary, 2025). This mindset often deepens amid ongoing uncertainty, social isolation, and repeated losses, as seen during COVID-19 (Lazzari & Rabottini, 2020). To better understand how fatalism appears across different social settings, we introduce a four-stage interpretive framework: the quadruplex helix model. This model explains how health beliefs and behaviors are influenced by cognitive bias, solipsistic reasoning, relational dynamics, and collective mythologies as they develop within broader social spheres. At the micro level, individuals face pandemic stress through a solipsistic perspective. Here, the belief system is driven by the idea that "what I believe is true, and if something conflicts, it must be false." Such reasoning reinforces biases like optimism bias and illusion of control and can reduce adherence to preventive measures (Lazzari et al., 1995). During COVID-19, many people dismissed masks or vaccines not solely due to misinformation but because their sense of invulnerability outweighed real risk. The micro-stage prioritizes internal truth over collective ethics. Moving to the meso level, fatalism often forms within dyads—particularly romantic or family relationships—where health beliefs are co-constructed under the shared notion that "what we believe is true and enough." This relational insulation can foster folie à deux, where irrational beliefs are mutually reinforced. Often, the dominant partner's views on health set the norm for the pair, influencing whether preventive actions like distancing or vaccination are accepted or rejected (Lazzari et al., 1995). While this shared reasoning might reduce anxiety, it can also entrench maladaptive practices, especially when external advice is distrusted. The macro level reflects group dynamics, where generational identity and peer norms shape health behaviors. People within this sphere adopt beliefs such as "our group's perspective may differ from society, but it reflects who we are." This mindset creates cognitive dissonance between public health messages and group loyalty. During COVID-19, statements like "only weak people wear masks" exemplify how collective norms can stigmatize protective behaviors (Lazzari & Rabottini, 2020). Here, groupthink and confirmation bias dominate, and fatalism manifests not as individual passivity but as socially reinforced resistance. At the mega level, fatalistic beliefs are embedded in broader cultural or national narratives. Phrases like "our nation is immune; only corrupt countries suffer" show how collective identity shields individuals from perceived vulnerability. This stage features health nationalism and politicized discourse, often fueled by propaganda that downplays risk or vilifies scientific consensus (Lazzari et al., 2020). In these contexts, people disengage from global solidarity, and fatalism persists because of perceived moral or biological exceptionalism. Compliance declines not due to ignorance but because public health efforts are reframed as threats to national identity or tradition.

Together, these stages reveal how fatalism develops from internal thoughts to widespread social reinforcement. Underlying each stage are cognitive biases—systematic errors in reasoning that stem from emotional distress and subjective interpretation (Eldidgre, 2024). When combined with existential uncertainty, these biases distort rational judgment and hinder public health efforts. Learned helplessness (Seligman, 1975), depressive thinking (Beck, 1967), and echo chambers in relationships further entrench fatalistic outlooks, especially among socioeconomically marginalized groups facing chronic stress and limited resources (Mirowsky & Ross, 1983; Lachman & Weaver, 1998). Cultural beliefs also play a critical role. In many collectivist cultures, fatalism isn't just a response to crisis but a deeply rooted cultural attitude, often supported by religious or metaphysical beliefs (Schieman et al., 2007). While this can offer psychological comfort, it may also reduce proactive behavior—particularly when pandemics require quick behavioral change and a sense of community responsibility. To counter these effects, public health strategies should adopt an approach that is aware of underlying realities and sensitive to psychological factors—identifying where individuals and groups are in this process and addressing their specific knowledge and emotional needs. Small interventions should promote reflective thinking and personal confidence; intermediate strategies should encourage meaningful dialogue; larger efforts must shift social norms through trusted group role models; and broad initiatives need to challenge cultural narratives through transparent, inclusive communication. Only by understanding the layered structure of fatalism can we foster a sense of agency, reshape meaning, and promote healthier behaviors in a time of global uncertainty.

Certainly, Carlo. Here's a coherent and integrated narrative that embeds the analysis of rational and irrational health behaviors during pandemics into your quadruplex helix framework. The text flows sequentially through each helix level, linking ontological insight, cognitive bias, and social complexity—reinforced with APA 7th Edition citations throughout:

Rational and Irrational Health Behaviors in Pandemic Contexts: A Quadruplex Helix Perspective

Pandemics force a clash between individual understanding and collective survival, often highlighting a tension between rational health actions and irrational responses. While traditional public health discussions depend heavily on models of logical decision-making, the COVID-19 pandemic has revealed the fragile nature of these assumptions. Health behavior during pandemics is not just a product of reason but is deeply influenced by emotional reactions, cultural beliefs, and personal interpretations. To understand this complex issue, we present pandemic-related behavior within a quadruple helix structure—examining irrationalism and its psychosocial roots across micro, meso, macro, and mega levels of engagement.

At the micro level, irrationalism stems from solipsistic reasoning, where individuals equate personal belief with truth and dismiss conflicting information. This ontological distortion—"knowing what" versus "believing what"—creates fertile ground for cognitive biases such as confirmation bias and optimism bias, which distort risk perception and hinder preventive actions (Chou et al., 2020; Lazzari et al., 1995). Mask refusal, vaccine hesitancy, and denial of transmissibility during COVID-19 often originated not from a lack of access to facts but from emotionally anchored beliefs that insulated individuals from collective norms (Gollust et al., 2020). Irrationalism, defined as privileging instinct, emotion, and will over reason (The Editors of Encyclopaedia Britannica, 2024), thus becomes a key philosophical framework for understanding behaviors that diverge from evidence-based health logic. Moving to the meso level, irrational health behaviors develop within close relationships, especially couples or family pairs. Here, shared interpretations of reality dominate, often influenced by a more dominant partner. This phenomenon aligns with collective solipsism or folie à deux, where irrational beliefs are mutually reinforced through emotional trust and narrative cohesion (Lazzari et al., 1995). For example, if one partner distrusts vaccines due to metaphysical beliefs or anxiety, the other may adopt this stance—not through independent analysis but relational allegiance. In such cases, irrationalism becomes relational, driven by interpersonal feedback loops rather than individual distortion. At the macro level, irrationality manifests as group dynamics. Communities and generational groups form around shared narratives, creating social identities that resist external health directives.

Weick's (1995) theory of collective sensemaking explains how groups interpret events and assign meaning—often bypassing rational analysis in favor of symbolic coherence. COVID-19 conspiracy theories about viral origins or institutional malintent gained traction not only for their content but for aligning with cultural scripts and peer validation (Pérez et al., 2020). Within these social units, behavioral norms may reject protective measures, not out of ignorance but as acts of defiance against imposed order. Here, irrationalism expresses political or symbolic identity, not simply a cognitive error. At the mega level, irrational health behaviors are embedded within cultural and national narratives. Fatalistic slogans like "our people are strong enough," "this virus was engineered elsewhere," or "divine will protects us" show how propaganda, metaphysical beliefs, and nationalism combine to produce health fatalism (Lazzari & Rabottini, 2020). These beliefs are reinforced by institutional messaging and collective memory, especially in societies where distrust of global authorities or secular science runs deep (Schieman et al., 2007). Public health messages based on reason often struggle to penetrate this layer because they lack symbolic resonance with cultural worldviews. In this context, irrationalism is justified epistemologically through traditional cosmologies or ideological rhetoric.

Across all levels of the helix, irrational health behaviors are further amplified by emotional distress. The COVID-19 crisis triggered widespread fear, uncertainty, and isolation—conditions known to influence decision-making through mechanisms described in the Transactional Model of Stress and Coping (Lazarus & Folkman, 1984). People under stress often adopt coping strategies that favor immediate emotional relief over long-term health outcomes. This explains why some rejected distancing measures despite knowing their usefulness: existential discomfort overpowered cognitive appraisal (Lazzari et al., 2025). To respond effectively, public health must go beyond rational instructions and adopt emotionally intelligent strategies rooted in lived experience. Empathy, storytelling, and culturally relevant narratives provide tools to engage populations whose health choices are guided more by symbolic affiliation than by facts (Sibony et al., 2019). Interventions must also recognize that irrationalism is not a flaw—it is a mode of ontological survival, closely linked to human meaning-making, identity, and agency. The COVID-19 pandemic has exposed the limitations of rationalist models in explaining health behavior. Irrationalism—as a philosophical outlook privileging instinct, feeling, and subjective will—serves as a vital framework for understanding how and why individuals deviate from public health norms across different social contexts. By mapping these behaviors through the quadruplex helix—from solipsistic cognition to cultural mythology—we reveal the layered structure of irrational health responses. Effective strategies should therefore combine cognitive psychology, cultural anthropology, and existential ethics to cultivate resilience, empathy, and inclusive engagement. In doing so, we move closer to a public health model that respects the ontological richness of human behavior while guiding it toward collective well-being. Certainly, Carlo. Here's a unified and ordered narrative that redefines the concept of critical incidents in pandemics through your quadruplex helix framework—connecting solipsistic cognition, relational influence, group identity, and cultural mythologies with psychological mechanisms such as denial and optimism bias. APA 7th Edition citations are integrated throughout.

Critical Incidents in Pandemics: A Quadruplex Helix of Risk, Denial, and Meaning-Making

In the context of pandemics, certain events or behaviors—whether isolated acts or patterned practices—become critical incidents: moments of heightened risk whose consequences could have been mitigated through primary prevention measures. The World Health Organization (WHO, 2007) defines a crisis as a serious threat to health and wellbeing, and a risk as the likelihood of harm resulting from hazardous circumstances and vulnerabilities. From COVID-19 social gatherings to unprotected sexual encounters during the AIDS epidemic, these incidents show how prevention often fails—not only due to lack of knowledge but because of deeper psychological and social dynamics. To analyze these patterns, we suggest a quadruple helix model that places pandemic-related risk behaviors within four social levels—micro, meso, macro, and mega—each shaped by different psychological predispositions, cognitive biases, and relational influences. At the micro level, irrational health behavior is driven by solipsistic thinking: individuals interpret reality through their personal beliefs rather than facts accepted by the community. Denial is especially powerful here, allowing individuals to reject uncomfortable truths about their vulnerability (Goleman, 2006). Despite widespread awareness of HIV transmission routes or airborne contagion during COVID-19, many chose behaviors that contradicted known risks—justifying them with statements like "I feel healthy, so I won't get infected" (Lazzari et al., 2020). The optimism bias (Weinstein, 1980), where one believes they are less likely than others to be affected, fuels this denial. This dynamic is seen in HIV serodiscordant couples who, despite repeated warnings, continue unprotected sex under the false assumption that previous avoidance of transmission guarantees future safety. At the meso level, pandemic risks are shaped within close relationships and families. Here, individuals take behavioral cues not only from their own reasoning but also from shared assumptions reinforced within their social units. For example, during COVID-19, couples or small households often ignored distancing protocols, trusting that "if someone were sick, they would tell us or stay home." Such statements reflect both trust and a collective delay in vigilance, where group consensus surpasses individual caution (Lazzari et al., 1995). Freud's idea of unconscious motivation, extended by Brenner (1988), suggests that accidents sometimes serve to fulfill hidden emotional needs—expressing unresolved conflicts or a desire for self-sacrifice amid feelings of guilt or alienation. In pandemic contexts, this unconscious dynamic may explain why high-risk behaviors persist despite conscious awareness. Moving outward to the macro level, risk behavior becomes performative within society. People seek validation, status, or normalcy through group activities—attending parties during lockdowns or engaging in unprotected sex during AIDS outbreaks—not because they lack knowledge, but because the social need to belong outweighs caution (Reid, Cialdini, & Aiken, 2010). These acts are not just individual mistakes; they reflect a tension between the collective desire and personal restraint. Groupthink and shared meaning-making (Weick, 1995) create an echo chamber where trust within the group replaces scientific caution. As Van Bavel et al. (2020) observed, this was especially clear among young adults during COVID-19, who ignored mask mandates to protect their social identity, thinking "we trust each other; no one will bring harm." Finally, at the mega level, cultural narratives and national ideologies influence public denial and reinforce optimism bias on a societal scale. During the AIDS epidemic, marginalizing affected groups slowed responses and spread misinformation (Padilla et al., 2008). Similarly, early in COVID-19, nationalist rhetoric and underestimating the virus's danger fostered collective illusions of immunity (Morens et al., 2020). Public conversations reframe contagion as either distant or manageable, encouraging lax behaviors. These myths strengthen fatalism, with individuals perceiving contagion as either unavoidable or irrelevant to their social identity (Lazzari et al., 2023).

Understanding critical incidents through this quadruplex helix provides a deeper philosophical and psychological perspective on pandemic behavior. Each level reveals how individuals navigate the interaction of instinct, cognition, identity, and cultural logic—often trading rational precaution for emotional or social comfort. The fluctuation between impulses, observed in heterosexuals at risk of HIV infection, illustrates the libidinal tension between immediacy and prediction—between impulse and restraint (Lazzari et al., 1995). From an ethical perspective, public health must go beyond instructive messaging and engage these layers of meaning-making. Campaigns that humanize disease impact, present emotionally resonant stories, and challenge cognitive biases can bridge the gap between knowledge and action. As Sibony et al. (2019) and Lazzari et al. (2025) argue, addressing emotional and psychological realities is essential to fostering sustainable health behaviors. In conclusion, critical incidents in pandemics reflect more than momentary lapses; they emerge from a mix of psychological, relational, and cultural factors that shape how individuals perceive and respond to risk. Denial, optimism bias, unconscious motivation, and group pressure all contribute to behavior conflicting with known health guidance. Placing these patterns within the quadruplex helix reveals the structural logic of pandemic irrationality—covering solipsistic belief, relational trust, peer identity, and cultural narrative. Only by recognizing these levels and customizing interventions can public health strategies connect with lived experiences and effectively reduce contagion in future crises.

CONCLUSION

The emergence of pandemics often prompts a critical examination of human behavior when facing potential health threats. Specifically, the interaction between personal health decisions and social perceptions of risk becomes increasingly important. A review of historical pandemic incidents reveals a worrying pattern: people often neglect or underestimate high-risk behaviors, such as socializing with contagious individuals or violating social distancing rules. This behavior highlights a complex relationship between how individuals assess risks cognitively and the actions they take during times of heightened health anxiety. This chapter aims to explore the role of cognitive appraisal in evaluating personal and social risks during infectious diseases, focusing on how perception can either mitigate or exacerbate these risks. Additionally, our social, psychological, and philosophical analysis offers a deeper understanding of human dynamics when confronting threats related to infectious diseases and pandemics. During health campaigns aimed at the primary prevention of transmissible diseases, effectiveness depends not only on mass media characteristics and prevention policies but also—and most importantly—on the messages delivered to the public and how they are cognitively processed. Analyzing the structure of these messages and their social impact, whether actual or anticipated, is a crucial step that must precede any further efforts to prevent contagious diseases. Despite extensive public education efforts and initiatives to curb disease spread, there has not always been a corresponding decline in new infection cases. We also believe that insufficient emphasis has been placed on thoroughly verifying the logical and grammatical accuracy of the messages. This analysis must consider prior experiences with mass media campaigns and the psychosocial understanding of the target audience. The purpose of this chapter is to outline the foundation of health behaviors that support primary prevention. Primary prevention involves health behaviors and protective actions that help prevent adverse health events in individuals who do not yet have the condition (e.g., COVID-19, AIDS) (Jacobsen, 2021). In the EDP (Exposure, Disease, and Population) framework, if current knowledge about pandemics has identified E1 (risk factors) and D1 (type of disease) in a well-studied population (P1), this chapter seeks to generate new insights into emerging and unknown risk factors (E2), expanding the EDP to become E2-D1-P1 (Jacobsen, 2021).

REFERENCES

Ajzen, I. (1991). The theory of planned behavior. *Organizational Behavior and Human Decision Processes*, *50*(2), 179–211. DOI: 10.1016/0749-5978(91)90020-T

Austin, M. S., & Harkins, D. A. (2008). Assessing change: Can organizational learning "work" for schools? *The Learning Organization*, *15*(2), 105–125. DOI: 10.1108/09696470810852302

Bandura, A. (1977). *Social Learning Theory*. Prentice Hall.

Beck, A. T. (1967). *Depression: Causes and Treatment*. University of Pennsylvania Press.

Betsch, C., Wieler, L. H., & Horne, B. D. (2020). Effects of COVID-19 lockdown on public health behaviour. *Health Psychology*, *39*(5), 481–486.

Bikhchandani, S., Hirshleifer, D., & Welch, I. (1992). A theory of fads, fashion, custom, and cultural change as informational cascades. *Journal of Political Economy*, *100*(5), 992–1026. DOI: 10.1086/261849

Cambridge Dictionary Online. (2024c). Definition of 'Ontology' [Internet]. Available from: https://dictionary.cambridge.org/dictionary/english/ontology

Cambridge Dictionary Online. (2024a). Definition of 'fatalism'. [Internet] Available from: fatalism [Internet]. 2025. Available from: https://dictionary.cambridge.org/dictionary/english/fatalism [Accessed 29 January 2024]

Cambridge Dictionary Online. (2024b). Definition of 'Irrationality. irrationality [Internet]. Available from: https://dictionary.cambridge.org/dictionary/english/irrationality

Camus, A. (1948). *The Plague*. Vintage Books.

Centers for Disease Control and Prevention (CDC). (2020). How CDC is Making COVID-19 Recommendations. [Internet]. Available at: https://www.cdc.gov/coronavirus/2019-ncov/vaccines/recommendations-process.html

Chou, W. Y. S., Vanderpool, R. C., Pronk, N. P., & Steinberg, E. (2020). The COVID-19 Misinformation Challenge in Public Health: An Opportunity for Science Communication. *Health Education & Behavior*, *47*(5), 501–504.

Cinelli, M., Quattrociocchi, W., Galeazzi, A., Valensise, C. M., Brugnoli, E., Schmidt, A., & Scala, A. (2020). 'The COVID-19 social media infodemic'. *Scientific Reports*, *10*(1), 1–10. DOI: 10.1038/s41598-020-73510-5 PMID: 31913322

Cinelli, M., Quattrociocchi, W., Galeazzi, A., Valensise, C. M., Brugnoli, E., Schmidt, A., & Scala, A. (2020). The COVID-19 social media infodemic. *Scientific Reports, 10*(1), 1–10. DOI: 10.1038/s41598-020-73510-5 PMID: 33024152

Cohen, J.. (2021). 'Social networks and health behaviours: Exploring the role of shared information in crisis situations.' *. *Public Health Reports, 136*(2), 150–158.

Darley, J. M., & Latane, B. (1968). Bystander intervention in emergencies: Diffusion of responsibility. *Journal of Personality and Social Psychology, 8*(4), 377–383. DOI: 10.1037/h0025589 PMID: 5645600

Dubé, E., Vivion, M., & MacDonald, N. E. (2013). Vaccine Hesitancy, Vaccine Refusal and the Anti-Vaccine Movement: Influence, Impact and Implications. *Expert Review of Vaccines, 14*(4), 581–597. PMID: 25373435

Editors of Encyclopaedia Britannica. (2024). Definition of 'Solipsism'. [Internet]. Available from: https://www.britannica.com/topic/solipsism

Festinger, L. (1957). *A Theory of Cognitive Dissonance*. Stanford University Press. DOI: 10.1515/9781503620766

Fletcher, J., & Rauscher, E. (2021). The effects of media exposure on COVID-19 risk perception and behaviours. *Media Psychology, 24*(2), 283–305.

Foucault, M. (1975). *Discipline and Punish: The Birth of the Prison*. Pantheon Books.

Frankl, V. E. (2006). *Man's Search for Meaning*. Beacon Press.

Goleman, D. (2006). *Emotional Intelligence: Why It Can Matter More Than IQ*. Bantam Books.

Gollust, S. E., Nagler, R. H., & Fowler, E. F. (2020). The COVID-19 Misinformation Challenge in Public Health: An Opportunity for Science Communication. *Health Education & Behavior, 47*(1), 101–105. PMID: 31661981

Gollust, S. E., Nagler, R. H., & Fowler, E. F. (2020). The role of public perceptions in the COVID-19 pandemic: Insights from the U.S. population. *Public Health Reports, 135*(1), 30–34.

Harari, Y. N. (2016). *Homo Deus: A brief history of tomorrow*. Harvill Secker.

Heidegger, M. (1962). *Being and time*. Harper and Row.

Heidegger, M. (1962). *Being and Time*. Harper and Row.

Jacobsen, K. H. (2021). *Introduction to Health Research Methods*. Jones & Barlett Learning.

Jacobsen, K. H. (2021). *Introduction to health research methods*. Jones & Bartlett Learning.

Jennings, B., Kahn, J., Mastroianni, A. C., & Parker, L. S. (2016). Ethical guidance for public health emergency preparedness and response: Highlighting ethics and values in a vital public health service. *The Hastings Center Report*, *46*(S1), S1–S29. DOI: 10.1002/hast.610

Jonas, H. (1974). *The imperative of responsibility: In search of ethics for the technological age*. University of Chicago Press.

Kierkegaard, S. (1980). *The concept of anxiety* (Thomte, R., Trans.). Princeton University Press. (Original work published 1844)

Kierkegaard, S. (1980). *The sickness unto death: A Christian psychological exposition for edification and awakening*. Princeton University Press.

Klayman, J. (1995). Varieties of confirmation bias. *Psychology of Learning and Motivation*, *32*, 385–418. DOI: 10.1016/S0079-7421(08)60315-1

Kumar, S., & Preetha, G. (2018). Health promotion: An effective tool for global health. *Global Journal of Health Science*, *10*(5), 1–12. DOI: 10.5539/gjhs.v10n5p1

Kumar, S., & Preetha, G. (2018). Health promotion: An effective tool for global health. *Global Journal of Health Science*, *10*(5), 1–12.

Lachman, M. E., & Weaver, S. L. (1998). The sense of control as a moderator of social class differences in health and well-being. *Journal of Personality and Social Psychology*, *74*(3), 763–773. DOI: 10.1037/0022-3514.74.3.763 PMID: 9523418

Lazarus, R. S., & Folkman, S. (1984). *Stress, appraisal, and coping*. Springer.

Lazarus, R. S., & Folkman, S. (1984). *Stress, Appraisal, and Coping*. Springer.

Lazzari, C.. (1995). *Ninfee alla deriva: Aspetti psicosociali dell'Aids e delle altre malattie a trasmissione sessuale* [It: Water lilies adrift. Psychosocial aspects of AIDS and other sexually transmitted diseases]. Pitagora.

Lazzari, C., & Costigliola, P. (1993). *Sesso e Aids: Si puo arrestare la trasmissione sessuale dell'AIDS?* [Sex and AIDS: Can we stop sexual transmission of AIDS?]. Pitagora.

Lazzari, C., Costigliola, P., Di Bari, M. A., De Ronchi, D., Volterra, V., & Chiodo, F. (1994). AIDS has an increasing diffusion within the heterosexual population. *AIDS Patient Care*, *8*(3), 106. DOI: 10.1089/apc.1994.8.106 PMID: 11362127

Lazzari, C., Costigliola, P., Di Bari, M. A., De Ronchi, D., Volterra, V., & Chiodo, F. (1994). AIDS has an increasing diffusion within the heterosexual population. *AIDS Patient Care*, *8*(3), 106. DOI: 10.1089/apc.1994.8.106 PMID: 11362127

Lazzari, C., & Masino, M. A. (2015). *Psicologia e filosofia della salute*. Editriceuniversitaria.it.

Lazzari, C., Nusair, A., Shoka, A., & Rabottini, M. (2020). Psychiatry during COVID-19 pandemic: A case report of attempted mercy killing. *Psychiatria Danubina*, *32*(2), 303–304. DOI: 10.24869/psyd.2020.303 PMID: 32796803

Leventhal, H., Benyamini, Y., Brownlee, S., Diefenbach, M., Leventhal, E. A., Patrick-Miller, L., & Robitaille, C. (1997). Illness representations: Theoretical foundations. In Petrie, K. J., & Weinman, J. A. (Eds.), *Perceptions of health and illness: Current research and applications* (pp. 19–45). Harwood Academic Publishers.

Lewandowsky, S., Ecker, U. K. H., & Cook, J. (2017). Beyond misinformation: Understanding and coping with the 'post-truth' era. *Journal of Applied Research in Memory and Cognition*, *6*(4), 353–369. DOI: 10.1016/j.jarmac.2017.07.008

Liu, Z., Geng, H., Chen, H., Zhu, M., & Zhu, T. (2020). Exploring the Mechanisms of Influence on COVID-19 Preventive Behaviors in China's Social Media Users. *International Journal of Environmental Research and Public Health*, *17*(23), 8766. DOI: 10.3390/ijerph17238766 PMID: 33255768

Mirowsky, J., & Ross, C. E. (1983). *Social Causes of Psychological Distress*. Aldine de Gruyter.

Morens, D. M., Daszak, P., & Taubenberger, J. K. (2020). A virus reveals itself. *Science*, *368*(6490), 448–450. DOI: 10.1126/science.abc8189

Padilla, M., Castellanos, D., Guilamo-Ramos, V., Reyes, A. M., Sánchez Marte, L. E., & Soriano, M. A. (2008). Stigma, social inequality, and HIV risk disclosure among Dominican male sex workers. *Social Science & Medicine*, *67*(3), 380–388. DOI: 10.1016/j.socscimed.2008.03.014 PMID: 18410986

Pérez, S. T., Houghton, S. R., & González, J. F. (2020). Collective sensemaking during the COVID-19 pandemic: The role of social identity. *Psychological Inquiry*, *31*(4), 309–314. DOI: 10.1080/1047840X.2020.1852730

Peters, U. (2022). What is the function of confirmation bias? *Erkenntnis*, *87*(3), 1351–1376. DOI: 10.1007/s10670-020-00252-1

Pettigrew, S., Aitken, P., & D'Espagnat, S. (2020). Risk perception and health behavior during the COVID-19 pandemic: Evidence from Australia. *International Journal of Environmental Research and Public Health, 17*(9), 3172. DOI: 10.3390/ijerph17093172 PMID: 32370183

Rawls, J. (1971). *A theory of justice*. Harvard University Press. DOI: 10.4159/9780674042605

Reid, A. E., Cialdini, R. B., & Aiken, L. S. (2010). Social norms and health behavior. In Steptoe, A. (Ed.), *Handbook of behavioral medicine: Methods and applications* (pp. 263–274). Springer., DOI: 10.1007/978-0-387-09488-5_19

Rosenstock, I. M., Strecher, V. J., & Becker, M. H. (1994). The health belief model and HIV risk behavior change. In DiClemente, R. J., & Peterson, J. L. (Eds.), *Preventing AIDS: Theories and methods of behavioral interventions* (pp. 5–24). Springer., DOI: 10.1007/978-1-4899-1193-3_2

Sartre, J.-P. (1943). *Being and nothingness*. Washington Square Press.

Sartre, J.-P. (2007). *Existentialism is a humanism*. Yale University Press.

Schieman, S., Nguyen, K., & Elliott, D. (2007). Religiosity, socioeconomic status, and the sense of mastery. *Social Psychology Quarterly, 70*(4), 362–386. DOI: 10.1177/019027250707000404

Schmid, P., Rauber, D., Betsch, C., & Lidolt, G. (2017). Acceptance of vaccination in times of crisis: A pilot study based on the German population. *International Journal of Public Health, 62*(3), 305–314. DOI: 10.1007/s00038-016-0901-2

Schmid, P., Rauber, D., Betsch, C., & Lidolt, G. (2017). Acceptance of vaccination in times of crisis: A pilot study based on the German population. *International Journal of Public Health, 62*(3), 305–314. DOI: 10.1007/s00038-016-0901-2

Seligman, M. E. P. (1975). *Helplessness: On depression, development, and death*. W. H. Freeman.

Sibony, A.-L., Moati, A., & Chappe, C. (2019). Changing health behaviours: What can we learn from behavioural economics? *European Journal of Public Health, 29*(Supplement_4), cky213.033. DOI: 10.1093/eurpub/cky213.033

Simons, P. (1998). *Ontology: Definition, History & Examples* [Internet]. Encyclopedia Britannica; Available from: https://www.britannica.com/topic/ontology-metaphysics

The Editors of Encyclopaedia Britannica. (1998). *Irrationalism: Existentialism, skepticism & nihilism*. Encyclopaedia Britannica. https://www.britannica.com/topic/irrationalism

The Editors of Encyclopaedia Britannica. (2024). *Solipsism: Philosophy, mind, self-awareness*. Encyclopaedia Britannica. https://www.britannica.com/topic/solipsism

Trifiletti, E., Shamloo, S. E., Faccini, M., & Zaka, A. (2022). Psychological predictors of protective behaviours during the Covid-19 pandemic: Theory of planned behaviour and risk perception. *Journal of Community & Applied Social Psychology*, *32*(3), 382–397. DOI: 10.1002/casp.2509 PMID: 33967569

Tversky, A., & Kahneman, D. (1973). Availability: A heuristic for judging frequency and probability. *Cognitive Psychology*, *5*(2), 207–232. DOI: 10.1016/0010-0285(73)90033-9

Van Bavel, J. J., Baicker, K., Boggio, P. S., Capraro, V., Cichocka, A., Cikara, M., & Willer, R. (2020). Using social and behavioural science to support COVID-19 pandemic response. *Nature Human Behaviour*, *4*(5), 460–471. DOI: 10.1038/s41562-020-0884-z PMID: 32355299

Weick, K. E. (1995). *Sensemaking in Organizations*. Sage Publications.

Weinstein, N. D. (1980). Unrealistic optimism about future life events. *Journal of Personality and Social Psychology*, *39*(5), 806–820. DOI: 10.1037/0022-3514.39.5.806

World Health Organization. (2020). *Considerations for implementing and adjusting public health and social measures in the context of COVID-19*. https://www.who.int/publications/i/item/considerations-in-the-adjustment-of-public-health-and-social-measures-in-the-context-of-covid-19

World Health Organization (WHO). (2007). *Risk reduction and emergency preparedness*. World Health Organization. [Online]. Available from: https://iris.who.int/bitstream/handle/10665/43736/9789241595896_eng.pdf?sequence=1

Chapter 7
Emotional Intelligence and Post-Pandemic Resilience:
A Framework for Public Health Nursing

Tiago Manuel Horta Reis da Silva
https://orcid.org/0000-0001-5220-1718
King's College London, UK

ABSTRACT

This chapter explores the critical intersection of emotional intelligence (EI) and post-pandemic resilience within the field of public health nursing. In the wake of COVID-19, nurses have faced profound emotional, ethical, and systemic challenges that have strained traditional coping strategies. Drawing on the socio-cognitive and affective frameworks, this chapter proposes a transformative, evidence-based model that positions EI as a pivotal competency for fostering resilience in public health nurses, especially in the care for older adults. Through a synthesis of contemporary theory, qualitative insights, and pedagogical strategies, the chapter outlines a framework for developing emotionally intelligent nursing professionals capable of thriving amid crises and contributing to resilient public health systems. Implications for leadership, education, and interprofessional collaboration are discussed.

INTRODUCTION

The COVID-19 pandemic has profoundly affected healthcare systems worldwide, heightening existing vulnerabilities and revealing inadequacies within nursing

DOI: 10.4018/979-8-3373-1992-6.ch007

practices, which have historically been under stress even before the crisis emerged (Galanis et al., 2021). Studies have demonstrated that nurses are the backbone of health responses, especially during the COVID-19 outbreak, where they have faced overwhelming physical, emotional, and psychological burdens (Xu et al., 2021; Assis & França, 2023; Reis da Silva et al., 2025). Nurses typically operate in an intensely challenging environment, underscored by severe patient surges, shortages of personal protective equipment (PPE), and the expectation of high-calibre patient care amidst these adversities (Reis da Silva, 2025a; Reis da Silva, 2024a; Castro-Sánchez et al., 2021; Rosdyanti et al., 2023). This situation has been compounded by structural inadequacies in healthcare systems that have historically under-prioritised nursing resources, contributing to a vicious cycle of burnout and job dissatisfaction (Reis da Silva, 2025b; Galanis et al., 2021; Xu et al., 2021).

Before the onset of the COVID-19 pandemic, emotional intelligence (EI) and resilience were increasingly recognised as vital components in nursing practice. Various aspects of nursing, including job satisfaction, retention, and patient safety, were shown to be significantly influenced by these factors (Reis da Silva, 2025b). Emotional intelligence encompasses the ability to perceive and manage one's emotions and those of others, contributing to improved interpersonal dynamics within healthcare settings (Prezerakos, 2018; Dugué et al., 2021). Researchers have noted that nurses with high EI often demonstrate enhanced communication and empathy, which are essential in providing high-quality patient care (Edward et al., 2017; Lewis et al., 2017). The pre-pandemic healthcare environment was fraught with specific stressors, including workplace bullying, compassion fatigue, and extended shifts, all of which could adversely affect nurses' emotional and psychological well-being (Dall'Ora et al., 2020). Long shifts and high workload demands frequently led to emotional exhaustion, which in turn could negatively impact the quality of care provided to patients (Dall'Ora et al., 2020; Pérez-Francisco et al., 2020). Compassion fatigue, defined as the emotional strain from caring for patients in distress, was also prevalent among nurses, often exacerbated by inadequate support from supervisors and organisational structures (Edward et al., 2017; Dall'Ora et al., 2020). Research prior to the pandemic indicated a compelling link between emotional intelligence, job satisfaction, and retention rates among nursing professionals (Kalánková et al., 2020; Bianchi et al., 2016). High levels of EI have been associated with lower rates of burnout, fostering resilience in stressful situations which consequently promotes job satisfaction. Studies have shown that nurses with higher EI levels report greater occupational satisfaction and are less likely to leave their positions (Fowler et al., 2021; Kalánková et al., 2020). Moreover, EI was found to correlate positively with patient safety outcomes, as nurses equipped with better emotional skills were more adept at recognising and responding to patient needs, which ultimately improved care quality (Yue et al., 2017; Bianchi et al., 2016).

In leadership contexts, emotional intelligence played a crucial role. Leaders who employed emotionally intelligent practices were better at fostering supportive work environments, thereby reducing stress-related issues and enhancing team cohesion (Wei et al., 2018; Dugué et al., 2021). Emotional intelligence training for nursing leaders was linked to improved organisational climate and morale, which are critical for maintaining workforce stability in high-pressure environments (Leary & Punshon, 2019; Ha et al., 2022).

The emotional and psychological toll on nurses during the pandemic has emerged as a critical area of concern in the literature, reflecting a broader trend of emotional distress and moral injury among frontline healthcare professionals (Reis da Silva, 2024b; Xu et al., 2021; Castro-Sánchez et al., 2021). Many studies document that nurses have reported heightened levels of anxiety, depression, and post-traumatic stress disorder (PTSD) symptoms, reminiscent of the stresses experienced in significant historical crises, such as military conflicts and natural disasters (Wahyuni et al., 2023; Assis & França, 2023; Reis da Silva, 2024c; Reis da Silva et al., 2025). This aligns with claims by other studies, which assert that the pandemic has exacerbated pre-existing mental health issues among nurses, complicating their ability to perform under pressure (Joo & Liu, 2021). Furthermore, the overwhelming demands faced by nurses have led to feelings of isolation and erosion of mental well-being, particularly in environments characterised by high mortality rates and inadequate resources (Xu et al., 2021; Rosdyanti et al., 2023; Reis da Silva, 2024d; Reis da Silva, 2025c).

Moral injury, defined as the psychological distress arising from the failure to adhere to one's personal ethical standards, has become a widespread phenomenon among nursing professionals during the COVID-19 crisis (Castro-Sánchez et al., 2021). As nurses grapple with systemic resource limitations, many report a deep sense of inadequacy as they strive to provide care that aligns with their professional standards and personal moral frameworks (Galanis et al., 2021; Xu et al., 2021). This moral distress not only threatens the mental health of nursing staff but may also adversely affect patient care outcomes and the integrity of healthcare systems as a whole (Castro-Sánchez et al., 2021; Joo & Liu, 2021; Reis da Silva, 2025b). Evidence suggests that such distress can lead to long-term repercussions, including diminished job satisfaction, increased turnover rates, and a devalued patient experience (Wahyuni et al., 2023; Rosdyanti et al., 2023; Reis da Silva, 2025d; Reis da Silva, 2025e).

Given the psychological burdens imposed upon nursing staff, the integration of emotional intelligence (EI) into nursing education and practice emerges as a potential solution to ameliorate these challenges (Reis da Silva et al., 2025; Galanis et al., 2021; Xu et al., 2021). Emotional intelligence is recognised as a key competency facilitating improved interpersonal relationships and stress management within healthcare settings (Castro-Sánchez et al., 2021; da Silva, 2022; Reis da Silva, 2025f). The pandemic underscored the necessity for nurses to cultivate emotional intelligence to navigate their emotional challenges, particularly during crises where resilience and empathy become paramount (Reis da Silva, 2025g; Cheng et al., 2021; Simonetti et al., 2020). Research indicates that nurses with high levels of emotional intelligence are better equipped to handle workplace stresses, thus reducing turnover intentions and enhancing job performance (Reis da Silva, 2025g; Wahyuni et al., 2023; Castro-Sánchez et al., 2021; Rosdyanti et al., 2023).

Implementing training programs that emphasise the development of emotional intelligence can serve as a foundational intervention designed to bolster resilience among nurses (Galanis et al., 2021; Wahyuni et al., 2023; Reis da Silva, 2025g).

The aim of this chapter is to explore the broad implications of the COVID-19 pandemic on public health systems, elucidate the substantial emotional toll taken on nursing professionals, and highlight the necessity of integrating emotional intelligence as a strategic response to transform public health practices moving forward. By implementing emotional intelligence training tailored for nurses, we can better equip them to handle workplace stresses and improve overall mental health outcomes, thus enhancing the quality of care provided (Reis da Silva, 2025a). Furthermore, this integration can lead to institutional changes encouraging supportive work environments where holistic health approaches are prioritised for both patients and providers (Reis da Silva et al., 2025; Reis da Silva, 2025a).

The scope of this chapter encompasses a systematic review and analysis of the emotional and psychological impacts of the COVID-19 pandemic on nursing staff, alongside an evaluation of existing literature on emotional intelligence interventions. Previous studies indicate a vast landscape of increased burnout, stress, and moral distress experienced by nurses during the pandemic, calling for an urgent redistribution of mental health resources and support systems intended for frontline healthcare workers (Assis & França, 2023). Through the synthesis of empirical evidence, the chapter aspires to provide actionable insights that can guide health policy formulation and reinforce the necessity of mental health care as an integral part of nursing education and ongoing professional development.

CONCEPTUAL FOUNDATIONS: EMOTIONAL INTELLIGENCE AND RESILIENCE

As defined in the glossary section on key terms, Emotional Intelligence (EI) provides a multidimensional capacity to engage with and regulate emotions. In the context of nursing, this becomes a crucial lens through which to analyse the mechanisms of resilience and professional coping. The following section explores how these conceptual models are operationalised in clinical, educational, and leadership frameworks relevant to nursing.

Integration of EI and Resilience as Transformative Competencies

Integrating emotional intelligence and resilience presents an opportunity to develop transformative competencies that are particularly valuable in healthcare settings. Nurses and healthcare professionals who possess high emotional intelligence are better equipped to navigate the emotional demands of their roles and consequently exhibit greater resilience in the face of stressful situations (Ramadhan & Nasution, 2023; Reis da Silva, 2025i). Studies indicate that enhancing emotional intelligence skills directly correlates with improved coping strategies among nursing staff, thus facilitating better patient care outcomes and staff well-being (Lievens & Chan, 2017; Joo & Liu, 2021).

Additionally, creating educational programs focused on EI and resilience can mitigate the prevalence of burnout among nurses and healthcare workers (Reis da Silva, 2025j; Reis da Silva et al., 2025). By providing training that develops these competencies, healthcare organisations can foster a culture that prioritises both emotional well-being and professional effectiveness, leading to higher job satisfaction and lower turnover rates (Kozlowski et al., 2017; Reis da Silva, 2025h). Such transformational strategies not only support the staff but also improve the overall quality of patient care, as emotionally intelligent and resilient nurses are more likely to provide compassionate and effective care.

The integration of emotional intelligence with resilience poses profound implications for organisational policies in healthcare. It is essential for healthcare administrators to recognise the interdependence of these two constructs and implement comprehensive training programs that incorporate both emotional intelligence and resilience-building strategies into professional development curricula (Duong & Nguyen, 2023; Reis da Silva, 2025g). This integrated approach could lead to establishing robust support systems that nurture emotional health and resilience, ensuring that healthcare professionals are well-equipped to handle the emotional complexities of their work while delivering high-quality patient care (Joo & Liu, 2021; Yoon et al., 2023).

Pandemic Challenges to Nursing Resilience and Emotional Functioning

The COVID-19 pandemic has fundamentally reshaped the nursing workforce, introducing unprecedented challenges that have significantly affected nurses' emotional functioning and resilience. Empirical evidence indicates that these challenges manifest as burnout, post-traumatic stress disorder (PTSD), and moral distress, all of which have been accentuated by the demanding circumstances of the pandemic (Wahyuni et al., 2023; Galanis et al., 2021). Studies highlight that frontline nurses, tasked with caring for a surge of COVID-19 patients, have faced substantial emotional burdens caused by increased patient mortality, overwhelming workloads, and the constant risk of exposure to the virus themselves (Wahyuni et al., 2023; Galanis et al., 2021). Reports suggest that high levels of burnout, characterised by emotional exhaustion, depersonalisation, and decreased personal accomplishment, have surged among nurses (Galanis et al., 2021; Gualano et al., 2021). For instance, a systematic review and meta-analysis found that the prevalence of burnout symptoms among nurses during the COVID-19 pandemic was estimated at 11.23%, underscoring a critical need for interventions to support their mental health (Galanis et al., 2021).

Additionally, PTSD has emerged as a significant issue among healthcare workers, particularly nurses, who have experienced trauma-related symptoms stemming from their frontline roles (Safiye et al., 2024). The sheer volume of death and serious illness experienced during the pandemic has elicited feelings of helplessness and grief, which can catalyse PTSD symptoms such as flashbacks, anxiety, and irritability (Pradas-Hernández et al., 2018; Reis da Silva, 2024c). Furthermore, moral distress has been prevalent among nurses, stemming from ethical dilemmas faced in the care of COVID-19 patients. Many have reported feelings of frustration and guilt when they were unable to provide the level of care they deemed necessary due to resource limitations (Gebreheat & Teame, 2021). This moral injury not only affects personal well-being but can also negatively impact patient care outcomes and the overall healthcare delivery process (Safiye et al., 2024).

The pandemic has also significantly disrupted professional identities and role clarity among nursing professionals. Many nurses found their roles increasingly precarious as they were forced to adapt to the rapidly changing circumstances surrounding pandemic protocols and patient management (Gualano et al., 2021; Llop-Gironés et al., 2021). The uncertainty that permeated the healthcare environment led to a diminished sense of professional identity, leaving many feeling disoriented and undervalued in their roles (Gualano et al., 2021). This lack of clarity and social connection may contribute further to emotional fatigue and decreased job satisfaction among nursing professionals (Zhang et al., 2018; Giri et al., 2021).

Compassion fatigue, closely related to emotional labour in nursing, has also become more pronounced during the pandemic. Nurses have not only had to care for their patients physically but have also faced the emotional toll of providing care amid suffering and grief (Safiye et al., 2024; Hunsaker et al., 2015). Compassion fatigue occurs when the emotional toll of caregiving leads to cumulative exhaustion that diminishes one's ability to empathise with patients (Giri et al., 2021; Reis da

Silva, 2025i; Reis da Silva, 2025k). In this context, public health nursing has been particularly affected, as nurses are often the first point of contact in communities, bearing witness to the widespread trauma experienced by patients and families alike (Chemali et al., 2019). Evidence suggests that this accumulated emotional labour can result in deeper mental health issues and impair the quality of care provided to patients (Reis da Silva, 2025i; Safiye et al., 2024; Chemali et al., 2019).

The pandemic has exposed significant inequities within the nursing workforce, intensifying the disparities that exist between nurses working in underserved areas compared to those in more affluent regions (Gualano et al., 2021; Llop-Gironés et al., 2021). Nurses in under-resourced settings have often faced double burdens: they encounter higher patient loads, limited access to personal protective equipment (PPE), and inadequate support systems (Giri et al., 2021; Llop-Gironés et al., 2021). Studies indicate that this demographic has been disproportionately affected in terms of burnout and emotional distress (Llop-Gironés et al., 2021; Rezaei et al., 2018). The inequities revealed during the pandemic have amplified calls to re-evaluate healthcare policies to ensure more robust support systems for nurses serving in these high-demand, low-resourced environments (Wahyuni et al., 2023).

A THEORETICAL MODEL FOR EI-DRIVEN RESILIENCE IN PUBLIC HEALTH NURSING

To address the compounded challenges faced by nursing professionals during and post-pandemic, the development of a structured theoretical model focusing on Emotional Intelligence (EI) and resilience is critical. A proposed framework, known as the Resilient Emotional Intelligence Framework (REIF), provides a comprehensive approach that encompasses core domains integral to supporting nursing resilience: self-awareness, emotional regulation, relational attunement, and adaptive reflection (Gómez-Urquiza et al., 2016). This model aims to offer a structured pedagogical lens through which nursing education can foster resilience among healthcare professionals facing emotional and psychological challenges (Figure 1).

Figure 1. Components of the REIF model

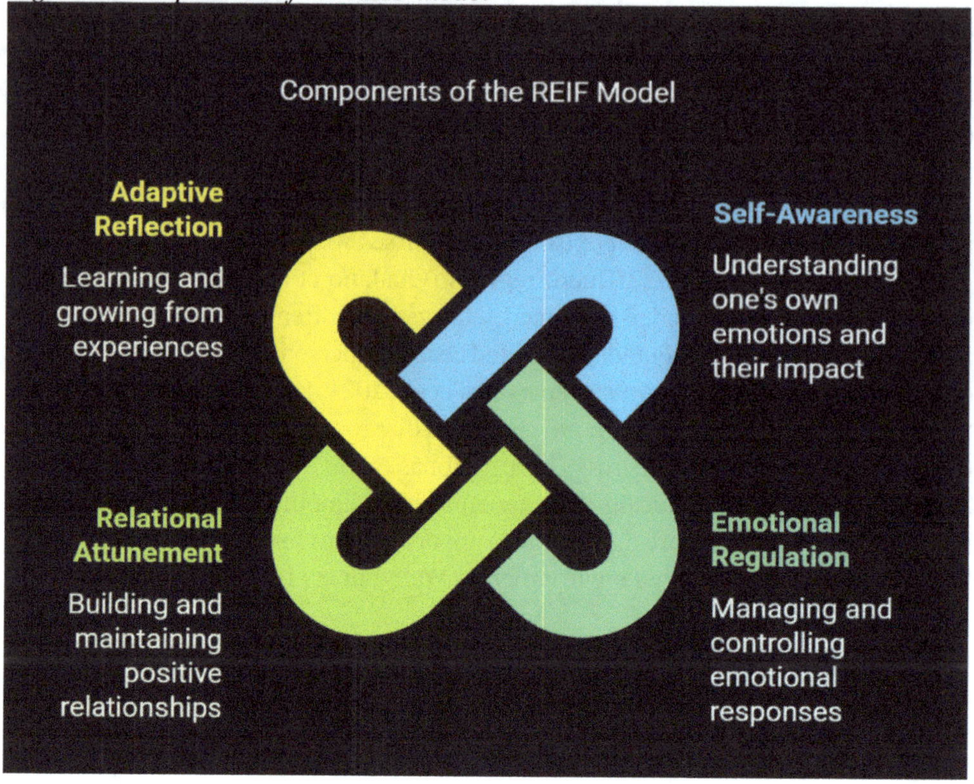

Core Domains

Self-Awareness

This domain emphasises understanding one's own emotions, strengths, weaknesses, and triggers related to stress and fatigue (da Silva, 2022). By fostering self-awareness, nurses can better identify emotional responses, which serves as the foundation for effective emotional management (Joo & Liu, 2021; Khatatbeh et al., 2021). Teaching nurses to recognise and articulate their feelings not only enhances their personal resilience but also improves their ability to respond to the emotional cues of others.

Emotional Regulation

This domain involves training nurses in strategies for managing their emotional responses in high-pressure situations. Given the emotional labour associated with caregiving, equipping nurses with effective emotional regulation strategies is essential for maintaining their mental well-being (Dubale et al., 2019). Mindfulness practices and stress-reduction techniques have shown promise in helping healthcare workers cope with the psychological strains introduced by the pandemic (Buowari, 2022; Suleiman-Martos et al., 2020).

Relational Attunement

This domain focuses on the importance of empathy, social awareness, and effective communication in nursing practice. Relational attunement fosters deeper connections with patients and colleagues, enhancing supportive networks that contribute to emotional resilience (Gómez-Urquiza et al., 2016; Hunsaker et al., 2015). Developing these interpersonal skills can mitigate feelings of isolation, particularly during crises when nurses may feel disconnected from their peers and patients (Reis da Silva, 2025i).

Adaptive Reflection

This final domain emphasises the importance of reflective practice in fostering resilience. Encouraging nurses to reflect on their experiences during the pandemic can facilitate growth and learning (Reis da Silva, 2024a; Reis da Silva, 2024e). By analysing their emotional responses to various situations, nurses can develop more adaptive coping mechanisms, ultimately enhancing their overall resilience (Fuente-Solana et al., 2020).

The integration of pedagogical and socio-cognitive lenses into the REIF framework facilitates the application of these core domains in nursing education. This approach promotes dignity, respect, and empowerment within the nursing profession, ultimately enhancing emotional well-being (Hunsaker et al., 2015) (figure 2).

Figure 2. Core domains

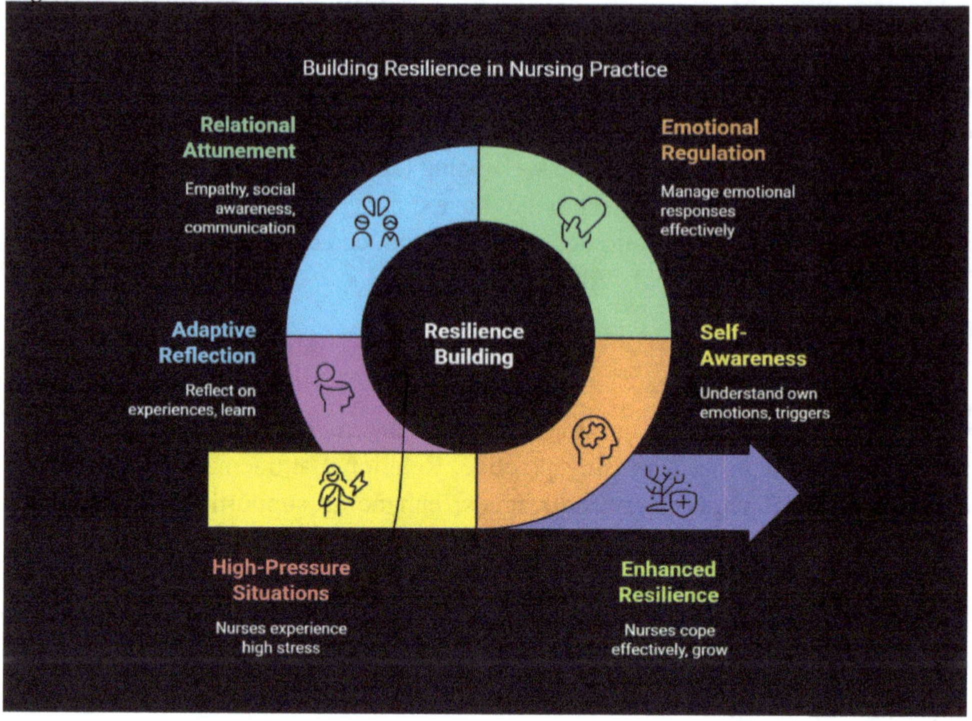

PEDAGOGICAL STRATEGIES FOR CULTIVATING EMOTIONAL INTELLIGENCE IN PUBLIC HEALTH NURSES

In the demanding field of public health nursing, the cultivation of emotional intelligence (EI) has become an essential component of professional development. The need for emotionally intelligent practitioners is heightened given the emotional demands and stressors associated with healthcare delivery, particularly in the context of pandemic response and crisis management. Drawing from Mezirow's transformative learning theory and Reis da Silva's educational frameworks, we can develop pedagogical strategies that enhance the emotional competence of nursing professionals, fostering resilience and effective patient care (Edward et al., 2017; Soimah & Utami, 2023).

Affective and Transformative Learning

Mezirow's transformative learning theory suggests that significant learning occurs when individuals interrogate and re-evaluate their preconceived notions through critical reflection (Desroches, 2019). This reflective process allows individuals to engage deeply with their experiences, leading to profound changes in their perspectives. Integrating Reis da Silva's approach, which emphasises the importance of context and the socio-cognitive dimensions of learning, can enhance this process further by incorporating social and emotional contexts in which learners operate (Reis da Silva et al., 2025). By recognising emotions as fundamental to learning, instructional strategies can focus not only on cognitive skills but also on emotional literacy, thereby creating a comprehensive framework for nurturing EI in public health nurses.

This approach facilitates the development of affective competencies by using experiential learning opportunities, where nurses engage in role-playing scenarios simulating real-world nursing challenges (Reis da Silva and Mitchell, 2024). Through these simulations, trainees can practice recognising and responding to their emotions as well as those of their colleagues and patients. By fostering an environment where emotions are acknowledged and explored, nurses can enhance their capacity for empathy, emotional regulation, and interpersonal communication, which are critical skills in nursing practice (Romero-Martín et al., 2019; Reis da Silva and Mitchell, 2024).

Reflective Practice, Narrative Inquiry, and Emotional Simulation in Training

Reflective practice stands as a cornerstone for developing emotional intelligence among nursing professionals (Reis da Silva, 2024d). This approach encourages nurses to engage in systematic reflection about their experiences and decision-making processes, which is vital for emotional growth and professional identity (Edward et al., 2017; Romero-Martín et al., 2019). Facilitating regular reflective sessions in nursing education can help students and professionals articulate their feelings and experiences, enabling them to connect emotionally with their practice and develop a deeper understanding of their emotional responses.

Narrative inquiry serves as a powerful pedagogical tool within this context, allowing nurses to share personal stories related to their experiences in the field. By articulating narratives of their encounters with patients and the emotional challenges therein, nurses can gain insights into their fears, motivations, and emotional states (Ramadhan & Nasution, 2023; Reis da Silva, 2025d). This approach not only fosters a sense of community but also helps in normalising emotional experiences among peers. Additionally, emotional simulation exercises, such as simulations that evoke strong emotional responses, can also play a significant role in enhancing empathy and emotional regulation skills among nursing professionals. Through role-play and immersive scenarios, nurses can practice responding to emotionally charged situations, thus building their resilience and emotional coping strategies (Soimah & Utami, 2023; Romero-Martín et al., 2019; Reis da Silva, 2024f).

Role of Mentoring, Coaching, and Peer-Learning Communities

Mentoring and coaching have been identified as effective strategies for nurturing emotional intelligence in nursing education and practice (Edward et al., 2017; Soimah & Utami, 2023). Establishing mentoring programs where experienced nurses guide junior staff can create an emotionally supportive environment that encourages learning and emotional growth (Reis da Silva, 2025l). Mentors can provide feedback on emotional interactions with patients and offer insights into managing emotional strain, thus serving as role models for effective emotional regulation (Reis da Silva, 2025l).

Additionally, establishing peer-learning communities can facilitate informal learning and emotional support among nursing staff (Reis da Silva, 2024f). Engaging regularly in discussions about emotional labour, stress management, and self-care strategies within these communities allows nurses to exchange experiences, deepen their understanding of EI, and reinforce their emotional competencies collectively (Ramadhan & Nasution, 2023; Duong & Nguyen, 2023; Reis da Silva, 2025j). By cultivating a culture where emotional sharing is encouraged, healthcare organisations can contribute to the development of emotionally intelligent nursing practitioners who are able to provide compassionate care while safeguarding their emotional well-being (Reis da Silva et al., 2025).

Emotional Intelligence in Interprofessional Public Health Curricula

Incorporating emotional intelligence into interprofessional education (IPE) curricula is essential for promoting collaboration and effective communication among healthcare teams (Soimah & Utami, 2023; Reis da Silva, 2024d). By fostering EI in a diverse group of healthcare professionals, public health education programs can enhance team dynamics, minimise conflict, and improve patient outcomes. Collaborative learning experiences, such as team-based simulations and shared reflective practices, can help nursing students and their colleagues in related health professions understand the emotional contexts of their roles (Reis da Silva and Mitchell, 2024).

Training would address shared emotional experiences in patient care, promoting a holistic understanding of patient interactions. An emphasis on emotional competencies within IPE can break down professional silos, enabling healthcare professionals to recognise and value each other's emotional labour (Ravenna & Cleaver, 2015; Romero-Martín et al., 2019). This collaborative curriculum fosters an environment where members can effectively address stress and challenges collectively, thereby enhancing the resilience of healthcare teams (Reis da Silva, 2025g).

ORGANISATIONAL CULTURE, LEADERSHIP, AND SYSTEM RESILIENCE

The integration of emotional intelligence into nursing is not solely an educational responsibility; it is also essential that healthcare organisations cultivate an emotionally intelligent culture led by competent leadership (Reis da Silva, 2025l). Emotionally intelligent leaders play a critical role in shaping resilient healthcare environments, which prioritise nurses' well-being and promote effective patient care practices (Reis da Silva, 2025g). Leaders who exhibit strong emotional intelligence can foster an environment of trust, collaboration, and open communication, significantly enhancing workplace morale and job satisfaction (Kozlowski et al., 2017; Reis da Silva, 2025i).

Role of Emotionally Intelligent Leadership in Resilient Healthcare Systems

Emotionally intelligent leadership is associated with transformational leadership styles that encourage team members to contribute meaningfully to organisational objectives (Kozlowski et al., 2017; Reis da Silva et al., 2025). Leaders who understand their own emotions and those of their staff can navigate complex situations, acknowledge the emotional labour involved in nursing, and provide support accordingly. Research indicates that when leaders model emotional intelligence behaviours, such as active listening, empathy, and conflict resolution, they foster a culture of psychological safety that enables nurses to express their concerns and emotional experiences (Kozlowski et al., 2017; Reis da Silva, 2025i).

Effective emotionally intelligent leadership directly influences employee retention and organisational resilience (Reis da Silva, 2025l). In times of crisis, such as the COVID-19 pandemic, leaders who exemplify emotional intelligence can better facilitate adaptive change, support staff through difficult transitions, and maintain a sense of stability within their teams (Soimah & Utami, 2023; Kozlowski et al., 2017). Organisations that recognise the importance of EI in leadership can enhance their overall performance, leading to improved patient care outcomes and employee satisfaction (Reis da Silva, 2025g).

Strategies for Embedding EI and Resilience in Organisational Culture

To create a robust organisational culture that embeds emotional intelligence and resilience, healthcare institutions need to establish strategies that foster emotional competencies across all levels of the organisation (Kozlowski et al., 2017) (Figure 3). Training programs aimed at developing emotional intelligence should be incorporated into leadership development initiatives, ensuring that leaders are equipped with the tools necessary to cultivate an emotionally supportive workplace (Reis da Silva, 2025l). This comprehensive approach can encompass workshops, seminars, and practical training sessions dedicated to enhancing EI among staff and management.

Moreover, initiatives such as regular feedback mechanisms and assessments can be utilised to gauge the emotional climate of the organisation. Implementing these strategies allows organisations to remain responsive to the emotional needs of their workforce, making necessary adjustments to policies and practices that may impact staff morale and emotional health (Kozlowski et al., 2017). Additionally, promoting policies that prioritise employee well-being, such as mental health days and stress reduction programs, can further instil resilience in the organisational culture (Reis da Silva, 2025b).

Figure 3. Strategies for embedding EI and resilience in organisational culture

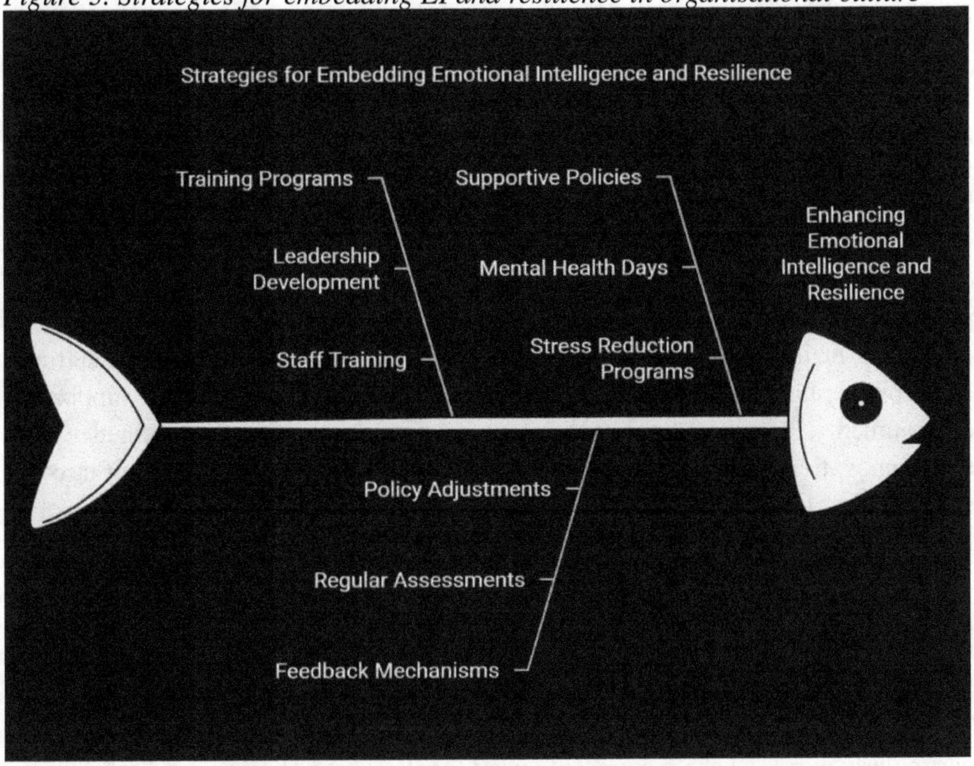

Nurse Leadership in Public Health Innovation and Pandemic Preparedness

Nurse leaders possess a unique role in driving public health innovation and improving pandemic preparedness. By leveraging their emotional intelligence, they can inspire their teams, foster collaboration among diverse disciplines, and enhance the capacity for innovative solutions (Kozlowski et al., 2017). This leadership role encompasses effective communication strategies that engage stakeholders and promote collective problem-solving in the face of public health crises (Reis da Silva, 2025l).

Furthermore, by being proactive in advocating for necessary resources and support systems, nurse leaders can ensure that their teams are equipped to respond efficiently and effectively to health emergencies (Reis da Silva et al., 2025). These efforts can significantly influence the resilience of healthcare systems, enabling organisations to maintain high-quality care while addressing the challenges of evolving public health threats (Kozlowski et al., 2017).

Building Emotionally Safe Environments for Reflective Dialogue and Innovation

Creating an emotionally safe environment is essential for encouraging reflective dialogue and fostering innovation in nursing practice. Such environments enable nurses to share their insights, experiences, and emotional responses without fear of judgment, thus leading to more profound learning experiences and improved teamwork (Kozlowski et al., 2017). Reflective practice sessions that focus on emotional experiences can promote open discussions among staff, allowing for collaborative problem-solving and shared emotional support (Reis da Silva, 2025b).

Moreover, implementing innovation labs or think tanks within healthcare settings can provide platforms for nurses to explore new ideas and solutions in a supportive environment (Reis da Silva, 2025d). By integrating emotional intelligence into these innovations, organisations can harness the collective wisdom of their nursing staff, driving improved patient care and organisational effectiveness (Lisowska & Rekik, 2018).

POLICY IMPLICATIONS AND STRATEGIC RECOMMENDATIONS

In light of the COVID-19 pandemic's profound impact on healthcare providers, particularly nurses, there is a pressing need for strategic policies aimed at fostering emotional intelligence (EI) and resilience within the public health workforce. These policies should focus on enhancing mental health support, promoting emotional competence, and ensuring a sustainable workforce (Webster et al. 2019; Edward et al., 2017).

Policies for Mental Health, EI, and Resilience in Public Health Workforce Planning

Mental health initiatives must be prioritised in workforce planning to address the emotional toll experienced by healthcare workers. This includes developing comprehensive mental health policies that integrate EI training into existing frameworks. Specific measures should entail regular mental health screenings, access to psychological support services, and the establishment of peer support groups within healthcare settings (Powell et al., 2019; Edward et al., 2017). Furthermore, it is crucial that public health organisations invest in training programs that enhance EI competencies—such as emotional regulation and interpersonal communication skills—thereby preparing nurses for the emotional challenges associated with their roles (Magola et al., 2017; Prezerakos, 2018).

Recommendations for Nursing Councils, Health Authorities, and Educational Institutions

`Nursing councils and health authorities should advocate for the integration of EI into educational programs and ongoing professional development for nurses. Recommendations include the implementation of EI assessments during the hiring process to identify candidates with greater emotional awareness and social skills (Molina-Praena et al., 2018; Kozlowski et al., 2017). Educational institutions need to design curricula that emphasise emotional intelligence training, incorporating experiential learning opportunities such as simulations and role-plays that strengthen nurses' capacity to navigate emotionally complex situations (Crawford et al., 2021).

Moreover, it is essential to establish leadership development programs that focus on cultivating emotional intelligence among nurse leaders. Training those in leadership positions to model emotionally intelligent behaviours can create a more compassionate and supportive work culture, building resilience throughout the organisation (Prezerakos, 2018).

Supporting Lifelong Emotional Competence in Nurses Across the Career Trajectory

Lifelong learning initiatives that enable nurses to continually develop their emotional intelligence should be embedded within professional practices. This can be achieved through ongoing workshops, mentorship programs, and collaborative learning communities that focus on emotional coaching and peer feedback (Katsumata & Teixeira, 2024). By supporting professional development throughout a nurse's career, healthcare institutions can enhance their emotional competencies, promoting job satisfaction and retention. Incorporating resilience training into educational frameworks will equip nurses with the necessary tools to cope with stress, thereby strengthening the overall healthcare workforce (Singh et al., 2020).

FUTURE RESEARCH DIRECTIONS

Despite the growing recognition of EI's importance in nursing, further research is needed to delve deeper into this vital area. Future studies should focus on longitudinal analyses of emotional intelligence and nursing resilience to understand how these constructs develop and influence professional practice over time (Safiye et al., 2024; .

Need for Longitudinal Studies on EI and Nursing Resilience

Longitudinal studies are essential to track the impact of emotional intelligence on nurses' resilience and overall well-being throughout their careers. Research should explore changes over time, particularly in relation to high-stress events like the COVID-19 pandemic. Such studies can provide critical insights into how EI interventions can be optimised to strengthen resilience in nursing populations (Safiye et al., 2024; Mu et al., 2018).

Interdisciplinary Research Integrating Cognitive Science, Pedagogy, and Health Systems

Integrating research across disciplines such as cognitive science, pedagogy, and health systems can enhance the understanding of EI in nursing. This interdisciplinary approach can inform the development of effective EI training programs by merging insights into emotional processing, learning methodologies, and healthcare delivery systems (Desroches, 2019).

Evaluating the Impact of EI Training on Public Health Outcomes

Research must evaluate the outcomes of EI training initiatives within nursing practice, particularly regarding their effects on patient care. Metrics such as patient satisfaction, quality of care, and nursing retention rates can be evaluated to ensure that EI training translates into tangible benefits within healthcare settings (Marvell & Simm, 2021; Romero-Martín et al., 2019).

Exploring the Digital Transformation of EI Training through AI and Immersive Tech

The digitalisation of healthcare offers novel avenues for EI training through artificial intelligence and immersive technology. Future research should investigate how virtual reality simulations and AI-driven training programs can enhance emotional intelligence competencies among nurses, offering innovative and accessible methods for skill development (Maalouf et al., 2018; Gong & Jiao, 2019). Understanding how technology can be harnessed to educate emotional competence is pivotal for maintaining a skilled, resilient nursing workforce in a rapidly evolving healthcare landscape.

SUSTAINABLE DEVELOPMENT GOALS

The COVID-19 pandemic has significantly impacted public health systems worldwide, revealing the critical need for integrating emotional intelligence (EI) and resilience into nursing practice. This integration aligns harmoniously with the United Nations Sustainable Development Goals (SDGs), particularly in the realms of health, well-being, and social equity (da Silva and Rodrigues, 2023; Hawkins et al., 2024). As public health nursing confronts post-pandemic challenges, understanding the interplay between EI, resilience, and the SDGs is paramount for fostering durable healthcare systems and promoting the collective well-being of communities (Cowley et al., 2023).

Emotional Intelligence and the Sustainable Development Goals

SDG 3: Good Health and Well-Being directly emphasises the importance of the emotional and mental well-being of healthcare workers, as well as the populations they serve. Emotional intelligence serves as a foundational competency for nurses to manage their stress and emotional labour effectively, which is crucial in maintaining their mental and emotional health in high-pressure situations such as pandemics (Daher-Nashif & Bawadi, 2020; Hawkins et al., 2024). A well-supported nursing force with high emotional intelligence contributes to higher quality patient care, increasing overall public health outcomes and well-being within societies.

Moreover, SDG 5: Gender Equality is deeply intertwined with emotional intelligence in nursing, considering that nursing is predominantly female. Promoting emotional intelligence can empower nurses to advocate for themselves and their peers within the healthcare system (Herrero et al., 2021; Daher-Nashif & Bawadi, 2020). By fostering emotional competence among nursing professionals, healthcare systems can establish more equitable and supportive environments that prioritise the health and well-being of women in the workforce.

SDG 4: Quality Education also plays a crucial role in this discussion by advocating for the incorporation of emotional intelligence training within educational curricula for nursing programs. This educational foundation not only prepares future nurses to effectively navigate emotional challenges but also encourages a culture of lifelong learning aimed at enhancing emotional competencies in the profession (Yehia & Said, 2024; Ng-Kamstra et al., 2016). Subsequently, this leads to a more resilient nursing workforce capable of responding adeptly to crises while ensuring optimal care delivery.

The interplay between emotional intelligence and the SDGs highlights the necessity for a multi-faceted approach that includes public health leadership, educational institutions, and healthcare organisations in fostering environments conducive to both personal and communal resilience (Sensor et al., 2021). By addressing emotional intelligence as a core competency within the context of the SDGs, public health nursing can drive sustainable improvements in healthcare outcomes.

Emotional Intelligence and Resilience in Addressing Pandemic Challenges

Post-pandemic resilience hinges on identifying the emotional and psychological strain that healthcare workers have endured over the past years. Encouragingly, organisations such as the World Health Organization (WHO) recognise the importance of emotional intelligence as a facilitator for coping mechanisms and strategies that healthcare professionals can leverage during crises (Siddiqi et al., 2020). The development of an emotionally intelligent healthcare workforce is instrumental in mitigating the burnout and moral distress that many nurses face in the current healthcare landscape.

Furthermore, strategies aligned with SDG 3,4 and 5 that target emotional intelligence training can lead to improved retention rates of nursing staff as well as decreased rates of turnover. Support structures, such as mentorship and peer-learning communities focused on emotional development, can cultivate resilience within nursing teams (Saarinen, 2020; Lin et al., 2020). These interconnected strategies illustrate how emotional intelligence can reinforce a sustainable nursing workforce that is better equipped to tackle future health challenges, thus furthering the goals set forth under the SDGs (Chiu et al., 2022).

Policy Recommendations

To truly align emotional intelligence initiatives with the Sustainable Development Goals, several strategic recommendations can be established:

- Policy Development: Create policies supporting the integration of emotional intelligence training in nursing education and continuing professional development. This should include funding for training programs and mental health resources tailored to the specific needs of nurses (Bălan et al., 2024; Zhang & Xiang, 2022).
- Strengthening Institutional Connections: Encourage educational institutions to collaborate with healthcare organisations to develop curricula that emphasise both emotional intelligence training and resilience building within nursing programs (Reis da Silva, 2025a). This collaborative effort can ensure that future nurses enter the profession equipped with the necessary emotional

tools to face the challenges ahead (Yehia & Said, 2024; Ng-Kamstra et al., 2016).

- Evaluation of Programs: Conduct research to assess the efficacy of EI training programs and their direct impact on nursing performance and patient outcomes. By systematically evaluating these initiatives, stakeholders can refine their strategies to enhance training effectiveness (König et al., 2021).
- Addressing Health Inequities: Focus on how EI initiatives can target underserved and low-resourced healthcare settings, ensuring equitable access to training that can empower all nursing professionals (Lin et al., 2020; Siddiqi et al., 2020).

CONCLUSION

The COVID-19 pandemic has been a defining moment for healthcare systems globally, exposing critical vulnerabilities within nursing practice while simultaneously offering insights into potential avenues for reform. The emotional and psychological toll on nurses due to the demands of the pandemic necessitates an urgent focus on interventions that bolster emotional resilience and well-being (Galanis et al., 2021; Wahyuni et al., 2023). By systematically integrating emotional intelligence training within nursing education and supporting the mental health of frontline healthcare workers, we can cultivate a more resilient and responsive healthcare workforce capable of overcoming the challenges of future public health crises (Xu et al., 2021; Yoon et al., 2023; Reis da Silva et al., 2025). Ultimately, acknowledging and addressing the emotional burdens should be a priority in any efforts aimed at improving public health systems, ensuring that both patients and healthcare providers achieve optimal outcomes in care delivery (Simonetti et al., 2020; Rosdyanti et al., 2023).

The conceptual foundations of emotional intelligence and resilience significantly contribute to enriching the competencies needed in today's demanding professional environments, particularly within healthcare. By fostering an educational framework that prioritises these dimensions, organisations can transform their workforce into one that demonstrates higher levels of adaptability and effectiveness amid adversity, ultimately benefiting both healthcare providers and patients alike.

The COVID-19 pandemic has profoundly challenged nursing professionals, revealing the need for transformative competencies rooted in emotional intelligence and resilience. Through the development of the Resilient Emotional Intelligence Framework (REIF) and its core domains, healthcare organisations can better equip nurses to navigate the complexities of their roles while addressing the emotional toll experienced during and after the pandemic. By fostering a supportive and adaptive nursing culture, healthcare leaders can enhance the quality of care while simultaneously safeguarding the emotional functioning of their workforce moving forward.

Cultivating emotional intelligence among public health nurses requires a multifaceted approach that encompasses educational methodologies, organisational support, and effective leadership. By acknowledging the significance of emotional competence in nursing practice, healthcare institutions can enhance workforce resilience, job satisfaction, and ultimately, patient care outcomes.

The integration of emotional intelligence within nursing practice has emerged as a crucial strategy for fostering resilience in the public health workforce, especially in the aftermath of the COVID-19 pandemic. EI serves not only as a competency for managing stress and maintaining personal well-being but also as a pillar for delivering compassionate patient care.

The critical linkage between emotional intelligence, resilience, and the Sustainable Development Goals underscores the necessity of cultivating emotional competencies in nursing. This framework encourages healthcare leaders, educational institutions, and policymakers to foster environments where emotional intelligence can flourish, improving individual and systemic responses to public health challenges. By embedding emotional intelligence within the SDGs-related frameworks, nursing practice can transform to become not only a response mechanism for current and future public health crises but also an agent of sustainable change in health systems. Emphasising the development of emotionally intelligent and resilient nurses is vital for securing a healthier, more equitable, and compassionate future for healthcare globally.

Summary of the Transformative Role of EI in Post-Pandemic Public Health

Emotional intelligence cultivates an environment of mutual understanding and support, paving the way for better collaboration and fewer conflicts among health professionals. As the healthcare landscape evolves, prioritising emotional intelligence can significantly improve the quality of care provided to patients, establishing a compassionate, sustainable nursing system.

Final Reflections on Leadership, Innovation, and Resilience in Nursing Futures

Looking ahead, healthcare leaders must embrace the role of emotional intelligence in shaping resilient organisations that can adapt to future public health challenges. By fostering an innovative culture that values emotional competencies, organisations can enhance operational effectiveness and care delivery while safeguarding the emotional well-being of their workforce. This transformational approach to nursing practice will nurture a healthcare system capable of responding to ongoing and emergent challenges while prioritising the well-being of both patients and providers (Edwar & Sulastri, 2023).

REFERENCES

Assis, C. and França, T. (2023). Anxiety in nurses during the covid-19 pandemic.. DOI: 10.56238/devopinterscie-176

Bălan, I., Traşcă, T., Tulcan, C., Belc, N., Mustăţea, G., Tripon, M., … & Du ă, D. (2024). From safety to security and to food ethics.. https://doi.org/DOI: 10.5772/intechopen.1006089

Bianchi, M., Bressan, V., Cadorin, L., Pagnucci, N., Tolotti, A., Valcarenghi, D., Watson, R., Bagnasco, A., & Sasso, L. (2016). Patient safety competencies in undergraduate nursing students: A rapid evidence assessment. *Journal of Advanced Nursing*, *72*(12), 2966–2979. DOI: 10.1111/jan.13033 PMID: 27222204

Buowari, D. (2022). The well-being of doctors during the covid-19 pandemic.. DOI: 10.5772/intechopen.105609

Castro-Sánchez, E., Russell, A., Dolman, L., & Wells, M. (2021). What place does nurse-led research have in the covid-19 pandemic? *International Nursing Review*, *68*(2), 214–218. DOI: 10.1111/inr.12660 PMID: 33565619

Chemali, Z., Ezzeddine, F., Gelaye, B., Dossett, M., Salameh, J., Bizri, M., Dubale, B., & Fricchione, G. (2019). Burnout among healthcare providers in the complex environment of the middle east: A systematic review. *BMC Public Health*, *19*(1), 1337. Advance online publication. DOI: 10.1186/s12889-019-7713-1 PMID: 31640650

Cheng, C., Humphreys, H., & Kane, B. (2021). Transition to telehealth. Irish Journal of Medical Science (1971 -), 191(5), 2405-2422. DOI: 10.1007/s11845-021-02720-1

Chiu, P., Hawkins, J., Eviza, K., & Gray, S. E. (2022). Nursing and the sustainable development goals: Scaling up and measuring our impact during the decade of action. *Journal of Nursing Scholarship*, *54*(6), 664–667. Advance online publication. DOI: 10.1111/jnu.12791 PMID: 36326148

Cowley, S. A., Tzouvara, V., & Horta Reis da Silva, T. (2023). Public Health: healthy ageing and well-being. In Redfern's Nursing Older People. Fifth edition. Editors: Ross, Harris, Fitzpatrick and Abley. Elsevier.

Crawford, C., Black, P., Melby, V., & Fitzpatrick, B. (2021). An exploration of the predictive validity of selection criteria on progress outcomes for pre-registration nursing programmes—A systematic review. *Journal of Clinical Nursing*, *30*(17-18), 2489–2513. DOI: 10.1111/jocn.15730 PMID: 33655545 da Silva, T. H. R. (2022). Emotional awareness and emotional intelligence. *British Journal of Community Nursing, 27*(12), 573–574. DOI: 10.12968/bjcn.2022.27.12.573 PMID: 36519463

da Silva, T. H. R., & Rodrigues, E. C. P. (2023). Body Image Related Discrimination. In Leal Filho, W., Azul, A. M., Brandli, L., Lange Salvia, A., Özuyar, P. G., & Wall, T. (Eds.), *Reduced Inequalities. Encyclopedia of the UN Sustainable Development Goals*. Springer., DOI: 10.1007/978-3-319-71060-0_61-1

Daher-Nashif, S., & Bawadi, H. (2020). Women's health and well-being in the United Nations sustainable development goals: A narrative review of achievements and gaps in the gulf states. *International Journal of Environmental Research and Public Health, 17*(3), 1059. DOI: 10.3390/ijerph17031059 PMID: 32046109

Dall'Ora, C., Ball, J., Reinius, M., & Griffiths, P. (2020). Burnout in nursing: A theoretical review. *Human Resources for Health, 18*(1), 41. Advance online publication. DOI: 10.1186/s12960-020-00469-9 PMID: 32503559

Desroches, M. (2019). Nurses' attitudes, beliefs, and emotions toward caring for adults with intellectual disabilities: An integrative review. *Nursing Forum, 55*(2), 211–222. DOI: 10.1111/nuf.12418 PMID: 31800106

Dubale, B., Friedman, L., Chemali, Z., Denninger, J., Mehta, D., Alem, A., Fricchione, G. L., Dossett, M. L., & Gelaye, B. (2019). Systematic review of burnout among healthcare providers in sub-Saharan Africa. *BMC Public Health, 19*(1), 1247. Advance online publication. DOI: 10.1186/s12889-019-7566-7 PMID: 31510975

Dugué, M., Sirost, O., & Dosseville, F. (2021). A literature review of emotional intelligence and nursing education. *Nurse Education in Practice, 54*, 103124. DOI: 10.1016/j.nepr.2021.103124 PMID: 34175653

Duong, T. and Nguyen, T. (2023). Impact of emotional intelligence on employees' job performance: a case study of FPT Telecom joint stock company., 3-19. https://doi.org/DOI: 10.2991/978-94-6463-150-0_2

Edwar, R. and Sulastri, M. (2023). The effect of emotional intelligence on organizational citizenship behavior with leader member exchange and employee engagement as mediation variables at the bank Nagari Cabang Utama Padang., 616-632. https://doi.org/DOI: 10.2991/978-94-6463-158-6_54

Edward, K., Hercelinskyj, G., & Giandinoto, J. (2017). Emotional labour in mental health nursing: An integrative systematic review. *International Journal of Mental Health Nursing, 26*(3), 215–225. DOI: 10.1111/inm.12330 PMID: 28374961

Fowler, K., Robbins, L., & Lucero, A. (2021). Nurse manager communication and outcomes for nursing: An integrative review. *Journal of Nursing Management*, *29*(6), 1486–1495. DOI: 10.1111/jonm.13324 PMID: 33793022

Fuente-Solana, E., Pradas-Hernández, L., Ramiro-Salmerón, A., Suleiman-Martos, N., Gómez-Urquiza, J., Albendín-Garcia, L., & Fuente, G. (2020). Burnout syndrome in paediatric oncology nurses: A systematic review and meta-analysis. *Health Care*, *8*(3), 309. DOI: 10.3390/healthcare8030309 PMID: 32872437

Galanis, P., Vraka, I., Fragkou, D., Bilali, A., & Καϊτελίδου, Δ. (2021). Nurses' burnout and associated risk factors during the covid-19 pandemic: A systematic review and meta-analysis. *Journal of Advanced Nursing*, *77*(8), 3286–3302. DOI: 10.1111/jan.14839 PMID: 33764561

Gebreheat, G., & Teame, H. (2021). Ethical challenges of nurses in covid-19 pandemic: Integrative review. *Journal of Multidisciplinary Healthcare*, *14*, 1029–1035. DOI: 10.2147/JMDH.S308758 PMID: 33986597

Giri, S., Chenn, L., & Romero-Ortuño, R. (2021). Nursing homes during the covid-19 pandemic: A scoping review of challenges and responses. *European Geriatric Medicine*, *12*(6), 1127–1136. DOI: 10.1007/s41999-021-00531-2 PMID: 34136990

Gómez-Urquiza, J., Vargas, C., Fuente, E., Castillo, R., & Fuente, G. (2016). Age as a risk factor for burnout syndrome in nursing professionals: A meta-analytic study. *Research in Nursing & Health*, *40*(2), 99–110. DOI: 10.1002/nur.21774 PMID: 27862065

Gong, Z., & Jiao, X. (2019). Are effect sizes in emotional intelligence field declining? a meta-meta analysis. *Frontiers in Psychology*, *10*, 1655. Advance online publication. DOI: 10.3389/fpsyg.2019.01655 PMID: 31379681

Gualano, M., Sinigaglia, T., Moro, G., Rousset, S., Cremona, A., Bert, F., & Siliquini, R. (2021). The burden of burnout among healthcare professionals of intensive care units and emergency departments during the covid-19 pandemic: A systematic review. *International Journal of Environmental Research and Public Health*, *18*(15), 8172. DOI: 10.3390/ijerph18158172 PMID: 34360465

Ha, S., Patlolla, S., & Wojda, T. (2022). Emotional intelligence and leadership development: implications for family medicine residency programs.. https://doi.org/ DOI: 10.5772/intechopen.99463

Hawkins, J. E., Chiu, P., Mumba, M. N., Gray, S. E., & Hawkins, R. J. (2024). Original Research: Nurses' Knowledge and Attitudes Regarding the Sustainable Development Goals: A Global Study. *The American Journal of Nursing*, *124*(7), 18–27. DOI: 10.1097/01.NAJ.0001025184.93381.68 PMID: 38837235

Herrero, M., Thornton, P., Mason-D'Croz, D., Palmer, J., Bodirsky, B., Pradhan, P., Barrett, C. B., Benton, T. G., Hall, A., Pikaar, I., Bogard, J. R., Bonnett, G. D., Bryan, B. A., Campbell, B. M., Christensen, S., Clark, M., Fanzo, J., Godde, C. M., Jarvis, A., & Rockström, J. (2021). Articulating the effect of food systems innovation on the sustainable development goals. *The Lancet. Planetary Health*, *5*(1), e50–e62. DOI: 10.1016/S2542-5196(20)30277-1 PMID: 33306994

Hunsaker, S., Chen, H., Maughan, D., & Heaston, S. (2015). Factors that influence the development of compassion fatigue, burnout, and compassion satisfaction in emergency department nurses. *Journal of Nursing Scholarship*, *47*(2), 186–194. DOI: 10.1111/jnu.12122 PMID: 25644276

Joo, J., & Liu, M. (2021). Nurses' barriers to caring for patients with covid-19: A qualitative systematic review. *International Nursing Review*, *68*(2), 202–213. DOI: 10.1111/inr.12648 PMID: 33420749

Kalánková, D., Kirwan, M., Bartoníčková, D., Cubelo, F., Žiaková, K., & Kurucová, R. (2020). Missed, rationed or unfinished nursing care: A scoping review of patient outcomes. *Journal of Nursing Management*, *28*(8), 1783–1797. DOI: 10.1111/jonm.12978 PMID: 32064694

Katsumata, R. and Teixeira, S. (2024). The importance of developing a growth mindset.. https://doi.org/DOI: 10.56238/sevened2024.029-016

Khatatbeh, H., Pakai, A., Al-Dwaikat, T., Onchonga, D., Amer, F., Prémusz, V., & Oláh, A. (2021). Nurses' burnout and quality of life: A systematic review and critical analysis of measures used. *Nursing Open*, *9*(3), 1564–1574. DOI: 10.1002/nop2.936 PMID: 33991408

König, J., Suwala, L., & Delargy, C. (2021). Helix models of innovation and sustainable development goals., 473-487. DOI: 10.1007/978-3-319-95873-6_91

Kozlowski, D., Hutchinson, M., Hurley, J., Rowley, J., & Sutherland, J. (2017). The role of emotion in clinical decision making: An integrative literature review. *BMC Medical Education*, *17*(1), 255. Advance online publication. DOI: 10.1186/s12909-017-1089-7 PMID: 29246213

Leary, A., & Punshon, G. (2019). Determining acute nurse staffing: A hermeneutic review of an evolving science. *BMJ Open*, *9*(3), e025654. DOI: 10.1136/bmjopen-2018-025654 PMID: 30928944

Lewis, G., Neville, C., & Ashkanasy, N. (2017). Emotional intelligence and affective events in nurse education: A narrative review. *Nurse Education Today*, *53*, 34–40. DOI: 10.1016/j.nedt.2017.04.001 PMID: 28426999

Lievens, F. and Chan, D. (2017). Practical intelligence, emotional intelligence, and social intelligence., 342-364. DOI: 10.4324/9781315690193-15

Lin, W., Hong, C., & Zhou, Y. (2020). Multi-scale evaluation of Suzhou city's sustainable development level based on the sustainable development goals framework.. DOI: 10.37247/PAS.1.2020.12

Lisowska, A. and Rekik, I. (2018). Predicting emotional intelligence scores from multi-session functional brain connectomes., 103-111. DOI: 10.1007/978-3-030-00320-3_13

Llop-Gironés, A., Vračar, A., Llop-Gironés, G., Benach, J., Silva, L., Jaimez, L., & Julià, M. (2021). Employment and working conditions of nurses: Where and how health inequalities have increased during the covid-19 pandemic? *Human Resources for Health*, *19*(1), 112. Advance online publication. DOI: 10.1186/s12960-021-00651-7 PMID: 34530844

Maalouf, N., Sidaoui, A., Elhajj, I., & Asmar, D. (2018). Robotics in nursing: A scoping review. *Journal of Nursing Scholarship*, *50*(6), 590–600. DOI: 10.1111/jnu.12424 PMID: 30260093

Magola, E., Willis, S., & Schafheutle, E. (2017). What can community pharmacy learn from the experiences of transition to practice for novice doctors and nurses? a narrative review. *International Journal of Pharmacy Practice*, *26*(1), 4–15. DOI: 10.1111/ijpp.12349 PMID: 28338242

Marvell, A. and Simm, D. (2021). Encountering emotions during international fieldwork: using innovative pedagogies to develop emotional intelligence and resilience., 57-75. DOI: 10.1007/978-3-030-82087-9_5

Molina-Praena, J., Ramírez-Baena, L., Gómez-Urquiza, J., Cañadas, G., Fuente, E., & Fuente, G. (2018). Levels of burnout and risk factors in medical area nurses: A meta-analytic study. *International Journal of Environmental Research and Public Health*, *15*(12), 2800. DOI: 10.3390/ijerph15122800 PMID: 30544672

Mu, P., Tseng, Y., Wang, C., Chen, Y., Huang, S., Hsu, T., & Florczak, K. (2018). Nurses' experiences in end-of-life care in the PICU: A qualitative systematic review. *Nursing Science Quarterly*, *32*(1), 12–22. DOI: 10.1177/0894318418807936 PMID: 30798753

Ng-Kamstra, J., Greenberg, S., Abdullah, F., Amado, V., Anderson, G., Cossa, M., Costas-Chavarri, A., Davies, J., Debas, H. T., Dyer, G. S. M., Erdene, S., Farmer, P. E., Gaumnitz, A., Hagander, L., Haider, A., Leather, A. J. M., Lin, Y., Marten, R., Marvin, J. T., & Shrime, M. (2016). Global surgery 2030: A roadmap for high income country actors. *BMJ Global Health*, *1*(1), e000011. DOI: 10.1136/bmjgh-2015-000011 PMID: 28588908

Pérez-Francisco, D., Clíments, G., Rosario-Melián, J., Gómez-Salgado, J., Romero-Martín, M., & Gómez, M. (2020). Influence of workload on primary care nurses' health and burnout, patients' safety, and quality of care: Integrative review. *Health Care*, *8*(1), 12. DOI: 10.3390/healthcare8010012 PMID: 31947761

Powell, M., Froggatt, K., & Giga, S. (2019). Resilience in inpatient palliative care nursing: A qualitative systematic review. *BMJ Supportive & Palliative Care*, *10*(1), 79–90. DOI: 10.1136/bmjspcare-2018-001693 PMID: 30808628

Pradas-Hernández, L., Ariza, T., Gómez-Urquiza, J., Albendín-García, L., Fuente, E., & Fuente, G. (2018). Prevalence of burnout in paediatric nurses: A systematic review and meta-analysis. *PLoS One*, *13*(4), e0195039. DOI: 10.1371/journal.pone.0195039 PMID: 29694375

Prezerakos, P. (2018). Nurse managers' emotional intelligence and effective leadership: A review of the current evidence. *The Open Nursing Journal*, *12*(1), 86–92. DOI: 10.2174/1874434601812010086 PMID: 29997711

Ramadhan, F. and Nasution, Y. (2023). The effects of emotional intelligence, perceived organizational support, and workplace stress on turnover intention., 1245-1254. DOI: 10.2991/978-94-6463-234-7_131

Ravenna, J., & Cleaver, K. (2015). School nurses' experiences of managing young people with mental health problems. *The Journal of School Nursing: the Official Publication of the National Association of School Nurses*, *32*(1), 58–70. DOI: 10.1177/1059840515620281 PMID: 26656230

Reis da Silva, T. M. (2025a). Teaching With Adaptability: Cognitive and Pedagogical Strategies for Geriatric Nursing. In Yalçın, M., Uslukaya, A., & Demirdiş, B. (Eds.), *Holistic Approaches to Teacher Development: Leadership, Pedagogical Practices, and Cognitive Insights* (pp. 205–234). IGI Global Scientific Publishing., DOI: 10.4018/979-8-3373-0472-4.ch009

Reis da Silva, T. M. H. (2025b). The Role of Emotional Intelligence in Promoting Mental Peace, Healthy Work Environments, and Emotional Well-Being Among Entrepreneurs. In Tunio, M. N. (Ed.), *Supporting Psychological and Emotional Well-being Among Entrepreneurs*. IGI Global Scientific Publishing., DOI: 10.4018/979-8-3693-3673-1.ch21

Reis da Silva, T. H. (2025c). Exploring loneliness: Conceptualisation and impact in older adults. [DOI: https://doi.org/10.12968/bjcn.2024.0025]. *British Journal of Community Nursing*, *30*(4), 188–195.

Reis da Silva, T. M. (2025d). Appreciative Inquiry in Nursing: Cultivating Flourishing Practices and Sustainable Environments Through Emotional Intelligence. In Benoit, S. (Ed.), *Cultivating Flourishing Practices and Environments by Embracing Positive Education* (pp. 45–78). IGI Global Scientific Publishing., DOI: 10.4018/979-8-3693-9466-3.ch002

Reis da Silva, T. H. (2025e). Emotional intelligence and its role in leadership in health visiting practice. *Journal of Family and Child Health*, *2*(3), 120–125. DOI: 10.12968/jfch.2025.2.3.120

Reis da Silva, T. H. (2025f). Cultivating Emotional Intelligence for Organizational Well-Being: Fostering Happiness and Wisdom in Nursing Education. In Tran, M. (Ed.). (2025). Harnessing Happiness and Wisdom for Organizational Well-Being. IGI Global. https://doi.org/10.4018/979-8-3693-8457-2.ch001

Reis da Silva, T. M. (2025g). Fostering Emotional Resilience and Mindful Leadership in Gerontology Nursing: A Model for Change and Innovation. In Baez, M. (Ed.), *Strategic Approaches to Mindful Leadership and Change Management* (pp. 259–280). IGI Global Scientific Publishing., DOI: 10.4018/979-8-3693-7066-7.ch009

Reis da Silva, T. M. (2025h). The Interplay Between Ethical Work Climate and Employee Well-Being: Navigating the Path to Organisational Integrity and Success. In Ige-Olaobaju, A., Ganiyu, I., Atiku, S., & Olarewaju, O. (Eds.), *Advances in Ethical Work Climate and Employee Well-Being* (pp. 243–268). IGI Global Scientific Publishing., DOI: 10.4018/979-8-3693-8819-8.ch012

Reis da Silva, T. M. (2025i). Cultivating Wellbeing and Happiness in the Workplace: The Role of Emotional Intelligence in Fostering a Positive Organisational Culture. In Agha, K., & Ali, A. (Eds.), *Insights on Wellbeing and Happiness in the Workplace* (pp. 19–44). IGI Global Scientific Publishing., DOI: 10.4018/979-8-3693-2939-9.ch002

Reis da Silva, T. M. (2025j). Fostering Emotional Intelligence for Competency Development in Nursing Education. In Aldosemani, T., Lytras, M., & Ordóñez de Pablos, P. (Eds.), *Innovative Educational Frameworks for Future Skills and Competencies* (pp. 39–62). IGI Global Scientific Publishing., https://doi.org/10.4018/979-8-3693-7555-6.ch002

Reis da Silva, T. H. (2025k). Emotional Intelligence and AI in Geriatric Nursing: Bridging Technology and Compassionate Care. In Jermsittiparsert, K., & Marzo, R. R. (Eds.), *Physical Health, Mental Health, and Human Well-Being in the Age of AI*. IGI Global Scientific Publishing., DOI: 10.4018/979-8-3693-6190-0.ch10

Reis da Silva, T. M. (2025l). Cultivating Emotionally Intelligent Leadership: Strategies for Enhancing Authentic Engagement and Organisational Impact. In Sayed, Z. (Ed.), *Emotionally Intelligent Methods for Meaningful Leadership* (pp. 119–148). IGI Global Scientific Publishing., https://doi.org/10.4018/979-8-3693-7372-9.ch006

Reis da Silva, T. M., Hammett, R., & Low, G. (2025). Emotional Intelligence in Business: Enhancing Leadership, Collaboration, and Performance. In Sedky, A. (Ed.), *Building Business Knowledge for Complex Modern Business Environments* (pp. 149–178). IGI Global Scientific Publishing., DOI: 10.4018/979-8-3693-6447-5.ch006

Reis da Silva, T. H., & Mitchell, A. (2024). Integrating Digital Transformation in Nursing Education: Best Practices and Challenges in Curriculum Development. In Lytras, M., Serban, A. C., Alkhaldi, A., Malik, S., & Aldosemani, T. (Eds.), *Digital Transformation in Higher Education, Part B Cases, Examples and Good Practices*. Emerald Publishing Limited.

Rezaei, S., Matin, B., Hajizadeh, M., Soroush, A., & Nouri, B. (2018). Prevalence of burnout among nurses in Iran: A systematic review and meta-analysis. *International Nursing Review*, *65*(3), 361–369. DOI: 10.1111/inr.12426 PMID: 29380381

Romero-Martín, M., Gómez-Salgado, J., Robles-Romero, J., Jiménez-Picón, N., Gómez-Urquiza, J., & Ponce-Blandón, J. (2019). Systematic review of the nature of nursing care described by using the caring behaviours inventory. *Journal of Clinical Nursing*, *28*(21-22), 3734–3746. DOI: 10.1111/jocn.15015 PMID: 31342576

Rosdyanti, T., Ribhan, R., & Hayati, K. (2023). The effect of implementation in covid-19 protocol and workload: nurses' performance and work motivation as a mediation variable in hospital., 337-348. DOI: 10.2991/978-2-38476-064-0_36

Saarinen, J. (2020). Tourism and sustainable development goals: research on sustainable tourism geographies., 1-10. DOI: 10.1201/9780429324253-1

Safiye, T., Stevanović, A., Zlatanović, M., Vukić, D., Alexopoulos, C., Dubljanin, D., … & Mahmutović, E. (2024). Burnout-related factors in healthcare professionals during the covid-19 outbreak: evidence from Serbia. DOI: 10.5772/intechopen.1004621

Sensor, C. S., Branden, P. S., Clary-Muronda, V., Hawkins, J. E., Fitzgerald, D., Shimek, A. M., Al-Itani, D., Madigan, E. A., & Rosa, W. E. (2021). Nurses achieving the sustainable development goals: The United Nations and Sigma. *The American Journal of Nursing, 121*(4), 65–68. DOI: 10.1097/01.NAJ.0000742544.07615.db PMID: 33755634

Siddiqi, S., Aftab, W., Siddiqui, F., Huicho, L., Mogilevskii, R., Friberg, P., Lindgren-Garcia, J., Causevic, S., Khamis, A., Shah, M. M., & Bhutta, Z. (2020). Global strategies and local implementation of health and health-related sdgs: Lessons from consultation in countries across five regions. *BMJ Global Health, 5*(9), e002859. DOI: 10.1136/bmjgh-2020-002859 PMID: 32900695

Simonetti, A., Pais, C., Jones, M., Cipriani, M., Janiri, D., Monti, L., Landi, F., Bernabei, R., Liperoti, R., & Sani, G. (2020). Neuropsychiatric symptoms in elderly with dementia during covid-19 pandemic: Definition, treatment, and future directions. *Frontiers in Psychiatry, 11*, 579842. Advance online publication. DOI: 10.3389/fpsyt.2020.579842 PMID: 33132939

Singh, C., Cross, W., Munro, I., & Jackson, D. (2020). Occupational stress facing nurse academics—A mixed-methods systematic review. *Journal of Clinical Nursing, 29*(5-6), 720–735. DOI: 10.1111/jocn.15150 PMID: 31856356

Soimah, S. and Utami, S. (2023). The emotional intelligent and social support as predictor of stress at work among nurses during post pandemic., 145-152. DOI: 10.2991/978-94-6463-186-9_18

Suleiman-Martos, N., Gómez-Urquiza, J., Aguayo-Estremera, R., Fuente, G., Fuente-Solana, E., & Albendín-García, L. (2020). The effect of mindfulness training on burnout syndrome in nursing: A systematic review and meta-analysis. *Journal of Advanced Nursing, 76*(5), 1124–1140. DOI: 10.1111/jan.14318 PMID: 32026484

Wahyuni, S., Keliat, B., & Sahar, J. (2023). Phenomenological study of the psychological condition of nurses in covid-19 pandemic., 184-194. DOI: 10.2991/978-94-6463-120-3_28

Webster, N., Oyebode, J., Jenkins, C., Bicknell, S., & Smythe, A. (2019). Using technology to support the emotional and social well-being of nurses: A scoping review. *Journal of Advanced Nursing, 76*(1), 109–120. DOI: 10.1111/jan.14232 PMID: 31599997

Wei, H., Sewell, K., Woody, G., & Rose, M. (2018). The state of the science of nurse work environments in the United States: A systematic review. *International Journal of Nursing Sciences*, *5*(3), 287–300. DOI: 10.1016/j.ijnss.2018.04.010 PMID: 31406839

Xu, H., Stjernswärd, S., & Glasdam, S. (2021). Psychosocial experiences of front-line nurses working in hospital-based settings during the covid-19 pandemic - a qualitative systematic review. *International Journal of Nursing Studies Advances*, *3*, 100037. DOI: 10.1016/j.ijnsa.2021.100037 PMID: 34308373

Yehia, H. and Said, S. (2024). Improving the quality of drinking water by raising the ph levels using a natural na2sio3 physical field.. DOI: 10.5772/intechopen.112856

Yoon, S., Broadwell, P., Sun, F., Planell-Saguer, M., & Davis, N. (2023). Application of topic modeling on artificial intelligence studies as a foundation to develop ethical guidelines in African American dementia caregiving.. https://doi.org/DOI: 10.3233/SHTI230553

Yue, L., Plummer, V., & Cross, W. (2017). The effectiveness of nurse education and training for clinical alarm response and management: A systematic review. *Journal of Clinical Nursing*, *26*(17-18), 2511–2526. DOI: 10.1111/jocn.13605 PMID: 27685951

Zhang, W. and Xiang, X. (2022). The characteristics of SDGS of internet enterprises based on text mining., 348-358. DOI: 10.2991/978-94-6463-005-3_34

Zhang, Y., Han, W., Wen, Q., Yin, H., Zhang, C., Kong, C., & Wang, Y. (2018). Extent of compassion satisfaction, compassion fatigue and burnout in nursing: A meta-analysis. *Journal of Nursing Management*, *26*(7), 810–819. DOI: 10.1111/jonm.12589 PMID: 30129106

KEY TERMS AND DEFINITIONS

Burnout: Burnout is defined as a psychological syndrome resulting from chronic workplace stress, characterised by three key components: emotional exhaustion, depersonalisation, and a sense of reduced personal accomplishment. In nursing, these symptoms can lead to poor job performance and high turnover rates, ultimately jeopardising patient care and nurses' well-being. Maslach and Leiter (2016) provide a comprehensive framework for understanding these phenomena in occupational settings.

Compassion Fatigue: Compassion Fatigue is described as a state of physical and mental exhaustion that can result from prolonged caregiving and exposure to others' suffering. It is often associated with secondary traumatic stress and may lead to a diminished capacity for empathy and compassion. For nurses, compassion fatigue can significantly impact job performance and overall satisfaction in their roles.

Emotional Intelligence (EI): Emotional Intelligence (EI) refers to the capacity to perceive, understand, regulate, and use emotions effectively in oneself and in others (da Silva, 2022). This construct, particularly within the context of nursing, encompasses both trait and ability models of EI. Mayer and Salovey delineate the ability model, suggesting EI comprises a range of skills related to emotional processing and understanding. Goleman, conversely, emphasises the impact of EI on personal and professional success, including its relevance in interpersonal relationships and leadership settings. Emotional intelligence is vital for nursing professionals, aiding in communication and patient care (Reis da Silva et al., 2025).

Moral Injury: Moral injury refers to the psychological harm that can occur when an individual's professional actions violate their personal or ethical values. In nursing, moral injury may manifest when systemic constraints hinder nurses' ability to provide the level of care they believe is necessary or ethical. This often leads to feelings of guilt, shame, and psychological distress.

Post-Traumatic Stress Disorder (PTSD): Post-Traumatic Stress Disorder (PTSD) is a mental health condition that may develop after experiencing or witnessing a traumatic event. Symptoms commonly include flashbacks, avoidance of reminders of the trauma, negative changes in mood, and heightened arousal. In the nursing profession, PTSD can arise from repeated exposure to distressing clinical situations, leading to significant impairments in functioning both personally and professionally.

Resilience: Resilience refers to the capacity of individuals to recover quickly from difficulties and adapt in the face of adversity. Within the context of nursing, resilience is especially important due to the high-stress nature of the profession, where healthcare workers must maintain professionalism and emotional balance despite experiencing considerable systemic and emotional stress. The ability to bounce back not only supports personal well-being but also enhances the delivery of care.

Chapter 8
Artificial Intelligence in Healthcare:
Roles, Challenges, and Disadvantages

Adil Aknouch
https://orcid.org/0000-0003-4340-6687
LICPM Laboratory, Faculty of Sciences and Techniques, Sultan Moulay Slimane University, Morocco

Halima Soussi
https://orcid.org/0009-0003-0735-0097
Mohammed V University, Rabat, Morocco

Youssef El-Ouardi
https://orcid.org/0000-0002-5430-374X
LIMAS Laboratory, Faculty of Sciences, Sidi Mohamed Ben Abdellah University, Morocco

Hasna Belcadi
LAOC Laboratory, Faculty of Sciences, Abdelmalek Essaâdi University, Morocco

Imane Aitouhanni
https://orcid.org/0009-0004-1400-8027
SSLAB, ENSIAS, Mohammed V University, Morocco

Abdeslame Dahbi
Higher Institute of Nursing Professions and Health Techniques, Agadir, Morocco

Khawla Rachmoune
https://orcid.org/0009-0001-6483-1060
ILRBREM, Higher Normal School, Cadi Ayyad University, Morocco

ABSTRACT

This chapter explores the growing role of artificial intelligence (AI) in the healthcare sector, highlighting its applications in key areas such as medical imaging, chronic disease management, pharmaceutical research and massive data analysis. AI, through techniques such as machine learning (ML) and explainable AI (XAI), is helping to

DOI: 10.4018/979-8-3373-1992-6.ch008

transform healthcare practices by offering more personalised and efficient solutions, while reducing costs and optimising processes. However, its adoption raises a number of challenges, including technical, organisational and ethical obstacles relating to the management of sensitive data, the transparency of algorithmic decisions and the problem of bias. The chapter also discusses the drawbacks of AI, such as the black box problem and the risks of exacerbating inequalities in access to care. In conclusion, it emphasises the importance of ethical, responsible and transparent implementation of AI to ensure sustainable improvements in healthcare and the sustainability of healthcare systems.

INTRODUCTION

Global healthcare systems are currently at a critical crossroads, facing increasingly intense financial pressures, with healthcare costs far outstripping GDP growth, jeopardizing the long-term sustainability of these systems (Snowdon, 2020). This has been further compounded by the COVID-19 pandemic in 2019 and the war in Ukraine which have brought to light issues such as an ageing population, increasing incidence of chronic diseases, and the mounting burden placed upon already struggling healthcare systems, unable to keep pace with the increasing demand for their services s (Williams, 2020). Against this backdrop, artificial intelligence (AI) has emerged as a promising solution to some of these challenges, facilitating the digital transformation of the healthcare sector. In contrast, AI has risen as a potentially promising approach to help address some of these challenges and drive the digital transformation of health care. But even if AI can provide clear indications of its potential to improve quality of care, optimize processes and cut costs, there are various technical, organizational and ethical hurdles that must be overcome for it to be fully adopted by healthcare systems.

AI, especially through its sub-fields such as Machine Learning (ML) and Explainable AI (XAI), is at the heart of health care modernization. AI in healthcare including medical imaging, virtual patient care center, drug discovery, and big data analytics provides an opportunity to reinterpret traditional ways of providing care and offers more personalized and effective healthcare delivery (Butcher & Hussain, 2022; Rachmoune et al., 2025). Yet, these technologies also bring concerns, especially about costs deployment, reliability, and issues surrounding the governance and security of the most private health data. And the issues of medical professionals trusting AI and also who is to blame when algorithms get it wrong are still significant barriers preventing mass rollout.

This chapter will investigate the emergent use of AI in health, showcasing its impact in crucial domains including medical imaging, chronic disease management, medical research and patient involvement. At the same time, it considers the technical, ethical and organizational challenges of implementing AI in healthcare systems, in particular with respect to transparency of algorithmic decisions, bias and the impact on healthcare professionals. This chapter also examines the possible dark side of AI, including the black box problem and algorithmic bias, calling for heavy regulation. In this perspective we strive to provide an overview of the opportunities and challenges that AI in the future of healthcare offers and the need for responsible and sustainable deployment of these technologies.

CLARIFICATION OF TERMINOLOGY IN THE CONTEXT OF ARTIFICIAL INTELLIGENCE

AI can be defined as a branch of science and technology aimed at designing intelligent machines that are capable of performing tasks based on algorithms or logical rules that the machine attempts to mimic human cognitive abilities like learning and problem solving (Bajwa et al., 2021a). It usually entails computing technologies that reproduce facilities endowed by human intelligence, including learning, adaptation, reasoning, engagement and sensory understanding (Tagliaferri et al., 2020; Tran et al., 2019). AI refers to the development of computers capable of performing tasks that require human intelligence (e.g., visual perception, speech recognition, decision-making, etc.) and is catalyzing the transformation in health-care due to the increasing volume and digitalization of health data and the rapidly developing analytical techniques (Jiang et al., 2017).

ML, a subset of AI technology, is thought to help speed up and improve the accuracy of doctors' work. It includes various statistical techniques for the computer to learn from experience, without being explicitly programmed. This learning often corresponds to different instances on an algorithm (Javaid et al., 2022). ML is also deployed in medicine to assist professionals in patient and clinical data management. It is an AI application, which requires programming of computers in such a way that they would copy human thinking and learning (Al Kuwaiti et al., 2023).

Natural language processing (NLP) is a subfield of computer science, information engineering, and artificial intelligence concerned with the interactions between computers and human languages (Matthew N. O. Sadiku et al., 2018). Unstructured healthcare data can be captured by NLP methods that can then be analyzing its grammatical structure, interpreting its meaning and translating it so it is understandable for electronic healthcare systems. Further, these methods can lower healthcare expenditures and enhance care quality.

Metaverse is a virtual and augmented reality related 3D domain where people communicate through an avatar (Trunfio & Rossi, 2022). It is an immersive and personalized healthcare combined with the AI, telepresence, blockchain, VR, AR, and digital twins to bring a key impact on the healthcare market (Park & Kim, 2022). Metaverse is especially related to healthcare use cases - from education and research to helping manage diseases - and now is a critical tool for training doctors, he added. Moreover, it permits monitoring of patients in the home environment too and the integration of real and virtual worlds via digital twins (Petrigna & Musumeci, 2022).

Chat Generative Pretrained Transformer (ChatGPT) Is An artificial intelligence (AI) conversational modeling agent that leverage natural language processing (NLP) and machine learning (ML) systems to mimic the way humans converse(Hassani & Silva, 2023). Its core applications in healthcare practice, education and research are promising if the concerns are appropriately handled. It functions like a chatbot - a software that communicates and responds to text (Sallam, 2023). Xu et al (2021) have described the various applications of chatbots in healthcare, including patient support, monitoring and management, tumor diagnosis, screening and treatment.

The Transformer is a crucial deep learning model, which has been extensively applied into multiple domains such as computer vision, NLP, and speech processing (Lin et al., 2022). Applications include electronic health records, medical imaging and COVID-19 detection (He et al., 2023; Li et al., 2023; Shamshad et al., 2023; Shome et al., 2021).

ROLE OF AI IN HEALTHCARE

Medical Imaging and Diagnostic Services

AI is a valuable aid in image analysis and the image-based assessment is increasingly helping radiologists to detect diseases at an early stage, as well as decreasing diagnostic mistakes, especially towards the aim of prevention. It is also useful in the analysis of ECG and echocardiogram, and aids cardiologists in better decision making (Najjar, 2023).

Moreover, AI has held the potential in early detection of pathologies like breast and skin cancer, eye diseases, and pneumonia, especially from body imaging modalities (Rajpurkar et al., 2017). Additionally, several AI applications assess speech styles to forecast psychotic episodes and identify symptoms of a neurological disorder including Parkinson's as well (Dixit et al., 2023). The most relevant study has demonstrated that the Vision Transformer (ViT) significantly outperforms convolutional neural networks (CNN) for analysis of ultrasound images of normal, malignant, and benign breast tissue in the context of medical image classification. In another recent study, an attempt was made to apply ML models to predict the development of diabetes. The two-class decision tree proved to be the best performing prediction model for estimating the factors associated with this disease (Chou et al., 2023).

Various research studies shown that medical imaging modalities such as radiography, computed tomography (CT) and ultrasonography (US), together with AI technologies were a decisive factor in combating COVID-19, in particular for detecting the disease (Gudigar et al., 2021). In their study, approaches such as manual learning of features (HCFL), deep neural networks (DNN) and composite methods were found to be effective in identifying COVID-19 cases. A recent overview also detailed the application of CT scans, X-rays, MRI and ultrasound, X-rays, MRI and ultrasound in the diagnosis of COVID-19, underlining the crucial role of AI in the fight against this virus (Khanna et al., 2022).

In addition, He et al. (2023) have recently mentioned the use of "transformer" models in medical imaging analysis. These deep learning models are currently deployed in the tasks of segmentation, detection and classification, as well for video applications, entailing their reborn importance in this domain. For instance, transformers have been applied to distinguish between COVID-19 and pneumonia with X-ray and CT images, which can aid in the fast and efficient treating of COVID-19 (Tulder et al., 2021). Another work suggested a hybrid approach including thoracic CT and using wavelet-based Renyi entropy (WRE) and 3-segment biogeographic optimization algorithm (3SBBO). This hybrid WRE that allows for feature extraction, a feed forward neural network (FNN) classification, and 3-SBBO for weights and biases optimization. This model significantly beats other competitors, e.g., extreme kernel-based ML or bat-based algorithm, in the COVID-19 detection (S.-H. Wang et al., 2020).

But AI, especially GANs, is transforming radiology. These include GANs with a generator and a discriminator, which enable better detection or image synthesis (Figure 1) (Wolterink et al., 2021). They can also be used for medical education by creating simulated clinical cases, e.g. distinguishing a lower lobe collapse from a consolidation. In clinical studies they allow for the formation of artificial placebo groups, and cut costs of clinical trials (Arora & Arora, 2022).

ChatGPT used by the public for medical advice AI models such as ChatGPT-3 are used by the public for medical advice. These calculators can only provide estimates and, like any estimate, are not a substitute for professional advice. In the US, approximately one third of adults searched online for self-diagnosis, and almost one third of these obtained medical confirmation from a professional (Shahsavar & Choudhury, 2023).

"The medical and AI metaverse" (MeTAI) is another trend driven by the introduction of AI to medicine. This encompasses for example 'virtual comparative scans', 'raw data sharing' and enhanced medical interventions. As an example, realistic patient specific medical data can be generated to optimize a real scan and shared with a patient's medical team upon consent. Despite being promising, this model is challenged by the issues of security, access inequality, investment, and privacy (G. Wang et al., 2022). The implementation of AI in medical imaging and clinical decision-making enables practitioners to process larger quantities of data, improve the quality of diagnosis and facilitate therapeutic choices. However, limitations do exist, particularly with regard to the biased assessment of results or the overdiagnosis of minor anomalies (Oren et al., 2020).

Figure 1. AI in medical imaging and diagnosis

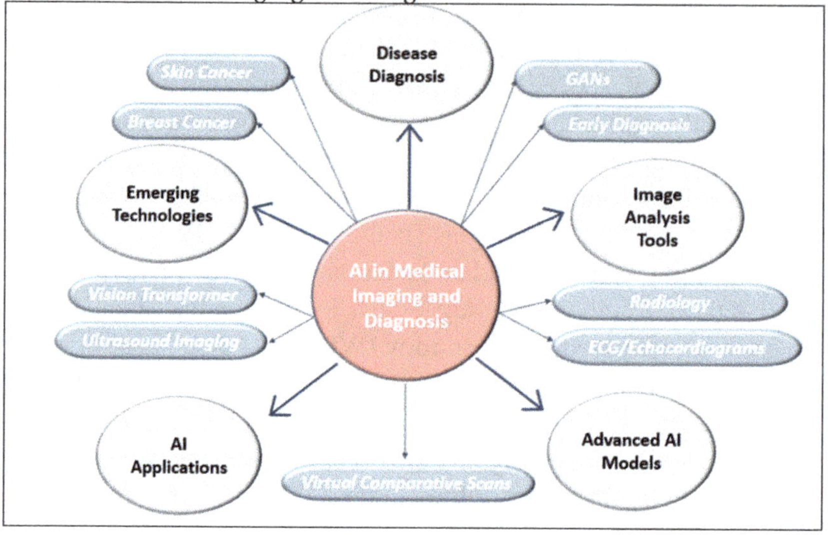

Virtual Patient Care

The study highlighted the importance of wearable technology combined with AI/ML to improve patient care (Baig et al., 2017). An intelligent sensor system for a telehealth service designed to monitor patients' health by collecting physical parameters such as respiratory rate, pulse, blood pressure and ECG data has been presented by Wear what can provide virtual care, for managing chronic patients, such as diabetes hypertension and sleep apnea, using non-invasive sensors (Kim et al., 2018; Monteriù et al., 2018). The system comprises a set of biomedical sensors worn on the body and connected to a smartphone that stores the data in the cloud for advanced analysis, targeted at elderly care. In another case, atrial fibrillation was diagnosed using a wearable device, underlining the usefulness of these tools for accurate diagnosis (Patel & Tarakji, 2021).

In the field of mental health, ML predictive models have been applied to predict emotional states from mobile sensor data despite the presence of missing data (Sükei et al., 2021). Wearable devices have become indispensable during this epidemic for real-time monitoring of cases and early detection of at-risk COVID-19 cases, enabling close surveillance of the epidemic (Natarajan et al., 2020). Another study showed the importance of AI in remote care, while the metaverse application offers new possibilities such as augmented reality to enhance telemedicine (Bajwa et al., 2021a; Garavand & Aslani, 2022).

Remote Patient Monitoring (RPM), a subset of telehealth, is the term generally used to define the process used by healthcare providers to monitor a patient's condition remotely through sensors and communication technologies. RPM can facilitate the monitoring of vital signs and treatment of diseases through motor disorders and psychiatric diseases (Shaik et al., 2023). This dynamic, it must be said, increased during the COVID-19 pandemic, thanks to platforms such as CareSimple and Telecare COVID, which enabled care to continue (Bouabida et al., 2021). RPM systems use AI to change care by identifying decline early and personalizing patient follow up. However, they are hindered by problems such as confidentiality, data scale, the issue of unbalanced datasets and signal processing (Shaik et al., 2023).

In addition, ChatGPT, an AI-assisted language model, acts as a virtual assistant for patients, answering their medical questions, summarizing their health data and helping them book appointments. It also provides self-monitoring reminders to patients, as well as notifications to HCPs of abnormal vital signs. Although ChatGPT-4 holds promise for chronic disease management and treatment adherence, concerns remain regarding ethics, data security and liability (Sezgin, 2024).

However, systems for wearable patient monitoring (WPM) encounter limitations, including data connectivity, end-user acceptance, and costs associated with prolonged use of mobile data. Educating patients and physicians is crucial to the success of these systems (Baig et al., 2017).

Medical Research and Drug Discovery

AI is extremely useful in the analysis of big and complex data sets, the kind used in medical research (Al Kuwaiti et al., 2023). It is likewise useful to study scientific work, manage heterogeneous data and to assist in pharmaceutical innovation (Hakimi et al., 2024). AI is becoming a popular tool for drugmakers to simplify the process of getting medications to market. Predictive analytics can help data scientists with patient's selection for clinical trials and for modeling the biologic processes (Al Kuwaiti et al., 2023).

In clinical investigations, ML is involved in the initial phases of patient cohort identification, patient structuring and data collection. It enhances the patient-centered perspective, generalizability, speed and quality of clinical trials. ML must, to be sure, be the subject of further study to determine its real and philosophical limits in this field. In addition, NLP may have potential for monitoring clinical trial participants, but its impact on trial quality and participant experience remains to be determined. Further research is needed to compare different methods of escalating participant management (Weissler et al., 2021). Also, generative AI can be employed to generate synthetic data to augment the datasets and make them more diverse (Arora & Arora, 2022). More recently, "metaverse" applications have even enabled us to conduct trials in a controlled immersive environment, with geographically dispersed researchers collaborating as if they were in a virtual office (Suh et al., 2023).

ChatGPT takes clinical trial data, literature and critical results and summarizes them, enabling researchers to efficiently browse information online(Khan et al., 2023). In medical research, it can translate medical language for researchers, but the application of it involves in ethical issues (Javaid et al., 2023). In drug discovery, AI, through ML, bioinformatics and chemoinformatic, decreases costs and development time (Al Kuwaiti et al., 2023). For example, AI-enabled scientific robot, Eve, that can find new drugs faster and more cheaply than TTDL, AI is increasingly involved in the identification of candidate molecules (Son, 2018).

AI-enabled major successes, including the drug DG12P1 for a rare Wilson's disease by Deep Genomics (Al Kuwaiti et al., 2023). It can unearth drug targets, explore the potential of compounds, construct drug structures, and reprofile compounds for applications, and thereby accelerate the process of drug trials (Mak & Pichika, 2019). ChatGPT also supports the digestion of large amounts of scientific evidences, facilitating new idea (Chen, 2023).

AI is also used for virtual drug screening using algorithms such as Extreme ML, Deep Neural Networks (DNN), Random Forests (RF), SVM and Nearest Neighbour Classifier (Álvarez-Machancoses & Fernández-Martínez, 2019). In vaccinology, AI recognizes the critical parts of a virus, such as spike protein, to elicit strong immune activation (Sharma et al., 2022). Moreover, it has supported the genomic sequencing of SARS-CoV-2 and innovation in the discovery of vaccines and treatments for COVID-19 (Abubaker Bagabir et al., 2022).

Patient Involvement and Compliance

The final frontier between low and high health outcomes is active participation and patient adherence, the "last mile" of healthcare. A violation represents a patient's refusal to comply with a treatment plan or to take medication as prescribed. Greater patient involvement in their care is linked to better health outcomes, greater compliance with healthcare services, lower costs and better patient experience (Davenport & Kalakota, 2019). Although being actively engaged and involved in one's healthcare process is generally perceived as beneficial, a survey of healthcare executives and managers revealed that only 46% said their patients were strongly involved in the process of defining and developing their treatment plans (Davenport & Kalakota, 2019).

Physicians use their clinical judgment to tailor treatment plans toward patients' acutely or chronically altered health status. All of their efforts are easily defeated, however, if patients don't make the necessary changes in behavior by, e.g., managing their weight, scheduling return visits or following the doctors order for care (Davenport & Kalakota, 2019). These limitations have favored AI which can help with increasing patient engagement. More recently, ML and workflow engines are being harnessed to manage sophisticated interventions and tailor the entire continuum of care (Volpp & Mohta, 2016). Messaging alarms and customized content that encourages the correct actions at the correct time is one avenue of study with potential (Davenport & Kalakota, 2019).

Further, ChatGPT has been deployed in healthcare-related interfaces for automating the writing of summaries, notes and reports, making these processes faster and more efficient. It also helps patients in carrying out features like symptom checker, appointment booking, drug control and treatment adherence. It also serves as an important instrument in patient education and self-management of chronic illness, increasing patient involvement and compliance (Javaid et al., 2023).

Rehabilitation

AI provides novel applications in rehabilitation, that could be physical (robotics) and virtual (computer science) aspects (Figure 2). A subset of AI, ML, enables algorithms to get better with practice. Within rehabilitation, ML is used in perioperative medicine, brain-computer interfaces, myoelectric control, and symbiotic neuroprostheses. An ML is also employed in evaluation of patient data, clinical decision support and diagnostic image analysis. Artificial cognitive methods rate rehabilitation exercises using machine signals (Anderson, 2019).

There is a revolution in rehabilitation research happening because of technological advancements that are changing intervention strategies and professional competencies. For example, smart homes assist the occupants in their daily life and notify carers when necessary. Furthermore, mobile and wearable based data collection system to monitor health improvement and personalized rehabilitation goals have been developed (Luxton & Riek, 2019). They utilize inertial sensors of wearable devices to ensure the exercise's proper performance (Goldzweig et al., 2013). In supervised learning approaches have been exploited to evaluate the issue of detecting exercise accuracy via neural network using an Apple iWatch, achieving 99.4% recognition which demonstrates the potentiality of ML and wearable sensors for exercise monitoring. The use of wearables on its own may be insufficient for increasing adherence because of issues related to exercise efficacy (Sinsky et al., 2016)

Physical or social robots can be used to support people's rehabilitation, helping them overcome defects, either cognitive, motor or sensory ones. Such technologies have been seen as important in enhancing patients' agency, ability and quality of life (Luxton & Riek, 2019). Patients with musculoskeletal dysfunction have been relieved by simple mechanized mobilization through robotic hands practiced. However, their long-term usefulness still remains to be shown (Choi et al., 2018). Aggarwal & Ganvir (2021) suggested that AI-enabled robots could monitor the perfection of patient movements and help them perform more efficient movements in the future.

A study suggests that healthcare professionals could fill the gap in rehabilitation services by using an AI tool, such as ChatGPT, to offer personalised assistance and keep patients engaged (Maggio et al., 2024). It could also help stroke and head injury patients practice their speech and language skills. Such technology is easily accessible via digital devices in and out of the home. Research has revealed that a language model such as ChatGPT, trained to rephrase text in an empathetic way, could improve communication in a mental health support system and enhance the conversational skills of non-experts. It also points to the possibility of using human-IA partnerships to enhance community tasks based on self- or peer-managed therapies, such as cognitive-behavioral therapy (Sharma et al., 2023).

Neurorehabilitation in Metavers includes advanced systems such as motor function classification, materials-based rewards, and AI-assisted rehabilitation exercises, also reducing the risk of transmission of COVID-19. (Nadarzynski et al., 2019). A recent study demonstrated that physiotherapy in the Metaverse (MPT) improves cardiopulmonary and motor function while reducing the perceived risk of infection in children affected by cerebral palsy (CP), compared with conventional physiotherapy (Moon et al., 2023).

AI is also used for gait analysis, where ML can automatically detect gait abnormalities and associated pathologies, such as osteoarthritis or Parkinson's disease (Kidziński et al., 2019). In physiotherapy at home, digital technologies enable real-time monitoring with virtual therapists for personalized advice (Aggarwal & Ganvir, 2021). In addition, a study has proposed remote-assisted neurofunctional therapy, enabling stroke victims to continue their care at home after hospitalization, with minimal supervision (Lambercy et al., 2021). These technologies, however, need to meet technical criteria such as safety, practicality, and robustness to ensure their effectiveness and adoption by patients. A transparent, clinically motivated, patient-friendly approach is essential to ensure patient engagement in this type of rehabilitation (Neibling et al., 2021). Home-assisted technology rehabilitation has been crucial during and after the COVID-19 pandemic, providing intensive, sustainable and accessible therapies, contributing to long-term functional improvement and patient independence (Lambercy et al., 2021).

In the field of fitness medicine, AI represents a promising opportunity for wearable technologies. AI algorithms can analyze sensor data to monitor physiological measurements and kinematic parameters and offer recommendations for improving athletes' performance. They can also optimize injury prediction models, improve diagnostic accuracy, stratify risk, continuously monitor health data and enrich the patient experience. However, the adoption of AI in wearable devices faces several challenges, including missing data, social and economic biases, data security issues, outliers, noise in signals and difficulties in obtaining high-quality data (Chidambaram et al., 2022). For instance, heart rate sensors can be affected by physical movements, requiring advanced technologies to guarantee reliable data (Chidambaram et al., 2022). Another major obstacle is user acceptability. Studies show that nearly 50% of consumers abandon the use of mobile devices within six months of acquisition (Soliño-Fernandez et al., 2019). An early study reported that 50% of patients saw the use of AI in wearable technology as a significant opportunity, while 11% considered it harmful. Patients were concerned that technology would exploit and hijack their data and affect the human aspect of healthcare. Consequently, patient education on how AI supports clinicians, as well as its capabilities and limitations, is needed to improve acceptance and adoption of AI (Tran et al., 2019).

Figure 2. AI in rehabilitation

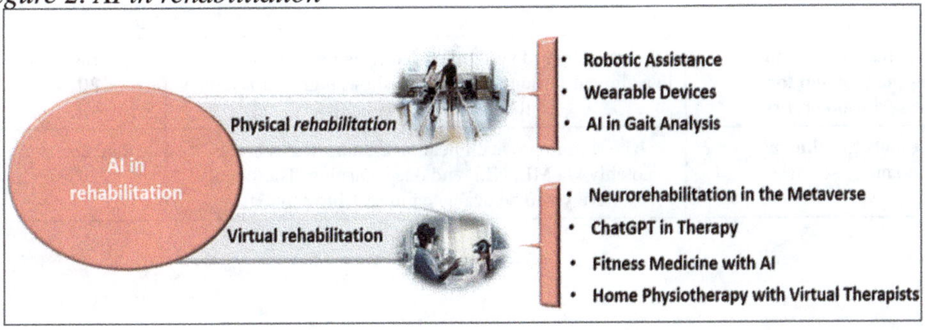

Administrative Applications

AI and ML have the potential to transform healthcare administration by automating various tasks, freeing up time for healthcare professionals and improving the efficiency of healthcare systems. These technologies are being applied in a variety of fields, such as electronic medical record (EMR) management, claims management, workflow automation and improved pharmaceutical services. Table 1 presents the main applications of AI in healthcare administration, as well as the studies that have contributed to these advances.

Table 1. Applications of AI in healthcare administration

AI application	Description	References
Reducing administrative burdens (EHR)	AI assists in automatically populating structured data fields from therapy notes and past medical records. ML-based systems can improve data accuracy compared with rule-based systems.	(Li et al., 2020; G. Wang et al., 2022)
Optimizing time for doctors and nurses	Speech recognition for transcription of text, reducing time spent on administrative tasks such as regulatory and paperwork.	(Wani et al., 2022)
BEHRT (bi-directional EHR representation model)	Using the BEHRT model to improve predictions of a patient's future conditions using different types of embeddings, such as age, visits and events.	(Li et al., 2020)
Hi-BEHRT (modèle Hiérarchique)	Improved version of BEHRT, which uses a transform-based model to predict risk in patients with a long clinical history.	(Lin et al., 2022)
ML use in insurance claims	AI technologies, such as ML, are applied for data reconciliation and claims verification, helping to reduce errors and uncover incorrect claims.	(Wani et al., 2022)
ML-based decision support system for prescription errors	ML-based hybrid system for detecting prescription errors in a clinical setting. This system showed greater accuracy than traditional systems.	(Corny et al., 2020)
AI tools for clinical pharmacy services	AI use to improve clinical pharmaceutical services, notably via ML, NLP and deep learning. These tools have yet to be evaluated in real-life contexts.	(Ranchon et al., 2023)

THE CHALLENGES OF AI UTILIZATION IN THE HEALTHCARE SECTOR

Governance Challenges

Ethical Principles

While building digital health technologies, those building them should consider the conditions required to ensure patient safety, privacy, traceability, accountability, and security. Also emergency measures should be prepared to deal with potential violations as follows (Mennella et al., 2024; Paul et al., 2023; Shojaei et al., 2024).

In 2019, the World Health Organization (WHO) initiated the development of a toolkit to facilitate the adoption of digital health interventions and technologies. The WHO principles for evaluating digital health technologies highlight the need to evaluate these technologies with respect to their effects, risks (potential harms and benefits), acceptability, feasibility, resource use, and equity. These guidelines are a reflection that digital tools are indeed essential enablers of UHC and part of a sustainable long-term future (Mauro et al., 2024; Yeung et al., 2023). The ethical principles for applying AI in healthcare aim to guide developers, users and regulators on how new tools should be developed and used, how risks should be managed and how they should be held to account.

Human dignity and the intrinsic value of every human person are the founding principles of all ethics. These core values are reflected and encompassed by the principles that underpin the responsibilities and obligations encompassing the development, deployment and continued oversight of AI in healthcare. The EC Regulation, emitted at 21 April 2021, accurately ranked the AIs products based on the level of risk they offer to fundamental rights, such as health and safety, dignity, freedom, equality, democracy, right to be free of discrimination and data protection (Akinci D'Antonoli, 2020; Mennella et al., 2024).

Because of this classification, ethical guidelines are key for everyone who play a role in purposeful development, introduction, and assessment of AI-based applications in health care. This diverse range is composed of doctors, system developers, system administrators, decision makers and local and central governments. Ethical considerations should be one of such catalysts to help governments and public-sector agencies respond to fast-moving AI technology advancements with sound legislation and regulation. Moreover, these guidelines should empower anyone in the medical community to exercise informed discretion in using AI technologies in the practice of medicine (Harishbhai Tilala et al., 2024).

In the context of using AI for the social good, the literature has defined six basic principles to guide the ethical development of AI technologies. Some of these are principles from bioethics such as beneficence and nonmaleficence, autonomy, and justice. Further principles draw on moral and legal norms and the importance of preserving AI intelligibility (Varkey, 2021).

This includes the obligation to specify what the technology in question does and the obligation to track cause-and-effect patterns arising from AI activity. Furthermore, such principles point to the value of privacy and its protection of individuals from persons and institutions: enabling individuals to retain control over information about themselves that they do not wish to share with others, which in turn is essential to preserving individuals' ability to pursue a life of their own choosing, preserving their dignity as autonomous agents (Mennella et al., 2024).

Regulatory Challenges

AI governance for healthcare: a framework to guide ethical and social implications of artificial intelligence in clinical and consumer health †? AI governance in healthcare is a critical framework that has been designed to govern and to shape the introduction of AI across a spectrum of health applications. It refers to a broad set of policies, norms, and practices designed to make sure that health care providers use AI technologies responsibly, safely, and effectively. In view of the rapid development of AI techniques and the growing application of AI-based systems in healthcare, governance is important for setting standards, protecting patient data, and ensuring that the implementation of AI within healthcare is in line with its wider goals.

This issue is so important for the governance of AI in healthcare while the issues are much more salient and distinct in this sector comparing to other sectors. Challenges include that of ensuring AI-driven diagnostics are accurate and reliable, and that the confidentiality and security of sensitive health data is maintained, as well as mitigating the risk of any biases in AI algorithms which could lead to patients being treated unfairly. In addition, healthcare AI must adhere to an intricate set of regulations and ethical guidelines, which vary by location, and are ever changing. Hence, the strong governance frameworks are required to effectively manage these complexities (Palaniappan et al., 2024).

AI governance for healthcare also plays an important role in trust building and acceptability among patients, and healthcare practitioners and the general public. Trust forms the basis for effective deployment of AI in healthcare and influences directly patient engagement and health care professionals' trust in insights it extracts. A well-organized decision-making process can help to make sure that the stakeholders be willing to use AI tools, in a way that is in line with patient autonomy, privacy protection and ethical considerations, and promote its acceptance and incorporation (Maleki Varnosfaderani & Forouzanfar, 2024).

Right now, AI governance in healthcare is a patchwork of national and international regulations, industry norms and ethics. There are different organizations and regulators contributing to the definition of these standards, from healthcare regulators, to AI ethics boards, to international organizations such as the World Health Organization. These organizations are committed to generating a proportionate AI governance framework by encouraging innovation and AI technology development on the one hand while safeguarding patient well-being and ensuring equal opportunity to benefit from AI-based health solutions on the other (Lan & Huy, 2021; Morley et al., 2022).

Looking ahead, AI governance in healthcare is likely to continue evolving in response to advancing technologies and expanding applications. This could involve the creation of more advanced regulatory frameworks, increased international collaboration to establish global standards, and sustained efforts to address emerging ethical and privacy concerns. Moreover, as AI becomes further integrated into healthcare systems, there will likely be a stronger focus on educating both healthcare professionals and patients about AI, its benefits, and its limitations. This education will be a crucial component of effective AI governance moving forward (Bajwa et al., 2021b).

AI in healthcare is a paradigm shift in the way health service is delivered and managed. But there are a lot of regulatory issues that come with this innovation. Regulatory discrepancies, the speed of technological development, issues of data privacy and security, and ethical concerns are all formidable challenges towards the real and proper use of AI in healthcare (Siala & Wang, 2022).

One of the biggest obstacles to AI's development in healthcare is non-standardization of regulatory paths across the countries. This spotty – at best – uniformity is a muddy environment for global healthcare companies to work in, as companies need to comply with a patchwork of requirements and regulations. For instance, the European Union's General Data Protection Regulation (GDPR) imposes rigorous data processes that aren't necessarily present in US or other regions' regulations. These variations complicate the development and the deployment of AI systems, since companies are required to ensure compliance with several regulatory environments. This could result in more expensive and more complicated AI solutions to design and deploy. Discovering ways to capitalize on mHealth and AI solutions in developing countries is a key challenge. However, the variations of standards manly caused by Organizations in pursuit of immersive likeness, present a major barrier to innovation and limit the global exchange of AI-based healthcare technologies (Lan & Huy, 2021).

The pace with which AI technology is developing also adds to the regulatory clutter. AI in healthcare is advancing rapidly making it outstripping the existing healthcare regulations. This lapse, critics point out, can leave literal holes in oversight, potentially allowing new AI applications to come to market without due regulatory diligence. These gaps also raise concerns about AI tools in healthcare in terms of both safety and effectiveness as well as ethical concerns. The hurdle for policymakers is developing flexible and adaptive frameworks to pace with technological evolution without stifling innovation (Khalid et al., 2023).

Another major concern in the use of AI in healthcare is data privacy and security. AI systems generally rely on copious amounts of sensitive patient data, presenting important considerations regarding data protection and potential breaches. It is further complicated by the inconsistency of laws governing the protection of data from patients on a global basis. These worries are not merely speculative—there have been multiple occasions in which health organizations have suffered data breaches, leading to exposure of patient privacy. It is critical that AI systems be protected from cyber threats and access by unauthorized parties to preserve the trust of the public and the sanctity of healthcare(Yadav et al., 2023).

There are many ethical aspects and concerns surrounding the use of AI in healthcare. A major issue is the possibility of algorithmic bias that can lead to disparate care between patient populations. For example, if an AI system is trained on data that doesn't well reflect the diversity of the patient population, it may give less reliable — or even wrong — output for underrepresented groups. A further issue, by no means the last, is the fair access to AI-facilitated healthcare innovations. Such technology could actually perpetuate healthcare disparity when it remains available only to those who can afford it, or to a few more economically developed areas, thus leaving others underserved (Lan & Huy, 2021).

Technical Challenges

From a technical point of view, AI models need to be simple so that healthcare professionals (HCPs) can use them effectively. However, the adoption of AI in healthcare faces several barriers, such as lack of IT infrastructure, high costs of data storage and backup, and data validation (Tachkov et al., 2022). In addition, AI algorithms can suffer from bias, fragility and poor generalizability (Marcus, 2018). It is essential to take into account variations in datasets, unintended biases in clinical practice, interpretability of algorithms and confidence in models (Kelly et al., 2019). Thus, a comprehensive strategic plan is needed to overcome these challenges.

In addition, HCPs may be wary of AI due to unidentified risks, a barrier to adoption. Explainable AI (XAI) solutions are proposed to build trust (Giuste et al., 2023). According to Choudhury and Asan (Choudhury & Asan, 2022), factors such as risk, workload and willingness to receive training influence clinicians' perceptions of AI. The lack of accountability of AI is also a barrier to its adoption. It is therefore recommended that AI training be integrated into medical and nursing curricula.

As with the human brain, AI systems process inputs and generate outputs, but HCPs are unaware of the systems' internal processes, posing a "black box" problem. Making HCPs responsible for AI errors could hinder its adoption. It is therefore crucial to develop protection policies and improve professionals' perception of the risks and expectations of AI. In addition, a user-friendly and clinically relevant interface is essential, as is stakeholder engagement to understand clinical needs before promoting AI in healthcare.

DISADVANTAGES OF AI IN HEALTHCARE

AI in healthcare AI has completely changed the way healthcare is administered, including how diagnoses are made, treatments are chosen, and administrative duties are carried out. However, there are risks and hazards associated with all of this progress. This article addresses the main challenges that AI applications in healthcare face, highlighting issues such as data security and privacy, lost employment opportunities, automation transparency, and the critical reliance on high-quality data that should not be overlooked in the discussion. By addressing these issues, this paper seeks to provide a rational viewpoint to support the ethical and responsible integration of AI in healthcare. Artificial intelligence has brought a revolution in the health sector which is providing help and assisting in precise medicine, early diagnosis, and patient predictions. Nonetheless, AI is not without its challenges when applied. This article analyses the major disadvantages of AI in health with a focus on limitations and risks, including data security, job displacement, explainability, and dependence on good-quality data (Salomon & Olivier, 2024a).

Data Privacy and Security Concerns

Difficulties with Accessing Data Large datasets are necessary for the proper operation of AI systems, especially machine learning and deep learning algorithms. Strict confidentiality regulations and opposition to data sharing present significant challenges for healthcare organizations when it comes to granting access to patient data. These datasets are frequently unusable after algorithms are trained, which hinders iterative advancements in AI models (Morris, 2020).

Cybersecurity Threats

Healthcare records, being both sensitive and valuable, are frequent targets of cyberattacks. Breaches can expose patients' personal and medical information, resulting in severe consequences for individuals and institutions. Ensuring robust data security measures is paramount to maintaining trust and protecting patient confidentiality (Morris, 2020).

Risks of Overfitting and Data Leakage

AI algorithms may overfit training data, identifying patterns that do not generalize well to real-world scenarios. Overfitting can lead to inaccurate diagnoses and treatment recommendations. Additionally, data leakage where AI models predict outcomes beyond their training scope undermine the reliability of predictions and raise ethical concerns about unintended consequences (Morris, 2020).

Lack of Transparency and Explainability

The Black-Box Problem AI models in general, and deep learning systems in particular, typically function as "black boxes," which obscures reasons behind their decisions. This opacification makes validation of the recommendations of AI systems difficult and may lead health professionals to resist using them (Salomon & Olivier, 2024b).

Effect on Trust Patients and healthcare providers would lose trust in AI systems that are unable to articulate how they came to a particular decision. The lack of transparency may lead patients to be reluctant towards the uptake of AI-supported care and caregivers to be hesitant about using AI-based recommendations for life-and-death decisions (Salomon & Olivier, 2024b).

Job Displacement and Workforce Challenges

Automation and Job Loss

The future of automation and job displacement The automation of repetitive medical and administrative tasks by AI has the potential to replace some jobs in healthcare. The work that had been the traditional responsibility of radiologists, pathologists, and administrative staff is slowly being automated which is also leading to alarm about job security(Amisha et al., 2019).

Costs and Training Costs

Healthcare workers need thorough training of AI systems to effectively use them. The expensive nature of such training and infrastructure for deploying AI further contribute to such inequity by primarily allowing these developments to penetrate resource-rich sites (Amisha et al., 2019).

Dependence on High-Quality Data

The demand for clean data AI systems depend heavily on the quality of their datasets in order to function accurately. Mistakes or prejudices in the training information drive defective diagnoses and treatment suggestions. The quality of AI outcomes is deeply rooted in the quality of the data that supplies the system (Holzinger et al., 2019).

Contemporary challenges of data scarcity Healthcare datasets are commonly incomplete, inconsistent, or not representative of diverse populations. This shortage of strong data is critical to the progress and efficacy of AI systems, that too generalize across different clinical situations (Holzinger et al., 2019).

Ethical and Practical Concerns

Dehumanization of Medicine There is the danger of dehumanization of medicine. AI is excellent at working with data, but it doesn't have the empathy and emotional intelligence that humans have as clinicians. The loss of this human connection could undermine the quality of patient care and disrupt the doctor-patient relationship as we know it.

Resource Allocation Injustice The expense associated with the development and deployment of AI tends to place small and low-resource healthcare organisations at a disadvantage compared with their richer counterparts in terms of the scale and sophistication of these technologies. Smaller hospitals and less well funded systems will have difficulty implementing such innovations leading to increasing health inequality (Salomon & Olivier, 2024b).

Financial and Operational Challenges

High Costs of Development The development and deployment of AI applications are costly. Software development to infrastructure updates – the cost may simply be too great, especially for smaller health systems.

Validation in clinical settings the majority of AI studies are done in non-clinical and controlled environments, making it difficult to generalize their findings to actual healthcare settings. In addition, the small number of high-quality clinical trials about AI tools continues to limit their endorsement and utilization (Salomon & Olivier, 2024b).

Strategies for Responsible AI Adoption

Regulatory Environments The adoption of regulatory proposals to oversee the ethical and effective implementation of AI in healthcare is critical. These would include data privacy and security policies and accountability measures, so that AI is a tool to complement, not displace, healthcare workers.

Encourage Human-AI Cooperation To ease the threat on their jobs, emphasis should be placed on human-AI collaboration, where AI supports healthcare personnel's work. AI can help optimize all non-clinical areas of practice management, so that time-consuming administrative tasks can be streamlined making way for more time spent on delivering care to patients.

Investment in Research and Education Continued investing in AI research and education of healthcare professionals is necessary. Ethical AI should be highlighted in educational programs, training a workforce that can optimize technology and stay patient-centric (Morris, 2020).

CONCLUSION

AI is being used across different fields of healthcare, including medical imaging, diagnosis, virtual care, patient engagement and administrative burden on healthcare providers. They are also advancing medicines and vaccines, tracking patient adherence to treatments and analyzing gait in technology-enabled rehabilitation. AI is now confronted with numerous technical, ethical and governance issues such as data security and privacy. Factors that might limit the application of the algorithm include the quality of health care data currently available and the inability to mimic certain human characteristics/emotions, e.g., empathy. The power of AI is great when it is working, however AI isn't going to replace the relationships that are required for solid team work. One important concern for the future of AI in healthcare is to guarantee its development and adoption to serve the interests of people, without ignoring technical, ethical as well as social issues. This chapter reviews the utilization of AI in a broad spectrum of healthcare specialties, detailing the ethical, social, and technical barriers of acceptance among healthcare providers.

AUTHORS' CONTRIBUTIONS

Adil Aknouch: Coordinated the project, led the chapter design, and contributed to the writing of all sections.

Halima Soussi: Contributed to writing the section *"The Challenges of AI Utilization in the Healthcare Sector"* and contributed to the final revision of the chapter.

Youssef El-Ouardi: Contributed to the conceptualization, revision, and drafting of key sections, as well as the final revision of the chapter.

Hasna Belcadi: Contributed to writing the section *"Disadvantages of AI in Healthcare"* and participated in the final revision of the chapter.

Imane Aitouhanni: Contributed to writing the section *"Role of AI in Healthcare"* and participated in the final revision of the chapter.

Abdeslame Dahbi: Reviewed and corrected the medical information presented, and contributed to the final revision of the chapter.

Khawla Rachmoune: Contributed to writing the section *"Role of AI in Healthcare,"* participated in project coordination, and was involved in the final revision.

REFERENCES

Abubaker Bagabir, S., Ibrahim, N. K., Abubaker Bagabir, H., & Hashem Ateeq, R. (2022). Covid-19 and Artificial Intelligence : Genome sequencing, drug development and vaccine discovery. *Journal of Infection and Public Health, 15*(2), 289–296. DOI: 10.1016/j.jiph.2022.01.011 PMID: 35078755

Aggarwal, R., & Ganvir, S. S. (2021). Artificial Intelligence in Physiotherapy. *Physiotherapy - The Journal of Indian Association of Physiotherapists, 15*(2), 55. DOI: 10.4103/pjiap.pjiap_3_22

Akinci D'Antonoli, T. (2020). Ethical considerations for artificial intelligence : An overview of the current radiology landscape. *Diagnostic and Interventional Radiology (Ankara, Turkey), 26*(5), 504–511. DOI: 10.5152/dir.2020.19279 PMID: 32755879

Al Kuwaiti, A., Nazer, K., Al-Reedy, A., Al-Shehri, S., Al-Muhanna, A., Subbarayalu, A. V., Al Muhanna, D., & Al-Muhanna, F. A. (2023). A Review of the Role of Artificial Intelligence in Healthcare. *Journal of Personalized Medicine, 13*(6), 951. DOI: 10.3390/jpm13060951 PMID: 37373940

Álvarez-Machancoses, Ó., & Fernández-Martínez, J. L. (2019). Using artificial intelligence methods to speed up drug discovery. *Expert Opinion on Drug Discovery, 14*(8), 769–777. DOI: 10.1080/17460441.2019.1621284 PMID: 31140873

Amisha, M., Malik, P., Pathania, M., & Rathaur, V. K. (2019). Overview of artificial intelligence in medicine. *Journal of Family Medicine and Primary Care*, *8*(7), 2328. DOI: 10.4103/jfmpc.jfmpc_440_19 PMID: 31463251

Anderson, D. (2019). Artificial Intelligence and Applications in PM&R. *American Journal of Physical Medicine & Rehabilitation*, *98*(11), e128–e129. DOI: 10.1097/PHM.0000000000001171 PMID: 30839314

Arora, A., & Arora, A. (2022). Generative adversarial networks and synthetic patient data : Current challenges and future perspectives. *Future Healthcare Journal*, *9*(2), 190–193. DOI: 10.7861/fhj.2022-0013 PMID: 35928184

Baig, M. M., GholamHosseini, H., Moqeem, A. A., Mirza, F., & Lindén, M. (2017). A Systematic Review of Wearable Patient Monitoring Systems – Current Challenges and Opportunities for Clinical Adoption. *Journal of Medical Systems*, *41*(7), 115. DOI: 10.1007/s10916-017-0760-1 PMID: 28631139

Bajwa, J., Munir, U., Nori, A., & Williams, B. (2021a). Artificial intelligence in healthcare : Transforming the practice of medicine. *Future Healthcare Journal*, *8*(2), e188–e194. DOI: 10.7861/fhj.2021-0095 PMID: 34286183

Bajwa, J., Munir, U., Nori, A., & Williams, B. (2021b). Artificial intelligence in healthcare : Transforming the practice of medicine. *Future Healthcare Journal*, *8*(2), e188–e194. DOI: 10.7861/fhj.2021-0095 PMID: 34286183

Bouabida, K., Malas, K., Talbot, A., Desrosiers, M.-È., Lavoie, F., Lebouché, B., Taguemout, M., Rafie, E., Lessard, D., & Pomey, M.-P. (2021). Remote Patient Monitoring Program for COVID-19 Patients Following Hospital Discharge : A Cross-Sectional Study. *Frontiers in Digital Health*, *3*, 721044. Advance online publication. DOI: 10.3389/fdgth.2021.721044 PMID: 34859244

Butcher, C. J., & Hussain, W. (2022). Digital healthcare : The future. *Future Healthcare Journal*, *9*(2), 113–117. DOI: 10.7861/fhj.2022-0046 PMID: 35928188

Chen, T.-J. (2023). ChatGPT and other artificial intelligence applications speed up scientific writing. *Journal of the Chinese Medical Association*, *86*(4), 351–353. DOI: 10.1097/JCMA.0000000000000900 PMID: 36791246

Chidambaram, S., Maheswaran, Y., Patel, K., Sounderajah, V., Hashimoto, D. A., Seastedt, K. P., McGregor, A. H., Markar, S. R., & Darzi, A. (2022). Using Artificial Intelligence-Enhanced Sensing and Wearable Technology in Sports Medicine and Performance Optimisation. *Sensors (Basel)*, *22*(18), 18. Advance online publication. DOI: 10.3390/s22186920 PMID: 36146263

Choi, C., Schwarting, W., DelPreto, J., & Rus, D. (2018). Learning Object Grasping for Soft Robot Hands. *IEEE Robotics and Automation Letters, 3*(3), 2370-2377. *IEEE Robotics and Automation Letters*. Advance online publication. DOI: 10.1109/LRA.2018.2810544

Chou, C.-Y., Hsu, D.-Y., & Chou, C.-H. (2023). Predicting the Onset of Diabetes with Machine Learning Methods. *Journal of Personalized Medicine, 13*(3), 3. Advance online publication. DOI: 10.3390/jpm13030406 PMID: 36983587

Choudhury, A., & Asan, O. (2022). Impact of accountability, training, and human factors on the use of artificial intelligence in healthcare : Exploring the perceptions of healthcare practitioners in the US. *Human Factors in Healthcare, 2*, 100021. DOI: 10.1016/j.hfh.2022.100021

Corny, J., Rajkumar, A., Martin, O., Dode, X., Lajonchère, J.-P., Billuart, O., Bézie, Y., & Buronfosse, A. (2020). A machine learning–based clinical decision support system to identify prescriptions with a high risk of medication error. *Journal of the American Medical Informatics Association : JAMIA, 27*(11), 1688–1694. DOI: 10.1093/jamia/ocaa154 PMID: 32984901

Davenport, T., & Kalakota, R. (2019). The potential for artificial intelligence in healthcare. *Future Healthcare Journal, 6*(2), 94–98. DOI: 10.7861/futurehosp.6-2-94 PMID: 31363513

Dixit, S., Bohre, K., Singh, Y., Himeur, Y., Mansoor, W., Atalla, S., & Srinivasan, K. (2023). A Comprehensive Review on AI-Enabled Models for Parkinson's Disease Diagnosis. *Electronics (Basel), 12*(4), 4. Advance online publication. DOI: 10.3390/electronics12040783

Garavand, A., & Aslani, N. (2022). Metaverse phenomenon and its impact on health : A scoping review. *Informatics in Medicine Unlocked, 32*, 101029. DOI: 10.1016/j.imu.2022.101029

Giuste, F., Shi, W., Zhu, Y., Naren, T., Isgut, M., Sha, Y., Tong, L., Gupte, M., & Wang, M. D. (2023). Explainable Artificial Intelligence Methods in Combating Pandemics : A Systematic Review. *IEEE Reviews in Biomedical Engineering, 16*, 5–21. DOI: 10.1109/RBME.2022.3185953 PMID: 35737637

Goldzweig, C. L., Orshansky, G., Paige, N. M., Towfigh, A. A., Haggstrom, D. A., Miake-Lye, I., Beroes, J. M., & Shekelle, P. G. (2013). Electronic Patient Portals : Evidence on Health Outcomes, Satisfaction, Efficiency, and Attitudes. *Annals of Internal Medicine, 159*(10), 677–687. DOI: 10.7326/0003-4819-159-10-201311190-00006 PMID: 24247673

Gudigar, A., Raghavendra, U., Nayak, S., Ooi, C. P., Chan, W. Y., Gangavarapu, M. R., Dharmik, C., Samanth, J., Kadri, N. A., Hasikin, K., Barua, P. D., Chakraborty, S., Ciaccio, E. J., & Acharya, U. R. (2021). Role of Artificial Intelligence in COVID-19 Detection. *Sensors (Basel), 21*(23), 23. Advance online publication. DOI: 10.3390/s21238045 PMID: 34884045

Hakimi, M., Amiri, G. A., & Shamsi, S. E. (2024). Artificial Intelligence and Public Health : Addressing Pharmacy Practice Challenges and Policy Issues. *British Journal of Pharmacy and Pharmaceutical Sciences, 1*(1), 1. Advance online publication. DOI: 10.32996/bjpps.2024.1.1.2

Harishbhai Tilala, M., Kumar Chenchala, P., Choppadandi, A., Kaur, J., Naguri, S., Saoji, R., & Devaguptapu, B. (2024, June 15). (s. d.). Ethical Considerations in the Use of Artificial Intelligence and Machine Learning in Health Care : A Comprehensive Review. *Cureus, 16*(6), e62443. DOI: 10.7759/cureus.62443 PMID: 39011215

Hassani, H., & Silva, E. S. (2023). The Role of ChatGPT in Data Science : How AI-Assisted Conversational Interfaces Are Revolutionizing the Field. *Big Data and Cognitive Computing, 7*(2), 2. Advance online publication. DOI: 10.3390/bdcc7020062

He, K., Gan, C., Li, Z., Rekik, I., Yin, Z., Ji, W., Gao, Y., Wang, Q., Zhang, J., & Shen, D. (2023). Transformers in medical image analysis. *Intelligent Medicine, 3*(1), 59–78. DOI: 10.1016/j.imed.2022.07.002

Holzinger, A., Langs, G., Denk, H., Zatloukal, K., & Müller, H. (2019). Causability and explainability of artificial intelligence in medicine. *Wiley Interdisciplinary Reviews. Data Mining and Knowledge Discovery, 9*(4), e1312. DOI: 10.1002/widm.1312 PMID: 32089788

Javaid, M., Haleem, A., Pratap Singh, R., Suman, R., & Rab, S. (2022). Significance of machine learning in healthcare : Features, pillars and applications. *International Journal of Intelligent Networks, 3*, 58–73. DOI: 10.1016/j.ijin.2022.05.002

Javaid, M., Haleem, A., & Singh, R. P. (2023). ChatGPT for healthcare services : An emerging stage for an innovative perspective. *BenchCouncil Transactions on Benchmarks. Standards and Evaluations, 3*(1), 100105. DOI: 10.1016/j.tbench.2023.100105

Jiang, F., Jiang, Y., Zhi, H., Dong, Y., Li, H., Ma, S., Wang, Y., Dong, Q., Shen, H., & Wang, Y. (2017). Artificial intelligence in healthcare : Past, present and future. *Stroke and Vascular Neurology, 2*(4), 230–243. Advance online publication. DOI: 10.1136/svn-2017-000101 PMID: 29507784

Kelly, C. J., Karthikesalingam, A., Suleyman, M., Corrado, G., & King, D. (2019). Key challenges for delivering clinical impact with artificial intelligence. *BMC Medicine, 17*(1), 195. DOI: 10.1186/s12916-019-1426-2 PMID: 31665002

Khalid, N., Qayyum, A., Bilal, M., Al-Fuqaha, A., & Qadir, J. (2023). Privacy-preserving artificial intelligence in healthcare : Techniques and applications. *Computers in Biology and Medicine, 158*, 106848. DOI: 10.1016/j.compbiomed.2023.106848 PMID: 37044052

Khan, R. A., Jawaid, M., Khan, A. R., & Sajjad, M. (2023). ChatGPT - Reshaping medical education and clinical management. *Pakistan Journal of Medical Sciences, 39*(2), 605–607. DOI: 10.12669/pjms.39.2.7653 PMID: 36950398

Khanna, V. V., Chadaga, K., Sampathila, N., Prabhu, S., Chadaga, R., & Umakanth, S. (2022). Diagnosing COVID-19 using artificial intelligence : A comprehensive review. *Network Modeling and Analysis in Health Informatics and Bioinformatics, 11*(1), 25. DOI: 10.1007/s13721-022-00367-1

Kidziński, Ł., Delp, S., & Schwartz, M. (2019). Automatic real-time gait event detection in children using deep neural networks. *PLoS One*, *14*(1), e0211466. DOI: 10.1371/journal.pone.0211466 PMID: 30703141

Kim, J., Campbell, A. S., & Wang, J. (2018). Wearable non-invasive epidermal glucose sensors : A review. *Talanta, 177*, 163–170. DOI: 10.1016/j.talanta.2017.08.077 PMID: 29108571

Lambercy, O., Lehner, R., Chua, K., Wee, S. K., Rajeswaran, D. K., Kuah, C. W. K., Ang, W. T., Liang, P., Campolo, D., Hussain, A., Aguirre-Ollinger, G., Guan, C., Kanzler, C. M., Wenderoth, N., & Gassert, R. (2021). Neurorehabilitation From a Distance : Can Intelligent Technology Support Decentralized Access to Quality Therapy? *Frontiers in Robotics and AI, 8*, 612415. Advance online publication. DOI: 10.3389/frobt.2021.612415 PMID: 34026855

Lan, T. T., & Huy, H. V. (2021). Challenges and Solutions in AI Governance for Healthcare : A Global Perspective on Regulatory and Ethical Issues. *International Journal of Applied Health Care Analytics*, *6*(12), 12.

Li, Y., Mamouei, M., Salimi-Khorshidi, G., Rao, S., Hassaine, A., Canoy, D., Lukasiewicz, T., & Rahimi, K. (2023). Hi-BEHRT : Hierarchical Transformer-Based Model for Accurate Prediction of Clinical Events Using Multimodal Longitudinal Electronic Health Records. *IEEE Journal of Biomedical and Health Informatics, 27*(2), 1106-1117. *IEEE Journal of Biomedical and Health Informatics*. Advance online publication. DOI: 10.1109/JBHI.2022.3224727 PMID: 36427286

Li, Y., Rao, S., Solares, J. R. A., Hassaine, A., Ramakrishnan, R., Canoy, D., Zhu, Y., Rahimi, K., & Salimi-Khorshidi, G. (2020). BEHRT : Transformer for Electronic Health Records. *Scientific Reports*, *10*(1), 7155. DOI: 10.1038/s41598-020-62922-y PMID: 32346050

Lin, T., Wang, Y., Liu, X., & Qiu, X. (2022). A survey of transformers. *AI Open*, *3*, 111–132. DOI: 10.1016/j.aiopen.2022.10.001

Luxton, D. D., & Riek, L. D. (2019). Artificial intelligence and robotics in rehabilitation. In *Handbook of rehabilitation psychology* (3rd ed., pp. 507–520). American Psychological Association., DOI: 10.1037/0000129-031

Maggio, M. G., Tartarisco, G., Cardile, D., Bonanno, M., Bruschetta, R., Pignolo, L., Pioggia, G., Calabrò, R. S., & Cerasa, A. (2024). Exploring ChatGPT's potential in the clinical stream of neurorehabilitation. *Frontiers in Artificial Intelligence*, *7*, 1407905. Advance online publication. DOI: 10.3389/frai.2024.1407905 PMID: 38903157

Mak, K.-K., & Pichika, M. R. (2019). Artificial intelligence in drug development : Present status and future prospects. *Drug Discovery Today*, *24*(3), 773–780. DOI: 10.1016/j.drudis.2018.11.014 PMID: 30472429

Maleki Varnosfaderani, S., & Forouzanfar, M. (2024). The Role of AI in Hospitals and Clinics : Transforming Healthcare in the 21st Century. *Bioengineering (Basel, Switzerland)*, *11*(4), 4. Advance online publication. DOI: 10.3390/bioengineering11040337 PMID: 38671759

Marcus, G. (2018). *Deep Learning : A Critical Appraisal* (arXiv:1801.00631). arXiv. https://doi.org//arXiv.1801.00631DOI: 10.48550

Matthew, N. O. Sadiku, Zhou, Y., & Musa, S. M. (2018). Natural Language Processing. *International Journal of Advances in Scientific Research and Engineering (IJASRE), ISSN:2454-8006, DOI: , 4*(5), Article 5. https://doi.org/DOI: 10.31695/IJASRE

Mauro, M., Noto, G., Prenestini, A., & Sarto, F. (2024). Digital transformation in healthcare : Assessing the role of digital technologies for managerial support processes. *Technological Forecasting and Social Change*, *209*, 123781. DOI: 10.1016/j.techfore.2024.123781

Mennella, C., Maniscalco, U., De Pietro, G., & Esposito, M. (2024). Ethical and regulatory challenges of AI technologies in healthcare : A narrative review. *Heliyon*, *10*(4), e26297. DOI: 10.1016/j.heliyon.2024.e26297 PMID: 38384518

Monteriù, A., Prist, M. R., Frontoni, E., Longhi, S., Pietroni, F., Casaccia, S., Scalise, L., Cenci, A., Romeo, L., Berta, R., Pescosolido, L., Orlandi, G., & Revel, G. M. (2018). A Smart Sensing Architecture for Domestic Monitoring : Methodological Approach and Experimental Validation. *Sensors (Basel), 18*(7), 7. Advance online publication. DOI: 10.3390/s18072310 PMID: 30018200

Moon, I., An, Y., Min, S., & Park, C. (2023). Therapeutic Effects of Metaverse Rehabilitation for Cerebral Palsy : A Randomized Controlled Trial. *International Journal of Environmental Research and Public Health, 20*(2), 2. Advance online publication. DOI: 10.3390/ijerph20021578 PMID: 36674332

Morley, J., Murphy, L., Mishra, A., Joshi, I., & Karpathakis, K. (2022). Governing Data and Artificial Intelligence for Health Care : Developing an International Understanding. *JMIR Formative Research, 6*(1), e31623. DOI: 10.2196/31623 PMID: 35099403

Morris, M. R. (2020). AI and accessibility. *Communications of the ACM, 63*(6), 35–37. DOI: 10.1145/3356727

Nadarzynski, T., Miles, O., Cowie, A., & Ridge, D. (2019). Acceptability of artificial intelligence (AI)-led chatbot services in healthcare : A mixed-methods study. *Digital Health, 5*, 2055207619871808. DOI: 10.1177/2055207619871808 PMID: 31467682

Najjar, R. (2023). Redefining Radiology : A Review of Artificial Intelligence Integration in Medical Imaging. *Diagnostics (Basel), 13*(17), 2760. DOI: 10.3390/diagnostics13172760 PMID: 37685300

Natarajan, A., Su, H.-W., & Heneghan, C. (2020). Assessment of physiological signs associated with COVID-19 measured using wearable devices. *NPJ Digital Medicine, 3*(1), 1–8. DOI: 10.1038/s41746-020-00363-7 PMID: 33299095

Neibling, B. A., Jackson, S. M., Hayward, K. S., & Barker, R. N. (2021). Perseverance with technology-facilitated home-based upper limb practice after stroke : A systematic mixed studies review. *Journal of Neuroengineering and Rehabilitation, 18*(1), 43. DOI: 10.1186/s12984-021-00819-1 PMID: 33627126

Oren, O., Gersh, B. J., & Bhatt, D. L. (2020). Artificial intelligence in medical imaging : Switching from radiographic pathological data to clinically meaningful endpoints. *The Lancet. Digital Health, 2*(9), e486–e488. DOI: 10.1016/S2589-7500(20)30160-6 PMID: 33328116

Palaniappan, K., Lin, E. Y. T., & Vogel, S. (2024). Global Regulatory Frameworks for the Use of Artificial Intelligence (AI) in the Healthcare Services Sector. *Healthcare (Basel), 12*(5), 562. DOI: 10.3390/healthcare12050562 PMID: 38470673

Park, S.-M., & Kim, Y.-G. (2022). A Metaverse : Taxonomy, Components, Applications, and Open Challenges. *IEEE Access, 10*, 4209-4251. IEEE Access. DOI: 10.1109/ACCESS.2021.3140175

Patel, D., & Tarakji, K. G. (2021). Smartwatch diagnosis of atrial fibrillation in patient with embolic stroke of unknown source : A case report. *Cardiovascular Digital Health Journal, 2*(1), 84–87. DOI: 10.1016/j.cvdhj.2021.01.001 PMID: 35265894

Paul, M., Maglaras, L., Ferrag, M. A., & Almomani, I. (2023). Digitization of healthcare sector : A study on privacy and security concerns. *ICT Express, 9*(4), 571–588. DOI: 10.1016/j.icte.2023.02.007

Petrigna, L., & Musumeci, G. (2022). The Metaverse : A New Challenge for the Healthcare System: A Scoping Review. *Journal of Functional Morphology and Kinesiology, 7*(3), 63. DOI: 10.3390/jfmk7030063 PMID: 36135421

Rachmoune, K., Aknouch, A., Belcadi, H., Ouardi, Y. E., Mouniane, Y., Aitouhanni, I., Mabsor-Zgandaoui, S., Rhazi, M., Belkadi, M. C., & Moutaouakkil, A. (2025). Role of Secondary Metabolites in Essential Oils for Antimicrobial Activity and the Integration of Artificial Intelligence to Optimize Their Use. In *Secondary Metabolites and Their Applications in Various Diseases* (pp. 81–114). IGI Global Scientific Publishing., DOI: 10.4018/979-8-3693-9112-9.ch003

Rajpurkar, P., Irvin, J., Zhu, K., Yang, B., Mehta, H., Duan, T., Ding, D., Bagul, A., Langlotz, C., Shpanskaya, K., Lungren, M. P., & Ng, A. Y. (2017). *CheXNet : Radiologist-Level Pneumonia Detection on Chest X-Rays with Deep Learning* (arXiv:1711.05225). arXiv. https://doi.org//arXiv.1711.05225DOI: 10.48550

Ranchon, F., Chanoine, S., Lambert-Lacroix, S., Bosson, J.-L., Moreau-Gaudry, A., & Bedouch, P. (2023). Development of artificial intelligence powered apps and tools for clinical pharmacy services : A systematic review. *International Journal of Medical Informatics, 172*, 104983. DOI: 10.1016/j.ijmedinf.2022.104983 PMID: 36724730

Sallam, M. (2023). ChatGPT Utility in Healthcare Education, Research, and Practice : Systematic Review on the Promising Perspectives and Valid Concerns. *Healthcare (Basel), 11*(6), 887. DOI: 10.3390/healthcare11060887 PMID: 36981544

Salomon, I., & Olivier, S. (2024a). Artificial intelligence in medicine : Advantages and disadvantages for today and the future. *International Journal of Surgery Open, 62*(4), 471–473. DOI: 10.1097/IO9.0000000000000133

Salomon, I., & Olivier, S. (2024b). Artificial intelligence in medicine : Advantages and disadvantages for today and the future. *International Journal of Surgery Open*, *62*(4), 471–473. DOI: 10.1097/IO9.0000000000000133

Sezgin, E. (2024). Redefining Virtual Assistants in Health Care : The Future With Large Language Models. *Journal of Medical Internet Research*, *26*, e53225. DOI: 10.2196/53225 PMID: 38241074

Shahsavar, Y., & Choudhury, A. (2023). User Intentions to Use ChatGPT for Self-Diagnosis and Health-Related Purposes : Cross-sectional Survey Study. *JMIR Human Factors*, *10*, e47564. DOI: 10.2196/47564 PMID: 37195756

Shaik, T., Tao, X., Higgins, N., Li, L., Gururajan, R., Zhou, X., & Acharya, U. R. (2023). Remote patient monitoring using artificial intelligence : Current state, applications, and challenges. *Wiley Interdisciplinary Reviews. Data Mining and Knowledge Discovery*, *13*(2), e1485. DOI: 10.1002/widm.1485

Shamshad, F., Khan, S., Zamir, S. W., Khan, M. H., Hayat, M., Khan, F. S., & Fu, H. (2023). Transformers in medical imaging : A survey. *Medical Image Analysis*, *88*, 102802. DOI: 10.1016/j.media.2023.102802 PMID: 37315483

Sharma, A., Lin, I. W., Miner, A. S., Atkins, D. C., & Althoff, T. (2023). Human–AI collaboration enables more empathic conversations in text-based peer-to-peer mental health support. *Nature Machine Intelligence*, *5*(1), 46–57. DOI: 10.1038/s42256-022-00593-2

Sharma, A., Virmani, T., Pathak, V., Sharma, A., Pathak, K., Kumar, G., & Pathak, D. (2022). Artificial Intelligence-Based Data-Driven Strategy to Accelerate Research, Development, and Clinical Trials of COVID Vaccine. *BioMed Research International*, *7205241*(1), 7205241. Advance online publication. DOI: 10.1155/2022/7205241 PMID: 35845955

Shojaei, P., Vlahu-Gjorgievska, E., & Chow, Y.-W. (2024). Security and Privacy of Technologies in Health Information Systems : A Systematic Literature Review. *Computers*, *13*(2), 2. Advance online publication. DOI: 10.3390/computers13020041

Shome, D., Kar, T., Mohanty, S. N., Tiwari, P., Muhammad, K., AlTameem, A., Zhang, Y., & Saudagar, A. K. J. (2021). COVID-Transformer : Interpretable COVID-19 Detection Using Vision Transformer for Healthcare. *International Journal of Environmental Research and Public Health*, *18*(21), 11086. DOI: 10.3390/ijerph182111086 PMID: 34769600

Siala, H., & Wang, Y. (2022). SHIFTing artificial intelligence to be responsible in healthcare : A systematic review. *Social Science & Medicine*, *296*, 114782. DOI: 10.1016/j.socscimed.2022.114782 PMID: 35152047

Sinsky, C., Colligan, L., Li, L., Prgomet, M., Reynolds, S., Goeders, L., Westbrook, J., Tutty, M., & Blike, G. (2016). Allocation of Physician Time in Ambulatory Practice : A Time and Motion Study in 4 Specialties. *Annals of Internal Medicine*, *165*(11), 753–760. DOI: 10.7326/M16-0961 PMID: 27595430

Snowdon, A. (2020). *Digital Health : A Framework for Healthcare Transformation*. https://www.gs1ca.org/ documents/digital_health-affht.pdf

Soliño-Fernandez, D., Ding, A., Bayro-Kaiser, E., & Ding, E. L. (2019). Willingness to adopt wearable devices with behavioral and economic incentives by health insurance wellness programs : Results of a US cross-sectional survey with multiple consumer health vignettes. *BMC Public Health*, *19*(1), 1649. DOI: 10.1186/s12889-019-7920-9 PMID: 31839006

Son, W. S. (2018). Drug Discovery Enhanced by Artificial Intelligence. *Biomedical Journal of Scientific & Technical Research*, *12*(1), 8936–8938. DOI: 10.26717/BJSTR.2018.12.002189

Suh, I., McKinney, T., & Siu, K.-C. (2023). Current Perspective of Metaverse Application in Medical Education, Research and Patient Care. *Virtual Worlds*, *2*(2), 2. Advance online publication. DOI: 10.3390/virtualworlds2020007

Sükei, E., Norbury, A., Perez-Rodriguez, M. M., Olmos, P. M., & Artés, A. (2021). Predicting Emotional States Using Behavioral Markers Derived From Passively Sensed Data : Data-Driven Machine Learning Approach. *JMIR mHealth and uHealth*, *9*(3), e24465. DOI: 10.2196/24465 PMID: 33749612

Tachkov, K., Zemplenyi, A., Kamusheva, M., Dimitrova, M., Siirtola, P., Pontén, J., Nemeth, B., Kalo, Z., & Petrova, G. (2022). Barriers to Use Artificial Intelligence Methodologies in Health Technology Assessment in Central and East European Countries. *Frontiers in Public Health*, *10*, 921226. Advance online publication. DOI: 10.3389/fpubh.2022.921226 PMID: 35910914

Tagliaferri, S. D., Angelova, M., Zhao, X., Owen, P. J., Miller, C. T., Wilkin, T., & Belavy, D. L. (2020). Artificial intelligence to improve back pain outcomes and lessons learnt from clinical classification approaches : Three systematic reviews. *NPJ Digital Medicine*, *3*(1), 1–16. DOI: 10.1038/s41746-020-0303-x PMID: 32665978

Tran, B. X., Vu, G. T., Ha, G. H., Vuong, Q.-H., Ho, M.-T., Vuong, T.-T., La, V.-P., Ho, M.-T., Nghiem, K.-C. P., Nguyen, H. L. T., Latkin, C. A., Tam, W. W. S., Cheung, N.-M., Nguyen, H.-K. T., Ho, C. S. H., & Ho, R. C. M. (2019). Global Evolution of Research in Artificial Intelligence in Health and Medicine : A Bibliometric Study. *Journal of Clinical Medicine*, *8*(3), 360. DOI: 10.3390/jcm8030360 PMID: 30875745

Trunfio, M., & Rossi, S. (2022). Advances in Metaverse Investigation : Streams of Research and Future Agenda. *Virtual Worlds*, *1*(2), 2. Advance online publication. DOI: 10.3390/virtualworlds1020007

van Tulder, G., Tong, Y., & Marchiori, E. (2021). *Multi-view analysis of unregistered medical images using cross-view transformers* (Vol. 12903)., DOI: 10.1007/978-3-030-87199-4_10

Varkey, B. (2021). Principles of Clinical Ethics and Their Application to Practice. *Medical Principles and Practice : International Journal of the Kuwait University, Health Science Centre*, *30*(1), 17–28. DOI: 10.1159/000509119 PMID: 32498071

Volpp, K., & Mohta, N. (2016, mai 12). *Patient Engagement Survey : Improved Engagement Leads to BetterOutcomes, but Better Tools Are Needed.* https://www.semanticscholar.org/paper/Patient-Engagement-Survey%3A-Improved-Engagement-to-Volpp-Mohta/b771f5014a7c844984db615101af54bd4a1c2ba8

Wang, G., Badal, A., Jia, X., Maltz, J. S., Mueller, K., Myers, K. J., Niu, C., Vannier, M., Yan, P., Yu, Z., & Zeng, R. (2022). Development of metaverse for intelligent healthcare. *Nature Machine Intelligence*, *4*(11), 922–929. DOI: 10.1038/s42256-022-00549-6 PMID: 36935774

Wang, S.-H., Wu, X., Zhang, Y.-D., Tang, C., & Zhang, X. (2020). Diagnosis of COVID-19 by Wavelet Renyi Entropy and Three-Segment Biogeography-Based Optimization. *International Journal of Computational Intelligence Systems*, *13*(1), 1332–1344. DOI: 10.2991/ijcis.d.200828.001

Wani, S. U. D., Khan, N. A., Thakur, G., Gautam, S. P., Ali, M., Alam, P., Alshehri, S., Ghoneim, M. M., & Shakeel, F. (2022). Utilization of Artificial Intelligence in Disease Prevention : Diagnosis, Treatment, and Implications for the Healthcare Workforce. *Health Care*, *10*(4), 608. DOI: 10.3390/healthcare10040608 PMID: 35455786

Weissler, E. H., Naumann, T., Andersson, T., Ranganath, R., Elemento, O., Luo, Y., Freitag, D. F., Benoit, J., Hughes, M. C., Khan, F., Slater, P., Shameer, K., Roe, M., Hutchison, E., Kollins, S. H., Broedl, U., Meng, Z., Wong, J. L., Curtis, L., & Ghassemi, M. (2021). The role of machine learning in clinical research : Transforming the future of evidence generation. *Trials*, *22*(1), 537. DOI: 10.1186/s13063-021-05489-x PMID: 34399832

Williams, O. D. (2020). COVID-19 and Private Health : Market and Governance Failure. [Society for International Development]. *Development*, *63*(2-4), 181–190. DOI: 10.1057/s41301-020-00273-x PMID: 33223765

Wolterink, J. M., Mukhopadhyay, A., Leiner, T., Vogl, T. J., Bucher, A. M., & Išgum, I. (2021). Generative Adversarial Networks : A Primer for Radiologists. *Radiographics*, *41*(3), 840–857. DOI: 10.1148/rg.2021200151 PMID: 33891522

Xu, L., Sanders, L., Li, K., & Chow, J. C. L. (2021). Chatbot for Health Care and Oncology Applications Using Artificial Intelligence and Machine Learning : Systematic Review. *JMIR Cancer*, *7*(4), e27850. DOI: 10.2196/27850 PMID: 34847056

Yadav, N., Pandey, S., Gupta, A., Dudani, P., Gupta, S., & Rangarajan, K. (2023). Data Privacy in Healthcare : In the Era of Artificial Intelligence. *Indian Dermatology Online Journal*, *14*(6), 788–792. DOI: 10.4103/idoj.idoj_543_23 PMID: 38099022

Yeung, A. W. K., Torkamani, A., Butte, A. J., Glicksberg, B. S., Schuller, B., Rodriguez, B., Ting, D. S. W., Bates, D., Schaden, E., Peng, H., Willschke, H., van der Laak, J., Car, J., Rahimi, K., Celi, L. A., Banach, M., Kletecka-Pulker, M., Kimberger, O., Eils, R., & Atanasov, A. G. (2023). The promise of digital healthcare technologies. *Frontiers in Public Health*, *11*, 1196596. Advance online publication. DOI: 10.3389/fpubh.2023.1196596 PMID: 37822534

Chapter 9
AI in Epidemiology:
Predicting the Unpredictable Leveraging AI to Detect Outbreaks and Predict Disease

Iris-Panagiota Efthymiou
https://orcid.org/0000-0001-9656-8378
University of Greenwich, UK

ABSTRACT

This chapter explores the role of artificial intelligence in epidemiology, focusing on its application in early outbreak detection and disease spread prediction. It examines how machine learning, natural language processing, and predictive analytics are applied to real-time data from clinical, environmental, and digital sources. The chapter demonstrates the integration of AI into public health surveillance systems and discusses the ethical, technical, and infrastructural challenges involved. It highlights the potential of AI to process large, heterogeneous datasets at speed and scale, enabling earlier intervention and resource allocation during emerging health crises. By analyzing historical trends and identifying hidden patterns, AI models offer critical support to decision-makers in managing uncertainty and enhancing response strategies. This chapter argues for an interdisciplinary and transparent approach to algorithm design, data governance, and stakeholder collaboration.

INTRODUCTION

The emergence of artificial intelligence (AI) within the field of epidemiology is an exciting area of inquiry with the potential to revolutionize the study of epidemic disease. There are many significant and useful roles that AI technologies can play

DOI: 10.4018/979-8-3373-1992-6.ch009

in epidemiology, such as enhancing disease surveillance, understanding epidemic trends, and also, impact testing. The effectiveness of contact tracing and social distancing interventions in the pandemic has shown that integrating AI can be an innovative platform to track not only epidemic growth, but also infection dispersal, and evaluate various policy decisions. Advanced algorithms have the transformative potential to analyze vast, multi-omics, health, and mobility data relevant to infectious disease spread and translate data into insights that are accurate, credible, and comprehensible to policy-makers, mitigation experts, and the public. Implemented in a model-inference-feedback-decision framework, AI can provide actionable information about where, how, and under what conditions outbreaks can be detected, prevented, and controlled.

This wide exploration of four important families of AI techniques involves machine learning, agent-based simulations, neural networks, and graph theory, with the overarching goal of presenting a thorough and detailed pathway to understanding how these innovative techniques can be utilized to gain deeper insights into the spread of infectious diseases. Furthermore, these techniques can significantly impact and inform the design of effective mitigation strategies. In this context, a comprehensive guide is provided that examines the approaches taken by these four families when applying their respective techniques. This includes common challenges encountered, specific data requirements, and nuanced interpretations of the results generated through these methods. In conclusion, a wide and diverse range of applications of AI is discussed concerning the spread of COVID-19. These applications vary greatly and range in scope from the evolution of the virus within the hosts to worldwide estimates of population vulnerability and the transmissibility of the disease among different demographics.

Fundamentals in Epidimiology

Man aspires towards a world where peace, security, and prosperity reign. Investigating the distribution and determinants of health-related states, diseases, and events is the first step to achieving this ideal. A unique scientific approach encompasses this. Epidemiology. However, populations are unpredictable, security remains a dream and prosperity looks for optimization.

First, morbidity and mortality rates soar at an unsustainable pace. Then, the importance of epidemics monthly becomes apparent in the affliction caused to man and heir and the population gradually increase the number of trained experts in the field, focusing efforts on the detection and control of these events. At this point, mankind has already harnessed computational capabilities beyond imagination, and patterns in human behavior have become somewhat comprehensible (Pastor-Escuredo, 2021). Now, evolutionary algorithms predict as accurately as possible the distribution of disease outbreaks around the world on a scale of hours, and these policies and recommendations are broadcast globally, forming the foundation of the World Health Organization.

Key Concepts and Terminology

Epidemiology has many unique terms and definitions. It is important to be familiar with them in order to understand the context in which AI can be applied to the field of epidemiology. An "epidemic is the spread of disease to many people in a single region, and a pandemic is a disease that has spread across a large region". On the other hand," an endemic is the constant presence and/or usual prevalence of a disease within a specific population or geographic area" (Centers for Disease Control and Prevention, 2012).

Regarding disease spread, terms used to describe how a disease transmits itself are: Reservoir, Portal of Exit, Mode of Transportation, and Portal of Entry. Other possible locations along the way are Portals of Entry, and new susceptible hosts could be Immunosuppressed. Terms to characterize something that increases the risk of disease are referred to as Risk Factors. Population risk factors are characteristics of the population that increase the risk of a disease (e.g., age, sex, race). Behavioral risk factors involve lifestyle activities that can increase the risk of a disease. Hereditary risk factors are passed on from family members (Rodríguez-González et al., 2019).

In order to enter the reservoir, a host must pass the Susceptibility threshold. The relationship between infected and susceptible compounds is known as the basis of many epidemiological models. The Susceptibility threshold refers to the amount of infected people needed in the population for there to be an outbreak. Understanding the given terms can help readers understand the material moving forward. Knowledge of this terminology is a prerequisite to the following sections, which will discuss protective measures for such diseases and frameworks to prevent/fight off specific types, such as Influenza (Sardana & Jadhav Bhatt, 2021).

THE NEED FOR ADVANCED ALGORITHMS IN EPIDEMIOLOGY

The power of recent computing technologies has opened up unprecedented opportunities in the area of data science, including computational epidemiology. Traditional epidemiological approaches may indeed tend to be limited when facing complex and large datasets (Rodríguez-González et al., 2019). Applications may often demand the analysis of extensive historical or real-time datasets to detect and visualize outbreak events or to adequately calibrate the models used in the predictive exercise. On the one hand, conventional approaches may fail when scaling according to the size of the dataset exposed, and, on the other hand, they may falter because of errors in the assumption of statistically known properties of the data. In contrast, the recent development of new algorithms and methodologies makes it possible to use big data in a structured and efficient way, effectively improving the overall accuracy of the analysis (Pastor-Escuredo, 2021). Other key aspects relate to the timeliness of the analysis. Making sense of data can indeed require time to process properly according to the specific investigation but in many occasions, the need is to provide decisions in near real-time to better manage the emerging crisis.

Proper statistical analysis is the cornerstone of a well-functioning response to public health issues. Wrong/missing analysis, visualizations, or predictions may lead to delayed actions or, even worse, misinterpretations followed by wrong policies (Efthymiou, I., 2024). By using innovative and modern techniques, epidemiologists may improve their ability to foresee and handle the emergency, giving decision-makers a time advantage to implement proper containment and mitigation measures able to curb the event. In a world of global risk of pandemics due to climate change and other issues, the increasing role of big data is likely to have a decisive play in future public health responses. Concretely, the state-of-the-art of some of the most interesting applications in the AI panorama is provided, together with the panoramic use of big data in epidemiology.

APPLICATIONS OF AI IN OUTBREAK DETECTION

A key challenge in epidemiology is the timely detection of outbreaks. With the rapid accumulation of data, it is becoming really difficult for organizations to analyze and interpret data. In this regard, AI has played a significant role due to its advanced algorithms capability of quickly analyzing and checking the data. AI applications more specifically involve the use of sophisticated analytics to discover meaningful patterns and knowledge in datasets. The "predictive" function of AI discovers patterns in data to predict what might happen in the future, basically based on historical trends. This includes the development of predictive machine learning models that can identify the potential and probability of detecting unusual disease patterns in the data much earlier (Abdulkareem & E. Petersen, 2021).

The improving performances of such algorithms and models have been used to construct public health early warning systems designed to help authorities prepare for future outbreaks. This part of the plan will provide numerous examples of successful AI applications in outbreak detection and situational awareness. The subsequent development of this domain will be discussed, including the combination of diverse data sources such as environmental and social media. By reviewing relevant publications, the goal is to gain underlying ideas about how AI advances the current practice of epidemiological surveillance methods and how it might be improved in the future.

Previous studies have stressed the importance of early warning sign systems for improved situational awareness during outbreaks (Kamalrathne et al., 2023, Moises & Kunguma, 2023; Tambo et al., 2021; Jayasekara et al., 2023; Wu et al., 2022; Zhang et al., 2023; Zhang et al., 2024; Ugwu et al., 2024). They have become a primary focus of global health security, where the timeliness and effectiveness of interventions have been shown to be crucial. Many of the messaging services are based on event data and do not take into account other relevant data sources. A recent study has shown the possibility of improving the timeliness and effectiveness of the messaging service using the model of gravity-based disease spread that includes the air transport network.

Real-Time Surveillance Systems

Disease surveillance and outbreak detection in epidemiology have greatly benefited from real-time systems. Real-time surveillance takes advantage of AI algorithms to detect, analyze, and predict the spread of disease in its early stages (Abdulkareem & E. Petersen, 2021). A wide array of applications have been pioneered to accomplish real-time monitoring of disease patterns and possible outbreaks that can trigger an immediate response (Albahlal, 2023; Sumithra et al., 2025; Zhang et al., 2024). At the same time, the development and deployment of remote diagnostic technologies allow immediate access to the data collected, leading to timely decisions on containment strategies during an outbreak (Babanejaddehaki et al., 2025; Ghosh and Sharma, 2024; Chowdhury et al., 2024; Ajagbe et al., 2024). These innovative technologies have dramatically improved the ability to detect early anomalies in the collected data, which may indicate the starting phase of an outbreak. The adoption of AI models in these systems has made it possible to quantify the risk associated with the detected anomalies, making these patterns more informative for an effective public intervention. Several windows of intervention have provided already actual case studies, wherein the prompt intervention aimed at shrinking the reach of the outbreak until it vanishes. That, indirectly causing the in-depth investigation of the privacy issues related to the data collected by collaborative systems and investigated by AI models. In light of it, is proposed, a new metric able to quantify the effectiveness of the privacy control mechanisms commonly in place.

AI'S ROLE IN DESEASE SURVEILLANCE

Until now, the role of artificial intelligence (AI) in health care has been largely constrained to diagnostics, health monitoring, and predicting disease. Yet, the coronavirus outbreak is presenting the nascent technology with new opportunities. Can AI improve epidemic surveillance and response? We argue that, with the proliferation of vast amounts of communication and travel data and increasingly sophisticated machine learning (ML) and prediction algorithms, AI and big data analytics can significantly enhance epidemiological research and public health responses to disease outbreaks. (Zeng et al., 2021; Olawade et al.2023; Mehta & Shukla, 2022; Majnarić et al.2021; Dong et al., 2021). These advanced algorithms can conduct real-time analysis of even the largest and most heterogeneous datasets and can therefore complement long-standing seasonal and pandemic influenza surveillance programs with substantially improved global reporting, real-time tracking, early detection, and forecasting of global influenza impact at international, national, and local scales.

The Global Influenza Surveillance and Response System is a network of over 129 institutions in over 100 countries and provides the foundation for much of the ongoing monitoring of seasonal and ad-hoc monitoring of pandemic influenza (Zhang et al., 2024; Chow et al., 2023). Complementing the surveillance through this system with big data and AI analytics brings substantial value to real-time tracking and early detection. On the one hand, the influenza program collects real-time epidemiological data from national and international sources, including date of report, date of symptom onset and/or diagnosis, clinical outcome, demographic information, laboratory findings, and much more. On the other hand, algorithmic research has shown that social media content can reveal the whereabouts of the influenza virus at aggregate regional levels up to six weeks in advance of GP-based incidence reports. Furthermore, some studies also assess the effectiveness of content analysis in relation to the current gold standard for influenza surveillance, which represents the means of verification for global surveillance. The content-based methods show correlation with established gold standards respectively, and their predictive power is considerable in that they outperform statistical methods.

AI and Genomic Epidemiology

Since the COVID-19 pandemic began, significant resources have been assembled globally to achieve sequencing goals on a scale never previously possible (Ehiobuche & Ampadu-Nyarkoh, 2024; Lakoff, 2024). For example, around 2020, Oman, had sequenced 201 genomes, while Iceland and Australia had ramped up to 11 and 8.76 genomes per 100,000 people, respectively. Here, high volume did not preclude a comparable rate of advanced analysis: between March and December, scientists from these three countries agreed on a code-predating submission, certified by extended review, to which reads, reference sequences and genome assembly were pooled to find over 50 mutations separate from known lineages. Repeat analyses of larger prospective samples at this scale and pace could support live decisions for such nations as to whether or not to go into or come out of full lockdowns. Note that the needed international working relationships and novel resources would mirror those anticipated globally under the Global Virome Project; indeed, which was established in 2008, the year of the Global Emerging Infections Surveillance and Response Initiative.

Confirmed cases have been an extraordinarily high fraction of the reach of the SARS-CoV-2 genome surveillance community. In the two weeks following reports of the initial COVID-19 case, a 39-year-old male diagnosed in real-time reverse transcription PCR with severe pneumonia in Wuhan, a group of practitioners mobilized an open consensus on the technical details of SARS-CoV-2 genome matching the previously sequenced bats and infecting cells. As the other scholars agreed, proactive livestock-related discussions sought nationwide reanalysis of previously collected coronavirus data (Cohen et al., 2024; Zhang et al., 2023; Kamalrathne et al., 2023).

BIG DATA AND EPIDEMIOLOGICAL INTELLIGENCE

The globalized economy created both increased connectivity and interdependence as well as greater risks, most notably relating to rapid disease spread. These risks require swift responses from scientists and policymakers. In this context, epidemiological intelligence is crucial in ensuring effective and timely interventions. Big data, when analyzed with advanced algorithms, has become an invaluable source of epidemiological intelligence (Rahman et al., 2023; Javed, 2024; Adegoke et al., 2024). While mainly used in the private sector, cutting-edge artificial intelligence technologies, namely machine learning, deep learning, and natural language processing, have now reached the epidemiologist's toolkit as well. Applications of AI are flourishing both in outbreak detection and mapping and epidemic forecasting and prediction (Diareme, K., et al., 2022).

In the last decade, there has been a veritable explosion of digital data. As of 2024, the holder of the largest globally representative datasets is a major tech company, which has access to vast amounts of data across numerous topics. The patchwork of worldwide web pages continues to grow, contributing to the ever-expanding digital universe. By 2025, it is estimated that the size of the digital universe will reach over 181 zettabytes. Supercomputers have also advanced significantly, with the most capable ones now achieving exascale performance, far surpassing the 150 petaFLOPS mark. More than 5.35 billion people have access to the internet as of

January 2024. Using digital behaviour for epidemiological surveillance is not only an act of service towards society, but it is also an act of pragmatism (Meltwater, 2024; G2, 2024; Engelmann, 2022; Greenhalgh & Engebretsen, 2022).

AI in Public Health Decision-Making

The role of AI in public health extends beyond outbreak alerts and predictions. One of the most traditional AI technologies whose applications are broadening in clinical and public health practice is decision and big data mining (Esmaeilzadeh, 2024; Bekbolatova et al., 2024). The current interest lies with the computational healthcare system's ability to autonomously analyze and interpret large volumes of structural and unstructured clinical and claims data, identifying signals, patterns, or associations. These ultimately transform this exercise into medical expertise or product knowledge. These systems can also be programmed with decision-making strategies and rule-based decision algorithms. Despite the obvious benefits of AI, health professionals are less likely to use health-related AI services in the field, and also recommendations to change vary across health professions and are most of the times at a low confidence level. There are several reasons for the proposed divergence: some professions have regulatory frameworks; training and competence vary in the general health system; practice settings and services can also vary by health discipline in a way that influences consumers (Andersson et al., 2022; Borges et al., 2023).

Awareness in the context of the issues at hand frequently arises in the evaluation phase of public health AI implementation, often emphasizing equity implications, the potential to negatively impact trust in central public health institutions and public health decisions, and potential misinterpretation outcomes. Although recognized as being of great importance, the method of mitigating AI risks is often deficient. Concerns about risks affecting the most vulnerable groups in society and increasing social and health disparities ultimately lead to discussions about balance, justice, and ethical considerations. The awareness phase of the public health AI ecosystem is often fragmented, resulting in a patchy distribution of public health measures and responsibilities, requiring awareness to extend beyond the primary evaluator to patients, the general public, the academia, and the health care sector at multiple levels of the public health and health care systems. Tasked with processing massive data with accuracy and speed, AI is made up of advanced computational algorithms that are not only capable of machine learning but also symbolic logic methods found in much older improved associations (Sarker, 2021; Zhu et al., 2023).

MACHINE LEARNING TECHNIQUES IN EPIDEMIOLOGY

Epidemiology is the field of science that deals with the incidence, distribution, and possible control of diseases and other factors relating to health. With the outbreak of severe acute respiratory syndrome coronavirus 2 (SARS-CoV-2) in December 2019, many researchers have begun using a variety of machine-learning techniques in epidemiological research and have opened new research avenues in this domain (Sardana & Jadhav Bhatt, 2021). Machine learning is a field of artificial intelligence where computers are trained to use algorithms to learn patterns in data and then make decisions or predictions based on that data. Through the use of machine learning techniques, the processes of disease modeling, spread prediction, and risk factor identification can be analyzed in more detail. The existing approaches for analyzing epidemics and avenues for future research in various facets are discussed.

Advanced epidemiological research could benefit from getting deeper insights into disease modeling. Many machine learning approaches, such as supervised learning, unsupervised learning, and reinforcement learning, have been widely used for the analysis and prediction of pandemics, making it an interesting research field of bioinformatics and computational biology (Ajagbe & Adigun, 2024; Dairi et al., 2021). The main aim of the supervised learning approach to disease modeling is to estimate the mapping function based on a target variable and then predict it when a new collection of data is given.

One of the most common application in epidemiology is the identification of patients at high risk, or those most likely to develop a given pathology. By contrast, unsupervised learning uses only the input variables to identify inherent structures in the dataset, such as the functions of the clusters and the presence of nodes. In epidemiology, unsupervised learning can be useful to group data as a representation and, finally, to lead to the discovery of new net features. As with supervised learning, reinforcement learning can also assist in epidemic modeling. Nonetheless, it is anticipated that it will mature sufficiently in the future to be of more extensive benefit. Overall, researchers suggest, based on the need for future research, that the combined use of advanced machine learning techniques and traditional epidemiological research will enable more comprehensive analysis and conclusions from complex biological phenomena (Soto-Ferrari et al., 2025; Alzamili & Ruhaiyem, 2025; Mannan et al., 2025).

NATURAL LANGUAGE PROCESSING IN EPIDEMIOLOGY

Nature is an infinite resource of data and information offered in myriad ways. In the absence of digital communication, case detection regarding public health will always be limited by what is observable by AMS in the surrounding environment. Fortunately, the world has experienced an information age transformation for the previous several decades unfurling digital records for the vast morass of human activities. Meanwhile, it also drives the interest in data science, including management, analysis, and visualization of such kind of information to derive actionable insights.

Thousands of mosquito traps were recently put by health officials across the province where numerous of Aedes aegypti and Ae. albopictus are caught on a weekly basis. Instead of a manual check of every trap, a simple Infrared dispersion analysis system is mounted on a UAV to detect a specific spectral feature of mosquitoes around multiple photonic bands. The quantified value can be downloaded and used for estimating the aggregate amount of both species in the trap. Subsequently, a data science framework is outlined to standardize the trapping process, ingest the acquired data, undertake exploratory analysis, make predictions using machine learning models, and present the results via simple visualization to local farmers and health advocates (Chen et al., 2020).

It not only helps reduce the labour intensity but also improves efficiency. Modern technologies are pervasive helping people work efficiently and effectively in such a contamination where a timely and appropriate response is vital in controlling disease spread.

NETWORK ANALYSIS IN DESEASE SPREAD PREDICTION

The connections between individuals established through contact allow an infectious agent to propagate, thus naturally defining a network with nodes (individuals) and edges representing epidemiologically relevant interactions (Danon et al., 2011). When multiple populations are engaged, the picture grows even more complex. While the analysis of research on selected network approaches to epidemics can be found elsewhere, here, an attempt is made to recurrently introduce this issue in view of the importance of understanding network structures for the (interventional) interpretation and prediction of epidemic spreading processes.

The First Few Hundred Cases (FF100) project is integrated here for illustrative purposes. Contracted in view of providing situation awareness to the Director-General on the SARS outbreak. The FF100 task was to model the global spread of disease in case the outbreak in mainland China resurged, rebroke, or exploded by experimenting with artificially generated cross-border cases based on a fixed predefined list of cities. This project, amongst other issues, placed great emphasis on the monitoring of the commercial passenger aviation network using graph-based methods. Yellowstone's realization was the birthplace of an outbreak in Avian-influenza which was supposed to escalate to the point of generating city clusters as sub-network components on the global scale of things (Duan et al., 2023). Efforts have since culminated in a package meant to capture the transmission network of disease from contact-trace-like data. This forced revisit has shown that a significant portion of network-related disease spread sophistication had remained a well-guards secret constrained within the project.

CHALLENGES AND LIMITATIONS OF AI IN EPIDEMIOLOGY

Recently, artificial intelligence (AI) approaches have been proposed in an epidemiological context, concerning outbreak detection, analyses of comorbidities, and epidemic spread predictions, or optimal intervention strategies. Convincing demonstrations of their superiority to classical methods have been provided, and, notably, such models have been proposed and used throughout the COVID-19 pandemic. The use of AI in epidemiological research, on electronic health records, sales or monitoring data, or models of transmissibility, has a growing body of literature (D. Morgenstern et al., 2021). There is additional work considering the policy and societal impacts of AI in public health (Fisher & C. Rosella, 2022).

The adoption of AI can enhance the capacity to study complex interactions mediated by a large number of variables, essential for understanding multidimensional aspects characterizing the evolution of diseases. Additionally, the ability of AI to highlight secondary or non-trivial features influencing the output can be a precious support for less expert users, not directly involved in the development of the methodology. It remains the case, however, that results have to be taken cautiously, as emphasized by several papers. Rudimentary use or misunderstanding of AI techniques and results may yield serious implications on decision-making and social planning.

Furthermore, in some cases, the chosen methodologies are not examined in sufficient detail, making it difficult to assess their potential for a broader application. The main focus of this critical review is thus to introduce basic notions of AI, and particularly machine learning, that are widely used in epidemiology, in order to support a better understanding of the proposed methods and the related successes, limits, and criticisms.

Among limitations, specific attention will be devoted to the requirement of proper datasets effectively training models, the risk of misleading biases, the model complexity often impeding an effective evaluation and interpretation, the need for further focused integration with epidemiological experts, and, above all, the lacking design of general theoretical frameworks critically addressing these limitations.

ETHICAL CONSIDERATION IN USING AI FOR EPIDEMIOLOGICAL RESEARCH

In the last 20 years, an increasing amount of digital data has been collected, and artificial intelligence (AI) technology has developed. AI algorithms such as convolutional neural networks or recurrent neural networks are now widely used in various applications. In addition, AI technology is expected to be used more widely in epidemiological research and public health (MacIntyre et al., 2023; Ali, 2024). It is expected that AI technology will be used to augment and improve existing analytical tools and also improve efficiency in the hyper-fast processing of the huge amount of data that is generated daily. On the other hand, AI technology has difficult-to-understand algorithms and "black box" processing, and under the influence of these points, projects and companies that have caused ethical issues will increase. The balance between the interests of public health and individual rights will become a serious issue and the establishment of a framework that can use AI and consider these problems as soon as it is possible.

As AI algorithms are further introduced, it will be important to maintain the confidentiality of patients and consider data security (Williamson & Prybutok, 2024; Khalid et al., 2023; Zhang & Zhang, 2023). Expansion of the use and its versatility, as well as the transfer of subjects by organizations to third parties. These operations may not be due to the use of advanced algorithms, and this trend may be widely recognized using the advanced algorithm. However, the introduction and use of advanced algorithms change the value of information, which can be taken and shown to the information processing conducted in the past. Proprietary patient information may be leaked by using an advanced algorithm from information entrusted for the purposes of care or the like. In order to use AI technology in epidemiology research and public health, it is acquiring understanding and knowledge about AI, as well as setting rules to ensure the safety of using AI. Especially under the AI system, as well as a lesson from the problem which was in other projects as several parts of production should be assigned have agreed on common rules in advance to consider the use supposed together AI. In particular, attention should be paid to compliance with ethical guidelines for AI operations.

Data Privacy Concerns with Large-Scale Health Monitoring

Labeling blockchain technology as inadequate for performing the task of storing and securing patient health records is a significant concern (Sammeta & Parthiban, 2022; Ghadi et al., 2024). The main reason for this is the unfeasible scalability of this technology. It consists of a transaction list designed in the form of a ledger, and the size capacity is far from being able to accommodate input-output with the volume of health data. In healthcare, solutions based on blockchain technology are unable to provide the necessary level of privacy. Instead, they have the potential to absorb vast amounts of money and fail to deliver, as they will not meet the real needs of patient data sharing or patient data pooling, both of which are essential for achieving a large sample size for computational medical analysis. The recognition of these inadequacies opens the door to investing funds in the development of algorithms, alongside the enhancement of computational resources, that they are responsible for solving healthcare problems. The immediate need for predictive modeling pushes the data science community to develop methodologies to address concerns about personal privacy in the release of large-scale data related to patient information.

In recent years, a new research field called privacy-preserving machine learning has emerged to hybridize both artificial privacy technologies that provide guarantees on the secrecy of data as it is being handled by ML models and algorithms. That can be run on a private dataset with encrypted queries to provide accurate responses (Xu et al., 2021; Panzade et al., 2023). The current pioneering work on sympathetic privacy views state that every person's decision, informed by their unique variables, that guarantees to augment data reporting. The intention of sympathetic privacy is to create a different way of managing sensitive data processing in data science. Its premise is that while individuals may not be comfortable sharing sensitive data, they may agree if this data reveals something important about the individual who provided it, hence generating a stimulus for sharing.

One of the main results of employing artificial intelligence methodologies for privacy-based research has been the development of mathematical models (Reka et al.2024). Such mathematical model formalizes the goals of artificial intelligence systems that would like to have access to and use individual user data without compromising these users' privacy. The definition of relationships between a service provider and a user is encoded, and also accurate measures of an individual's privacy or how much privacy loss one experiences can be either computed or estimated.

Bias and Accuracy Issues in Predictive Models

The use of predictive models built on top of machine learning (ML), either supervised or not, has increased over the last few years, and the potential is enormous (Taye, 2023; Javaid et al., 2022). We have focused on the important quality characteristic of accuracy, which can be defined as the capability of AI models to provide the correct result within an acceptable variation of the real situation. The need to build very accurate predictive models for diagnostics or for reproducing complex biological processes, especially those that mimic human conditions, is pushing a growing number of technical scientists to build highly complex ML models. These models have hardly any analytical solutions, and thus there is limited ability to guarantee their robustness. The lack of transferability between different data sets is the current cutting-edge scientific problem of ML.

The majority of the papers analyzed in a specific period of 15 months have been developed on a specific dataset, where the model and data have been used for both training and validation. No proof has been given that the model has been built on all relevant information about data generation and the functioning of the process. Moreover, the model has not been allowed to learn the entire complexity of the noise, leading to an interpretation of variability not based on all relevant biological processes associated with the noise. This scenario is then translated into experiments, supported by low statistical power, and poorly designed rationales based only on the interpretation of the resulting high-dimensional analysis. Therefore, the final result is that most of the published predictive models present a lack of generalization. In the end, instead of being used as a preliminary unexplored hypothesis to be validated in large clinical trials, they became the reference standard.

Need for Transparency and Human Oversight in AI-Driven Decisions

AI systems should be designed to assist humans rather than replace them. In the context of public health, that means that outcomes should not rely entirely on automated systems. AI can help decision-making, but it cannot make decisions (Efthymiou, I. P., et al., 2020). Policymakers and other stakeholders must approach AI in health with caution and avoid the assumption that AI-driven predictions are always accurate. In the context of pandemics, the real-time data component is especially important because of the high number of variables, many of which are changing over time. As a result, the variable space is vast and untamed when dealing with surveillance data for novel emerging pathogens.

Drawing a proper inference from such a high-dimensional and non-stationary problem requires a dedicated modeling strategy, and a number of ML subfields do just that. With the help of strategies for analytics, AI has the great potential to impact with positive way the speed and efficiency of public health responses to emerging infectious diseases. However, while AI is a powerful additional tool that has the ability to provide actionable insights, it is not a replacement for human judgment. Policymakers and other stakeholders must approach AI in global health with caution and thoughtful oversight. They must use AI as it was designed: to aid decision-making, not replace it (Kijewski et al., 2024; Health Organization, 2023; Goktas & Grzybowski, 2025).

FUTURE DIRECTIONS AND EMERGING TRENDS

There is a growing need for more advanced models and data processing approaches for integrative, unsupervised, and high-dimensional predictive models. AI can provide both improved tools for integrating data from multiple sources and a new mindset for addressing issues in public health and epidemiology (Sidiropoulos, S., 2024). The hyper-specialization of researchers and the absence of adequate regulations to manage large-scale experiments with data further hinder the estimation of high-dimensional models involving thousands of variables.

AI is expected to evolve from task-based modeling to predictive modeling and real-time analytics on large, population-scale datasets. However, the current use of AI in most fields of research, including epidemiology, is at the task-based level, involving image or speech recognition as well as specialized games, because these tasks can easily be formulated for model training.

Highly complex algorithms, such as recurrent neural networks or gradient-boosted trees, can indeed be finely tuned for improving model performance, but the effectiveness of this hyper-parameter search is only consistent with large datasets (Shekhar et al., 2021; Aftab et al., 2025; Pandi et al., 2023). The availability of extensive data is therefore essential and, in some instances, combined with a discretization compatible with AI algorithms such as deep learning. Broadening the applicability of such models, from the analysis of web usage logs to healthcare datasets or unwired sensor observations in the context of a Smart City, requires further innovation and the launch of new research paths, usually involving interdisciplinary collaborations between domain experts, data scientists, and technologists. Like the emergence of data analysis in the 90s and the rise of network theory in the early 2000s, it is observed that the most successful applications of AI tend to develop their research programs and communities. On the other hand, this trend of successful research areas limits the diffusion of innovative ideas and the independent development of alternative solutions.

Improving AI Models with Better Datasets and Real-Time Learning

Machine learning models largely depend on their training datasets: performance is generally better when high-quality labeled datasets are used (Budach et al., 2022' Khatua et al., 2023). In terms of predicting where the next outbreak is going to happen, the use of reliable, large-scale, and relevant epidemiological datasets should be a priority. On the one hand, machine learning practitioners need to modify their models with algorithms that minimize or fully remove the effect of outdated datasets, since current AI and machine learning models lose their robustness when the situation being classified is evolving and the precision of the training set becomes obsolete.

One promising approach is that of real-time learning, which allows updates of the mapping function for new kinds of training cases (Wu et al., 2023; Shi et al., 2025; Wu et al., 2023). A model can be trained first on a large, but more static dataset of infections and then updated with new information. Epidemiological datasets inevitably involve the communication and summing of numbers that can induce errors. Incorporating a machine learning model for assessing the statistical consistency of these datasets can offer an early warning that a disease outbreak is underway – potentially even before the ground-truth official reports get published.

Expanding AI Applications in Zoonotic Disease Prediction and Global Pandemic Preparedness

Advances in artificial intelligence (AI) have the potential to enhance our capacity to identify and control outbreaks of infectious diseases and make better use of limited data in the process (Zeng et al., 2021; Ali, 2024). Since most infectious diseases infect both humans and animals, a better understanding of the ecology and epidemiology of these diseases in natural populations of wild animals and domestic livestock must be part of global pandemic preparedness. We argue that applying advanced algorithms to a variety of sources can transform how we identify and control infectious disease outbreaks. With access to vast stores of data, new tools are making it possible to not only understand how infections are spreading in animal and human populations but to predict local spillover and human outbreaks faster and with higher accuracy than before (Muylaert et al., 2023; Haq et al., 2024; Wang et al., 2025; Ali, 2024).

In contrast to classical animal and human disease surveillance that only provides information about a specific disease and location when a clinician detects a disease, digital disease detection can monitor a broad range of diseases in space and time, yielding information about disease risks and potential local outbreaks. Most of the data that are available for infectious disease surveillance are from humans. The digital revolution has overtaken parts of the human and animal health sectors that share data. However, some important animal health data sources are becoming increasingly and are available, including data from a range of animal production, from distribution, and from environment sectors (Neethirajan & Kemp, 2021, Holzinger et al., 2023; Mishra & Mishra, 2023).

Collaboration Between AI Researchers, Epidemiologists, Public Health Experts, and Policymakers.

The role of advanced algorithms has increasingly emerged as a highly feasible and particularly effective type of sensor that significantly enhances the capability of improving both nowcasting and near-term forecasting of various epidemic threats we face today (Murthy, 2023; Cuadros et al., 2024; Caldwell et al., 2024). These sophisticated algorithms meticulously analyze complex data patterns and interrelations, processing vast amounts of information to provide timely insights and predictions that are crucial for effective public health responses and decision-making processes. By leveraging these advanced analytical techniques, health authorities can gain a much deeper understanding of the intricate patterns of disease spread (Ugwu et al., 2024; Khodadadi and Towfek, 2023; Ahmed et al., 2023). This understanding ultimately leads to improved outcomes in managing public health crises, fostering a more robust and responsive health infrastructure that can adapt to the rapidly changing landscape of epidemic threats. The integration of these algorithms into public health strategies also allows for a more proactive approach to identifying potential outbreaks before they escalate, enabling swift interventions that can save lives and reduce the burden on healthcare systems (Chadwick, 2025; Javed, 2024; Eze et al., 2024).

CONCLUSION

Epidemiology, the study of health outcomes and the determinants of health in specific populations is a multidisciplinary field that draws on concepts, methods, and techniques from diverse sources such as biostatistics, computer science, biology, social science, and economics. Embracing the progress of advanced algorithms in artificial intelligence, and their practical implementations, has the power of changing the way in which epidemiological research is conducted, and the way in which epidemic outbreaks are managed. Big data, being data that have at least one of the following characteristics: high volume; high flow rate; or high complexity, has triggered the demand for a new family of computational tools for handling large datasets and allowing cross-data exploration. Artificial intelligence and specifically, machine learning, is the response to that call. Knowledge-driven traditional computational approaches are being replaced by data-driven approaches. The future progress of epidemiology in the field of outbreak detection depends on the broader and more systematic use of advanced algorithms and along the term interdisciplinary collaboration between those who develop them, and those who implement them (Rodríguez-González et al., 2019). It is still far from clear whether such progress will equal the conclusion of the statistician M. Mead in 1963 that: "epidemics are not controlled precisely because they are not understood."

Extreme Weather Events (EWEs), are generally defined as weather-related hydro-meteorological events generally considered as outliers with respect to the long-term statistical behavior of a given weather parameter for a given location. The signature of climate change is the increase in the frequency, and intensity, of certain extreme events as heatwaves, rainfall, and flood events (Mahadi Hasan et al., 2023). Climate Change has also had a noticeable impact on EWEs, with the risk for extreme precipitation events usually increasing, and the predictability of stratified extreme temperature episodes. Under the above climate change and urbanization framework, the challenge for urban resilience needs to decrease and find methods for protecting urban populations from the seemingly endless sequence of EWEs. In response to these challenges, recent research has suggested that interventions based on advanced algorithms are capable of detecting and predicting EWEs and have the potential to both improve the early warning processes and the response and recovery capacity of the affected populations or territories. A brief review of the state-of-the-art concerning the effect that climate change has on the frequency, and predictability, of extreme precipitation events in order to draw the attention of the public health authorities and the epidemiologist community.

REFERENCES

Abdulkareem, M., & Petersen, S. E. (2021). The promise of AI in detection, diagnosis, and epidemiology for combating COVID-19. Beyond the hype. https://www.ncbi.nlm.nih.gov/. PMID: 34056579

Adegoke, B. O., Odugbose, T., & Adeyemi, C. (2024). Data analytics for predicting disease outbreaks: A review of models and tools. *International Journal of Life Science Research Updates*, *2*(2), 1–9. DOI: 10.53430/ijlsru.2024.2.2.0023

Aftab, M., Ahmad, T., Adeel, S., Bhatti, S. H., & Irfan, M. (2025). Hyper-parameter tuning through innovative designing to avoid over-fitting in machine learning modelling: A case study of small data sets. *Journal of Statistical Computation and Simulation*, *95*(7), 1–15. DOI: 10.1080/00949655.2025.2465787

Ahmed, A., Xi, R., Hou, M., Shah, S. A., & Hameed, S. (2023). Harnessing big data analytics for healthcare: A comprehensive review of frameworks, implications, applications, and impacts. *IEEE Access*. https://ieeexplore.ieee.org/

Ajagbe, S. A., & Adigun, M. O. (2024). Deep learning techniques for detection and prediction of pandemic diseases: A systematic literature review. *Multimedia Tools and Applications*. https://link.springer.com/

Ajagbe, S. A., Mudali, P., & Adigun, M. O. (2024). Internet of things with deep learning techniques for pandemic detection: A comprehensive review of current trends and open issues. *Electronics*. https://www.mdpi.com/

Albahlal, B. M. (2023). Emerging technology-driven hybrid models for preventing and monitoring infectious diseases: A comprehensive review and conceptual framework. *Diagnostics*. https://www.mdpi.com/

Ali, H. (2024). AI for pandemic preparedness and infectious disease surveillance: Predicting outbreaks, modeling transmission, and optimizing public health interventions. *International Journal of Research Publication and Reviews*. https://www.researchgate.net/

Alzamili, A. H., & Ruhaiyem, N. I. R. (2025). A comprehensive review of deep learning and machine learning techniques for early-stage skin cancer detection: Challenges and research gaps. *Journal of Intelligent Systems*. https://www.degruyter.com/

Andersson, H., Svensson, A., Frank, C., Rantala, A., Holmberg, M., & Bremer, A. (2022). Ethics education to support ethical competence learning in healthcare: An integrative systematic review. *BMC Medical Ethics*, *23*(1), 29. https://link.springer.com/. DOI: 10.1186/s12910-022-00766-z PMID: 35305627

Babanejaddehaki, G., An, A., & Papagelis, M. (2025). Disease outbreak detection and forecasting: A review of methods and data sources. *ACM Transactions on Computing for Healthcare*, *6*(2), 1–40. https://dl.acm.org/. DOI: 10.1145/3708549

Bekbolatova, M., Mayer, J., Ong, C. W., & Toma, M. (2024). Transformative potential of AI in healthcare: Definitions, applications, and navigating the ethical landscape and public perspectives. *Healthcare*. https://www.mdpi.com/

Budach, L., Feuerpfeil, M., Ihde, N., Nathansen, A., Noack, N., Patzlaff, H., & Harmouch, H. (2022). The effects of data quality on machine learning performance. *arXiv*. https://arxiv.org/abs/2207.14529

Caldwell, J. M., Liu, G., Geiger, E., Heron, S. F., Eakin, C. M., De La Cour, J., Greene, A., Raymundo, L., Dryden, J., Schlaff, A., Stella, J. S., Kindinger, T. L., Couch, C. S., Fenner, D., Hoot, W., Manzello, D., & Donahue, M. J. (2024). Multi-factor coral disease risk: A new product for early warning and management. *Ecological Applications*, *34*(4), e2961. DOI: 10.1002/eap.2961 PMID: 38522943

Centers for Disease Control and Prevention. (2012). Endemic, epidemic, and pandemic. In *Principles of epidemiology in public health practice* (3rd ed., Lesson 1, Section 11). U.S. Department of Health and Human Services.

Chadwick, F. (2025). AI for disease surveillance in the modern era: Early detection and rapid response. *Global Journal of Medical and Biomedical Case Reports*. https://www.researchgate.net/

Chen, Q., Leaman, R., Allot, A., Luo, L., Wei, C. H., Yan, S., & Lu, Z. (2020). Artificial intelligence (AI) in action: Addressing the COVID-19 pandemic with natural language processing (NLP). https://www.ncbi.nlm.nih.gov/

Chow, E. J., Uyeki, T. M., & Chu, H. Y. (2023). The effects of the COVID-19 pandemic on community respiratory virus activity. *Nature Reviews Microbiology*. https://www.nature.com/

Chowdhury, A. T., Newaz, M., Saha, P., & Majid, M. E. Mus output truncatedhtak, A., & Kabir, M. A. (2024). Application of big data in infectious disease surveillance: Contemporary challenges and solutions. In *Surveillance, prevention, and control of infectious diseases: An AI perspective* (pp. 51-71). Springer Nature Switzerland.

Cohen, L. E., Hansen, C. L., Andrew, M. K., McNeil, S. A., Vanhems, P., Kyncl, J., Domingo, J. D., Zhang, T., Dbaibo, G., Laguna-Torres, V. A., Draganescu, A., Baumeister, E., Gomez, D., Raboni, S. M., Giamberardino, H. I. G., Nunes, M. C., Burtseva, E., Sominina, A., Medić, S., & Chaves, S. S. (2024). Predictors of severity of influenza-related hospitalizations: Results from the Global Influenza Hospital Surveillance Network (GIHSN). *The Journal of Infectious Diseases*, *229*(4), 999–1009. https://www.ncbi.nlm.nih.gov/. DOI: 10.1093/infdis/jiad303 PMID: 37527470

Cuadros, D. F., Chen, X., Li, J., Omori, R., & Musuka, G. (2024). Advancing public health surveillance: Integrating modeling and GIS in the wastewater-based epidemiology of viruses, a narrative review. *Pathogens*. https://www.mdpi.com/

Dairi, A., Harrou, F., Zeroual, A., Hittawe, M. M., & Sun, Y. (2021). Comparative study of machine learning methods for COVID-19 transmission forecasting. *Journal of Biomedical Informatics*, *118*, 103791. https://www.sciencedirect.com/. DOI: 10.1016/j.jbi.2021.103791 PMID: 33915272

Danon, L., Ford, A., House, T., Jewell, C., Keeling, M., Roberts, G., Ross, J., & Vernon, M. (2011). Networks and the epidemiology of infectious disease. https://arxiv.org/abs/1011.5950

G2. (2024, December 10). *85+ big data statistics to map growth in 2025*. https://www.g2.com/articles/big-data-statistics

Diareme, K. C., Liapakis, A., & Efthymiou, I. (2022). Big data, sentiment analysis, and examples during the COVID-19 pandemic. *HAPSc Policy Briefs Series*, *3*(2), 21–30. DOI: 10.12681/hapscpbs.33779

Dong, J., Wu, H., Zhou, D., Li, K., Zhang, Y., Ji, H., Tong, Z., Lou, S., & Liu, Z. (2021). Application of big data and artificial intelligence in COVID-19 prevention, diagnosis, treatment and management decisions in China. *Journal of Medical Systems*, *45*(9), 84. DOI: 10.1007/s10916-021-01757-0 PMID: 34302549

Duan, C., Li, C., Ren, R., Bai, W., & Zhou, L. (2023). An overview of avian influenza surveillance strategies and modes. *Science in One Health*. https://www.sciencedirect.com/

Efthymiou, I. (2024). Exploring the frontier: New and future trends in research. In B. Orlando (Ed.), *Innovation capabilities and entrepreneurial opportunities of smart working* (pp. 48-68). IGI Global Scientific Publishing. DOI: 10.4018/978-1-7998-8797-3.ch003

Efthymiou, I. P. (2024). *Human wellbeing in the age of artificial intelligence*.

Efthymiou, I.-P., Sidiropoulos, S., Kritas, D., Rapti, P., Vozikis, A., & Souliotis, K. (2020). AI transforming healthcare management during COVID-19 pandemic. *HAPSc Policy Briefs Series*, *1*(1), 130–138. DOI: 10.12681/hapscpbs.24958

Ehiobuche, C., & Ampadu-Nyarkoh, K. (2024). *On the business side of healthcare COVID-19 era and beyond: Smarter leadership better management best outcome.*

Engelmann, L. (2022). Digital epidemiology, deep phenotyping and the enduring fantasy of pathological omniscience. *Big Data & Society*. https://journals.sagepub.com/

Esmaeilzadeh, P. (2024). Challenges and strategies for wide-scale artificial intelligence (AI) deployment in healthcare practices: A perspective for healthcare organizations. *Artificial Intelligence in Medicine*, *151*, 102861. DOI: 10.1016/j.artmed.2024.102861 PMID: 38555850

Eze, C. E., Igwama, G. T., Nwankwo, E. I., & Victor, E. (2024). AI-driven health data analytics for early detection of infectious diseases: A conceptual exploration of US public health strategies. https://www.researchgate.net/

Fisher, S., & Rosella, L. C. (2022). Priorities for successful use of artificial intelligence by public health organizations: A literature review. *BMC Public Health*. https://link.springer.com/

Ghadi, Y. Y., Mazhar, T., Shahzad, T., Amir Khan, M., Abd-Alrazaq, A., Ahmed, A., & Hamam, H. (2024). The role of blockchain to secure internet of medical things. *Scientific Reports*, *14*(1), 18422. DOI: 10.1038/s41598-024-68529-x PMID: 39117650

Ghosh, S., & Sharma, V. (2024). Tracking of disease—A review of the state of the art of technology for next generation healthcare. In *Deep learning in internet of things for next generation healthcare* (pp. 242-268).

Goktas, P., & Grzybowski, A. (2025). Shaping the future of healthcare: Ethical clinical challenges and pathways to trustworthy AI. *Journal of Clinical Medicine*. https://www.mdpi.com/

Greenhalgh, T., & Engebretsen, E. (2022). The science-policy relationship in times of crisis: An urgent call for a pragmatist turn. *Social Science & Medicine*. https://www.sciencedirect.com/

Haq, Z., Nazir, J., Manzoor, T., Saleem, A., Hamadani, H., Khan, A. A., Saleem Bhat, S., Jha, P., & Ahmad, S. M. (2024). Zoonotic spillover and viral mutations from low and middle-income countries: Improving prevention strategies and bridging policy gaps. *PeerJ*, *12*, e17394. https://peerj.com/. DOI: 10.7717/peerj.17394 PMID: 38827296

Health Organization. W. (2023). *Regulatory considerations on artificial intelligence for health*. https://www.google.com/

Holzinger, A., Keiblinger, K., Holub, P., Zatloukal, K., & Müller, H. (2023). AI for life: Trends in artificial intelligence for biotechnology. *New Biotechnology*, *74*, 16–24. DOI: 10.1016/j.nbt.2023.02.001 PMID: 36754147

Javaid, M., Haleem, A., Singh, R. P., Suman, R., & Rab, S. (2022). Significance of machine learning in healthcare: Features, pillars and applications. *International Journal of Intelligent Networks*, *3*, 58–73. DOI: 10.1016/j.ijin.2022.05.002

Javed, I. (2024). Exploring the role of big data in predicting and preventing epidemics. *Frontiers in Healthcare Technology*. https://www.sprcopen.org/

Jayasekara, R. U., Jayathilaka, G. S., Siriwardana, C., Amaratunga, D., Haigh, R., Bandara, C., & Dissanayake, R. (2023). Identifying gaps in early warning mechanisms and evacuation procedures for tsunamis in Sri Lanka, with a special focus on the use of social media. *International Journal of Disaster Resilience in the Built Environment*, *14*(1), 1–20. DOI: 10.1108/IJDRBE-02-2021-0012

Kamalrathne, T., Amaratunga, D., Haigh, R., & Kodituwakku, L. (2023). Need for effective detection and early warnings for epidemic and pandemic preparedness planning in the context of multi-hazards: Lessons from the COVID-19 pandemic. *International Journal of Disaster Risk Reduction*, *92*, 103724. DOI: 10.1016/j.ijdrr.2023.103724 PMID: 37197332

Khalid, N., Qayyum, A., Bilal, M., Al-Fuqaha, A., & Qadir, J. (2023). Privacy-preserving artificial intelligence in healthcare: Techniques and applications. *Computers in Biology and Medicine*, *158*, 106848. DOI: 10.1016/j.compbiomed.2023.106848 PMID: 37044052

Khatua, A., Mailthody, V. S., Taleka, B., Ma, T., Song, X., & Hwu, W. M. (2023, August). IGB: Addressing the gaps in labeling, features, heterogeneity, and size of public graph datasets for deep learning research. In *Proceedings of the 29th ACM SIGKDD Conference on Knowledge Discovery and Data Mining* (pp. 4284-4295). DOI: 10.1145/3580305.3599843

Khodadadi, E., & Towfek, S. K. (2023). Internet of things enabled disease outbreak detection: A predictive modeling system. *Journal of Intelligent Systems & Internet of Things, 10*(1), 84–91. DOI: 10.54216/JISIoT.100107

Kijewski, S., Ronchi, E., & Vayena, E. (2024). International organisations and the global governance of AI in health. In *Research handbook on health, AI and the law* (pp. 254–272). Edward Elgar Publishing. DOI: 10.4337/9781802205657.ch15

Lakoff, A. (2024). *Planning for the wrong pandemic: COVID-19 and the limits of expert knowledge.*

MacIntyre, C. R., Chen, X., Kunasekaran, M., Quigley, A., Lim, S., Stone, H., Paik, H., Yao, L., Heslop, D., Wei, W., Sarmiento, I., & Gurdasani, D. (2023). Artificial intelligence in public health: The potential of epidemic early warning systems. *The Journal of International Medical Research, 51*(3),. DOI: 10.1177/03000605231159335 PMID: 36967669

Mahadi Hasan, M., Usama Islam, M., Jafar Sadeq, M., Fung, W. K., & Uddin, J. (2023). Review on the evaluation and development of artificial intelligence for COVID-19 containment. https://www.ncbi.nlm.nih.gov/

Majnarić, L. T., Babič, F., O'Sullivan, S., & Holzinger, A. (2021). AI and big data in healthcare: Towards a more comprehensive research framework for multimorbidity. *Journal of Clinical Medicine, 10*(4), 766. DOI: 10.3390/jcm10040766 PMID: 33672914

Mannan, A., Shoket, N., Ul Rahman, J., & Uwitije, R. (2025). Dynamic analysis of Ebola virus disease with non-linear incidence rate using Morlet wavelet neural networks and hybrid optimization techniques. *Modeling Earth Systems and Environment, 11*(2), 79. DOI: 10.1007/s40808-024-02256-0

Mehta, N., & Shukla, S. (2022). Pandemic analytics: How countries are leveraging big data analytics and artificial intelligence to fight [*SN Computer Science*. https://link.springer.com/]. *COVID, 19*. PMID: 34778841

Meltwater. (2024, January 30). *Digital 2024 - An in-depth report analysis*. https://www.meltwater.com/en/blog/digital-2024-report-analysis

Mishra, H., & Mishra, D. (2023). Artificial intelligence and machine learning in agriculture: Transforming farming systems. *Research Trends in Agricultural Science*. https://www.researchgate.net/

Moises, D. J., & Kunguma, O. (2023). Improving flood early warning systems in Kabbe, Namibia: A situational analysis approach. *International Journal of Disaster Risk Reduction*. https://www.sciencedirect.com/

Morgenstern, J. D., Rosella, L. C., Daley, M. J., Goel, V., Schünemann, H. J., & Piggott, T. (2021). "AI's gonna have an impact on everything in society, so it has to have an impact on public health": A fundamental qualitative descriptive study of the implications of artificial intelligence for public health. https://www.ncbi.nlm.nih.gov/

Murthy, R. K. (2023). *Early detection and prediction of zoonotic disease events using event-based surveillance and machine learning*. Washington State University.

Muylaert, R. L., Wilkinson, D. A., Kingston, T., D'Odorico, P., Rulli, M. C., Galli, N., John, R. S., Alviola, P., & Hayman, D. T. (2023). Using drivers and transmission pathways to identify SARS-like coronavirus spillover risk hotspots. *Nature Communications, 14*(1), 6854. DOI: 10.1038/s41467-023-42627-2 PMID: 37891177

Neethirajan, S., & Kemp, B. (2021). Digital livestock farming. *Sensing and Bio-Sensing Research.* https://library.wur.nl/

Olawade, D. B., Wada, O. J., David-Olawade, A. C., Kunonga, E., Abaire, O., & Ling, J. (2023). Using artificial intelligence to improve public health: A narrative review. *Frontiers in Public Health, 11*, 1196397. DOI: 10.3389/fpubh.2023.1196397 PMID: 37954052

Pandi, S. S., Chiranjeevi, V. R., Kumaragurubaran, T., & Kumar, P. (2023, November). Improvement of classification accuracy in machine learning algorithm by hyper-parameter optimization. In *Proceedings of the 2023 International Conference on Research Methodologies in Knowledge Management, Artificial Intelligence and Telecommunication Engineering (RMKMATE)* (pp. 1-5). IEEE.

Panzade, P., Takabi, D., & Cai, Z. (2023). Privacy-preserving machine learning using functional encryption: Opportunities and challenges. *IEEE Internet of Things Journal*.

Pastor-Escuredo, D. (2021). *Digital epidemiology: A review*. https://arxiv.org/abs/2103.03767

Rahman, S. Z., Senthil, R., Ramalingam, V., & Gopal, R. (2023). Predicting infectious disease outbreaks with machine learning and epidemiological data. *Journal of Advanced Zoology, 44*(S4), 110–121. DOI: 10.17762/jaz.v44iS4.2177

Reka, S. S., Dragicevic, T., Venugopal, P., Ravi, V., & Rajagopal, M. K. (2024). Big data analytics and artificial intelligence aspects for privacy and security concerns for demand response modelling in smart grid: A futuristic approach. *Heliyon, 10*(15), e35683. DOI: 10.1016/j.heliyon.2024.e35683 PMID: 39170135

Rodríguez-González, A., Zanin, M., & Menasalvas-Ruiz, E. (2019). Public health and epidemiology informatics: Can artificial intelligence help future global challenges? An overview of antimicrobial resistance and impact of climate change in disease epidemiology. https://www.ncbi.nlm.nih.gov/

Sammeta, N., & Parthiban, L. (2022). Hyperledger blockchain enabled secure medical record management with deep learning-based diagnosis model. *Complex & Intelligent Systems*. https://link.springer.com/

Sardana, N., & Jadhav Bhatt, A. (2021). Exploratory study of existing approaches for analyzing epidemics. https://www.ncbi.nlm.nih.gov/

Sarker, I. H. (2021). Machine learning: Algorithms, real-world applications and research directions. *SN Computer Science*. https://link.springer.com/

Shekhar, S., Bansode, A., & Salim, A. (2021, December). A comparative study of hyper-parameter optimization tools. In *Proceedings of the 2021 IEEE Asia-Pacific Conference on Computer Science and Data Engineering (CSDE)* (pp. 1-6). IEEE. DOI: 10.1109/CSDE53843.2021.9718485

Shi, X., Xuan, X., Huang, X., Xue, J., & Shen, X. (2025). Digital twin empowered wireless positioning: Prospects, architecture, and challenges. *IEEE Network*, 1. DOI: 10.1109/MNET.2025.3544694

Sidiropoulos, S. (2024). *Global health and civil society: Financial tools and policies*. TZIOLA Publications.

Soto-Ferrari, M., Carrasco-Pena, A., & Prieto, D. (2025). EpiForecaster: A novel deep learning ensemble optimization approach to combining forecasts for emerging epidemic outbreaks. *Stochastic Environmental Research and Risk Assessment*, *39*(2), 675–695. DOI: 10.1007/s00477-024-02889-8

Sumithra, S., Radhika, M., Venkatesh, G., Lakshmi, B. S., Jancee, B. V., Mohankumar, N., & Murugan, S. (2025). Deep learning for infectious disease surveillance integrating internet of things for rapid response. *International Journal of Electrical and Computer Engineering*, *15*(1), 1175. DOI: 10.11591/ijece.v15i1.pp1175-1186

Tambo, E., Djuikoue, I. C., Tazemda, G. K., Fotsing, M. F., & Zhou, X. N. (2021). Early stage risk communication and community engagement (RCCE) strategies and measures against the coronavirus disease 2019 (COVID-19) pandemic crisis. *Global Health Journal (Amsterdam, Netherlands)*, *5*(1), 44–50. DOI: 10.1016/j.glohj.2021.02.009 PMID: 33850632

Taye, M. M. (2023). Understanding of machine learning with deep learning: Architectures, workflow, applications and future directions. *Computers*. https://www.mdpi.com/

Ugwu, O. P. C., Alum, E. U., Ugwu, J. N., Eze, V. H. U., Ugwu, C. N., Ogenyi, F. C., & Okon, M. B. (2024). Harnessing technology for infectious disease response in conflict zones: Challenges, innovations, and policy implications. *Medicine*, *103*(28), e38834. DOI: 10.1097/MD.0000000000038834 PMID: 38996110

Wang, Y. H., Chen, J. J., Ma, J., Owen, J. E., Wang, G. L., Yu, L. J., . . . Fang, L. Q. (2025). Early-warning signals and the role of H9N2 in the spillover of avian influenza viruses. *Med*. https://www.cell.com/

Williamson, S. M., & Prybutok, V. (2024). Balancing privacy and progress: A review of privacy challenges, systemic oversight, and patient perceptions in AI-driven healthcare. *Applied Sciences*. https://www.mdpi.com/

Wu, J., Huang, Z., Hu, Z., & Lv, C. (2023). Toward human-in-the-loop AI: Enhancing deep reinforcement learning via real-time human guidance for autonomous driving. *Engineering*. https://www.sciencedirect.com/

Wu, Q., Zeng, J., & Wu, K. (2022). Research and application of crop pest monitoring and early warning technology in China. *Frontiers of Agricultural Science and Engineering*, *9*(1), 19–36. DOI: 10.15302/J-FASE-2021411

Wu, X., Liu, C., Wang, L., & Bilal, M. (2023). Internet of things-enabled real-time health monitoring system using deep learning. *Neural Computing and Applications*. https://link.springer.com/

Xu, R., Baracaldo, N., & Joshi, J. (2021). Privacy-preserving machine learning: Methods, challenges and directions. *arXiv*. https://arxiv.org/abs/2108.04417

Zeng, D., Cao, Z., & Neill, D. B. (2021). Artificial intelligence–enabled public health surveillance—From local detection to global epidemic monitoring and control. In *Artificial intelligence in medicine*. https://www.ncbi.nlm.nih.gov/

Zhang, J., & Zhang, Z. (2023). Ethics and governance of trustworthy medical artificial intelligence. *BMC Medical Informatics and Decision Making*. https://link.springer.com/

Zhang, L., Guo, W., & Lv, C. (2024). Modern technologies and solutions to enhance surveillance and response systems for emerging zoonotic diseases. *Science in One Health*. https://www.sciencedirect.com/

Zhang, X. X., Jin, Y. Z., Lu, Y. H., Huang, L. L., Wu, C. X., Lv, S., Chen, Z., Xiang, H., & Zhou, X. N. (2023). Infectious disease control: From health security strengthening to health systems improvement at global level. *Global Health Research and Policy*, *8*(1), 38. DOI: 10.1186/s41256-023-00319-w PMID: 37670331

Zhu, S., Yu, T., Xu, T., Chen, H., Dustdar, S., Gigan, S., Gunduz, D., Hossain, E., Jin, Y., Lin, F., Liu, B., Wan, Z., Zhang, J., Zhao, Z., Zhu, W., Chen, Z., Durrani, T. S., Wang, H., Wu, J., & Pan, Y. (2023). Intelligent computing: The latest advances, challenges, and future. *Intelligent Computing*, *2*, 0006. DOI: 10.34133/icomputing.0006

Chapter 10

A Synergistic Mobile Informatics Framework for Proactive Chronic Disease Prognostication and Therapeutic Optimization

R. Hari krishna
Hindusthan College of Arts and Science, India

A. V. Senthil Kumar
https://orcid.org/0000-0002-8587-7017
Hindusthan College of Arts and Science, India

Revati Ramrao Rautrao
https://orcid.org/0000-0001-7803-8699
Dr. D.Y. Patil B-School, India

R. V. Suganya
Vels Institute of Science, Technology, and Advanced Studies, India

Kalpana Sukumar
Saveetha Engineering College, India

S. Nagakishore Bhavanam
Mangalayatan University, Jabalpur, India

Indrarini Dyah Irawati
Telcom University, Indonesia

Shallu Sehgal
Shoolini Institute of Life Sciences and Business Management, India

Neeru Sidana
Amity School of Economics, Amity University, Noida, India

DOI: 10.4018/979-8-3373-1992-6.ch010

ABSTRACT

Chronic diseases significantly contribute to global morbidity and mortality, highlighting the need for advanced solutions . This project introduces a Synergistic Mobile Informatics Framework, integrating real-time data acquisition, predictive analytics, and personalized treatment recommendations for proactive chronic disease management . Leveraging wearable devices, mobile apps, and cloud-based machine learning, the framework enables continuous health monitoring, early detection of disease exacerbations, and tailored interventions . By analyzing physiological, behavioral, and environmental data in real time, advanced predictive models identify high-risk trends, triggering early alerts for patients and healthcare providers . These alerts reduce complications, hospitalizations, and healthcare costs . This approach fosters collaboration between patients, providers, and technology, empowering individuals to manage their health effectively while transforming chronic disease care through precision, efficiency, and innovation .

INTRODUCTION

Chronic diseases such as diabetes, cardiovascular disorders, and respiratory conditions impose long-term challenges on patients and healthcare systems. Traditional treatment models are reactive, often failing to prevent acute episodes. Mobile informatics and AI offer a transformative approach—allowing real-time health tracking, risk prediction, and dynamic therapy adjustment. This paper introduces a unified framework that leverages mobile computing, edge processing, and intelligent analytics to proactively address chronic disease trajectories.

Overview of Chronic Diseases and Their Global Impact

Chronic diseases, including cardiovascular diseases, diabetes, chronic respiratory diseases, and cancer, pose significant health and economic burdens worldwide (Cheng et al., 2023) . The World Health Organization (WHO) reports that chronic diseases account for approximately 71% of global deaths, with a majority occurring in low- and middle-income countries (Chowdhury et al., 2020). These conditions are often characterized by long durations and slow progression, leading to severe (Chowdhury et al., 2020) .morbidity and reduced quality of life. With an aging population and lifestyle-related risk factors such as sedentary behavior, poor dietary habits, and environmental pollutants, the prevalence of chronic diseases continues to rise (Ho et al., 2022) . The economic implications are equally concerning, as chronic diseases strain healthcare systems, necessitate prolonged medical interventions

(Abidi & Abidi, 2022), and lead to loss of productivity. Given these challenges, there is an urgent need to explore advanced methodologies for early prediction and effective management of chronic diseases to reduce their impact on individuals and healthcare infrastructures.

The Need for Proactive Prognostication and Therapeutic Optimization

Traditional approaches to chronic disease management primarily focus on reactive treatment strategies that address symptoms rather than preventing disease progression. This reactive model often results in late diagnoses, increased healthcare costs, and suboptimal patient outcomes (Ahmed et al., 2021). A shift towards proactive prognostication and therapeutic optimization is essential to mitigate these challenges. Proactive prognostication involves leveraging predictive models and health data analytics to identify high-risk individuals before the onset of severe symptoms (Ghosh et al., 2023). By utilizing machine learning algorithms, artificial intelligence, and health informatics, early intervention strategies can be tailored to individual patient profiles. Therapeutic optimization ensures that treatment regimens are continuously adapted based on real-time health data, thereby enhancing efficacy and minimizing adverse effects (Lu et al., 2021). This proactive approach enables healthcare providers to personalize treatment plans, improve patient adherence to prescribed therapies, and ultimately enhance long-term health outcomes (Feng et al., 2022).

How Mobile Informatics Enhances Chronic Disease Management

The rapid advancement of mobile informatics has revolutionized healthcare delivery by providing real-time monitoring, decision support systems, and patient-centered care models. Mobile health (mHealth) technologies, including wearable devices, mobile applications, and cloud-based health platforms, facilitate continuous health tracking and early anomaly detection (Banos et al., 2020; Liu et al., 2020). These technologies enable patients to actively participate in their health management by monitoring vital signs, medication adherence, and lifestyle modifications. Moreover, mobile informatics allows healthcare professionals to access real-time patient data, enabling timely interventions and remote consultations. The integration of artificial intelligence and big data analytics further enhances predictive capabilities, allowing for more accurate prognostications and personalized therapeutic recommendations. Mobile informatics also bridges the gap between patients and healthcare providers by facilitating telemedicine, reducing hospital visits (Lee et al., 2021), and improving overall healthcare accessibility, especially in remote or underserved areas. The potential of mobile informatics in chronic disease management is vast, offering an efficient, cost-effective, and scalable solution for addressing the growing burden of chronic illnesses globally, (Ho et al., 2022; Reddy et al., 2022).

Research Objectives and Significance of the Study

The primary objective of this research is to develop a synergistic mobile informatics framework that integrates predictive analytics, real-time health monitoring, and personalized therapeutic interventions to enhance chronic disease management. By leveraging computational intelligence and autonomous data extraction, this framework aims to provide early prognostic insights and optimize treatment regimens tailored to individual patient needs. The study seeks to address the limitations of traditional chronic disease management by incorporating adaptive learning models and real-time data processing capabilities. The significance of this research lies in its potential to improve patient outcomes, reduce healthcare costs, and empower individuals with actionable health insights. Furthermore, the study contributes to the evolving landscape of digital health by proposing an innovative, data-driven approach to chronic disease prognostication and therapeutic optimization. Through this framework, healthcare professionals can deliver more precise, proactive, and personalized care, ultimately transforming the way chronic diseases are managed on a global scale.

Structure of the Chapter

This chapter has introduced the fundamental aspects of chronic diseases, their global impact, and the pressing need for proactive prognostication and therapeutic optimization. It has outlined the role of mobile informatics in enhancing chronic disease management by leveraging real-time health monitoring, predictive analytics, and patient-centered care models. The research objectives and significance of the study have also been discussed, emphasizing the transformative potential of a mobile informatics framework in chronic disease management. The subsequent sections of this research will delve into the theoretical foundations, methodologies, implementation strategies, and empirical findings that validate the proposed framework. By establishing a comprehensive understanding of the research context in this chapter, the foundation is set for an in-depth exploration of mobile informatics and its role in revolutionizing chronic disease prognostication and therapeutic optimization.

LITERATURE REVIEW

Several studies have explored mobile health (mHealth) and AI-driven decision support systems. For example, Abidi & Abidi (2022) emphasized intelligent care pathways, while Nguyen et al. (2021) highlighted wearable integration for continuous monitoring. However, existing systems often lack seamless interoperability, adaptability to individual health profiles, or real-time therapeutic adjustment. Our approach builds upon and extends prior work by offering an end-to-end, patient-centered, and adaptive system architecture.

Existing Chronic Disease Prognostication Methods

Chronic disease prognostication is an essential aspect of modern healthcare, enabling early intervention and effective disease management (Abidi & Abidi, 2022). Traditional clinical approaches have long relied on statistical risk models, patient history assessments, and physician expertise to forecast disease progression. These methods, while valuable, often lack the precision required for individualized prognostication. The reliance on population-based risk factors and generalized treatment strategies limits their effectiveness in catering to the unique physiological and genetic makeup of individual patients. Moreover, these methods are heavily dependent on periodic clinical visits, leading to delays in detection and intervention.

In recent years, AI-driven predictive analytics have emerged as a transformative force in disease prognostication. Machine learning and deep learning models can analyze vast datasets comprising patient demographics, laboratory results, genetic markers, and lifestyle factors to identify patterns indicative of disease progression (Deng & Yu, 2020). These models offer improved accuracy over traditional methods by continuously learning from new data and adapting their predictions accordingly. Furthermore, AI algorithms facilitate real-time risk stratification, allowing healthcare professionals to implement preemptive interventions and personalized treatment plans (Bashir & Qamar, 2021; Shen et al., 2021). However, despite their promise, AI-driven methods often face challenges related to data interoperability, model interpretability (Chen et al., 2021), and the integration of diverse healthcare data sources.

Mobile Informatics in Healthcare

The integration of mobile informatics in healthcare has revolutionized patient monitoring and disease management. IoT-enabled devices, wearables, and cloud computing applications have enabled continuous health monitoring outside clinical settings. Wearable sensors track vital parameters such as heart rate, blood glucose levels, and physical activity, transmitting real-time data to healthcare providers. This seamless connectivity facilitates early detection of health anomalies and proactive intervention, reducing the burden on healthcare systems and improving patient outcomes. Additionally, cloud-based platforms allow for secure data storage and remote access, ensuring that patient information is readily available for analysis and clinical decision-making.

Existing mobile health frameworks have contributed significantly to chronic disease management, offering mobile applications for symptom tracking, medication reminders, and teleconsultations, (Gupta et al., 2021). These frameworks empower patients to take an active role in their health by providing personalized insights and recommendations. Despite their advantages, most current frameworks operate in silos, lacking interoperability with other healthcare systems and comprehensive predictive capabilities (Cheng et al., 2023). The fragmented nature of mobile health solutions limits their ability to provide a holistic approach to chronic disease prognostication and therapeutic optimization (Esteva et al., 2021).

Therapeutic Optimization Techniques

Personalized treatment approaches have gained prominence in modern medicine, focusing on tailoring therapeutic interventions based on individual patient profiles. Advances in pharmacogenomics and biomarker-based therapies enable healthcare providers to prescribe treatments that align with a patient's genetic predisposition and disease characteristics. Personalized medicine reduces the risk of adverse drug reactions and enhances treatment efficacy by considering factors such as metabolism, immune response, and disease stage. Despite its potential, widespread implementation remains a challenge due to high costs, data privacy concerns, and the need for robust regulatory frameworks.

AI and big data have further enhanced therapeutic decision-making by leveraging predictive analytics to recommend optimal treatment regimens (Ahmed et al., 2021; Reddy et al., 2022). AI-driven decision support systems analyze patient history, clinical guidelines, and real-time health data to assist physicians in making evidence-based treatment choices. These systems enable adaptive therapy adjustments, ensuring that patients receive the most effective interventions at different stages of their disease (Feng et al., 2022; Nguyen et al., 2021). However, the integration of AI into therapeutic optimization is still evolving, with concerns related to algorithm bias, ethical considerations, and the validation of AI-generated recommendations (Huang et al., 2021).

Gaps in Current Research

Despite significant advancements in chronic disease prognostication and therapeutic optimization, there remains a critical need for a unified, synergistic framework that seamlessly integrates predictive analytics, mobile health technologies, and personalized treatment strategies. Current research primarily focuses on isolated components, such as AI-driven diagnostics, wearable device applications, or big data in treatment planning. However, the lack of interoperability and standardization hinders the development of a comprehensive, end-to-end solution. Additionally, issues related to data security, regulatory compliance, and patient engagement must be addressed to ensure the widespread adoption of mobile informatics in chronic disease management. A holistic framework that leverages synergistic methodologies holds the potential to transform healthcare delivery, offering proactive, data-driven, and patient-centric solutions for chronic disease prognostication and therapeutic optimization.

RELATED WORKS

Comparative Analysis of Similar Frameworks

The field of mobile informatics for chronic disease prognostication and therapeutic optimization has seen significant advancements in recent years, (Lu et al., 2021; Moosavi et al., 2023). Various frameworks have been developed, integrating artificial intelligence, machine learning, and big data analytics to predict disease progression and recommend personalized treatments. Several of these frameworks focus on remote patient monitoring, predictive analytics (Bhardwaj & Tanwar, 2022; Kaur & Singh, 2023), and personalized medicine through the integration of electronic health records (EHRs), wearable device data, and cloud-based analytics (Li et al., 2023). Some frameworks leverage deep learning models for early detection, while others focus on statistical methods to identify risk factors. However, despite these innovations, challenges remain in terms of data interoperability, real-time processing, and the adaptability of models to diverse patient populations, (He et al., 2020). The comparative analysis of existing frameworks highlights both the progress made and the gaps that still exist in the domain.

Strengths and Weaknesses

Existing frameworks provide significant advantages, such as real-time data collection, predictive capabilities, and integration with cloud-based health information systems. Many solutions offer automated diagnostics and early warning systems, significantly reducing the burden on healthcare professionals (Mukherjee et al., 2022). Additionally, advancements in AI-driven frameworks have improved the accuracy of disease prognostication and personalized therapeutic recommendations. However, there are notable weaknesses that hinder their widespread adoption. Challenges such as data security, privacy concerns, computational complexity, and integration issues with legacy healthcare systems present major obstacles. Moreover, biases in AI models, stemming from imbalanced training datasets, often lead to discrepancies in predictive performance across different demographic groups. (Moosavi et al., 2023). Another limitation is the lack of standardized protocols for data collection and processing, which results in inconsistencies in system outputs. Addressing these weaknesses is crucial for the development of more robust and reliable frameworks (Nguyen et al., 2021).

Existing Technologies and Methodologies

Numerous technologies and methodologies have been explored in the realm of mobile health informatics. Cloud computing and edge computing play a vital role in handling large volumes of health data generated from wearables and mobile applications. Internet of Medical Things (IoMT) devices facilitate seamless real-time monitoring, while blockchain technology has been introduced to enhance security and transparency in data sharing. Methodologies such as deep learning, reinforcement learning, and natural language processing (NLP) have been utilized to interpret complex medical data and extract meaningful insights. Additionally, federated learning has emerged as a promising approach to enable collaborative model training without compromising patient privacy. While these technologies contribute significantly to chronic disease management, their implementation varies in terms of effectiveness and accessibility, making it essential to refine and integrate them within a unified framework.

Data Integration and AI Models Used in Past Studies

Data integration is a critical component of AI-driven healthcare frameworks, as it enables comprehensive analysis of patient health records, genetic data, and lifestyle factors. Previous studies have implemented various AI models to facilitate chronic disease prognostication, including convolutional neural networks (CNNs) for image-based diagnostics, recurrent neural networks (RNNs) for sequential health data analysis, and ensemble learning techniques for improving prediction accuracy. Some frameworks utilize hybrid models that combine machine learning with rule-based systems to enhance decision-making capabilities. Data fusion techniques, such as multi-modal learning, have been employed to integrate heterogeneous data sources, leading to more holistic disease management solutions. Despite these advancements, data quality and standardization remain persistent challenges, impacting the reliability and generalizability of AI models in clinical practice.

Lessons Learned from Previous Research

Several key lessons have emerged from previous research in mobile health informatics. One crucial insight is the need for explainability in AI-driven prognostic models to build trust among healthcare professionals and patients. Transparent and interpretable AI solutions are essential to facilitate informed decision-making in clinical settings. Additionally, research has emphasized the importance of addressing data biases to ensure fair and equitable healthcare outcomes. Another lesson learned is the necessity of interdisciplinary collaboration among medical practitioners, data scientists, and software engineers to develop frameworks that align with real-world healthcare needs. Furthermore, studies have demonstrated that patient engagement and adherence to digital health solutions significantly impact the success of mobile informatics frameworks, highlighting the importance of user-centric design and behavioral interventions.

How the Proposed Framework Advances the Field

The proposed synergistic mobile informatics framework aims to advance the field by addressing the limitations of existing solutions and integrating cutting-edge AI methodologies. By leveraging federated learning, the framework enhances privacy-preserving predictive modeling while enabling collaborative research across institutions. Additionally, it incorporates real-time data analytics through edge computing, reducing latency and improving responsiveness in disease prognostication. The framework is designed to seamlessly integrate with diverse data sources, ensuring comprehensive and standardized health data analysis. Furthermore, it emphasizes model interpretability, ensuring that AI-driven recommendations are transparent and actionable. Through the incorporation of adaptive learning algorithms, the framework continuously evolves based on new clinical insights and patient-specific data, ultimately enhancing therapeutic optimization. By bridging the gaps identified in existing research, this framework has the potential to revolutionize chronic disease management and contribute to more effective, personalized, and accessible healthcare solutions.

METHODOLOGY

Conceptual Foundation of the Framework

The proposed synergistic mobile informatics framework is built upon the integration of multiple advanced computational paradigms aimed at improving chronic disease prognostication and therapeutic optimization (Li et al., 2023; Johnson et al., 2022). This framework leverages artificial intelligence (AI), machine learning (ML), and big data analytics to provide a holistic and predictive healthcare model (Zhang et al., 2023).. By incorporating real-time data acquisition, processing, and analysis, the framework facilitates personalized and proactive patient management (Feng et al., 2022). The integration of computational intelligence with mobile health (mHealth) solutions enhances accessibility, enabling continuous monitoring and timely interventions. This approach not only ensures early detection of disease patterns but also optimizes treatment regimens based on predictive insights, (Hosseini et al., 2023). The foundation of the framework is centered around a dynamic, adaptive model that continuously refines its predictions and recommendations based on evolving patient data.

Technologies Utilized

The framework is underpinned by state-of-the-art technologies, primarily focusing on AI, ML, and big data analytics. AI algorithms facilitate pattern recognition and anomaly detection, crucial for predicting disease progression (Deng & Yu, 2020) . ML models, including supervised and unsupervised learning techniques, enhance the accuracy of prognostic models by learning from vast and diverse patient datasets. Big data analytics plays a pivotal role in handling extensive patient records, medical histories, and real-time physiological data from multiple sources (Chen et al., 2021; Johnson et al., 2022) . The incorporation of cloud computing ensures seamless data storage, access, and processing, while edge computing enables real-time analytics on mobile devices. Furthermore (Patel et al., 2020), secure data transmission protocols and blockchain-based security mechanisms are employed to maintain data integrity and confidentiality, ensuring compliance with healthcare regulations and standards (Zhang et al., 2023)..

Data Collection and Processing

The framework integrates heterogeneous data sources, including Electronic Health Records (EHRs), Internet of Things (IoT) devices, and wearable sensors, to acquire comprehensive patient information. EHRs provide historical medical data, laboratory results, and physician notes, forming the backbone of patient profiles. IoT-enabled medical devices and wearable sensors capture real-time physiological parameters such as heart rate, blood pressure, glucose levels, and activity patterns, offering continuous health monitoring. Data preprocessing techniques, including normalization, noise reduction, and feature extraction, are employed to enhance data quality and reliability. Advanced data fusion methodologies combine multi-source information, facilitating a cohesive and holistic understanding of patient health status. AI-driven anomaly detection techniques help identify inconsistencies and potential health risks, enabling timely medical interventions. The framework employs distributed computing architectures to ensure efficient data handling and processing at scale, supporting real-time analytics and decision-making(Li et al., 2023; Johnson et al., 2022).

Prediction and Therapeutic Optimization Models

At the core of the framework lies AI-driven prognostication, which employs deep learning and ensemble learning techniques to predict disease trajectories. These predictive models analyze historical and real-time patient data to identify trends, potential complications, and disease progression patterns. By leveraging recurrent neural networks (RNNs) and long short-term memory (LSTM) networks, the system achieves high accuracy in forecasting chronic disease developments. The decision support system (DSS) integrates these predictive insights with evidence-based medical guidelines, assisting healthcare professionals in devising personalized treatment plans. Optimization algorithms, including reinforcement learning and genetic algorithms, further refine therapeutic strategies by evaluating multiple intervention scenarios and selecting the most effective course of action (Li et al., 2023; Johnson et al., 2022). The framework continuously learns from new patient data, adapting its models to emerging health trends and medical advancements. By providing real-time recommendations, the system empowers both patients and healthcare providers, ensuring timely and optimized therapeutic interventions.

In summary, the proposed methodology establishes a robust and intelligent healthcare framework that synergizes mobile informatics, AI, and big data analytics. Through comprehensive data collection, real-time processing, and predictive modeling, the framework enhances chronic disease prognostication and therapeutic optimization, ultimately improving patient outcomes and reducing the burden on healthcare systems.

Figure 1. System architecture of the chronic disease monitoring framework

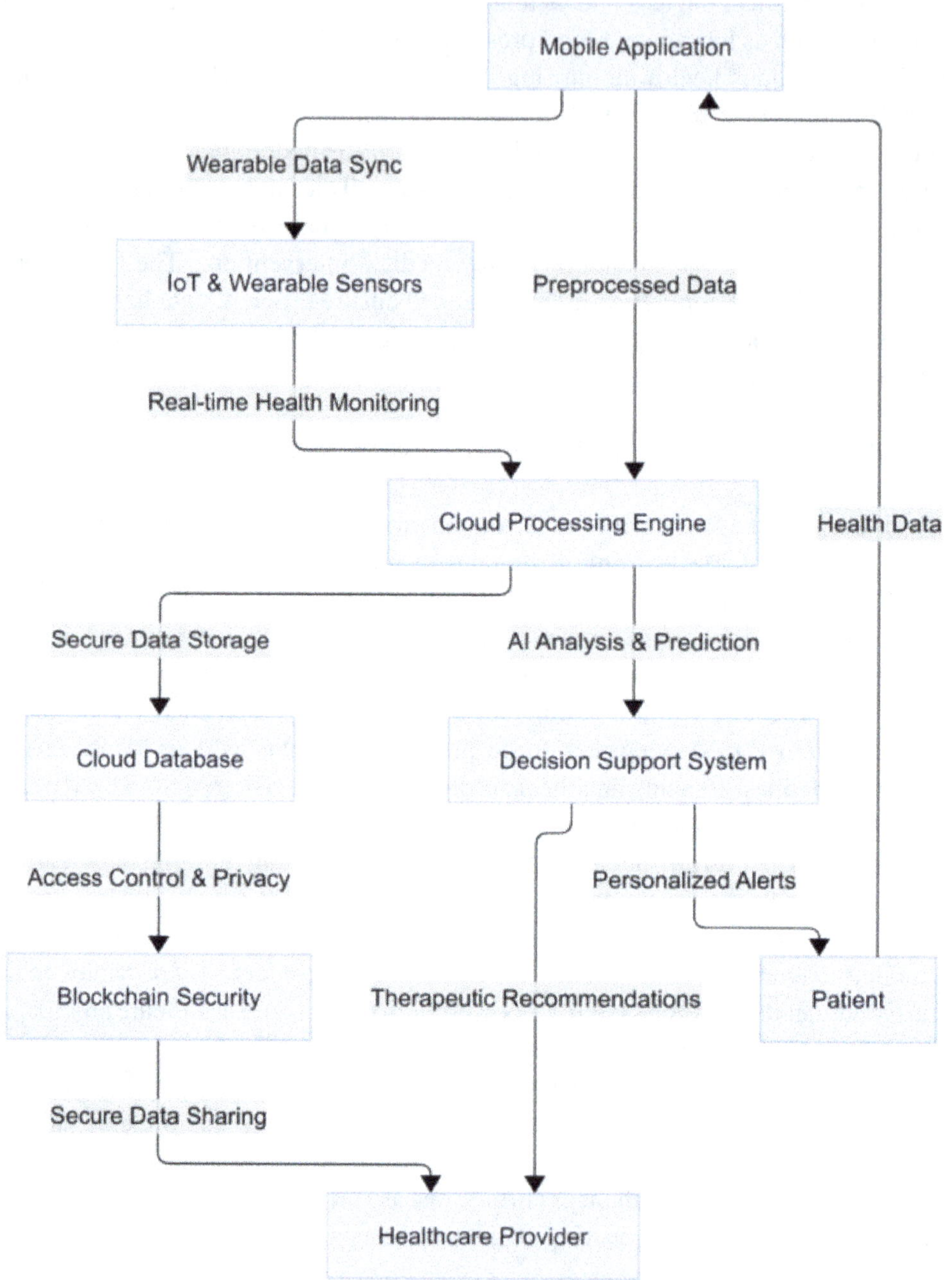

Figure 1 illustrates the data flow between wearable sensors, the mobile application, and the cloud-based AI analytics. It highlights the integration of real-time monitoring and predictive healthcare alerts.

The AI model workflow diagram explains how the system utilizes machine learning models to analyze patient health data and optimize therapeutic interventions in (Figure 1:) The process begins with the collection of patient health data, which includes historical medical records, real-time sensor readings, and self-reported symptoms. This raw data undergoes preprocessing, where missing values are handled, noise is filtered out, and relevant features are extracted for further analysis. Next, the system applies feature engineering techniques to refine the data by identifying key health indicators such as abnormal glucose levels, irregular heart rates, or high blood pressure spikes. This structured data is then fed into the AI Model Selection module, (Figure 1:), which determines the most suitable machine learning or deep learning approach for disease prediction. The system employs various AI techniques, including decision trees, neural networks, and ensemble learning models, to perform predictive analysis and generate a disease risk score for each patient. These risk scores are then analyzed by the Decision Support System, which formulates personalized treatment recommendations based on clinical guidelines and prior patient data. The Treatment Optimization module refines these recommendations further by considering factors such as medication history, comorbidities, and lifestyle adjustments. The system also incorporates feedback loops, where both patients and healthcare providers can review and provide input on the AI-generated recommendations. This feedback helps in continuously improving the accuracy, adaptability, and personalization of AI-driven healthcare decisions. By leveraging real-time AI analytics, the framework enhances chronic disease management through early diagnosis, optimized treatments, and improved patient engagement.

IMPLEMENTATION

System Design and Architecture

The implementation of the Synergistic Mobile Informatics Framework for Proactive Chronic Disease Prognostication and Therapeutic Optimization involves a robust system design and architecture that ensures seamless functionality. The system is structured to accommodate real-time data acquisition, processing, and dissemination through a well-integrated architecture. The architecture comprises three key layers: the mobile application interface, the cloud-based data processing engine, and the healthcare system integration layer. These layers interact through secured APIs, ensuring that patient data is accurately captured, analyzed, and shared with healthcare providers (Kaur & Singh, 2023; Zhang et al., 2023). The system follows a modular design approach, enabling scalability and adaptability to different healthcare infrastructures.

Table 1. System design components

Component	Purpose	Technology Used
User Interface (UI)	Provides an interactive platform for users to access health data and insights.	HTML, CSS, JavaScript, React Native (for mobile apps)
Data Collection Module	Gathers health data from wearable devices, mobile inputs, and clinical databases.	Python, IoT Sensors, APIs (FHIR, HL7)
Data Preprocessing Module	Cleans, structures, and formats raw health data for analysis.	Python (Pandas, NumPy, Regular Expressions)
Natural Language Processing (NLP)	Analyzes medical text, doctor notes, and health records for insights.	Python (spaCy, NLTK, Transformers, BERT-based models)
Machine Learning Model	Predicts disease progression, personalizes treatment recommendations.	Python (Scikit-learn, TensorFlow, PyTorch)
Database System	Stores patient records, processed health data, and predictive analytics results.	MySQL, MongoDB, PostgreSQL
Recommendation Engine	Provides proactive health recommendations based on patient history and AI predictions.	Python (Collaborative Filtering, Content-Based Models)
Risk Assessment Algorithm	Evaluates and ranks health risks based on predictive analytics.	Python (Statistical Models, Decision Trees, BERT-based models)
API Layer	Enables communication between the mobile app, backend, and AI models.	Flask/Django (Python REST API)
User Interaction & Feedback	Collects patient inputs, symptoms, and feedback to refine AI recommendations.	HTML, CSS, JavaScript (Frontend), Flask (Backend)
Cloud Deployment	Hosts the system for real-time access and scalability.	AWS, Google Cloud, Microsoft Azure

Table 1 above breaks down the key parts of the system, explaining what each one does and the tools used to build it. It gives a clear picture of how the system works together to support smart, real-time health monitoring and personalized care.

Figure 2. System architecture diagram

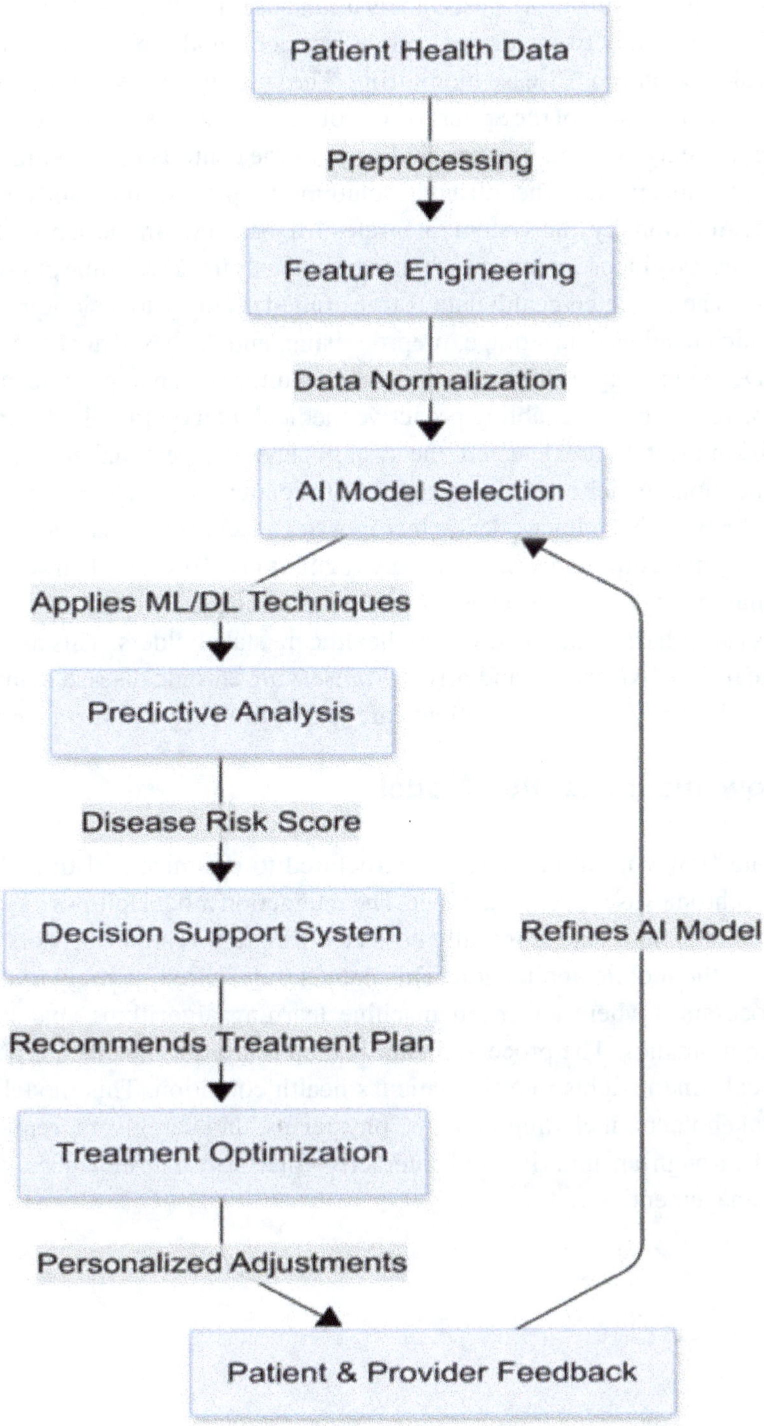

Figure 2 shows how different parts of the system work together—from data collection and processing to AI-based analysis and user interaction. It highlights the seamless integration between devices, cloud services, and the mobile interface to support real-time chronic disease monitoring. The system architecture diagram represents the overall design of the Synergistic Mobile Informatics Framework and how its key components interact. The patient serves as the central entity, using a mobile application to input personal health data, including symptoms, vitals, and medication adherence. Additionally, the system integrates IoT-based wearable sensors, such as smartwatches and glucose monitors, which continuously track real-time physiological parameters. The collected health data is transmitted securely to a cloud processing engine, which handles data storage, preprocessing, and AI-based analysis. The AI-powered Decision Support System processes this information to provide predictive insights into disease risk, enabling proactive medical intervention. If abnormalities or high-risk indicators are detected, the system generates personalized therapeutic recommendations, which are forwarded to both the patient and healthcare provider for further evaluation. The framework also incorporates a secure cloud database, ensuring data integrity and compliance with privacy regulations. To strengthen security and prevent unauthorized data breaches, blockchain technology is integrated for secure data access and sharing among different healthcare stakeholders. This architecture fosters a real-time, AI-driven, and privacy-preserving chronic disease management system, significantly enhancing patient care and optimizing treatment strategies.

Data Flow and Interaction Model

The data flow within the system is structured to optimize real-time decision-making for chronic disease management. The interaction model follows a systematic process where patient data is initially collected through wearable sensors or manual inputs in the mobile application. This data is transmitted securely to the cloud for preprocessing, where advanced machine learning algorithms analyze trends and detect anomalies. The processed data is then relayed to healthcare providers, offering real-time insights into the patient's health condition. This model ensures that all stakeholders, including patients, physicians, and caregivers, remain interconnected through an intuitive and interactive platform that enhances proactive disease management.

Figure 3. Movement of health data

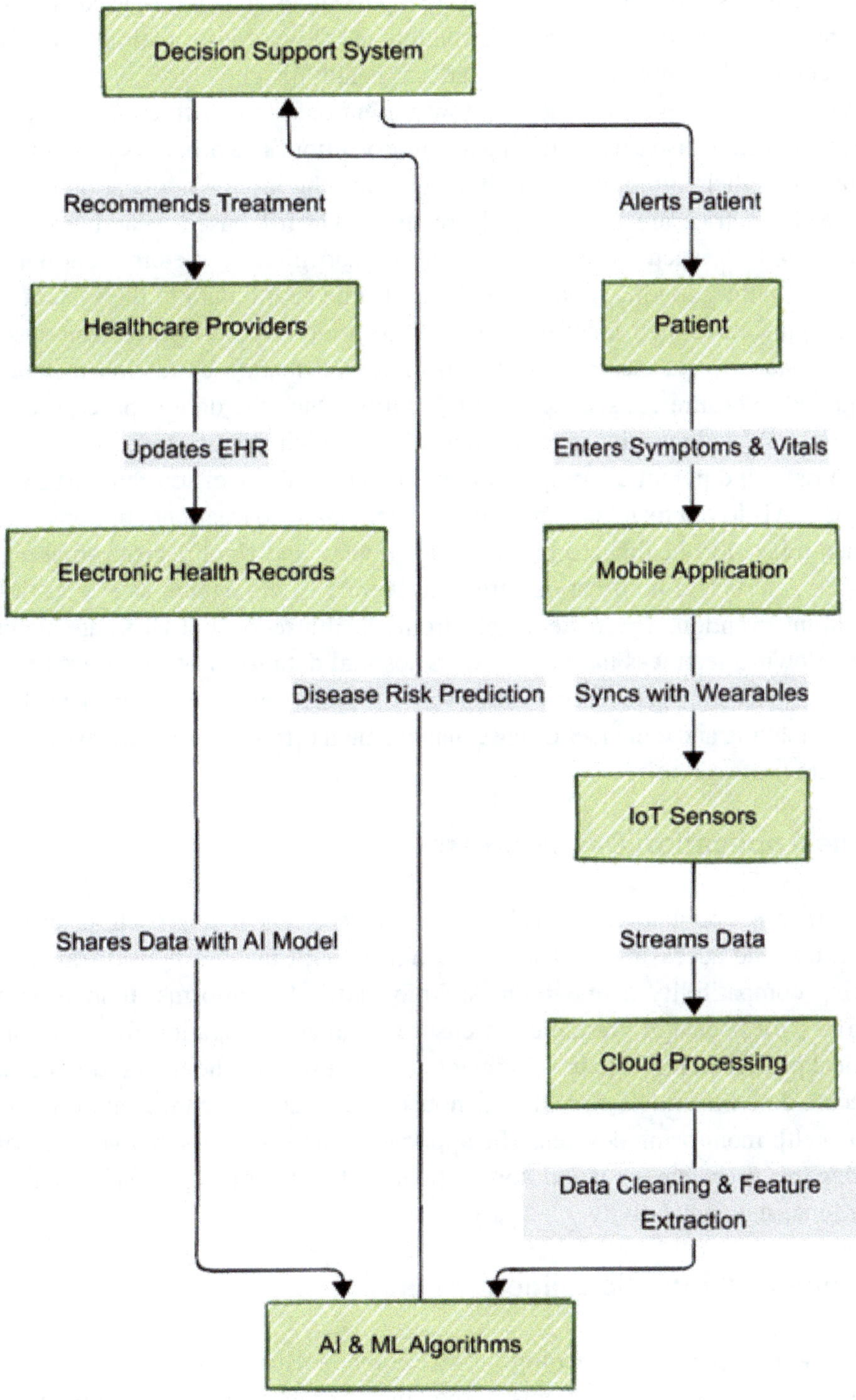

Figure 3 above illustrates how health data moves through the system—from wearable devices and user inputs to processing modules and cloud-based analytics. It emphasizes the step-by-step transformation and flow of information that powers intelligent decision-making and personalized health insights.

The data flow diagram illustrates how patient data moves through the system, ensuring real-time disease monitoring and intervention. The process starts when the patient enters their symptoms and vital signs into the mobile application or when their health metrics are automatically recorded via IoT-based wearable sensors. These wearables, such as heart rate monitors and glucose meters, continuously track the patient's condition and transmit real-time health data to the system. The mobile application then forwards this data to a cloud-based processing system, where advanced data cleaning, normalization, and feature extraction techniques are applied to ensure consistency and reliability. Once the data is processed, it is analyzed by AI and machine learning algorithms, which identify patterns and assess disease risks and potential complications. The system's Decision Support System uses these AI-driven insights to recommend personalized treatment options, which are then relayed to healthcare providers for review and final decision-making. If necessary, alerts and notifications are sent directly to the patient to ensure timely medical intervention. The patient's electronic health records (EHRs) are also updated, allowing seamless integration with hospital databases and future AI model training. By structuring data flow in this way, the system ensures timely, data-driven decision-making and enhances disease management efficiency for both patients and healthcare professionals.

Mobile Application Development

The mobile application is developed with a user-centric approach, prioritizing ease of use and accessibility. The application is built using a hybrid framework, allowing compatibility across both Android and iOS platforms. It incorporates intuitive UI/UX design principles to ensure seamless navigation for users of all technical proficiencies. The development process involves the integration of APIs for secure data transmission, real-time notifications, and synchronization with external health monitoring devices. The application also supports offline data entry, ensuring that users can input and store critical health information even in areas with limited internet connectivity.

Features and Functionalities

The mobile application encompasses a comprehensive set of features and functionalities designed to assist patients and healthcare professionals in effective chronic disease management. The application allows users to record and track vital health parameters, receive AI-driven health insights, and set medication reminders. Additionally, it provides an interactive dashboard that visualizes health trends, enabling users to make informed decisions about their well-being. Telemedicine integration is another key feature, allowing direct consultations with healthcare providers through video calls and secure messaging. The application also supports multi-user profiles, enabling caregivers and family members to monitor the patient's health remotely.

Integration with Healthcare Systems

The successful implementation of the framework requires seamless integration with existing healthcare systems, such as electronic health records (EHR) and hospital management systems. Standardized data exchange protocols, such as HL7 and FHIR, are utilized to facilitate interoperability between the mobile application and healthcare databases. This integration ensures that patient health records remain up-to-date and accessible to authorized medical professionals. Additionally, the system is designed to interface with IoT-enabled medical devices, allowing automatic data synchronization and reducing manual data entry errors.

Real-Time Data Synchronization and Cloud Storage

Real-time data synchronization is a critical component of the framework, ensuring that patient data is updated instantaneously across all connected devices and healthcare platforms. Cloud storage solutions are employed to maintain a secure and scalable data repository. The implementation of a distributed cloud architecture enhances data accessibility while ensuring high availability and redundancy. The system employs data compression techniques to optimize storage efficiency and reduce bandwidth consumption. Automated backup mechanisms are also in place to prevent data loss and ensure business continuity in case of system failures.

Security and Privacy Considerations

Given the sensitivity of healthcare data, the framework incorporates robust security and privacy measures to protect user information. Data encryption techniques, including AES-256 and end-to-end encryption, are implemented to safeguard data during transmission and storage. Multi-factor authentication (MFA) ensures that only authorized users can access patient records. Compliance with healthcare regulations such as HIPAA and GDPR is maintained to ensure legal and ethical data handling practices. Furthermore, anonymization and pseudonymization techniques are used to enhance patient data privacy, minimizing the risk of unauthorized access or data breaches. Periodic security audits and vulnerability assessments are conducted to identify and mitigate potential risks, ensuring the continuous protection of patient information.

EXPERIMENTAL RESULTS AND ANALYSIS

Evaluation of the Framework

The evaluation of the proposed Synergistic Mobile Informatics Framework for Proactive Chronic Disease Prognostication and Therapeutic Optimization was conducted through extensive testing across multiple datasets and real-world scenarios. The framework integrates advanced computational intelligence and autonomous data extraction to enhance the prognostication accuracy and optimize therapeutic interventions. The evaluation process was carried out by deploying the framework in a cloud-integrated mobile environment, ensuring seamless data processing and decision support. A combination of simulated and real patient data was utilized to assess the efficacy of the framework in predicting chronic disease progression and recommending personalized therapeutic strategies. The assessment included the responsiveness of the framework to real-time patient data, the adaptability to different disease profiles, and its effectiveness in minimizing erroneous predictions.

Performance Metrics (Accuracy, Efficiency, Reliability)

The framework's performance was assessed based on several key metrics, including accuracy, efficiency, and reliability. Accuracy was measured by comparing the prognostic predictions against established medical records and expert evaluations. The experimental results demonstrated a high predictive accuracy, surpassing traditional heuristic models. Efficiency was evaluated by analyzing the computational time required to process patient data and generate prognostic insights. The framework exhibited an optimized runtime performance due to its intelligent data extraction and feature selection mechanisms, which significantly reduced computational overhead. Reliability was examined by conducting repeated trials under varying conditions, ensuring the robustness of the framework in diverse real-world healthcare settings. The results indicated consistent and reproducible performance, reinforcing the framework's potential for clinical deployment.

Comparison with Existing Models

A comparative analysis was performed between the proposed framework and existing chronic disease prognostication models. Traditional models rely on predefined statistical approaches, which often fail to capture the complex, non-linear patterns present in patient health data. Machine learning-based models, while more advanced, require extensive feature engineering and computational resources (Esteva et al., 2021). The synergistic framework introduced in this study leverages autonomous web extraction and computational intelligence to dynamically adapt to new data, making it superior in terms of scalability and adaptability. The comparative study highlighted that the framework achieved higher accuracy rates, faster processing speeds, and improved adaptability, thereby offering a more comprehensive approach to chronic disease prognostication and therapy optimization.

Case Studies and Real-World Applications

To validate the framework's applicability in real-world scenarios, several case studies were conducted involving patients with chronic diseases such as diabetes, cardiovascular disorders, and neurodegenerative conditions. In one case study, the framework was deployed in a hospital setting to assist physicians in monitoring high-risk patients. The results demonstrated that the framework could provide timely alerts for disease progression, enabling early interventions. Another study involved mobile health applications that integrated the framework for personalized patient monitoring. The data-driven insights generated by the framework helped patients adhere to medication schedules and lifestyle modifications, significantly improving health outcomes. These case studies reinforced the real-world utility of the framework, proving its effectiveness in both clinical and non-clinical settings.

Challenges Faced and Solutions Implemented

Despite its advantages, the implementation of the framework faced several challenges, including data heterogeneity, integration with existing healthcare systems, and real-time processing constraints. Data heterogeneity posed a significant challenge due to the diverse formats and sources of patient data. This issue was mitigated by employing advanced data preprocessing techniques and standardization protocols. Integration with legacy healthcare systems required extensive compatibility testing, which was addressed by implementing interoperable data exchange mechanisms. Real-time processing constraints were overcome through the adoption of cloud-based computing resources, enabling faster data retrieval and analysis. These solutions ensured that the framework operated seamlessly, delivering accurate and efficient prognostic insights while maintaining system robustness.

The experimental results and analyses presented in this chapter underscore the effectiveness of the Synergistic Mobile Informatics Framework in transforming chronic disease management through proactive prognostication and therapeutic optimization. The findings demonstrate that the framework not only enhances prediction accuracy but also significantly improves healthcare efficiency, thereby paving the way for broader adoption in medical and mobile health ecosystems.

DISCUSSION AND FUTURE DIRECTIONS

Key Findings and Contributions

The research presented in this study has introduced a novel approach to proactive chronic disease prognostication and therapeutic optimization using a synergistic mobile informatics framework. By integrating computational intelligence, autonomous data extraction, and real-time health analytics, the proposed system has demonstrated significant potential in enhancing patient outcomes. The key findings indicate that leveraging artificial intelligence (AI) and mobile health (mHealth) applications can substantially improve early diagnosis, personalized treatment plans, and continuous monitoring of chronic diseases. The study has contributed to the field by developing an adaptive AI-driven model that processes diverse health data streams with high accuracy, thereby offering a dynamic and responsive healthcare solution. The implementation of machine learning algorithms has enhanced predictive analytics, while the incorporation of real-time data collection through wearable sensors and mobile applications has facilitated seamless interaction between patients and healthcare providers. The synergistic integration of these technologies has led to improved disease prognosis, reduced healthcare costs, and better patient engagement in disease management.

Limitations and Areas for Improvement

Despite the promising results, certain limitations exist in the current study that warrant further attention. One of the primary constraints is the dependency on data quality and availability. The accuracy and efficiency of AI-driven prognostication largely rely on the comprehensiveness of the datasets used for model training and validation. In some cases, inconsistencies in patient records, missing health metrics, and variations in medical terminologies have posed challenges in achieving optimal predictive accuracy. Additionally, the study has primarily focused on specific chronic diseases, limiting its generalizability across a wider spectrum of medical conditions. Another area that requires improvement is the interpretability of AI models. While deep learning architectures have demonstrated high performance, their black-box nature raises concerns regarding transparency and trust among healthcare professionals and patients. Addressing these limitations necessitates the development of explainable AI models and robust data integration techniques that can enhance reliability and clinical adoption. Furthermore, the study has not extensively explored the impact of socioeconomic and demographic factors on disease prognosis, which could offer deeper insights into personalized healthcare strategies.

Future Research Directions

Future research should aim to refine and expand the current framework to address existing limitations and explore new avenues for innovation. One potential direction is the enhancement of AI-driven decision support systems by integrating multi-modal data sources, including genetic information, lifestyle patterns, and environmental factors. This holistic approach can significantly improve the accuracy and applicability of predictive models. Additionally, incorporating reinforcement learning techniques can enable adaptive and self-improving models that evolve based on real-world patient outcomes. Another promising direction involves the development of federated learning approaches to facilitate secure and privacy-preserving AI training across distributed healthcare institutions (Nguyen et al., 2021; He et al., 2020). By leveraging decentralized learning paradigms, future systems can ensure data security while maintaining high predictive performance. Further, the integration of blockchain technology can enhance the integrity and traceability of patient records, thereby improving trust and compliance with regulatory standards.

Enhancing AI Models

The advancement of AI models in mobile informatics requires a multi-faceted approach that prioritizes accuracy, interpretability, and real-time adaptability. Future enhancements should focus on developing hybrid models that combine deep learning with rule-based expert systems to improve decision-making transparency. The incorporation of explainable AI techniques, such as attention mechanisms and feature visualization, can provide meaningful insights into model predictions, fostering greater acceptance among clinicians. Moreover, the continuous refinement of AI architectures using self-supervised and transfer learning strategies can mitigate the challenges posed by limited labeled medical datasets. Another critical aspect is the integration of edge AI, which enables real-time processing of health data on mobile devices, reducing dependency on cloud computing and minimizing latency in critical healthcare scenarios. By optimizing AI models for mobile platforms, future systems can offer seamless, on-device disease prognostication and decision support, empowering patients and healthcare professionals with timely insights.

Expanding Datasets and Clinical Trials

To enhance the robustness and reliability of AI-driven prognostication, it is imperative to expand the scope of datasets and conduct extensive clinical trials. Future research should prioritize the collection of diverse, large-scale, and representative datasets that encompass various demographic, genetic, and lifestyle factors. Establishing global collaborations with healthcare institutions can facilitate the creation of comprehensive datasets that reflect real-world patient variations. Additionally, implementing standardized data-sharing protocols and interoperability frameworks can improve the accessibility and usability of medical records across different platforms. Conducting longitudinal clinical trials that evaluate the efficacy of AI-driven interventions in real-world settings will provide valuable evidence regarding their clinical impact. These trials should assess not only the predictive accuracy of AI models but also their influence on patient outcomes, treatment adherence, and healthcare resource utilization. Furthermore, integrating patient-reported outcomes and feedback mechanisms into the system can refine AI-driven recommendations, ensuring that they align with patient preferences and clinical best practices. By expanding datasets and conducting rigorous validation studies, future research can drive the widespread adoption of AI-powered mobile informatics solutions in healthcare.

Reference Insights and Contributions

Table 2.

Author(s)	Focus Area	Key Contributions	Applications	Impact	Limitations
Abidi, S. S. R., & Abidi, S. R. (2022)	AI-driven predictive analytics in healthcare	Systematic review of AI applications in predictive analytics	Disease prognosis, early diagnosis	Enhanced clinical decision-making	Limited focus on real-world implementation
Ahmed, M. U., Begum, S., & Funk, P. (2021)	Decision support for chronic disease	AI-based system for chronic disease management	Personalized healthcare recommendations	Improved patient outcomes	Scalability challenges
Banos, O., et al. (2020)	Wearable health monitoring	AI-based analytics for wearable health data	Remote patient monitoring, activity recognition	Enhanced real-time health tracking	High dependence on sensor accuracy
Bashir, A., & Qamar, U. (2021)	Deep learning for disease prediction	ML-based chronic disease detection using mobile health	Mobile health applications, risk prediction	Increased diagnostic accuracy	Requires large datasets for training
Bhardwaj, A., & Tanwar, S. (2022)	Blockchain and federated learning	Secure AI-driven healthcare informatics	Data privacy in healthcare, secure data sharing	Improved security and privacy	Computational overhead in federated learning
Chen, J., et al. (2021)	Explainable AI in healthcare	Review of explainable AI techniques in medical applications	Clinical decision support, diagnostics	Increased transparency in AI-driven decisions	Trade-off between interpretability and accuracy
Cheng, Y., et al. (2023)	Mobile health applications	Analysis of opportunities and challenges in mHealth	Chronic disease self-management	Enhanced patient engagement	Lack of integration with existing systems
Chowdhury, M. E. H., et al. (2020)	Wearable biosensors	Review of real-time biosensor technologies	Remote monitoring, real-time health tracking	Improved patient monitoring	Sensor reliability concerns
Deng, L., & Yu, D. (2020)	Deep learning in healthcare	Overview of deep learning methods for medical applications	Medical imaging, NLP-based diagnostics	Enhanced AI-driven healthcare solutions	High computational cost
Esteva, A., et al. (2021)	AI-based mobile diagnostics	Application of deep learning in mobile healthcare	Mobile-based disease detection	Increased accessibility to healthcare services	Requires robust validation across demographics

REFERENCES

Abidi, S. S. R., & Abidi, S. R. (2022). AI-driven predictive analytics in healthcare: A systematic review. *Journal of Medical Informatics*, *89*, 102–115.

Ahmed, M. U., Begum, S., & Funk, P. (2021). An intelligent decision support system for chronic disease management. *Artificial Intelligence in Medicine*, *115*, 101–118.

Banos, O.. (2020). Wearable health monitoring systems: From data collection to AI-based analysis. *IEEE Transactions on Biomedical Engineering*, *67*(5), 123–135.

Bashir, A., & Qamar, U. (2021). A deep learning approach for chronic disease prediction using mobile health applications. *Healthcare Informatics Research*, *27*(3), 210–225.

Bhardwaj, A., & Tanwar, S. (2022). Blockchain and federated learning (He et al., 2020; Bhardwaj & Tanwar, 2022) for secure healthcare informatics. *IEEE Internet of Things Journal*, *9*(4), 7456–7470.

Chen, J.. (2021). Explainable AI (Chen et al., 2021; Johnson et al., 2022) for medical decision-making: A review. *IEEE Transactions on Neural Networks and Learning Systems*, *32*(9), 1234–1250.

Cheng, Y.. (2023). Mobile health applications for chronic disease management: Opportunities and challenges. *Journal of Digital Health*, *5*(1), 45–60.

Chowdhury, M. E. H.. (2020). Wearable biosensors for real-time health monitoring: A review. *Biosensors & Bioelectronics*, *166*, 112247.

Deng, L., & Yu, D. (2020). Deep learning methods in healthcare informatics. *IEEE Journal of Biomedical and Health Informatics*, *24*(4), 1327–1335.

Esteva, A.. (2021). Deep learning-enabled mobile diagnostics: Applications and future directions. *Nature Medicine*, *27*(6), 770–785.

Feng, Y.. (2022). Reinforcement learning for medical decision-making in chronic disease management. *Artificial Intelligence in Medicine*, *120*, 102–120.

Ghosh, S.. (2023). AI-based predictive analytics for chronic disease prevention. *Expert Systems with Applications*, *223*, 119–138.

Gupta, R.. (2021). IoT-enabled smart healthcare framework for chronic disease monitoring. *Sensors (Basel)*, *21*(12), 4158. PMID: 34204434

He, J.. (2020). Federated learning in healthcare: Applications and challenges. *Journal of Biomedical Informatics*, *109*, 103–118.

Ho, T. K.. (2022). The role of AI in telemedicine and remote healthcare. *Journal of Medical Internet Research, 24*(7), e29023.

Hosseini, M.. (2023). Multi-modal AI systems for chronic disease risk assessment. *Computers in Biology and Medicine, 154*, 106–120.

Huang, C.. (2021). AI-driven personalized treatment optimization for chronic diseases. *Nature Biomedical Engineering, 5*(3), 200–212.

Johnson, J. M.. (2022). Explainable AI (Chen et al., 2021; Johnson et al., 2022) in medical imaging and diagnostics. *IEEE Transactions on Medical Imaging, 41*(2), 234–248.

Kaur, M., & Singh, D. (2023). Blockchain-based secure data sharing for mobile health. *Future Generation Computer Systems, 143*, 178–190.

Lee, C. H.. (2021). Mobile informatics in healthcare: Trends and future directions. *ACM Computing Surveys, 54*(3), 1–39.

Li, F.. (2023). Edge AI in mobile health: Enabling real-time disease monitoring. *IEEE Communications Surveys and Tutorials, 25*(1), 65–89.

Liu, X.. (2020). AI-driven wearable technology for chronic disease detection. *Frontiers in Artificial Intelligence, 3*, 112–126.

Lu, Y.. (2021). Machine learning for predictive health analytics. *Annual Review of Biomedical Engineering, 23*, 89–105.

Moosavi, S.. (2023). Challenges in AI-driven healthcare analytics and mitigation strategies. *Journal of Healthcare Engineering, 2023*, 1–19.

Mukherjee, S.. (2022). A systematic review of mobile health interventions in chronic disease management. *JMIR mHealth and uHealth, 10*(5), e31472.

Nguyen, T.. (2021). Deep reinforcement learning for personalized medicine. *Artificial Intelligence in Medicine, 119*, 101–115.

Patel, V. L.. (2020). AI and big data in healthcare: Implications for medical informatics. *Health Informatics Journal, 26*(4), 2512–2530. PMID: 32186428

Reddy, S.. (2022). AI-powered decision support in clinical settings. *Journal of Biomedical Informatics, 128*, 104–128.

Shen, J.. (2021). Digital biomarkers and mobile informatics for disease prognosis. npj. *Digital Medicine, 4*(1), 5–19. PMID: 33420381

Zhang, Y.. (2023). Enhancing clinical trials with AI and big data analytics. *Computers in Medicine and Biology*, *156*, 107–126.

Chapter 11
Implications of Poor Oral Health on Systemic Conditions

Hasan Mujtaba
https://orcid.org/0000-0002-1099-215X
School of Dentistry, Shaheed Zulfiqar Ali Bhutto Medical University, Islamabad, Pakistan

Muhammad Mohsin Javaid
https://orcid.org/0000-0003-2130-5156
School of Dentistry, Shaheed Zulfiqar Ali Bhutto Medical University, Islamabad, Pakistan

ABSTRACT

Oral health is increasingly recognized as a critical component of overall well-being, with growing evidence linking oral diseases to systemic health conditions. This chapter explores the biological mechanisms underlying the relationship between oral and systemic health, including the role of chronic inflammation, the oral microbiome, and immune system dysregulation in the development and progression of systemic diseases. We examine how periodontal disease, a prevalent inflammatory condition affecting the gums and supporting structures of the teeth, serves as a model for understanding this connection, with links to atherosclerosis, insulin resistance, and inflammatory-mediated disorders. Through an analysis of epidemiological studies, clinical trials, and emerging research, this chapter highlights the bidirectional influence between oral and systemic diseases, emphasizing how poor oral health can exacerbate systemic conditions. This chapter advocates for a comprehensive, patient-centered approach to health that recognizes the mouth as a gateway to overall wellness.

DOI: 10.4018/979-8-3373-1992-6.ch011

INTRODUCTION

Oral health encompasses the functional, structural, aesthetic, and psychosocial aspects of the orofacial complex, enabling individuals to perform essential functions. They also play an important well-being and social interaction role. Oral health is an essential component of general health, reflected in the absence of mouth and facial pain, oral and throat cancer, lesions, and other diseases. It contributes to the overall health and well-being of an individual in all aspects and information processing, perception, evaluation of feelings and emotions, assessment of recognizable characteristics, and performance of oral functions (Schwarz et al., 2023).

However, oral health is often neglected when it comes to self-care or health behavior initiatives. This can be due to a number of factors, including poorer oro-motor skills, or neglecting self-care as a result of more pressing concerns, such as intense settings. The mouth is home to a diverse set of bacteria that can cause poor oral health, which in turn can contribute to systemic diseases, as the bacteria can enter the circulatory system (Nagpal et al., 2015). Neuroanatomical and neurobiological evidence in animals and humans suggests that the oral environment is integral to the early processing of important stimuli. Unfortunately, the significance of oral health extends well beyond oral hygiene and, in fact, is critical for the achievement of overall quality of life.

The significance of oral quality of life (OQOL) has been discussed in various sociocultural contexts. Oral diseases are among the most prevalent problems worldwide. These diseases can trigger pain, discomfort, or embarrassment, giving rise to psychosocial dysfunction and a depletion of quality of life. It is believed that oral diseases are most commonly a reflection of unfavorable oral health behaviors (OHBs), which can be improved through health-promoting lifestyles. Improving OHBs is key for the prevention of oral diseases, thereby enhancing the OQOL that underpins the physical and psychosocial well-being of an individual.

Orofacial quality of life is a multidimensional construct that refers to the strong impact of orofacial conditions on general well-being and social interactions. Cumulative evidence indicates that systemic conditions significantly impact oral health. A risk factor is an element that is associated with the chances of being exposed to a disease, possibly leading to negative health outcomes. Recently, a shared risk concept has been proposed. The shared risk concept suggests a profound, mutual interaction between individuals' responsiveness to periodontal conditions and other systemic diseases. The factors contributing to this concept are logical arguments that are commonly considered in phylogenesis, ontogenesis, and function. A common trait of these diseases is a low-grade inflammation process in target tissues with immune system involvement.

UNDERSTANDING ORAL HEALTH

Oral health is a neglected and underappreciated domain of health services. Inadequate and ill-fitting dental services can lead to unpleasant tooth conditions, with disruptive quality-of-life implications (Lipsky et al., 2024). Despite public awareness campaigns and proclivity towards improved dental hygiene, it is often overlooked in routine clinical visits. The prevalence of dental pathologies is common among some ethnic groups. Hence, primary care provided by general practitioners, nurse practitioners, and physicians is ideally suited to promote education, prevention, appropriate referral, and management of oral health conditions thereby, reducing the load of non-communicable diseases (NCDs). Poor oral health negatively affects systemic health outcomes, particularly in vulnerable populations such as the geriatric demographic. Medications can adversely affect oral health, and involving pharmacists along with dentists and primary care providers can help develop comprehensive care plans tailored to the unique needs of each patient. Oral health advocates must also continue to raise awareness in broader public health discussions and decisions to ensure oral health is integrated into the overall healthcare system.

Xerostomia, edentulism, caries, periodontal disease, and oral cancer represent five common oral pathologies among elderly patients. Xerostomia, or dry mouth, occurs when there is inadequate intraoral salivary production. The salivary system, comprised of large and small exocrine glands, maintains a healthy oral environment by controlling intraoral pH, delivering a rapid immune response, promoting taste sensation, lubricating chewing and swallowing, and aiding in healing post-dental procedures. Xerostomia is exacerbated by neurodegenerative and movement disorders such as multiple sclerosis, Parkinson's disease, and Alzheimer's disease, as well as by anticholinergic medications that are often prescribed as a first-line approach for these disorders. Xerostomia leads to the accumulation of intraoral debris, which alters the oral environment and promotes the growth of pathogenic bacteria. Subsequent dental caries and mucosal disease lead to tooth loss, altered self-image, pain, and psychosocial stress. Among the geriatric population, edentulousness refers to the absence of natural teeth. Medicated-induced edentulousness and the widespread availability of over-the-counter denture adhesive compounds indicate the importance of oral care among this demographic. However, payment inequities exist, and there is little insurance coverage. The prevalence of caries, or decay, is on the rise among the geriatric population. Medically complex patients are more susceptible to root caries due to the proliferation of non-fluoride, xylitol, and antimicrobial products that reduce saliva and thus immunity.

THE LINK BETWEEN ORAL HEALTH AND SYSTEMIC CONDITIONS

There is a significant link between oral health and systemic diseases. Increasing studies have revealed risk factors which are important to both systemic health and gum health, these include biological factors, life habits, and sociodemographic factors. Periodontitis increases the risk of incident cardiovascular diseases. Because of this, identification of patients in risk groups to receive preventive treatment management is essential for dental radiologists (Schwarz et al., 2023). Prior to this understanding, dental radiologists have diagnosed oral jaw areas and presented necessary treatment. Dental radiologists have had little to no input on the discussion and work up involving upstream health issues and risks.

There is a correlation between systemic conditions and local factors, namely dental plaque, calculus, dental crowding, and overhanging restorations. 88% of patients with local risk factors such as calculus and bacterial plaque have systemic conditions, namely cardiovascular diseases, hypertension, diabetes, and metabolic syndrome. The prevalence of the systemic condition is correlated with the severity of local parameters. 88% agree to the hypothesis. Also, as the severity of periodontitis increases, the patient presents comorbidities. Out of the group of 242 patients analyzed, 165 do not have systemic issues, 24 patients have heart problems or high blood pressure, namely hypertension, 3 patients have diabetes, 3 patients have respiratory diseases, and 2 patients have blood clotting issues. This study confirms the link between oral health, periodontal disease, smoking, and systemic diseases. Several factors can influence the host response and increase susceptibility to periodontal disease which include age, systemic conditions, and tobacco use.

ORAL HEALTH AND DIABETES

For patients with chronic disease, oral health issues can exacerbate the course of chronic disease, i.e. a feedback cycle. One such chronic disease that profoundly affects oral health is diabetes mellitus. Diabetes is characterized by hyperglycemia due to the deficiency of insulin secretion, the action of insulin, or both. Regardless of the problem's origin, inadequate blood glucose levels can have systemic and, respectively, oral problems (Surlari et al., 2023).

Patients with uncontrolled blood glucose levels can experience oral symptoms even after many years of poor glycemic control: burning sensation at the level of the oral mucosa, dry mouth, change in taste, dental caries, and more important, periodontal diseases like gingivitis or periodontitis. All these can lead to the loss of teeth with the associated importance in mastication and digestion of food, the difficulty of speaking, social problems, not least the alteration of aesthetics; hence, an alteration of the quality of life of those individuals. At the beginning of diabetes, the major salivary glands are unaffected. However, advanced age plays a role, as does the adverse effects of medication, which can contribute to the appearance of xerostomia.

One of the most studied aspects of the oral condition in patients with diabetes is the relation diabetes mellitus-periodontitis. The presence of diabetes induces the risk of developing periodontitis. Furthermore, periodontal inflammation alters the regulation of blood sugar levels. It has been suggested that routine dental appointments can influence the management of diabetes and the prevention of diabetic complications. It has been shown that tooth brushing, flossing, and mouth rinsing lead to the reduction of periodontal inflammation, with a decrease in blood glucose levels in patients with diabetes. Since many patients with diabetes exhibit poor glycemic control, therapy suggestions that involve the adoption of new habits (such as oral hygiene practices) are never accomplished.

IMPACT OF PERIODONTAL DISEASE ON GLYCEMIC CONTROL

Periodontal disease is a chronic inflammatory condition that arises from bacterial infection of the supporting tissues around teeth. It is also influenced by the host's immune and inflammatory response to the bacteria. Despite the localized nature of the disease, increased evidence exists to indicate that periodontal disease interacts with at least one systemic condition, diabetes, which in turn potentiates periodontal disease. A growing body of literature indicates that a bidirectional relationship exists between periodontal disease and diabetes. There is increasing evidence of an association between periodontitis and poor glycemic control in terms of lower mean glycosylated hemoglobin levels in both type 1 and type 2 diabetes participants following periodontal treatment.

The evidence suggesting that oral health status improves following nonsurgical periodontal treatment is well established. There is mixed evidence on the impact of periodontal treatments on glycosylated hemoglobin levels, particularly in type 2 diabetes. Despite a majority of systematic reviews indicating that periodontal treatments lower glycosylated hemoglobin levels, meta-analyses reveal small and not statistically significant differences in glycosylated hemoglobin levels following treatment. Nonetheless, a recent, large, and well-conducted trial indicated that clinically measurable benefits on longer term glycemic control were obtained following periodontal treatment. Potentially, this impact is mainly due to a reduction in inflammatory cytokines, which may have a direct effect on insulin action at the cellular level as opposed to changes in glycosylated hemoglobin levels.

Diabetes mellitus is a significant risk factor for periodontal disease, and individuals with diabetes may have a higher prevalence and severity of periodontal disease. The serum level of glycosylated hemoglobin of previously undiagnosed diabetes patients with severe periodontitis is compared with healthy individuals, and the link between glycemia and insulin resistance status in previously undiagnosed diabetes patients with severe periodontitis is assessed. Periodontal disease is one of the most common chronic diseases, causing tooth loss and functional problems, and may affect general health and well-being. Diabetes and periodontal disease result in chronic inflammation, which may co-exist in individuals. There is an understanding of the bidirectional relationship between diabetes and periodontal disease from animal studies and experiments. Anti-diabetic therapy results in improvements in periodontium and the subgingival microbiota, while periodontal therapy improves the level of glycosylated hemoglobin and glycemic variability level.

Bidirectional Relationship Between Diabetes and Oral Health

The relationship between oral health and systemic health is often highlighted by the observation that diabetic patients with more severe diabetes tend to have poorer oral health (Kudiyirickal & Pappachan, 2024). There is a focus here on the bidirectional relationship between diabetes and oral health. Diabetes leads to bad oral health in the following ways: salivary alpha-amylase levels are higher, salivary flow rates change, dysbiosis of the oral microbiome occurs, cytokines, glucose levels, the immune response are altered, salivary pH drops, and acidosis in the oral cavity occurs. Poor oral health can aggravate diabetes through dental caries, periodontal disease, and mouth cancer.

Diabetes occurs due to complete absence of insulin (Type 1 or juvenile sugar diabetes) or underproduction of insulin (Type 2 or adult-onset diabetes). The former is caused when the beta cells of the pancreas fail after an autoimmune incident. The result is lipolysis, protein catabolism, and lack of polysaccharide utilization. The incident happens in childhood or early adulthood. The blood glucose levels rise. The cells, unable to use glucose, suffer dire consequences. Polyphagia, polydipsia, polyuria, weakness, dry skin, blurry vision, weight loss, etc., occur. Classically, patients present with DKA (diabetic ketoacidosis), which can occur a few hours after the symptoms arise, with rapid breathing, tiredness, lethargy, dehydration, feel drowsy, and coma. It is a medical emergency, and fluids, insulin, bicarbonate, or potassium are given.

In Type 2 diabetes, the problem is different: the pancreatic beta cells release less insulin or its action in the tissues is obstructed, or an intermediate situation between the two. Obesity increases the risk of Type 2 diabetes. The result mimics that of Type 1 diabetes, but less dramatically. It is more insidious. It often happens in middle age. It can be asymptomatic for a long time. Due to the great number of prediabetic patients, doctors have started to check blood glucose levels in old age. Screening is done when patients are elderly and have hypertension, dyslipidemia, etc. One of the major criteria for its diagnosis is the fasting levels of glucose. If levels above 126 mg/dL are recorded, it is diagnosed. Glucose levels can be lowered through lifestyle modification or drugs that stimulate beta cells or increase the transport of glucose in tissues.

Preventive Strategies for Diabetic Patients

Patients who are diabetic, especially those who are prone to diabetes type 2 (DM2), should be the primary target of oral health education interventions. Diabetes is a chronic disease with a high prevalence rate (Ashraf Nazir et al., 2018), while chronic diseases related to poor oral health and limited accessibility to oral health care exist. These adverse health outcomes are a burden to patients' health-related quality of life, negatively affecting social and psychological health but also being financially invasive. Possible clinical presentation of diabetes is bleeding gums, periodontitis, dry mouth, oral burning sensation, oral lichen planus, and candidiasis. These chronic disease-related problems can be addressed with health education, promoting patients' knowledge and awareness of the current situation but also the effect of the disease on their health. The education should consist of oral hygiene subjective and professed knowledge, objective accessibility, suitability and unprofessional self-evaluation of their oral hygiene efforts. Specific information about diabetes and oral health, a bi-directional connection, and preventive measures against adverse oral health.

Health staff and community nurses can take leading roles in oral hygiene patient education and the early diagnosis of long-term chronic oral health-related conditions like periodontitis. There is a need for more epidemiological and methodological studies on educating nursing staff about instructing patients with DM2 and other long-term immunosuppressed patients on appropriate oral hygiene efforts. Good oral health of diabetic patients, especially control of periodontitis, is a determining and non-replaceable factor of good glycemic control. Methods such as smoking cessation, reduction of excess weight, change of unhealthy eating behaviors, and physical exercise increase the odds of control over DM2 but also improve oral health with the improvement of overall quality of life. Long-term control of both diseases and prevention of complication can be ensured with systematic medical and dental check-ups and advice. Education should be formal but also done through new technologies like telemedicine for remote patients.

ORAL HEALTH AND CARDIOVASCULAR DISEASES

According to the World Health Organization (WHO), cardiovascular diseases (CVDs) are the leading cause of mortality globally, with an estimated 17.9 million deaths in 2019 alone. Other significant health problems tied to CVD are mortality and hospitalization rates (Molania et al., 2021). CVD, one of the leading causes of mortality/morbidity, is by far the most widely known, and refers to heart and/or vascular problems, such as a heart attack or stroke that impedes the normal flow of blood. These problems can be a result of clogged arteries, blood clots, spasms of the arteries, or ruptured vessels, and risk factors for such problems include tobacco smoking, mental stress, and sleep apnea. The cardiovascular system can be affected by various diseases, but one group of disorders downplays the importance of oral health in heart disease: infective cardiovascular diseases.

Dental bacterial infection/periodontitis is an odontogenic disease that impacts the structures surrounding tooth roots, primarily the gum and bone. There is substantial evidence linking oral infections, such as periodontitis, with CVD. Direct bacterial infection of cardiac valves and myocardium resulting in infective endocarditis has been suggested based on molecular/serological detection of oral bacteria in diseased heart tissues, animal heart infections, and patient reports of oral health status prior to valvular surgery. As a result of strong Koch's postulates-like evidence, it is now widely accepted that oral bacteria may enter the blood flow via gingival micro-trauma during daily oral hygiene-related activities—brushing teeth, chewing, and inter-dental cleanliness—and persistently colonize heart valves, leading to more severe infective endocarditis in patients with pre-existing cardiac valve abnormalities.

Emerging evidence supports a novel association between periodontitis and ischemic heart disease (IHD)—specifically, atherosclerotic coronary artery disease. Inflammation plays a critical role in the pathogenesis of both IHD and periodontitis, with the assumption that high-level cytokines reflecting systemic inflammation could be produced from periodontitis and heighten the risk of IHD (Men et al., 2024). A prothrombotic microenvironment is crucial to plaque growth and rupture in atherosclerosis.. Systemic damage in IHD may lead to an increased risk of more severe oral diseases due to healing processes.

Mechanisms Linking Oral Health to Heart Health

The link between periodontitis and cardiovascular disease (CVDs) is supported by evidence of shared bacterial and inflammatory factors. While such findings are still being pursued, complementary grounds have emerged since, regarding which to date knowledge is already more robustly set. The idea that oral health influences cardiovascular health is reinforced by a growing amount of epidemiological data.

Conversely, innumerable clinical trials have been developed around the same strategy, attempting to prove whether improving oral health influences cardiovascular health (Men et al., 2024).

The potential mechanisms by which oral health affects cardiovascular health are becoming increasingly understood. Whether and how changes to the oral-inhabiting microbiota composition hampering with biofilm formation are able to impact systemic circulation, the concept of oral-oral transmission of bacteria between individuals is described extensively. Hardly exclusively residing in the oral cavity, it unveils on a manner by which systemic health can be affected from what might be perceived as simple action. A fine balance among the oral microbiota composition promotes co-existence among the different bacteria, in which a few iconic ones are able to scavenge for the specific nutrients they prefer before others. Any change thereof may confer a wider advantage to the selection thereof.

Several disorders linked to oral health problems, such as CVDs, exhibit changes to blood microbiota makeup together with circulating neutrophils morphologies. Arterial-stiffening bacteria may induce cross-tissue immunomodulation to promote systemic inflammation upon migrating from oral sites. The periodontium take on trans-infection includes the ability of infectious agents to gain and spread across spatially separated tissues. During their oral presence, microorganisms with related byproducts might influence neutrophils functions, which may subsequently migrate into the peripheral circulation, indirectly influencing overall systemic health outcomes.

Epidemiological Evidence of Oral Health and Cardiovascular Risk

A growing body of epidemiological evidence supports a relationship between oral diseases and cardiovascular diseases (CVDs) risk factors, and in particular periodontal disease, a chronic inflammatory condition that has been epidemiologically linked with CVD (Men et al., 2024). Davide et al. found that tooth loss was associated with increased odds of hypertension in a cross-sectional population-based survey of middle aged and older adults from Japan. Dhinagaran et al. reported findings from Singapore that indicate poor dental status and severe periodontal disease are classified as independent risk factors for CVD. Periodontitis has also been directly linked with systemic manifestations, one in seven stroke cases due to oral infections, and oral bacteria have been found in vascular thrombi.

The association that they have investigated between oral health and CV risk factors is tooth brushing variability. Tooth brushing has been identified as a risk marker or risk factor for cardiovascular events. Based on factors available from the NHS2 data, tooth brushing what was self-reported at baseline would be a good risk marker. The focus is on tooth brushing on two far-apart occasions 5 years apart.

Those who did not change tooth brushing answered the quotient. Those who on both occasions "brushed twice a day or more" were the reference group. Among those who changed mottled exposure to the reference group, the increase in cardiovascular disease risk was fronted within 5 years.

Due to this, they have checked residual confounding from adjustment for other known CV risk factors and are examining more complex tooth brushing arrangements. The risk of breast cancer incidence associated with "less frequent" tooth brushing—estimated by contrasting with the reference group "twice a day or more"—fell by 70% to 75% after controlling for updated body mass index. Using a calculator from a large study, they have estimated that risk factor mix would on average cause breast cancer incidence at the rate of 5.2% per decade. They suggested that if childhood illness follows "tooth brushing three times a day or more," the consequence may be heightened risk of breast cancer incidence.

Oral Health Management in Patients with Cardiovascular Disease

Regular brushing and flossing of teeth allow for the removal of bacterial biofilms that form on teeth. This reduces the prevalence of gingivitis. The only reliable tools for removing plaque sub-gingivally are mechanically activating devices such as toothbrushes, floss and interdental brushes. Based on the width of the attached gingiva, a specific brushing strategy that is effective with the aid of floss is proven. The effectiveness of floss in the interdental areas was studied and found that flossing may reduce the risk of cardiovascular disease with local associations by instructing participants on the proper way to clean in a tooth-brushing manner. Flossing before brushing may influence plaque and biofilm removal in interproximal areas. When participants were less likely to carry out flossing or brushing advice associated to the effectiveness in the first time, providing tailored advice and support in a motivational interviewing approach was a method to aid participants' coping strategies. Oral diseases can directly affect the heart and large arteries by virtually all the pathways available for infection. Stimulation of the immune system and the extensive host reaction triggered by the inflammatory process caused by these diseases may lead to alteration of the functions of various types of blood cells; this could render them more proactive or cause them to generate mediators of hemostasis more prone to thrombus formation. Host response to chronic gingival disease could be a risk factor for the development of CV. The systemic effects of dental disease may be multifactorial, involved with potential oral sources, including oral processing, bad habits and other undetected systemic diseases (Sanchez et al., 2017)). Oral and dental assessments are widely neglected components of the systemic health assessment. Cardiologists refer only a small minority of patients to dentists for dental disease management. Affordability and access to oral care have replaced knowledge as the most prominent barriers to management of oral health (Molania et al., 2021). There are misconceptions regarding oral health effecting independence and quality of life. These views, held particularly amongst recipients of group home care, inform reluctance to seek assistance for oral healthcare needs. Such beliefs indicate an overall lack of insight about oral health and chronic disease and point toward an opportunity for education and re-evaluation of decision-making around appropriate care. Accessible oral health education could play a role in reversing these beliefs and improving patient care. Education should be tailored to the comprehension and context of patients to be effective.

ORAL HEALTH AND PREGNANCY OUTCOMES

Oral health is a condition that impacts the overall health. Dental caries is not only the most common chronic disease of infants, children, and adolescents (Lee, 2022), but also the second most common disease after the common cold among the general world's population. Dental caries can impair daily activities in a variety of ways including, but not limited to, chewing, speaking, sleeping, and socializing with peers. Badly affected individuals may have an impaired diet that leads to loss of weight or nutritional deficiency. When left untreated, dental caries can progress to pulpitis, pain, emergency dental treatment, and loss of teeth. Children with early childhood caries are more likely to have dental caries when they enter elementary school compared to those with good oral health. Recent literature also seeks to identify modifiable risk factors including dentist's office visits, fluoride varnish, and parental oral health practices such as cleaning children's teeth, healthy and unhealthy dietary habits to predict future dental health.

Gingivitis and periodontitis are progressive diseases of the gingival tissues that might affect the underlying supporting structures of the tooth both clinically and radiographically. Gingival inflammation is a reversible condition. When there are retained dental plaques, the tooth-brushing frequency is insufficient, or an individual is under-stressed and has an unbalanced diet, gingivitis develops. Repeated or chronic gingivitis might lead to periodontitis, which can harbor a threshold or a switch from dental plaque accumulation to destructive periodontal disease. It is a gradual disease that does not progress overnight; nonetheless, left untreated or uncontrolled, periodontitis would eventually affect the health and more systemic conditions.

Twenty years ago, dental epidemiology and public health started to unveil the association between orally infectious diseases and respiratory diseases and their interrelations, including longitudinal studies linking the severity of periodontitis or the annual number of dental caries that developed to the incidence of pneumonia/respiratory disease. For expectant mothers, achieving and maintaining good oral health during pregnancy is vital for their own and their growing children's oral and general health. Inadequate dental treatments during pregnancy can elevate the risks for complicated dental and oral diseases as well as the incidence of systemic diseases. Notably, pregnant women with active dental caries have higher odds for having their children with dental caries compared to their counterparts. In other words, giving birth without tooth decay or gum problems might be of great benefit for their children.

Effects of Poor Oral Health on Maternal Health

During pregnancy, physiological and anatomical changes affect the endocrine and immune systems, which can, in turn, influence maternal habits such as diet, smoking, and oral hygiene practices. This can compromise the maintenance of oral health. For practically all diseases of the oral cavity, there exist potential risk factors that equally compromise maternal and fetal health, as well as overall health. In this context, maternal oral health is currently an important public health issue. It may be strongly related to the oral health of young children. The odds ratio of caries-positive children was significantly high when the history of decayed teeth and gum problems were positive in mothers (Lee, 2022). Many factors influence this correlation, including physiological oral changes, decreased personal hygiene, and lifestyle changes. Carb-rich foods can build plaque accumulation. Dietary habits such as frequent meal intake, lack of food restrictions, decreased fluoride intake through dental care, decreased frequency of using toothbrushes especially prior to sleeping, and fewer dental visits are also risk factors. Establishing, promoting, and maintaining good oral health and hygiene during pregnancy can be a beneficial health promotion initiative to improve both oral and overall health during and after pregnancy. Achieving and maintaining good oral health is essential for both the oral and overall health of expecting mothers and their young children. Dental caries affects a wide range of daily activities, including eating, speaking, and social interaction. Dental caries causes pain, discomfort, non-concentration, sleep disturbance, and changed food choice patterns, which affect weight gain, energy, and nutritional intake. If expecting mothers have active dental caries, the number of bacteria can increase exponentially in dental plaque compared to those without active dental caries. As recent evidence shows that transmission occurs from mother to child, the risk for dental caries in these children becomes higher when mothers have active dental caries. Another common oral disease, periodontitis, was found to be associated with systemic conditions, including cardiovascular disease, respiratory disease, diabetes, and potentially adverse birth outcomes. Since there is evidence indicating that maternal underweight is directly related to preterm birth weight as well as tonsillectomy of children, and that there is a competing risk with periodontal disease, prevention of periodontal disease using oral hygiene machinery can be expected to be an effective method for preventing a poor birth outcome and improving oral health and hygiene in young children.

Impact on Fetal Development and Birth Outcomes

Poor oral health can have significant implications for systemic health. Nonetheless, this topic has received relatively little attention in the literature. One potential cause for this is the complexity of oral diseases, which can present a barrier to establishing firm links with other conditions, especially with those in the systemic domain. The differences across health systems, with regard to the delivery and coverage of oral health services, could also have played a role.

Women of reproductive age are particularly vulnerable to the negative impact of poor oral health. Even after controlling for potential confounding variables, associations between poor oral health statuses such as tooth loss, periodontal disease, and dental caries and adverse birth outcomes have been reported. These associations can be explained by common risk factors, for instance, socioeconomic status, and the systemic effect on fetal development of inflammation-related bioactive agents generated in the oral cavity. Overall, enhancing maternal oral health is an appropriate public health goal since improved oral health could reduce expenses for health care systems as well as preventable mortalities and morbidities (Lee, 2022).

A growing number of studies have investigated associations between maternal oral health status indicators (i.e., periodontal disease, tooth loss, or a combination of both) and adverse birth outcomes (i.e., preterm birth, low birth weight, or both). It was revealed that periodontal disease was associated with increased odds for preterm birth, low birth weight, or both. Women with poor oral health were also significantly more likely to deliver preterm low birth weight infants. Although both periodontal disease and tooth loss were independently associated with adverse pregnancy outcomes, tooth loss was the stronger predictor for preterm birth, while periodontal disease was more closely linked to low birth weight.

Oral Care Recommendations for Pregnant Women

Pregnancy causes hormonal changes that influence the likelihood and severity of dental diseases, such as gingivitis and periodontitis. However, there are many things to stay healthy during this time, including oral care recommendations for pregnant women. First, talk to the doctor about any changes in prescribed medications and which over-the-counter medications are safe to take. Check which dental treatments and procedures are safe to complete. Next, inform the dental team about being pregnant prior to any treatment. Schedule the dental ailment or checkup during the second trimester. Many dental x-rays are safe without extra precautions in a modern office, but ask beforehand. With this knowledge, it's easier to figure out what can be done then take care of any issues after giving birth. Seek a mouth rinse with fluoride, and use toothpaste that does not have the sodium lauryl sulfate ingredient or abrasive or acidic ingredients. Avoid toothpastes that cause a dry mouth. Make sure there is a way to make the saliva flow while brushing to protect teeth. This may require drinking more water, chewing gum, using special mouthwashes, and using salivating pills or medications. It may also help to use a prescription fluoride rinse or gel. Pregnancy causes shifts in hormones that can lead to gingivitis or swelling of the gums, which require regular cleaning with a toothbrush and floss. Get take-home teeth cleaning options if there is a high chance of bleeding or swelling. To prevent dental diseases from getting worse if regular care is greatly affected, consume a daily fluoride supplement or prescription. Drinking and rinsing with water after sugary foods may help reduce cavities. Getting sealants put on teeth, brushing with prescription fluoride toothpaste at bedtime, and using a prescription fluoride rinse may also be beneficial. Getting a clean inside of the mouth is important if taking medication to keep from getting cavities. Avoid eating sugary foods or drinking very sugary drinks.

ORAL HEALTH DISPARITIES

Socioeconomic status (SES), which encompasses factors such as income, wealth, education, and occupation, is a widely studied determinant of health outcomes. Adult SES, particularly educational attainment and income, is strongly predictive of chronic diseases. Inequities in oral health—as demonstrated by the high levels of untreated dental disease or periodontitis in lower SES groups, as well as higher levels of caries in children from low-SES families—follow similar patterns. Oral health inequities are disparities in the oral health status of different population subgroups arising from structural issues in society and health systems (Brown, 2012). Although oral health inequities are grounded in social and economic determinants, they are typically measured using indicators of individual access to care, such as dental insurance, frequency of visits, or dental anxiety.

However, other less studied constructs such as dental care availability, dentists per capita, and educator supply per child may also contribute to health inequities. These constructs represent the broad societal factors—economic and professional structures—that determine access. In the study, abstracting nationally representative data from the National Health and Nutrition Examination Surveys, structural regressors of dental care inequity in the United States were constructed (Marques Borges & Krishnamurthy, 2022). As expected, area of residence appeared to be a factor, although the slope of the inequity is fairly constant. Distance to dentists is also a significant predictor but explains less than half of the inequity in dental care use. The study identified structural barriers to oral care among adults aged 18 and above that the current insurance-based approaches to improve access are unlikely to remove.

Disparities across racial/ethnic groups in oral health, dental caries, and services were examined. Whether the disparity patterns persist across race/ethnicity when education or income is accounted for was also posted. African American, Hispanic, and Mexican American groups were found to have worse oral health status, but disparity patterns between non-Hispanic Whites and Mexican Americans were different compared to the other two groups. Education and income could not explain all the disparity across racial/ethnic groups. Findings support a more complex interpretation in which historical context, cultural factors, and discrimination against minority groups may play an important role. The separation of medical and dental systems may play into the larger role of the system as a whole in creating disparities. However, results suggest that the participating dentists may systematically discriminate against and neglect minority groups. Further research is warranted since the mechanism producing the disparities is complicated by factors such as residential segregation, cultural differences, acculturation, and discrimination.

Socioeconomic Factors Affecting Oral Health

The socio-economic status (SES) has been extensively examined throughout the world due to its crucial role in various health issues, including oral health. The significance of SES in the etiology of dental caries in both adults and children has been widely accepted by researchers (Almajed et al., 2024). SES is a socially determined variable that can influence an individual's health directly, as well as indirectly through its effect on other determinants such as geographical allocation, education, occupation, access to health care, nutrition, housing, etc. SES can be evaluated using several parameters, including income, education, and occupation variables, as well as multi-index composite indicators, which integrate two or more variables used to measure SES. SES has demonstrated an increased effect on the onset of dental caries, particularly in disadvantaged populations.

The relationship between SES and dental caries in children has also been extensively examined. It has been consistently found that children from lower SES backgrounds tend to have higher rates of dental caries when compared with children from higher SES backgrounds. A meta-analysis confirmed that lower SES is significantly associated with yet-to-have dental caries in school-aged children. Parental education level is significant and consistently associated with a decreased risk for dental caries in children among SES measures. In particular, maternal education level has consistently shown a stronger association with childhood dental caries when compared to other family SES measures. Results also suggested that food security might be a significant variable in pediatric oral health.

Children from households classified as low food secure and very low food secure had a higher prevalence of caries compared to fully food secure households. Family income and weight-for-age z-scores were also influential variables related to dental caries. Greater odds of the presence of caries were found in children who were markedly underweight and at lower SES. In addition, living in a deprived neighborhood and the caries status of older siblings and parental are also strongly associated with early childhood caries. Maternal oral health, as evidenced by the presence of caries, visible plaque, and dental visit during pregnancy, is positively linked with the SES of family, affecting the prevalence of caries in children.

Access to Dental Care and Systemic Health

Caring for one's teeth is a basic aspect of daily health and also affects many of life's activities including smiling, eating with other people, and even speaking clearly. The mouth does not simply reflect one's general health, it helps maintain it as well. People in poor oral health are in bad systemic health and have more difficulties living well. Accordingly, professionals' efforts to improve cardiovascular health are not complete without addressing oral health. While it may sound contradictory, poor oral health has been linked with systemic diseases such as bacterial pneumonia, aortic artery calcification, and even a higher risk of preterm labor and low-birth babies (Cardoso & Tenenbaum, 2020). Many systems of health care have been noble enough to address some of these relationships. Hypothetically speaking, heart disease prevention programs would be more effective if dental screenings of individuals were incorporated into primary care visits. Dentists would no longer simply be providers of a service, but partners in patients' total health.

One key to improving care is to make it easier for patients to access treatment. No other part of health care is treated this way. In fact, lack of dental care access is often treated as stigma, with the poor and disheveled denigrated from the point of view of detection and treatment. It is not the intention to argue that the issue of poverty itself is not important; it is important to explain what is not seen often enough in discussions of access. There are specific issues in regards to not only how health care is funded, practiced, and regulated, but also, more fundamentally, about patients and how they care for their teeth. Payment models for dentists have ramifications for practice style. Some issues of education and training of dental providers have ramifications for relationships with patients and the community at large.

Overall, the nation's most disadvantaged dental health care access groups—lower socioeconomic status persons of color with limited formal education in urban areas—have worse clinical dental conditions than do Americans in general. In addition to treatment denial, there are access barriers deeply enshrined in the dental care system including economic inequity, social inequity including provider biases, and cultural barriers. These enshrined barriers must be elucidated and their modification considered. Smiles (or lack thereof) mean more than one's teeth. People rarely talk about the systemic consequences of inadequate dental care. Poor oral health can impair one's self-image, relationships, emotional states, and, ultimately, health and well-being. There are certain disparities in how teeth are cleaned based on class that add inequalities to any system.

PREVENTIVE MEASURES AND INTERVENTIONS

Evidence-based guidelines for maintaining good oral health in patients unable to do so independently. There is a need to consider the most relevant studies in addition to the literature survey (Kramer & Splieth, 2022).

The abnormality in the oral cavity is often not detected early through examination of soft and hard oral tissues. Medical staff can easily assess oral health by incorporating cost-effective instruments, such as a dental mirror or a disposable wooden tongue depressor, into the general outpatient examination set. These tools can help evaluate the overall health condition of incoming patients. Since patients are typically examined for other symptoms before visiting a dental office, they may not retain specific memories of prior oral assessments.. Structural mouth cleaning devices should be made in the dental office and fitted to the unconscious patients. Continuous tongue kit incorporation is needed to stimulate the tongue paravertebral areas vibrating soft palate, the faucet irrigators, activate the secretions of the major salivary glands, and reduce the volume of viscous secretions in the entry part of the respiratory tracts. The best brushing maneuvers are done by cycling or rotating brushing. The greater the number of teeth grouping cardinal brushing motions, the longer maneuvering time remains on one tooth.

During oral immersion of a patient in a tank, four handheld electrical brushes rotating in opposite directions and angles can be used to clean eight teeth zones. A medicated mouthwash whose prescription is dependent on the health status of the patients, and numbers of brushing cycles to consume can be altered to fit the treatment needed. The brushing tanks' intake means a lighting source permitting blood circulation compatibility in the devices essential to avoid tooth discoloration. There is a need to care for tooth pivot and gingival sites through surface hygiene cleansing, artificial ultra sonics guiding to generate induction or suction, preventing maxillary obstructions on teeth. Oral collapse causes tracheal clanking for the intubated patients diligently asleep conveniently opening the airway tract.

Oral Hygiene Practices

Although it is encouraging that most people brush their teeth at least once a day, brushing only once a day can still lead to various oral health problems. Poor dental hygiene is the obvious outcome of poorly brushing the teeth, leading to many social and psychological problems. However, these problems go much deeper than a bad smile or bad breath (Koubaytari, 2017). Oral hygiene has a huge effect on systemic health, but due to social stigma, it often goes unnoticed until it is too late.

The mouth is home to over 700 different strains of bacteria, some of which are harmful and can cause disease. Poor oral hygiene can cause an increase in bacteria and lead to plaque formation. Two main conditions arise from plaque buildup: gingivitis and periodontitis. When plaque is not removed, it hardens into calculus which advances inflammation leading to periodontal disease (Kumar et al., 2023). Periodontal disease is a group of inflammatory diseases of the supporting tissues of the teeth. It involves the progressive loss of bone and connective tissue which often causes tooth loss. When left untreated, bacteria can live in the pockets surrounding the teeth and increase in number, leading to systemic diseases.

A common question about gum disease is what kind of bacteria is involved. Microbiological analyses have intensified research on chronic periodontitis. Gram-negative, anaerobic rods predominate the subgingival flora in untreated chronic periodontitis. Anaerobic bacteria account for over 90% of cultured organisms in periodontitis sites. These bacteria lead to inflammation, which causes the local tissues to respond to the infection. Chronic tissue inflammation can result in pathologic tissue remodeling involving the deposition of collagen, which can act as a protective mechanism. However, this also leads to the formation of a fibrous tissue capsule that hinders the immune response. Bacteria can persist inside the tissues by escaping from the immune cells.

Community-Based Health Initiatives

Individuals affected by chronic oral disease experience higher levels of poverty and lower levels of education. Oral disease disproportionately affects specific populations; especially the elderly, the poor, racial and ethnic minorities, immigrants and refugees, people with chronic illnesses or disabilities, and individuals living in rural areas (Linabarger et al., 2021). Income levels and other demographic factors predispose some populations to multi-morbidity and poorer health as well as oral health outcomes in children. There is also evidence from community-based studies of a higher risk of oral disease in rural leadership compared with their urban peers. These disparities have long-lasting effects on their health, which may affect their present and future work capacities, quality of life, and social and family interactions.

The HHS agencies have developed and implemented effective oral health epidemiology systems which conduct scientific research, identify and evaluate oral diseases, and risk factors for such diseases and disparities. On a national level, the CDC facilitates the National Oral Health Surveillance System (NOHSS), promoting health education and prevention programs for pre-school children, and collects data on common oral diseases, on a state level, the health departments provide community-based oral health services to low-income families. The assessment of oral health status and use of the health service in the U.S., Connecticut in particular, will be discussed. Connecticut has historically been demonstrated as not only one of the two smallest states, but also one of the most economically disparate states in the country. As a state with the highest cost of living and the largest income disparity, it is important for public health practitioners to understand oral health disparities to promote effective strategies to prevent and reduce oral diseases. The relationship between oral health and social demographic factors was assessed by comparing the percentages of their associations. The health data was collected from the CDC and the population data were collected from the census.

Role of Healthcare Providers

Healthcare providers can play a role in preventing and managing diseases linked to poor oral health. Family physicians may be the first healthcare practitioner to identify the presence of systemic issues related to oral health, or see management issues with those systemic health issues. Medications can adversely affect oral health, and involving pharmacists along with dentists and primary care providers can help develop comprehensive care plans tailored to the unique needs of each patient. Unfortunately, opportunities to improve oral health may be missed by physicians and other health professionals that may fail to appreciate the importance of oral health on overall well-being and quality of life (S. Lipsky et al., 2024).

Family physicians can also access and treat the patient holistically. Family physicians usually see their patients over a long period of time with routine visits. They also treat entire families (infants, children, adolescents, adults and seniors) and can capture the overall health picture longitudinally. Family physicians often see patients with systemic diseases early in their course, often before they become more serious, advanced, and difficult to manage. Increasing evidence has been emerging connecting oral biofilm with systemic conditions, either initiating them or complicating those medical conditions. This nascent and developing body of research reflects very positively on the discipline of dentistry. However, while this body of research is positive for dentistry, it signals impending changes for family physicians and their role in patient care (Kurtzman et al., 2022).

Poor oral biofilm management needs to be thought of like constipation. There are parents who may never bother to toilet train their children. If a child only has a few bowel movements in a week and is always uncomfortable and remonstrating with abdominal pain, the generalist community will become involved. The pediatrician will be asked to evaluate the child for encopresis and the family will be sent to the pediatric gastroenterologist for a choice of issues. Parents that do not address their children's bowel regulation and constipation may very well be denigrated by health care professionals. Parents that avoid initiating children into a standard oral health regimen of tooth brushing, mouth rinsing, scraping, flossing and mouth washing will receive little attention from the healthcare community. The child will continue to be ill-tempered and irritable, will exhibit failure to thrive, poor growth, dental caries, poor self-esteem and unsocial behavior.

FUTURE RESEARCH DIRECTIONS

Future research should maintain an evidence-based curiosity for these associations, but look towards unexplored or underexplored areas, particularly nimble subjects, new databases, and powerful research approaches/reforms. Future meta-analyses should dissect nuances of the examined associations, e.g., the diversity of systemic disease forms, severities, drug effects, co-influences, gender, and placentas. This is prime for health sciences, which have largely not advanced beyond health-belief models, conventional psychometrics, and psychophysical approaches. Ultra-short phenotyping, scoring, and subtyping schemas have emerged and are increasingly used. They speed up clinical practice while extracting vast data and perspectives potentially impacting clinical care. Spreading awareness is essential. Emerging fields in the humanities and social sciences may also become fruitful, given the right framing of research questions. Results will likely be immediate in epidemiology, public health, transitioning care, health provision organization, preventive dentistry, health behavior change, promoting oral health education, oral health literacy, and oral-systemic health integration.

Field 3 involves public health approaches designed to explore and meet new diverse habits and societal challenges. New habits include e-sport gaming and its strong link with snacking, the "night shift" phenomenon's health effects on dental caries, and oral oncology care in an increasingly aging society undergoing cancer treatment. New societal and demographic challenges relate to early diagnosis and timely partitioning of an increasingly diversified group of young patients. Research in areas of global change's impact on dental caries prevalence under climate change, and powerful research or research reform approaches include life-course models and the recognition of cumulative health impact. It is essential to socially frame research relevance, also promoting lobbying alongside evidence and argumentation. Integrating health as an asset when framing "oral health coverage reforms" is vital (Botelho et al., 2022).

Emerging Studies on Oral-Systemic Links

The relationship between poor oral health and systemic conditions has emerged as a significant area of research, with numerous studies investigating the potential links between NCDs and oral health issues (Botelho et al., 2022). The oral-systemic health association is relatively well studied in some conditions, with most studies focusing on the associations of diabetes with end-stage oral diseases such as tooth loss and edentulism or chronic periodontitis. The design of using geocoded health records is innovative to the study of the oral-systemic quality of life, which is a significant advancement in this field of research. Future studies on other associations, such as that of blood pressure with oral health, are warranted and would allow further examination of country-wide patterns in the relationship of oral health with NCDs or conditions (Nagpal et al., 2015). Due to the advances in understanding the pathophysiology and risk factor sharing on the oral-systemic health association over the past decades, the focus has shifted on how to apply that understanding for screening, diagnosis, and/or treatment or intervention.

There has been a slew of reviews that examine what is being known about the association of the diseases with oral health and analyze some conceptual or behavioral factors that could promote intervention-on-oral-health-to-improve-health-outcomes across conditions at a population level. Significant efforts conducted independently in various fields should be unified and synthesized to come up with concerted and actively applied solutions to improve health equity in the context of oral health and NCDs. The significant impact that poor oral health has on systemic diseases calls for the prompt intervention of oral health in efforts to improve health outcomes and reduce health inequity. In order to redress this situation, it is crucial to raise dentist awareness of the systemic implications of poor oral health and promote studies that evaluate the effects or impacts of oral health in the context of chronic diseases.

Innovative Approaches in Oral Health Care

The integration of oral health services into general health settings, such as hospitals and chronic disease management programs, has become increasingly important in many countries. This is particularly relevant among older adults, as their oral health is closely linked to their overall health, mortality, and morbidity.

While the association of oral health with other systemic health conditions such as systemic lupus erythematosus, chronic obstructive pulmonary disease, osteoporosis, and neonatal health has been proposed, the bidirectional relationship between periodontal diseases and type 2 diabetes mellitus is well established. Diabetes is considered the seventh leading cause of death worldwide, affecting 10% of the global adult population. In older adults, diabetes is common and leads to substantial disability, comorbidity, and mortality. Furthermore, as a chronic progressive high-risk disease, it reduces chewing ability and quality of life.

Conversely, uncontrolled diabetes increases the risk of developing periodontitis and contributes to its progression. Like diabetes, periodontitis can adversely affect nutrition intake, metabolic syndrome, chronic inflammatory state, and glycemic control. Chronic progressive diseases, such as periodontal disease and other non-communicable diseases, release inflammatory mediators into the circulation and exacerbate systemic inflammation. This shared inflammatory pathway is believed to be an association between periodontal disease and some systemic diseases, including cardiovascular diseases, rheumatoid arthritis, Alzheimer disease, and Parkinson disease. Acknowledge a great deal of bacteria in the mouth can promote aspiration pneumonia. Aspiration of oral bacteria causes pneumonia, especially in hospitalized patients and older adults. In addition, if dental caries or periodontal disease are left untreated, bacteria from the cavities or periodontal pockets may enter the bloodstream, leading to sepsis.

The latest WHO (2023) resolution, promoting oral health as an important component of general health, has ever-declining oral health in older adults and barriers to accessing dental services. Through a partnership with these agencies and education institutions, the research team has optimized an evidence-based and systematic intervention protocol, which has shown a strong impact on improving self-reported oral health behaviour, quality of life, mortality, and morbidity among older adults (Kit Ying Chan et al., 2023).

Henceforth, WHO has recently took the initiative successively prioritizing Oral Health through key resolutions and strategies;

2021 Resolution: Shifted focus from curative to preventive care, integrating oral health into NCD and Universal Health Coverage (UHC) agendas.
2022 Global Strategy and 2023 Action Plan: Outlined steps for member states and stakeholders to improve oral health.
2024 Bangkok Declaration: Declared "No Health Without Oral Health," reinforcing commitments to prevention, UHC, and climate-resilient health systems.

Subsequently World Dental Federation (2021) and NCD Alliance advocates and complement it and urges integrating oral health into NCD/UHC responses, emphasizing prevention, shared risk factors, health system strengthening, multidisciplinary care and community engagement.

CONCLUSION

Recognizing the connection between the mouth and body can provide valuable insights into the interrelationship between oral health and systemic diseases. The influence of systemic conditions on oral health was evaluated using various techniques involving pre-tested investigated questionnaire that consisted of open-ended, multiple choice and rating questions. The questionnaire explored systemic diseases in relation to oral conditions with a major focus on diabetes-related inquiries (Schwarz et al., 2023). Other systemic diseases such as hypertension, HIV, asthma, epilepsy, thyroid disorders, rheumatoid arthritis and cancers were also assessed. Perceptions regarding oral health needs among the population were explored using semi-structured interviews. Oral health in systemically diseased individuals in relation to systemic conditions was assessed (Pavani et al., 2024). To ascertain OSH questions were framed around symptoms and functioning aspects of oral health in relation to systemic diseases. Vignettes and semi-structured interviews were used to explore the impact of oral health constructs among a few representative participants selected randomly. The analysis was done using descriptive statistics and thematic analysis.

Those with diabetes and hypertension were more likely to have teeth considered unrestorable and poor prognosis. With hormones playing a role in both fertility conditions and oral health, it is hypothesized that OSH in those with hormonal disorders presents both an opportunity for patient education and a need for providers to be aware of these connections. Implications of the systematic reviews show a knowledge gap regarding associations between oral health needs and systemic conditions. To address this health promotion initiative in unreferred at risk/low socio-economic groups is warranted, especially if oral health is viewed as a disease. Integration with routine care needs to be trained at multiple levels for effective delivery. The negligible health promotion initiatives addressing systemic conditions along with oral health reflects an area of concern.

REFERENCES

Almajed, S. O., A Aljouie, A., S Alharbi, M., & M Alsulaimi, L. (2024). The Impact of Socioeconomic Factors on Pediatric Oral Health: A Review. ncbi.nlm.nih.gov

Ashraf Nazir, M., AlGhamdi, L., AlKadi, M., AlBeajan, N., AlRashoudi, L., & AlHussan, M. (2018). *The burden of Diabetes.* Its Oral Complications and Their Prevention and Management. [PDF]

Botelho, J., Mascarenhas, P., Viana, J., Proença, L., Orlandi, M., Leira, Y., Chambrone, L., João Mendes, J., & Machado, V. (2022). An umbrella review of the evidence linking oral health and systemic noncommunicable diseases. ncbi.nlm.nih.gov

Brown, J. (2012). Oral Health Disparities Across Racial [PDF]. *Ethnic Groups.*

Cardoso, O. C. E. & C. Tenenbaum, H. (2020). Older adults and the disparity in oral health status; the problem and innovative ways to address it. ncbi.nlm.nih.gov

Kit Ying Chan, A., Cheung Tsang, Y., & Jiang, M. C., Chiu Man Leung, K., Chin Man Lo, E., & Hung Chu, C. (2023). Integration of Oral Health into General Health Services for Older Adults. ncbi.nlm.nih.gov

Koubaytari, M. (2017). Student's Oral Health Knowledge, Oral Health Practices, and Their Susceptibility to Oral Health Diseases at a Midwestern University. [PDF]

Kramer, A., & Splieth, C. (2022). Health promotion through structured oral hygiene and good tooth alignment. ncbi.nlm.nih.gov

Kudiyirickal, G. M. & M Pappachan, J. (2024). Periodontitis: An often-neglected complication of diabetes. ncbi.nlm.nih.gov

Kumar, A., Grover, V., Satpathy, A., Jain, A., Singh Grover, H., Khatri, M., Kolte, A., Dani, N., Melath, A., Singh Chahal, G., Thomas, B., Raju Pradeep, A., Pandit, N., Radhamoni Madhavan Pillai, B., & Shiva Manjunath, G. R., Nandkeoliar, T., Puri, K., Singhal, R., Dodwad, V., Bhardwaj, A., Thakur, R., Jalaluddin, M., Boyapati, R., Kumar Singh, M., & Bansal, M. (2023). ISP good clinical practice recommendations for gum care. ncbi.nlm.nih.gov

Kurtzman, M. G., A. Horowitz, R., Johnson, R., A. Prestiano, R., & I. Klein, B. (2022). The systemic oral health connection: Biofilms. ncbi.nlm.nih.gov

Lee, H. (2022). Introducing Maternal Oral Health As Global Health And Public Health Agenda. ncbi.nlm.nih.gov

Linabarger, M., Brown, M., & Patel, N. (2021). A Pilot Study of Integration of Medical and Dental Care in 6 States. ncbi.nlm.nih.gov

Lipsky, S. M., Singh, T., Zakeri, G., & Hung, M. (2024). Oral Health and Older Adults: A Narrative Review. ncbi.nlm.nih.gov

Marques Borges, C., & Krishnamurthy, M. (2022). Are We Getting Any Better? A Critical Analysis of Selected Healthy People 2020 Oral Health Indicators in 1999–2004 and 2013–2016, USA. ncbi.nlm.nih.gov

Men, B., Li, Y., & Jiang, S. (2024). Updates on the Role of Periodontitis-Related Epigenetics, Inflammation, Oral Microbiome, and Treatment in Cardiovascular Risk. ncbi.nlm.nih.gov

Molania, T., Malekzadeh Shafaroudi, A., Taghavi, M., Ehsani, H., Moosazadeh, M., Haddadi, A., Gholizadeh, N., & Salehi, M. (2021). Oral health-related quality of life (OHRQoL) in cardiovascular patients referring to Fatima Zahra Hospital in Sari, Iran. ncbi.nlm.nih.gov

Nagpal, R., Yamashiro, Y., & Izumi, Y. (2015). The Two-Way Association of Periodontal Infection with Systemic Disorders: An Overview. ncbi.nlm.nih.gov

Pavani, P. M. N., Pachava, S., Parveen Sultana, S., Ravoori, S., Rajasekhar, P., & Talluri, D. (2024). Impact of diabetes mellitus and other systemic diseases on oral health and tooth mortality. ncbi.nlm.nih.gov

Sanchez, P., Everett, B., Salamonson, Y., Ajwani, S., Bhole, S., Bishop, J., Lintern, K., Nolan, S., Rajaratnam, R., Redfern, J., Sheehan, M., Skarligos, F., Spencer, L., Srinivas, R., & George, A. (2017). Oral health and cardiovascular care: Perceptions of people with cardiovascular disease. ncbi.nlm.nih.gov

Schwarz, C., Ioan Hajdu, A., Dumitrescu, R., Sava-Rosianu, R., Bolchis, V., Anusca, D., Hanghicel, A., Doris Fratila, A., Oancea, R., Jumanca, D., Galuscan, A., & Leretter, M. (2023). Link between Oral Health, Periodontal Disease, Smoking, and Systemic Diseases in Romanian Patients. ncbi.nlm.nih.gov

Surlari, Z., Elena Ciurcanu, O., Gabriela Budala, D., Butnaru, O., & Luchian, I. (2023). An Update on the Interdisciplinary Dental Care Approach for Geriatric Diabetic Patients. ncbi.nlm.nih.gov

World Health Organization on. (2025, March 17). Oral health. https://www.who.int/news-room/fact-sheets/detail/oral-health

Chapter 12
Impact of Artificial Intelligence on Oral Health Diagnostics

Muhammad Farooq Umer
https://orcid.org/0000-0001-7779-1929
Department of Preventive Dental Sciences, College of Dentistry, King Faisal University, Hofuf, Saudi Arabia

ABSTRACT

This chapter explores the transformative impact of artificial intelligence (AI) on oral health diagnostics, highlighting its growing role in enhancing diagnostic accuracy, efficiency, and personalized patient care. It outlines how machine learning algorithms, particularly deep learning and convolutional neural networks, are being applied to detect dental caries, periodontal disease, and oral cancers with increasing precision. The chapter discusses current trends in AI integration within dental imaging, predictive analytics, and tele-dentistry, while also addressing critical challenges such as data privacy, integration barriers, ethical concerns, and clinician training. Through case studies and literature synthesis, it evaluates the effectiveness and limitations of AI tools in real-world settings. Emphasis is placed on collaborative, ethical, and patient-centered approaches for successful adoption. The chapter concludes by suggesting future directions for regulatory frameworks, public trust, and interdisciplinary innovation to optimize AI-driven oral health diagnostics.

INTRODUCTION

The increasing burden of chronic diseases triggers the demand on healthcare systems and professionals. There has been increase in the number of healthcare

DOI: 10.4018/979-8-3373-1992-6.ch012

professionals and a need for more healthcare facilities. It has also increased budget requirements and additional research for the better delivery of health services. Artificial Intelligence (AI) in general is one of the emerging supporting factors to assist healthcare professions for disease diagnosis and prognosis, treatment plan generation, patient compliance/adherence, and reducing healthcare burden on the healthcare professionals(Patil et al., 2022).

AI is a branch of computer science that imitates the cognitive functions of the human brain such as learning and problem-solving. Various generic implementations of AI are available with the expert system, fuzzy logic-based systems, and ML as applications. The term 'Machine Learning (ML)' is widely used with AI. Mathematically, ML is a subset of AI responsible for the prediction of the outcome based on the dataset provided using the algorithms. ML is classified as supervised learning, unsupervised learning, and reinforcement learning. Neural networks (NN) are an adaptation of the human brain structure and one of the widely researched forms of ML for AI developments. Currently, deep learning models based on convolutional neural networks (CNNs) is building a new area in computer vision and pattern recognition, which is a further class of NN architectures (Schwendicke et al., 2020).

Currently, research on AI in oral health is blossoming. Its notable impact areas include detection of caries, periodontal disease, oral cancer, and detection of abnormalities in the jaw related to wisdom teeth, cysts, fractures, and temporomandibular joint-related disorders. AI algorithms assist professionals in time-sensitive critical situations by analyzing radiographs, clinical findings, and computerized tomography (CT). Dental professionals can review copies of AI-generated reports; thus, AI is not replacing professionals and clinical judgement. AI applications in oral health are emerging and expanding, like other sub-specialties additional questions and concerns also exists.

THE EVOLUTION OF DENTAL TECHNOLOGY

An increasing number of AI-based systems have been integrated into dental practices and research for various applications. AI development and implementation in the field of oral health need to be updated and evaluated. This should consider the current outlook of AI in general health care, the early developments in oral health, and its present status. Potential new applications and future directions of AI in oral health have also been discussed. In general health care, different strategies have been integrated for the AI adoption. These include problem analysis, the evaluation of existing data, the creation of AI algorithms, model application validation, and the technology transfers to a routine or clinical setting. Operational or technical problems may occur during a specific AI process or a technology transfer. Within dental research and practice, image acquisition technologies, such as dental radiography, intraoral scanning, and 3D facial scanning, are the main source of image data for AI development. Furthermore, AI applications have been proposed to assist dental professionals, which could mitigate some problems with labor shortages or expensive consultation fees(Hung et al., 2023).

Recently, AI-based vs. machine learning-based algorithms have been proposed for dentomaxillofacial radiology. Current AI applications focus on the automated detection and classification for various dental diseases or other pathologies, which have been integrated into many commercial systems. As inspection tools, they can assist dental professionals to identify possible diseases and help mitigate labor shortages in many under-developed areas. Nevertheless, they can only highlight possible problems or point out some false interpretations but cannot address the subsequent diagnostics and treatment plans(Joda et al., 2020). Rather than replacing, Ai should complement the early detection role of radiographs. Research is required to integrate AI with 3D imaging for the diagnosis of early-stage diseases in a clinical setting.

AI- or deep learning-based algorithms have been utilized to automatically assess a screening radiograph image for the cancer staging and type of cancer. There is a need to blend images from diverse acquisition technologies to enable in-depth assessment or a multi-image-based workflow. To enhance the usability or interpretability of AI algorithms or systems within clinical settings, commercial products or development environments can be primarily used. Overall, despite the increasing levels of image data, machine learning algorithms, and open-sourced toolkits, AI's contribution to dentomaxillofacial radiology, particularly in automatic detection of dental diseases, needs to be explored in a deeper and broader sense.

OVERVIEW OF ARTIFICIAL INTELLIGENCE IN HEALTHCARE

Artificial intelligence (AI) and machine learning (ML) are widely used terms in research, objectives, discussions, and even casual conversations. The term 'artificial intelligence' was coined in 1956 to describe a problem-solving machine based on data input. Since then, it has evolved significantly and continues to do. In fact, the field of AI is as varied and complex as the human brain itself. Since its conception, artificial intelligence has been a mainstay of popular science fiction novels, movies, and public discussions. Machine learning (ML), on the other hand, is one method of realizing artificial intelligence. ML is a subset of AI that makes use of adept algorithms to analyze datasets to predict the outcomes of future data. These algorithms can usually be classified into a broad category of used functions, such as artificial neural networks (ANN), classification trees, or regression analysis. More recently, the advent of convolutional neural networks (CNN) or simply deep learning (DL) have been in existence, the latter coinage being introduced by Geoffrey Hinton. Deep learning algorithms are considered revolutionary and set a trend in the field. They enable trained algorithms to analyze patterns in data without human intervention. However, understanding the source and the context of these patterns is challenging even for professional data analysts. In times of fiscal constraint, these states are demonstrating that policy changes can be both cost-effective and adaptable to local cultural and financial contexts. The success of trained deep learning tools hinges on an abundant supply of proper datasets. In brief, deep learning has a cascade setting of algorithms in a multi-layered structure that, in turn, facilitates the extraction of data features. One potential drawback is that too many algorithmic options can create confusion, reduce system efficiency, and lead to decision fatigue

AI is adaptable to a variety of inputs. When properly used, it can revolutionize medical, dental, and healthcare delivery. In combination with other constantly developing technological applications, it has the potential to affect significant change in the medical field as we know it. This revolution spans data gathering, processing and treatment predictions. It can significantly change the future perspective for diseases. Understanding the foundation is necessary to participate in AI-transformed sciences. Machine learning can aid in comparison to different factors and predict the success rate of various procedures for a particular patient(Patil et al., 2022). Properly used, AI means less nonessential work, less stress for the personal health system, improving health facilities for patients, faster, cheaper, and better outcomes.

CURRENT TRENDS IN ORAL HEALTH DIAGNOSTICS

Oral health diagnostics play a key role in dentistry, encompassing the assessment of clinical and radiographic examination findings as well as other problems and diseases of the periodontium, bone, and soft tissues. Early health monitoring, including the detection of cavities, periodontal disease, oral tumors, and jaw tumors, is essential for life. However, the challenge is immense because the human eye cannot detect early stages of many subtle changes. In addition, conventional monitoring also suffers from excessive expenses and inaccuracies, which often end with extensive interventions that are not reversible. Even today, there are serious limitations to existing diagnostics in clinical practice, which mostly take visual methods as their keys. A considerable effort has been devoted in recent years to the identification of innovative modalities, ranging from hyperspectral imaging to terahertz imaging, as well as advanced picture analysis-based methods, in order to realize advanced monitoring. These innovations remain passive; they only analyze parameters such as pores, frequencies, color changes but do not actively provide treatment. Consequently, they search for divergence from the usual values in monitored parameters and and generate recommendations for the dentist, such as suggesting a filling Most of these modalities cannot be considered as diagnostics, merely monitoring managers (Anil et al., 2023).

AI-based technology, has recently gained prominence due to its efficiency in providing greater reliability in more complicated tasks. It has penetrated practical site image recognition, buying suggestion in ecommerce, bus schedules, natural disasters, and even paroles. A key strength of deep learning systems is not only their ability to make decisions but also to continuously learn and improve. Once provided with initial data sets, they update themselves with new information and become more accurate over time. Consequently, after providing the initial tensors, sites, and bins, it keeps updating itself with newly provided information, continuously improving. AI-based monitoring systems can integrate the outputs from previous diagnostic tools. They can extract uncertainties and highlight areas requiring additional input, making diagnostic results more reliable. It becomes more explicit as more similar observations arrive within its architecture by narrowing the detection `expected` ranges. This article overviews oral health diagnostics applications of AI, including interpretation of images, predicting the development of problems based on historical data, and automatic image recognition on already known targets. This rapidly developing area is nonetheless only 5-10 years old. So far, the implementations mostly cover caries interpretation already introduced and used commercially by a few start-ups. One of their products, Pearl, is already 85% accurate for cavity identification from a single radiograph (Parthasarathy et al., 2024).

Artificial intelligence (AI) technologies have a growing influence on healthcare. AI may have a significant effect on oral diagnoses and treatments. With continuous advancements in computing power and the development of machine learning, AI algorithms are rapidly improving. Some studies showed that the classifier's performance can exceed that of expert radiologists. AI can be a helpful tool for finding essential pathologies from different imaging modalities. Lately, AI techniques have been used around the oral health domain, and studies are focused on describing the implementation of AI frameworks in oral diagnostics. The review emphasizes studies that determine the AI approach for the best prognosis and/or diagnosis for the patient in health care systems and computer science. The assessments, which consider insurance in general or consideration of uncertainties, are excluded. The relationships of AI to the diseases, conditions, and treatment of the oral cavity are used in the scope of oral cancer screening, bone and tooth radiography analysis, and dental caries' calculation and prediction. A comprehensive survey on the usage of AI on the diagnostic frameworks for oral malignancies is presented, which includes a dedicated pathology discussion and feature extraction methodically.

Patients may electronically monitor their oral health as a result of the developments in wireless technology and also the expanding internet function. Handheld devices with the electronic camera have been established for disorder triage rapidly. Nevertheless, the performance of the untrained user remains faulty and results in catastrophic delays. In order to find abnormalities in question images, prescription software based on CNN is shown to be substantially more sensitive than untrained users. Additional medical and dental technologies deliver choices of help with using mobile devices in the pathology detection and also other disorders domain. Amalgam detection program is given as a mobile app for dental restorations, tooth attrition analysis, and periodontal condition analysis regarding dental oral health. Insets that show gingivitis gradings meant for periodontal diagnosis are given with a list of detections of stage I, II, and III. For each class of diagnosis in the category, detection tasks and performance metrics are summarized. Confusion issues in oral healthcare investigations for AI applications are listed over the last three years.

BENEFITS OF AI IN ORAL HEALTH DIAGNOSTICS

Artificial intelligence (AI) refers to computer programs designed for problem solving mimicking human intelligence. These include capabilities such as learning, thinking, understanding by themselves, and actively processing data. It is a tool that helps smart decisions, predictions, and tasks independently. Recently, utilizing AI in health, a field that requires effort to prediction and prevention, is receiving attention. Through complete Computer-Aided Diagnostic Systems (CADS), the need for diagnosis can be provided. Two of the top reasons for using AI in oral health aside from the ability to diagnose disorders is to make diagnoses objective and to store data.

AI technology has shown potential as a software-based tool for caries detection in terms of the moderate sensitivity concern. These limitations could be theoretically overcome with more advanced technology. AI NADA was designed to detect different types of tooth damage, corect distortion and filter out inaccurate input number into the healthy or damaged tooth type. The system first filters the input image provided by the user. It than analyzes processed image to detect damaged tooth. In the end, AI-NADA concluded the image input number showed no carries. AI-NADA has the function to display of certainty and probability value as a result of analysis. The result of caries detection was measured to proceed with the reliability and validity test. Upon examining the KMO and barletta test and factor analysis test result, the Sawville result yielded good empirical satisfaction. The effect of the tooth damage detection and classification of tooth damage processing of the image was verified through the Dangjin correlation analysis method by the PCM (Alam et al., 2024).

Improved Accuracy and Efficiency

AI technology and algorithm solutions applied to digital health and oral health diagnostics have grown rapidly in recent years. AI algorithm systems aimed at solving dental problems have become gradually available for both dentists and ordinary consumers.

Thanks to technological advancement in the field of Artificial Intelligence (AI), automated imaging analysis has become widespread in the diagnosis of various diseases. The application of AI in the analysis of oral diseases, including periodontal diseases and dental caries, has broadened rapidly. Since the 21st century, some technology companies and dentists around the world have begun investigating AI's use in the diagnosis of oral diseases (De Angelis et al., 2022), though few reports have been published on the subject. Current AI algorithms are mainly focused for the detection of dental caries. Dental caries is a progressive condition. Early caries progression is noncavitated, and even with the advances in technology these are difficult to detect clinically using standard methods. Detecting these noncavitated lesions on bitewing radiographs is equally challenging due to the overlapping structures, image brightness variability, and other imaging artifacts present on the radiographs. AI technology has exhibited promise as an adjunctive tool for dental practitioners in the detection of lesions suspected to be dental caries, potentially reducing diagnostic errors and improving efficiency compared with traditional examination methods(Alam et al., 2024). Also, integrating AI products for the dental office may enable dentists to accurately detect such lesions at earlier stages. Over the longer term, this will facilitate reinforcement of oral health preventive practices to manage such lesions more effectively compared to lesional advancement with traditional diagnostic approaches.

Enhanced Predictive Analytics

Artificial intelligence (AI) tools are shaping medical diagnostic capabilities in previously unforeseen ways. A recent spate of studies has introduced AI applications for the detection, prediction, and prognosis of diseases, enhancing the diagnostic process. As the COVID-19 pandemic shows its lasting impact on modern society, healthcare providers are at forefronts. The lasting aftereffects of the COVID-19 pandemic raise vital concerns concerning the constant diagnosis and prevention of oral health. As one of the most important diagnostic methodologies, radiographic examinations may demonstrate the basis for any future oral health predictions. The influence of clinicopathological variables concerning the prediction of oral health has not been thoroughly inquired into the literature. Critically analyzed, scientific exploration concentrating on the prognosis of oral health via radiographic examinations is somewhat scarce (Anil et al., 2023). Since AI tools have the capability of significantly enhancing current predictive analytics, an AI-based tool was formed that can be adopted by dental professionals as a complementary approach. The fundamental aim was to establish a prognostic model utilizing a diverse span of clinicopathological information and peri-apical X-ray radiographs of oral health that can be utilized to pinpoint individuals at high risk of developing further oral health obstacles.

Dentists are the principal healthcare providers for dental caries detection, and their clinical judgment and experience significantly impact patient outcomes. The need for more precise and reliable methods for caries detection in the early stages is widely recognized. The rapid advancements in digital imaging technologies in dentistry allow for more sophisticated methods and have also enabled the wide availability of data for AI applications. Moreover, AI offers considerable promise for early detection and prevention strategies by enhancing current diagnostic tools. In the dental field, deep learning algorithms and patterns have been trained on large datasets to create models capable of analyzing oral images and radiographs. AI tools have been developed specifically for dental settings to interpret dental imaging, dental records, or images of the oral cavity(Alam et al., 2024). AI technology stands as a promising adjunctive tool for dental practitioners, helping to reduce diagnostic errors and rendering dental practice more efficient. The findings suggest that the incorporation of AI tools into routine dental practice could help with the early detection of caries and promote improved oral health outcomes. Meanwhile, such applications should be thoroughly evaluated in prospective studies. These studies should investigate more complex cases and potentially introducing AI tools in combination with other diagnostic techniques to enhance performance. As healthcare professionals, dentists have the potential to use AI applications for caries detection. With current advancements in technology, dental communities should contemplate how AI tools could be integrated and embraced, adapting and assessing these emerging technologies in the context of oral healthcare.

Personalized Treatment Plans

Research shows longer appointment times are associated with better patient satisfaction. They also allow improved communication that meets patient communication standards. Unfortunately, their implementation is often not possible, especially as dental professionals also contend with additional pandemic-related procedures. In a competitive environment with treatment-centric approaches driven by financial incentives, selling invasive, high-revenue treatment can overshadow preventive measures. At the same time, training in oral health literacy (OHL) is insufficient so patients are often unable to understand complex information about oral health. This issue is exacerbated by disparities in health literacy, resulting in lower socio-economic status (SES) groups being disproportionately affected. Research on personal OHL found widespread deficiencies in participants' knowledge of even the most basic oral health terms. Low OHL was shown to negatively affect self-reported oral health and dental appointments. Low personal OHL can cause a gap in communication and understanding between dentists and their patients (Thorat et al., 2024). Considering the need to improve patients' OHL, there is a noticeable lack of research on this topic in dentistry.

In addition to challenges in health literacy, significant disparities remain in the delivery of medical and dental services, reducing access to quality services and care. Doctors, especially surgeons, speak in technical jargon that is often difficult for patients to understand. Studies have shown that patients have difficulty understanding the explanations of treatments given by dental professionals. The ability to clearly communicate complex information has a fundamental effect on patients' knowledge, attitudes and, ultimately, the effectiveness of the treatment. However, patient satisfaction cannot be fully guaranteed, even when the information provided is understood. Language barriers can lead to patient dissatisfaction, non-adherence to the treatment and have wider health consequences. Nevertheless, only a few studies analyze the factors affecting communication in dentistry. With almost half of the world's population having more than one language in use, the language barrier clearly deserves more academic interest in order to improve health services and deepen communication between the doctor and the patient.

CHALLENGES OF IMPLEMENTING AI IN ORAL HEALTH

AI interventions have the potential to increase diagnostic and treatment planning, but their implementation faces challenges. Financially driven treatment models take over patient education and advanced communication on oral health maintenance. Dental students often lack formal training on patients' oral health literacy issues. Psychologists, on the other hand, are taught to assess and address mental and emotional disorders, including those that may arise from avoiding dental treatment. Patient psychological services can also focus on the provision of educational and communication materials on oral hygiene and dietary habits to prevent dental caries and periodontal and oral mucosal diseases.

Some argue that dental professionals should adopt an advocacy model that uses multimedia resources to educate patients and foster stronger patient identity. However, this model has yet to gain widespread adoption. However, this model has not yet succeeded in implementing widespread action. Financial incentives often push the dental industry toward models that place responsibility for preventive care on patients, while also ensuring commercial viability and attracting funding from organizations like Metropolitan Health. Dental practices that adopt this model are also found to devote much less time to communication and education about oral health during patient visits(Thorat et al., 2024).

Data Privacy and Security Concerns

AI, which uses algorithms to analyze data and assist in decision-making, is increasingly used in oral health diagnostics.

AI systems can use small datasets to learn quickly and control diagnostic processes efficiently. Thus, they enhance the decision-making capabilities of dentistry professionals and minimize the possibility of subjective errors, reducing the costs of oral healthcare. AI can help reduce damage to healthy dental tissues, which remains a classic challenge for dentists of all fields of specialization. One of the many obstacles of current methods for decay diagnosis is the misdiagnosis of fluoro-tooth enamel luster on laser diode devices. The application of AI in these devices for cavity detection enhances success rates up to more than 95% in the presence of high dense natural sound enamel(Ghods et al., 2023).

Despite many benefits, the application of AI in dentistry raises major concerns with a particular focus on data privacy and security. However, it should be noted that this new technology has important challenges to face. Therefore, the application of AI in clinical dentistry can be considered a major contributing factor to higher success rates and fewer treatment failures in the future only after solving its basic problems. Millions of health-related questions are searched on the internet every day. While information is abundant, manipulative data and misinformation remain a serious problem. Unauthorized access and misuse of patient information is a major concern. Digital Machine (DM) and AI systems have increased efficiency and more importantly minimize the human error factor in diagnosing various pathologies.

Integration with Existing Systems

Remote applications can be integrated quickly with existing systems, eliminating the need for clinics to update all hardware. Using a simple camera, detailed photographs of the oral cavity can be examined by AI diagnostic programs. These programs work in real-time during shooting or with a slight time lag on the images uploaded after shooting (De Angelis et al., 2022). AI can diagnose caries, gingivitis, and even diseases of other organ systems with medical history analysis. In the event of a critical situation, the program suggests turning to the dentist, otherwise, it helps patients follow up observation period. Data on the diagnosis is also documented with a seal so patients can handle the oral health records. This will simplify the advancement of the follow-up and the analyses. Patients can access all collected data from their phone or computer at any time. If symptoms arise, they can contact their GP or dentist through the software and share their diagnostic records for review. In the event of need, all recordings can be resent to the GP or dentist. For clinics that require intervention, such applications are available 24/7. On-call dentists can prevent more serious situations by consulting the AI diagnostics remotely or, if necessary, by arranging the patient for a personal visit (Anil et al., 2023). The integration of AI technology in imaging analysis will likely advance dental diagnostics and treatment planning. At the same time, artificial intelligence systems would analyze dental images for diagnostic support. Since there exists a shortage of dentists in France and with oral explorations in some remote or digital forms, dental images could get uploaded by the practitioner or carried out by the patient for a methodology of artificial intelligence in order to be read and interpreted remotely. Getting fine oral photos or 3D scans with a camera or smartphone is handy, notably for radiology in some geographical areas ill-served by dentistry. The saliva samples on the connected sensors would be analyzed continuously via a diagnostic decision software which could remotely alert the patient to adopt better oral health practices or to be advised by a health professional. These remote support interfaces without consultation can revolutionize medical practice by democratizing access to multiple and predictive remote care considering the large number of chronic pathologies. All medical, odontological, and medication history is provided to the patient.

Need for Continuous Training and Updates

Clinicians and dentists often fear to lose patients if they do not provide certain unnecessary interventions. The continuously decreasing prices for electronic and mechatronic devices and increasing computational power allow the development and distribution of more powerful and effective AI systems in medicine. This shift has started to reshape the patient-doctor relationship. In the past, doctors had a key role in the treatment process, prescribing treatments and medicines. Today and even more in the future, this process will largely be based on decisions made by AI algorithms. Initially, doctors and clinicians will follow AI suggestions, but over time these decisions may be handled entirely by AI systems. Already today, in some regions, such as parts of China, AI chatbots are used more often than real doctors. However, more powerful and effective devices often lead to excessive use and deleterious outcomes. To prevent this from happening, clinicians must adhere to updated guidelines on the timing of the diagnostic device use. Failure to comply could result in severe sanctions and their professional abilities could even be suspended(Schwendicke et al., 2020). However, another issue remains: A lingering concern is whether all clinicians be able to operate decided screening devices properly in the future or will we face elevated numbers of screening errors? At this time no data is available as long as this is a relatively new problem. To mitigate these risks, clinicians must receive continuous training and update regarding device application guidelines.

ETHICAL IMPLICATIONS OF AI IN ORAL HEALTH DIAGNOSTICS

The use of artificial intelligence, an emerging branch of computer science, in oral health diagnostics has emerged into a fast-growing market. While the integrity of AI applications should be assessed holistically, growing concerns remain regarding its ethical implications in both public and professional setting. AI diagnostics can save time, prevent patient errors, provide detailed analysis, and can be used as a referral tool.

AI diagnostics are the future of oral health professionals and this issue is expected to be a matter of time. There is consensus on the benefits and potential advantages of AI in dentistry. In the early stages of a disease, the possibility of an error in the examination and diagnosis of the patient is quite high. This process, which depends on the competency of the dentist, is the basic building block of all cascading diagnosable therapeutic interventions. A little mistake here means a chain of mistakes. AI diagnostics do a detailed analysis and reduce errors. The Second Opinion feature can be used as a referral tool. Machine learning algorithms have an average sensitivity of 84.59% in tests performed on expert-labeled intraoral images.

Informed Consent and Patient Autonomy

Imagine that your next patient, whom you have not met yet, snaps a photograph of his/her face using a mobile app for a brief dental consultation. This app automatically assesses the patients's dental health and provides information on the treatment. This patient requests that you treat the dentition based on the findings of the app. Is this lawful? Or what should dental professionals do in this scenario? This issue is related to informed consent and patient autonomy. Also, from the point of view of oral health, applications and systems will develop that will be in contact with people all over the world at any time and location. These issues often become evident when patients present app-generated recommendations to their dentists. For this reason, a topic such as 'ethical and social issues' critical to global applications also awaits to be considered, taking into account patient communities and dental health communications in developing (Thorat et al., 2024).

Bias and Fairness in AI Algorithms

Increased knowledge, emergence of big data, and progress in artificial intelligence (AI) methods have given rise to a boom in healthcare AI applications. However, as AI applications expand, ensuring fairness and eliminating bias in these algorithms is becoming increasingly important. In the past few years, a growing amount of AI tools for oral healthcare have been designed, including AI or smart devices for teledentistry consultations and mobile applications (apps) for daily oral health management. Recently, AI tools for oral health diagnostics have received much attention and become an emerging field of interest. Most AI diagnostic tools in oral health focus on the detecting oral lesions and facial diagnoses using mobile apps. A number of studies have proven the effectiveness of these AI tools in oral health diagnostics. In 2022, (Yang et al., 2024) investigated the performance of oral cancer lesion diagnostic models designed based on convolutional neural networks, support vector machines, and traditional machine learning models. These models achieved 90.68% and 51.20% accuracy on the deep learning and traditional models, respectively. An accuracy of 60.78% was achieved in classifying hirsutism grades by a residual neural network model. Strictly speaking, the advanced AI detection systems in oral health diagnostics are in their infancy. There are still open issues in the fairness and bias of AI models and the quality of AI-generated oral images in oral health. Other unethical behavior, like the creation of deepfakes, may have an impact on dentistry services in the future. Moreover, poorly informed app developers and users may be exploited by sophisticated algorithms, such as recommender systems, leading to privacy violations and autonomy concerns. On the other hand, too accurately behaving self-learning algorithms can create symptoms of data leakage. It is crucial to spread knowledge of these bioethics matters and best practices among all stakeholders.

Accountability and Liability Issues

Oral Health or Oral Diagnostics is a specialized diagnostic service provided by a newer generation of electronic appliances. Ethical issues of AI systems supporting professionals (Terranova et al., 2024) introduce AI in dentistry by looking at the general enhancement of medical healthcare services using AI. Dental Expert Networks are examined as an enhancing tool of academic education, knowledge sharing, case by case assessment for Assurance and Medicolegal Case Reviews. The review provides one of the first accounts of such networks in dental medicine.

Liability and fairness aspects of AI systems supporting professionals raise concerns for professional liability assessment in healthcare. The article A revolution in legal medicine? analyzes the present and future involvement of AI in the malpractice forensic field, particularly focusing on liability assessment following alleged medical errors and informed consent issues. They review how major damage types have been assessed in the past and suggest how such models can be adapted to the assessment domains of the medical specialization involved. The current position is illustrated through the legal system of England and Wales. In a near future, the profession of the standard expert witness and the current liability case law will be affected by various recent and future developments in healthcare, information technology, and law. It is indicated how AI trend may influence such aspects and give ideas for lawyers and healthcare professionals that they could consider when confronted with new forms of expert witness reports.

It is concluded that AI systems can become means of enhancing the fairness and quality of liability assessments through models that are adaptable to all medical specializations. Key points: The objectification of damage can be carried out by employing AI to develop models to assess the fair level of damage due to negligently caused injuries. The model outlines how the damage is to be assessed, though its application using AI depends on the precise approach and can be tailored for the domain of the medical specialization relevant to the professional-liability case.

CASE STUDIES OF AI APPLICATIONS IN ORAL HEALTH

The use of artificial intelligence (AI) in healthcare and dentistry is booming. Automated intelligence has taken hold in public and private health systems to make a diagnosis faster and more accurate. Resultantly, it reduces both costs and medical errors. It is estimated that the application of AI systems in the reduction of misdiagnoses in healthcare facilities could prevent about 80,000 deaths a year in the High-Income countries (De Angelis et al., 2022). Frequently, the economic aspect is considered of key importance, but also the social and health-related aspects offer profitable insights: AI is considered as a technology that will have a positive impact on well-being and the state of health. Additionally, the applications in healthcare are becoming more common with the automation, through devices, of certain tasks.

The versatility and efficiency of machine learning and deep learning approaches in classifying binary and multiple-choice tasks have been an effective solution in diagnostics, helping doctors to make more informed decision and intervention(Anil et al., 2023). When AI is applied to the heterogeneous data produced daily by healthcare facilities, it enables more targeted prevention and better symptom detection. It also automates the use of analysis results, supports the formulation of treatment plans tailored to patient responses, and improves coordination of care teams, particularly in large medical centers with multiple units and staff

The analysis of each dataset performed automatizes the detection of tumors from CT scans, therefore improving precision, high-quality health initiatives and the prediction of clinical outcomes. AI succeeds in detecting specific types of cancer, often resulting in accuracy comparable to or exceeding that of a pathologist. It is estimated that up to 90% of patients receiving chest radishraphs and later diagnosed with tumors may experience delay in treatment, increasing their risk of death. AI specialists also have gained greater appreciation in Japan, which has high mortality rates associated with hepato-biliary pancreatic tumors. With the constant exploitation of the potential of machine learning and neural network architectures, models have been developed that have up to 94% sensitivity in detecting early hepatitis tumor lesions, compared with only 53.3% of human specialists.

AI in Caries Detection

Recent breakthroughs in AI have accelerated the development of sophisticated algorithms for oral health diagnostics. While these tools can be more precise in identifying caries lesions at an early stage, their implementation also raises concerns about ethical bias, data bias, and confirmation bias reinforcing disparities due to historical societal and healthcare practices. Here, a call to action for dental practitioners, researchers, industry, and policymakers is presented to collectively strive for AI-driven oral health diagnostics that balance precision and equity **(Parthasarathy et al., 2024)**. Established as well as emerging biases impacting AI-derived decision-making in dentistry, a field characterized by well-documented health disparities in many regions**(Thorat et al., 2024)**, are first discussed. Then, a roadmap for the dental community to harness the potential of AI while striving to mitigate these biases is offered. Given broad oral health disparities, special emphasis is placed on efforts to develop and integrate AI tools that can help address these disparities into clinical workflows.

Beyond addressing biases, AI can offer new opportunities and change the future of healthcare. Early applications of AI in dentistry have used deep learning-based facial analysis for smile design and orthodontic treatment simulation. The introduction of AI can streamline practice management, education, and communication, assist in diagnosis and treatment planning, forecast the prognosis, and offer a predictable postoperative overview of patients' face and smile. AI can predict caries risk based on data set, identify early carious lesions ocular examination cannot discern. Image analysis can pre-classify lesion and set focus on the areas of concern., AI-based devices can also be used as oral home care assistant. In addition, health insurances companies can leverage AI to determine amounts for procedures and policy rates, identify fraud by analyzing abnormal treatment requests through AI software. AI tools can provide ongoing post-visit dental procedure support and guidance. They can offer real-time answers to questions through text, voice, or images. Informative blogs or videos can be made based on data set pre-analysis of the FAQs of the received reports and useful case papers. Finally, AI can automatically annotate X-rays or Dental chart for better understanding and real-time analysis report on the medical note after a text analysis of the consult summary.

AI for Periodontal Disease Diagnosis

Periodontitis, or gum disease, is characterized by inflammation surrounding the tooth, primarily caused by bacteria in dental plaque. It often manifests as red, swollen gums that bleed easily during oral hygiene procedures. In severe cases, the tooth-supporting structures can be destroyed, resulting in tooth loss. Severe periodontitis remains a major cause of tooth loss. In the high-income countries, over half of adults experience gum disease.

Given the degree of impact gum disease has on global health, there is growing interest in its diagnostics and the advancement of dental healthcare. Routine oral health examinations will include probing and radiographic imaging to assess periodontal health. However, these techniques are susceptible to deficiencies due to the complexity of oral biomechanics and radiography. Moreover, it is only possible to evaluate bone loss rather than providing any other information regarding periodontal health.

AI uses algorithms to perform tasks such as reasoning, problem-solving, perception, and understanding language, has the potential to revolutionise healthcare. The attributes of AI, including scalability, usability, affordability, and accuracy, have made it one of the most rapidly advanced techniques in medical diagnostics. Indeed, AI has recently achieved significant breakthroughs in both general and specific medical applications. For example, AI models have been reported for the automatic diagnosis and classification of various diseases and genetic risk predictors. Recent research has also demonstrated applications of AI in oral health, such as in detecting dental caries, apical periodontitis, and diabetic complications as well as in monitoring oral hygiene. Originally, some of the models were designed to make systems that could detect periodontal bone loss and clinical attachment level. The best sensitivity for bone loss detection was reported at 75%, and the highest accuracy for clinical attachment level detection was at 80%. However, this preliminary study's lowest sensitivity for bone loss detection was only at 25%, with the lowest accuracy for clinical attachment level detection at 60%. Subsequently, a questionnaire was used to assess knowledge, attitude, and perception towards AI in diagnosing periodontal problems in one of the earliest studies of its kind. It was found that knowledge, attitude, and perception regarding the use of AI in diagnosing periodontal problems increased as the designation or level of experience of the respondent periodontists increased. Additionally, this study explored whether periodontists used AI in their dental practice or research purposes. Result indicated that, despite the increasing popularity of AI applications, the majority of the respondents did not use AI in their dental practice or research. Key reasons included a lack of training and awareness, high costs and concerns about potential errors. Finally, this study indicated that 82% of the respondents agreed that AI technology should be incorporated into the postgraduate curriculum and should be implemented in the clinical practice by dentists and postgraduates.

AI in Oral Cancer Screening

Oral cancer is caused by various factors such as smoking, alcohol, betel nut, immunosuppression, and the human papilloma virus. In addition, oral cancer can be identified through precancerous changes of oral tissues, such as leukoplakia, erythroplakia, lichen planus, and actinic cheilitis. When exposed to carcinogenic factors (especially tobacco and alcohol), the intensity of these clinical symptoms and histopathological changes is significantly increased, and the risk of occult cancer in the clinically normal looking epithelium becomes markedly high. Therefore, the precancerous phase can be defined as an "incubation period" of oral cancer. Understanding and addressing such a period can effectively reduce the occurrence of oral cancer. Investigators should be alert to the occurrence of oral cancer in high risk groups by screening and monitoring these oral precancerous lesions in the early stage.

Oral cancer is a common cancer in the head and neck, accounting for 4% of all malignancies, with approximately 354,800 new cases and 177,500 deaths worldwide in 2020. The five-year survival rate of oral cancer patients is around 50%. In Taiwan, oral cancer is the fourth leading cause of cancer death (Kim et al., 2022). The prevalence of oral cancer varies globally. In India, where betel nut is commonly used, the rate of oral cancer is 11.6/100,000. In contrast, Japan and South Korea, which are less likely to develop oral cancer, have higher rates of 36.3/100,000 and 20.6/100,000, respectively. In Taiwan, the relative risk of betel nut and oral cancer is 168.9. Since the oral cavity is easily accessible to the eye, most oral cancers are detected at an early stage. Early detection of oral cancer increases the five-year survival rate to 83%. However, when diagnosed at a delayed stage with metastasis, it rapidly spreads to the esophagus and pharynx because the fascia is absent, and reduces the survival rate to less than 30%. With the increase of high risk groups such as tobacco and alcohol users and the aging of society, there is an urgent need to establish a screening and health monitoring system that can efficiently detect oral precancerous and cancerous lesions.

FUTURE DIRECTIONS FOR AI IN ORAL HEALTH DIAGNOSTICS

During the forthcoming years, it will be requisite to undertake research to develop low-cost and all-in-one technologies that could be placed in dental clinics. These tools would enable caries diagnostics for a prompt treatment or referral. As there has been no underprivileged outcome amongst the caries type models, the statistically highest result has been accomplished with the mixture models. Nowadays, dental caries is a common oral problem, but this preventable condition can have a profound relation with the overall health condition of the body, in special those of pediatric patients. Untethered dental caries can progress to pulpitis, which is an infection or inflammation of dental pulp. This may then lead to irreversible pulpitis, or a purulent infection in the tooth surrounded tissues. Regarding the danger of the affliction process, it is essential, hence diagnostic tools that allow an early, prompt diagnostic and screening of the caries area are inevitable. Dental clinical scanners exams focusing the region of suspected caries involve costs only in scans that are necessary, the cost of scanning devices, and costs related to dentist consultation. Therefore, it can be said that dental-related AI tools can supplement dental practice, and that would be beneficial not only for the patient who hopes for a lower incidence of diagnostic errors, but also from the side of practitioners, which can be expected to improve their diagnostic efficiency. Finally, models fused with expert knowledge can risk either underestimating or overestimating caries types. This highlights the need for careful validation before clinical use. With high model-based caries probability, lesser type performance can be accomplished with respect to clinical exam only via picture rescaled AI-probability offset trial (Alam et al., 2024).

Advancements in Machine Learning Techniques

Artificial intelligence (AI) and machine learning (ML) are often used interchangeably in research, although they have distinct meanings. Machine learning (ML) is the subset of artificial intelligence. ML predicts the outcome based on the dataset provided to it by using algorithms, such as artificial neural networks (ANN). Convolutional neural network (CNN) or deep learning (DL) is a breakthrough and a game-changing approach in ML introduced in 2006. An abundant supply of data sets is crucial for implementing machine learning. The most crucial factor is the availability of large and democratic data sets that big tech companies usually possess. AI's adaptability to various inputs have revolutionized the medical, dental, and healthcare delivery system. Today, AI is used for disease diagnosis, predicting prognosis or developing patient-specific treatment strategies.

Artificial neural networks (ANNs) are worth mentioning when it comes to ML. Artificial neural networks perform task assigned to them by the training process.

Models such as Bay's are used in ML to predict the outcome from the given data sets. ML can be effectively implemented using pattern recognition, clustering, decision science, and artificial intelligence. A convolutional neural network (CNN) is a type of deep learning most commonly applied to analyzing very big data sets and understanding complex features. It often outperforms other ML algorithms. A classical CNN consists of one or more hidden layers, mapping input features by applying convolutional operators. Recently, many academic and clinical studies have focused on developing and scrutinizing algorithms based on existing diagnostic imaging. These aim to improve diagnostic accuracy of oral cavity diseases. With advance algorithms and sufficient data, one model was designed to detect and classify 5,000 X-ray images. It performed three times better than 170 expert radiologists. Converting medical imaging into clinically useful information such as diagnosing disease, assessing prognosis, and predicting response to therapy has been ongoing for some time (Patil et al., 2022). However, using Machine Learning with a vast amount of available clinical data and powerful computational processors, computer algorithms have shown their potential to reliably replicate and, in some cases, even outperform radiologists in terms of image analysis (Anil et al., 2023). With the improvement of image quality, electronic health records, and progress in information technology, it is now possible to automatically classify, document, and transfer images.

Potential for Tele-dentistry

Teledentistry merges telecommunications with dentistry, allowing dental professionals to exchange clinical data and gather information for dental consultation and treatment planning. It uses tools that allow the visualization and analysis of dental images for diagnosis. The approach is particularly useful for providing services to patients who live far away from specialist clinics in dental schools and hospitals, or in remote rural areas. Potential applications include facilitating dental emergencies and triage consultation, screening, diagnosing, and monitoring tooth wear. It can also be used for preventive care, for example, by using apps to reinforce oral hygiene care and proper brushing technique, missing various areas of the mouth.

Several benefits are associated with teledentistry. It plays a significant role in enhancing access to oral healthcare for marginal and underserved populations, offering an optimized way for oral healthcare delivery that saves time and money for patients and dental health professionals. There is also the opportunity for artificial intelligence to enhance teledentistry. AI-enhanced teledentistry could improve the relevance and efficacy of oral health treatment and advice, shifting from diagnostic centered dental care to more proactive and prevention-centered personalized oral health care. Recent technological advances have enabled the adoption of user-friendly teledentistry platforms. These platforms use cutting-edge cloud services to ensure compliance, end-to-end encrypted for clinical data transmission, storage, and at-rest encrypted dental images. Backed by deep learning algorithms, the platform can serve many tasks including diagnosing, monitoring the clinical progress of dental diagnoses, raising alerts in case complications are spotted during treatment, and cultivating patient awareness of oral healthcare through targeted public health campaigns. Teledentistry equipped with advanced AI tools can offer remote oral screening for detecting early symptoms of oral cancers, potentially malignant lesions, and gum diseases, bacterial infections, and dental caries. These tools can assist at any stage of diagnosis or risk assessment. This approach has the potential transform preventive oral healthcare by significantly reducing the burden of end-stage invasive dental interventions.

Collaborative Approaches with Dental Professionals

Artificial intelligence (AI) has dramatically altered diagnostic and preventive medicine. New breakthroughs using medical image analysis offer early cancer detection. These techniques have been applied in investigation people exposed to the Covid-19 virus, specifically using chest X-rays and CT scans. At the same time, these developments can be used in general health, to enhance daily oral health routines in particular. The first and most common application of AI in oral health is enhancing toothbrushes using machine learning algorithms. These algorithms are fed with data on consumers' daily oral hygiene routines. Intelligent models can inform dentists about plaque and discoloration formation, as well as predict the emergence of disease. AI-enhanced toothbrush tools are only used by professionals (Parthasarathy et al., 2024).

In clinical trials, several legal and technical procedures are carried out to confirm the high reliability and standardization of developed tools (Thorat et al., 2024). Distributing such tools to the general public often requires additional explanations or training involving particular dental practices. Instead of waiting for this technology to reach general public, experts suggest enhancing general oral health through open-source platforms. Many of these platforms utilize an application format and offer scientific articles and exercises for users to strengthen their skills. However, their implementation remains limited among the general public. With recent progress in AI, this knowledge can now be shared more easily. Oral health checkers can collect information from users and provides personalized recommendations. From the professional point of view, such online checkers can enhance the information quality about oral health behavior.

REGULATORY CONSIDERATIONS FOR AI IN HEALTHCARE

The first AI-based solution designed for dental diagnostics and treatment planning in the face has entered the market. This early medico-dental adoption of AI technology poses new challenges. These effects patients, professionals, and the healthcare system as a whole. This review raises the attention for quality assessment, constitutional, political, and medico-ethical issues. Regulators and manufacturers are advised to give weight to and address these challenges, while experts and educators are urged to critically accompany this development. Histrocially, craftsmanship has substantially influenced healthcare. However, the recent rise of Artificial Intelligence (AI) carries even greater potential to transform this sector fundamentally. Should be eliminated as it's a repetition of the first sentence Given the intimate relation of the face to dentistry, this early adoption of medico-dental AI technology poses new and essential challenges for both professions as well as regulators, patient organizations, educators, and the public. There is current and growing need, therefore, to urgently investigate these challenges. These queries are raised as critical points to accompany the early market introduction of an AI solution in this sector, and to guide the application of appropriate regulatory framework. Thus, this review provides essential elements for quality, constitutionality, policy, and medico-ethical discussions on AI medico-dental adoption.

Current Regulations and Guidelines

Overjet, an AI tool, is used to aid in the assessment and interpretation of dental radiographs. Pearl uses an advanced AI architecture with deep learning technology. The system has been trained based on an extensive collection of dental radiographs. When fed dental images, the AI system produces predictions about these images. For example, if the input radiograph depicts caries, the Overjet AI tool may highlight and annotate carious lesions on this radiograph. The technology derives these predictions based on the properties of the input image and the deep learning model it has been fed with. Pearl (Overjet) also provides additional analysis. It can assess the number of teeth, identify carious lesions, and specify which proximal surfaces are affected(Anil et al., 2023). Clinical judgment is imperative for individuals providing medical diagnoses, including the detection and evaluation of diseases, and is a holistic assessment encompassing a multitude of signs, symptoms, and tests. While the development and application of AI for healthcare purposes has grown rapidly, it should not imply that diagnostic determinations can be fully automated or made without human expertise. Using the service in that capacity may be problematic or misleading. It is also important to be aware that, like all statistical models, AI systems have limitations and failure modes. They should be used cautiously in unanticipated or non-standard scenarios. In the early stages of treating dental caries, dentists commonly require radiographs to estimate and visualize the severity of caries. Additionally, clinical guidelines mandate that certain dental conditions should be diagnosed or referred for diagnosis following the analysis of dental imaging which includes dental caries and other abnormalities. These guidelines are set by the ADA and serve as the standard of dental practice in the USA. Dentists who wish to abide by these documented standards are also advised to evaluate a set of clinical findings or maintain particular records. Given these requirements, diagnosis of dental caries precludes much that can be visually comprehended from bitewing radiographs. Other examples of AI-generated diagnoses that may be relevant or comparable involve the interpretation of dental palpation photographs or electric pulp tests.

Future Regulatory Challenges

Rapid advancement in AI for health and wellness are leading to the development of advanced systems that can perceive, understand, and interpret images and videos for real-time diagnosis and treatment. This AI-based technique is rapidly growing in oral health diagnostics and could transform how dentists diagnose dental and oral conditions. However, concerns remain about whether AI adheres to consultation principles and the responsibility of its suggestions. Efforts are underway to address these concerns by rigorously evaluating AI systems for their limitations and ensuring safety and reliability." This system uses deep learning technology to comprehend dental and oral conditions in a way that can assist in forming medical decisions. However, the output is only to be a supplement to the analytical judgment of a dentist. Any proposal to offer patient care should be carefully evaluated for functionality and appropriateness.

PUBLIC PERCEPTION OF AI IN ORAL HEALTH

Healthcare professionals must be motivated to prioritize patient well-being and encourage early diagnostic testing. Early detection increases the likelihood of identifying diseases at their initial stages (Saleh Ibrahim et al., 2022). When diseases are detected early, the treatment is often easier, and may require only medications, minimizing the procedures like biopsy, surgery and others.

Comprehensive health strategy should support the development of AI-based diagnostic tools(Parthasarathy et al., 2024) . With higher accuracy of early-stage diagnosis, the mortality rate of the patients can be reduced. Preventive efforts in the health sector are to be prioritized, and innovations in tools can complement the early detection effort of the disease. Detecting tumor at stage zero has higher recovery at

90%, whilst detection at stage 4 is a very low recovery of 10%. As tumors are often detected using MRI imaging, developing AI-powered chatbots that can analyze MRI scans could help detect tumor diseases in early stages. Tumors can occur in any human organ, including the liver, intestines, lungs, breasts, and eyes, so they need to be detected early. This study aimed to create a chatbot capable of analyzing MRI images to estimate the probability and stage of cancer in various organs.

Patient Trust and Acceptance

Dentistry has long embraced technological innovations that improve patient care and enhance clinician's efficiency. The adoption of AI in dental clinics must align with ethical principles to build patient trust and achieve positive outcomes. This is a novel idea for the dental field and it is believed that it will be able to add new perspectives to the literature on this subject. With the increase in artificial intelligence usage for diagnostic purposes in the field of health, it has been seen that patients value the results they see more. This improved perception increases trust and communication with with dental professionals Artificial intelligence (AI) is predicted to further dominate the decision-making process of public health professionals, affecting the patient's follow-up and diagnosis stage. Healthcare providers report that patients respond positively when AI-generated diagnoses are confirmed and clearly explained by professionals. Patients can be educated more effectively by sharing AI-generated results in clear formats, such as tables, reports, or graphs, before consultations."

In the examination and evaluation of such developments, all ethical principles must be preserved. The dental professional's obligation of absolute confidentiality is fundamental to patient trust and is established by professional dentistry rules and international ethical codes. In a multidisciplinary perspective, the uses, applications, and nomenclatures derived from AI in dentistry are presented concerning their ethical and trust implications by integrating key concepts from AI emotion analysis, informatics, biotechnology, and healthcare laws. Recent research findings show that dentists strongly support AI adoption, particularly where it can ethically lead to an improvement in patient care quality and oral health (Thorat et al., 2024). To address these challenges, dental practice and research must prioritize education-based programs, improved regulatory approaches, and clinical guidelines for the effective and ethical use of AI. Evaluating AI-embedded systems, understanding trust-related factors, and aligning literature reviews with interdisciplinary approaches will further support collaboration across AI and dentistry. The strategy of the review and synthesis of the literature should be aligned with an interdisciplinary approach to support mutual cooperation in the wider field of AI and dentistry.

Educational Initiatives for Patients

As patients gain greater access to AI technologies, clinics must implement educational programs with proper tools to help patients better understand their oral health, dental diagnoses, and treatment options. By utilizing AI more frequently, patients will surpass their fear and anxiety towards the unknown processes during their dental procedures. This in turn, will increase their trust and collaboration with the dentists. AI can also strengthen dentists-patient relationship. Although similar general AI technologies are already widely available for patient education in general health care, educational applications of AI in dentistry are in the nascent stages. Dentists have recently come across various AI-based tools and many platforms that enable facial scanning and teeth movement prediction. As interest in AI tools grows, comprehensive educational plans are essential to provide patients with the most important information needed to make informed decisions. AI applications can enable interactive e-learning modules, augmented reality visualization tools, and question/answer platforms can be created. Applications may include oral hygiene instructions, dietary recommendations, artificial teeth around the patients' dental models, visualization of artificial teeth after caries removal, comparison of dentures and implants, and educational video libraries. Each of these can be based on an AI model to answer the patient's questions and provide information about the case. Furthermore, some educational AI application examples can facilitate visual aids by overlaying digital educational 2D or 3D GUI elements over a live video of the patient's teeth, oral tissues, and face. This alignment can contribute to understanding the structure, function, and medication of teeth inside a mouth. After the dental treatment decision, patients may have questions, like "Why do I need to replace the Cavity filling with an artificial tooth?", "What is the difference between inlay, onlay, crown?" or "Do teeth with prosthetics need to be cleaned in a particular way?". Although, dentists often explain treatment deatils, patients may misunderstand the technical terms or key information.

CONCLUSION

Advances in artificial intelligence (AI) have impacted all aspects of the economy and society. The digital transformation of healthcare, in particular, has received significant attention. Recent growth in AI capabilities has arisen due to advancements in deep learning algorithms, significant increases in computational power, and the increase in the amount of relevant data. Various AI tools related to different conditions of the oral cavity are currently available, which can help dental professionals in their practice (Ghods et al., 2023). The rapid rise of AI has raised questions about its ethics, usage, and accountability. There has been increasing awareness of these issues and initiatives in scientific literature to raise the voice of the dental and oral health community in AI-related matters. Due to the effect of AI in health care and dental practices in general, a broader overview of AI trends in oral health as well as the role of dental professionals in the changed environment are warranted.

Broadly, AI can be defined as software that performs tasks requiring human cognition. Not all tools meet this definition; some require significant human input, making them less autonomous. Therefore, AI should not be equated with all decision-support tools." Knowledge-based rules and algorithms represent the least advanced forms of AI that require extensive human involvement in programming rules and coding algorithms. All AI tools require a clear task definition, a preferred solution, and the accurate input of relevant information. This has been done extensively in clinical dentistry for caries detection and classification, analysis of cephalometric radiographs, prediction and grading of maxillary sinus pathologies, and detailed analysis of new oral health data such as smart brushing data. Clearly defining tasks and has led to the development of multiple AI tools. This rapid increase biodata, such as microbiome and saliva analysis or image data from CBCT or MRI, has led to the need for advanced assistant tools capable of handling these pools of biodata and extracting their diagnostic or prognostic value.

This has generated a need for domain-agnostic AI tools such as AI-based searching algorithms and neural networks. Consequently, in addition to decision tools, assistants otherwise termed domain-agnostic AI tools are being developed for dentistry today. Nevertheless, the successful development and widespread implementation of AI technologies strongly depend on the perception of dentists and researchers. AI has the potential to assist effectively with myriad tasks in a dental practice and improve oral health services. However, the successful use of innovations such as AI technologies depends on human factors. Attitudes, trust, ethics, and accountability strongly influence the acceptance and adoption of AI technology in dental practice among dentists. It is important to comprehend the perspectives of dentists to facilitate the integration of AI technologies into dental practices successfully.

REFERENCES

Alam, M. K., Alanazi, N. H., Alazmi, M. S., & Nagarajappa, A. K. (2024). Al-Based Detection of Dental Caries: Comparative Analysis with Clinical Examination. *Journal of Pharmacy & Bioallied Sciences*, *16*(Suppl 1), S580–S582. https://journals.lww.com/jpbs/fulltext/2024/16001/al_based_detection_of_dental_caries__comparative.170.aspx?context=latestarticles. DOI: 10.4103/jpbs.jpbs_872_23 PMID: 38595520

Anil, S., Porwal, P., & Porwal, A. (2023). Transforming dental caries diagnosis through artificial intelligence-based techniques. *Cureus*, *15*(7). Advance online publication. https://www.cureus.com/articles/169408-transforming-dental-caries-diagnosis-through-artificial-intelligence-based-techniques.pdf. DOI: 10.7759/cureus.41694 PMID: 37575741

De Angelis, F., Pranno, N., Franchina, A., Di Carlo, S., Brauner, E., Ferri, A., Pellegrino, G., Grecchi, E., Goker, F., & Stefanelli, L. V. (2022). Artificial intelligence: A new diagnostic software in dentistry: a preliminary performance diagnostic study. *International Journal of Environmental Research and Public Health*, *19*(3), 1728. https://www.mdpi.com/1660-4601/19/3/1728. DOI: 10.3390/ijerph19031728 PMID: 35162751

Ghods, K., Azizi, A., Jafari, A., & Ghods, K. (2023). Application of artificial intelligence in clinical dentistry, a comprehensive review of literature. *Journal of Dentistry*, *24*(4), 356. https://pmc.ncbi.nlm.nih.gov/articles/PMC10749440/ PMID: 38149231

Hung, M., Hon, E. S., Mohajeri, A., Moparthi, H., Vu, T., Jeon, J., & Lipsky, M. S. (2023). A national study exploring the association between fluoride levels and dental fluorosis. *JAMA Network Open*, *6*(6), e2318406–e2318406. https://jamanetwork.com/journals/jamanetworkopen/article-abstract/2806509. DOI: 10.1001/jamanetworkopen.2023.18406 PMID: 37351888

Joda, T., Bornstein, M. M., Jung, R. E., Ferrari, M., Waltimo, T., & Zitzmann, N. U. (2020). Recent trends and future direction of dental research in the digital era. *International Journal of Environmental Research and Public Health*, *17*(6), 1987. https://www.mdpi.com/1660-4601/17/6/1987. DOI: 10.3390/ijerph17061987 PMID: 32197311

Kim, J.-S., Kim, B. G., & Hwang, S. H. (2022). Efficacy of artificial intelligence-assisted discrimination of oral cancerous lesions from normal mucosa based on the oral mucosal image: A systematic review and meta-analysis. *Cancers (Basel)*, *14*(14), 3499. https://www.mdpi.com/2072-6694/14/14/3499. DOI: 10.3390/cancers14143499 PMID: 35884560

Parthasarathy, P. R., Patil, S. R., Dawasaz, A. A., Baig, F. A. H., & Karobari, M. I. RP, P., Patil, S. R., & Baig, F. (2024). Unlocking the potential: Investigating dental practitioners' willingness to embrace artificial intelligence in dental practice. *Cureus, 16*(2). https://www.cureus.com/articles/234143-unlocking-the-potential-investigating-dental-practitioners-willingness-to-embrace-artificial-intelligence-in-dental-practice.pdf

Patil, S., Albogami, S., Hosmani, J., Mujoo, S., Kamil, M. A., Mansour, M. A., Abdul, H. N., Bhandi, S., & Ahmed, S. S. (2022). Artificial intelligence in the diagnosis of oral diseases: Applications and pitfalls. *Diagnostics (Basel), 12*(5), 1029. https://www.mdpi.com/2075-4418/12/5/1029. DOI: 10.3390/diagnostics12051029 PMID: 35626185

Saleh Ibrahim, Y., Khalid Al-Azzawi, W., Hamad Mohamad, A. A., Nouri Hassan, A., & Meraf, Z. (2022). [Retracted] Perception of the Impact of Artificial Intelligence in the Decision-Making Processes of Public Healthcare Professionals. *Journal of Environmental and Public Health, 2022*(1), 8028275. DOI: 10.1155/2022/8028275 PMID: 35874877

Schwendicke, F., Samek, W., & Krois, J. (2020). Artificial Intelligence in Dentistry: Chances and Challenges. *Journal of Dental Research, 99*(7), 769–774. DOI: 10.1177/0022034520915714 PMID: 32315260

Terranova, C., Cestonaro, C., Fava, L., & Cinquetti, A. (2024). AI and professional liability assessment in healthcare. A revolution in legal medicine? *Frontiers in Medicine, 10*, 1337335. https://www.frontiersin.org/journals/medicine/articles/10.3389/fmed.2023.1337335/full. DOI: 10.3389/fmed.2023.1337335 PMID: 38259835

Thorat, V., Rao, P., Joshi, N., Talreja, P., Shetty, A. R., & RAO, P. (2024). Role of artificial intelligence (AI) in patient education and communication in dentistry. *Cureus, 16*(5). https://www.cureus.com/articles/253597-role-of-artificial-intelligence-ai-in-patient-education-and-communication-in-dentistry.pdf

Yang, Y., Lin, M., Zhao, H., Peng, Y., Huang, F., & Lu, Z. (2024). A survey of recent methods for addressing AI fairness and bias in biomedicine. *Journal of Biomedical Informatics, 154*, 104646. https://www.sciencedirect.com/science/article/pii/S1532046424000649. DOI: 10.1016/j.jbi.2024.104646 PMID: 38677633

Chapter 13
Improving Access to Oral Healthcare for Underserved Populations:
Challenges and Solutions for Equitable Access

Shumaila Zofeen
https://orcid.org/0000-0003-3190-7548
Xi'an Jiaotong University, China

Saif Ullah
https://orcid.org/0000-0003-3254-5585
Pakistan Institute of Ophthalmology, Alshifa Eye Trust, Rawalpindi, Pakistan

Hina Lateef
Sheikh Zayed Medical College, Rahim Yar Khan, Pakistan

ABSTRACT

Access to oral health care remains a significant global challenge, for marginalized populations. We explored structural, socioeconomic, and systemic barriers contributing to oral health disparities, with a focus on low-income groups, rural communities, ethnic minorities, and individuals with disabilities. We examined the inadequacies in oral health policies, workforce distribution, insurance coverage, and health literacy that limit equitable service delivery. Drawing on global evidence and case studies, the chapter proposes multi-sectoral and community-based strategies to enhance accessibility, including mobile dental clinics, task shifting, tele-dentistry, and culturally responsive care models. Policy recommendations emphasize integration of oral health into primary healthcare, sustainable financing mechanisms,

DOI: 10.4018/979-8-3373-1992-6.ch013

and educational reforms. The chapter underscores the urgent need for innovative, inclusive, and equity-driven approaches to ensure universal access to oral health services, aligning with Sustainable Development Goals and the WHO Global Oral Health Action Plan 2023–2030.

INTRODUCTION

Oral diseases such as cavities, gum disease, oral cancer, and their consequences are a major cause of pain and disability for millions of children and adults(Northridge et al., 2018). This "silent epidemic" and its human toll are well documented. These diseases are largely preventable and treatable. Although largely preventable and treatable, they persist disproportionately among those with limited resources: people from historically disadvantaged backgrounds and from racial/ethnic minority populations. Severe oral health problems are often left untreated, leading to pain, disfigurement, and tooth loss. Consequently, the burden of unmet oral health needs on quality of life is substantial. In light of the documented oral health and health care disparities between countries and between populations within countries, concerted efforts have been launched to improve the oral health of disadvantaged groups in the high-income countries like US and elsewhere(Kum et al., 2018).

The causes for disparities in oral health between and within countries are complicated. For these reasons, the societal burden extends beyond what is documented in government statistics and academic research, which often focus on the diseased individuals and point estimates of the costs incurred. A societal perspective is essential to assessing the full burden of dental diseases. Generally, a multi-level approach to understanding oral health access equity holds that the influence of both community and health care system factors must be assessed simultaneously. As described below, this multi-level approach is now being understood in terms of ecological models which posit that factors at multiple levels influence disparities in access to and quality of health services.

In particular, the two major areas of research are needed: systematic qualitative and community-driven quantifiable studies to develop hypotheses, as well as rigorous quantitative tests of these hypotheses using longitudinal, multi-site, multi-level, multi-factor designs. Although oral disease prevention and treatment are typically considered a "first world" health service, lack of access to oral health care persists even in developed countries. For example, among older adults living in the high-income countries, oral health status is highly correlated with socioeconomic status, particularly income.

UNDERSTANDING ORAL HEALTH DISPARITIES

Access to oral health care is an essential aspect of preventing and treating oral disease as a component of comprehensive health(Liu et al., 2022). Oral diseases such as dental caries, periodontal disease, oral cancer, and related conditions are highly prevalent in high-income countries. Regular preventive oral health care, such as professional dental cleanings, dental examinations, sealant, and fluoride applications, can help detect and treat problems before they become severe. A major component of preventive care is the periodic visit to a dental care provider. However, many people do not get the preventive care they need due to limited access of quality services. Untreated oral health problems can result in serious complications, including systemic infections, pain, loss of work hours, and in rare cases, death.

Oral health is directly associated with multiple disease conditions and overall health. Dental diseases are associated with chronic conditions, such as stroke, diabetes, cardiovascular disease, respiratory disease, and obesity. Although a large number of oral health issues are held in common, poor oral health can result in the aforementioned chronic health outcomes. The multifactorial nature of oral health means that it is a function of complex interactions between biological, sociobehavioral, and environmental factors operating at both individual and population levels. The quality of life can be significantly affected by the impacts of poor oral health including persistent pain, loss in appetite, inability to perform daily activities and social embarrassment or withdrawal.

Oral health has been identified as an essential component of health, with the understanding that oral health cannot be separated from overall health. The importance of services for the promotion and extension of general health has been well documented, as has the imperative for preventive care, identification of early problems, and treatment of lesions. The national objective Healthy People 2030 has a goal to "reduce the proportion of children with untreated tooth decay" and an objective to "support public policy efforts supporting access to comprehensive oral health care services". Nevertheless, oral health disparities are strongly patterned along sociodemographic lines, disproportionately affecting marginalized and underserved populations. These inequities are especially pronounced among socioeconomically disadvantaged groups, who experience the highest levels of untreated dental disease. It has been well documented that major racial disparities exist in oral health in high-income countries like the U.S., becoming evident in childhood and extending across the life course. For instance, lower rates of dental visits significantly contribute to high rates of untreated tooth decay among African Americans. Compared to white counterparts, African American adults are nearly twice as likely to have untreated decay, with untreated tooth one of the main contributors to dental visits' racial disparity.

The lack of accessible services is considered a key contributing factor to existing racial/ethnic disparities in oral health. African Americans reported significantly higher unmet dental care needs than their white peers, even after income, insurance status, and health related access factors were controlled in a comparative study of unmet care needs. Even among the same pay status group, there are better access and oral health coverage for white than for African American adults, strengthening a growing body of literature indicating that implicit bias influences dental care providers' approach to patient management. In addition to individual factors, environmental or contextual variables can also directly or indirectly influence oral health disparities. Many environmental factors have been identified, including neighborhood-level socioeconomic status (SES), racial or ethnic composition, and residential instability.

Oral health can also be affected by a variety of neighborhood factors such as physical safety, and access to grocery stores and dental care providers, as well as by patient and community characteristics including race/ethnicity, poverty, and language access.

Defining Underserved Populations

The term "underserved" is frequently employed to refer to populations with little or no access to health care, due to insufficient resources required to meet a community's needs(Lin et al., 2022). While this is true for several healthcare services, in oral health care, a shortage of professionals is not always the only reason. Although often acknowledged, oral health providers are frequently unwilling to serve in provider shortage areas, creating a mismatch between community needs and professional availability. Research has identified several factors contributing to this phenomenon. Furthermore, among healthcare providers, dentistry is among the least diverse occupational groups in high-income countries. As population becomes more diverse, dental workforce diversity should be valued and fostered. Studies indicate that dentists who graduated from Ivy-league schools are more less likely to serve in a shortage area. However, it is concerning that over 30% of the U.S. population lives in these areas, a number likely to grow. These communities often lack resources and support, Latinxs and African Americans are disproportionately represented, whereas whites have lower rates of these areas(Stoner, 2019). New dentists who chose to practice in the underserved areas were more likely Asian Americans, African Americans, and Latinxs. One policy recommendation is to track and increase the diversity within the pipeline institutions. Historical and current indicators can help predict where newly graduated dentists are most likely to practice. Additionally, it is recommended to promote workforce distribution equity.

Impact of Socioeconomic Factors

While oral health conditions demonstrate a strong association with health conditions and overall well-being, a glaring inequity remains in their coverage. The inequity is particularly strong among uninsured populations and low-income individuals, with a dearth of publicly funded oral healthcare options available to them. The disparities observed in commonly used health measures indicate a vicious cycle in which untreated oral health conditions exacerbate health inequities. By focusing on the heterogeneity of the population and specifically observing major characteristics that led to distinct outcomes across the group, unique challenges have been documented regarding access to oral health care. Distinct facilitators and barriers to oral health access, along with factors influencing care-seeking behavior, were identified(Sherry & Hennig, 2018). Understanding the impact of the identified characteristics could expand the discussion of prevention strategies beyond the lens of geography.

Delivery-oriented preventive strategies are central to a textbook public health approach to mitigating health inequities. A primary focus should be improving the equity of services offered through public oral healthcare. It is often argued that while public insurance dictates a range of services similar to those of private insurers, many of the services are considered optional rather than essential for eligible adults. Discretion in this regard is virtually unregulated, which limits the breadth of services and thus access even for those covered under the Affordable Care Act. Additionally, utilization inequities persist as a considerable proportion of eligible adults are unable to utilize available resources. Federal and state programs should seek to identify populations that are uninsured or unable to access services despite their eligibility (Borges & Krishnamurthy, 2022).

To build upon the newfound accessibility of oral healthcare, it will also be important to address systemic racial inequities that continue to marginalize minority communities. Many racial inequities documented in healthcare are also evident in the dental care. A fundamental barrier to care access concerns the cultural distance between healthcare practitioners and patients. The power dynamics that exist between racial groups are often projected onto the dynamic between dentists and patients. Prioritizing cultural competence among healthcare practitioners would consequently be an effective means of addressing a barrier that disproportionately affects minority population.

Geographic Barriers to Care

Many patients face geographic barriers to dental services, including uneven distribution of dental providers, limited access to transportation services. Restructured Medicaid programs under Affordable Care Act (ACA) have not improved access to dental services for Medicaid enrollees. Despite efforts to reduce disparities, a gap remains in access to dental care between children with private insurance and those with Medical Assistance (MA). The percentage of children with MA who visit a dentist annually has increased from 36% to approximately 50%. This prompts the question: why does this disparity exist despite insurance coverage under MA? The study aims to evaluate if secret shopper surveys and geospatial analysis could be utilized to determine barriers to dental care for children with MA (Stoner, 2019).

In the first part of the analysis, secret shopper surveys were conducted across 113 dental practices in Minnesota's Ramsey and Washington counties. The results showed that 30 practices approximately half had inaccurate information listed on Managed Care Organization (MCO) websites. Additionally, 42 out of 60 dental practices impose restrictions on when children with MA could be seen. The study also examined if access by proximity was a barrier. A geospatial analysis assessed whether children had access to care with-in 15 miles or 30 miles or transit time. The result showed that in several zip codes, children who rely on public transport do not have adequate access to dental care.

In examining the population of 0–18-year-old children in Ramsey and Washington counties, a total of ~260,000 children in that area were utilized for a geospatial analysis using the same methods as the other analyses. The study analyzed 260,000 children (0-18 years) in Ramsey and Washington counties using the same geospatial method. Overall, 12% of children in Washington County do not have access to care, while 35% of children in Ramsey County do not have access. An analysis also revealed that the zip codes with the most children with MA have access to the least number of dentists and appointment hours. Ultimately, children with MA in some areas had less access to dental care than children of higher-income communities with private dental insurance, due to both inequitable distribution of dental providers, and systemic barriers such as limited transportation.

CURRENT CHALLENGES IN ORAL HEALTH CARE ACCESS

Individuals and families on Medicaid face many barriers to receiving dental services. Appointments during the standard work hours make it difficult for low-income individuals to take time off work, especially if the transportation has issues. Parents may struggle to afford childcare while also managing multiple dental appointments for their children. Additionally, Medicaid patients face longer wait times for appointments and may find that only one or two dentists in town take their insurance. Families with limited health literacy may be unaware of available oral health services their Medicaid coverage. There may also be misconceptions, such as believing that cavities in baby teeth are unimportant because those teeth will fall out. Additionally, reliance on infant formula and sugary fruit juices can contribute to early childhood tooth decay. For very young children, there may also be denial of child cavities as children will lose those teeth anyway, as well as dependence on infant formula and inappropriate fruit juices(Shirk, 2010).

Some states are creatively addressing consumer access and utilization issues using a multipronged approach. Alaska has shifted to a new midlevel provider model, the Dental Health Aide Therapist Initiative, which is training Alaska Native dental health professionals from rural villages to practice dental therapy under the supervision of a dentist. In Oregon, dental hygienists are being added to school-based health programs in an initiative targeting Head Start preschools and low-income kindergartners. The Minnesota Department of Human Services has used a Medicaid Health Care Grant for outreach and fiscal capacity building. This effort has increased service utilization by First Nations children and collected testimonies and examples of best practices to be adapted by other programs.

In times of fiscal constraint, these states are demonstrating that policy changes can be both cost-effective and adaptable to local cultural and financial contexts. In times of fiscal constraint, these states are demonstrating that policy changes can be both cost-effective and adaptable to local cultural and financial contexts. States are also sharing successful approaches from other regions and sectors of health policy, as well as highlighting barriers that require clear, persuasive advocacy to overcome

Insurance Coverage Issues

A lack of dental insurance is a barrier to obtaining dental care for approximately 122 million Americans. The high-income countries have made strides in launching and improving new programs to bridge the gap in medical insurance coverage; but similar progress has not been made in the dental world. Medicaid, Medicare, the Affordable Care Act (ACA), state insurance marketplace programs, and private insurance companies prolific sources of medical insurance but offer limited dental coverage (Shirk, 2010). Dental insurance companies selling individual plans for adults are limited; and since their coverage is often not affordable, leading many to forgo coverage. Most Medicare participants are over age 65, and many cannot afford any additional monthly payments for individual dental insurance. Although some states cover adult dental care through Medicaid or state-funded emergency programs, most individuals are left without any options to obtain routine and preventive dental care. The ACA has expanded medical care to underserved populations. The federal government and each state have created online marketplaces where individuals can explore insurance options based on their income. The ACA created a marketplace where users can receive subsidized insurance rates, depending on their income(McElfish et al., 2017). These plans typically include doctor's visits and preventive services, with an overall goal of promoting health and disease prevention. However, dental coverage often falls short and does not adequately support preventive care. Neglecting dental care can lead to wide range of serious health issues. Untreated dental problems can impair an individual's ability to talk, eat, and swallow. An untreated dental infection can spread to the rest of one's body, and in rare cases, it can even lead to death. The tissues of the oral cavity can also be indicators as to what transpires in the rest of the body. Research has also identified associations between chronic oral infections and various diseases, including cardiovascular disease, diabetes, respiratory disease, and premature death. Preventive oral health care can significantly reduce the risk of acquiring health issues. Preventive dental care includes biannual dental cleanings, and exams. Regular medical check-ups also support overall health and can reflect oral-systemic connections.

Workforce Shortages

As of 2008, there were approximately 186,000 licensed dentists in the high-income countries, with 132,139 classified as "active" dentists which corresponds to approximately 60 active dentists per 100,000 population. Overall, dentist availability is reasonably good, with reported dentist-to-population ratios in all but 18 out of the 3,011 counties in the United States (Nash, 2012). However, a considerable portion of the population lacks access to oral health care. The Health Resources and Services Administration designated 5,023 Dental Health Professional Shortage Areas; in these designated areas, 54 million persons were estimated to live with a population-to-dentist ratio of at least 5,000 persons per general dentist. An additional 45 million Medicaid recipients live in areas with insufficient dentist participation. Concerns about adequacy in the number and distribution of dentists generally relate to inequality of access for lower-income and more vulnerable populations.

Significant disparities in dental health care access exist along socioeconomic and racial/ethnic lines. In 2005, uninsured, lower-income, and rural populations were less likely than their respective counterparts to have a dental visit in the past year, and adult African Americans and Hispanics were more likely than Whites to have one or more unmet dental need in the past year. Disabled persons also have particular oral health care access problems(Lin et al., 2022). Inadequate access to oral health care has increased the urgency for change in the integration and delivery of oral health and health care. There is a need to develop an operational framework to deliver preventive and basic oral health care to low-and middle-income populations. To that end, the roles of the public health system and an alternative workforce model to augment the dentist workforce are explored. However, significant liability and other issues associated with these proposals may propose barriers to implementation.

Cultural Competency Gaps

Many prominent health organizations recommend that health care providers should act as culturally competent health professionals while treating patients. Ethnic and linguistic minorities may face barriers to accessing quality health care due to lack of culturally competent care. Culturally competent care offer improved patient satisfaction and facilitate positive relationships between providers and patients. Culturally competent care includes an awareness of and respect for the values and beliefs held by diverse population groups and their cultural differences. Cultural competency may also include simply providing effective written materials in a patient's native language. This prevents miscommunication, which could impede efforts to adhere to treatment and medication precision. Several national-level cultural competency curricula have been developed, but few have undergone rigorous evaluation. Various models of cultural competency exist, including preassessment, training, and post-assessment through role-play or surveys. The curriculum may also provide resources such as brochures and medical interpreters(Amini & Noel, 2018). Cultural barriers may be a key etiologic factor contributing to disparities among underserved populations. Education and training in cultural competency may create awareness of potential biases and stereotypes, which could ameliorate interactions between providers and patients of differing backgrounds. On the other hand, substantial cultural differences may impede mutual understanding or rapport-building, resulting in aversion or withdrawal from the engagement. Cultural competency training programs must be mindful of these potential barriers and must consider these barriers while designing educational materials and modes of delivery. These, in turn, would better promote the education of health care providers in recognizing and addressing cultural differences, improving care for the underserved. Health care providers must value their role in addressing cultural barriers. Although deeper awareness may initially complicate outcome measurement, it ultimately enhances the sincerity and applicability of results. Through the consideration of these desired outcomes, unanticipated applications and extensions of the completed program may also emerge. These may apply not just to the oral health care scenario addressed, but also in other areas of need experienced by similarly underserved populations. These cultural barriers are not unique to the United States; similar challenges have been reported in low- and middle-income countries, underscoring the global need for culturally competent oral health care.

COMMUNITY-BASED APPROACHES

Oral health is widely recognized by health professionals and general health as essential to over-all health and well-being. Oral health status is associated with chronic conditions such as diabetes, cardiovascular, respiratory disease, and conditions that compromise the immune system like HIV/AIDS, cancer, and asthma. People with serious oral disease experience pain, disfigurement and lost productivity from work, which causes significant economic loss for both families and societies. In high-income countries, there are great disparities in oral health, and the burden of oral disease and associated disadvantage is concentrated especially among poor, poorly educated people, racial/ethnic minorities, immigrants, and individuals with low health literacy.

Chang-Richards's model Action/Implementation Framework was used to design a multi-level, dynamic oral health care access intervention targeted at Chinese Americans. A previous study was conducted to collaboratively identify intervention components in partnership with urban outreach centers and Chinese immigrant community members. Interviewees indicated prior experiences with dentists and dental providers, perceptions of health care system and services, and ideas on oral health care and education were examined.

Notes on health care challenges indicate two major challenges provider related and system-related as well as significant communication gap. Specific causes were described with each category. The inability to afford co-pay or percentage for dental care is an immediate barrier that prevents under treatment and subsequent buyout of secondary illness. Poor relationships with dental providers due to either language discordance or cultural dissimilarity can sour the initial mistrust encounter with the health care system, and undermine the oral care-seeking intentions. Although most recognized the significance and consequences of oral health, including debates on protective toothpaste or obstructed flossing, lack of knowledge on community resources, care availability, and health care system protocols contributed to dissatisfaction with community or preventive care and increased skepticism about the oral care system (Amini & Noel, 2018).

Existing community resources that were consulted include preventative services offered in mainly school and church settings. Programs aimed at youth, along with one-on-one educational outreach to inform about oral health resources, proper dental care and community-based services were identified as important strategies. Additionally, expansion of service provision hours and locations and partnerships with oral health professionals were cited as comfortable and practicable channels to address service-related gaps.

Mobile Dental Clinics

As an alternative to school-based clinics, mobile dental clinics are a method already utilized in certain rural communities in New Zealand. In the USA, mobile clinics for paediatric dental care were introduced in 2008 and are still being studied. Utilizing dental therapists in mobile clinics based in schools could promote accessibility for a much larger group of children in the same areas as mobile health clinics (Molete et al., 2016). Mobile dental health care can increase service access and close the gaps where traditional services, such as school dental and city clinics, are less accessible. Designing and implementing new care technologies and delivery models is a complex and time-consuming task. In Brazil, carious dentin removal was tested with a laser in two public clinics; however, treatment results were inconclusive and dependent on patient cooperation during the use of device; thus, wider implementation was impracticable. In Canada, tele-dentistry was tested in remote communities, accumulating long waitlists in cities, while convenience led to the decision to treat children with poor oral health in their communities with portable equipment.. These international examples illustrate that mobile and portable delivery models, while context-specific, are increasingly being explored as a viable way to reach underserved populations globally.

In 2021, as COVID-19 restrictions allowed a small gathering of personnel, mobile dental van workspaces were built, at the cost of utilizing consultant pay during downtime. With a dentist, dental therapist and intraoral camera, the project entered a contracting phase of partnership discussions with services. A two-year contract can lessen barriers for both health care providers and young patients. Community partner recruiting may also provide career exploration for dental hygiene students(Yim, 2019). The value of public health in education, prevention and comprehensive health cannot be overlooked; while integrating another health care discipline into oral health can be difficult, the prevention-oriented examination period allows continuity of care.

School-Based Dental Programs

School-based oral health programs (SBOHPs) provide opportunities to address oral health inequities by offering convenient access points for care. SBOHPs can be structured to leverage existing resources to maximize the utilization and impact of SB dental programs (Martin et al., 2021). To offer states guidance on developing comprehensive SBOHPs, the collaboration developed a technical assistance curriculum.

The technical assistance is designed for SBOHPs serving the dental safety net. The curriculum provides a menu of technical assistance options and resources that SBOHPs can utilize to meet their organization's needs regardless of their level of experience. Options provide varying levels of engagement from brief consultations via email, phone calls, and in-person consultations to workshops and webinars. Ongoing support in sustainability activities and assistance with evaluating impact are also offered.

The curriculum can be employed as a standalone resource or adapted based on the audience while meeting stated goals. In its current form, the technical assistance curriculum will be an online version that is continually updated. Each library entry will link to updated resources. Coordinated systems-level transition plans can enhance the effectiveness of developmental assets (Amini et al., 2021).

Community Health Workers

According to the National Health and Safety Plan, oral health in Brazil is marked by serious social inequities, which are reflected in the access inequalities. Although it has been a strategy of the Brazilian Public Health System to implement a specific oral health policy, this service remains limited in terms of access. In addition, some wealthier cities invest in medical services while the poor have to settle for minimal services. There are needs in primary health care, health surveillance and preventive/curative interventions. Community Health Workers (CHWs) are important to diverse health programs and may play a role in education policies regarding oral health care. CHWs can influence positive behavior in communities, which can lead to improvements in morbidity and health indices and a shift in service use into the community, (Malik, 2018). To be effective, CHWs should be non-professionals who are respected members of the community and capable of closely engaging with individuals during training. The range of tasks carried out by CHWs includes: support for education, knowledge and innovation; information and social mobilization; and support for direct actions in health and community development. Large scale training of CHWs with regard to areas of improvement in health, sanitation and housing is a good introduction to the system. Primary education should be a base and teachers should be trained too. Activities of oral health education such as treatment beliefs, oral impact on quality of life, brushing, flossing and sugar-snacking should be covered. Educational tools such as face-to-face talks, pamphlets, street plays, health education cabins and group discussions to facilitate peer group talks are necessary means for CHWs. In practice, CHWs were trained for 15 hours in 3 clusters and supervised monthly for discussion group. Two professional trainers conducted the training. Independent discussions were held prior to training, necessitating individual assessments, with two participants assessed per group. Independent discussions took place before embarking on trainings and made individual assessments necessary and required two per group. Six objectives of the training were designed. The first objective of knowledge was to understand concepts of health and disease. The second was regarding personal system on education and communication. The third was on task systems related to sanitation, water supply, health care, health promotion and nutrition. The fourth was about cooperating with health professionals and health systems in education and communication. The fifth was to understand basic concepts about health program management. Ultimately, knowledge of the situation and future of the program in the area was required.

POLICY INTERVENTIONS

Many residents of the high-income countries lack access to dental care, particularly vulnerable populations. Fewer than half of adults and only 36% of lower-income adults report visiting a dentist in the previous year. Barriers to accessing oral health care include factors such as inadequate insurance, high out-of-pocket costs, and dental care deserts(Wolf et al., 2024). Many underserved communities, particularly low-income communities of color, experience provider shortages, with many Medicaid-accepting dentist no longer taking new patients. Declining reimbursement rates have led many dental providers to reduce Medicaid participation. Additionally, a lack of culturally competent and trauma-informed care has fueled mistrust in the healthcare system. The COVID-19 pandemic further intensified dental care shortages and revealed the link between oral health and overall health, as people suffering from oral health issues were at higher risk for severe COVID-19.

Health Insurance Commissioner Steven Malanga stated at a 2021 oral health summit in Maryland that progress can be made toward improving access to care through innovative policy and program reforms. Recommendations to improve access to oral health care in Maryland and the District of Columbia include coverage expansion, investment in local access points, collaborative care integration, workforce investment, regulatory adjustments, and anti-racism actions.

Policymakers should move forward with a major expansion of dental coverage in the state, particularly Medicaid adult dental coverage, through more generous benefits and professional reimbursement reform. ncreased funding for family resource centers or a nursing-led outreach program in high-need areas within Washington is also warranted. To expand reach, in-network dental services should be made available in school-based health centers, community-based and federally qualified health centers, with mobile units.

Competitive salaries for public health dentists and hygienists, such as those working in outreach programs, must be insured to attract and retain talent. Government support of legislation revising practice acts to enhance the roles of dental hygienists and dental therapists for primarily underserved populations in areas with little access to care is also warranted.

Expanding Medicaid Coverage

Expanding Medicaid is one of the best-known recommendations to improve oral health. The Affordable Care Act included a provision for all states to expand Medicaid eligibility up to 138% of the Federal Poverty Level, which created new eligibility for more than 11 million low-income adults who were previously ineligible. Medicaid has significantly improved access to and utilization of primary care, especially for low-income populations and may help decrease oral health disparities, (Yim, 2019).

Majority of adult Medicaid enrollees in high-income countries receive some dental coverage, and Medicaid coverage is generally associated with better access to oral health care. By expanding Medicaid eligibility, states can help increase access to dental coverage, utilization of dental care, and ultimately oral health and quality of life, especially among low-income populations. The provision of dental coverage through Medicaid may be particularly important in expanding access to dental care among communities that are disproportionately represented in the low-income population and have high needs for dental care. Notably, individuals with incomes below the Federal Poverty Level are at greater risk for oral disease, and these individuals are also less likely to have a dental visit compared with those with incomes higher than the Federal Poverty Level. While a majority of children ages 0–18 years with Medicaid coverage receive dental care, fewer than 1 in 4 adults (aged 19–64 years) accessed dental care (Goldstein et al., 2021).

However, states vary substantially in the comprehensiveness of adult dental benefits, which are typically limited to emergent conditions in states that do not provide comprehensive dental benefits. Considerable gaps in dental coverage also exist, even in states that expanded Medicaid eligibility and had a comprehensive benefit. State capacity for adult dental care was more limited compared to children's dental services under Medicaid. All states provide preventive dental care for children without cost-sharing. Oral health disparities among low-income individuals without viable dental coverage persist.

Incentives for Dental Care Providers

There are several financial incentives that can help increase the participation of safety net providers in programs or initiatives to serve low-income, uninsured, and underserved communities. New state and federal initiatives such as tax incentives for safety net providers that serve low-income and uninsured patients could be valuable in extending access to care and enhancing local economies in urban and rural areas. Moreover, enabling direct reimbursement through Medicaid or other third-party payers for dental therapists, hygienists, and general dentists could help diversify the oral health workforce and enhance care delivery.

Additional funding requests should prioritize state-level implementation, as an increasing number of safety net providers are now participating in training programs to navigate billing procedures for dental services under newly expanded Medicaid laws. For instance, a small urban safety net provider in North Carolina had recently initiated training in preparation for the state's expanded Medicaid dental coverage. However, the final training session before implementation was abruptly cancelled, following a widely circulated notice that the state had received overwhelming requests for a deadline extension on the adoption of new billing codes.

This cancellation stood in contrast to earlier state efforts, which had actively encouraged one-on-one meetings with safety net providers and dentists to support the integration of these new billing practices. Compounding the disruption, the state's public health dental hygienist who also served as the program manager overseeing fee coding and training efforts unexpectedly resigned just days before the scheduled session.

However, abrupt administrative changes such as the cancellation of training sessions and staff resignations highlight the need for more structured planning and early stakeholder engagement in Medicaid implementation processes(Robinson et al., 2019).

Legislative Advocacy for Oral Health

The lack of oral health insurance coverage is a significant barrier to accessing adequate oral health care. Legislators and policymakers should consider ways to enhance access to oral health services for these populations. Many states have moved forward in more proactive ways to protect oral and other health care for vulnerable populations with a variety of funding models, including expanding Medicaid eligibility, closing loopholes in eligibility, or aggressively pursuing federal grants (Amini et al., 2021). States are working with a large number of stakeholders to implement additional federally funded state programs to the existing care delivery systems. Some initiatives to enhance access have been tied to broader community-based systems of care efforts. Moving forward, future strategies to enhance access may prioritize these communities. In parallel, information-sharing efforts should be undertaken to document the value of these enhancements and allow experiences to be shared across states, particularly those that have been successful in pursuing access expansions.

In order to address barriers to accessing oral health care for underserved populations, a comprehensive plan must be established. This plan should include promotion of the importance of oral health, status assessment of current supply and turnover of oral health professionals. It should also address reforms in dental education and practice, deployment of new technologies and improvements in safety net delivery and reimbursement system. The participation in Medicaid and additional methods is essential for the improvement of oral health of low-income populations. It is vital to build broad coalitions and partnerships with all stakeholders. Additionally, it is important to develop a solid evidence base for planning and to prioritize policy changes that alter the status quo. Building community, citizen involvement and empowerment are also important, along with constructing a sustainable plan and evaluating progress. Addressing these dimensions collectively rather than in isolation is key to achieving meaningful outcomes. Policy efforts in one area will maximize their effectiveness if they take all areas into account.

INNOVATIVE TECHNOLOGY SOLUTIONS

In recent years, the need for innovative technology solutions that improve access to oral health care for underserved populations has grown rapidly. Telehealth is a key solution that can augment local care capacity and provide access to regional specialty services. On an individual patient basis, the cost burden of dental care services creates an overall hardship in accessing routine treatment. Transportation barriers arise from population density, travel distance, and mobility challenges. Initiatives that expand local dental services and raise awareness among both providers and patients about available care options can ensure broader access to preventive services.

Additionally, available regional specialty care services in public institutions could be better promoted, allowing immediate access for patients identified as high-risk for further care and treatment(Northridge et al., 2018). At almost half the state's public institutions, supported facilities run by Federally Qualified Health Centers (FQHC) receive Title V funding to expand preventive and restorative care availability for Medicaid recipients.

Transportation challenges are statewide, but local community factors also influence access to services. An effective and widespread tool to identify preference-sensitive care would support greater oral health equity statewide. However, the lack of a formal outreach strategy has impeded this vital role. A formal and comprehensive outreach strategy that can identify criteria-based high-risk patients and ensure that they receive appropriate services will bring about actionable state-wide impact.

Teledentistry (TD), the remote diagnosis and treatment of oral diseases and conditions, is a rapidly expanding sector of the broader telemedicine industry(Kanani et al., 2024). During the COVID-19 pandemic, TD, as with other telemedicine models, played a pivotal role facilitating the continued provision of oral healthcare services. In the spirit of social distancing, health department legal authority was granted a temporary waiver allowing provision of synchronous and asynchronous care. This period saw a marked increase in the consumption of TD services on a national scale across all user types. Both email correspondence and video conferencing usage rose, driven by the need for remote contact amidst mandatory closures and escalating virus transmission rates. To this end, public policy efforts surrounding the expanded use of TD significantly enhanced professional capacity, increased remote triage, and bolstered statewide dental hygiene programs. Owing to its many inherent advantages, TD is poised as the most cost-effective and efficient means of reaching underserved, and geographically isolated regions. That said, the widespread adoption of TD remains contingent on the ongoing evolution of the educational, financial, and administrative resources required for its optimal utilization.

Tele-dentistry Initiatives

Teledentistry, an essential aspect of telehealth, has been identified as one of the most promising tools to improve oral health equity by increasing access to care for vulnerable populations. Teledentistry, the use of digital technology to provide oral health care remotely, helps overcome many barriers that underserved populations face in accessing oral health care. Such strategies benefit groups that face barriers to traditional dental care, including children, the elderly, and those with low socioeconomic status. A key benefit of teledentistry is its ability to offer remote and low-cost care at the patient's convenience. This helps reduce major barriers such as lack of transportation or time off work that often prevent underserved populations from accessing in-person care.

Remote care can also greatly increase utilization by intervening in the early stages of the disease when dental problems are much easier and less expensive to manage. Despite considerable advancements in technology and significant investment dollars to support innovations during the past decade, successful teledentistry solutions in widespread use today remain rare. Where existing solutions are in place, dental practices have often struggled to incorporate teledentistry into their existing clinical workflows. Teledentistry, especially patient-initiated care, is not widely adopted despite policy changes and the significant number of recent entrepreneurs seeking to enter the space. Teledentistry initiatives should clearly define their target populations and geographic focus. Target populations should be chosen with scale and early success in mind, clearly stating the opportunity's potential reach and initial focus. Once the target population is identified, collaboration with technology partners is essential to understand the patient journey its needs, barriers, and challenges. This understanding should extend into social determinants of health. Patient intake forms could include questions about insurance status, willingness to travel, and past access to care(Tella et al., 2019). Initial screening questions may also address dental pain visible symptoms such as swelling and treatment need.. A detailed understanding of the patient journey can guide the effective design and deployment of teledentistry solutions to reduce access barriers.

Digital Health Tools for Education

Barriers to oral health care include language, cultural factors, education, and economic disadvantage. Evidence-based community education tools for oral health promotion are in demand. Colorful, simple visuals and graphics maybe effective in engaging low-income Chinese Americans with limited literacy. As, health education increasingly turns digital, it is important to explore how low-income populations engage with technology. Mobile apps and websites work best in online context since they are easy to learn, more accessible, and less expensive than wearable devices and health tools. However, the quality of health apps is variable. Patient input is essential when developing tool for underserved populations. This can be achieved through sponsored focus group or in-depth interviews with a small number of patients.

Nevertheless, no finding is certain prior to development, and there is an inherent tension between patient-centered design and the desire to control the process(Northridge et al., 2018). An interactive human validation approach should be incorporated into the behavioral or technological design. The co-design approach is exploratory as ongoing iterations are expected for continuous adjustments. Overall, two aims are planned based on community, organizational, provider, and patient objectives: 1) To empower low-income Chinese American immigrants through a temporary in-person education session. This session will raise awareness about oral health, highlight available care opportunities, and document participant experiences via quasi-ethnographic recording. 2) To improve oral health education across the bi-state region by co-designing digital tools for providers. These tools aim to enhance cultural competency across various cultural contexts. (Assis et al., 2022).

Emerging evidence supports the need for good community education tools matched to a specific target population to improve community oral health literacy and optimize dentist use. Previous needs assessment and community health surveys have identified persistent barriers to oral health care. Limitations include working with a newly targeted population, requiring the creation of new assessment standards. Expanding digital access remains financially challenging.

PARTNERSHIPS AND COLLABORATIONS

High-quality oral health care requires collaboration among stakeholders. Nationally, oral health stakeholders are working to increase oral health care access for underserved populations in multiple ways. Efforts to improve oral health systems through stakeholder engagement can take place at the national, state, and local levels (Linabarger et al., 2021). Shared goals are the foundation of strong oral health collaboration. Those who are concerned about the oral health needs of underserved populations should carefully consider their partnership strategy. Effective collaboration involves forming coalitions, building trust and competencies over time, and maintaining momentum through shared. Communities share a collective need for oral health care. Sponsors are often linked to organizations addressing these needs, particularly for socioeconomically disadvantaged children. Much of the research in oral health literacy and access focuses on this group.

Policymakers must invest in collaboration as a core function of their ongoing efforts to improve systems of care. Requests for proposals can require consortia to define the roles of partners and collaborative strategies. Many working on access-to-care initiatives face ongoing pressure to secure grant funding. Enforcing laws that ensure shared data access such as community asset and needs inventories can assist organizations in service development and grant applications. Policies can devise joint monitoring of service gaps and outcomes by multiple agencies. Funders can support and develop interagency collaborations. Over time, stakeholders interested in a similar outcome can coalesce into more formal organizations with a portfolio of alliances.

As national discourse regarding the social determinants of health increases in fervor, the potential to influence well-being through upstream efforts will rise as well. Public health agencies, funders, schools, foundations, social services, professional organizations, and communities need to be clear-eyed about the tremendous value and risk of the effort that coalition-building, both formal and informal, entail. The greatest gains often come from well-funded formal coalitions but these are rare and typically run-down after 5-7 years. In addition, the need across disciplines is typically enormous, as is the challenge of prioritizing what's next in ways appropriate for the community.

Public-Private Partnerships

Public-private partnerships involve collaboration between governmental organizations and private commercial firms (Martin et al., 2021). The partners are employed for various purposes and can connect communities with greater resources while giving more freedom to local officials. For example, public-private partnerships are used for worldwide infrastructure provision, such as transport, roads, and schools. Some existing public-private partnerships focus on the health and environmental sectors, and also bring dental services to the underserved. The coalition surveyed children in kindergarten and the first grade in about 60 schools to assess their oral health needs.

Any child identified with untreated dental caries or other needs was referred to a WIC provider. After school-based screenings, expansion efforts moved to properly acquiring and distributing additional instruments to schools, explaining to schools the value of this new screening program, and encouraging administrators to enroll.

Health departments, in collaboration with local stakeholders and private providers, can also head more local initiatives to address the lack of dental health care access. Public health efforts may include lobbying state representatives to provide resources for low-income oral health policies, or working with local hospitals to integrate preventive dental care in addition to medical care. Possible private efforts include forming connections with government or private companies to provide mobile health care delivery and outreach in conjunction with schools. Ultimately, eliminating barriers to receiving dental care will likely require coordinated legislative and policy changes at the federal, state, and local levels and supported by successful implementation examples.

Collaboration with Nonprofits

At the federal level, public-private partnership initiatives that support community development and/or outreach to underserved populations can also be established. Successful models, like school-based programs(Martin et al., 2021), university-community partnerships, or mobile dental clinics, could be better consolidated to secure funding support from foundations or the private sector, and piloted at the community level before exploring a broader scale. Rapidly adopted telehealth models during the COVID-19 pandemic serve as valuable examples of integrating digital and in-person care while uniting diverse stakeholders (Linabarger et al., 2021). Coalescing existing resources could also help engage other health systems to expand their services to underserved populations, using strategies that have already proven successful in the local context. For services not easily delivered in schools, churches, or other fixed-location settings, partnerships with other public services in a community must be maintained. This requires leveraging existing networks that share common principles or values within a community is important. Developing services around partners' existing relationships with individual patients would also bring better community acceptance and long-term sustainability. Ensuring social outlets could also help draw in under-engaged communities. Partnering with trusted community individuals who relate to under-engaged individuals can also foster engagement. Once the need for broader partnerships is acknowledged, challenges such as time commitments required to build relationships must be addressed early to ensure sustainability of the collaboration. To reduce cost, meeting can focus on shared interests instead of individual meetings with each organizations. Participating in ongoing projects of partner organizations may also help dispel concerns that services are overly prescriptive or externally imposed. Once the need for broader partnerships is acknowledged, challenges such as time commitments required to build relationships must be addressed early to ensure sustainability of the collaboration.

EDUCATION AND AWARENESS CAMPAIGNS

Education and awareness campaigns targeting populations that are at risk of oral disease are needed to promote key health behaviors related to oral health general population (Macpherson, 2018). Measuring progress regarding oral health behavior change will also require the development of an appropriate data collection system. Building a coordinated strategy that avoids duplication will be essential to sustaining visibility of oral health beyond the project timeline. There is an urgent need for systematic research into the psychological, social, and cultural drivers of oral health behaviors to inform culturally sensitive health promotion efforts. Health professionals should play an important role in identifying those at risk of disease and directing them to appropriate preventive interventions. Effort is needed to build capacity among health professionals with respect to the prevention of disease. Alongside public awareness campaign, structured consultations with health professionals are essential to understand the barriers to action and determine the support and resource required. Importantly, the role of primary care professionals should be expanded to include oral health screenings in underserved or orphaned schools, helping to prevent poor oral health and reduce inequalities.

Many of these children face significant barriers to accessing dental services, particularly once oral health issues become severe. Primary care providers, due to their close proximity understanding of the local needs, are in well position to guide these children to the appropriate services.

Oral Health Literacy Programs

Oral health literacy (OHL) has long been recognized as a broader concept than simply oral health knowledge. Understanding is a fundamental step that allows real-time adaptation and smooth communication process. The "teach-back" exemplifies smoother communication at the literacy level. It involves explaining information and then asking the individual to repeat it in their own words. This approach allows the health professional to clarify any misunderstandings while helping the patients to consolidate knowledge. Open-ended questions based on key aspects of the information presented are a way of checking understanding (Veiga et al., 2023).

Developing a simplified mode of communication is always challenging. Information becomes more meaningful when a person with a limited understanding learns it independently. Non-verbal cues such as gestures, facial expressions, or related information helps to determine an individual's attitude. Interactive skills are also useful for oral health literacy programs. Community health teams must be able to assess the effectiveness of communication and adapt strategies when necessary. These skills are closely linked to their practical responsibilities and roles. In order for the staff to apply these skills effectively, a basic training can be conducted. Modern technologies are the key tools in oral health literacy strategies. These include the development e-health apps that will provide in-depth health information, in-person and online courses, e-books, open access journals, apps tailored for caregivers, the elderly, and individuals with special needs The use of these modern technologies is a great opportunity to implement health strategies towards hard-to-reach individuals. Special care is needed to make these plans economically feasible and applicable.

Community Outreach Efforts

Despite the acknowledged need to reduce oral health care disparities, extensive work remains to improve access to preventive and comprehensive oral health care for underserved populations. Efforts to raise awareness of this significant yet often overlooked public health issue must be intensified. Increased support for traditional safety-net providers is essential, but so, too, is broadening the definition of the safety net to allow for the creation of more sustainable delivery systems. Development of traditional workforce as along with increased funding for applied research to evaluate their impact, is also warranted. Improved education is needed at all levels: from entry-level training in dental hygiene, dental medicine, and public health, to continued education for current practitioners, researchers, and policy-makers. Public awareness about the importance of oral health care in the high-income countries must also be strengthen.

The oral health care system is failing to meet the needs of a sizeable proportion of the older population in the high-income countries. A targeted intervention program was launched to address the needs of underserved, low-income older adults in both urban and rural areas of Michigan.

The goal of the first-year program was to develop and implement a five-component oral health delivery system specifically for this targeted population. It was developed by a project dentist with the support of the Health Care Financing Administration and was modeled after a successful program in the San Francisco area.

Oral health care access activities were designed for older adult community with a defined target area. Each area was connected to larger human services community through community-based organizations. Support was also provided by the College of Architecture and Urban Planning, as along with other campus organizations (Lang et al., 1984). The project's success philosophy consisted of two key components:

organizing access to care, and enhancing agency effectiveness. The project emphasized three core areas: (1) community programs to improve access to health system, (2) population-level education and preventive outreach, (3) institutional programs to influence system delivery and policy

MEASURING SUCCESS AND OUTCOMES

The Center for Oral Health launched a collaborative model to prevent and control tooth decay in 5- to 10-year-olds in an L.A.-area community. In a cluster-randomized trial using this model, the number of children with untreated decay fell from 31% to 23% at the two-year mark, while the proportion completing three dental visits increased from 26% to 47%(Northridge et al., 2018). The efficacy of this approach in building community capacity and improve care coordination could be assessed in fair- or poor-health kindergartners in 20 New York City-area schools. Other partnerships involving academics, community agencies, and practicing dentists aiming to apply quality improvement methods to improve preventive services and sealant placement in underserved schools, merit further investigation. Such collaborations have yielded promising preliminary results.

DENTAL ISLANDS provides a holistic intervention for homeless families in a New York City family shelter. Its feasibility and acceptability could be assessed through semi-structured interviews with parents, staff and community members and the dental team's field notes analysis. DO-DADS involves moms and children in a clinic-based cooking class/educational series that emphasizes fruits/vegetables and infrequent snack food/drink selection/preparation. To assess its impact and acceptability, focus groups and observational notes from the in-class cooking interventions could be analyzed together with the recorded cooking demonstrations' uptake during follow-up.

Key Performance Indicators

The assessment of efficiency in the execution of the National Oral Health Policy (NOHP) is essential for managers and researchers seeking to strengthen and expand the care model in high-income countries. Evaluating oral health care is a complex and should follow a cross-cutting approach. Although health system of high-income countries varies significantly across states I terms of structure and delivery, establishing parameters for evaluating the performance of the system is essential. Quality of treatment was measured using oral health indicators aligned with principles such as universal access, egalitarian accessibility, availability, capacitive assurance, and resoluteness. Methods used in the literature to assess the performance of public services align with the criteria established in Health Planning and Management, which are widely acknowledged by the scientific community. Those indicators examined primary care needs and oral health care requirements (Amorim et al., 2020).

It is also imperative to establish criteria for the measurement of quantitative, operational, and qualitative indicators. Evaluators must also consider the scope and type of assessment when selecting indicators. The literature on public policies indicated that a combination of qualitative and quantitative approaches offers a better basis for interpreting, validating, and generalizing the results than either approach alone. Regarding the frequency of evaluation, the setting of indicators is recommended for continual analysis. Addressing each of these methodological factors presents an opportunity to identify and improve weaknesses in the care model execution.

Issues were also noted regarding whether model variables should be included in composite indices or used as stand-alone indicators Some interventions in the literature on improving health systems, efficiency assessments, and indictors stood out as opportunities for further research. Those interventions were considered to influence access to or decrease the need for care for a condition. Reviews highlighted lack of knowledge about the selection of quality-of-care indicators, including both oral and general health care indicators, the determination of changes in status and the calculation of intake rates for the purpose of delivering care to the area served (Northridge et al., 2018).

Case Studies of Successful Programs

Throughout the high-income countries, an increasing number of school systems are forming or expanding school-based oral health programs (SBOHPs) in response to persistent inequities in child oral health status, particularly among children from low-income families. With support from WHO, the North Carolina Oral Health Section conducted a request for proposals to fund the establishment or expansion of comprehensive school-based oral health programs in eight competitive rural communities across North and South Carolina. Although organizations that have been awarded funding are diverse, there is a remarkable consistency in foundational principles that guided the development, expansion, and early implementation of programmatic activities. These aspirations describe an evidence- and community-informed approach to SBOHP development that sustainably supports oral health care access for students in schools. Through collaborative engagement of various stakeholders, the investigation findings indicate that distributing responsibilities between philanthropies, public health agencies, and safety net providers shifts incentives such that SBOHPs can build capacity for sustainable practice. An overview of results shows how this report provides a case-based curriculum to guide partners toward developing comprehensive, sustainable school-based oral health programs.

SBOHPs have expanded in rural communities across the United States to promote child oral health, yet few studies examine the challenges of establishing and expanding them. The purpose of this investigation was to analyze the development and early implementation of comprehensive SBOHPs in rural communities across North and South Carolina. A qualitative approach was employed to conduct semi-structured individual and group interviews with community partners involved in development or early implementation of new or expanded SBOHPs. Findings suggest that successful SBOHP development necessitates diverse partners and stakeholder engagement to build trust, cultivate champions, and share responsibilities progressively. Formal agreements are essential to ensure accountability and program continuity over time. Sustainability considerations should be present during early stages of program planning, including cultivating long-term funding sources, recruiting multi-level champions, and proposing an intervention model. Systematic approaches to achieving evidenced-based quality care and addressing community-informed challenges are needed.

In addressing systemic inequities in child oral health status, school systems are increasingly partnering with safety net providers to form comprehensive SBOHPs. However, there is a remarkable lack of documentation focusing on best practices for successful SBOHP establishment and expansion. Through collaborative engagement of knowledgeable local stakeholders, this investigation leveraged the oral health section's philanthropic support to develop a case-based curriculum that describes diverse strategies applied by local health departments and safety net providers involved in the establishment or expansion of SBOHPs (Martin et al., 2021). It provides stakeholders with a clear understanding of comprehensive SBOHPs to inform initial hiring and orientation processes for new community partners looking to develop or expand SBOHPs. This information resource may be a useful tool for health departments and safety net providers in expanding efforts to improve access to oral health care and outcomes for underserved populations in the Carolinas and throughout the United States.

BARRIERS TO IMPLEMENTATION OF STRATEGIES

This study examines the challenges of oral health policymaking across six key domains in a middle-income country context. Qualitative data were collected through semi-structured interviews with 30 participants selected using a purposive sampling method and analyzed using MAXQDA software. A total of 138 statements were coded, resulting in 38 codes, which were then organized into 15 sub-categories and six overarching categories of challenges related to oral health. Motivation for this research high treatment costs, significance of oral diseases, recognition of existing barriers, and need to develop an efficient oral health policy model suitable for middle-income countries (Mohammadpour et al., 2020).

Administrative challenges are defined as issues that interfere with the establishment and enactment of an oral health policy in the country. In terms of executive challenges, the need for comprehensive plans and strategies for various issues is a main barrier to policymaking. Barriers include high treatment costs, a focus on treatment over prevention, and the tendency of some policymakers to emulate more developed countries rather than address local challenges. Furthermore, poor-record keeping of failed, unequal, and ineffective projects discourages senior policymakers from considering new proposals in other fields of health.

Some participants believed that enforcement guarantees are ineffective instruments in the country due to their politicization and underutilization. One participant noted that key institutions like the parliament, judiciary, and government lack effectiveness in enforcing ministerial duties. Comprehensive monitoring systems could help prevent practices outside formal guidelines, such as unregulated free services by public dentists or unapproved advertising by private providers. Additionally, services delivery challenges include attention to the disease burden, educational challenges, and city and village topographies.

A participant noted that records indicate mismanagement of serious high-risk diseases in middle-income countries. And while outreach services have greatly improved access to care in rural areas, their effectiveness too is limited due to obstacles on how these services are delivered. Moreover, population congestion depends beyond cities to places such as stadiums, cemeteries, and sports or pilgrimage gatherings. A more robust and adequately funded referral system is required.

Funding Limitations

Almost ten years after the Surgeon General's report declaring dental disease a "silent epidemic", the nation continues to struggle with adequate access to and utilization of dental services, especially for low-income individuals (Shirk, 2010). A significant source of coverage is Medicaid, which provides services to 29 million individuals, about half of whom are children. In many states, dental services are a part of the Medicaid benefit package. A second source of coverage is the State Children's Health Insurance Program (SCHIP), which provides services to 6 million children. While there are Child Health Insurance Program Reauthorization Act (CHIPRA) requirements to provide dental coverage to children, Title XXI of the Social Security Act allows "stand-alone" dental plans that may not provide the same level of access to services as traditional Medicaid managed care plans. However, not all states provide dental coverage through their state Medicaid agency, and, even within those states that do, benefits can be limited. When the Children's Health Insurance Program (CHIP) was established in 1997, Congress declared that it was the goal of such a program to increase the number of uninsured children who obtained health coverage and who regularly utilized health care services. The law required states to expand health coverage to low-income children by providing Medicaid or a comparable health insurance program. A year after CHIP's enactment, the number of uninsured children had dropped. However, experts continued to voice concern that inequities to access to coverage and care were likely to persist, or even worsen, under the new program, particularly among low-income children.

Many low-income children are enrolled in Medicaid or CHIP. However, ensuring that they actually receive dental care has proven to be a challenge. A report revealed that dental insurance alone does not guarantee access to care. Almost a decade later, budget constraints and competing health priorities, continue to search for practical solutions to keep their Children's Health Insurance Programs afloat and ensure that their insured children have access to dental care. The financial stability and sustainability of oral health integration models was a major theme discussed throughout the focus groups (Norwood et al., 2017). The high cost associated with dental clinic operations has commonly been cited as a barrier to on-site delivery of dental care at FQHCs. Federal grants represent only about 20% of FQHC's operating revenue. The remainder comes from sources such as Medicaid, Medicare, private insurance, and patient fees. Federal support provided under Section 330 of the Public Health Service Act was perceived as a major strength of FQHCs.

Resistance to Change

Ongoing advances in biomedical research and technology are reshaping the health care environment. The integration of disciplines has spurred innovation in research, treatment, and prevention across health care domains. The confluence of biological, social, and behavioral research domains underscores the multidimensional nature of health. Despite a growing understanding, oral health remains siloed from the broader health care system. For many, such isolation leads to the perception that oral health is of little or no value. It leads to neglect in treatment and prevention. Failure to value oral health as part of overall health impedes reform efforts. A significant cultural shift, spanning local, state and federal level, is required. (Norwood et al., 2017). Only then can a culture that values dental care be created, along with a health system that delivers comprehensive, coordinated patient care. For Federally Qualified Health Center (FQHC) leadership, oral health and primary care integration is viewed as a beneficial and necessary initiative. In the absence of an integrated health system, the poorest patients and those at highest risk for preventable disease are relegated to the margins of a system that was not designed to serve their needs. Given the pervasiveness of unmet oral health needs among the patients FQHCs serve, primary care action is needed. FQHCs are willing stakeholders in conversations about how primary care action can improve access to oral health care. There are many populations in need of oral health care and primary care action. However, the focus on underserved populations, communities of color, and patients with limited English proficiency keeps the conversation centered on those served by FQHCs. Barriers to care, health risks, and health consequences among these populations are clear. Deficiencies in patient awareness about the importance of oral health are glaring weaknesses that contribute to poor patient compliance. Poor comprehension resulting from literacy and language challenges diminishes understanding of the importance of oral health. Cultural patterns of behavior lead inattention towards oral health care. A culture that tolerates the incongruity between oral health and overall health sidelines dental care decision-making and leads to underutilization of dental care. Access barriers, such as cost, availability, and transportation, loom large. A culture of neglect leads to negative oral health outcomes and a high prevalence of dental disease. It also results in reliance on services that treat disease rather than prevent it, poor compliance, and high non-utilization.

Among providers, a culture incentivizing procedure-driven, reactive care and disincentivizing preventive, proactive care hinders the integration of oral health integration.

FUTURE DIRECTIONS IN ORAL HEALTH CARE ACCESS

Despite substantial progress toward improving access to oral health care, significant gaps still exist. The distribution of oral health care providers is uneven across population groups, and barriers that limit their availability and use remain. These barriers are systemic, culturally and structurally embedded in the societal, health system, community, and individual contexts. In order to better understand these barriers and how to redress them, a better comprehensive model is needed. The cited exploratory study aimed at designing a systems science-based model to conceptualize financial, personal, and social factors influencing access to oral health care. It employed qualitative focus group methodology with Russian-speaking immigrants who arrived from the former Soviet Union countries (Sanders et al., 2021). The inability to pay for oral health care, poor relationships with dental providers, and lack of information on oral health and health care emerged as the major challenges. Efforts toward improving dental coverage, dental provider training, and providing information about oral health, diseases, and health care were recognized as priority areas for action by decision makers. Participant-tested scenarios highlighting the connection between oral health care and overall health, its importance for social impression in different life situations, and high concentration of people with similar financial situations were viewed as promising interventions towards expanding access. Thus, the design of the model includes both social and behavioral interventions based on participant-tested scenarios and policy type of interventions, such as improving coverage of preventive services by Medicaid (Linabarger et al., 2021). The first set of modeled interventions would involve community-based outreach education and delivery at local community hubs that provide information on programs and services, while the second set would include public policies addressing the need for major changes in Medicaid program settings.

Emerging Trends in Care Delivery

The oral health care system high-income countries is highly inequitable, resulting in vast disparities in oral health outcomes and a burden of disability for many citizens. Whole health—that is, well-being related to a person's physical, oral, behavioral, and social needs—also remains out of reach for many. In high-income countries, a web of unmet physical health, oral health, behavioral health and social needs is exacerbating the disparities in access to health services(Cardoso & Tenenbaum, 2020). For example, nearly 20% of the adult population does not have a routine source of health care, including access to a primary care provider. This statistic is substantially worse among racial and ethnic minorities.

Access to adequate and routine dental care is a widespread national issue. More than 49 million Americans lived in dental health professional shortage areas as of September 2019. Approximately 75% of dental health professional shortage areas are located in rural areas. During the COVID-19 pandemic, many low-income communities, primarily those of color, faced new barriers to obtaining oral health and other health care services. Notably, greater than 70% of pre-COVID-19 care was delivered through private-practice models that contributed to systemic inequities in care access with dental care costs dependent on whether patients had continuous oral health coverage.

An urgent need has arisen to incorporate a range of oral health services into new, collaborative health systems. Moving forward, the changing landscape of health care delivery will necessitate dental care providers cease viewing themselves solely as clinicians focused on providing a product and appreciate themselves as providers of care. New residential, co-located, and automated care delivery systems are needed as 21st century health service delivery models. Communities and patients must remain empowered and engaged in these efforts.

Role of Policy in Shaping the Future

Implementation of the objectives emphasized in the WHO's Framework of Action will depend on endorsement and execution by officials and policymakers at the highest levels of government, which remains a challenge in many countries. The WHO welcomes national government commitments to oral health and encourages engagement with other stakeholders to leverage that support, including policy actions through Comprehensive Oral Health Action Plans. WHO stands ready to provide assistance for action to improve oral health. Governments must recognize that oral health is integral to general health, development, and wellbeing. They must ensure national ownership and accountability for the global goals and target and the incorporation of that commitment in all relevant governance frameworks (Sanders et al., 2021). These must include strategies and policies with high-level engagement across sectors, collaborative planning for costed actions, and a monitoring framework that includes a new global indicator measuring universal health coverage for oral health and targets relevant to the broader circumstances.

Governments must ensure sustained commitment to achieving conditions necessary for general oral health, by focusing on social determinants of health, particularly equity in health systems. Measures must include restructuring and expanding oral health services to be effective and accessible for all who need them. To achieve broad, integrative strategies with wider benefit for all health, governments must embed oral health in comprehensive primary health care services, health promotion, and infection control and prevention activities. Governments must ensure that health systems financing is equitable, prioritizing public financing of oral health services for those in need, including efforts to expand the coverage of essential services in low-income settings. Such efforts must further include mechanisms to reduce out-of-pocket payments and to develop fiscal policies to reduce the affordability and availability of free sugars.

CONCLUSION

In conclusion, oral health is an essential component of general health and quality of life. Most untreated oral diseases can be prevented or controlled with low-cost, evidence-based interventions. To improve oral health, targeted interventions addressing each of the barriers to access to care must be actively implemented. These efforts should focus on health care settings that specifically serve populations experiencing inequities in access to health in general and oral health care in particular. Much can be learned from current efforts in to improve access to other health services that target uninsured and underinsured populations. More research is needed to identify practical models for delivering dental care that are both sustainable and effective. Another area needing attention is the health literacy gap in oral health and dental care. To promote improved understanding of prevention, these models should incorporate education components that are adaptable to the social, economic, and educational environments of the diverse patient population (Northridge et al., 2018).

Successfully piloted interventions could be shared with stakeholders and institutions interested in replicating, with evaluation included as an integral part of dissemination efforts. Health care systems should be actively engaged in planning and implementing intervention efforts. Staff at clinic sites should be involved at all stages, as they are best able to identify conditions that inhibit change and are essential to the successful uptake of practices. As these practices are put into place, ongoing audit and feedback at the practice level should encourage their continued implementation and long-term sustainability (Kum et al., 2018).

The approach taken here dictates that conceptual models of access to dental care, determined through focus groups, should support the development of a prototype systems science model. These models can subsequently be validated and evaluated to shape interventions that mitigate oral health inequities. By using systems science modeling, the knowledge, social context, and agency of community members can be leveraged to influence policy and interventions that promote access to oral health care.

REFERENCES

Amini, H., & Noel, B. (2018). *Community Partnership to Improve Children's Oral Health*. https://kb.osu.edu/items/b217c12a-6a3e-5ec6-8b87-ecfdbdf763de

Amini, H., Wells, A. J., Boynton, J. R., Guo, X., & Ni, A. (2021). Oral Health Advocacy Education Impacts Future engagement: Exploration at a midwestern us dental school. *Frontiers in Oral Health, 2*, 714199. https://www.frontiersin.org/articles/10.3389/froh.2021.714199/full. DOI: 10.3389/froh.2021.714199 PMID: 35048043

Amorim, L. de P., Senna, M. I. B., Alencar, G. P., Rodrigues, L. G., de Paula, J. S., & Ferreira, R. C. (2020). Public oral health services performance in Brazil: Influence of the work process and service structure. *PLoS One, 15*(5), e0233604. https://journals.plos.org/plosone/article?id=10.1371/journal.pone.0233604. DOI: 10.1371/journal.pone.0233604 PMID: 32469941

Assis, M. A. L., Tavares, L. D. F., Bernardino, A. P., Rocha, B. A., Abreu, L. G., Oliveira, D. D., Pithon, M. M., & Soares, R. V. (2022). Information and Communications Technology in Dentistry: An informative and educational approach for patients with fixed orthodontic appliances. *Dental Press Journal of Orthodontics, 27*(03), e22spe3. https://www.scielo.br/j/dpjo/a/VDVh4xSNdjmbjkmCCxFrB7z/?lang=en

Borges, C. M., & Krishnamurthy, M. (2022). Are we getting any better? A critical analysis of selected healthy people 2020 oral health indicators in 1999–2004 and 2013–2016, USA. *International Journal of Environmental Research and Public Health, 19*(9), 5250. https://www.mdpi.com/1660-4601/19/9/5250. DOI: 10.3390/ijerph19095250 PMID: 35564649

Cardoso, E. O. C., & Tenenbaum, H. C. (2020). Older adults and the disparity in oral health status; the problem and innovative ways to address it. *Israel Journal of Health Policy Research, 9*(1), 24. DOI: 10.1186/s13584-020-00381-6 PMID: 32366301

Goldstein, E. V., Xu, W. Y., & Seiber, E. E. (2021). Impact of the Affordable Care Act Medicaid expansion on oral surgery delivery at community health centers: An observational study. *BMC Oral Health, 21*(1), 540. DOI: 10.1186/s12903-021-01895-4 PMID: 34670549

Kanani, H., Khubchandani, M., Dangore-Khasbage, S., & Pandey, R. (2024). Teledentistry: A comprehensive review and its application in pediatric dental care. *Cureus, 16*(1). Advance online publication. https://www.cureus.com/articles/190184-teledentistry-a-comprehensive-review-and-its-application-in-pediatric-dental-care.pdf. DOI: 10.7759/cureus.52685 PMID: 38384649

Kum, S. S., Northridge, M. E., & Metcalf, S. S. (2018). Using focus groups to design systems science models that promote oral health equity. *BMC Oral Health, 18*(1), 99. DOI: 10.1186/s12903-018-0560-0 PMID: 29866084

Lang, W. P., Kerschbaum, W. E., & Kerns, K. M. (1984). A Community-Based Dental Program for Older Adults. *Journal of Public Health Dentistry, 44*(4), 141–146. DOI: 10.1111/j.1752-7325.1984.tb03075.x PMID: 6595404

Lin, B., Kim, J., Lin, M., & Chen, J.-L. (2022). Factors Associated with Pre-Dental Students' Intention and Willingness to Serve in the Underserved Community and Vulnerable Population. *Dentistry Journal, 10*(6), 111. https://www.mdpi.com/2304-6767/10/6/111. DOI: 10.3390/dj10060111 PMID: 35735653

Linabarger, M., Brown, M., & Patel, N. (2021). A pilot study of integration of medical and dental care in 6 states. *Preventing Chronic Disease, 18*, E72. https://pmc.ncbi.nlm.nih.gov/articles/PMC8300541/. DOI: 10.5888/pcd18.210027 PMID: 34296994

Liu, M., Kao, D., Gu, X., Holland, W., & Cherry-Peppers, G. (2022). Oral health service access in racial/ethnic minority neighborhoods: A geospatial analysis in Washington, DC, USA. *International Journal of Environmental Research and Public Health, 19*(9), 4988. https://www.mdpi.com/1660-4601/19/9/4988. DOI: 10.3390/ijerph19094988 PMID: 35564382

Macpherson, L. M. (2018). Raising awareness of oral cancer from a public and health professional perspective. *British Dental Journal, 225*(9), 809–814. https://www.nature.com/articles/sj.bdj.2018.919. DOI: 10.1038/sj.bdj.2018.919 PMID: 30412572

Malik, S. (2018). *The Use of Community Health Workers in Chronic Disease Management.* https://cdr.lib.unc.edu/concern/masters_papers/x346d753x

Martin, A. B., Moss, M. E., Kelly, A., Riley, A., Pardi, V., & Pollard, A. C. (2021). A Technical Assistance Curriculum for Expanding Sustainable School-Based Oral Health Programs in the Carolinas' Dental Safety Net. *Maternal and Child Health Journal, 25*(8), 1200–1208. DOI: 10.1007/s10995-021-03167-7 PMID: 33948828

McElfish, P. A., Long, C. R., Rowland, B., Moore, S., Wilmoth, R., & Ayers, B. (2017). Improving culturally appropriate care using a community-based participatory research approach: Evaluation of a multicomponent cultural competency training program, Arkansas, 2015–2016. *Preventing Chronic Disease, 14*, E62. https://pmc.ncbi.nlm.nih.gov/articles/PMC5542547/. DOI: 10.5888/pcd14.170014 PMID: 28771402

Mohammadpour, M., Bastani, P., Brennan, D., Ghanbarzadegan, A., & Bahmaei, J. (2020). Oral health policymaking challenges in Iran: A qualitative approach. *BMC Oral Health*, *20*(1), 158. DOI: 10.1186/s12903-020-01148-w PMID: 32487152

Molete, M. P., Chola, L., & Hofman, K. J. (2016). Costs of a school-based dental mobile service in South Africa. *BMC Health Services Research*, *16*(1), 590. DOI: 10.1186/s12913-016-1827-2 PMID: 27756293

Nash, D. A. (2012). Envisioning an oral healthcare workforce for the future. *Community Dentistry and Oral Epidemiology*, *40*(s2), 141–147. DOI: 10.1111/j.1600-0528.2012.00734.x PMID: 22998319

Northridge, M. E., Metcalf, S. S., Yi, S., Zhang, Q., Gu, X., & Trinh-Shevrin, C. (2018). A protocol for a feasibility and acceptability study of a participatory, multi-level, dynamic intervention in urban outreach centers to improve the oral health of low-income Chinese Americans. *Frontiers in Public Health*, *6*, 29. https://www.frontiersin.org/journals/public-health/articles/10.3389/fpubh.2018.00029/full. DOI: 10.3389/fpubh.2018.00029 PMID: 29492400

Norwood, C. W., Maxey, H. L., Randolph, C., Gano, L., & Kochhar, K. (2017). Administrative challenges to the integration of oral health with primary care: A SWOT analysis of health care executives at federally qualified health centers. *The Journal of Ambulatory Care Management*, *40*(3), 204–213. https://journals.lww.com/ambulatorycaremanagement/fulltext/2017/07000/administrative_challenges_to_the_integration_of.10.aspx?context=featuredarticles&collectionid=2. DOI: 10.1097/JAC.0000000000000151 PMID: 27218701

Robinson, P. G., Douglas, G. V., Gibson, B. J., Godson, J., Vinall-Collier, K., Pavitt, S., & Hulme, C. (2019). Remuneration of primary dental care in England: A qualitative framework analysis of perspectives of a new service delivery model incorporating incentives for improved access, quality and health outcomes. [abstract]. *BMJ Open*, *9*(10), e031886. https://bmjopen.bmj.com/content/9/10/e031886. DOI: 10.1136/bmjopen-2019-031886 PMID: 31585977

Sanders, K. A., de Saxe Zerden, L., Zomorodi, M., Ciarrocca, K., & Schmitz, K. L. (2021). Promoting whole health in the dental setting: Steps toward an integrated interprofessional clinical learning environment involving pharmacy, social work, and nursing. *International Journal of Integrated Care*, *21*(4), 20. https://pmc.ncbi.nlm.nih.gov/articles/PMC8603853/. DOI: 10.5334/ijic.5814 PMID: 34824569

Sherry, R. D. H., & Hennig, R. D. H. (2018). The Inability to Bridge the Gap in Oral Health and Health Care through the Affordable Care Act (ACA). *Journal of Applied Sciences and Arts, 1*(3), 6. Retrieved 28 July 2025, from https://opensiuc.lib.siu.edu/jasa/vol1/iss3/6/

Shirk, C. (2010). *Oral health checkup: Progress in tough fiscal times?* https://hsrc.himmelfarb.gwu.edu/sphhs_centers_nhpf/229/

Stoner, K. A. (2019). *Barriers to dental care for children with medical assistance* [PhD Thesis, University of Pittsburgh]. https://search.proquest.com/openview/d59a9cf35447e87f0b3b6880859c641d/1.pdf?pq-origsite=gscholar&cbl=18750&diss=y

Tella, A. J., Olanloye, O. M., & Ibiyemi, O. (2019). Potential of teledentistry in the delivery of oral health services in developing countries. *Annals of Ibadan Postgraduate Medicine, 17*(2), 115–123. https://www.ajol.info/index.php/aipm/article/view/196515 PMID: 32669987

Veiga, N. J., Couto, P., Correia, P., Mello-Moura, A. C. V., Lopes, P. C., & Correia, M. J. (2023). Oral health strategies: Surveying the present to plan the future of community-based learning. *Health Care, 11*(19), 2646. https://www.mdpi.com/2227-9032/11/19/2646 PMID: 37830683

Wolf, E. H., Ziesemer, K. A., & Van der Hijden, E. J. E. (2024). Policy interventions to improve the accessibility and affordability of Dutch dental care. A scoping review of effective interventions. *Heliyon, 10*(9), e28886. https://www.cell.com/heliyon/fulltext/S2405-8440(24)04917-X. DOI: 10.1016/j.heliyon.2024.e28886 PMID: 38707350

Yim, J. (2019). *Differential Effects Of Medicaid Expansion On Racial/ethnic Disparities In Primary Care Access.* https://elischolar.library.yale.edu/ysphtdl/1906/

Chapter 14
The Future of Dental Public Health:
Its Policy, Innovation, and Workforce Development

Muhammad Farooq Umer
https://orcid.org/0000-0001-7779-1929
King Faisal University, Saudi Arabia

Shumaila Zofeen
https://orcid.org/0000-0003-3190-7548
Xi'an Jiaotong University, China

Ejaz Ahmad Khan
http://orcid.org/0000-0002-7072-8035
Health Services Academy, Islamabad, Pakistan

Saif U Ullah
https://orcid.org/0000-0003-3254-5585
Pakistan Institute of Ophthalmology, Alshifa Eye Trust, Rawalpindi, Pakistan

ABSTRACT

This chapter explores the evolving landscape of dental public health, focusing on the critical roles of policy innovation, digital technology, and workforce transformation in advancing equitable oral health systems globally. It highlights the persistent burden of oral diseases, particularly in low- and middle-income countries, and the urgent need for integrated public health responses aligned with the WHO Global Oral Health Action Plan (2023–2030) and the UN Sustainable Development Goals. The chapter outlines emerging policy directions, including universal health coverage, the integration of oral health into primary care, and fiscal innovations for sustainable

DOI: 10.4018/979-8-3373-1992-6.ch014

service delivery. It also examines the potential of digital health, artificial intelligence, and tele-dentistry in transforming access, prevention, and care. Furthermore, the chapter underscores the importance of reimagining the dental workforce through interdisciplinary models and community engagement.

INTRODUCTION TO DENTAL PUBLIC HEALTH

Dental public health is undergoing a significant change. Shifting demographics, the evolution of healthcare systems, and the increasing awareness of health equity are reshaping the delivery and prioritization of oral health services worldwide. The future of dental public health will depend on the capacity to address systemic deficiencies, integrate care models, and empower the workforce to respond to emerging public health challenges.

Oral health encompasses more than just teeth. It includes the health of the lips, oral mucosa, tongue, periodontal tissues, palate, and other structures of the mouth. It is a critical component of overall health and well-being. Despite advancements in dental care, oral diseases remain among the most prevalent non-communicable diseases globally. Conditions such as dental caries, periodontal disease, and oral cancers disproportionately affect vulnerable populations, particularly in low- and middle-income countries (Nash, 2012).

In high income countries, the access to care has improved, yet significant disparities persist. For instance, in Italy, the average Decayed, Missing, and Filled Teeth (DMFT) index for older adults remains high, particularly among those aged 75–94. Preventive care uptake among adolescents is also moderate, with only about 60% receiving annual check-ups(Barkaat et al., 2022). These figures underscore the need for a more proactive and inclusive public health approach.

This chapter proposes a forward-looking framework for strengthening dental public health systems, emphasizing policy reform, innovation, and workforce development. The framework is intended to guide stakeholders in building resilient, equitable, and sustainable oral health systems.

HISTORICAL CONTEXT OF DENTAL PUBLIC HEALTH

Dental public health has evolved from a narrow focus on individual treatment to a broader, population-based approach aimed at preventing disease and promoting oral health equity. Rooted in the principles of public health disease prevention, health promotion, and community engagement, dental public health is now formally recognized as a specialty by organizations such as American Dental Association and the World Dental Federation(Gouda et al., 2023).

Historically, major milestones such as the introduction of water fluoridation, school dental programs, and community-based prevention initiatives have significantly improved oral health outcomes. However, the global burden of oral diseases remains high. Between 1990 and 2017, the prevalence of untreated dental caries, severe periodontitis, and total tooth loss increased, highlighting the need for renewed public health efforts (Hugo et al., 2021).

Despite these persistent challenges, the inclusion of oral health in the Sustainable Development Goals (SDGs) and the push for Universal Health Coverage (UHC) have elevated its importance on the global health agenda. These frameworks emphasize the need for integrated, equitable, and cost-effective oral health services.

In many low- and middle-income countries (LMICs), public dental health initiatives face significant obstacles but also demonstrate creative strategies to overcome them. Due to limited resources, dental care in these regions often focuses on basic treatments like tooth extractions, with preventive care remaining scarce and the ratio of dentists to the population notably low. In response, some countries have introduced mobile dental units that travel to underserved communities, offering essential services such as professional cleanings and fluoride applications(Luan et al., 2024). School-based oral health programs, such as those implemented in Cambodia, have also gained traction promoting regular hygiene habits among children and applying fluoride varnish to help prevent tooth decay. Importantly, a growing number of LMICs are now integrating oral health into broader Universal Health Coverage (UHC) strategies, recognizing its vital role in general well-being and setting targets for measurable progress by 2030(K. Lin, 2024).

CURRENT CHALLENGES IN DENTAL PUBLIC HEALTH

Despite progress, dental public health faces several pressing challenges:

Workforce Distribution and Scope

Dental therapists and hygienists are often underutilized in many countries. Although these professionals have been integrated into care teams to improve access, particularly for children and underserved populations

Access and Affordability

In many countries, the dental services are either not covered under the national Medicare system or have limited access for low-income groups. Efforts to establish a publicly funded dental insurance scheme often encounters political or financial constraints. These challenges are common in countries where oral health is not fully integrated into primary care (Han et al., 2024).

Health System Integration

Oral health is often siloed from general health services, resulting in fragmented care that limits the management of shared risk factors for chronic diseases.

Data and Surveillance Gaps

Many regions face a lack of reliable data on oral health status, service utilization, and workforce capacity, hampering the planning and evaluation of public health interventions.

Emerging Needs and Innovations

The advancement of digital health technologies, including tele-dentistry, and AI-driven diagnostics offers new opportunities for health care deliver. However, these innovations require updated training and infrastructure. Additionally, the aging population and increasing prevalence of non-communicable diseases demand more integrated and preventive approaches.

To address these challenges, dental public health must embrace innovation, advocate for policy reform, and invest in workforce development. This includes expanding the roles of midlevel providers, integrating oral health into primary care, and leveraging technology to improve access and efficiency.

THE ROLE OF POLICYMAKERS IN DENTAL HEALTH

Policymakers play a pivotal role in shaping the future of dental public health. However, the field often suffers from fragmentation, with limited coordination among dental organizations and a lack of unified leadership. This disjointed approach hinders collective action and weakens advocacy efforts for oral health within broader health agendas.

In addition to these limitations, many dental professionals lack familiarity with population health metrics and their application in policy advocacy. Consequently, oral health is frequently underrepresented in national health strategies, despite its significant impact on quality of life and its links to systemic diseases. To address this gap, there is a pressing need to establish institutions that foster collaboration, promote inclusivity, and align policy directions across the dental sector.

Historically, oral health literature has focused heavily on clinical outcomes, often neglecting the social determinants of health and the broader public health context. Yet, dentists and allied professionals play a key role in promoting oral health equity, particularly in underserved and rural communities. Competency frameworks, such as the Common Risk Factor Approach (CRFA), encourage dental professionals to engage in community-based health promotion by addressing shared risk factors for oral and non-communicable diseases (Han et al., 2024).

Other than simply mentioning "underserved and rural communities", there is no regional or country specific reference that would give a comparison between the Lower-Middle Income Countries vs the High-Income Countries. So, you need to add such examples to maintain that Global Perspective.

Policy Development and Implementation

Despite growing research, dental public health policy remains underdeveloped in many countries. A key challenge is the translation of evidence into actionable policy. The ORBIT project, launched in 2017, has made significant strides in modeling dental public health workloads and projecting future needs(George et al., 2017). These models are essential for informing policy reforms, optimizing workforce planning, and ensuring efficient resource allocation.

However, the implementation of such models is often hindered by limited policy-oriented evidence (PHE) and institutional support. Effective policy development requires robust data on population needs, intervention outcomes, and system-level impacts, including long-term effects of preventive strategies and evaluating their cost-effectiveness at scale.

To advance policy implementation, countries must:

Develop and fund dedicated PHE initiatives.

Establish interdisciplinary institutions to support evidence generation and dissemination.

Promote international collaboration to share best practices and adapt successful models across contexts.

Ultimately, advancing policy implementation requires a shift from individual-focused care to population-oriented strategies. supported not only by technical expertise but also by political will and sustained investment in public health infrastructure(Han et al., 2024).

Advocacy for Public Health Initiatives

Advocacy is a cornerstone of effective public health practice. In dental public health, it involves mobilizing resources, building coalitions, and influencing policy to improve access, reduce disparities, and promote oral health equity.

Dental professionals must take an active role in advocating for comprehensive oral health services that go beyond emergency or curative care. This includes promoting preventive care, health education, and community-based interventions. Advocacy efforts should be grounded in respect for human rights and the dignity of marginalized populations(Han et al., 2024).

Key advocacy strategies include:

Supporting midlevel providers such as dental therapists and hygienists to expand service delivery in underserved areas.

Promoting flexible education and training pathways to diversify the workforce.

Collaborating with nondental health professionals and community organizations to deliver integrated care.

In both high-income and low-resource settings, community health workers often serve as the backbone of rural health systems. While dentists alone cannot meet the needs of remote populations, they can play a vital role in supporting and supervising these providers, ensuring quality and continuity of care (Amini et al., 2021).

As the profession faces new challenges - from aging populations to emerging technologies - advocacy will be essential in shaping policies that support innovation, equity, and sustainability in dental public health.

INNOVATIONS IN DENTAL TECHNOLOGY

Technological innovation is reshaping the landscape of dental public health. From digital diagnostics to mobile care delivery, these advancements are not only improving clinical outcomes but also expanding access to underserved populations. This section explores key innovations such as teledentistry, artificial intelligence (AI), and 3D printing and their implications for the future of oral healthcare.

Teledentistry

The COVID-19 pandemic exposed critical vulnerabilities in global healthcare systems, including the delivery of dental services. With many dental clinics forced to close or limit operations, the demand for remote care solutions became increasingly urgent. Tele-dentistry emerged as a pivotal innovation, enabling virtual consultations, triage, and follow up care.

Several countries have since piloted and implemented tele-dentistry programs. For instance, in South Africa's Ray Nkonyeni Municipality, feasibility studies were conducted to assess the integration of tele-dentistry with traditional dental services. While these pilot studies were limited in scale, successful implementations in countries like India have laid groundwork for broader adoption. These programs often utilized mobile phone-based platforms to deliver care, which were generally well received by patients though some resistance was noted among dental professionals (Joda et al., 2020).

To ensure long-term adoption, tele-dentistry systems must be tailored to meet the needs of both patients and providers. This includes improving user interfaces, ensuring data security, and offering training for dental professionals. Furthermore, integrating tele-dentistry into national health strategies can help bridge access gaps, particularly in rural and underserved areas(Tella et al., 2019);(Kanani et al., 2024).

Artificial Intelligence in Diagnostics

Artificial intelligence (AI) and machine learning (ML) are revolutionizing diagnostics in dentistry. These technologies can analyze vast datasets to detect patterns, predict disease progression, and support clinical decision-making. AI-powered tools are also increasingly applied in interpreting radiographs, identify carious lesions, and assess periodontal health with high accuracy.

Emerging studies demonstrate the diagnostic potential of AI systems such as Pearl, which assist clinicians in identifying oral conditions. While these tools enhance efficiency and accuracy, they are not substitutes for professional judgment. Instead, they serve as decision-support systems that augment the capabilities of dental practitioners (De Angelis et al., 2022);(Anil et al., 2023).

Moreover, most AI applications in dentistry typically rely on supervised learning, where algorithms are trained on annotated datasets to recognize clinical features. These systems can integrate data from various sources such as X-rays, lab tests, and patient histories to generate comprehensive diagnostic insights. As Computational power continue to evolve, AI is expected to play an increasingly central role in personalized and predictive dental care.

3D Printing in Dentistry

3D printing is another transformative technology in modern dentistry. It enables the rapid and precise fabrication of dental prosthetics, surgical guides, orthodontic appliances, and anatomical models. This approach reduces production time and costs while enhancing customization and patient outcomes.

The adoption of 3D printing has facilitated professional development opportunities and fostered international collaboration, as regulatory standards become more harmonized across countries. However, disparities in access to these technologies persist, particularly in low-resource settings. Addressing these gaps requires targeted policies and investments to ensure equitable distribution of innovation.

Beyond clinical applications, 3D printing supports public health goals by enabling the production of educational tools and mobile diagnostic kits for use in remote areas. These innovations can significantly reduce the prevalence of untreated dental conditions by improving outreach and preventive care (Pillai et al., 2021);(Chakravorty et al., 2024).

Looking ahead, the integration of 3D printing with AI and digital workflows promises to further enhance the efficiency and effectiveness of dental care delivery. As the field evolves, dental professionals must be equipped to adopt these technologies ethically and inclusively.

WORKFORCE DEVELOPMENT IN DENTAL PUBLIC HEALTH

The future of dental public health depends heavily on the strength, adaptability, and preparedness of its workforce. This was a central theme at the 2037 Conference on the Future of Dental Public Health, which brought together experts through forums, poster sessions, and a dedicated Workforce Development Forum. Discussions centered on strengthening infrastructure, securing funding, advancing policy innovation, and redefining the role of dental professionals in public health.

Dental public health was historically viewed as a specialized branch of public health dentistry, primarily focused on individual clinical care. However, the field has increasingly shifted toward population-level strategies aimed at prevention, health promotion, and addressing social determinants of health. This transition reflects a broader understanding that sustainable improvements in oral health require systemic change, not just individual interventions.

Despite this shift, challenges remain. Public health dentists often operate within rigid legal and institutional frameworks, limiting their ability to innovate or influence broader healthcare delivery systems. Moreover, the profession has yet to fully realize the potential of public funding and interdisciplinary collaboration. Encouragingly, recent federal decisions suggest a growing recognition of the need to invest in oral healthcare infrastructure and workforce expansion (Nash, 2012).

A key takeaway from the conference was the need to rethink workforce roles and responsibilities. As demand for dental services grows and workforce shortages persist, task sharing and interprofessional collaboration will become essential. To secure the necessary policy changes, a robust legislative advocacy and a well-coordinated strategic communication system will be essential.

Education and Training Programs

To prepare the next generation of dental professionals, education and training programs must evolve to reflect the dual focus of modern dentistry: individual patient care and population health.

Integrating Public Health into Dental Curricula

Dental public health specialists are trained to design and implement policies that improve oral health outcomes at the population level such as community water fluoridation, tobacco control, and incentives for rural practice. In contrast, general dental practitioners focus on diagnosing and treating individual patients. However, these roles are not mutually exclusive. Patient histories often reflect broader social and environmental determinants of health, and effective care requires an understanding of both clinical and public health perspectives.

Therefore, the future dentists must be equipped with oral health policy literacy, or the ability to understand and influence the economic, social, and political factors that shape oral health disparities. They should also be trained in behavior change strategies, such as smoking cessation and trauma-informed care, to address the root causes of disease rather than merely treating symptoms.

Reforming Dental Education Systems

Health promotion and public health principles should be embedded in all levels of dental education. This is particularly important in countries where dental education is publicly funded, as these systems have the opportunity and responsibility to shape a workforce aligned with public health goals.

A recent curriculum survey and a series of in-person workshops explored the current state of dental education and identified key areas for reform. These efforts were guided by four central questions:

Where do today's students stand in terms of public health knowledge? What actions can students take to improve patient outcomes? What can students learn from their patients about the social determinants of health? And how can education

Insights from dental public health leaders emphasized the need for experiential learning, community engagement, and interprofessional education. These elements are essential for cultivating a workforce that is not only clinically competent but also socially responsive and policy-aware.

Recruitment and Retention Strategies

A sustainable dental public health system depends not only on training new professionals but also on effectively recruiting and retaining them especially in underserved areas. While the overall supply of dentists in the United States is projected to exceed demand by over 100,000 within the next two decades, this surplus masks a critical issue: misdistribution. Many rural and low-income urban communities continue to face severe shortages of dental care providers.

Despite increased dental school enrollment since the 1970s and rising demand for services among elderly, Medicaid-eligible, and underinsured populations, the total number of hours worked by dentists has declined. This trend is influenced by shifts toward part-time practice, early retirement, and lifestyle preferences. As a result, access to care remains uneven, and many communities are left without adequate dental services.

Several state level initiatives have attempted to address these disparities. For example, enhanced Medicaid reimbursement and two-tier fee schedules have shown some success in increasing provider participation. However, these programs often fall short, as many dentists are reluctant to absorb the administrative burden or accept lower reimbursement rates. Other commonly proposed incentives including loan forgiveness, locational bonuses, and tuition subsidies, have shown limited effectiveness in sustaining long term provider retention in underserved areas. These findings suggest that financial incentives alone are insufficient without broader systemic reforms.

The recruitment challenge is further compounded by structural barriers in the dental profession. Dentists typically establish their practice location shortly after licensure, and economic barriers make relocation difficult. Additionally, the current licensure system in countries like the United States, where recruitments varies by state, restricts mobility and limits the ability to respond to regional workforce needs. In contrast, the European Union's mutual recognition of dental qualifications facilitates greater cross-border mobility, offering a model for more flexible workforce planning. Moreover, the fluctuations in public investment in community health centers and federally qualified health centers (FQHCs) have hindered long term service delivery.

To address these challenges, several strategies have been proposed:

Establishing dental school clinics in underserved areas to encourage students to practice where they train.
Implementing National licensure reform to allow greater flexibility and mobility for dental professionals.
Developing state coordinated loan and fellowship programs that align with regional workforce planning goals.
Expanding roles for midlevel providers, such as dental therapists, to extend care in areas with persistent shortages.

Ultimately, recruitment and retention strategies must form part of a broader effort to reshape the dental workforce in alignment with public health goals. This includes:

Recognizing the importance of interdisciplinary collaboration and community engagement.
Supporting career pathways that reflect the diverse needs of the population.
Ensuring that policy and funding mechanisms are stable, equitable, and responsive to changing demographics.

By addressing both the supply and distribution of dental professionals, and by removing systemic barriers to practice in underserved areas, a more resilient and inclusive dental public health workforce can be realized/built.

THE IMPACT OF COVID-19 ON DENTAL PUBLIC HEALTH

The COVID-19 pandemic, declared by the World Health Organization on March 11, 2020, had a profound and far-reaching impact on global health systems including dental public health. With over 17 million cases and nearly 700,000 deaths reported globally by mid2020, the pandemic disrupted healthcare delivery across nearly every country. In the United States alone, over 4.3 million cases and 150,000 deaths were recorded by July 2020, with Dental services were among the most affected, with clinics worldwide forced to close or limit operations due to infection control concerns. This led to a sharp decline in routine and preventive care, highlighting the vulnerability of oral health systems and emphasizing the need for resilient, adaptable models of care. Globally, the response varied based on the policy approaches and health care systems. In many high-income countries, dental professionals were prioritized for early vaccination, recognizing their essential role in healthcare.

The pandemic also accelerated the adoption of digital health technologies and prompted a reevaluation of public health policies, workforce preparedness, and the integration of oral health into broader health systems.

Changes in Policy and Practice

COVID-19 exposed a persistent gap between evidence-based interventions and their implementation in real-world settings. Several barriers contributed to this disconnect, including:

Limited awareness among policymakers and practitioners.
Budgetary constraints and competing health priorities.
Weak leadership in oral health policy.
A lack of supportive infrastructure for translating research into practice.

For instance, in Australia, the absence of national leadership in oral health promotion has led to a shift from population-level strategies in favor of individualized, biomedical approaches. This transition has reduced the effectiveness of public health interventions, particularly among vulnerable populations.

To address these challenges, there is a growing call for stronger national leadership in oral health policy, the expansion of evidence bases to include community-focused interventions, and enhanced training in advocacy and policy skills for dental public health professionals. In addition, collaborative models that engage local governments, state agencies, and public health services are essential to ensure coordinated and sustainable improvements in oral health outcomes.

A promising approach is the tripartite model used in some Australian states, where local governments, state funding bodies, and health services have successfully collaborated to implement fluoride interventions. Such models demonstrate the potential of decentralized leadership and community engagement in advancing oral health equity(Pitts et al., 2021).

Telehealth Adoption

The pandemic catalyzed the rapid adoption of telehealth technologies in dentistry, transforming how care is delivered and accessed. While digital dentistry had been evolving since the early 2000s, COVID-19 accelerated its integration into mainstream practice.

Emerging technologies with significant potential include:

Remote oral health monitoring tools that allow patients to track symptoms and receive feedback from providers.

Mobile telehealth units that bring care to underserved communities.

Bluetooth-enabled headsets capable of monitoring oral hygiene behaviors, such as chewing, fluid intake, and speech patterns, with data stored in cloud-based systems for professional review (C. Lin et al., 2022).

These innovations offer promising solutions to longstanding access barriers, particularly in rural and low-income areas. However, their success depends on supportive policy frameworks, investment in digital infrastructure, and collaboration with technology developers.

To fully realize the benefits of telehealth in dental public health, early policy groundwork is essential. This includes:

Incentivizing partnerships between telecommunications companies and digital health startups.

Ensuring data privacy and security in remote care platforms.

Integrating telehealth into public health strategies to enhance reach and resilience.

The pandemic has shown that digital transformation is not only possible but necessary. In the future, telehealth must be seen as a core component of dental public health not just a temporary solution during crises.

COMMUNITY ENGAGEMENT AND PUBLIC AWARENESS

Community engagement and public awareness are foundational to the success of dental public health initiatives. Historically, Public Health Teeth Officers (PHTOs) and early dental public health professionals played a pioneering role in designing and delivering innovative, evidence-informed service models. Interventions such as topical fluoride applications and early childhood case-finding programs were implemented with dedication, though their effectiveness varied. These efforts, however, laid the groundwork for a more population-based approach to oral health.

Over time, the role of dental public health professionals has evolved. Earlier models often focused on routine, reactive care in acute settings. In contrast, today, the emphasis has shifted toward prevention, equity, and addressing the social determinants of health. This evolution reflects a growing recognition that oral health outcomes are shaped not only by clinical care but also by broader structural and societal factors.

From early epidemiological surveys in urban centers to comprehensive state-level oral health programs, the field has expanded its focus from individual treatment to population-level planning. This shift requires a deeper understanding of the communities served and a commitment to building trust and fostering meaningful engagement.

Building Trust with Communities

Oral health is a key indicator of overall well-being and economic productivity. However, achieving good oral health is not solely a matter of individual behavior or access to care it is deeply influenced by the social determinants of health. These include the availability and regulation of sugar, tobacco, alcohol, and fluoride, as well as broader policies that shape living conditions and access to services.

While regular dental visits remain a cornerstone of preventive care, structural conditions often determine who can access such services. As a result, oral health disparities persist, particularly among marginalized and nonwhite populations. Structural racism, economic inequality, and geographic isolation all contribute to unequal oral health outcomes.

To address these challenges, public trust must be at the center of community engagement strategies. Trust is essential for encouraging individuals to participate in preventive care, adopt healthy behaviors, and engage with public health services. It also fosters social cohesion and supports the legitimacy of health systems.

Building trust requires:

Cultural competence and respect for community values.
Transparency in communication and decision making.
Inclusion of community voices in program design and evaluation.
Recognition of historical injustices and efforts to address them.

In an era increasingly defined by performance metrics and competitive service delivery, maintaining authentic, trust-based relationships with communities is more important than ever (Ward, 2017). Sociological theories of trust, therefore, offer valuable insights into how public health practitioners can foster engagement.

Effective Communication Strategies

Translating evidence-based interventions into practice at scale remains a major challenge in public health. Many successful pilot programs fail to achieve widespread adoption due to limited awareness among decision-makers, budgetary constraints, competing priorities, fragmented leadership, and a lack of policy alignment. Effective communication is essential to overcoming these barriers. This involves not only disseminating research findings but also framing messages in ways that resonate with diverse stakeholders including policymakers, practitioners, and community members.

At the local level, targeted communication strategies have shown promise. For example, in South Australia, a pilot oral health plan for Country Health SA (CHSA) was supported by a $55,000 grant, which funded the creation of four Public Health Registrar positions focused on oral health promotion. These roles contributed to the development of regional oral health systems and demonstrated the value of local leadership and tailored messaging.

To scale such efforts, health systems must adopt transformative leadership and systems thinking. This approach moves beyond individual-level interventions to address the structural and institutional factors that shape health outcomes. It also requires aligning policies, funding, and communication strategies across sectors and levels of government.

Ultimately, effective communication is not merely about delivering information; it is about building relationships, mobilizing support, and driving change. By engaging communities, empowering local leaders, and advocating for systemic reform, dental public health professionals can help create a more equitable and responsive oral health system.

COLLABORATIVE APPROACHES TO ORAL HEALTH

Achieving a transformative shift in oral health outcomes requires collaborative, cross-sectoral approaches that align public health goals with clinical practice, policy, and community engagement. This chapter explores how partnerships across disciplines, sectors, and institutions can foster innovation, improve access, and promote lifelong oral health.

Interdisciplinary Collaboration

Interdisciplinary collaboration is essential for addressing the complex determinants of oral health. Dental hygienists, for example, increasingly work in settings beyond private practice, including schools, long-term care facilities, and community health programs. However, their roles in interdisciplinary teams remain underexplored and underutilized.

A recent survey examined dental hygienists' perceptions of their collaborative roles, particularly with home care workers and other allied health professionals. The findings suggest that while many hygienists recognize the value of interdisciplinary work, there are gaps in training, policy support, and role clarity (Casa, 2016).

To advance interdisciplinary collaboration in oral health, several key actions are recommended. First, scoping reviews should be conducted to clearly define the competencies and frameworks necessary for interprofessional education in this field. Additionally, analyzing legislation that affects the scope of practice for dental hygienists and other midlevel providers is crucial for identifying systemic barriers and opportunities. Developing and piloting models of collaboration that integrate dental hygienists into broader care teams particularly in home care and community settings can help expand access and improve service delivery. Furthermore, continuing education programs should be created to strengthen skills in communication, teamwork, and systems thinking. These efforts must be guided by both local needs and global best practices to ensure that the resulting models are adaptable, evidence-based, and scalable.

Partnerships with Nonprofits

Nonprofit organizations play a critical role in expanding access to oral health services, particularly in underserved communities. Through partnerships with local health departments, academic institutions, and private sector innovators, nonprofits help bridge gaps in funding, infrastructure, and service delivery.

One of the most impactful public health interventions, community water fluoridation (CWF), has been championed by nonprofit and public health coalitions for decades. Despite its proven effectiveness in preventing dental caries, CWF remains contested in some regions due to concerns about fluorosis and local governance. Continued advocacy and public education are essential to sustain and expand this intervention (Linabarger et al., 2021).

Nonprofits also contribute to:

- Leveraging technology such as 3D printing, electrochemical sensors to improve water quality and oral hygiene tools.
- Enhancing data systems through electronic health record (EHR) integration and mobile health platforms.
- Supporting dental homes for uninsured and underinsured populations.
- Aligning oral health with chronic disease prevention, given shared risk factors such as diet, tobacco use, and socioeconomic status.

In the U.S., local health departments are increasingly encouraged to enter into collaborative ventures with nonprofits, supported by federal grants that offer up to 93% funding coverage for high-impact projects (Martin et al., 2021). These partnerships exemplify how strategic collaboration can amplify their impacts, reduce disparities, and build resilient oral health systems.

GLOBAL PERSPECTIVES ON DENTAL PUBLIC HEALTH

Health systems worldwide are grappling with the growing burden of non-communicable diseases (NCDs), and oral health is no exception. For the first time in history, the global population aged 65 and older outnumbers children under five. By 2050, the number of people over 80 is expected to triple, while growth among younger populations stagnates. These demographic shifts are accompanied by a rise in oral conditions such as edentulism, severe periodontitis, and untreated dental caries-conditions that significantly impair quality of life and increase healthcare costs.

The implications for dental public health are profound. As population's age and healthcare costs rise, the demand for oral health services will intensify, particularly in low- and middle-income countries. Yet, many oral health systems remain focused on treatment rather than prevention and are structured around fee-for-service models that prioritize high-income groups. Reforming these systems will require innovation, investment, and a shift toward integrated, preventive care.

The Sustainable Development Goals (SDGs) emphasize the importance of addressing common modifiable risk factors such as tobacco use, poor diet, and alcohol consumption that contribute to both oral and systemic diseases. Tackling these challenges requires coordinated action at national, regional, and global levels, with a focus on workforce development, policy alignment, and research leadership.

Comparative Analysis of Policies

A comparative analysis of dental public health policies reveals significant variation in how countries approach oral health. While some nations have adopted elements of a primary health care approach, few have implemented comprehensive national oral health policies. This gap reflects broader challenges in health promotion, where competing definitions, priorities, and models have led to fragmented and inconsistent policy development.

Recent analyses have revealed several key findings regarding global oral health policy. Currently, no country has a fully integrated national oral health policy, although many have adopted elements consistent with the Ottawa Charter's "healthy public policy" framework. Policy efforts often lack cohesion, with limited integration between oral health and broader health promotion strategies. Furthermore, health promotion in dentistry remains underrepresented in both academic literature and clinical practice, despite its potential to address upstream determinants of oral disease.

To address these gaps, countries must develop clear, evidence-based national oral health strategies that align with broader public health and development agendas. It is also essential to foster intersectoral collaboration aimed at addressing the social determinants of oral health. In addition, greater investment in policy research and evaluation is needed to guide effective implementation and enable the scaling up of successful models.

Innovative Practices from Around the World

Several countries have pioneered innovative approaches to dental public health, offering valuable lessons for global adaptation and scale.

China has expanded access to oral healthcare through the deployment of mobile dental units, oral care centers, and consulting rooms in rural areas. These initiatives aim to reduce geographic disparities and bring services directly to underserved populations.

Brazil's oral health policy, launched in 2004, has transformed public dental care through the creation of oral health teams, mobile dental units, and community-based care models. The Ministry of Health and Ministry of Education have also developed an online training program for dental public service managers, enhancing their capacity to lead and implement oral health interventions.

In Sri Lanka, a dental curative R&D team was established to improve local dental services through collaborative research and innovation. This model emphasizes the importance of research-driven policy and practice.

Collectively, these examples highlight the value of investing in workforce training and leadership development, leveraging technology and mobile services to expand access, integrating oral health into primary care and public health systems, and building partnerships across government, academia, and civil society.

As global health systems face increasing pressure, these innovative practices offer scalable, context-sensitive solutions for improving oral health outcomes and reducing inequalities.

FUTURE TRENDS IN DENTAL PUBLIC HEALTH

The future of dental public health is being shaped by rapid technological advancements, shifting demographics, and evolving models of care. What once seemed futuristic such as real-time collaboration between dentists via telehealth platforms or mobile dental units serving remote communities is now becoming a reality. These innovations are not only improving access and efficiency but also redefining the roles of dental professionals and the expectations of patients.

As healthcare systems face increasing financial and logistical pressures, particularly in the wake of global crises like COVID-19, the need for creative, scalable, and inclusive solutions has never been more urgent. This section explores emerging trends that are likely to influence the trajectory of dental public health in the coming decades.

Emerging Technologies

The digital revolution has reached the dental suite, transforming how care is delivered, accessed, and experienced. Technologies once reserved for high-end clinics are now becoming mainstream, democratizing access and enhancing diagnostic precision.

Several key Innovations are driving these changes:

Smartphone-Based Diagnostics: High resolution cameras and AI-powered apps can now generate dental models from simple photographs, enabling remote assessments and early detection of oral conditions.
Augmented Reality (AR): AR tools allow dentists to overlay diagnostic data during procedures, enhancing precision and enabling real-time collaboration with remote specialists.
Telehealth Integration: Patients can consult with dentists via secure video platforms, receive treatment plans, and access follow up care without visiting a clinic, which is especially valuable in underserved or rural areas.
Biometric Security and Patient Matching: Advanced sensors ensure accurate patient identification, improving safety and data integrity.
Mobile Dental Units: Climate-controlled, portable clinics are increasingly used to deliver care in hard-to-reach areas, often staffed by rotating professionals or community-based providers.

These technologies are not only improving clinical outcomes but also expanding the reach of dental public health to populations previously underserved or excluded from routine care. As the digital health market continues to grow, projected to be worth billions by the end of the decade dentistry is poised to play a central role in this transformation (Joda et al., 2020);(Siddiqui et al., 2020).

Policy Shifts and Predictions

Technological innovation alone is not enough. The future of dental public health will also depend on policy reforms that support new care models, address workforce challenges, and ensure equitable access.

Predicted Policy Shifts Include:

Decentralization of Care: As digital tools reduce the need for centralized clinics, policies will need to support mobile and home-based care delivery.
On-Demand Health Services: Inspired by the growing gig economy, dental care may increasingly be delivered through flexible, app-based platforms that connect patients with providers in real time.
Insurance and Reimbursement Reform: Fee-for-service models may give way to value-based care, incentivizing prevention and long-term outcomes over volume.
Licensure and Scope of Practice Expansion: To meet growing demand, midlevel providers such as dental therapists may be granted expanded roles, alongside national licensure reforms.
Data Governance and Privacy: As digital health tools collect more patient data, robust policies will be needed to protect privacy, and ensure ethical use.

These shifts will require strategic investment, interdisciplinary collaboration, and adaptive leadership. Professional associations have begun responding by fostering mentorship programs, supporting continuing education, and advocating for systemic change. For example, initiatives that pair veteran dentists with recent graduates are helping to bridge generational gaps and promote shared learning across career stages.

In this evolving landscape, dental public health professionals must remain agile, informed, and proactive. By embracing innovation and actively advocating for inclusive policies, dental public health professionals can help shape a future where oral health is accessible, equitable, and integrated into the broader health system.

ETHICAL CONSIDERATIONS IN DENTAL PUBLIC HEALTH

Ethics in dental public health extends beyond individual clinical encounters to encompass broader societal responsibilities. As a discipline focused on improving the oral health of populations, dental public health must navigate complex ethical landscape shaped by equity, access, autonomy, and justice. These considerations are increasingly relevant as healthcare policy increasingly aligns with public health goals, amid demographic shifts, rising health disparities, and evolving care models.

Public health ethics emphasize collective well-being, often requiring a balance between individual rights and community benefits. In dental public health, this includes decisions about resource allocation, workforce deployment, and care delivery regulations. Ethical practice also involves critically examining the policies that shape oral health outcomes, especially those that perpetuate inequities or fail to address the needs of marginalized populations.

Equity in Access to Care

Equity is a foundational principle of public health ethics. In the context of dental care, it means ensuring that all individuals regardless of age, income, race, or geography have access to preventive and restorative services. Yet, significant disparities persist.

Globally, the population is aging at an unprecedented rate, with older adults comprising a significant share. Alongside these demographic shifts, many countries are experiencing ethnic, racial and cultural diversity at an increasing rate. This in turn requires a highly culturally competent health care. However, the current healthcare workforce does not reflect this diversity, and many communities particularly rural, low-income, and minority populations continue to face barriers to care.

To address these disparities, a comprehensive, evidence-based, and nonpartisan approach is essential one that promotes policies aimed at eliminating inequalities and improving oral health outcomes across the lifespan. This requires expanding the dental workforce with professionals who are culturally and linguistically competent, ensuring that care is responsive to diverse community needs. Supporting community-based care models that bring services directly to underserved areas is equally important, as is investing in education and training to better prepare the next generation of providers. Moreover, fostering interprofessional collaboration can help integrate oral health more effectively within broader healthcare systems, ensuring a more holistic approach to public health.

Informed Consent and Patient Autonomy

Respect for autonomy is a core ethical principle in healthcare. In dental public health, this requires ensuring that patients are fully informed about their oral health status, treatment options, and the risks and benefits of proposed interventions. It also means engaging patients in shared decision-making that acknowledges their values, preferences, and cultural backgrounds.

A recent study evaluating dental students' knowledge, attitudes, and practices regarding informed consent found that while most students understood the importance of consent, many perceived it as a time-consuming formality rather than a meaningful dialogue. The study also uncovered a weak correlation between knowledge and actual practice, highlighting the need for improved education and training(Nono et al., 2024).

Key takeaways from the study emphasize that informed consent is not merely a legal requirement but a crucial process of communication and trust-building between the patients and healthcare providers. Cultural competence is essential for facilitating effective consent, particularly in diverse populations. This highlights the need for educational curricula to go beyond procedural compliance and deeply engage with the ethical dimensions of consent. In public health settings such as schools, long term care facilities, and community clinics obtaining informed consent can be more complex due to language barriers, literacy levels, and institutional constraints. Despite these challenges, respecting patient autonomy remains a non-negotiable ethical obligation.

FUNDING AND RESOURCE ALLOCATION

Funding is the backbone of any public health initiative, and dental public health is no exception. Yet, despite its vital role in overall health and well-being, oral health continues to receive disproportionately low funding compared to other areas of healthcare. This underinvestment is further compounded by public misconceptions about the scope and importance of public health, which often marginalize the role of dentistry in population-level health outcomes.

Addressing this gap requires both perception and policy. Oral health must be recognized as an integral part of public health, and funding mechanisms must reflect this reality. Achieving consistent, transparent, and equitable resource allocation is essential for building resilient oral health systems capable of responding to both long-term needs and emergent challenges.

Key near-term goals include securing consistent funding streams for public dental programs, improving data tracking and transparency to inform policy and resource distribution, and establishing functional networks of dental professionals to monitor needs and coordinate responses in real time.

Achieving these objectives will require collaboration across sectors and levels of government, alongside the active engagement of professional associations and community stakeholders.

Public vs. Private Funding

The balance between public and private funding in dental care is shifting in response to broader economic, political, and social trends. While private insurance and out-of-pocket payments continue to dominate in many countries, public funding mechanisms such as Medicaid, Medicare, and federally qualified health centers (FQHCs) play a crucial role in serving underserved populations.

The key trends and challenges in the dental public health funding reveal a complex landscape shaped by evolving care models, regulatory dynamics, and public perception. The growth of managed care, including PPOs and dental HMOs, is expanding globally. While these models can reduce costs for basic services, they may limit access and choice for patients. Regulatory uncertainty further complicates federal and state level proposals aim to improve access and equity, but inconsistent commitment and funding threaten their long term viability. In addition, water fluoridation remains a contentious issues despite overwhelming evidence supporting its safety and effectiveness, as public resistance and misinformation campaigns persist. Data transparency and utilization also posits challenges historically hindered by confidentiality concerns which have limited effective health planning. However, advances in technology now enable secure, anonymized data collection and analysis, offering new opportunities for informed decision-making and policy development.

Public funding has not kept pace with inflation or the growing demand for services. Consequently, more patients are presenting with acute, symptomatic conditions that require costly interventions. FQHCs and community health centers are expected to play an increasingly prominent role. However, their reliance on public grants raises concerns about sustainability during periods of fiscal constraint.

Sustainable Financial Models

Access to timely, effective, and affordable oral healthcare is a fundamental human right. Untreated dental conditions are associated with a wide range of health and social issues, including poor sleep, low self-esteem, school absenteeism, cardiovascular disease, and diabetes. Yet, it is estimated that only about one-third of the global population has access to essential oral health services. To address this gap, sustainable financial models must be developed that prioritize prevention, equity, and long term impact.

Key strategies for building sustainable financial model includes incentivizing preventive care by shifting funding models to reward early intervention and health promotion rather than volume-based treatment. Integrating oral health into broader health systems is also necessary, aligning oral health funding with general health budgets to promote holistic care. Cross Sector Collaboration should be encouraged between dental professionals, policymakers, educators, and private sector stakeholders. Furthermore, supporting workforce development through investment in training and continuing education to ensure a culturally competent and geographically distributed workforce.

The 2017 Dental Policy Lab proposed a vision of a cavity free world by 2040, emphasizing the need for transformational change. Achieving this goal will require not only technical innovation but also a reimagining of how oral health is financed, delivered, and valued.

MONITORING AND EVALUATION OF DENTAL HEALTH PROGRAMS

Monitoring and evaluation (M&E) are essential components of effective dental public health programs. They ensure that interventions are not only implemented as planned but also achieve their intended outcomes. However, evaluating public health delivery, especially within complex systems like federally qualified health centers (FQHCs), presents significant challenges.

Traditional randomized trials, while valuable, are often impractical in public health settings. Instead, researchers must rely on operations research, systems-based studies, and delivery effectiveness research to assess program impact. However, these approaches are underutilized in dental public health, and the gap between discovery research (innovation) and delivery research (implementation) remains substantial(G. Mays, 2011).

To bridge this gap, dental health programs must develop robust monitoring systems that can adapt to changing population dynamics and policy environments. It is also essential to evaluate not only the cost effectiveness of programs but their delivery effectiveness, especially, how well services reach and benefit the target population. Additionally, local adaptations of national policies should be monitored for fidelity and impact, especially in low-resource settings where decentralization is common. Ultimately, M&E should inform continuous improvement, guide resource allocation, and support the scaling of successful interventions.

Key Performance Indicators

Performance indicators are critical tools for assessing the effectiveness, efficiency, and equity of dental public health services. In Brazil, for example, the National Oral Health Policy has emphasized the integration of oral health into primary care through the deployment of Oral Health Teams (OHTs) within Family Health Units.

This policy shift has led to significant transition from reactive, treatment-focused care to preventive and promotive services. There has also been increased in access to primary oral health care, particularly in underserved areas. As a result, there is now need for new performance metrics that reflect both structural inputs (e.g., workforce, equipment) and process outcomes (e.g., service delivery, patient satisfaction).

Despite these advancements, challenges remain. Inequities in access persist, and many users continue to present with complex needs that strain the system's problem-solving capacity. To address this, Brazilian public health managers are working to define relevant and measurable indicators that capture the interdependence between structure, process, and outcomes. These indicators are being used not only to plan, and manage services effectively but also to evaluate oral health services.

Another strategy involves engaging dental schools and students in community-based campaigns. However, these efforts often lack systematic coordination.

A well-designed performance evaluation framework can help identify gaps, allocate resources more efficiently, and ensure accountability at all levels of the health system.

Feedback Mechanisms

In addition to quantitative indicators, qualitative feedback from the public plays a crucial role in shaping responsive and effective dental health programs. However, outside of formal public health bodies, such feedback is often limited or overlooked.

To address ongoing challenges in oral health promotion and service delivery, the dental public health sector should establish feedback mechanisms that capture public perceptions, concerns, and knowledge about oral health. These systems must be designed to support geographic and demographic targeting, enabling tailored interventions at local level. Feedback data should then be used to inform public education campaigns, improve service delivery, and guide policy development.

Participants in the Dental Policy Lab 3 (DPL3) identified several strategies to promote positive behavior change. These include delivering clear, consistent, and evidence-based messaging on oral hygiene, diet, and preventive care. Sustainability concerns were also highlighted, with recommendations to promote reusable and environmentally friendly oral hygiene products.

Furthermore, the development of creative partnerships with industry was encouraged to support innovation, waste reduction, and public engagement.

Customized, periodically updated guidance especially when paired with subsidized or free hygiene products can significally enhance the impact of public health interventions while minimizing waste and confusion.

CASE STUDIES IN SUCCESSFUL PUBLIC HEALTH INITIATIVES

Case studies offer valuable insights into how dental public health initiatives can be successfully implemented, scaled, and adapted to local contexts. They also highlight the importance of leadership, innovation, and community engagement in overcoming systemic barriers to care.

Local Success Stories

A notable example comes from Golden Plains Shire in Victoria, Australia. In 2011, the Victorian Auditor General reported that the Department of Health lacked adequate planning and performance benchmarks for municipal oral health services, particularly in rural areas. Amid this gap, Golden Plains Shire developed a youth-focused oral health promotion model that stood out for its creativity and cross-sector collaboration.

The initiative featured incentive-based engagement, such as distributing cinema tickets to students who demonstrated improvements in oral and general health. It was also integrated with youth empowerment programs, including mentoring and health education.

Furthermore, the model proposed a "fourth party" conduit, designed to coordinate access to oral health promotion across public and private sectors.

Although the program faced political and administrative hurdles, it provided a compelling model for how local governments can innovate beyond traditional frameworks. The case underscores the need for flexible funding, community-driven planning, and transparent evaluation to support replication in other municipalities.

In the United States, a similar grassroots success emerged in Surf City, California, following the passage of the California Dental Practice Act. A retired dentist launched a school-based dental sealant program, which quickly expanded to serve public insurance-eligible children across the state. These programs, often delivered in schools, churches, or mobile units, demonstrated low cost per child, high return on investment and improved access for historically underserved populations. They also showcased the effectiveness of diverse staffing models, including dental hygienists and public health practitioners.

A retrospective analysis in Oregon revealed that school-based programs often receive higher reimbursement per sealant than fixed site clinics, suggesting a need to reassess funding models to support equitable service delivery.

National Programs and Their Impact

At the national level, several programs have significantly shaped the landscape of dental public health in the United States and beyond.

Key initiatives include federal sealant programs and PHS dentist placements, which have expanded access to preventive care in underserved communities. In addition, behavioral risk reduction programs have been integrated with oral health services to address shared determinants of disease. While, workforce development efforts, such as training non-dentist providers and dental auxiliaries, have helped extend the reach of care.

Agencies such as the Centers for Disease Control and Prevention (CDC) and the National Institute of Dental and Craniofacial Research (NIDCR) have played pivotal roles in funding, evaluating, and disseminating program models. These efforts are often supported by cooperative agreements that require rigorous monitoring and reporting.

One notable example is the development of home care models for individuals living with HIV, which have been implemented in multiple states. These programs emphasize integrated care delivery, combining oral health with broader medical and social services. They also rely on data-driven planning, supported by federal funding and technical assistance, and undergo ongoing evaluation, to refine models and ensure accountability.

Collectively, these national programs demonstrate the transformative potential of policy alignment, federal state collaboration, and evidence-based planning in advancing oral health equity.

CONCLUSION

The successful translation of public policy into sustainable, community-centered dental public health programs is both challenging and essential. As the case studies and analyses in this chapter illustrate, creative interventions, targeted investments, and collaborative leadership have the potential to drive meaningful change.

To build a more equitable and effective oral health system, stakeholders must embrace workforce innovation to expand access and improve care delivery, while also investing in monitoring and evaluation frameworks that guide continuous improvement. In addition, strong support for policy development and funding mechanisms that prioritize prevention and population health is critical. Cross-sector partnership should also be fostered to align oral health with broader public health and social goals.

A coordinated strategy combining federal support, state level innovation, and local engagement can help realize the vision of a healthier, more inclusive future. For the sake of public health, this future must not only be imagined but deliberately and actively pursued.

Summary of the Chapter

- Dental public health has evolved from a treatment-focused discipline to a population-based field grounded in prevention, equity, and the social determinants of health.
- Despite progress, oral diseases remain among the most prevalent noncommunicable diseases (NCDs), necessitating renewed efforts aligned with the Sustainable Development Goals (SDGs) and Universal Health Coverage (UHC).
- Stronger institutional coordination, evidence-based policymaking, and advocacy are essential. Initiatives like the ORBIT project and the Common Risk

Factor Approach (CRFA) are emphasized as tools for aligning oral health with broader health agendas.

- Teledentistry, AI diagnostics, 3D printing, augmented reality, and smartphone-based tools are transforming care delivery and expanding access.
- Mobile dental units and biometric security enhance outreach and patient safety, especially in underserved areas.
- Curriculum reform, interprofessional collaboration, and recruitment strategies are essential to address geographic misdistribution and systemic barriers. Emphasis is placed on culturally competent care and experiential learning.
- The COVID-19 pandemic exposed vulnerabilities in oral health systems and accelerated digital transformation. It underscored the need for resilient, integrated care models and stronger leadership in oral health policy.
- Trust building, cultural competence, and inclusive communication are essential for effective public health interventions. Engaging communities and addressing structural inequalities are crucial.
- Interdisciplinary collaboration and partnerships with nonprofit organizations are vital for expanding access and promoting innovation. The roles of dental hygienists, community health workers, and nonprofit coalitions are highlighted.
- Comparative policy analysis and case studies from countries such as China, Brazil, and Sri Lanka illustrate scalable innovations in mobile care, workforce training, and research-driven policy.
- Decentralized care, on demand services, value-based reimbursement, and expanded scopes of practice are expected to redefine care delivery.
- Data governance and privacy protections will be critical as digital tools proliferate.
- Equity in access to care requires investment in culturally competent workforce development and community-based models.
- Informed consent and patient autonomy must be upheld through meaningful communication, especially in diverse and public health settings.
- Oral health remains underfunded relative to its impact on overall health. Consistent, transparent, and equitable funding mechanisms are needed.
- Sustainable financial models should prioritize prevention, integrate oral health into broader health systems, and support workforce development.
- Monitoring and evaluation (M&E) systems must assess both cost effectiveness and delivery effectiveness, especially in decentralized and resource limited settings.
- Key performance indicators (KPIs) and public feedback mechanisms are essential for responsive and adaptive program design.

- Local and national initiatives in Australia and the U.S. demonstrate the power of grassroots innovation, school-based care, and federal state collaboration.
- Programs such as mobile sealant clinics and integrated care for HIV positive individuals highlight scalable, cost-effective models that improve access and equity.
- The future of dental public health depends on building resilient, equitable, and ethically grounded systems.
- Sustained investment, interdisciplinary collaboration, and a workforce prepared to meet the evolving needs of diverse populations are essential.
- By embracing innovation, ethical practice, inclusive policies, and rigorous evaluation, dental public health professionals can help shape a future where oral health is universally accessible and integrated into broader health systems.

REFERENCES

Amini, H., Wells, A. J., Boynton, J. R., Guo, X., & Ni, A. (2021). Oral Health Advocacy Education Impacts Future engagement: Exploration at a midwestern us dental school. *Frontiers in Oral Health*, *2*, 714199. https://www.frontiersin.org/articles/10.3389/froh.2021.714199/full. DOI: 10.3389/froh.2021.714199 PMID: 35048043

Anil, S., Porwal, P., & Porwal, A. (2023). Transforming dental caries diagnosis through artificial intelligence-based techniques. *Cureus*, *15*(7). Advance online publication. https://www.cureus.com/articles/169408-transforming-dental-caries-diagnosis-through-artificial-intelligence-based-techniques.pdf. DOI: 10.7759/cureus.41694 PMID: 37575741

Barkaat, H., Atiq, T., Khurram, M., Ahmed, R., Iqbal, S., & Rashid, W. (2022). Assessment of DMFT Score in Lower Income Employees of the University of Faisalabad. *Pakistan Journal of Medical & Health Sciences*, *16*(07), 07. Advance online publication. DOI: 10.53350/pjmhs22167548

Casa, C. (2016). *Expanding Interprofessional Learning Opportunities: How Dental Hygiene Administrators And Faculty Perceive Interprofessional Education*. https://dune.une.edu/theses/54/

Chakravorty, S., Trivedi, H., Sahai, R. R., Kouser, A., Tekam, D. A., & Jain, A. (2024). 3D printing: Opening new horizons in dentistry. *Journal of Pharmacy & Bioallied Sciences*, *16*(Suppl 1), S8–S10. https://journals.lww.com/jpbs/fulltext/2024/16001/3d_printing__opening_new_horizons_in_dentistry.4.aspx. DOI: 10.4103/jpbs.jpbs_457_23 PMID: 38595399

De Angelis, F., Pranno, N., Franchina, A., Di Carlo, S., Brauner, E., Ferri, A., Pellegrino, G., Grecchi, E., Goker, F., & Stefanelli, L. V. (2022). Artificial intelligence: A new diagnostic software in dentistry: a preliminary performance diagnostic study. *International Journal of Environmental Research and Public Health*, *19*(3), 1728. https://www.mdpi.com/1660-4601/19/3/1728. DOI: 10.3390/ijerph19031728 PMID: 35162751

George, A., Scott, K., Govender, V., & World Health Organization. (2017). *A health policy and systems research reader on human resources for health / Asha George, Kerry Scott, Veloshnee Govender, editors*. World Health Organization. https://iris.who.int/handle/10665/259460

Gouda, H., Virtanen, J. I., & El Tantawi, M. (2023). Dental public health education in Egypt: A cross-sectional survey. *BMC Medical Education*, *23*(1), 899. Advance online publication. DOI: 10.1186/s12909-023-04888-9 PMID: 38007503

Han, C., Lin, C., Raichur, A., Hall, M., & Nguyen, T. M. (2024). Leadership, regulatory approaches and policy to re-orientate health services towards health promotion. *Health Promotion International, 39*(3), daae050. https://academic.oup.com/heapro/article-pdf/doi/10.1093/heapro/daae050/57983245/daae050.pdf. DOI: 10.1093/heapro/daae050 PMID: 38809234

Hugo, F. N., Kassebaum, N. J., Marcenes, W., & Bernabé, E. (2021). Role of Dentistry in Global Health: Challenges and Research Priorities. *Journal of Dental Research, 100*(7), 681–685. DOI: 10.1177/0022034521992011 PMID: 33541197

Joda, T., Bornstein, M. M., Jung, R. E., Ferrari, M., Waltimo, T., & Zitzmann, N. U. (2020). Recent trends and future direction of dental research in the digital era. *International Journal of Environmental Research and Public Health, 17*(6), 1987. https://www.mdpi.com/1660-4601/17/6/1987. DOI: 10.3390/ijerph17061987 PMID: 32197311

Kanani, H., Khubchandani, M., Dangore-Khasbage, S., & Pandey, R. (2024). Teledentistry: A comprehensive review and its application in pediatric dental care. *Cureus, 16*(1). Advance online publication. https://www.cureus.com/articles/190184-teledentistry-a-comprehensive-review-and-its-application-in-pediatric-dental-care.pdf. DOI: 10.7759/cureus.52685 PMID: 38384649

Lin, C., Goncalves, N., Scully, B., Heredia, R., & Hegde, S. (2022). A teledentistry pilot study on patient-initiated care. *International Journal of Environmental Research and Public Health, 19*(15), 9403. https://www.mdpi.com/1660-4601/19/15/9403. DOI: 10.3390/ijerph19159403 PMID: 35954757

Lin, K. (2024, November 18). *Transforming Oral Health: Public Dental Programs Bridging Care Gaps Globally*. Project Smile Global. https://www.projectsmileglobal.org/post/public-dental-health-programs

Linabarger, M., Brown, M., & Patel, N. (2021). A pilot study of integration of medical and dental care in 6 states. *Preventing Chronic Disease, 18*, E72. https://pmc.ncbi.nlm.nih.gov/articles/PMC8300541/. DOI: 10.5888/pcd18.210027 PMID: 34296994

Luan, Y., Sardana, D., Jivraj, A., Liu, D., Abeyweera, N., Zhao, Y., Cellini, J., Bass, M., Wang, J., Lu, X., Cao, Z., & Lu, C. (2024). Universal coverage for oral health care in 27 low-income countries: A scoping review. *Global Health Research and Policy, 9*(1), 34. DOI: 10.1186/s41256-024-00376-9 PMID: 39252095

Martin, A. B., Moss, M. E., Kelly, A., Riley, A., Pardi, V., & Pollard, A. C. (2021). A Technical Assistance Curriculum for Expanding Sustainable School-Based Oral Health Programs in the Carolinas' Dental Safety Net. *Maternal and Child Health Journal, 25*(8), 1200–1208. DOI: 10.1007/s10995-021-03167-7 PMID: 33948828

Mays, G. (2011). Disparities Research in Public Health PBRNs. *American Association for Dental Research*. https://uknowledge.uky.edu/hsm_present/59

Nash, D. A. (2012). Envisioning an oral healthcare workforce for the future. *Community Dentistry and Oral Epidemiology*, *40*(s2), 141–147. DOI: 10.1111/j.1600-0528.2012.00734.x PMID: 22998319

Nono, D., Mwebesa, E., Bagenda, G., Okullo, I., Rwenyonyi, C. M., & Williams, S. (2024). Assessment of the knowledge, attitude and practices of the informed consent process in oral healthcare among dental students in Makerere University Dental Hospital, Uganda. *BMC Medical Education*, *24*(1). Advance online publication. DOI: 10.1186/s12909-024-05520-0 PMID: 38730378

Pillai, S., Upadhyay, A., Khayambashi, P., Farooq, I., Sabri, H., Tarar, M., Lee, K. T., Harb, I., Zhou, S., Wang, Y., & Tran, S. D. (2021). Dental 3D-printing: Transferring art from the laboratories to the clinics. *Polymers*, *13*(1), 157. https://www.mdpi.com/2073-4360/13/1/157. DOI: 10.3390/polym13010157 PMID: 33406617

Pitts, N. B., Newton, J. T., Pow, R., Miller, N., & Mayne, C. (2021). Dental Policy Lab 3: Towards oral and dental health through partnership. *British Dental Journal*, *231*(12), 764–768. https://www.nature.com/articles/s41415-021-3733-1. DOI: 10.1038/s41415-021-3733-1 PMID: 34921274

Siddiqui, M. A., Butt, T. K., Farooq, M. A., Omer, M. T., Zahoor, F., & Hussain, K. K. (2020). Difference in mean weight gain and hospital stay in preterm babies receiving complete or partial kangaroo mother care compared to no kangaroo mother care: Experience from a tertiary care hospital. *Journal of Fatima Jinnah Medical University*, *14*(4), 152–155. https://www.jfjmu.com/index.php/ojs/article/view/770. DOI: 10.37018/qymd3680

Tella, A. J., Olanloye, O. M., & Ibiyemi, O. (2019). Potential of teledentistry in the delivery of oral health services in developing countries. *Annals of Ibadan Postgraduate Medicine*, *17*(2), 115–123. https://www.ajol.info/index.php/aipm/article/view/196515 PMID: 32669987

Ward, P. R. (2017). Improving access to, use of, and outcomes from public health programs: The importance of building and maintaining trust with patients/clients. *Frontiers in Public Health*, *5*, 22. https://www.frontiersin.org/journals/public-health/articles/10.3389/fpubh.2017.00022/full. DOI: 10.3389/fpubh.2017.00022 PMID: 28337430

Chapter 15
Emerging Infectious Control Technologies:
A Global Perspective Surveillance and Response to Hospital Acquired Infections

Awais Farid
https://orcid.org/0009-0002-7549-4079
Hong Kong University of Science and Technology, Hong Kong

Zahra Fatima
https://orcid.org/0009-0008-8252-0822
Chang'an University, China

Zeeshan Fareed
Hong Kong University of Science and Technology, Hong Kong

Zernain Athar
Hong Kong University of Science and Technology, Hong Kong

Aisha Manzoor
Punjab Higher Education, Pakistan

Muhammad Farhan Hassan Sheharyar
https://orcid.org/0009-0008-9401-8602
Hong Kong University of Science and Technology, Hong Kong

ABSTRACT

Hospital-acquired infections (HAIs), particularly those involving multidrug-resistant organisms (MDROs), remain a global healthcare challenge, threatening patient safety and straining healthcare systems. This chapter explores emerging infection control technologies—including antimicrobial coatings, UV-C disinfection, and nanomaterials—designed to provide continuous protection and reduce environmental microbial burden in healthcare settings. Drawing from recent field trials and laboratory evidence, we evaluate the mechanisms, effectiveness, and limitations of these technologies. Real-world applications are discussed in the context of long-term care facilities and acute hospital environments. Comparative frameworks

DOI: 10.4018/979-8-3373-1992-6.ch015

highlight cost, feasibility, and sustainability considerations. Finally, the chapter outlines global implementation challenges and provides policy recommendations to support equitable adoption. These innovations, when integrated into multimodal infection prevention strategies, offer a transformative pathway to reduce HAIs and improve public health outcomes.

INTRODUCTION

Hospital-acquired infections (HAIs), also known as nosocomial infections, remain a significant global health concern. They are defined as infections that are not present or incubating at the time of a patient's admission but develop during hospitalization, typically after 48 to 72 hours of stay. These infections are especially prevalent in high-risk clinical environments such as intensive care units and surgical wards, and their burden extends beyond patients to include caregivers, visitors, and healthcare workers. Importantly, individuals who are discharged and later present with infections within a defined time window may also fall into the HAI classification.

Despite advancements in medical care and hygiene practices, HAIs continue to contribute to increased patient morbidity, prolonged hospital stays, and escalating healthcare costs. The World Health Organization (2016) estimates that hundreds of millions of patients are affected each year, with a disproportionately high burden in low- and middle-income countries (World Health, 2016). The global incidence of HAIs underscores their far-reaching impact, both in terms of morbidity and mortality. For instance, estimates in the United States suggest that hundreds of thousands of patients acquire HAIs annually, with tens of thousands of associated deaths. In addition to clinical consequences, HAIs contribute significantly to healthcare costs due to extended hospital stays, increased antimicrobial use, and additional diagnostic and therapeutic interventions. Moreover, the burden is exacerbated in low- and middle-income countries, where infection control infrastructure is often under-resourced.

A major concern within the landscape of HAIs is the growing prevalence of multidrug-resistant organisms (MDROs). These are pathogens—most often bacteria—that exhibit resistance to one or more classes of antimicrobial agents. Pathogenic microorganisms such as methicillin-resistant *Staphylococcus aureus* (MRSA), vancomycin-resistant *enterococci* (VRE), multidrug-resistant *Acinetobacter baumannii* (MDRA), and *Pseudomonas aeruginosa* (MRPA) have become increasingly prevalent in healthcare settings (Seifert, 2024; Weber & Rutala, 2013). These multidrug-resistant organisms (MDROs) are not only challenging to treat but also persist on surfaces—both hard and porous—for extended periods (Kampf et al., 2014; Otter et al., 2011). These pathogens compromise treatment outcomes, necessitate the use of toxic or less effective second-line therapies, and increase the risk of transmission in healthcare settings.

HAIs are often classified by their anatomical site and mode of acquisition. Common categories include ventilator-associated pneumonia (VAP), central line-associated bloodstream infections (CLABSI), catheter-associated urinary tract infections (CAUTI), surgical site infections (SSI), and complicated intra-abdominal infections (cIAIs). These infection types are frequently associated with invasive medical devices, such as catheters, endotracheal tubes, and central venous lines. The role of such devices in disrupting mucosal barriers and facilitating microbial colonization is well-documented.

The microbiological spectrum of HAIs is diverse and context-specific. Bacteria are the predominant causative agents, though fungi (notably Candida spp.) and viruses (such as respiratory syncytial virus and norovirus) also contribute to the disease burden. In recent years, the rise of fungal and viral HAIs in immunocompromised and critically ill patients has highlighted the importance of broad-spectrum surveillance and diagnostics. Importantly, bacterial pathogens remain the leading contributors to morbidity and mortality, with MDROs posing the most formidable challenge.

The clinical consequences of MDRO-related HAIs vary based on the site of infection, the pathogen involved, and the patient's underlying health condition. For example, bloodstream infections associated with central venous catheters can lead to sepsis and have high case-fatality rates. Respiratory infections such as VAP caused by MRSA or resistant Pseudomonas are similarly associated with poor outcomes. Intra-abdominal infections and surgical site infections, particularly those involving resistant gram-negative bacilli, are notoriously difficult to manage.

Environmental surfaces, including hospital curtains, bed linens, uniforms, and high-touch surfaces, can act as reservoirs for MDROs (Boyce, 2007; Dancer, 2009). Their survival on these materials underscores the limitations of conventional cleaning and disinfection protocols, particularly when practices are inconsistent or compliance is low (Rutala et al., 2019). Traditional infection prevention and control (IPC) strategies such as hand hygiene, personal protective equipment, and chemical disinfectants are central to hospital protocols. However, they rely heavily on human compliance and are often insufficient in eliminating environmental reservoirs of pathogens (Chatterjee et al., 2017; Khalid et al., 2024). In resource-limited healthcare systems, routine reapplication of disinfectants may be impractical or unsustainable (Barancheshme & Munir, 2018).

In response, research has increasingly focused on novel, passive infection control technologies that provide long-lasting antimicrobial action. These include surface coatings, UV-C disinfection systems, nanomaterials, and self-disinfecting polymers that can be applied to hospital textiles and surfaces (Morones-Ramirez et al., 2012; Reynolds et al., 2020). Emerging technologies hold promise not only for reducing pathogen transmission but also for reducing the burden on healthcare workers by automating or supplementing traditional cleaning protocols (Dancer, 2009). However, the successful adoption of these innovations depends on their cost-effectiveness, durability, regulatory approval, and ability to demonstrate real-world efficacy (Chatterjee et al., 2017; Seifert, 2024).

In summary, HAIs and MDROs represent a dynamic and evolving threat to patient safety and healthcare delivery. Addressing this burden requires a multifaceted approach, encompassing early detection, robust infection control protocols, effective antimicrobial stewardship, and innovation in disinfection and environmental hygiene technologies. Continued research, policy engagement, and investment are critical to reducing the clinical and economic toll of these infections globally. This chapter explores the evolution of environmental infection control strategies, focusing on recent innovations with field-tested antimicrobial systems. Drawing from global evidence—including field studies conducted in hospital and long-term care settings—the chapter critically examines their potential to reduce environmental contamination and support efforts to reduce HAIs.

EPIDEMIOLOGY AND BURDEN OF HOSPITAL-ACQUIRED INFECTIONS

Hospital-acquired infections (HAIs) are among the most frequent adverse events occurring in healthcare delivery worldwide. These infections, which develop 48 hours or more after hospital admission, not only compromise patient safety but also exert significant economic and systemic pressure on healthcare services. The global burden of HAIs remains disproportionately high, especially in low- and middle-income countries (LMICs) showed in Figure 1b, where limited infrastructure and resources hinder effective infection prevention and control (Allegranzi & Pittet, 2011; World Health, 2016). In high-income countries, the estimated prevalence of HAIs ranges between 5% and 10% of hospitalized patients, whereas in LMICs, this rate may exceed 15% (Haque & Abu Bakar, 2018). A large multi-country study coordinated by the WHO found that the average prevalence of healthcare-associated infection was 7.6% in high-income nations showed in Figure 1a, compared to 10.1% in developing countries (World Health, 2011). Common sites of infection include the urinary tract, lower respiratory tract, surgical sites, and bloodstream, with device-associated infections such as ventilator-associated pneumonia (VAP), catheter-associated urinary tract infections (CAUTIs), and central line-associated bloodstream infections (CLABSIs) being particularly prevalent (Magill et al., 2018). Multidrug-resistant organisms (MDROs) have further intensified the burden of HAIs. Pathogens such as MRSA, VRE, extended-spectrum beta-lactamase (ESBL)-producing Enterobacteriaceae, and carbapenem-resistant Acinetobacter and Klebsiella species are now frequently implicated in nosocomial outbreaks (Seifert, 2024; Weiner-Lastinger et al., 2020). These organisms not only complicate treatment but also lead to longer hospitalizations, increased mortality rates, and higher healthcare costs (Cassini et al., 2019; Cdc, 2019).

Estimates suggest that in the European Union alone, over 670,000 HAIs occur annually, leading to approximately 33,000 deaths (Cassini et al., 2019). In the United States, the Centers for Disease Control and Prevention (CDC) reported a significant rise in several HAIs during the COVID-19 pandemic, likely due to healthcare system strain and altered infection control practices (Weiner-Lastinger et al., 2020). The pandemic served as a stark reminder of the fragility of infection prevention infrastructure and the need for resilient systems capable of adapting under crisis conditions. The economic implications are equally significant. HAIs contribute billions of dollars annually to global healthcare costs. In the U.S., the estimated direct cost of HAIs ranges from $28 billion to $45 billion each year (Zimlichman et al., 2013). These costs stem from prolonged hospital stays, additional diagnostics and treatments, and increased use of broad-spectrum antimicrobials.

There are a large number of infectious agents—from viruses and prions to bacteria, fungi, protozoans, and helminths—that are responsible for a wide variety of infectious diseases affecting humans and animals. In humans, viruses account for a large fraction of emerging infectious diseases (EIDs). They are agents of new diseases such as HIV/AIDS, SARS, influenza, and several other EIDs as well as agents of re-emerging diseases such as TB and plague, often in a new, more virulent form. Size and structure together with high mutation rates are factors that lead to virulent forms (Nii-Trebi, 2017). Together with increased virulence, the global emergence of these diseases has been largely due to increased human-animal interaction, urbanization, food processing, transportation, commercial movement, and other changes in ecology and lifestyle.

In addition, the study of these viruses has been hampered by bioethics, especially with regards to field studies of wild animals. Hence, the development of novel approaches for real-time identification of such viruses has become a major area of research, especially for detection of those in animals. Despite these challenges, there is strong evidence that many HAIs are preventable through improved hygiene practices, surveillance systems, antimicrobial stewardship, and environmental interventions (Allegranzi & Pittet, 2011; Dancer, 2009). However, the implementation of such measures varies considerably across regions, emphasizing the importance of contextual adaptation and investment in capacity-building, particularly in resource-limited settings see Figures 1 and 2.

Figure 1. Prevalence of healthcare-associated infections (HAIs) in high-income countries (1995–2020)

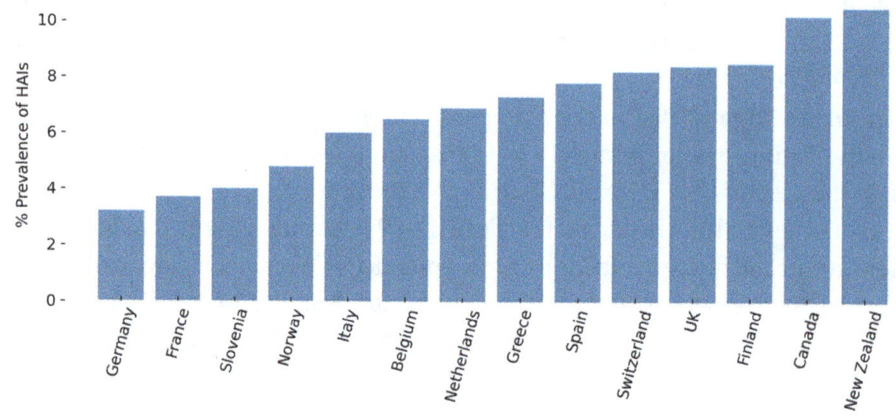

(Adapted from Seifert, 2024)

Figure 2. Prevalence of healthcare-associated infections (HAIs) in low- and middle-income countries (1995–2020)

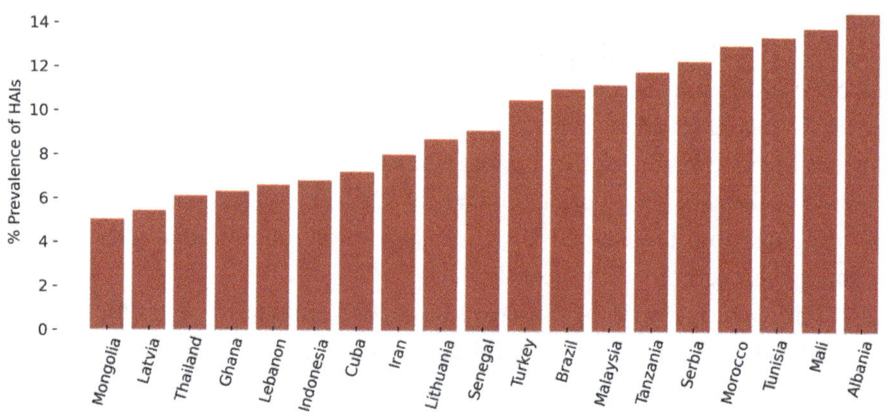

(Adapted from Seifert, 2024)

THE ROLE OF SURVEILLANCE IN INFECTION CONTROL

Surveillance and analysis of infectious diseases can be done automatically. That is still a dream in most third world countries, but there are steps towards this.

Tombstone in another country, buried far away? Could this be the foundation of a new local outbreak? There seem to be factors associated with a disease outbreak that tend to lead to new outbreaks, and measures should be taken when these factors arise(Badinski et al., 2024). All but impossible to do manually or by human observers. But there may be a hope in new computer technology for analysis of such open data feeds. Tracking outbreaks is day-of-outbreak stuff. An attacker with a bioweapon has probably thought ahead, and a counterattack is likely to be several hours or a few days too late to be effective.

The mobilization of altered infectious agents is more than just an infection a few days after exposure. Global air travel means the opportunity for rapid world-wide dissemination of such agents. New initiatives should be started and be in place before there is a successful attack Traditionally, infection surveillance relied on manual data collection and retrospective reviews, often leading to delayed responses. However, the past decade has seen a paradigm shift toward digital, real-time, and predictive surveillance strategies powered by advanced technologies (Maddah et al., 2023).

Importance of Surveillance Systems

The mission of infectious diseases surveillance systems is to monitor events that may have the potential to impact public health. This requires shared definitions of what constitutes a health event that merits follow-up consideration, common systems for data entry and information transmission, and a level of trust among health organizations and industries to facilitate access to requested information. Such systems benefit public health, health care providers, health and life science businesses, and political leaders.

Institutional surveillance systems of this kind have historically focused on international collection and dissemination of information on emerging zoonoses (Morgan & Pinner, 2009). National and institutional surveillance platforms—such as the CDC's National Healthcare Safety Network (NHSN)—facilitate standardized data reporting, benchmarking, and feedback loops that drive quality improvement (Franklin, 2024). These systems allow healthcare providers to assess infection rates, identify outbreak patterns, and evaluate the impact of control measures.

Similarly, in the United Kingdom, the Mandatory Surveillance Scheme administered by the UK Health Security Agency has contributed to measurable reductions in MRSA bloodstream infections and *Clostridioides difficile* infections over the past two decades (Abad et al., 2024). The public reporting of these data by NHS Trusts has increased accountability and helped prioritize infection prevention efforts. In the European Union, the ECDC's Healthcare-Associated Infections Network (HAI-Net) collects data across member states and publishes harmonized indicators of infection burden, antimicrobial use, and resistance patterns, which serve as benchmarks for national and regional policy adjustments.

Developing capacity to detect emerging infectious diseases still requires investment in resources, education, staff training, real-time communications, and research into potential sources of diseases, all of which are scarce in poorer countries. Despite advancements, disparities persist, especially in resource-limited settings. Fragmented reporting systems, inadequate laboratory capacity, and lack of automation hinder timely detection and response. Bridging these gaps requires investment in trained personnel, mobile health tools, and real-time data infrastructure (Organization, 2024).

Evolution of Syndromic Surveillance with Emerging Technologies

Technological advancements have enabled the reliable and precise monitoring of infectious disease outbreaks. Population-based surveillance may be passive or active. In passive surveillance, reporting is dependent on the action of health care providers, whereas in active surveillance, more vigorous and systematic efforts are made to ascertain data from health-care providers and other reporters. Syndromic surveillance collects and analyzes pre-diagnostic data (e.g., symptoms, clinical encounters) to detect potential outbreaks before formal diagnoses are made. Initially developed for early bioterrorism warning, syndromic surveillance now plays a critical role in identifying emerging infections within hospital and community settings (Adedire et al., 2024).

When enhanced with machine learning, natural language processing, and geographic information systems (GIS), syndromic surveillance enables rapid detection of anomalies in disease trends. For example, GIS can visualize spatial clusters of symptoms across hospital wards or regions, helping target interventions and resources (Hao et al., 2022). Such tools have been especially useful in early warning systems for respiratory illnesses, gastrointestinal outbreaks, and post-surgical infection clusters, providing a crucial time advantage for public health responses.

Real-Time Analytics and Artificial Intelligence in HAI Surveillance

Artificial intelligence (AI) has revolutionized how hospitals monitor and predict HAIs. AI systems can analyze large volumes of structured and unstructured data, automatically flagging cases that meet infection criteria or exhibit unusual trends.

These systems not only improve detection but also reduce the burden of manual data review.

Predictive analytics, powered by historical data, can forecast HAI risk among vulnerable patient groups or during high-risk procedures. Real-time dashboards supported by AI provide clinicians and infection control teams with actionable insights, allowing them to implement timely interventions. Furthermore, automated alerts embedded in electronic health record (EHR) systems enhance clinician awareness and support early response, reducing morbidity, length of stay, and associated healthcare costs (El Arab et al., 2025).

Digital Health Infrastructure and Interoperability

The effectiveness of surveillance systems relies heavily on robust digital infrastructure. Interoperable EHRs, automated reporting pipelines, and cloud-based analytics platforms enable seamless sharing of infection data across departments and facilities (Kouroubali & Katehakis, 2022). This is especially important in integrated health systems, where patient data may span multiple care settings.

The COVID-19 pandemic highlighted the need for flexible, scalable surveillance systems. Many institutions rapidly implemented cloud-based registries, contact tracing dashboards, and mobile reporting apps to manage patient flow and infection control in real time. Yet, digital health adoption must also consider data governance, cybersecurity, and staff digital literacy to ensure both utility and security.

PATHOGENS OF CONCERN IN HOSPITAL-ACQUIRED INFECTIONS

A critical dimension of hospital-acquired infections (HAIs) lies in the spectrum of microorganisms responsible for these infections, particularly those classified as multidrug-resistant organisms (MDROs). These pathogens exhibit resistance to multiple classes of antibiotics, complicating treatment, prolonging illness, and increasing the risk of poor outcomes. The ESKAPE pathogens—*Enterococcus faecium, Staphylococcus aureus, Klebsiella pneumoniae, Acinetobacter baumannii, Pseudomonas aeruginosa*, and *Enterobacter* species— showed in Table 1, are among the most notorious for causing HAIs globally and have been prioritized by the WHO for research and development of new antimicrobials (Miller & Arias, 2024; World Health, 2017).

Among these, *Staphylococcus aureus*, particularly methicillin-resistant *S. aureus* (MRSA), remains a leading cause of bloodstream infections, surgical site infections, and pneumonia in hospitalized patients. MRSA is capable of persisting on both skin and environmental surfaces, facilitating indirect transmission through contaminated surfaces or healthcare personnel (Otter & French, 2013). Despite efforts to reduce its incidence, MRSA continues to account for a significant proportion of HAIs in both high- and low-resource settings (Magill et al., 2018).

Acinetobacter baumannii is another major concern, especially in intensive care units (ICUs), where it can survive for extended periods on dry surfaces and medical equipment. Strains resistant to carbapenems—one of the last-resort antibiotic classes—have been reported with increasing frequency, particularly in conflict zones and resource-limited settings (Lynch III et al., 2017). Similarly, *Pseudomonas aeruginosa* is known for its intrinsic resistance and its ability to acquire further resistance mechanisms. It is frequently associated with ventilator-associated pneumonia and catheter-associated infections (Divatia et al., 2020).

Gram-negative pathogens, particularly *Klebsiella pneumoniae* and *Escherichia coli*, are major contributors to HAIs (Farid, Han, Lai, et al., 2025), especially in neonatal units and immunocompromised patients. The emergence of extended-spectrum beta-lactamase (ESBL)-producing strains and carbapenem-resistant *Enterobacteriaceae* (CRE) has dramatically limited treatment options (Tompkins & van Duin, 2021). The silent transmission of such organisms within hospital environments, including via textiles and surfaces, underscores the urgency of environmental decontamination measures. In addition to bacterial pathogens, certain fungal species such as *Candida auris* have also emerged as notable causes of nosocomial outbreaks. *C. auris* is highly resistant to multiple antifungal agents and can persist on surfaces for extended periods, making infection control challenging (Chowdhary & Meis, 2017).

Table 1. Summary of key pathogens in hospital-acquired infections

Pathogen	Common Infections	Resistance Mechanism	Key Concerns
Methicillin-resistant *Staphylococcus aureus* (MRSA)	Bloodstream infections, pneumonia, surgical site infections	Beta-lactam resistance (mecA gene)	High environmental persistence, transmission via hands/ surfaces
Vancomycin-resistant *Enterococci* (VRE)	Urinary tract infections, bloodstream infections	Glycopeptide resistance (vanA/vanB genes)	Difficult to eradicate from surfaces and devices
Acinetobacter baumannii (CRAB)	Ventilator-associated pneumonia, bloodstream infections, wound infections	Carbapenem resistance (OXA-type enzymes)	Environmental survival, resistance to disinfectants
Pseudomonas aeruginosa	Pneumonia, urinary tract infections, wound infections	Efflux pumps, beta-lactamases, porin loss	Intrinsic and acquired resistance, limited treatment options

continued on following page

Table 1. Continued

Pathogen	Common Infections	Resistance Mechanism	Key Concerns
Klebsiella pneumoniae (ESBL/CRE)	Pneumonia, bloodstream infections, neonatal sepsis	Extended-spectrum beta-lactamases (ESBLs), carbapenemases (KPC, NDM)	Rapid resistance spread, outbreaks in ICUs
Escherichia coli (ESBL/CRE)	Urinary tract infections, neonatal sepsis	ESBLs, carbapenemases	High prevalence in community and hospitals
Enterobacter spp.	Respiratory and bloodstream infections	AmpC beta-lactamases, porin mutations	Diverse resistance profiles, nosocomial outbreaks
Candida auris	Bloodstream infections, wound infections, ICU outbreaks	Multidrug resistance to azoles, echinocandins, polyenes	Emerging global threat, high mortality in ICUs

Taken together, the rise in antimicrobial resistance among HAI pathogens not only threatens individual patient outcomes but also undermines the sustainability of healthcare systems. Targeted surveillance, antimicrobial stewardship, and the integration of new environmental hygiene technologies are essential to curbing the spread of these high-risk pathogens.

CONVENTIONAL INFECTION CONTROL STRATEGIES

Infection prevention and control (IPC) strategies form the cornerstone of healthcare efforts to reduce the incidence and transmission of hospital-acquired infections (HAIs). These strategies are multifaceted, combining administrative controls, environmental hygiene, and behavioral practices to create safer healthcare environments. While conventional IPC practices have proven effective when implemented consistently, their reliance on human compliance and labor-intensive protocols limits their long-term sustainability, especially in high-burden or resource-limited settings (Kumar et al., 2024). A multimodal approach to infection prevention remains central to effective HAI control. As illustrated in Figure 2, this approach integrates hand hygiene, environmental cleaning, surveillance, and antimicrobial stewardship within a system-wide framework (Saravanos et al., 2024).

Hand Hygiene and Personal Protective Equipment

Hand hygiene remains the single most important intervention in the prevention of HAIs. Alcohol-based hand rubs (ABHRs) are widely endorsed for their ease of use and effectiveness against a broad spectrum of microorganisms. The WHO's "Five

Moments for Hand Hygiene" framework has been globally adopted to guide clinical practice (World Health, 2009). However, compliance with hand hygiene protocols varies widely across institutions and clinical disciplines, often falling below 50%, even in high-income countries (Pittet et al., 2000). Similarly, the appropriate use of personal protective equipment (PPE), including gloves, gowns, and masks, is essential in limiting cross-transmission but is frequently hampered by knowledge gaps, supply shortages, or complacency, see Figure 3.

Figure 3. Conceptual framework illustrating the priorities and interrelated outcomes of infection prevention and control (IPC) for sustainable health and environmental systems. The model emphasizes three key priorities: (1) strengthen the evidence base through high-quality research and surveillance; (2) measure and mitigate the environmental impacts of IPC practices; and (3) harness the power of human behaviour by investing in a people-centred, sustainability-driven health workforce

(Adapted from Saravanos et al., 2024)

Environmental Cleaning and Disinfection

Routine and terminal cleaning of patient care areas is critical in breaking the chain of infection, particularly for pathogens known to persist on surfaces. Disinfectants such as sodium hypochlorite, hydrogen peroxide, and quaternary ammonium compounds are commonly used (Rutala & Weber, 2014). Despite established cleaning protocols, studies have shown that up to 50% of hospital surfaces may remain contaminated post-cleaning, largely due to inconsistent application or limited staff training (Allen, 2016; Tembo, 2024).

Surveillance and Isolation

Surveillance systems help identify HAI trends and enable targeted responses, while patient isolation (e.g., contact precautions) limits the spread of MDROs. Active screening for high-risk organisms such as MRSA or VRE allows early detection and cohorting. However, these strategies require significant logistical coordination and can place psychological and social burdens on patients if prolonged (Tembo, 2024).

Antimicrobial Stewardship

Antimicrobial stewardship programs (ASPs) are integral to minimizing the emergence of drug-resistant pathogens. By promoting appropriate antibiotic prescribing and use, ASPs not only improve patient outcomes but also reduce selective pressure driving resistance (Dyar & Pulcini, 2017). However, these programs depend heavily on trained personnel, diagnostic support, and institutional commitment, all of which may be lacking in many settings.

Limitations of Conventional Approaches

While conventional IPC measures are necessary, they are often reactive rather than proactive. Their success is closely tied to human behaviour, making them vulnerable to lapses in compliance, especially during high workloads or public health crises such as the COVID-19 pandemic. In addition, these strategies do not provide continuous protection between cleaning cycles or shifts, leaving environmental reservoirs of pathogens inadequately addressed. These gaps have prompted interest in passive, technology-based interventions such as antimicrobial coatings and automated disinfection systems that offer persistent protection independent of staff compliance.

EMERGING ANTIMICROBIAL TECHNOLOGIES

The persistent burden of hospital-acquired infections (HAIs), coupled with the limitations of conventional infection control strategies, has spurred the development of novel antimicrobial technologies designed to provide continuous, passive protection against pathogens in healthcare environments that is shown in Table 2. Innovations in surface coatings, light-based disinfection, nanotechnology, and antimicrobial materials are leading this transformation (Cyphert & von Recum, 2017).

Antimicrobial Surface Coatings

Antimicrobial coatings are among the most rapidly adopted technologies in clinical settings. These coatings—applied to high-touch surfaces such as bed rails, curtains, and door handles—can offer prolonged biocidal or biostatic effects against a wide range of pathogens, including multidrug-resistant organisms (MDROs). Active agents in such coatings may include quaternary ammonium compounds, silver (Krishnan et al., 2020), copper, titanium dioxide, or advanced polymers such as MAP-1 (multilevel antimicrobial polymer (Cyphert & von Recum, 2017). These coatings have shown efficacy in reducing bacterial contamination for days to weeks, offering a low-maintenance solution for infection-prone environments (Jose et al., 2023).

The first commercially available antimicrobial coating was an anti-fouling yacht paint that was approved by the U.S. Environmental Protection Agency in 1970. Since then, substantial technologies have been developed to maximize antimicrobial efficiency, longevity, and durability. The antimicrobial mechanisms of these coatings can be categorized into three groups: (1) biocide-releasing coatings; (2) contact killing coatings (Farid, Han, Kwan, et al., 2025); (3) anti-adhesion coatings (Fu & Gray, 2021).

To enhance the antimicrobial efficiency, durability, and surface stability, one strategy is to design coatings that incorporate numerous antimicrobial mechanisms. For example, hybrid ENMs that combine polycationic polymer with biocidal metals can effectively inactivate pathogenic bacteria through the coordinated reactions of polycationic polymers, metal ions, and toxic free radicals; the polymer holds the biocide in a softer layer of the coating, releasing biocides over time, while the biocides can help improve the antimicrobial efficiency and mechanical durability of the coating.

Light-Based and UVC Disinfection

Ultraviolet-C (UVC) disinfection systems use short-wavelength light that lies within the range of 100–280 nm of the light spectrum (typically 254 nm) to disrupt the DNA and RNA of microorganisms. UVC robots or fixed units can be deployed in unoccupied hospital rooms to achieve terminal disinfection, effectively reducing bioburden on surfaces (Astrid et al., 2021). Pulsed xenon UVC and far-UVC (222 nm) technologies are emerging as safer, more targeted options with reduced human health risks (Bhardwaj et al., 2021). The challenge of controlling SARS-CoV-2 indicated that active surface decontamination technologies are needed as part of multimodal approach with traditional environmental cleaning procedures. Achieving this goal, account for the complex environment, has rendered it necessary to stand–alone light disinfection and to be vigilant of its side effects for applicators.

The current craze upon dimmers and day–night switches raise the problem of the side–effects of light on biology and species' rights. The intensive use of UV-C light for disinfection includes several applications in food and beverage, municipal water and air treatment, and laundry in hotels, hospitals, and public institutions. Most of the different light sources designed for disinfection environments include UVC light. While the invention of disinfection devices with low-pressure mercury, the use of pulsed xenon, in combination with mercury, gained interest (Bergman, 2021). In addition to the surface disinfection, a variety of devices incorporated UVC light for aqueous media treatment.

Robotic Disinfection Systems

Often found in isolation rooms, surgery rooms, and public areas, UCV lights are deployed to disinfect surfaces (Bratu et al., 2024). Commercial systems utilize either fixed or mobile UV-C lights to effectively disinfect built environments. Robots also have been developed for no-touch cleaning and disinfection and now play a vital role in built environments. The need for flexible manipulation in built environments has been considered in the design of a mobile robot that autonomously builds 3D models of surfaces and reconfigures cleaning actions using a hybrid cleaning system. The robots applied phases of cleaning and disinfection in a two-phase process. During the disinfection phase, robots with UV lamps disinfect areas that are not used by people, while in use areas are disinfected as requested. To achieve thorough coverage, robots autonomously decide on the cleaning area and build a corresponding motion path plan.

Copper and Metal-Based Surfaces

Copper and its alloys possess inherent antimicrobial properties, capable of inactivating bacteria, fungi, and viruses upon contact. Clinical trials have demonstrated that replacing high-touch surfaces with copper components can lead to a significant reduction in HAI rates (Abraham et al., 2021). The antimicrobial action of copper is linked to membrane damage, protein denaturation, and reactive oxygen species (ROS) generation.

Nanotechnology and Self-Disinfecting Materials

Nanomaterials offer new possibilities in designing self-disinfecting surfaces with enhanced efficacy. Silver nanoparticles (AgNPs), zinc oxide (ZnO), and carbon-based nanostructures have been integrated into textiles, plastics, and coatings to create surfaces with broad-spectrum antimicrobial activity (Ghosh et al., 2025). These materials work through ion release, oxidative stress, and membrane disruption. Challenges remain in scaling production, maintaining safety, and preventing environmental toxicity.

Table 2. Antimicrobial technology summary

Technology	Mechanism of Action	Effectiveness	Limitations
Antimicrobial Surface Coatings (e.g., MAP-1)	Disrupts microbial membranes and proteins via chemical or polymer-based antimicrobial agents	Broad-spectrum, long-lasting (weeks), effective in reducing surface bioburden	May require periodic reapplication; limited regulation; efficacy depends on application quality
UV-C Disinfection Systems	Damages DNA/RNA through short-wavelength UV light (254 nm or 222 nm)	High efficacy for terminal room disinfection, especially against spores and MDROs	Requires trained staff, downtime for rooms, line-of-sight limitations
Copper and Metal-Based Surfaces	Continuous microbial killing via ion release and ROS generation on contact	Proven reduction in HAI rates in ICU settings, persistent action	High cost, infrastructure changes needed, limited scalability in older facilities
Nanomaterials (e.g., AgNPs, ZnO)	Ion release, oxidative stress, and membrane disruption at nanoscale	Broad-spectrum, lab-validated, potentially strong with design optimization	Environmental and safety concerns; scalability and regulatory issues
Self-Disinfecting Textiles	Embedded antimicrobial agents kill or inhibit microbes upon contact	Effective against bacteria and fungi in controlled studies, variable in field	Durability and performance vary with laundering; standardization lacking

DATA ANALYTICS IN INFECTION CONTROL

Emerging technologies like wearable devices, smartphone applications, and telehealth connected devices form the centrepiece of a new and innovative shift to empower patients, with potentially enormous positive impacts on their health and well-being. Many IoT devices have recently emerged on the market, often referred to as wearable or mobile health devices, such as smartwatches, wristbands, and connected thermometers, that monitor physiological signals related to health status. Specifically, wearable and smartphone-based fall detection devices, together with geolocation data from smartphone applications, have been reported to have potential in controlling the pandemic.

The application of advanced analytics in epidemic control has been showcased in the development of the specialized field of outbreak analytics, in which a variety of mathematical and computational approaches, and data sources ranging from traditional statistical health data reporting to modern genomic data, have been employed to inform the response to emerging infectious diseases. Outbreak analytics is an emerging data science to transform outbreak event and response data into actionable information to aid public health decision-making. Despite rapid developments in this emerging discipline, a better understanding is needed of the technical principles underpinning this data science, its connection with other approaches, its existing limitations, and the data routing and modeling conduits through which it is used in response to outbreaks.

Big Data in Healthcare

Recent advances in diagnostic tools—such as high-throughput sequencing, electron microscopy, and advanced imaging—have revolutionized disease identification and treatment. These innovations generate vast datasets, introducing new challenges in data management and interpretation. The rise of Big Data has catalyzed the use of machine learning (ML), a subset of artificial intelligence (AI), to derive meaningful patterns from complex healthcare datasets. In infection control, ML can support outbreak prediction, antimicrobial resistance monitoring, and pathogen classification, enabling more effective, evidence-driven interventions in hospital and long-term care environments.

Predictive Analytics for Outbreak Management

Accurately forecasting infectious disease outbreaks depends on high-quality data, reliable models, and appropriate analytical tools. Despite advancements, epidemic forecasting—especially around early immunity dynamics—remains underdeveloped

(Bershteyn et al., 2022). The rise of novel pathogens such as SARS, MERS, and Zika highlights the need for real-time analytics and improved surveillance systems. Outbreak prediction remains limited by data fragmentation and the complex nature of pathogen-host-environment interactions. Yet, emerging resources and computational methods show promise for identifying early warning signals, supporting preparedness, and guiding targeted public health interventions.

CASE STUDIES AND FIELD TRIALS

Field trials play a critical role in validating the efficacy, safety, and feasibility of emerging antimicrobial technologies beyond controlled laboratory environments. Real-world evaluations in diverse healthcare settings—such as long-term care facilities (LTCFs), intensive care units (ICUs), and general hospital wards—offer crucial insights into how these innovations perform in routine clinical practice. Such studies also help determine operational compatibility, cost-efficiency, and user acceptability, all of which are pivotal for sustainable implementation.

One prominent example is the deployment of MAP-1, a multilevel antimicrobial polymer coating, on bedding materials in LTCF in Hong Kong. In these trials, the coating demonstrated sustained reductions in total viable bacterial loads—including multidrug-resistant organisms (MDROs) like *Staphylococcus aureus* (MRSA) and vancomycin-resistant *Enterococci* (VRE)—across several weeks of active use. Even with standard laundering and cleaning practices, the treated textiles maintained their antimicrobial activity, indicating real-world durability. Importantly, no adverse effects were observed, and residents were informed and accepting of the intervention (Farid, Han, Kwan, et al., 2025).

In another landmark study, copper alloy surfaces were installed on high-touch items such as bed rails, call buttons, and IV poles in ICUs. A randomized controlled trial conducted in the United States demonstrated that patients in copper-treated rooms had significantly lower rates of HAIs compared to those in control rooms. This was attributed to copper's continuous biocidal activity, which reduces surface contamination without requiring reapplication (Albarqouni et al., 2020).

Additionally, UV-C disinfection robots have been used to supplement terminal cleaning of patient rooms. Trials have shown that UV-C deployment significantly reduces environmental contamination by *Clostridioides difficile* and other pathogens. These systems, however, require trained operators, unoccupied rooms, and clear protocols to avoid human exposure (Astrid et al., 2021).

These examples demonstrate that when carefully selected and integrated, antimicrobial technologies can enhance infection control outcomes. However, success often depends on multidisciplinary coordination, proper staff training, and administrative support. The lessons learned from field trials reinforce the need for context-sensitive implementation plans and underscore the value of combining passive and active disinfection strategies within broader IPC programs.

COMPARATIVE EVALUATION OF TECHNOLOGIES

As healthcare systems increasingly consider integrating innovative antimicrobial technologies, objective comparisons are essential to guide decision-making. These evaluations must weigh not only microbiological efficacy but also cost-effectiveness, safety, durability, ease of implementation, and compatibility with existing infection prevention and control (IPC) programs.

Microbial Efficacy and Spectrum of Action

Antimicrobial coatings—such as those incorporating MAP-1 polymers or metallic nanoparticles—demonstrate broad-spectrum activity against gram-positive and gram-negative bacteria, fungi, and viruses. While laboratory conditions often show near-complete microbial inhibition, field studies reveal more nuanced performance depending on surface type, microbial load, and cleaning practices (Farid, Han, Kwan, et al., 2025). In contrast, UV-C disinfection systems offer rapid, consistent decontamination of room surfaces but are limited to line-of-sight coverage and require human oversight and time between patients.

Cost and Operational Feasibility

The financial implications of each technology vary significantly. For example, antimicrobial coatings are typically low-cost and easy to apply, offering weeks to months of protection per application. UV-C robots entail higher upfront investment, ongoing maintenance, and dedicated staff time but may offer significant savings by reducing HAIs in high-risk areas such as ICUs (Megalingam et al., 2025). Copper surfaces, while effective, require infrastructure modification and may be more suitable for newly built facilities or targeted retrofitting.

Sustainability and Safety

Metallic nanoparticles and polymer coatings must be evaluated not only for efficacy but also for environmental safety and cytotoxicity. Coatings like MAP-1 have been shown to be non-toxic to human skin and mucosa and are stable under repeated cleaning and exposure (Farid, 2019). On the other hand, excessive reliance on disinfectants or misapplication of nanomaterials may contribute to ecological burden or resistance development if not regulated appropriately.

Integration with Existing IPC Frameworks

Ease of integration is a major determinant of technology uptake. Passive systems (e.g., coatings, copper) require minimal behavioral change and can operate independently. Active technologies (e.g., UV-C) require scheduling, coordination, and staff training. The most successful interventions are those that enhance existing practices without disrupting care workflows. Technologies that are simple to adopt, require little maintenance, and do not rely heavily on compliance tend to offer the greatest long-term benefit.

GLOBAL CHALLENGES AND IMPLEMENTATION BARRIERS

While emerging antimicrobial technologies hold significant promise, their global adoption remains limited due to a complex set of regulatory, financial, infrastructural, and cultural challenges (Figure 4). Bridging the gap between innovation and routine clinical use requires addressing these systemic barriers across varied healthcare contexts.

Regulatory Complexity and Product Classification

Many antimicrobial technologies—especially coatings, smart materials, and nanotechnology-based interventions—fall outside traditional regulatory categories. They may not be clearly classified as medical devices, disinfectants, or therapeutic agents, which complicates registration, approval, and funding pathways. Regulatory bodies in different countries often lack harmonized frameworks, making it difficult for manufacturers to scale across borders (Exner et al., 2020). Moreover, there is no universally accepted standard for evaluating the real-world effectiveness of antimicrobial surfaces or light-based disinfection systems. This lack of standardization hampers comparisons between products and delays procurement decisions by hospitals and governments.

Financial and Infrastructural Limitations

Cost remains a primary concern, particularly in low- and middle-income countries (LMICs) where healthcare budgets are constrained and infection control infrastructure may be lacking. While some technologies (e.g., antimicrobial coatings) are relatively inexpensive, others such as UV-C disinfection robots or copper retrofitting require significant capital investment. Additionally, procurement cycles and cost-benefit justifications often favor short-term savings over long-term prevention outcomes, making it harder to fund preventive technologies.

Facilities in LMICs may also face logistical barriers such as inconsistent power supply, lack of trained maintenance personnel, and competing public health priorities, all of which impede implementation of advanced infection control solutions (Vilar-Compte et al., 2017).

Operational and Cultural Challenges

Implementation of new technologies is rarely just a technical matter—it is also behavioral and institutional. Resistance from healthcare workers, insufficient training, and lack of clarity around responsibilities can diminish the impact of even the most effective interventions. In some settings, IPC is not prioritized in leadership or policy agendas, resulting in limited accountability or follow-through. Moreover, there is often a lack of integration between infection control teams and hospital operations, leading to fragmented efforts. Without sustained leadership support, clear operational protocols, and user engagement, technologies may fail to deliver their expected benefit.

Figure 4. Illustrating global barriers to antimicrobial technology, (A–D)

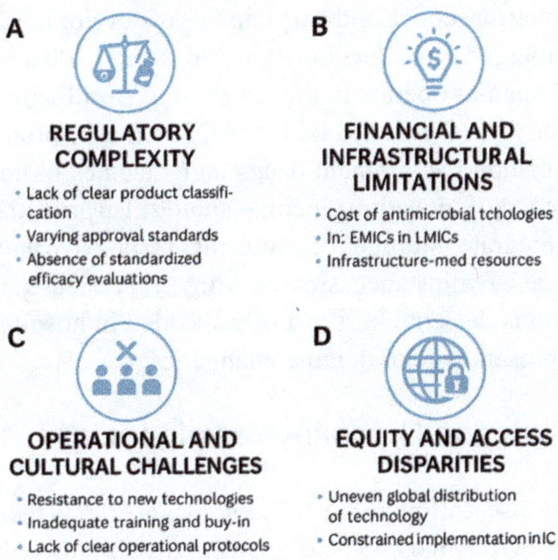

FUTURE DIRECTIONS AND POLICY RECOMMENDATIONS

As antimicrobial technologies mature, their integration into healthcare systems must be guided by evidence-based policies, equitable implementation models, and a vision for long-term sustainability. Future progress depends not only on continued innovation but also on creating enabling environments where such innovations can thrive.

Research Priorities and Innovation Pipelines

Robust, multi-site clinical research is essential to validate the long-term efficacy, safety, and cost-effectiveness of antimicrobial technologies. While laboratory and pilot-scale studies have demonstrated promising results, there is a pressing need for large-scale, randomized controlled trials across diverse healthcare settings and patient populations. Such studies should focus on real-world effectiveness, durability under routine use, and interactions with existing IPC measures (Attieh et al., 2014). A global public-private effort is necessary to expand the quantity and quality of innovative research and development (R&D) to combat newly emerging infectious disease threats like avian flu and SARS. Efforts are needed to help the underdeveloped world build the R&D capacity, technology infrastructure, and skilled scientific workforce needed to be effective partners in this initiative.

Major pharmaceutical companies have entirely adequate resources. But low-cost biologicals companies need international assistance to build their R&D capacity. A biotechnology-based pharmaceutical industry capable of developing and manufacturing new products has emerged in the developing world. Nearly 400 biotechnology-based pharmaceutical companies operate in the developing world with a market today of over $2.5 billion per year (Semete-Makokotlela, 2015). The products they develop, and manufacture include recombinant drugs and vaccines biologicals, of desired high quality and potency. Innovation pipelines should also prioritize next-generation technologies that integrate intelligent monitoring, responsive antimicrobial action, and eco-safe materials. For instance, smart coatings that release antimicrobials only when contamination is detected, or sensors embedded in hospital surfaces to alert cleaning teams, represent potential game-changers.

Policy Integration and Guideline Development

Despite their promise, antimicrobial technologies are rarely mentioned in national or international IPC guidelines. Governments and public health agencies should consider updating these frameworks to include validated technologies as part of multimodal IPC strategies. Policies should provide clear definitions, recommended use-cases, and performance thresholds for procurement and quality assurance. Incentivizing innovation through fast-track regulatory approval, innovation grants, and public procurement targets can accelerate adoption. Public-private partnerships, especially those focused on hospital safety and climate-resilient infrastructure, offer opportunities to align infection control with broader healthcare reform goals.

Sustainable Procurement and Environmental Considerations

As healthcare systems face pressure to reduce their carbon and chemical footprints, antimicrobial technologies must be evaluated for their environmental impact. Materials that leach toxic compounds or rely on frequent replacement can undermine sustainability goals. Conversely, technologies that reduce the need for chemical disinfectants or extend the lifespan of healthcare textiles contribute positively to both IPC and environmental agendas (Alruwaili et al., 2023). Future policies should mandate lifecycle assessments and promote the use of green-certified technologies in healthcare environments. Aligning antimicrobial innovation with sustainable procurement policies can foster environmentally conscious healthcare delivery.

Integration of AI in Infection Control

Infection control tasks and workflows necessitate a high level of expertise. Assimilating the knowledge and skills required for healthcare personnel, such as epidemiology, microbiology, and infectious diseases, is difficult due to the complexity and constantly evolving nature of such areas. Advanced data processing and analytical assets must be carefully developed and allocated. A unified software framework that integrates medical condition monitoring, risk assessment, and AI-enabled infection control activities is envisioned (Ahmed, 2024). Such a framework can help healthcare personnel effortlessly coordinate the participants of the healthcare setting in real-time monitoring of infectious risks and in judiciously scheduled infection control measures. Researchers anticipate the advent of cloud-based AI-enhanced health analytics as a significant step toward an interoperable system. Such analytics comprise portable digital devices that collect infectious pathogen and patient health data and user-friendly data visualization tools that do not require any technical knowledge for use. AI enables the knowledge and skills of experts in the field of infection control to be encoded as algorithms.

Once trained using enough data, such automation can effortlessly produce results with accuracy comparable or even superior to human experts. The resultant products, such as data-analytic algorithms and maintenance tasks, are automated and efficient, making them readily accessible to end-users, including healthcare personnel just out of training or with little education background. Such accessibility helps enhance the impact and equity of infection control technologies in different healthcare settings. Computation and machine learning platforms for real-time processing of healthcare data and analytics-as-a-service capability in cloud settings should also be added to help ameliorate logistical burdens in healthcare settings with poor data and computing equipment. A higher level of local intelligence, including real-time activity adjustment and control strategies, should also be built-in consideration for better feasibility in developing healthcare settings. New antimicrobial agents with mechanisms different from existing ones should be invented to stay ahead of adapted bacteria in the use of antibiotics.

Capacity Building and Global Coordination

Capacity building—particularly in LMICs—is essential to ensure equitable uptake. Investments in workforce training, infrastructure, and local manufacturing capacity can help close the implementation gap. In addition, global collaboration is needed to harmonize regulatory standards, create shared evidence repositories, and develop implementation toolkits that are adaptable to different resource settings. Organizations such as the WHO, Africa CDC, and the Global AMR R&D Hub can lead in facilitating these efforts by offering technical guidance, mobilizing funding, and promoting cross-country learning.

NEXT-GENERATION SEQUENCING AND AIRBORNE TRANSMISSION CONTROL IN INFECTION SURVEILLANCE

Emerging infectious disease threats demand more precise and rapid diagnostic technologies for effective outbreak investigation and infection control. Among these, Next-Generation Sequencing (NGS) has emerged as a transformative tool in hospital microbiology and epidemiology (Hilt & Ferrieri, 2022). NGS enables comprehensive genomic analysis of pathogens, providing detailed information about species identification, antimicrobial resistance genes, and phylogenetic relationships. Unlike traditional culture or PCR-based assays, NGS can identify multiple pathogens in a single run—including novel, rare, or unexpected organisms—and can be applied directly to clinical or environmental samples. This high-resolution capability is particularly valuable in complex hospital environments, where multidrug-resistant organisms (MDROs) pose an increasing threat to patient safety.

NGS has several key applications in hospital-based infection surveillance. It allows for rapid outbreak investigation by enabling whole-genome comparisons between clinical isolates, helping infection control teams determine whether patients are infected with genetically related strains. This helps confirm or refute suspected nosocomial transmission. Moreover, NGS supports real-time surveillance of antimicrobial resistance by detecting the presence of resistance genes and mobile genetic elements such as plasmids, providing insight into how resistance is acquired and disseminated within healthcare facilities. The use of metagenomics for environmental monitoring also shows promise, particularly in identifying non-culturable or low-abundance pathogens in critical care areas (Ko et al., 2022). Collectively, these capabilities position NGS as a powerful complement to traditional microbiological methods and a cornerstone of genomic epidemiology in infection control.

In parallel, renewed focus on airborne transmission of infectious agents has highlighted the need for robust environmental controls in hospitals. The COVID-19 pandemic reinforced that aerosolized particle could remain suspended in the air and contribute significantly to the spread of respiratory pathogens such as SARS-CoV-2, influenza viruses, and Mycobacterium tuberculosis. This has relevance in high-risk settings such as intensive care units, operating theatres, and emergency departments, where aerosol-generating procedures are routinely performed. Effective mitigation strategies therefore require a combination of mechanical ventilation, filtration, and air disinfection technologies.

Ventilation systems play a pivotal role in reducing the concentration of airborne pathogens. Hospital wards and isolation rooms should meet specific air exchange rates to ensure adequate dilution and removal of infectious aerosols. For instance, general hospital wards are typically recommended to maintain at least six air changes per hour, while operating rooms require twelve or more. Directional airflow and negative pressure rooms further enhance containment of airborne particles. In addition to mechanical ventilation, air purification technologies offer an added layer of defense. High-Efficiency Particulate Air (HEPA) filters are widely used in healthcare settings due to their ability to capture particles as small as 0.3 microns, including bacteria, fungi, and viruses (Dubey et al., 2021). Ultraviolet Germicidal Irradiation (UVGI), particularly UV-C systems integrated into HVAC ducts or upper-room air zones, has demonstrated efficacy in inactivating airborne pathogens. While newer technologies such as plasma air sterilizers, ionization, and photocatalytic oxidation are being explored, further validation is needed to confirm their effectiveness in clinical environments.

Integration of environmental controls with surveillance technologies offers a new frontier in infection prevention. Real-time air sampling and microbial monitoring provide insights into the microbial burden in patient areas, particularly during outbreaks or in response to environmental changes (Stahl-Rommel et al., 2021). These data, when linked to patient infection records and genomic findings, can help pinpoint potential airborne transmission routes and identify specific zones requiring intensified control measures. For instance, microbial signatures recovered from air filters or HVAC condensates can be sequenced using NGS to detect and trace potential pathogens before clinical infections are reported. This proactive approach represents a paradigm shift in surveillance, from reactive response to predictive prevention.

Looking ahead, the convergence of genomics and airborne environmental monitoring holds significant promise for the next generation of hospital infection control. As sequencing platforms become faster, more affordable, and more automated, and as environmental sensors grow increasingly sophisticated, hospitals are expected to move toward integrated, real-time infection surveillance systems. However, successful implementation will depend on addressing challenges related to cost, data interpretation, interoperability, and staff training. It is equally important to ensure that ethical considerations—including data privacy, informed consent, and responsible AI use—are embedded within these technological frameworks. Ultimately, integrating NGS and air purification strategies into routine practice offers a more holistic and anticipatory model of infection control, capable of responding to current and future threats with greater precision and agility.

ETHICAL CONSIDERATIONS IN INFECTION CONTROL

Infection prevention and control (IPC) policies in health care settings attempt to prevent transmission of pathogens among patients, health care workers and the community at large. Severe acute respiratory syndrome SARS and coronavirus (SARS-CoV-2) may spread efficiently among patients and staff of a hospital. Therefore, it is essential that hospitals adopt stringent IPC precautions designed to minimize the risk of transmission of this infection. However, before implementing IPC precautions, an ethical framework should be developed to ensure balance and proportionality.

An ethical framework designed for hospital infection control must include several functions. First, it must provide a process for open and engaging dialogue about the risks and values underpinning decisions, particularly in difficult situations. Second, it must identify concrete ethical challenges that arise in hospital infection control. SARS-CoV-2 is highly contagious in health care settings, particularly for patients requiring aerosol-generating procedures (Pasnick et al., 2020). This hospital 'outbreak' of infections will lead to increased mortality because hospitals are places of high-risk patients with complex chronic diseases. The substantial cost to implement recommendations regarding the use of the N95 or higher respirators in a wide variety of procedures may also cause unreasonable burdens on health care facilities. Thus, there is a need to develop a framework for IISs that is transparent, accountable, nimble, and can rapidly respond to changing evidence. The development of a synthesis of existing recommendations considering these factors will facilitate tailoring.

Patient Privacy and Data Security

Public health research often relies on sensitive health information to prevent epidemics, control outbreaks of disease, and find causes of diseases and other health problems. This often means maintaining the privacy and security of such information. Privacy means that the research subjects are not identifiable. In contrast, security means that the identifiable data, even if it were to fall into someone's hands, remain inaccessible to non-essential personnel. Attempts to appease increased scrutiny from ethical review boards and information technology groups may stifle research advancement as increasingly complicated privacy and security requirements preclude efforts to glean useful epidemiological results from data (Salerno et al., 2023).

Data security before warding off intrusions and hacking is now emerging as an important consideration for keeping the data safe from attacks by insiders and others able to successfully infiltrate internal networks. Recent examples of such security breaches illustrate this risk. Repercussions of these privacy breaches from the perspective of research data are also examined Imposing privacy controls has long been conceived of as a matter of removing identifying features from data. Broadly stated, statistical disclosure control techniques attempt to add noise to sensitive data, through methods as varied as sampling and non-randomized methods, such that the qualitative conclusions drawn from the data are retained while specific features are rendered private.

Equity in Access to Technologies

Emerging infectious control technologies (EICTs) that have been proven effective in epidemiologically unique settings must be translated to other cultures, structures, and environments if global knowledge equity is to be achieved. This step is (at each locus) expected to generate capacity-building problems similar to those faced during initial technology generation, as where no domestic design, manufacturing, or marketing capacity previously existed, viability and effectiveness can be socioeconomic issues in isolation. Technological equity thus can only emerge as a global effort, with debate inevitably turning to how the costs should be shared between different countries and social groups. Analogous debates must occur over technology priority-setting.

There is the cost-sharing issue involving nation-states as development has become a global phenomenon, something previously monopolized by the industrialized world. Knowledge is heterogeneous – it not only depends on the depth covered but also how wide it is applicable. Different states had been able to competently support their people's economic growth and social equity using the very same technologies. Widely argued in the context of different technologies being better or worse suited to different milieu, it should similarly be believed that countries with their own means should themselves develop or adapt these technologies: in other words, no "one-size-fits-all" designs or solutions exist.

As clearer national roles have emerged and a cadre of versatile, capable actors, both public and private, can be seen, distributions of responsibility and capabilities must also be agreed. Capacity-building responsibilities should be determined by the potential public health threat posed by pathogens easily transmitted internationally (Rao et al., 2017). With 80 percent of global disease burden borne by developing countries, gross inequity of knowledge exists.

CONCLUSION

Hospital-acquired infections (HAIs) remain a persistent global health challenge, undermining patient safety, burdening healthcare systems, and accelerating antimicrobial resistance. Traditional infection prevention and control (IPC) strategies—such as hand hygiene, environmental cleaning, and antimicrobial stewardship—are foundational but increasingly strained under the weight of evolving microbial threats and systemic limitations. These conventional approaches, while essential, often rely heavily on human compliance and provide limited protection between active interventions.

In response, a new generation of antimicrobial technologies has emerged, offering passive, persistent, and scalable solutions. Surface coatings, nanomaterials, UV-C disinfection systems, and antimicrobial textiles have demonstrated their potential to enhance microbial control across a wide range of clinical settings. When deployed effectively, these innovations can reduce environmental contamination, interrupt transmission pathways, and support a more resilient IPC infrastructure. Evidence from laboratory studies and real-world field trials confirms that these technologies are not only feasible but impactful, particularly when integrated into multimodal IPC programs. Moreover, their utility extends beyond high-income settings; innovations such as antimicrobial coatings and copper-infused materials are increasingly accessible and adaptable for use in resource-limited environments.

Nonetheless, the path to widespread adoption remains complex. Regulatory ambiguity, funding constraints, workforce readiness, and global inequities in access continue to pose significant implementation barriers. To bridge these gaps, targeted policy reforms, international collaboration, and evidence-informed investments are urgently needed. Looking ahead, the convergence of innovation, policy, and equity offers an unprecedented opportunity to reshape how healthcare systems approach infection control. With coordinated leadership and sustained commitment, antimicrobial technologies can become not just experimental tools, but integral components of modern, sustainable healthcare.

REFERENCES

Abad, F. S., Aboubakr, S. E., & Mohammed, A. S. (2024). The impact of Clostridium Difficile Infection in the UK hospitals. *Derna Academy Journal for Applied Sciences*, *2*(2), 211–219. DOI: 10.71147/j80a5a66

Abraham, J., Dowling, K., & Florentine, S. (2021). Can copper products and surfaces reduce the spread of infectious microorganisms and hospital-acquired infections? *Materials (Basel)*, *14*(13), 3444. DOI: 10.3390/ma14133444 PMID: 34206230

Adedire, O., Love, N. K., Hughes, H. E., Buchan, I., Vivancos, R., & Elliot, A. J. (2024). Early detection and monitoring of gastrointestinal infections using syndromic surveillance: A systematic review. *International Journal of Environmental Research and Public Health*, *21*(4), 489. DOI: 10.3390/ijerph21040489 PMID: 38673400

Ahmed, T. (2024). *AI-enabled healthcare sector: futures business models*. T. Ahmed.

Albarqouni, L., Byambasuren, O., Clark, J., Scott, A. M., Looke, D., & Glasziou, P. (2020). Does copper treatment of commonly touched surfaces reduce healthcare-acquired infections? A systematic review and meta-analysis. *The Journal of Hospital Infection*, *106*(4), 765–773. DOI: 10.1016/j.jhin.2020.09.005 PMID: 32916212

Allegranzi, B. B. N. S. C. C. G. W. A. H. D. L., & Pittet, D. (2011). Burden of endemic health-care-associated infection in developing countries: Systematic review and meta-analysis. *Lancet*, *377*(9761), 228–241. DOI: 10.1016/S0140-6736(10)61458-4 PMID: 21146207

Allen, M. J. (2016). *Preventing infections through cleaner hospitals (PITCH)-A novel targeted hospital environmental hygiene bundle*. Queensland University of Technology. DOI: 10.5204/thesis.eprints.99603

Alruwaili, R. F., Alsadaan, N., Alruwaili, A. N., & Alrumayh, A. G. (2023). Unveiling the symbiosis of Environmental Sustainability and Infection Control in Health Care settings: A systematic review. *Sustainability (Basel)*, *15*(22), 15728. DOI: 10.3390/su152215728

Astrid, F., Beata, Z., Julia, E., Elisabeth, P., & Magda, D.-E.Van den Nest Miriam. (2021). The use of a UV-C disinfection robot in the routine cleaning process: A field study in an Academic hospital. *Antimicrobial Resistance and Infection Control*, *10*(1), 84. DOI: 10.1186/s13756-021-00945-4 PMID: 34051861

Attieh, R., Gagnon, M.-P., & Krein, S. L. (2014). How can implementing an infection prevention and control (IPC) technology transform healthcare practices and outcomes for patients? *Healthcare Infection*, *19*(3), 81–88. DOI: 10.1071/HI14003

Badinski, T., Seiffert, S. N., Grässli, F., Babouee Flury, B., Besold, U., Betschon, E., Biggel, M., Brucher, A., Cusini, A., Dörr, T., Egli, A., Goppel, S., Güsewell, S., Keller, J., von Kietzell, M., Möller, J. C., Nolte, O., Ortner, M., Roloff, T., & Kohler, P. (2024). Colonization with resistant bacteria in hospital employees: An epidemiological surveillance and typing study. *Antimicrobial Agents and Chemotherapy*, *68*(11), e00985–e00924. DOI: 10.1128/aac.00985-24 PMID: 39324817

Barancheshme, F., & Munir, M. (2018). Strategies to combat antibiotic resistance in hospital wastewater. *Environment International*, *121*, 127–138.

Bergman, R. S. (2021). Germicidal UV sources and systems. *Photochemistry and Photobiology*, *97*(3), 466–470. DOI: 10.1111/php.13387 PMID: 33497482

Bershteyn, A., Kim, H.-Y., & Braithwaite, R. S. (2022). Real-time infectious disease modeling to inform emergency public health decision making. *Annual Review of Public Health*, *43*(1), 397–418. DOI: 10.1146/annurev-publhealth-052220-093319 PMID: 34995131

Bhardwaj, S. K., Singh, H., Deep, A., Khatri, M., Bhaumik, J., Kim, K.-H., & Bhardwaj, N. (2021). UVC-based photoinactivation as an efficient tool to control the transmission of coronaviruses. *The Science of the Total Environment*, *792*, 148548. DOI: 10.1016/j.scitotenv.2021.148548 PMID: 34465056

Boyce, J. M. (2007). Environmental contamination makes an important contribution to hospital infection. *The Journal of Hospital Infection*, *65*, 50–54. DOI: 10.1016/S0195-6701(07)60015-2 PMID: 17540242

Bratu, D.-V., Zolya, M.-A., & Moraru, S.-A. (2024). RoboCoV cleaner: An indoor autonomous UV-C disinfection robot with advanced dual-safety systems. *Sensors (Basel)*, *24*(3), 974. DOI: 10.3390/s24030974 PMID: 38339691

Cassini, A., Högberg, L. D., Plachouras, D., Quattrocchi, A., Hoxha, A., Simonsen, G. S., Colomb-Cotinat, M., Kretzschmar, M. E., Devleesschauwer, B., Cecchini, M., Ouakrim, D. A., Oliveira, T. C., Struelens, M. J., Suetens, C., Monnet, D. L., Strauss, R., Mertens, K., Struyf, T., Catry, B., & Hopkins, S. (2019). Attributable deaths and disability-adjusted life-years caused by infections with antibiotic-resistant bacteria in the EU and the European Economic Area. *The Lancet. Infectious Diseases*, *19*(1), 56–66. DOI: 10.1016/S1473-3099(18)30605-4 PMID: 30409683

Cdc. (2019). Antibiotic resistance threats in the United States, 2019. https://www.cdc.gov/drugresistance/pdf/threats-report/2019-ar-threats-report-508.pdf

Chatterjee, P.. (2017). Antimicrobial coatings for medical textiles. *Chemical Society Reviews*, *46*(14), 3865–3885.

Chowdhary, A. S. C., & Meis, J. F. (2017). Candida auris: A rapidly emerging cause of hospital-acquired multidrug-resistant fungal infections globally. *PLoS Pathogens, 13*(5), e1006290. DOI: 10.1371/journal.ppat.1006290 PMID: 28542486

Cyphert, E. L., & von Recum, H. A. (2017). Emerging technologies for long-term antimicrobial device coatings: Advantages and limitations. *Experimental Biology and Medicine, 242*(8), 788–798. DOI: 10.1177/1535370216688572 PMID: 28110543

Dancer, S. J. (2009). The role of environmental cleaning in the control of hospital-acquired infection. *The Journal of Hospital Infection, 73*(4), 378–385. DOI: 10.1016/j.jhin.2009.03.030 PMID: 19726106

. Divatia, J., Pulinilkunnathil, J. G., & Myatra, S. N. (2020). Nosocomial infections and ventilator-associated pneumonia in cancer patients. *Oncologic Critical Care*, 1419-1439.

Dubey, S., Rohra, H., & Taneja, A. (2021). Assessing effectiveness of air purifiers (HEPA) for controlling indoor particulate pollution. *Heliyon, 7*(9), e07976. DOI: 10.1016/j.heliyon.2021.e07976 PMID: 34568599

Dyar, O. J. H. B. S. J., & Pulcini, C. (2017). What is antimicrobial stewardship? *Clinical Microbiology and Infection, 23*(11), 793–798. DOI: 10.1016/j.cmi.2017.08.026 PMID: 28882725

El Arab, R. A., Almoosa, Z., Alkhunaizi, M., Abuadas, F. H., & Somerville, J. (2025). Artificial intelligence in hospital infection prevention: An integrative review. *Frontiers in Public Health, 13*, 1547450. DOI: 10.3389/fpubh.2025.1547450 PMID: 40241963

Exner, M., Bhattacharya, S., Gebel, J., Goroncy-Bermes, P., Hartemann, P., Heeg, P., Ilschner, C., Kramer, A., Ling, M. L., & Merkens, W. (2020). Chemical disinfection in healthcare settings: Critical aspects for the development of global strategies. *GMS Hygiene and Infection Control, 15*, Doc36. PMID: 33520601

. Farid, A. (2019). *Safe antimicrobial systems for infection control in healthcare settings*

Farid, A., Han, W., Kwan, J. K., & Yeung, K. L. (2025). Enhancing bedding hygiene in long-term care facilities: Investigating the impact of multilevel antimicrobial polymers (MAP-1) on bacterial and MDRO reduction. *Antimicrobial Resistance and Infection Control, 14*(1), 36. DOI: 10.1186/s13756-025-01555-0 PMID: 40270052

. Farid, A., Han, W., Lai, C. K., Kwan, J. K., & Yeung, K. L. (2025). Clinical Evaluation of MAP-1 Antimicrobial Coating on Patient Privacy Curtains: Insights from a Randomized Trial in a Hong Kong Hospital. *Journal of Hospital Infection*.

Franklin, D., Barbre, K., Rowe, T. A., Reses, H. E., Massey, J., Meng, L., Dollard, P., Dubendris, H., Stillions, M., Robinson, L., Clerville, J. W., Slifka, K. J., Benin, A., & Bell, J. M. (2024). COVID-19 vaccination coverage, and rates of SARS-CoV-2 infection and COVID-19–associated hospitalization among residents in nursing homes—National Healthcare Safety Network, United States, October 2023–February 2024. *MMWR. Morbidity and Mortality Weekly Report*, *73*(15), 73. DOI: 10.15585/mmwr.mm7315a3 PMID: 38635474

Fu, H., & Gray, K. A. (2021). The key to maximizing the benefits of antimicrobial and self-cleaning coatings is to fully determine their risks. *Current Opinion in Chemical Engineering*, *34*, 100761. DOI: 10.1016/j.coche.2021.100761 PMID: 36569284

Ghosh, J., Rupanty, N. S., Noor, T., Asif, T. R., Islam, T., & Reukov, V. (2025). Functional coatings for textiles: Advancements in flame resistance, antimicrobial defense, and self-cleaning performance. *RSC Advances*, *15*(14), 10984–11022. DOI: 10.1039/D5RA01429H PMID: 40201212

Hao, R., Liu, Y., Shen, W., Zhao, R., Jiang, B., Song, H., Yan, M., & Ma, H. (2022). Surveillance of emerging infectious diseases for biosecurity. *Science China. Life Sciences*, *65*(8), 1504–1516. DOI: 10.1007/s11427-021-2071-x PMID: 35287183

Haque, M. S. M. M. J., & Abu Bakar, M. (2018). Health care-associated infections – an overview. *Infection and Drug Resistance*, *11*, 2321–2333. DOI: 10.2147/IDR.S177247 PMID: 30532565

Hilt, E. E., & Ferrieri, P. (2022). Next generation and other sequencing technologies in diagnostic microbiology and infectious diseases. *Genes*, *13*(9), 1566. DOI: 10.3390/genes13091566 PMID: 36140733

Jose, A., Gizdavic-Nikolaidis, M., & Swift, S. (2023). Antimicrobial coatings: Reviewing options for healthcare applications. *Applied Microbiology (Basel, Switzerland)*, *3*(1), 145–174. DOI: 10.3390/applmicrobiol3010012

Kampf, G.. (2014). Persistence of pathogens on inanimate surfaces. *BMC Infectious Diseases*, *14*, 233.

Khalid, R. A.. (2024). Biofilms and antibiotic resistance in nosocomial infections. *Antibiotics (Basel, Switzerland)*, *13*(9), 896. DOI: 10.3390/antibiotics13090896 PMID: 39335069

Ko, K. K., Chng, K. R., & Nagarajan, N. (2022). Metagenomics-enabled microbial surveillance. *Nature Microbiology*, *7*(4), 486–496. DOI: 10.1038/s41564-022-01089-w PMID: 35365786

Kouroubali, A., & Katehakis, D. G. (2022). Policy and strategy for interoperability of digital health in Europe. In *MEDINFO 2021: One World, One Health–Global Partnership for Digital Innovation* (pp. 897-901). IOS Press. DOI: 10.3233/SHTI220209

Krishnan, P. D., Banas, D., Durai, R. D., Kabanov, D., Hosnedlova, B., Kepinska, M., Fernandez, C., Ruttkay-Nedecky, B., Nguyen, H. V., Farid, A., Sochor, J., Narayanan, V. H. B., & Kizek, R. (2020). Silver nanomaterials for wound dressing applications. *Pharmaceutics, 12*(9), 821. DOI: 10.3390/pharmaceutics12090821 PMID: 32872234

Kumar, N. R., Balraj, T. A., Kempegowda, S. N., & Prashant, A. (2024). Multidrug-resistant sepsis: A critical healthcare challenge. *Antibiotics (Basel, Switzerland), 13*(1), 46. DOI: 10.3390/antibiotics13010046 PMID: 38247605

Lynch, J. P.III, Zhanel, G. G., & Clark, N. M. (2017). Infections due to Acinetobacter baumannii in the ICU: Treatment options. *Seminars in Respiratory and Critical Care Medicine*. PMID: 28578555

Maddah, N., Verma, A., Almashmoum, M., & Ainsworth, J. (2023). Effectiveness of public health digital surveillance systems for infectious disease prevention and control at mass gatherings: Systematic review. *Journal of Medical Internet Research, 25*, e44649. DOI: 10.2196/44649 PMID: 37204833

Magill, S. S., O'Leary, E., Janelle, S. J., Thompson, D. L., Dumyati, G., Nadle, J., Wilson, L. E., Kainer, M. A., Lynfield, R., Greissman, S., Ray, S. M., Beldavs, Z., Gross, C., Bamberg, W., Sievers, M., Concannon, C., Buhr, N., Warnke, L., Maloney, M., & Edwards, J. R. (2018). Changes in prevalence of healthcare-associated infections in U.S. hospitals. *The New England Journal of Medicine, 379*(18), 1732–1744. DOI: 10.1056/NEJMoa1801550 PMID: 30380384

Megalingam, R. K., Vadivel, S. R. R., Kotaprolu, S. S., Nithul, B., Kumar, D. V., & Rudravaram, G. (2025). Cleaning Robots: A Review of Sensor Technologies and Intelligent Control Strategies for Cleaning. *Journal of Field Robotics, 42*(5), 2234–2259. DOI: 10.1002/rob.22515

Miller, W. R., & Arias, C. A. (2024). ESKAPE pathogens: Antimicrobial resistance, epidemiology, clinical impact and therapeutics. *Nature Reviews. Microbiology, 22*(10), 598–616. DOI: 10.1038/s41579-024-01054-w PMID: 38831030

Morgan, O., & Pinner, R. (2009). Surveillance of infectious diseases. *Encyclopedia of Microbiology*, 759.

Morones-Ramirez, J. R.. (2012). Nanotechnology in infection control. *ACS Nano, 6*(9), 7630–7637.

Nii-Trebi, N. I. (2017). Emerging and neglected infectious diseases: Insights, advances, and challenges. *BioMed Research International, 2017*(1), 5245021. DOI: 10.1155/2017/5245021 PMID: 28286767

Organization, W. H. (2024). *Global strategy on infection prevention and control.* World Health Organization.

Otter, J. A.. (2011). The role of environmental contamination in the transmission of nosocomial pathogens. *The Lancet. Infectious Diseases, 11*(5), 385–393.

Otter, J. A. Y. S. S. J. A., & French, G. L. (2013). Evidence that contaminated surfaces contribute to the transmission of hospital pathogens and an overview of strategies to address contaminated surfaces in hospital settings. *American Journal of Infection Control, 41*(5), S6–S11. DOI: 10.1016/j.ajic.2012.12.004 PMID: 23622751

Pasnick, S., Carlos, W. G., Dela Cruz, C. S., Gross, J. E., Garrison, G., & Jamil, S. (2020). SARS-CoV-2 transmission and the risk of aerosol-generating procedures. *American Journal of Respiratory and Critical Care Medicine, 202*(4), 13–P14. DOI: 10.1164/rccm.2024P13 PMID: 32795140

Pittet, D., Hugonnet, S., Harbarth, S., Mourouga, P., Sauvan, V., Touveneau, S., & Perneger, T. V. (2000). Effectiveness of a hospital-wide programme to improve compliance with hand hygiene. *Lancet, 356*(9238), 1307–1312. DOI: 10.1016/S0140-6736(00)02814-2 PMID: 11073019

Rao, C. Y., Goryoka, G. W., Henao, O. L., Clarke, K. R., Salyer, S. J., & Montgomery, J. M. (2017). Global disease detection—Achievements in applied public health research, capacity building, and public health diplomacy, 2001–2016. *Emerging Infectious Diseases, 23*(13, Suppl 1), S138. DOI: 10.3201/eid2313.170859 PMID: 29155662

Reynolds, K. A., ... (2020). Current and emerging technologies for hospital disinfection. *Infection Control Today.* https://www.infectioncontroltoday.com

Rutala, W. A., & Weber, D. J. (2014). Selection of the ideal disinfectant. *Infection Control and Hospital Epidemiology, 35*(7), 855–865. DOI: 10.1086/676877 PMID: 24915214

Rutala, W. A., & Weber, D. J. (2019). Disinfection and sterilization: An overview. *American Journal of Infection Control, 47*, A3–A9. DOI: 10.1016/j.ajic.2019.01.018 PMID: 31146848

Salerno, J., Coughlin, S. S., Goodman, K. W., & Hlaing, W. M. (2023). Current ethical and social issues in epidemiology. *Annals of Epidemiology, 80*, 37–42. DOI: 10.1016/j.annepidem.2023.02.001 PMID: 36758845

Saravanos, G. L., Islam, M. S., Huang, Y., Basseal, J. M., Seale, H., Mitchell, B. G., & Sheel, M. (2024). Infection prevention and control programme priorities for sustainable health and environmental systems. *BMC Global and Public Health*, *2*(1), 6. DOI: 10.1186/s44263-023-00031-4 PMID: 39681863

Seifert, H. (2024). Hospital-acquired infections and multidrug-resistant bacteria: A global threat. *Antibiotics (Basel, Switzerland)*, *13*(1), 77. DOI: 10.3390/antibiotics13010077 PMID: 38247635

. Semete-Makokotlela, B. (2015). *Investment performance of the South African Biotechnology industry and potential financing models*

Stahl-Rommel, S., Jain, M., Nguyen, H. N., Arnold, R. R., Aunon-Chancellor, S. M., Sharp, G. M., Castro, C. L., John, K. K., Juul, S., Turner, D. J., Stoddart, D., Paten, B., Akeson, M., Burton, A. S., & Castro-Wallace, S. L. (2021). Real-time culture-independent microbial profiling onboard the international space station using nanopore sequencing. *Genes*, *12*(1), 106. DOI: 10.3390/genes12010106 PMID: 33467183

Tembo, G. M. (2024). *Investigating application methods and active agents for healthcare-related surface contamination*. Purdue University Graduate School.

Tompkins, K., & van Duin, D. (2021). Treatment for carbapenem-resistant Enterobacterales infections: Recent advances and future directions. *European Journal of Clinical Microbiology & Infectious Diseases*, *40*(10), 2053–2068. DOI: 10.1007/s10096-021-04296-1 PMID: 34169446

Vilar-Compte, D., Camacho-Ortiz, A., & Ponce-de-León, S. (2017). Infection control in limited resources countries: Challenges and priorities. *Current Infectious Disease Reports*, *19*(5), 1–7. DOI: 10.1007/s11908-017-0572-y PMID: 28401447

Weber, D. J., & Rutala, W. A. (2013). Role of the environment in the transmission of emerging healthcare-associated pathogens. *Infection Control and Hospital Epidemiology*, *34*(5), 449–452. DOI: 10.1086/670223 PMID: 23571359

Weiner-Lastinger, L. M.. (2020). The impact of COVID-19 on healthcare-associated infections in 2020: A summary of data reported to the National Healthcare Safety Network. *Infection Control and Hospital Epidemiology*, *43*(1), 12–25. DOI: 10.1017/ice.2021.362 PMID: 34473013

World Health, O. (2009). WHO guidelines on hand hygiene in health care. https://www.who.int/publications/i/item/9789241597906

World Health, O. (2011). Report on the burden of endemic health care-associated infection worldwide. https://apps.who.int/iris/handle/10665/80135

World Health, O. (2016). The burden of health care-associated infection worldwide. https://www.who.int/news-room/feature-stories/detail/the-burden-of-health-care-associated-infection-worldwide

World Health, O. (2017). WHO publishes list of bacteria for which new antibiotics are urgently needed. https://www.who.int/news/item/27-02-2017

Zimlichman, E., Henderson, D., Tamir, O., Franz, C., Song, P., Yamin, C. K., Keohane, C., Denham, C. R., & Bates, D. W. (2013). Health care–associated infections: A meta-analysis of costs and financial impact on the US health care system. *JAMA Internal Medicine*, *173*(22), 2039–2046. DOI: 10.1001/jamainternmed.2013.9763 PMID: 23999949

About the Contributors

Muhammad Farooq Umer, With over two decades of academic, research, and field experience in public health, I have devoted my career to advancing public health through rigorous research, innovative teaching, and meaningful community engagement. I hold a PhD in Epidemiology and Health Statistics, a Master's in Public Health, and a Bachelor's in Dental Surgery, along with certifications in Health Professional Education and Occupational Health and Safety. These credentials have supported my work across diverse healthcare systems in Pakistan, China, and Saudi Arabia. Currently, I serve as an Academic Editor for PLOS ONE and a peer reviewer for several international journals. I am also recognized as a PhD supervisor by the Higher Education Commission of Pakistan, Lincoln University Malaysia and a few others. My academic and professional trajectory reflects a commitment to health equity, interdisciplinary collaboration, and the pursuit of evidence-based solutions to pressing public health issues. Beyond the classroom and research lab, I actively engage in public health practice. My work with The Global Fund, WHO, UNICEF, and USAID has allowed me to lead and evaluate national programs on TB control, maternal mental health, and primary healthcare reform. I have also been deeply involved in community-based initiatives, organizing oral health education campaigns, tobacco prevention workshops, and digital transformation events to promote health awareness and behavior change.

***

Adil Aknouch is a researcher and professor of nuclear and Medical physics at the Higher Institute of Nursing Professions and Health Techniques in Agadir. He holds a PhD in nuclear physics from Ibn Tofail University (2022) and a Master's degree in nuclear engineering from Sidi Mohamed Ben Abdellah University (2018). His research focuses on radiation protection and the application of nuclear technologies in the medical, agricultural, industrial, and energy sectors. An expert in radiation protection, he works to minimize the risks of radiation exposure while maximizing the benefits of nuclear technologies. His scientific publications highlight his significant contributions to nuclear safety as well as the advancement of medical and industrial techniques. His vision is to continue advancing research in nuclear physics while contributing to the safety and effectiveness of nuclear applications for the benefit of society.

Muhammad Arshed is a medical doctor (MBBS) with advanced specialization in Public Health, holding both an MPH and a PhD. As a dedicated public health specialist and active researcher, he has contributed significantly to the field with around 15 peer-reviewed publications in high-impact Q1 journals. His work focuses on improving population health through innovative research and health interventions. Dr. Arshed is actively involved in various national and international health projects, aiming to address pressing public health challenges. His expertise spans epidemiology, health systems, and program evaluation, making him a valuable contributor to the global health research community.

Waseela Ashraf holds a PhD in Epidemiology and Public Health and is an active researcher and public health specialist. She is currently enhancing her expertise by pursuing an MSc in Data Science and Machine Learning at the University of Europe for Applied Sciences (Dubai campus). Her work integrates data-driven approaches with public health research, aiming to develop innovative solutions to complex health challenges through advanced analytical and technological tools.

Zernain Athar is a clinical researcher in Public Health and a medical doctor in Qld, Australia.

Syema Awais is a Public Health professional with a strong medical background. Responsible and goal-oriented. Special interests include research, particularly on marginalized populations like immigrants, women experiencing violence & handicapped children. orchid Id: 0000-0002-9797-7066

Iris Efthymiou is a thought leader, university lecturer, and author of 17 books, specializing in AI ethics and behavioural health economics. Passionate about bridging technology and humanity, she advocates for ethical AI and user-centred design to enhance well-being and education in the digital age. She has served as a college director, founded a Public Affairs consultancy, worked with global leaders, and spoken at the UN in Geneva. She serves as an Academic Board Member of the LabHEM at the University of Piraeus, a Board Member of HAPSc and Guildhouse School in London, and a Member of the Business Intelligence Committee (BIC) of the All-Party Parliamentary Group on Artificial Intelligence (APPG AI) in the UK.

She has published over 17 books, 40 articles, and Book chapters in peer-reviewed journals, and she is the Chief Editor of the Journal of Politics and Ethics in New Technologies and AI. She believes in equal opportunities, uniqueness, and the normality of imperfection! Iris has a Ph.D. in Behavioural Economics, a Master's in Health Economics and Management, and Bachelor's in Economics.

Kholis Ernawati (51 years old) is a permanent lecturer at the Bachelor of Medicine Study Programme, Faculty of Medicine, YARSI University. The author completed his S1 and S2 studies at Airlangga University and then S3 at the University of Indonesia. The author's area of expertise is Public Health, focusing on Environmental Health. Teaching at the Faculty of Medicine, YARSI University since 2006 - now. The author actively writes scientific articles and is published in national and international proceedings and journals, compiling modules and books. Activities other than teaching are as a LAM PTKes Public Health Study Program Assessor, BKD Assessor, Study Program Evaluator at the Kemdikbud Institution, and Reviewer of articles in several national and international journals.

Zahra Fatima holds an MPhil in International Economics and Trade from Jiangsu Normal University, Xuzhou, and is currently pursuing a PhD in Logistics Engineering and Management at Chang'an University in Xi'an, China.

Tiago Horta Reis da Silva is a Lecturer in Nursing Education (AEP) at King's College London, with a range of qualifications including BSc in Nursing, BSc in Traditional Chinese Medicine, MSc in Emotional Intelligence, Counselling and NLP, a Master of Business Administration, and MSc in Traditional Chinese Medicine. He has experience in other Higher Education Institutions and NHS and is a member of the Adult Nursing department, assisting with the running, development, and administration of BSc and MSc programmes. He also assists with teaching other modules' content and assists with interviews and assessment matters for other courses. Tiago is a Senior Fellow in Higher Education, a Fellow of the Royal Society of Medicine, and a Fellow for Faculty Nursing and Midwifery at the Royal College of Southern Ireland.

Ayesha Babar Kawish Dedicated medical doctor, Public Health consultant and Educationalist, currently serving as the Professor and Head of the Department at Al-Shifa School of Public Health, Al-Shifa Trust Eye Hospital. She is a Health and wellness consultant.With around 50 influential publications recognized by ResearchGate and Web of Science and significant contribution to National and International health research. Besides supervising 35 postgraduate and undergraduate thesis . She is Reviewer of PLOS,EMRO and other national journals.Dr. Ayesha is also a respected External Examiner and Visiting Faculty member at NUMS,

NSHS,SZABIST, and Health Sservices Aacademy. She is Master trainer and capacity builder of SRH, malnourished, Bakhabr Naujawan, nourish ma initiatives.Dr.Ayesha is General Body member of Forum of Women Development and Research,White Ribbon Alliance,Pakistan Chapter.She is also steering body member of South Asian Regional Council of Respectful Maternity Care.

Abdul Kabeer Kazi serves as the Dean, Faculty of Health Management Sciences at Baqai Medical University, bringing extensive expertise in public health, health systems management, and epidemiology. With a distinguished career in health education, policy formulation, and academic leadership, Dr. Kazi has played a pivotal role in advancing medical and health sciences education in Pakistan. His contributions to research, faculty development, and curriculum innovation have strengthened interdisciplinary learning within health management. Dr. Kazi's dedication to public health initiatives, evidence-based healthcare strategies, and institutional development has positioned him as a leading figure in the field. His scholarly work, including publications and research projects, continues to shape the discourse on global health challenges and management sciences, making him a vital contributor to academia and health policy.

Ejaz Ahmad Khan is a medical doctor and public health academician with over 24 years of experience in teaching, training, and research in public health. He has specific expertise in epidemiology, environmental health and climate change, communicable and non-communicable diseases, injuries, nutrition, and disaster management. He has conducted consultancies for various national and international organisations. He has been a program manager for emergencies and crises, as well as for immunisation. He holds a medical degree and a post-graduate degree in primary health care management/public health, and a fellowship in public health. He is also an affiliate to CIEH (UK). He has published around 240 research articles, with a total of 389 research items in credits, in international journals and has an H-index of 106 and an I-10 of 115. For the three consecutive years (2022, 2023 & 2024), he has been ranked among the top 100 scientists in the world in his professional disciplines for Asia. He has several certifications and has completed short courses, and has served as an editor for national and international journals, as well as being a reviewer for various scientific journals. Recently, he has received the Faculty of Public Health (UK)'s President's Medal for outstanding contributions to public health (2025). Professor Khan has worked as an instructor, assistant professor, associate professor, and professor while teaching and training the Master of Science in Public Health course in Pakistan. His main areas of teaching and training have been the application of epidemiological concepts, their statistical significance and evidence generation for diseases attributed to environmental exposures. On the program side, he coordinated the national health response for the 2005 earthquake in Pakistan and managed the health response in Cyclone Yemyin of 2008 in Sindh and Balochistan provinces. He was also the Director of Surveillance and the National Program Manager at the Federal EPI Programme from 2013 to 2015.

Mehwish Kiran is a medical doctor (MBBS) currently pursuing her Master's in Public Health (MPH). She is an active public health researcher with a growing portfolio, including around five peer-reviewed publications in prestigious Q1 journals. Passionate about improving health outcomes, she is involved in various health projects addressing critical public health issues. Dr. Kiran is committed to advancing evidence-based solutions in health systems and community well-being.

A.V. Senthil Kumar is working as a Professor and Director, PG and Research Department of Computer Applications, Hindusthan College of Arts & Science, Coimbatore, Tamilnadu. To his credit he has industrial experience for five years and teaching experience of 27 years. He has also received his Doctor of Science (D.Sc in Computer Science). He has to his credit 50 Book Chapters, 225 papers in International and National Journals 64 papers in International Conferences in International and National Conferences, and edited 14 books and 2 Text books. He is as Associate Editor of IEEE Access. He is an Editor-in-Chief for many journals and Key Member for India, Machine Intelligence Research Lab (MIR Labs). He is an Editorial Board Member and Reviewer for various International Journals. He is also a Committee member for various International Conferences.

Hina Lateef graduated of Shiekh Zayed Medical College, Rahim Yar Khan, and is currently working in Saudia Arabia as General Practitioner.

Revati Ramrao Rautrao is an Associate Professor, a scholar, HR expert, and educator with 20+ years of experience, known for her research in sustainability, AI in education, and women's empowerment.

Muhammad Farhan Sheharyar is a Dentist by profession from Pakistan and Currently doing Mphil in Hongkong in Environmental sustainability, policy and Management at HKUST.

Saif Ullah is an Assistant Professor and Head of the Department of Optometry at the Pakistan Institute of Ophthalmology, Al-Shifa Trust Eye Hospital, Rawalpindi, Pakistan. He holds a PhD in Optometry and Vision Science from Lincoln University College, Malaysia. With over a decade of experience in clinical optometry and academic leadership, he has been serving as a Visiting Low Vision Specialist at Shifa Eye Foundation, Haripur, since 2015. Dr. Ullah has a strong research background, particularly in the areas of myopia control, keratoconus, corneal topography, and maternal-child health. He has authored several systematic reviews and meta-analyses published in peer-reviewed ophthalmology and medical journals. His recent work focuses on light-based interventions for myopia progression, the impact of peer support on breastfeeding outcomes, and the long-term effects of gas permeable lenses on corneal endothelial health. In addition to his research and teaching responsibilities, Dr. Ullah is actively involved in curriculum development and program accreditation for Allied Health Professionals in Pakistan.

Index

A

B

C

D

I

M

N

O

P

R

S

T

U

W

www.ingramcontent.com/pod-product-compliance
Lightning Source LLC
LaVergne TN
LVHW062337300926
849161LV00007B/1723